THE SECOND
GREAT WAR

AIR CHIEF MARSHAL SIR ARTHUR TRAVERS HARRIS, K.C.B., O.B.E., A.F.C.

THE SECOND GREAT WAR

A Standard History

Edited by

SIR JOHN HAMMERTON

Editor of The Great War, World War 1914–18, Europe's Fight for Freedom, etc.

Military Editor

Maj.-Gen. SIR CHARLES GWYNN, K.C.B., C.M.G., D.S.O.

Volume Seven

Pages 2589—3084

Published by

THE WAVERLEY BOOK COMPANY LTD.

in association with

THE AMALGAMATED PRESS LTD.

Farringdon Street, London, E.C.4

MADE AND PRINTED IN GREAT BRITAIN BY PURNELL AND SONS, LTD.
PAULTON (SOMERSET) AND LONDON

CONTENTS OF VOLUME SEVEN

LIST OF CHAPTERS

HISTORIC DOCUMENTS

(The number of the page on which each document appears is given in brackets)

MAPS AND PLANS

SPECIAL PLATES IN COLOUR

CHAPTERS CLASSIFIED ACCORDING TO SUBJECT—Vols. 1 to 7

7*

ix

CHAPTERS CLASSIFIED ACCORDING TO SUBJECT—Vols. 1 to 7 (Contd.)

JAPANESE WARSHIP RECEIVES ITS DEATH BLOW

As its oil trail indicates, this destroyer—already damaged—twisted and turned in a vain attempt to evade Allied air attack; the bombs which eventually sank it are seen bursting on its bows. The destroyer was one of the 22 ships in the ill-fated Japanese convoy every one of which was sent to the bottom by land-based Allied bombers in the Battle of the Bismarck Sea, March 2–3, 1943 (see page 2602). The enemy lost 12 troop transports, seven destroyers, and three cruisers, at least 72 planes, and all but 97 of 15,000 men. Allied losses were four aircraft. *Photo, Paul Popper*

BRITISH PRISONERS OF WAR HOME FROM GERMANY

As the result of two years' negotiations, the first exchange of Allied and German prisoners took place in October 1943, when some 5,400 British and Empire prisoners—3,000 seriously sick and wounded men, 1,200 doctors, chaplains, orderlies, etc., about 170 sick merchant seamen, and some 100 sick civilians—were exchanged for 5,000–6,000 Germans in similar categories. British hospital ships delivered German prisoners to Gothenburg in Sweden, and came back with Allied men : the photograph shows a tender arriving at the quayside at Leith on October 25 with some of the 3,351 men brought by the 'Empress of Russia' and the 'Drottningholm.' Next day the 'Atlantis' disembarked at Liverpool 764 men too badly disabled to be brought ashore in tenders. German ships picked up German prisoners at an Allied port in north-west Africa, and a British ship brought Germans from the Middle East to Barcelona and took back more than 1,000 men belonging to the forces of Australia, New Zealand, South Africa and other parts of the empire.

Photo, G.P.U.

Chapter 262

THE HOME FRONT IN BRITAIN DURING 1943

*Britain, the beleaguered fortress of 1940–41, had become by 1943 the centre
from which invasion of the Continent, with all this implied of organization,
training and provision of supplies, was being prepared. But even at this critical
time thought and planning for the post-war world was not lacking, as this
review shows. Consult also Historic Documents Nos. CCLXI and CCLXV.
Home front activities in the second half of 1942 were recorded in Chapter 239*

THE year 1943 in Britain may well be described as one of preparation for the Allied invasion of Western Europe. This it was intended to be in the Government's planning, so long-scale, so immensely vast in comprehension so intensely complex in its construction. In the middle of January Mr. Oliver Lyttelton, Minister of Production, set the keynote of all the year's activities when he told the House of Commons that 1943 would be a peak year in our war production; and six months later, in a speech to the U.S.A. on American Independence Day, he declared that we in Britain, while fully cognizant of America's vast contributions to the common cause by way of Lend-Lease, had mobilized our men and women for war to the full, tightening our belts, working the longest hours possible, and pressing every ounce of our strength into the offensive battle. We now lived on less than half of our pre-war imports, he reminded his hearers across the Atlantic; men in the munitions industry were working an average of over 55 hours a week and women over 50 hours; and Britain as a result was now producing a greater volume of goods than ever before, and the figures for munitions production showed a steady rise. About 17 per cent of the munitions production of the United Nations was contributed by Great Britain alone, and 22 per cent by the Empire as a whole.

By the summer the mobilization of the country's man- and woman-power was practically complete. Out of a population of 46,750,000 (mid-1942), of whom 9 millions were children under 14, and an " effective " population between 14 and 65 of 33,130,000 (15,900,000 males and 17,230,000 females) 15,200,000 males and 7,100,000 females (including 2,500,000 married women) were in the

Services or engaged in full-time paid employment, while the remaining 10 million women were married or occupied in necessary household duties. (Some 650,000 of these were also engaged in part-time jobs, and another million were engaged as voluntary workers.) Over a million more men were engaged in making munitions than in the last war, but the mobilization of women was on an unprecedented and unrivalled scale.

**NEW IDENTITY CARD ISSUED TO RESIDENTS IN
GREAT BRITAIN**

Under the National Registration Act, passed on September 1, 1939, identity cards were issued to each person resident in the United Kingdom on Sept. 30, 1939. These were recalled in 1943, when fresh ones of the pattern shown above were distributed with the new ration books (see illus., p. 2593).

In September a mass meeting of representative women workers in industry was called by the Government in the Albert Hall, London. Some 6,000 women attended, and addresses were

<table>
<tr><td colspan="2">~~~~~~~~~~~~~~~~~~~~~~~~~~~~~~~~</td></tr>
</table>

BRITAIN'S WAR PRODUCTION

The following figures were given by Mr. Oliver Lyttelton (Minister of Production) in the House of Commons, on March 8, 1944.

From the beginning of the war to the end of 1943 :

    83,000 tanks, armoured cars and carriers.
   115,000 guns of calibres larger than 20 mm.
150,000,000 rounds of gun ammunition.
  5,500,000 machine-guns, rifles, sub-machine-guns,
       and automatic pistols.
7,000,000,000 rounds of small arms ammunition.
  1,000,000 wheeled vehicles of unarmoured types.
    * 90,000 aircraft of all kinds (80% combat types).

* [*From an official report issued in Washington,
May 31, 1944, the number appears to have been even
larger*—95,305].

given by Mr. Churchill, Mr. Bevin, Lord Woolton, and other ministers. The Prime Minister said that " the war effort would not have been achieved if the women had not marched forward in millions and undertaken all kinds of tasks and work for which any other generation than our own—unless you go back to the Stone Age—would have considered them unfitted "; while Mr. Bevin, who as Minister of Labour could speak of women's work with unexampled authority, declared that the response, discipline, and output of British women had surpassed all expectations, and permitted of the most orderly and efficient mobilization of labour-power ever seen. Their effort had been vast, but " it would be a tough go during the winter and early spring," and the last great effort must now be made.

In spite of all that the U-boats had been able to achieve, the British people were still remarkably well fed—perhaps (indeed almost certainly) the best-fed people in Europe. The national larder continued to be well stocked with the produce of home agriculture and imports from abroad. Concerning the latter, Mr. Mabane, Parliamentary Secretary of the Ministry of Food, said pertinently enough on May 13 in the House of Commons that never had so much been carried in so little, a reference to the careful scheming and scientific developments that had enormously reduced the ratio of volume to value in shipping space. Eighty per cent of space had been saved by importing eggs dried instead of in shell, 25 per cent by boning and telescoping carcase meat; and by dehydration a thousand tons of vegetables, occupying 140,000 cu. ft., could be reduced to 40 tons and 1,500 cu. ft. Improved methods of dehydration of both meat and vegetables were constantly sought.

1. These cottages—two out of 3,000 promised for farm labourers by the Government—were 'opened' at Riding Lane, Hildenborough, Kent, on September 15, 1943, by the Rt. Hon. Ernest Brown, Minister of Health.
2. Volunteer land workers line up for their wages : many townsmen and women helped regular farm workers to get in the splendid harvest of 1943.

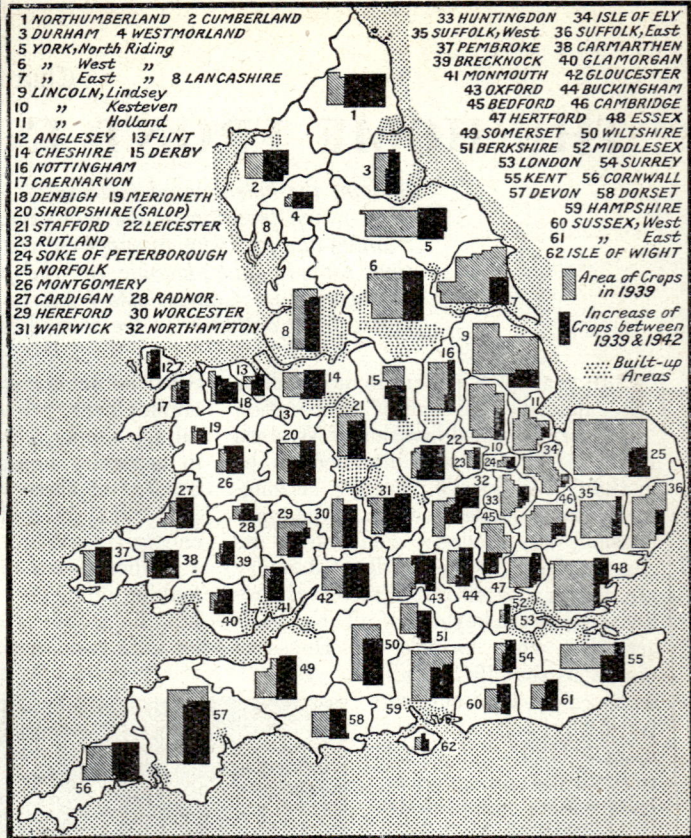

1 NORTHUMBERLAND	2 CUMBERLAND		33 HUNTINGDON	34 ISLE OF ELY
3 DURHAM	4 WESTMORLAND		35 SUFFOLK, West	36 SUFFOLK, East
5 YORK, North Riding			37 PEMBROKE	38 CARMARTHEN
6 " West "			39 BRECKNOCK	40 GLAMORGAN
7 " East "	8 LANCASHIRE		41 MONMOUTH	42 GLOUCESTER
9 LINCOLN, Lindsey			43 OXFORD	44 BUCKINGHAM
10 " Kesteven			45 BEDFORD	46 CAMBRIDGE
11 " Holland			47 HERTFORD	48 ESSEX
12 ANGLESEY	13 FLINT		49 SOMERSET	50 WILTSHIRE
14 CHESHIRE	15 DERBY		51 BERKSHIRE	52 MIDDLESEX
16 NOTTINGHAM			53 LONDON	54 SURREY
17 CAERNARVON			55 KENT	56 CORNWALL
18 DENBIGH	19 MERIONETH		57 DEVON	58 DORSET
20 SHROPSHIRE (SALOP)			59 HAMPSHIRE	
21 STAFFORD	22 LEICESTER		60 SUSSEX, West	
23 RUTLAND			61 " East	
24 SOKE OF PETERBOROUGH			62 ISLE OF WIGHT	
25 NORFOLK				
26 MONTGOMERY				
27 CARDIGAN	28 RADNOR			
29 HEREFORD	30 WORCESTER			
31 WARWICK	32 NORTHAMPTON			

Area of Crops in 1939

Increase of Crops between 1939 & 1942

Built-up Areas

HOW BRITAIN DEVELOPED HER AGRICULTURE

In 1943, 70 per cent more food was produced in England and Wales than in 1939—a rise due in large measure to the greatly increased area under the plough. From the map (compiled from information supplied by the Ministry of Agriculture) can be seen the increase in production county by county in 1942 ; it was higher still in 1943. Great expansion in the use of machinery helped: this combine harvester (3), adjusted to cut only the ears of corn, left behind the straw to be ploughed back into the soil to form humus.

NEW RATION BOOKS FOR OLD

The new ration books issued between May and July 1943 included personal points, used for the purchase of sweets and chocolate; coupons for all rationed foods (left); and clothing coupons (right). Personal points and food coupons came into use from July 25; clothing coupons from September 1. Personal points and clothing coupons were detachable from the food book, but their issue bound as one saved time and trouble in preparation and distribution.

Stocks of food had been steadily accumulated since 1939 so as to maintain a fair and consistent distribution. The supplies from India and Ceylon had sufficed to maintain the tea ration; and the loss of almost all our sources of rice had been compensated, at least in part, by increased production in Brazil and the U.S.A. Subsidies kept the price of food stable (during 1943 £205,800,000 was spent on food subsidies, including over £60 million on bread, flour, and oatmeal; £23 million on meat and £28 million on potatoes, £11 million on eggs, and nearly £11 million on milk, and the same on sugar), so that food prices were only 20 per cent above pre-war. This should be compared with the rise of 108 per cent in the spring of 1918, the fourth year of the last war. Many other interesting facts were revealed by Mr. Mabane. Fish zoning was saving about 7,000 train miles weekly, and milk rationalization about 25 per

cent of petrol; the scheme for moving seed potatoes from Scotland had saved about 250,000 tons of transport, and soft drink concentration had taken about 1,000 vehicles off the road. British Restaurants now numbered over 2,000 and were rapidly increasing;

SALMON GOES INTO COLD STORAGE

During the salmon season, many fish were put into cold storage on behalf of the Ministry of Food at Billingsgate Market, London. Here is a section of a freezing room with more fish being added to the freezing racks.

Photo, Topical Press

the number of meals served in these and works canteens, catering establishments, etc., was approximately 180 millions a week. The national loaf was the best, and the only unrationed bread in Europe, and at 2¼d. a pound the cheapest food in the world.

All this would not have been possible but for the devoted labours of the British farming industry. In March Mr. R. S. Hudson, Minister of Agriculture, appealed to farmers to plough up an additional million acres, and at the same time urged the growing of yet more vegetables in gardens and allotments. In three years British food production had increased 70 per cent, of which 60 per cent was due to increased output per man unit. By now, the Minister could proudly boast, the British farm worker was producing nearly three times more than the German, and incidentally substantially more than the worker in America. On May 26 Mr. Hudson outlined a four-year plan for agriculture in Britain which should increase food production and improve the land (*see* Historic Document No. CCLXV, page 2600).

TWENTY-THREE UNITS' WORTH OF UTILITY FURNITURE

Manufacture of domestic furniture was prohibited from November 1, 1942, except for Utility furniture, introduced from January 1, 1943. Free of purchase tax, it was obtainable under permit on a 'units' system, by newly married couples, bombed-out persons and—from March 26 —by families with children setting up house for the first time. Couples with no furniture were entitled to 60 units ; and an additional 15 units for each child. Units value of the furniture here shown was : sideboard, 8 ; table, 6 ; dining chairs, 1 each ; fireside chair, 5. Nursery furniture, when available, could be bought without restrictions. Inset, Board of Trade official stamp.

Photo, Sport & General

The Ministry of Agriculture issued on June 17 a statement giving particulars of the extraordinary progress that had been made in food production since 1939. Although the total cultivated area had diminished by 2 per cent, owing to the extension of land given over to military uses, the tillage acreage in 1942–43 exceeded that of 1939 by 52·8 per cent (*see* map, p. 2592). The area under wheat was up by 35·6 per cent, oats 72, potatoes 80·4, vegetables 55·1. In 1939 enough beet was grown at home to meet 23·9 per cent of our sugar requirements; now it was sufficient to meet 35 per cent, i.e., to cover the domestic ration. Another striking fact was that the number of farm tractors in use rose from 55,000 in 1939 to 150,000 in 1942. In spite of the great drop in imported foodstuffs, cattle increased by 4·6 per cent (showing the Government's practical increase in milk production), but sheep, pigs, and commercial poultry all showed a fall in numbers. Allotments had increased from 930,000 to 1,675,000 during the war, and the number of private gardens producing vegetables rose from two millions to five millions. On Farm Sunday, July 4, Mr. Hudson broadcast an appeal for a great army of volunteers to help the farmers, their regular

Progress in Food Production

workers, and the Women's Land Army, in raising a harvest which would mean the best part of a hundred million tons, produced on the soil of a Britain that had become one of the most fertile spots on earth. Tens of thousands of men and women, boys and girls, answered the Minister's call, and in all parts of the country there were agricultural camps for the volunteers. Without their aid what Mr. Hudson called "the toughest harvesting job of our history" could never have been performed.

On April 12 Sir Kingsley Wood, the Chancellor of the Exchequer, opened his Budget for 1943–44. The total expenditure for the year was estimated at £5,756,114,000 and the revenue at £2,907,500,000, leaving a gap of £2,848,614,000 to be filled by borrowing, etc. There were not many tax changes. Income tax was kept at 10s. in the £. The Purchase Tax on "luxury articles" was increased from 66⅔ to 100 per cent, and there were small increases in the taxes on drink and tobacco, and seats in theatres and cinemas over a shilling. In his speech Sir Kingsley Wood, after paying a wholehearted tribute to the working of the Lease-Lend scheme, recalled that the cost of the war had now risen to the stupendous total of £13,000,000,000, and that the total expenditure, including debt charges

and normal civil services throughout the war period, amounted to some £15,600,000,000. The daily war expenditure had been steadily increasing, and was now £15 million as against £5 million at the time of the 1940 Budget and £12,500,000 a year earlier. During the past financial year taxation had yielded the unprecedented sum of £2,483,000,000, and for the first time in history income tax exceeded £1,000 million. No less than 44 per cent of all our expenditure since the war began, whether at home or abroad, had been met out of current domestic revenue ; in 1940 it was 36 per cent, and in the last year of the 1914–18 war only 29 per cent.

This was, concluded the Chancellor, a magnificent achievement by all sections of British taxpayers. Seven million wage-earners had paid about £200 million in income tax during the year, and nearly every family in the land contained now at least one income tax payer. What the taxpayers had not contributed had been borrowed—34 per cent through long-term loans and 21 per cent by way of subscriptions to small savings. Shortly before the close of the financial year the total sum raised by the War Savings campaign exceeded £5,000 million.

On September 21 Sir Kingsley Wood died suddenly, and was succeeded as

Paying for the War

'BEVIN'S BOYS'

Mr. Bevin, Minister of Labour, announced on July 29, 1943 (see page 2599) that if insufficient men volunteered for work in the mines, mining would be added to the services to which men called up could be directed. This step was taken on October 12, the men to be chosen, explained Mr. Bevin on December 2, by ballot. The first ballot took place on December 14. Below is a group of conscripted youths from London and Glasgow receiving instruction in coal-getting.

Photo, Associated Press

Chancellor of the Exchequer by Sir John Anderson, whose place as Lord President of the Council was taken by Mr. Attlee. At the same time Lord Cranborne became Dominions Secretary, Lord Beaverbrook Lord Privy Seal, and Mr. R. K. Law (son of the former Prime Minister) a Secretary of State. As Chancellor, Sir Kingsley Wood had recognized that the Budget was no mere money-raising device, but a powerful instrument of economic and social policy, and it was during his term of office that such fiscal innovations as the purchase tax, deferred credits for taxpayers, tax-free utility goods (utility furniture was introduced from January 1—see p. 2594), and tax-reserve certificates were inaugurated.

Yet another substantial reform had received his keen attention—the system of "pay-as-you-earn" income tax. Sir Kingsley had intended to describe the proposals himself to the House of Commons on September 22, but owing to his sudden demise his place was taken by Mr. R. Assheton, Financial Secretary to the Treasury. A White Paper explaining the proposals was issued the same day. Briefly, it was proposed that in future income tax should be deducted from current earnings instead of being based on the earnings for the previous year. It was intended that originally the scheme should apply only to weekly wage-earners, but so great was the pressure brought to bear on the new Chancellor that before it came into operation (in April 1944) it was extended to cover all persons receiving incomes under Schedule E. The Bill became law on November 11.

'Pay-as-you-earn' Income Tax

Although the nation was stripped for war, there was plenty of thought for the morrow—for the days after the victory had been won. During 1943 such criticism of the Government as there was had a domestic rather than a strategical or military complexion. It was generally admitted that the Churchill administration was making a good job of the war, but there were many who doubted its ability to plan the society that should emerge as the aftermath of the gigantic struggle. Loud and frequent were the complaints that the famous Reports of the Barlow, Scott, and Uthwatt Committees (see Historic Documents CCLVI–CCLVIII, pp. 2370 and 2371), had been pigeon-holed in Whitehall and next to nothing done to implement their recommendations. A new Ministry of Town and Country Planning was established in February, with Mr. W. S. Morrison as its head, and a Town and Country Planning (Interim Develop-

ment) Act was passed bringing under public control such land as was not already covered by the earlier Act and increasing the control exercised by planning authorities while their plans were being prepared. The Beveridge Report (see p. 2369), was the subject of much discussion, and in February there was a four-day debate in the Commons on its proposals. Sir John Anderson, speaking for the Government, announced its acceptance of the Report's basic assumptions—full employment, a comprehensive national medical service, and a system of children's allowances—and

promised that in due course steps would be taken to embody the main proposals in legislative form. The promise was welcomed, but here again the critics showed some disinclination to be content with assurances. By way of demonstrating the Government's genuine concern for the post-war world Mr. Churchill came to the microphone on March 21 and broadcast to the nation and the world the outlines of a four-year programme of British social policy, to be prepared at once, and initiated at the earliest opportunity. (See Historic Document No. CCLXI, page 2599.)

CARGO SHIPS FROM BRITISH YARDS

Fast ships designed to carry special war freight and built in British yards began to come into use in September 1943. Spacious, clear decks suitable for the carriage of bulky, heavy, and large items; many wide hatchways; extensive cargo gear, including three big derricks, were outstanding features of these vessels. They had accommodation for 24 passengers. Above, men at work on the engines for a 10,000-ton cargo ship. Below, a 12,000-ton dead weight merchant vessel seen behind the bows of another under construction.

Photos, British Official ; Topical

One measure of domestic reform, at least, was put on the Statute Book : the Bill for the regulation of wages in the catering industry. Fathered by Mr. Bevin, the Minister of Labour, this was hotly opposed by a section of the Conservative party who accused the Minister of breaking the political truce by promoting a highly controversial issue. Mr. Bevin stuck to his guns. He wanted the Bill, he declared, because it was necessary to put a great industry on a satisfactory basis ready for the post-war rush of tourists and other visitors. The Bill became law in June, and the Wages Board authorized thereunder was soon after set up.

Another and far more important measure of reform was the Education Bill, the text of which was issued in **Educational Proposals** December, although the proposals it embodied were outlined in a White Paper published on July 17. The Bill was hailed as the greatest step in educational progress since the Fisher Act of a quarter of a century before. Under it the school-leaving age was to be raised to 15 on April 1, 1945, and to 16 as soon as practicable thereafter ; the school system was to be entirely remodelled on the plan of nursery schools for children under 5 (voluntary), primary schools for children in the 5–11 age groups, and secondary schools for children over 11. All these schools were to be free, and local education committees would be

LORD WAVELL LEAVES FOR INDIA

Field-Marshal Sir Archibald Wavell, appointed to succeed Lord Linlithgow as Viceroy and Governor-General of India on June 19, 1943, became Viscount Wavell of Cyrenaica and Winchester on July 1. Shortly before his departure he said, 'I have no illusions as to the difficulties and dangers of my task, but I have also a vision of the great possibilities in front of India.' He is seen here with Lady Wavell and their daughter Felicity leaving England for India, which he reached on October 17. He was installed as Viceroy at New Delhi on October 20.

Photo, G.P.U.

required to provide free medical treatment and inspection and would also receive new powers to provide meals and milk and, in cases of real need, free boots and clothing. For young

FIRST FAIR IN WINDSOR GREAT PARK

In 1943, as in 1942, the Government recommended that workers in industry should have a week's holiday during the year. But, to avoid non-essential travel and to prevent confusion and difficulty in food distribution, everyone was advised to spend holidays at home. Many local authorities provided open-air attractions in the form of concerts, dances, and other entertainments. H.M. the King permitted a fair to be held in Windsor Great Park as part of the ' holidays at home ' movement. *Photo, Planet News*

people up to the age of 18 not attending school full time there would be Young People's Colleges, part-time attendance at which would be compulsory. All primary and secondary schools would begin the day with an act of corporate worship, and Church schools would have the choice of being either aided (when they would meet half the cost of modernizing their buildings and continue to appoint their own teachers and retain control of religious instruction) or controlled, when full financial responsibility would be assumed by the Local Education Authority, but the managers would be consulted as to the appointment of head teachers and those teachers giving religious instruction.

More Cabinet changes were announced on November 11. Lord Woolton, who had been an outstanding success as Minister of Food, became Minister of Reconstruction, with a **New Minister of Food** seat in the War Cabinet. Col. Llewellin took his place at the Food Ministry. Mr. H. U. Willink became Minister of Health in place of Mr. Ernest Brown who was appointed Chancellor of the Duchy of Lancaster.

Lord Woolton's appointment encouraged those who were anxious to see some progress in the plans for post-war reconstruction ; in his statement on the subject in the Lords in December,

2596

he made it clear there would be no Ministry of Reconstruction with a large staff. As he envisaged his position, it was that of a co-ordinator of the plans put forward by other ministries and departments. This rather limited view of his powers and responsibilities chagrined some of his critics, who also regretted his statement that "for some years to come we shall be a nation poor in wealth," which, taken in conjunction with a somewhat similar utterance by Field-Marshal Smuts (in his speech to the Houses of Parliament on November 25, that after the war Britain "from a material economic point of view will be a poor country," since she had put her all into the struggle), fostered their fears that finance would make a strait-jacket in which the new post-war Britain would be cramped and stifled and unable to grow.

Throughout the year the Home Front was dominated by the problem of coal production. Coal lay at the bottom of

COASTAL AREAS CLOSED

From time to time areas in Britain, particularly on the coast, were closed to visitors. Bottom right is a warning notice at a London terminus. But life went on in these areas—even in bomb- and shell-scarred Dover. Right, a notice at a Dover omnibus stop : though a number of employees were killed, and many more wounded, by enemy action, the East Kent 'buses never stopped running, even during the Battle of Britain. Below, recent damage being roped off in a street under the shadow of Dover Castle.

Photos, Topical Press ; " Daily Mirror "

the country's life, it was the basis of its capacity to make war. Yet insufficient coal was being produced, and nothing that was tried seemed able to lift the figure to what was needed to supply the domestic hearths, the fighting forces, and the demands of our overseas allies and friends. When the year opened, a National Coal Board of coal-owners and miners, coal distributors and consumers, under the chairmanship of Major Gwilym Lloyd George, Minister of Fuel and Power, had just come into being. In April the Minister said that he was watching the production figures with serious concern : although there were at the moment over 5,000

more men in the industry than a year earlier, the production each week was nearly 10,000 tons less than in the same week of 1942, and absenteeism among miners was higher than it should be. In a broadcast on April 14 he said that though the gap of 11 million tons between production and consumption had been closed, the production position was far from satisfactory. In May a scheme of conciliation for the settlement of all disputes came into force. A National Conciliation Board was set up, consisting of owners' and workers' representatives in equal numbers, with two chairmen representing both sides, and a National Reference Tribunal of three permanent members, unconnected with the industry and appointed by the Master of the Rolls.

Still the fall in output remained unchecked, and in September the Government proposed to the miners' leaders that there should be more Saturday work, full time work on one Sunday in four, and clearing of the coal face at every shift so as to leave nothing over for the next shift to do before commencing work. These proposals were rejected by the Mineworkers'

These proposals, said Major Lloyd George, the Minister of Fuel, on October 12 in the House of Commons in the course of a debate on the coal situation, would be carefully considered; one immediate step (already foreshadowed by Mr. Bevin's speech of July 29—*see* Historic Document No. CCLXII, p. 2599), would be the call-up of men for the mines in the same way as for the armed services. On December 2 Mr. Bevin announced that the men conscripted for the mines would be chosen by ballot from amongst those born on or after January 1, 1918. Special arrangements would be made for the conscripts to be properly trained in their duties before going down the pit.

TOWN AND COAST HOME DEFENCES

1. 'Flak tower' of A.A. Command, one of many constructed round the coasts of Britain to counter 'sneak' air raiders. They brought down 59 enemy planes in 1943. 2. Home Guards on an A.A. gun site in the London area, where they went into action for the first time on the night of January 24, 1943. 3. Six-pounder twin coastal gun, specially designed for defence against light coastal motor-boats and small torpedo-boats. Mounted in pairs in turrets turning a full circle, these guns have a high muzzle velocity and a range of over 5,000 yards (about 3 miles).

Photos, British Official: Crown Copyright ; Keystone ; Central Press

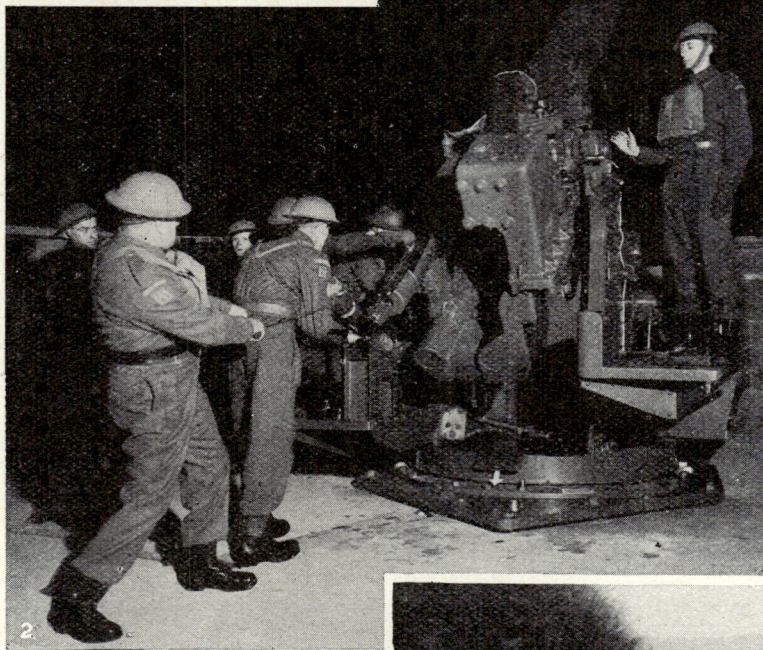

There were some important developments in the organization of the Civil Defence Services during the year. In January the first aid services were amalgamated with the rescue service; and in February the Fire Guards were recognized as a separate service, to be closely linked with the National Fire Service. To accomplish this new liaison a new Fire Guard Plan was devised, operative from September, making Fire Guards responsible for reporting to the N.F.S. fires from enemy action during the hours of black-out.

Federation, and a number of counter-proposals were submitted. These included the release of more miners from the forces, Civil Defence, and industry; abolition of dual control, and assumption by the State of full financial and operational control of the pits; accelerated mechanization and improved equipment; a minimum wage of £6 a week for underground workers and £5 10s. for surface workers; overhaul of transport arrangements; improvements in the holidays with pay scheme. Long-term proposals included immediate legislation governing post-war hours, Government control of the disposal and price of coal, continuation of the guaranteed week and national minimum wage, and comprehensive safety and welfare measures. The Federation concluded that there could be no final solution of the problems besetting the industry so long as its ownership remained in private hands.

'WE SHOULD MAKE AND PROCLAIM A 4 YEARS' PLAN'

By 1943 Allied victory soon or late seemed certain, and Mr. Churchill's broadcast of March 21 gave answer to a widespread feeling that attention should be given to post-war conditions. Mr. Bevin's decision to direct men between 18–25 into mining, and to register women up to 50, indicated clearly, however, that the stringencies of war were by no means at an end—a fact emphasized in the Premier's Mansion House speech.

MR. CHURCHILL, IN A BROADCAST ON MARCH 21, 1943, SPEAKS OF POST-WAR POLICY.

IT is our duty to peer through the mists of the future to the end of the war, and to try our utmost to be prepared by ceaseless effort and forethought for the kind of situations which are likely to occur. . . .

It would be our hope that the United Nations, headed by the three great victorious Powers, the British Commonwealth, the United States and Soviet Russia, should immediately begin to confer upon the future world organization which is to be our safeguard against further wars. . . . It is my earnest hope, though I can hardly expect to see it fulfilled in my lifetime, that we shall achieve the largest common measure of the integrated life of Europe that is possible without destroying the individual characteristics and traditions of its many ancient and historic races. . . . We must remember, however, that . . . it will not be given to any one nation to achieve the full satisfaction of its wishes. . . .

Coming nearer home . . . I am very much attracted to the idea that we should make and proclaim what might be called a Four Years' Plan. . . . We have five-year Parliaments, and a Four Years' Plan would give time for the preparation of a second plan. . . . A scheme for the amalgamation and extension of our present incomparable insurance system should have a leading place in our Four Years' Plan. I have been prominently connected with all these schemes of national compulsory thrift from the time when I brought my friend Sir William Beveridge into the public service 35 years ago. . . . The time is now ripe for another great advance. . . .

We must establish on broad and solid foundations a National Health Service. Here let me say that there is no finer investment for any community than putting milk into babies. . . . The care of the young and the establishment of sound, hygienic conditions of motherhood have a bearing upon the whole future of the race which is absolutely vital. Side by side with that is the war upon disease, which, so far as it is successful, will directly aid the national insurance scheme. . . .

The future of the world is to the highly educated races who alone can handle the scientific apparatus necessary for pre-eminence in peace or survival in war. . . . The facilities for advanced education must be evened out and multiplied. No one who can take advantage of a higher education should be denied this chance. You cannot conduct a modern community except with an adequate supply of persons upon whose education, whether humanitarian, technical or scientific, much time and money have been spent. . . .

We have one large and immediate task in the replanning and rebuilding of our cities and towns. . . . In the far-reaching scheme for reorganizing the building industry, prepared by the Minister of Labour and the Minister of Works, will be found another means of protecting our insurance fund from the drain of unemployment relief. . . .

It is necessary to make sure that we have projects for the future employment of the people and the forward movement of our industries carefully foreseen, and, secondly, that private enterprise and State enterprise are both able to play their parts to the utmost. A number of measures are being and will be prepared which will enable the Government to exercise a balancing influence upon development. . . . Our own efforts must be supported by international arrangements and agreements more neighbourlike and more sensible than before. . . . My solemn belief is that if we act with comradeship and loyalty to our country and to one another, and if we can make State enterprise and free enterprise both serve national interests and pull the national wagon side by side, then there is no need for us to run into that horrible, devastating slump or into that squalid epoch of bickering and confusion which mocked and squandered the hard-won victory which we gained a quarter of a century ago.

MR. ERNEST BEVIN, MINISTER OF LABOUR, ANNOUNCES NEW MEASURES FOR USING MAN-POWER TO THE FULL; HOUSE OF COMMONS, JULY 29, 1943.

GREAT though the expansion of the aircraft industry has been already, we must add still more to its labour force. This can only be done by the further recruitment of women, who will therefore not be available for the Women's Auxiliary Services, the Women's Land Army, and other services. . . . In addition . . . it has been decided to extend the age of registration of women for employment up to the age of 50. . . .

The man-power of the mining industry must be reinforced. . . . At the beginning of July the labour force in the coal-mining industry stood at 706,000. The net wastage is 20,000 a year; and the average man-power for the year up to next April, unless we change matters, will not exceed 700,000. An average labour force at this level will not be sufficient to meet our probable requirements. . . . I intend immediately to remove the age limit from the option to enter the mines which is given to men called up for the forces; at present this is limited to men under 25. If a sufficient number do not exercise this option my first line of approach will be to direct men between 18 and 25, who would otherwise be called up for the forces, to enter mining instead. Volunteers will also be accepted from among any suitable men who are not engaged on high priority work. But if these measures prove inadequate, I shall have no choice but to reduce the age for direction below 18. . . .

MR. CHURCHILL SPEAKS ON WAR DUTIES AT THE MANSION HOUSE, NOVEMBER 9, 1943.

WE and our Allies have had a year of almost unbroken victory on every front. British, Dominion, and U.S. armies have cleared Africa of the enemy. Together the British and U.S. forces have conquered Sicily, Sardinia, Corsica, and one-third of Italy. We have broken the back of the U-boat war, which at one time had seemed our greatest peril. We have inflicted, and are inflicting, shattering damage upon the German cities which are the centres of munitions production. . . . In the Pacific . . . many brilliant actions have been recorded. . . . But I gladly admit, and indeed proclaim, that the outstanding event of this famous year has been the victorious advance of the Russian armies. . . .

A great many people speak as if the end of the war in Europe were near. I hope they may prove right. . . . We should, however, be foolish and blameworthy if we allowed our plans and actions to be based on the prospect of an early collapse of Germany. . . . We must not lose for a moment the sense and consciousness of urgency and crisis which must continue to drive us, even though we are in the fifth year of war. . . .

Another tremendous and practical duty is involved in what is called winning the war. . . . I regard it as a definite part of the duty of this National Government to have its plans perfected in a vast and practical scheme to make sure that in the years immediately following the war food, work and homes are found for all. . . . On this far-reaching work H.M. Government are now concentrating all their energies that can be spared from the actual struggle with the enemy. . . .

It is a reasonable assumption that, unless we make some grave mistakes in strategy, 1944 will see the climax of the European war. Unless some happy event occurs, on which we have no right to count, and the hand of Providence is stretched forth in some crowning mercy, 1944 will see the greatest sacrifice of life by the British and American armies. . . . Sorrow will come to many homes in the United Kingdom and throughout the great Republic. . . . The supreme duty of all of us, British and Americans alike, is to preserve that good will that now exists throughout the English-speaking world, and thus aid our armies in their grim and heavy task. . . .

'IN THE MEDITERRANEAN WE HAD 3 CRUISERS LEFT . . .'

Only after the surrender of the Italian fleet on September 11, 1943, did the British Admiralty make public the desperate state of the Allied naval situation in the Mediterranean in the winter of 1941–42. The continuing need, in view of Allied shipping problems, for increased food production in Great Britain, and the Government's forward-looking policy for agriculture, were the theme of an important address made to the Council of Agriculture on May 26 by the Minister of Agriculture.

Mr. A. V. Alexander, First Lord of the Admiralty, Broadcasts on September 16, 1943, a Review of the Naval War in the Mediterranean from the Outbreak of War to the Surrender of the Italian Fleet.

In September 1939 the British and French fleets together were so superior to the German that there was no fear of our losing command of the seas. . . . In June 1940 the position was changed almost overnight. The French fleet went out and the Italian came in. . . . Fortunately, we had in the Mediterranean a C.-in-C. of great spirit and resource. . . . "Because of our weakness," said Admiral Cunningham later, "our policy had to be one of aggressiveness, and it paid handsome dividends." . . . It was decided to attack the Italian forces in harbour at Taranto by aircraft of the Fleet Air Arm. On November 11, 1940, the 19 Swordfish planes which took part in that remarkable attack succeeded in crippling the Italian battle fleet for a considerable period. . . . This was followed by a series of disasters which threatened our whole position at sea. . . . The crisis in our fortunes was reached in November and December 1941. On November 14 H.M. aircraft-carrier "Ark Royal" was torpedoed and sunk; on the 20th the Australian cruiser "Sydney" was sunk; on the 24th the cruiser "Dunedin"; on the 25th the battleship "Barham." Then came the treacherous attack on Pearl Harbor . . . followed almost immediately by the sinking of H.M.S. "Prince of Wales" and "Repulse." . . . Fortunately, the enemy did not know completely our precarious position, and for vital months we managed to conceal from him the damage to the "Queen Elizabeth" and "Valiant" and the sinking of the "Barham."

In the Mediterranean we had three cruisers left, yet our men fought on, working wonders. Our greatest problem was Malta. . . . Supplies were falling and at times could be measured in weeks. . . . A small convoy got through in January, but an attempt to get another through in February had to be abandoned. In March Admiral Vian, in command of the 15th Cruiser Squadron, was sent to make another attempt. He met the Italian fleet and the Luftwaffe, and his battle with them is one of the most brilliant in our naval history. . . . One of the four supply ships was sunk ten miles south of Malta, and another, the "Breconshire," was hit when almost home. . . . The other two were bombed in harbour, but most of their cargo was saved.

In June Admiral Vian was again on the Malta run. . . . The convoy did not get through. . . . However, a convoy had been simultaneously passed from the Western Mediterranean, and in the face of incessant attacks by the enemy air forces some of the ships reached Malta. The next convoy to Malta was in August. . . . Five ships only reached Malta. But Malta was saved by the supplies in those ships, which lasted until the victory of El Alamein. . . .

Offensive action against Rommel's supply lines was carried on, mainly by H.M. submarines and aircraft of the Fleet Air Arm and R.A.F. . . . H.M. submarines sank a total of 1,335,000 tons. These results are remarkable because the Mediterranean is perhaps the most difficult area in the world for successful submarine operations; 41 of our submarines were lost. In addition, the Fleet Air Arm . . . accounted for another 410,000 tons. Perhaps the most spectacular action by surface ships was the elimination of an enemy convoy of ten merchant ships and two destroyers by the cruisers "Aurora" and "Penelope" with the destroyers "Lance" and "Lively."

The advance of the army from El Alamein and the landing of the Anglo-American expedition in North Africa completely revolutionized the situation. Malta was relieved and became

an advanced offensive base, and from November onwards our grip on the inland sea has been steadily tightening. No large-scale enemy evacuation from Tunisia was allowed; there was little interference with our expedition to Sicily, and by the capture of Sicily the Italian fleet was irrevocably divided, one part at Taranto and the other at Spezia. . . .

Mr. R. S. Hudson, Minister of Agriculture, Announces a Four-Year Plan for Agriculture, at Middlesex Guildhall on May 26, 1943.

Last autumn I asked for an additional 600,000 acres of wheat. That was a stiff demand. Well, it has been achieved, nay, more than achieved. I now confidently expect to get well over half as much again. Indeed, this year we shall have doubled our pre-war wheat acreage. Nor is that all. Our acreage under other grains—and all kinds of corn are now used for your bread—also shows a substantial increase. That is a great achievement. . . .

So much for the present. . . . You are also wondering about the future. . . .

I said that we were at present working on a Four-Year Plan for agriculture . . . which would take us up to the harvest of 1947. . . . You may well ask, "When are your demands on us going to cease or let up?" Quite frankly, I can't tell you. It's unsafe in this world to prophesy. If you insist, however, on a guess, I should say not before 1947 at the earliest. For even if victory in Europe comes before then the demands for food from our own soil will not abate. Ships will still be needed for other vital purposes. The Japs must still be beaten. The starving peoples of Europe must be fed.

Please remember that there are still over ten million acres of permanent grass in England and Wales. Not all of this, of course, is ploughable. But a large part of it can and should be ploughed in the next few years. . . . Much of our present arable has given of its utmost and borne two, or even three, white straw crops in succession. It needs a rest. But our present tillage area must not drop. We must still go on producing the maximum amount of crops for human and animal consumption. We must therefore adopt a policy of turning over more grassland for cropping while gradually reseeding to leys of varying duration our more exhausted plough land. Such a policy is really common sense if we are to preserve the fertility of our soil. It is in fact the gradual implementation of the ley farming policy which I believe must be the future basis of British agriculture over a large part of the country. I want to see every farm in every county with a plan worked out so that by 1947 every acre of land that can and should be ploughed on that particular farm shall have been turned over.

What will be the effect? The most important will be that we shall have millions of acres of land under leys of varying duration one–six years old. Those leys will be vastly more productive than the millions of acres of permanent grass that they will have displaced.

That leads us directly to the other half of our Four-Year Plan—namely, our livestock policy. We shall require a larger head of both cattle and sheep to consume the additional grass. It is my ambition to see also a very material improvement in the quality of those cattle and sheep. . . .

Given ordinary luck in the weather (a factor I can't control) and reasonable supplies of fertilizers (a factor I hope to be able to control), we ought to be able, year by year, to increase the yield from the existing arable and tillage area. Add to that the improvement in livestock and livestock products which I visualize and I predict that when 1947 comes the agriculture of this country will never before have been so healthy and efficient. . . .

Chapter 263

NAVAL OPERATIONS IN THE PACIFIC: 1943

Allied naval weakness had enabled Japan to gain rapid ascendancy in the Pacific in 1942 ; but America's mounting output of craft and of trained crews, and the release of British ships after the surrender of Italy, made possible during 1943 that process of steady 'island-hopping' which was an essential preliminary to attack on Japan herself. Earlier phases in the Pacific naval war are recorded in Chapter 241

THE year 1943 began in the Pacific with the Japanese positions still very strong, although somewhat weakened through attrition and shipping losses due to Allied submarines and aircraft—a weakening which not only made it difficult for the Japanese to keep their garrisons in the south-west supplied but also reduced the flow of loot from the occupied territories to Japan, to the disappointment of both the public and the productions departments.

The Allies' first care was to maintain this pressure on lines of communication, and in the meantime to collect strength for the advance on Japan from both north and south. In all Pacific operations, the Allies' greatest difficulty was the enormous distances over which a prepared enemy of great strength had to be approached. The Japanese had been helped over these same distances by years of preparation, fifth-columnists in every territory, the element of surprise, and the weakness and overconfidence of the Allies.

Both sides adopted the policy of diffusing their opponent's strength and attention by carrying out numerous

Nuisance Raids by all Arms

nuisance raids by all arms, strong enough to force the other side to take them seriously, on shipping and land positions in widely separated areas. By the beginning of 1943 the enemy was making little attempt to advance farther to the south or west ; he seemed rather to be bent on making the occupied territories as defensible as possible and putting their products to the greatest use.

The main policy of the Allies was to tie down the Japanese forces in New Guinea, New Britain, and the Solomons by strong forces on land, supported by air and sea power, and then to work northward through the most easterly of the islands, the Gilbert and Marshall groups, and thus to turn the flank of the strong Japanese bases at Truk in the Carolines, and in Guam and the Philippines—the second and third taken from the U.S. since Pearl Harbour.

In the far north the Japanese were tied down to the most westerly of the Aleutian Islands by constant attacks along the chain. Canadian-American pressure on Kiska and others of the islands was maintained steadily, sometimes to the tune of eight and ten raids a day, until the Japanese finally evacuated them in August, after which the Allies maintained complete secrecy about them. Repeated Allied air attacks were also made on the Kuriles, leading to Japan proper, particularly on the naval base at Paramushiro.

In the Indian Ocean the strategical aim of the Japanese was to keep the British occupied and so prevent their joining the Americans in any great strength, but their nuisance operations in this area were not carried out in sufficient strength fully to accomplish

LAST MINUTES OF A JAPANESE DESTROYER

This dramatic photograph of a Japanese destroyer was taken by an Allied bomber flying mast-high over the ship just before bombing and sinking it. The victim was one of the 22 vessels in the Japanese convoy totally lost in the significant Battle of the Bismarck Sea (see page 2602). The logs piled up on the port side of the deck were part of the expedition's invasion equipment.

AMERICANS LAND ON ATTU ISLAND IN THE ALEUTIANS

A Japanese landing on Attu, westernmost of the Aleutians, was reported in June 1942. They abandoned it a little later, but reoccupied it in November of the same year. American warships bombarded enemy positions there in February 1943, and in May several landings were made, that shown here being on the black volcanic beach of Massacre Bay. By the end of May all organized resistance had ceased. Kiska, 196 miles to the east, was also occupied by the Japanese in June 1942; its reoccupation by American and Canadian forces in August 1943 brought the whole Aleutian chain once more under Allied control.

Photo, Associated Press

their purpose. In July it was announced that there had been no Japanese submarines in the Mozambique Channel for three months—their main surface strength was devoted to protecting their own supply line in Burma, where their forces were kept supplied almost entirely by sea.

The strong Japanese positions and naval bases in eastern New Guinea, New Britain, New Ireland, and the Solomon Group, attack on which had already started, were the first concern of the Allies at the beginning of the year. The enemy continued his unsuccessful efforts to regain Guadalcanal; after some big troopships had been sunk by aircraft, destroyers and small craft made repeated attempts to work inshore and were generally driven off with little difficulty, although their activities imposed a great strain on Allied units. In heavy sea and air fighting which started at the end of January, when the Japanese were covering the withdrawal of their troops from Guadalcanal, they claimed four American battleships, numerous cruisers, and other vessels; the loss of the cruiser "Chicago," a destroyer, and of three motor torpedo-boats was admitted. Several Japanese destroyers were believed sunk: the German official wireless said they had lost four battle-

Allies Occupy Guadalcanal

ships. In February Guadalcanal was fully occupied by the Americans. The U.S. Navy Department stated that Japanese losses in the Solomons campaign had been at least 50,000 men, 797 aircraft, 57 ships sunk (including at least one battleship and many heavy cruisers), seven probably sunk, and 102 damaged.

The harbour base at Rabaul, greatly strengthened by the Japanese, was kept under air attack almost without intermission, and a large number of enemy supply ships and men-of-war were sunk or damaged—they had little space in which to manoeuvre against attack from the air. Seriously damaged ships had to be taken to Singapore or Truk for repairs.

The most important Pacific action of the year, the Battle of the Bismarck Sea, developed out of the sighting, on March 1 by Allied reconnaissance planes, of a big Japanese fleet bound from Rabaul to New Guinea. The weather was bad, and the enemy possibly had hoped it would cover his movements. Seven transports, with four destroyers and three cruisers, made up the convoy. Next day these ships, shadowed by Australian Catalinas, were joined by five more transports and three more destroyers. For some little time past, concentrations of Japanese shipping at Rabaul had been reported, with the result that General MacArthur, Supreme

Commander of the United Nations Forces in the South-West Pacific, had assembled a striking force of all available American and Australian aircraft in the area. On March 2, Fortresses and Liberators of this force began an intensive attack on the augmented convoy. It went on all day in face of heavy A.A. fire and decreasing opposition from Japanese fighters, nine at least of the ships being sunk that day. The rest of the convoy steamed on into the Huon Gulf where, on March 3, the attack was continued. Fortresses, Liberators, Havocs, Beaufighters, Mitchells, Lightnings, Kittyhawks, Bostons, and Hampdens flew in at mast-head height, dropping over 100 tons of bombs. Transport after transport went down, packed with men and material, together with more destroyers. Action still went on against the burning remnant of the Japanese fleet; not a ship reached Lae.

The Battle of the Bismarck Sea—a naval victory won by air power directed by an army general—was, said General MacArthur on March 4, "a victory of such completeness as to assume the proportions

Battle of the Bismarck Sea

of a major disaster for the enemy. . . . His naval component consisted of 22 vessels . . . representing a tonnage estimated at approximately 90,000 tons. They have all been sunk or are sinking." Out of 15,000 soldiers and sailors, only 97 survived. American losses were one bomber and three fighters. This battle was the greatest victory achieved up to that date in air-sea warfare, and the first in which aircraft had attained complete success against so large a convoy.

In surprise dawn attacks on April 2, 3, and 4, 26 Fortresses, without loss, sank or badly damaged seven enemy warships, including two cruisers, and five other vessels off Kavieng, New Ireland. On the 7th, an Allied force near Guadalcanal was attacked in its turn, one U.S. destroyer, one tanker, and one New Zealand corvette being sunk at a price of 39 Japanese planes. Seven U.S. planes were lost.

Another phase in the Pacific operations started on June 29 with further American landings in the Solomons.

Two Actions in Kula Gulf This led to two actions in the Kula Gulf, which lies between Kolombangara Island and New Georgia, when the Japanese were reinforcing New Georgia : a day action on July 6, in which the Americans claimed six destroyers sunk and other ships damaged, for the loss of the cruiser " Helena " ; and a night action in which British ships took part, on the 12th–13th, when a Japanese light

MUSICAL WELCOME FOR U.S. SUBMARINE 'WAHOO'

The 'Wahoo,' returning to Pearl Harbour after a Pacific patrol during which she brought the total of her sinkings to eight, entered port with a broom lashed to her periscope as a symbol that she had made a clean sweep. On December 2 the U.S. Navy Department announced that she was overdue and must be presumed lost with her complement of about 65.

Photo, Keystone

cruiser and three destroyers were sunk, two more destroyers believed sunk, the survivors in the water refusing to be rescued by the Allied ships. The U.S. destroyer " Gwin," torpedoed in the action, later foundered while in tow. As was so often the case in high speed actions in the Pacific, conditions made it impossible to assess the Japanese losses accurately.

On August 6, Japanese warships packed with troops to reinforce Vila, the main Japanese base on Kolombangara, were intercepted off that island. A cruiser caught fire, blew up and sank ; two destroyers were claimed, with another damaged and believed sunk. Tokyo admitted one, with another damaged, and claimed an American— a claim not admitted by the U.S. Early in September Allied ships were busy covering several new landings in New Guinea. On October 6 nine Japanese destroyers were caught evacuating troops from Vella Lavella in the Central Solomons ; three were reported sunk.

Allied Progress in the Solomons

These actions on their wing, and the Allies' steady progress in the Solomons, were a serious embarrassment to any preparations the Japanese were making for an invasion of Australia from the islands to the north of it. In June Prime Minister Curtin considered that the Commonwealth was safe from invasion, though not from raids ; and in August Tokyo admitted that there was no longer any chance of invading.

In many of these operations in the South-West Pacific the American,

SURVIVORS FROM THE FIRST BATTLE OF KULA GULF

The only American loss in the Battle of Kula Gulf, July 6, 1943, when 10 Japanese warships (four cruisers and six destroyers) were sunk or damaged while escorting supply ships to the enemy garrison on Kolombangara in the Solomons, was the U.S. cruiser ' Helena ' (9,700 tons). Here some of the 600 survivors picked up by destroyers out of Kula Gulf crowd to the rail as they arrive in port. Another 161 of her complement of about 800 who reached an enemy-held island in the New Georgia group were rescued by U.S. destroyers after they had been in hiding a week.

Photo, Keystone

ALLIED AIRCRAFT CARRIERS IN THE PACIFIC

British, American, and Australian ships and aircraft of all types co-operated in the Pacific war zones. Here are the British aircraft carrier H.M.S. 'Victorious,' from whose decks U.S. Navy fighters and torpedo-bombers operated during her service with the U.S. Pacific Fleet during 1943, and beyond her the U.S. aircraft carrier 'Saratoga,' lying side by side in harbour at Noumea, New Caledonia. They formed part of a task force under Rear-Admiral Dewitt C. Ramsey, U.S.N.

Photo, Keystone

British, Australian, and New Zealand Navies worked in the closest co-operation, whose effectiveness increased steadily with improved knowledge of one another's systems. Air co-operation was also most satisfactory, and combined operations with the armies were brought to a very fine pitch of efficiency. The U.S. Navy made greatly increased use of the motor torpedo-boats which were being turned out in large numbers and manned by enthusiastic young volunteers; they found a happy hunting ground in the waters adjacent to innumerable inlets and bays in the Solomons and claimed a number of victims among enemy warships and supply vessels.

Attacks in narrow waters on the supply fleet became so effective that many of the enemy's land positions had to be revictualled at night by submarines, many of which were successfully attacked. The U.S. submarine fleet—conspicuously the "Wahoo" until she was sunk, the "Guardfish" and the "Gudgeon"—took a very heavy toll of supply ships also, sinking them not only far afield, but in home waters as well—occasionally even in

sight of the Japanese coast. Matters were made worse by repeated air attacks on all the dockyards and repair bases in Japanese hands. By September it was estimated that nearly a quarter of the tonnage with which Japan started the war had been sunk, including a large proportion of her best ships. As the year progressed the Japanese themselves admitted that the shortage of shipping was becoming very serious. Native labour in the occupied territories was impressed to build large numbers of wooden vessels of native type, but fitted with Japanese diesel engines. These improvised ships were considered to have a better chance of getting through than large vessels, but the state of positions captured on shore by the Allies suggested that the enemy supply service was far from satisfactory. Allied successes against Japanese communications were not achieved without a price—and there was a steady succession of Washington announcements of lost named U.S. submarines.

Having made themselves tolerably secure in the south-west, leaving the Japanese positions in the extreme west to take care of themselves for the time being, but having sufficient land forces in New Guinea, New Britain, and the Solomons to prevent any effective new moves, the Allies began to work northward through the eastern groups of islands. The occupation of the Ellice group was announced in April. Task forces consisting of all types of ships, but including numerous aircraft carriers, both regular and auxiliary, were used; the naval opposition encountered consisted in the main of numerous Japanese destroyers and occasional light cruisers. The U.S. destroyers generally proved themselves superior to the Japanese:

Allies Begin to Work Northward

THEY HELPED TO NEUTRALIZE WAKE ISLAND

A U.S. task force made a very heavy attack on Wake Island in the Central Pacific. It was begun at dawn on October 5, 1943, by warships and carrier aircraft, continued later in the day by land-based Liberators (which had to fly many hundreds of miles to reach the island), and completed on October 6 by further bombing from a carrier force. The island 'was effectively neutralized for months,' according to the report published in Pearl Harbour. Here men aboard a cruiser are loading the heated guns during the initial bombardment.

Photo, Planet News

RECAPTURE OF THE GILBERT ISLANDS

Between November 20 and 25, 1943, the Americans recaptured the Gilbert Islands in the Central Pacific. On Makin, the most northerly, their casualties were 65 killed and 121 wounded; but at Betio Island in the Tarawa atoll, the U.S. Marine Corps fought its bloodiest battle to date: 1,026 were killed and 2,557 wounded in this action. 1. Transferring to hospital ship men wounded in Tarawa landings. 2. Assault troops about to go ashore at Makin; the first wave has already reached land. 3. Naval guns blast Tarawa: 2,000 tons of shells were hurled at Betio Island, where the enemy had built strong defences. 4. Landing craft streaming towards Betio Island: coral reefs stopped them 800 yards from land, and the Marines had to wade that distance under murderous fire.

NIGHT ACTION OFF VELLA LAVELLA

An Allied warship, her engines damaged, hurls A.A. shells at Japanese bombers during the success-ful surprise American landing at Vella Lavella, northernmost island of the New Georgia group, on August 15, 1943. The Americans lost 12 men as the result of five enemy air raids during the operation; they took 350 Japanese prisoners. The capture of Vella Lavella made the reinforcement of the Japanese base at Vila on Kolombangara a very difficult problem for the enemy.

Photo, " New York Times " Photos

they were not only better sea boats and gun platforms, but their special short 5-inch gun proved ideal for high-speed actions. The standard of Japanese torpedo work was high.

In this way the tedious but necessary task of " island-hopping " proceeded steadily. The Japanese had spread their forces too widely to make an effective defence against attacks in any strength except at a few strong points. Many places attacked offered little or no resistance following a pre-liminary naval bombardment; in others the garrison fought desperately to the last man. Carrier-borne planes bombed Japanese positions in the Mariana Islands and Carolines, making the position of the base at Truk uncom-fortable. In May a submarine surfaced off Hokkaido, more northerly of the two large islands of Japan proper, and shelled the coast. In July carrier-borne planes attacked Aru on Ant Island (in the Carolines) and Wake Island in the Central Pacific. Wake Island was also bombarded in October by a strong squadron of U.S. surface ships.

On November 25, Chinese and American bombers, operating from China, attacked the Shinshiku air base on Formosa; while on November 1 a new American landing was made at Bougainville under powerful naval cover, the attack being preceded by an air bombardment of Rabaul which put the Japanese 8th Cruiser Squadron out of action. Ships were hurried south from Truk to replace it. Four cruisers and six destroyers put out from Rabaul, but made off; returning in the early morning with two more destroyers, they were intercepted 40 miles from the landing place and a cruiser and four destroyers were sunk. U.S. warships also beat off a daylight attack by 67 dive-bombers, shooting down 17 of them. The Japanese at first claimed to have sunk four American battle-ships, at least eight cruisers, and three destroyers. Then they added two more cruisers and another destroyer, with a battleship and an aircraft carrier dam-aged, and finally a large and two medium carriers, three cruisers, and another large warship. The Americans admitted the loss of two destroyers and another converted into a transport.

On November 20 bridge-heads were established in the Gilbert Islands in the Central Pacific, 1,000 miles north-east of the Solomons; the auxiliary aircraft carrier "Liscombe Bay," sunk by submarine attack on the 24th, was the only American ship lost in connexion with these landings. At the end of November, and for a large part of December, the Japanese made frantic attempts to get stores and reinforce-ments to their garrisons, generally by destroyers or under destroyer escort, but Allied light surface craft and air-craft intercepted many of these in the various channels, successfully adapting the Japanese tactics of earlier days.

On Boxing Day the Americans made a new landing at Cape Gloucester, New Britain, in the course of which one of their destroyers was sunk and one coastal transport damaged. While these extended operations were in progress, Rabaul continued to be sub-jected to incessant air raids, which did great damage, very much reducing its value to the Japanese Navy. In a spirited destroyer action off Rabaul on November 25, four Japanese ships were sunk and one damaged with no American loss. Early in December a successful attack by carrier task forces was made on two of the Marshall Islands, 500 miles north of the Gilbert group; and in the middle of the month Wash-ington reported that a task force had " trailed its coat " outside Truk, which lies 800 miles north of Rabaul, but had failed to tempt the Japanese out.

Allied Attack on the Gilberts

U.S. MARINES GO OVER THE SIDE TO LAND ON BOUGAINVILLE

On November 1, 1943, units of the U.S. Marine Corps, in a combined land-sea-air operation, made successful landings at Empress Augusta Bay, on Bougainville, the most northerly of the Solomon Islands. They met little ground opposition, and Japanese aircraft sent from Rabaul were driven off by Allied fighters. Here Marines are climbing down to a landing barge from the Coastguard-manned combat transport which brought them. Coastguardsmen also manned many of the craft which carried out landing operations in the Gilbert Islands (see page 2605). *Photo, U.S. Official*

FIRST ARMY INFANTRY MOVING UP UNDER FIRE NEAR BOU ARADA

In an effort to ease their position in Pont du Fahs, northern Tunisia, the Germans attempted in January 1943 to seize two hills on the edge of the plain that lay before it, 'Two Tree Hill' and the hill of Bou Arada. They captured 'Two Tree Hill' and advanced towards Bou Arada, but were held and eventually beaten back. Eighteen of their tanks were destroyed by Allied 25-pounders concealed in a wood and covering the plain over which the enemy had to move. British troops are here seen moving up under shell-fire during the operations on January 18 which prevented the capture of Bou Arada.

Photo. British Official : Crown Copyright

BREN-GUN CARRIERS OF THE GRENADIERS IN A TUNISIAN WADI

When the Germans followed up the Allied retreat through the Kasserine Pass in February 1943, the main Axis force—including heavy armour of the 10th Panzer Division—thrust to the outskirts of Thala, where it came into contact with 'Nicforce' (see page 2620). In the course of a fierce two days' battle the enemy was driven back towards the Kasserine Pass where, in the expectation that his armour would make a stand, two companies of Grenadiers took Bren-gun carriers (some of which are seen here coming down the stony bed of a dry rivulet or wadi) 10 miles across mountainous country in 5¾ hours—only to find the enemy in full retreat through the Pass under a rain of bombs from Allied aircraft.

Photo, British Official

To cover this discouraging train of events, Tokyo reported exaggerated Allied losses at sea—in October the Japanese navy was said to have sunk 25 Allied battleships, 15 aircraft carriers, 105 cruisers, and 114 destroyers, while two months later Tokyo claimed the sinking of the U.S. battleship " Wisconsin " in the Pacific within 48 hours of her launch at Philadelphia ! On the other hand, on December 13 Premier Tojo admitted that " It cannot be said that the Japanese Navy has the war situation under complete control."

More British Warships in the Far East

The surrender of Italy in September released a number of British warships for service farther east. H.M. aircraft carrier " Victorious " had served with the U.S. task forces in the Pacific for some time ; she and battleships which had been in European waters since the beginning of hostilities joined the Eastern Fleet. This constituted a serious threat to the Japanese Western wing and led to increased Japanese activity in the Indian Ocean. Carrier-borne planes raided the Indian and Ceylon coasts, and machines from Burma raided Chittagong and other ports in Bengal; while enemy submarines were spasmodically more active all over the Indian Ocean, achieving

some success and diverting Allied naval strength that could have been usefully employed elsewhere. But, despite enemy stories of operations by surface raiders in the same areas, there was no serious attempt to interfere with the control of the Indian Ocean by the British and Royal Indian Navies.

As the year progressed it became evident that the Japanese regarded the Pacific war as being separate from Germany's struggle in Europe. Badly needed supplies of rubber, tin, etc., were shipped to Europe in German blockade runners which had been sheltering in Japanese ports since 1939 ; many of them were intercepted and scuttled themselves to avoid capture. Liaison officers were sent to Bordeaux in a Japanese submarine and landed in very bad shape. But Tokyo made a special broadcast to the German people, telling them bluntly that they had their hands much too full to send any help to Europe ; and neither country hesitated to arrest and sentence the other's nationals for espionage.

On the technical side, the year in the Pacific was notable for the employment of a variety of landing craft carefully evolved for the varying conditions of different operations. The Allied landings in the Pacific (and in North Africa, Sicily, and Italy, too) were, in fact, largely made possible by the production of special types of landing craft, tank lighters, and similar vessels, such as the Higgins landing boats. Aircraft carriers, specially designed both for work with the fast task forces and for less exacting operations, also played a conspicuous part in Allied strategy. The enemy had made great use of converted carriers in his big southward sweep, but he appeared to find them too vulnerable once Allied sea and air power began to grow, and little was heard of these vessels in 1943. Certain corvettes and other small craft were specially adapted for work in the immense distances of the Pacific ; and the vulnerability in that ocean of ships of the cruiser type presented the naval designer with a number of problems to be solved.

RETURN FROM A BOMBING MISSION TO RABAUL

A Hamilton dive-bomber comes in to the U.S. aircraft carrier ' Saratoga ' after dropping its bombs on Rabaul, the Japanese-held port in New Britain, during a heavy raid by an American task force on November 5, 1943. Nineteen Japanese warships, including five heavy cruisers, had recently docked there. All the heavy cruisers were hit—one was seen to blow up—as well as two light cruisers. Twenty-four Japanese fighters were shot down, with 22 probables, for the loss of eight Allied aircraft. *Photo, U.S. Official*

ROYAL WEST KENTS IN TUNISIAN HILL-FIGHTING

The Queen's Own Royal West Kent Regiment arrived in Sfiana in January 1943 and at once moved eastward beyond Robaa (see map, p. 261?) to relieve a hard-pressed French unit on Djebel Bargou. After the enemy had been given a severe shelling by Allied 25-pounders (one of which is here seen in action), the West Kents pursued him in retreat until on January 29 they lost contact. The positions they regained were handed over to another French unit. Right, a wounded American being brought in ; he was out on patrol six miles ahead of the Royal West Kents' position when he was hit, once in the arm and three times in the stomach. He lay out in lonely country for three days before he was found by Moroccan troops, who carried him in in their blankets.

Chapter 264

ANGLO-AMERICAN OPERATIONS IN TUNISIA
DECEMBER 1942—FEBRUARY 1943

*Here, Mr. A. D. Divine continues from Chapter 256 his first-hand account
of the fighting in French North Africa, carrying the story of the campaign
in northern Tunisia up to the Battle for the Kasserine Pass at the end of
February 1943. Concurrent operations by the Eighth Army in southern
Tunisia after the fall of Tripoli are described in Chapter 265*

THE second portion of the Tunisian campaign divides itself naturally into three phases. The first was a phase of reorganization with, as its object, another thrust for Tunis. When that died stillborn under the dual influence of Longstop Ridge and the mud of the Tunisian winter, a second phase of consolidation began. It was apparent now to all concerned that the Germans had won, at least temporarily, the race for reinforcements. There was no hope of an easy thrust through to the twin seaports of the north, Tunis and Bizerta, and it was clear from the rate at which fresh reinforcement was coming in that the battle would be a long one and a hard. During this second phase, then, the Allies concentrated on securing the line that ran from the north by " Bald Hill " and " Green Hill " through the Djebels to the north of Medjez-el-Bab, across the Goubellat Plain and by Bou Arada down the long spine of the dorsale to Gafsa and the desert. That phase of consolidation may be said to have ended with the series of three defensive offensives initiated by the Germans, the culminating attack of which was that delivered in the Ousseltia valley against the French.

The third period was one of preparation and experiment, preparation for an attempt at a thrust through to the coast

**Preparation
and
Experiment**

in the extreme south of the fighting area— a thrust, that is, to Sfax or Gabes. It ended in the last of the great German offensive defensives—the Battle of Kasserine.

There was talk in England—even in Algiers during long stretches of this period—of static warfare. It was never static. There were points that remained stationary—fixed headlands in the coast of war—but over the rest of the line it was a coast subject to the flux and reflux of the tides of battle. It was a type of war that demanded enormous and fluid movements, marches that flung armoured brigades over a hundred miles of territory in a night to reinforce threatened points of the thinly held line of 250 miles. It is not even perhaps right to call it a line. It

was a series of points : garrisons on passes that commanded roads, on isolated hills that commanded plains, at salient points on rocky mountain ridges—a sort of defence in fluidity.

And it was conditioned throughout the whole of the northern section— inevitably the most important, because of its proximity to Tunis—by the atrocious mud of the Tunisian winter. The first lesson in the Tunisian mud was learnt by American Combat Command " B " in the battle for Medjez which closed the initial stage of the Tunisian operations. The Allied forces continued to learn that lesson at intervals for many months. Tunisia, contrary to the general belief as to North Africa, has in winter a wet and unpleasant climate. There is black cotton soil in the valleys and clay on the hillsides.

Save for three main lines of road, the communications are abominable, and under the influence of the winter rain

they failed at once to stand up to the necessities of tank and armoured car, of heavy lorry and of gun. And, with the roads, the air strips on which our strength depended failed. As far back as Oran the great aerodrome of Tafaroui was a vast and shallow sea of mud. At Algiers Maison Blanche, long-prepared, long-utilized by the French, became a horror of broken asphalt with mud pools oozing up through the cracks. In the forward areas Bône and Souk-el-Arba, the mainstays of our air position as far as the fighting line was concerned, were places of sheer nightmare. In considering the first two phases of this period, it is imperative always to bear this in mind.

During the reorganization phase of the second part of the Tunisian campaign, the losses in the first thrust (*see* Chapter 256) were made good. The brigade which had attacked through Medjez-el-Bab was partially rested,

GENERAL ALEXANDER DRIVES A JEEP
General Sir Harold Alexander, whose appointment as C.-in-C. Middle East was announced on August 18, 1942, became deputy to General Eisenhower in February 1943, in accordance with arrangements made at Casablanca. General Alexander is seen here arriving at an advanced brigade headquarters only four miles from the Tunisian front line. *Photo, British Official*

partially made up with fresh troops. Combat Command "B" was pulled clear out of the fighting area to the plain of Souk-el-Khemis, and there awaited new material. Into its place went part of the American 1st Infantry Division under General Terry Allen, including the two Combat Teams which had attacked at Oran from the east; and to replace Blade Force came the 6th Armoured Division, to strengthen Lieut.-General K. A. N. Anderson's infantry came the Guards Brigade and the Irish Brigade. Ancillary units of various kinds were brought into the fighting area. The force became a formidable one. To it, as the American material came up, was added the first American armour that could be spared.

By the middle of December 1942 plans were complete for the new attack. It was designed much on the lines of the old one—to follow a pattern conditioned by the fact that there were two dependable roads springing out of Medjez to the port of Tunis.

But there was a preliminary obstacle which had to be overcome. Immediately north of Medjez-el-Bab, above the

Battle of Longstop Ridge farm that had been the headquarters of Combat Command "B" in the first fight, was a ridge that was called by the natives Djebel Ahmera. When we fell down the road from Tebourba it was one of many "Djebels." We had not strength enough nor men enough to hold them all. When

BATTLE OF LONGSTOP RIDGE

Djebel Ahmera—christened by the British, Longstop Ridge—was the strategic key to the roads leading to Tunis. The story of the attempt of a battalion of the Guards to dislodge the Germans from it in December 1942 is given in this page. Right, mortar-carriers go into action on the heather-clad slopes of Longstop. Below, Guards attack Longstop at dusk.

Photos, British Official : Crown Copyright

the Germans fell back from their main attack on Medjez they left a garrison upon it. It was a ridge jutting out from the main massif of the Djebel el Ang and the Djebel Lanserine, in itself hardly more prominent, in no way more remarkable, than any of a score of the tortured hills that rose along that road. But close examination of it showed that it was the last high hill on the way to Tunis except the companion mound of the Djebel Bou Aoukaz, opposite on the Tunis side of the river valley. Its military value for that reason was obvious and enormous.

The summit of Longstop Ridge, as our men christened it immediately, was the strategic key to the roads which led to Tunis. From that summit it was possible to observe and indeed to maintain a degree of artillery control over the main road from Beja to Medjez-el-Bab. It was equally possible to observe and direct artillery fire over the road which led from Medjez-el-Bab to Tunis,

and the subsidiary road which led south-east to Goubellat. The Medjerda road, which led through Tebourba to Tunis, ran close beneath it. No move could be made save at night on any of those roads without direct and easy observation : no move could be made in Medjez town. The bridge over the Medjerda was in the range of the guns that stood along the ridge, and they plastered impartially traffic movements whether of tanks or trucks, men or material.

It was clear that before we could hope to make a successful attack along the roads the strong-point would have to be eliminated. A battalion of the Guards was detailed to throw the Germans off the hill on the night of December 22–23. The weather was good : it had been dry for some days, the night was clear and the moon was only a few days past full. Early in the first darkness the Guards began their assault. We had learnt primary lessons in the art of hill warfare on the northern road at

"Bald Hill." We had picked up secondary ones during the Tebourba fighting. But Longstop Ridge was to give us a new conception of "Djebel" warfare.

The attack went admirably at the start, but shortly it became obvious that the position was not the simple one that it had appeared from the distance. Folds of the ground too insignificant to be marked on contour maps or to be picked out through field glasses gave the Germans one defensive position after another. The Germans had well-sited machine-guns covering these re-entrants. The Guards lost considerably on the way. They had to fall back at one point and reorganize themselves for a second attack before they reached what appeared to be the last summit, but with great gallantry they made the last rise, established themselves in the half-light, and waited. Their task had been to seize the hill, and the position was then to be taken over by an American battalion.

The Americans came in and the Guards went down, but unfortunately the summit that had been occupied was not the final summit. There was very little difference—so little that it was impossible to see in the treacherous moonlight—but there was a higher level, and from it, when the Americans were consolidating, the Germans poured heavy machine-gun fire. The Guards, who had arrived back at their own positions by this time, had to turn round and march back again. Meanwhile, the Germans were bringing up reinforcements and a serious counter-attack developed.

But there was something more important than the counter-attack. On

made fresh attacks—five of them altogether in 48 hours—and, with the help of the Americans and the Tirailleurs Algériens, they clawed in and hung on throughout Christmas Day. But on the 26th they were forced to fall back on Medjez-el-Bab again.

The second thrust for Tunis was abandoned. It might be that if the weather had held we should have thrust more force into the attack on Longstop Ridge, but with the roads difficult and the open ground impassable, any hope of the 6th Armoured Division breaking through to Tunis had now to be given up. We had to wait upon dry ground, and it was a long time coming. The first phase of the new period was over.

During the consolidation phase, as troops became available, the Allies were able to make their long-drawn line almost tangible. For practical purposes at the end of the initial dash for Tunis (described in Chapter 256) there had been three occupied areas in Tunisia :

the hill complex in the north with Medjez as its heart ; the area of the dorsale about Pichon, which lies in one of the gaps, and which was occupied in somewhat doubtful strength by the pathetically ill-equipped French troops ; and Gafsa on the edge of the desert, which was occupied by a mixed force of French, American parachutists, and American Tank Destroyers.

Now, as new men and new material came up, fresh points were occupied, fresh areas developed. A link-up of the line took place in theory if not in actual fact. The British held the sector from Cap Serrat through the Djebels to the Medjerda **Disposition of Allied Forces** by Medjez and out across the Goubellat Plain to the hills above Pont du Fahs. The French held the area south of the Robaa road (which leads to Pont du Fahs) and along the great ridge of the dorsale past Ousseltia and Pichon to the road from Sbeitla to Kairouan. South of that area came American-held territory. These are not hard and fast divisions. There were French both in back areas and in the front line in the north as in the south. There were Americans in all three sectors. And the Derbyshire Yeomanry, in some sort of military parallel of the loaves and fishes, appeared to stretch their thin force over the whole of the 250 miles of the front. Wherever

ACTION NEAR BOU ARADA

An intended British attack on German positions in hills in the Bou Arada-Goubellat area (seen in the background of the photograph, left) was forestalled by a German attack on January 17, 1943, which continued through the 18th. But a number of 25-pounders which had been moved up preparatory to the intended British advance knocked out 18 German tanks (these among them) at 1,800 yards. Below, a Vickers' machine-gun post on 'Two Tree Hill ' (see map p. 2617) : the Germans captured this hill, but failed to take Bou Arada.

the morning of Christmas Eve it rained —the heavy, indignant Tunisian rain. As the Guards went back to stem the German threat, the main purpose of their attack was dissolving behind them as the red clay mired the roads. With tremendous *élan* they went through and re-established themselves on what appeared to be the summit at four o'clock on the afternoon of Christmas Eve. But once more there was a higher ridge beyond, and once more the batteries of heavy machine-guns drove them out. That night, and again early in the darkness of Christmas morning, they

KEEPING A WATCH ON ENEMY PATROL MOVEMENTS
This French machine-gunner in a lonely hill outpost of the Allied line in Tunisia is watching the movements of a German patrol after a bombardment of enemy positions by Allied mortars. Bomb holes can be seen in the low-lying country ahead of the post.

Photo, Planet News

road to Bizerta, was held chiefly by the Barenthin Regiment, under Broich, with a tank force and ancillary troops. In the centre was the Kampf Gruppe Tunis, under Lederle, which consisted of the best of the German Infantry plus the 10th Panzer Division. The southern section was Italian, consisting of the Piedmontese Division (the 10th Bersaglieri and the 1st and 92nd Italian Infantry) with the 131st Armoured Division. The whole was under the tactical command of General Walter Nehring, who had been in command of the armour of Rommel's Afrika Korps.

The first active move of this period, apart from the establishment of the line, was an Allied attack on the "Green Hill"-"Bald Hill" area. On January 5, 1943, it got under way. It was made with a mixed force consisting of a parachute battalion, a commando and two infantry battalions, and massed artillery preparation was used for the first time. About 50 guns carried out a heavy obliteration attack on the summit of "Green Hill." They ranged from 25-pounders to American 155-mm. and British heavies. The attack succeeded and failed. The parachutists and the Buffs got to the top of "Green Hill" and could not consolidate. It was impossible to keep them supplied with ammunition and stores on that deplorable summit under the fire of the German heavy machine-guns. We fell off "Green Hill" and returned to the *status quo*.

The next area of activity was at the junction of the French and the British sectors near Pont du Fahs. The Germans held that town, but they were not comfortable in it. Comfort could be assured by the seizure of two hills at the edge of the broad plain that led to it—"Two Tree Hill," and the hill of Bou Arada. About a week after the "Green Hill" action the Germans pushed across the plain. It was drier there than in the main hills; tanks could be used to support the infantry, and a bitter but small-scale action developed along the ridges. The Germans captured "Two Tree Hill," but they failed in the attempt on Bou Arada and the Allies prepared a limited offensive to drive them back across the plain whence they had come.

That offensive was forestalled. There were numerous—too numerous—occasions on which the Germans forestalled Allied thrusts. The Allied attack was fixed for the morning of January 18. As usual, the Derbyshire Yeomanry were deputed to open the ball. An armoured car of theirs ran into a German motor

the Germans were about to attack, wherever the Allies were about to probe, there seemed somehow to be a little screen of this superb steel cavalry in the critical eye of no man's land.

But gradually the Intelligence maps became intelligible, and gradually the Allies acquired knowledge of the German forces against them. Major-General Juergen von Arnim was now in command. To supplement his Barenthin Regiment and his parachutists he had the Hermann Goering Division, and for his spearhead

in attack he had now the whole of the 10th Panzer Division and the Potsdam Grenadiers. (The 10th Panzers had been the spearhead of the force that broke Gen. Corap on the Meuse: *see* Chapter 145.) He had a new mountain division as well, and a strong force of Italians.

This force was mainly disposed in three sectors which, however, did not quite coincide with those of the Allies. The first in the extreme north, which occupied itself principally with the coast cyclist, shot him, went on, and discovered that he was the scout for a force of a dozen tanks. The armoured car just managed to get clear and give the warning. The Germans attacked at three points on the front of about 25 miles. Thirty tanks attempted to cross the Bou Arada–Goubellat road, another 30 headed straight for Bou Arada itself, and German and Italian infantry plus Italian tanks attacked the French on the hills of the Robaa valley. Unfortunately for the enemy, the Allies had gathered together considerable strength in artillery to cover their attack and, under the massed guns, the German thrust broke: they lost more than half the tanks of the Bou Arada attack and failed to cross the Goubellat road.

On the 19th they attacked in the next valley to the south, the valley of Ousseltia. Through Ousseltia runs the road to Kairouan, the Holy City of the plains. It was an im-

Attack on French Positions

portant, possibly even a vital, gap in the line of the dorsale. And it was held, and the valley behind it also, lightly by French, Foreign Legion, Goum and other troops. The attack there was mainly a demonstration. It was cleverly done, and it was designed to deceive the French authorities and General Alphonse Juin. It is probable that its success depended entirely on the success of the attack to the north; but the French, with their outposts pushed back and a thrust apparently developing up the valley, assumed that this was the point of the major break. It was necessary to reinforce them at once.

Combat Command "B," which had by this time been rehabilitated, had moved south to Sbeitla in the near-desert country. In the early evening the Command was put on the alert and by nine o'clock it had begun a march first over the broad road towards Le Kef and then over excruciating roads through Maktar to the Ousseltia valley. When Combat Command "B" reached the valley there was no serious enemy to fight. The German tank force was small but energetic, endeavouring apparently, according to plan, to indicate that it was much larger. When Combat Command "B" attacked, it withdrew. The Americans swept up the valley practically without loss, and American infantry from another force, turning right-handed along the Kairouan road, wiped the rearguard out of the pass. The rearguard was Italian.

The period might be said to have terminated finally in the lengthy fighting which went on about this mountain corner, and ended with some advantage

SCENE OF THE TUNISIAN CAMPAIGN

The difficulty of the country is clearly indicated in this relief map of northern and central Tunisia, over which much of the Tunisian campaign was fought. Here are shown the relative positions of the strategic key points around which were waged the final stages in the Allies' successful struggle to throw Axis forces out of North Africa. Principal roads are marked by white lines, and railways by black.

Specially drawn for THE SECOND GREAT WAR *by Félix Gardon*

to the Germans in the capture of the Djebel Mansour in the head of the Robaa valley. It was something, but it was not enough. The Germans had hoped in this fighting to consolidate in their turn the corner of mountain peaks to which they would obviously eventually have to retire. It was only a partial consolidation.

But there was one more move of some significance. At the beginning of February, the 6th Armoured Division made a tank sweep of the Goubellat Plain with the object of testing the German defences and at the same time testing the quality of the ground. There had been no rain for five days, but at the end of the sweep two tanks were bogged in no man's land on ground that to the ordinary eye looked perfect. The last hope of tank operations before the rains ended vanished with that sweep.

The third phase covered the attempt on Sfax and Gabes. The policy of this

CHURCHILL TANKS IN ACTION IN TUNISIA

Coldstream and Grenadier Guards repulsed a strong German tank and infantry attack near Sbiba on February 19, 1943. Following this success, a unit of the 6th Armoured Division went in with its Churchill tanks. After very heavy fighting the German thrusts towards Thala and Tebessa were halted at all points. Above, a few hundred yards behind the Guards' positions, crews of the Churchills give their weapons a final check as zero hour approaches. Below, the Churchills carry forward men of a Field Coy. of the R.E., whose job it was to lift enemy mines and clear a way for the armour. (See also illus., page 2549.) *Photos, British Official: Crown Copyright*

Whether that would have been possible can scarcely be decided now. There is, however, small question that the Allies could have reached it in the early days had they attacked as soon as force became available. The objection to carrying this attack out in insufficient strength was that a small force might be left suspended between two millstones—the retreating Rommel on the south and Von Arnim on the north. It was finally decided, therefore, that the Allies would gather strength at Tebessa, and would not move forward until dumps of ammunition, food and other supplies had been prepared in the neighbourhood of the ancient city sufficient to maintain a force strong enough to overcome the objections.

When Combat Command "B" was recalled from Sbeitla a move had been planned which had for its main object the seizure of country ahead of the Faïd Pass. This move was cancelled. Instead, a strong combat force was assembled in the magnificent Bou Chebka pine-woods in the hills beyond Tebessa, and in conjunction with a second force, which had been assembled in Sbeitla and about Sidi-bou-Sid, moved in to the attack.

Allied Thrust towards Sfax

The object of this attack was in a measure nebulous. If it overran the opposition, it was to thrust clean through in an attempt to reach Sfax. Its course was then to be determined largely by the reaction of the enemy.

The move was made from Bou Chebka on the night of Saturday, January 30. Down the superb road

was decided at a meeting between Lieut.-General Anderson, General Alfrey, Brigadier Eveleigh and the American commanders. General Oliver was in favour of a swift thrust before the German's increasing strength could make it possible to defend the wide areas of this southern plain. The obvious strategic objective was the narrow bottle-neck between the great Chott Djerid and the sea, a little to the north of Gabes. The salt lake of Djerid is an enormous basin which thrusts out a narrow arm of shallow water almost to the coastline. Even where the shallows cease there is marshland. While the Chott itself was not an absolutely impassable barrier (there were roads and tracks across it at various points after dry weather), it was an important obstacle, and for a variety of reasons it could have been made sufficient to stop the junction of Rommel and Von Arnim provided the Allies held and could maintain the bottle-neck in strength.

through Thelepte to Gafsa the whole Command moved at high speed. Long before dawn it was beyond Gafsa, nearly 80 miles away, and by dawn the sweep up the valley towards Maknassy began. It was checked at Station Sened in a brisk two-day battle in which casualties on either side were moderate, but in which green American troops suffered heavily from the air. Station Sened was carried and the line pushed beyond it to the ridge which commanded Maknassy town.

The Germans had been present in greater strength than Intelligence had anticipated, but in the northern sector, the section of the Faïd Pass, their

German Strength at Faïd Pass

strength was greater still. The attack from that end failed to develop. It was held on the edge of the Pass, and the southern arm of what was to have been a pincer movement was left in the air. The Americans had to withdraw from Station Sened with little to show for a well-executed operation but a few hundred prisoners and the destruction of a store of German and Italian material.

It was clear that the time for an easy slash across the hamstrings of the German body was past. The period of building up began afresh at an increased pace. The whole of the American 1st Armoured Division was now moved into the area with infantry and ancillary troops to match. The dumps at Tebessa covered square

PACK ANIMALS OF THE FIRST ARMY
In the difficult country of French North Africa, the First Army was glad to call to its aid for transport those old friends of armies on the march, the horse and the mule. Here is a string of pack animals loaded with supplies for Allied troops, moving through the hills of Tunisia in January 1943.
Photo, British Official: Crown Copyright

miles of ground and the Germans allowed them to accumulate unmolested. Allied air power was rapidly achieving something more than parity. This southern area was out of the winter rainfall zone, and there were good aerodromes around Tebessa and at Thelepte and Feriana.

For a while there was quiet—suspicious quiet. Rommel was falling rapidly back to the Tunisian frontier, and it was clear that the quiet could not long continue. If the Allies were ever to achieve the Gabes gap, the hour was very nearly upon them. In the north quiet was still enforced by the rains. There was fighting—some of it bitter —but though the lines moved from one grove to another here, though they surged back between valley and valley there, there was no major movement. Only in the south

was the earth dry enough for battle— and in the south it came.

Again the Allies were forestalled— neatly, dangerously. The American 1st Armoured Division had moved through Tebessa and Bou Chebka down the road to Sbeitla, and was established in the ancient Roman town. Their line was held by the American Combat Command " A."

Combat Command 'A' in Action

In reserve was Combat Command " C." Combat Command " B " was still at Maktar, standing by against another possible German incursion in the Ousseltia valley. The rest of the reserve and headquarters lay behind Sbeitla. At midnight on Saturday, February 13, the Command was put on the alert, warned of a possible attack at dawn. But dawn was quiet. Not until an hour or so after first light did the Germans show their hand, but after that hour they acted with amazing speed and vigour. They swept through the Faïd Pass, isolating the forward Allied infantry. They swept up other roads about the Lessouda Mountain on which was a mixed force guarding the left flank of Combat Command " A," and they threatened the little white town of Sidi-bou-Sid itself. The Allies were forced to abandon the town and withdrew by the one road which still lay open. And on that road they were challenged by a fresh German tank force coming up from the direction of Station Sened. Fighting an action on parallel courses that had much of the elements of naval warfare,

AXIS COMMANDER-IN-CHIEF IN TUNISIA
Generaloberst Juergen Baron Sixt von Arnim, one of Germany's foremost specialists in building defences against tanks, was appointed to succeed General Nehring as commander-in-chief of Axis troops in Tunisia in January 1943. This was the first photograph of him to reach England ; it shows him shaking hands with a German shock troop leader. He was captured on May 12 and reached England shortly afterwards as a prisoner.
Photo, Associated Press

ALLIED AND ENEMY HEAVY ARMOUR

One of the reasons for the apparent slow progress of the Tunisian campaign was the mud produced by the winter rains, which made movement of tanks impossible; but in February, in the battle for the Kasserine Pass, they were able to play their part. Above, Shermans moving up in the advance on Kasserine. Below, German 62-ton 'Tiger' (Mark VI) tank—one of 70 tanks which supported a heavy attack towards Thala on February 21, 1943. Armed with an 88-mm. gun and two 7.82-mm. machine-guns, the 'Tiger,' though no larger, was nearly twice as heavy as the Mark IV (see illus., page 2236), owing to the great thickness of its armour (7–8 inches).

Photos, British Official : Crown Copyright

25-pounders and the 5th/16th Lancers. The main force, meanwhile, had broken through the narrow Kasserine Pass, and again it split. The going had been too easy. As before when opposition had been slight, the Germans decided to seek more than the first plan had allowed for. Once more they split, trying with a force adequate for one task to break through both to Tebessa, and also up behind the British First Army to Le Kef, and perhaps the valley of the Kroumerie.

The force which attacked towards Tebessa was the weaker. It was met again by Combat Command "B" and American infantry, and defeated. The main attack went up the broad Thala valley. It was met there by the defiantly named "Vicforce," a scratch handful consisting of a battalion of infantry, the 17th/21st Lancers, the Lothian and Border Horse, and sixteen 25-pounder guns. The Lothian and Border Horse fought a superb delaying action while the rest of Vicforce dug itself in.

the remnants of Combat Command "A" reached the main Sbeitla valley.

On Sunday, the 14th, the Germans contented themselves with consolidating their gains, and on Monday, the 15th, Combat Command "C" was thrust in in an attempt to restore the position, to free the men on the Lessouda Mountain and to free the infantry still holding out on the hills above the Pass itself. Combat Command "C" flung its whole tank force, following it up with soft-shelled vehicles, across the wadi-seamed plain towards Sidi-bou-Sid. They were new to warfare, and particularly to the ingenious warfare of the German. They neglected reconnaissance on their flanks and walked into a tank trap set with absolute genius. The whole of their tank force was lost in the space of an hour, and only the last-minute turning of the German counter-attack from the right flank saved the remnants of their soft-shelled vehicles.

Americans Walk into Tank Trap

Two Combat Commands were out of action, and the situation was critical in the extreme. Meanwhile Combat Command "B," the veterans of the American fighters, had been called down from Maktar. They bivouacked outside Sbeitla, and were given a position to hold on the low hills where attack was anticipated.

On the Tuesday General Ward began to withdraw his base elements from the olive groves on the enemy side of Sbeitla. By Tuesday night the German attack had swept up to the edge of those groves. All through that night

the 1st Armoured Division withdrew along the road to Kasserine and through the Kasserine Pass. Gafsa had been abandoned in conformity. The Allies were in process of giving up their forward aerodromes at Thelepte and Feriana. The whole force was swinging back into the Tebessa area.

A magnificent stand by Combat Command "B's" tanks outside Sbeitla saved the retreat of the American 1st Armoured Division, but that stand was not enough. The Germans came on. They made a thrust at once up the straight road that leads towards Le Kef, dividing their force, while the second arm continued west for the Kasserine. The northward thrust was probably a feint. It was met and defeated by part of the Guards Brigade with a few

On Sunday, the 21st, the real Battle of Thala began. It continued until Tuesday, the 23rd. The tiny Vicforce lost heavily, but it held the 10th Panzer Division. It did more—it broke it. Moreover, the work of the Americans to the westward began to place pressure on the German lines of communication and withdrawal. By Tuesday evening there was no German left on the wrong side of the Kasserine Pass. By Thursday the Allies were through the Pass again. The Battle of Kasserine was over, and any hope that Von Arnim may have had of disrupting the First Army in time to expand the walls of his box before Rommel joined him had gone. But with it had gone also our hopes of preventing the junction of the two German armies.

THE BATTLE FOR THE KASSERINE PASS

After making a thrust towards Sfax, the Allies in Tunisia were in mid-February 1943 forced to withdraw through the Kasserine Pass towards Tebessa. But in following them, the Germans overreached their strength, and on February 25 British and American infantry, supported by tanks, completely reoccupied the Pass. 1. U.S. troops examining the remains of German tanks blown to pieces by American gunfire. 2. Maj.-Gen. Terry Allen, commanding the 1st Infantry (New York) Division of U.S. forces in Tunisia. 3. American 37-mm. anti-tank gun and crew; in the background can be seen shell bursts from enemy artillery in the Kasserine gap. 4. 25-pounder shells landing among German positions and tanks in the Pass.

Chapter 265

EIGHTH ARMY'S ADVANCE FROM TRIPOLI TO THE WADI AKARIT

Anglo-American operations in northern Tunisia up to the battle for the Kasserine Pass towards the end of February 1943 were described by Mr. A. D. Divine in Chapter 264. The scene here shifts to southern Tunisia, where he records the Eighth Army's continued victorious advance, their great assault on the Mareth Line and the forcing of the Wadi Akarit.

IN the last days of January 1943 patrols of the Eighth Army crossed the borders of southern Tunisia. The topographical disposition of the German Army of Tunisia at this time is described in Chapter 264. Now the situation of the German Army of Egypt—Field-Marshal Rommel's army—has to be considered. Part of it—his best armoured divisions—had been in Tunisia for some considerable while, rehabilitating themselves on the southern coastal plain and assimilating reinforcements of men and material. But the bulk of the Army of Egypt, having crossed the indefensible desert frontier between Tripolitania and Tunisia, withdrew to the Mareth Line. There were thus two enemy armies of Tunisia, one of the north and one of the south. The great Tunisian coastal plain, which stretches from Enfidaville to the southern frontier, is divided into two unequal areas by the Chott Djerid.

THEY ROLLED UNOPPOSED INTO BEN GARDANE

Armoured cars of the Eighth Army's advance guard crossed the Tunisian frontier from Tripolitania on January 29, 1943. Sappers had to bridge the swampy lakes which lie about the frontier before the main body of the army could get through to occupy Ben Gardane, 20 miles inside the border, without opposition on February 15. Here are Valentine tanks of the Eighth Army—their drivers smiling—entering Ben Gardane. *Photo, British Official*

For the primary phases of the operation now to be described, the southern army was south of the Chott Djerid and south of the narrows of the Gabes gap where the Chott Djerid runs almost to the sea. (*See map, p. 2624.*)

There were two possibilities before Rommel and the German High Command : one was to stand on the Mareth Line—that Maginot rampart of Africa ; the other to give battle on the Gabes gap where the narrows—the areas of marsh and the wadis that run down to the sea—offer a holding line of considerable natural strength. The decision, taken possibly after the failure of the American attempt to push through to the coast (*see p. 2619*), was to stand at Mareth.

The earliest date of importance in this new phase of the North African campaign is February 15, when the Eighth Army occupied Ben Gardane. This is the first town in southern Tunisia, and from it springs the beginning of the Tunisian road network. Rommel made his first serious attempt to check the swift forward movement of the Eighth Army at Medenine. That strange city of mysterious tunnelled houses fell to the Eighth after a vigorous action on Saturday, the 20th. The Germans had stood on strong positions, well supported by artillery, following the failure of a tank attack the previous day. The Eighth thrust through the olive groves a powerful force of tanks supported by 25-pounders and 4.5-inch guns in considerable numbers. Visibility was bad owing to dust, and while the guns kept the German front bitterly occupied, the Allies carried out a very swift movement on the left flank of the position. By the late afternoon armoured cars and tanks had swung round to the rear of the main position and were imperilling the line of the German retreat along the Gabes road. Though the Germans threw in considerable numbers of dive-bombers in an attempt to retrieve their position, they failed, and under cover of the darkness the enemy pulled out. This was the first round of the Battle of Mareth.

Occupation of Ben Gardane

2622

Subadar L. THAPA
Awarded the V.C. for conspicuous gallantry in leading men of the 2nd Gurkha Rifles, Indian Army, in an attack on the Rass-Ez-Zouai position (Wadi Akarit area) during the night of April 5–6, 1943. He killed four of the enemy with his kukri and two others with his revolver.

Pte. E. ANDERSON
At Wadi Akarit on April 6, 1943, Pte. Eric Anderson, a stretcher bearer with the East Yorkshire Regiment, went out three times under intense fire and brought in wounded comrades. Going out a fourth time, he was hit and mortally wounded; he was posthumously awarded the V.C.

Maj. D. A. SEAGRIM
Led the Green Howards under heavy enemy fire over a scaling ladder across an anti-tank ditch 12 ft. wide and 8 ft. deep to a vital position in the Mareth Line (March 20–21, 1943), which they held against severe counter-attack. He died of wounds, and was posthumously awarded the V.C.

Lieut. M. NGARIMU
Lt. Moana - Nui - a - Kiwa Ngarimu, a Maori serving with the New Zealand forces, 'killed on his feet, facing the enemy with his tommy-gun at his hip' while leading his men against the enemy at Djebel Tabarga (near El Hamma), March 26, 1943; he was posthumously awarded the V.C.

Maj. L. M. CAMPBELL
Major (temp. Lt.-Col.) Lorne MacLaine Campbell, Argyll and Sutherland Highlanders, was awarded the V.C. for his gallantry in forming a bridge-head for a brigade of the 51st (Highland) Division on the Wadi Akarit positions on April 6, 1943, and subsequently capturing six hundred prisoners.

Photos, New Zealand Official : Associated Press ; Vandyk ; Keystone

The battles of the north and of the south were interdependent, even as were the German armies of the north and of the south. It is essential to preserve a picture of the whole situation in considering the movements of the Eighth Army. In the north, while these things were happening, Von Arnim's army—which included some of Rommel's armour, those units that had been rebuilt in South Tunisia—was attempting two things. Along the line of the eastern dorsale it was striving to break the threatened American thrust to the Gabes gap. Along the line of the northern foothills it was attempting to widen the box into which Rommel's army must eventually withdraw.

German Armies of Tunisia

This period from Sunday, February 14, to Friday, February 26, was the period of the Kasserine battles (described in page 2621). On the morning of the 26th the German northern offensive up the Sidi Nsir valley opened (*see* map in page 2547). This had as its objective Beja and the main roads which communicated with Medjez in the south and Sedjanane and the "Bald Hill" area in the north. In a correlated attack, Colonel Witzig, who commanded the German parachute troops of the north, pushed through atrocious thorn country between "Green Hill" and the coast, and thrust down towards Sedjanane. At the other end of the foothill line the enemy attacked in the area of Bou Arada.

If the German intention was to push the Allies back to the next line of the Tunisian hills, it failed. But they had minor successes. The Allies lost their positions about the "Green Hill" pass and were forced down the valley almost to Djebel Abiod beyond Sedjanane.

The Germans occupied the lower part of the Sidi Nsir valley. Their tanks were badly mauled in the strange and bloody little action near Hunt's Gap —the following description of which

PREPARING THE ASSAULT ON THE MARETH LINE

The main attack on the Mareth Line began on the night of March 20–21, 1943, but it had been preceded by much preliminary work, both in field reconnaissance and in the study of this line of fortifications built by the French, strengthened by the Italians and the Germans, and linked with strong points in the Matmata Hills to the west. Here is an officer explaining with the aid of a map the dispositions and the plan of attack just prior to the opening of the battle.

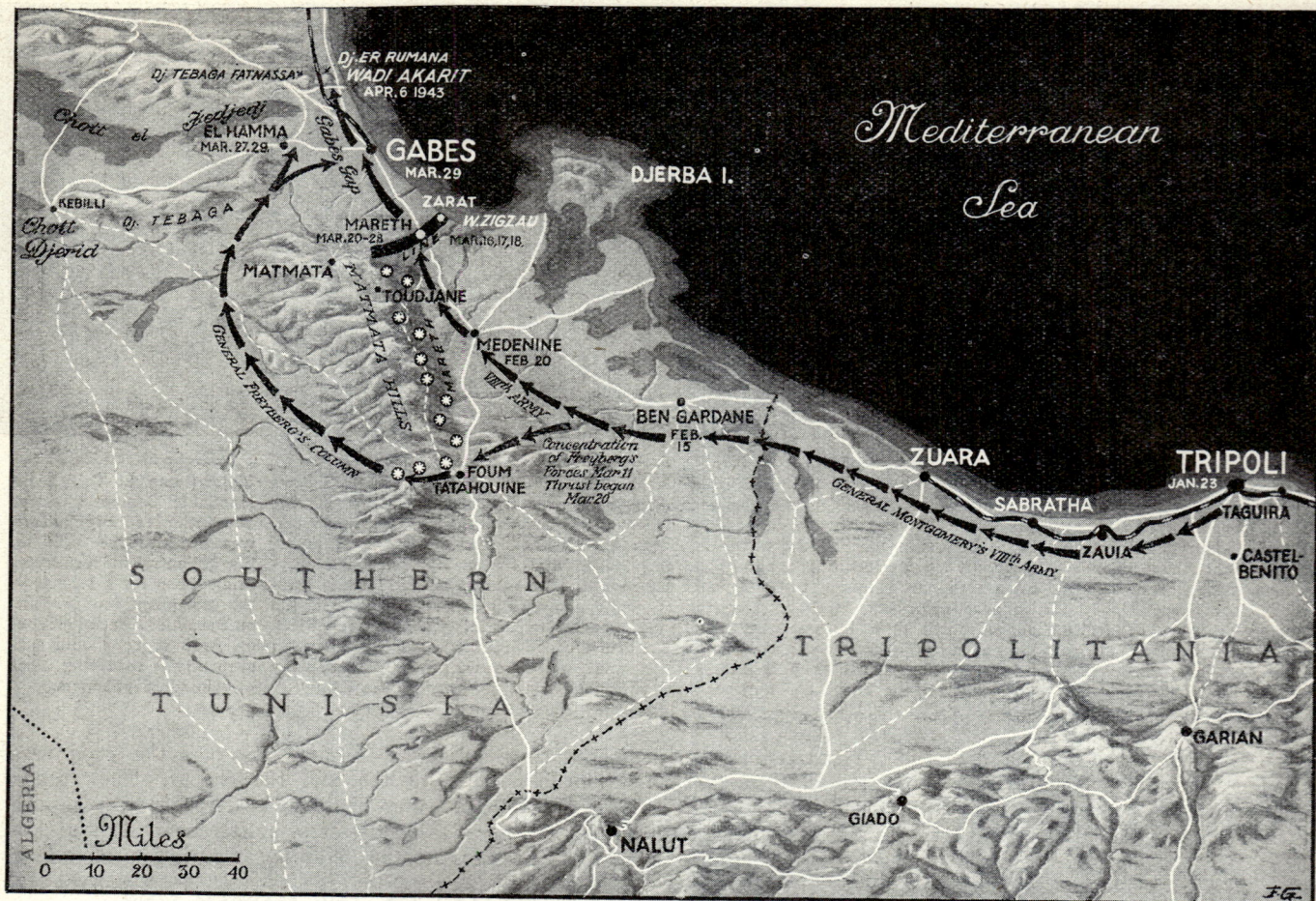

EIGHTH ARMY'S ADVANCE INTO TUNISIA

While the mixed British, American, and French forces in north Tunisia were struggling towards Tunis against Von Arnim's armies (see Chapter 264), General Montgomery and the Eighth Army were driving Rommel's retreating Afrika Korps through Tripolitania and south Tunisia. This map illustrates the Eighth Army's advance after the fall of Tripoli to the battle of Wadi Akarit.

Specially drawn for THE SECOND GREAT WAR *by Félix Gardon*

is taken from the official report :

Sidi Nsir lies in the hills 12 miles east of Hunt's Gap, near Beja. It was held by the 155th Field Battery R.A. and the Hampshires. Their orders were to gain time. On the evening of February 25 no signs were visible of any movement. But during the night Verey light signals began to go up, and at 6.30 next morning heavy mortar fire opened on the British guns.

After 45 minutes' shelling, German tanks drove down the road from Mateur. Four 25-pounders leapt into action, No. 1 firing over open sights. Three tanks were hit, and the road was blocked. Checked in their initial thrust, the enemy sent in lorried infantry who turned the battery's southern flank under cover of a hill. Eight Messerschmitts swooped down on the guns and raked each in turn and repeatedly with machine-gun and cannon fire.

By midday 30 German tanks, with self-propelled guns and infantry in support, were within 600 yards. At 3 o'clock strong detachments of infantry were across the road and no more ammunition could pass.

About 3.30 a column of enemy tanks raced along the road into the heart of the battery position. Thirteen other tanks gave covering fire from hull-down position. A Mark VI led the attack. This was holed three times in the turret by shells from No. 1 gun of "F" Troop. A Mark IV tried to pass round the wreckage, but it also was knocked

out by No. 1 gun. The same gun set on fire another tank. Then the surviving tanks drew back and shelled and machine-gunned both "F" and "E" Troops, concentrating on one gun at a time. When all seemed finished, the Germans advanced again. But No. 1 gun of "F" Troop destroyed the leading tank. A moment later a direct hit killed all the survivors. Nos. 2, 3 and 4 fought on to the last man and the last round.

At 5.30 the Germans, heavily mauled, moved on to crush "E" Troop. At nightfall one 25-pounder and several Bren guns were still engaging German tanks smothering the last resistance.

When the battle began, there were nine Officers and 121 Other Ranks in the position. Nine survived, of whom two were wounded.

Thereafter, the enemy flooded over the hills of the Djebel el Ang and dominated the Beja road. In the Bou Arada sector their gains were less obvious, but even there they improved their positions. (*See* map, p. 2547.)

None the less it was not enough. The fault perhaps lay with the German High Command, which lacked sufficient flexibility of mind to reorganize itself to the new situation. The southern

claw of the great pincer movement to the east had broken off short with Rommel's retreat. The German High Command had two alternatives : to reinforce Von Arnim and Rommel in sufficient strength to enable the claw to re-extend itself ; or to get out as many men as possible as early as possible. The German Command did neither of these things. It continued the policy of reinforcement on a scale which merely added to the numbers finally surrendered. Allied naval and air interference at sea played a part that perhaps is not generally recognized even now in this consummation. Once again the German incapacity to understand the implications of sea-power was to cost them a bitter price.

Half-hearted German Policy

The Battle of Mareth is the most important single event in the history of the southern section of the campaign, for with Mareth broke any hope the Germans had of holding the wider bridgehead that the southern plan implied.

The history of the Mareth Line is a curious one. It was built in the Maginot period as a defence against Italian ambition from the east. It occupied a series of wadi edges and hillocks across

2624

1

BATTLE FOR THE MARETH LINE OPENS

The Mareth Line, supported on the west by the natural difficulties of the Matmata Hills and on the east by those of wadi-seamed country stretching to the coast, formed a strong defence zone in which Rommel made his last African stand. Montgomery's attack on the Line began with an intense night barrage (March 20–21, 1943) from heavy guns (1). But many ground obstructions, natural and artificial, had to be overcome: a working party (2) goes forward under shell-fire to plant dynamite in the banks of a wadi which formed an effective natural tank trap; the resulting explosion (3) levelled the wadi banks, and enabled Eighth Army armour to take up its zero hour positions. *Photos, British Official*

2

3

the plain until it reached the slopes of the Matmata Hills, and in those hills it ended. It was assumed that the desert and the difficulties of the country would prevent an enemy from turning its western flank. After the Franco-Italian Armistice of June 1940, Italians took over the line, and with forethought and ingenuity they essayed to reverse its direction in so far as that was possible. Much of it could not be reversed and some of it was demolished. Subsequently, in the German occupation, it was refurbished, and on the approach of Rommel's army a considerable amount of work was put into improving the old French fortifications. The strongest part of the artificial line ended about 10 miles from the sea. Between that and the coast the French had relied on the intolerable natural difficulties of the wadi-seamed country, strengthened by occasional pillboxes, wire and minefields.

There was a pause after Medenine while General Montgomery built up his forces. That pause lasted until the middle of March, though there was intermittent fighting.

On the night of March 16, the 50th (Northumbrian) Division was given the task of breaching what by then had become perhaps the most formidable defensive position that the Eighth Army had ever faced. The line at the point selected ran on the northern bank of the Wadi Zigzau, a steep, mud-bottomed ravine, which offered incredible

AFTERMATH OF THE ACTION AT SIDI NSIR

One of seven German tanks knocked out by the 155th Field Battery, R.A., at Sidi Nsir (near Hunt's Gap, in northern Tunisia), on February 26, 1943. In this gallant and memorable action nine officers and 121 other ranks held their position against dive-bombing, mortar fire, and tanks until all their guns were destroyed. Only nine survivors (two wounded) got back to the British lines. Some others were taken prisoner. *Photo, British Official: Crown Copyright*

DEATH TRAPS SET IN A FIELD OF FLOWERS

By February 19, 1943, the Eighth Army, advancing from Tripolitania, had cleared the enemy from nearly all south-east Tunisia—an area of between 2,000 and 3,000 square miles—and were in contact with the Afrika Korps in the neighbourhood of Medenine, which was occupied on February 20.   The Axis forces left many deadly mementoes behind them : sappers are seen here searching for and finding mines sown in a flower-strewn field outside Medenine.   *Photo, British Official : Crown Copyright*

BARBED WIRE ENTANGLEMENTS ON THE MARETH LINE

Infantry section of the Eighth Army advancing through a wired position in the Mareth Line, the battle for which began on March 20, 1943. Both the town of Mareth and the Line were in Allied hands by March 28. General Montgomery's successful plan of action involved a direct attack on the Line itself, and a simultaneous left-flanking movement, led by Lt.-General Sir Bernard Freyberg, V.C., away to the west of the Matmata Hills, towards El Hamma. Below, observers spotting from a captured enemy post in the Mareth Line.   *Photos, British Official*

EIGHTH ARMY BREAKS THROUGH TO GABES AND BEYOND

The successful outflanking thrust west of the Matmata Hills executed by Freyberg's column forced Gen. Messe out of the Mareth Line, which was captured by the Eighth Army on March 28, 1943 (see map, page 2624). The Allies then pushed on to Gabes, which they occupied on March 29 after overcoming strong enemy rearguard opposition. New Zealand troops, some of whom are seen above in positions near the Gabes Gap, were the first to enter the town of Gabes. Below, a battalion of the Black Watch being piped through the town on its way to more heavy fighting in the Gabes Gap. *Photos, British Official : Crown Copyright*

2 X

PRELUDE TO THE MEETING OF TWO BATTLE-WORN ARMIES

The Eighth Army, pushing northward in Tunisia after storming the Wadi Akarit line on April 6, 1943, linked up in the coastal plain with patrols of the Second American Corps of the First Army, advancing from Gafsa towards Gabes, on April 7. Thereafter, the two armies combined to go 'forward to Tunis and drive the enemy into the sea,' to quote a message issued by General Montgomery on April 10.

Photo, Pictorial Press

difficulties. In a preliminary series of attacks on the nights of March 16 and 17 the Green Howards and the East Yorkshire Regiment drove back the enemy from the outposts on the south side of the wadi. By the 18th our foremost troops were within a thousand yards of the ravine itself. By this time, though the Eighth Army did not know it, Rommel had left for Europe, a sick man, and the Italian General Messe was in command of Axis defence at Mareth. On the night of March 20–21 the main attack began. Again the Green Howards, led by small fighting patrols, formed the spearhead of the advance. Their commanding officer helped to place the first scaling-ladder in position and was first over the anti-tank ditch.

It was a major battle. Losses were heavy on both sides, but when the Durham Light Infantry came in in the main attack a foothold was established in the line. In a series of heroic assaults a bridgehead was secured on the farther side of the wadi, a roadway of fascines was built across the mud bottom and the beginning of a path for the armour was opened. But the line was strong. It was also deep, and Messe was hanging on to it with the energy of desperation. We pierced it; we crossed the formidable trough of the Zigzau, and we were held upon the farther side.

But the assault on the Wadi Zigzau was a part only of the Battle of Mareth; there was a wider movement. On a number of occasions in the North Africa campaign General Montgomery had exploited what came to be known as the "left hook."

Another Montgomery 'Left Hook'

Attacking on or near the coast with his main force, he would swing a subsidiary force south and west of the position he was assaulting to take it in the rear. He had employed it as recently as Medenine. He exploited it again here. West of the Matmata Hills General Sir Bernard Freyberg, V.C., was leading a mixed and powerful column of British armour and New Zealand infantry, with a very strong artillery group under Brigadier Weir, plus General Leclerc's Fighting French column and men of the Royal Greek Army. The New Zealand corps began to concentrate on March 11; by March 18 it was complete. The force as a whole was self-contained and carried 11 days' food, water and ammunition, and petrol for 350 miles. Enemy Intelligence located the concentration, and on March 20, while the frontal assault was in progress at Mareth, it was decided to throw in the formation.

The Matmata Hills run roughly north-west almost to the little town of

MONTGOMERY USES THE 'LEFT HOOK' AGAIN

General Montgomery used his 'left hook' strategy again in Tunisia when N.Z. troops with British armour, advancing rapidly to El Hamma along the western slopes of the Matmata Hills, forced the Axis armies under Messe to abandon the Mareth Line. Top, Eighth Army tanks and self-propelled guns moving up for the attack on El Hamma (March 29, 1943). Above, Allied vehicles passing through El Hamma. Below, General Montgomery congratulates his troops on the success of their outflanking movement.   *Photos, British Official: Crown Copyright*

FORCING A WAY THROUGH THE GABES GAP

After capturing Gabes, the Eighth Army pursued the Axis forces through hastily constructed defences in the Gabes Gap to Oudref, which they captured on March 30, 1943. Left, Valentine tanks of the Eighth pushing their way through the Gabes Gap. Above, sappers marking off with signs and white tape the part of the road which has been cleared of mines. Below, a road blown up by the enemy under repair by R.E. sappers as Allied armour and supply trucks rumble past.

Photos, British Official : Crown Copyright

AMERICAN ARMOUR ENTERS MAKNASSY

On March 21, 1943, the American Fifth Army launched a three-pronged drive from Gafsa towards the coast. One column captured Sened on the 21st, Maknassy on the 22nd, and continued to advance in the direction of the sea. A second made for Gabes through El Guetar, while the third penetrated into the hilly country between. Above, a tank of the U.S. First Armoured Division rolls into Maknassy. Right, armoured car at Sened Station. Below, observation post in the hills above El Guetar.

Photos, Pictorial Press

BRIDGING THE WADI ZIGZAU BEFORE THE MARETH LINE

Among the natural features which helped to strengthen the position of the Mareth Line was the difficult, muddy-bottomed Wadi Zigzau. The Royal Engineers succeeded in making tracks across it with trees, sandbags, brushwood, and fascines ; over these British infantry fought their way on March 21, 1943, in face of fierce enemy opposition. After 36 hours of bitter hand-to-hand fighting, more intense than anything in the Battle of Egypt, they had driven a bridgehead into the Line between Mareth and Zarat some 5,000 yards wide and 1,500 yards deep, and taken 2,000 prisoners. *Photo, British Official : Crown Copyright*

El Hamma, which stands at the end of the arm of the Chott Djerid and the beginning of the Gabes gap. The purpose of the flank attack was two-fold : its first object was to turn the Mareth flank and thereby to force the Axis to relinquish its grip on that bloody line ; the second was to break through to the coast across the line of withdrawal from Mareth, cut off the retreating enemy and force him to battle or surrender in open country. Brilliantly led, moving with almost incredible speed, General Freyberg's column reached El Hamma in six days. The first object was superbly achieved. Messe was forced out of the Mareth Line.

This was a battle of many facets. One of the new features which played a very considerable part in the decision, particularly in the tank clashes of El Hamma, was the use of Hurricanes as tank-busters. Throughout the operation the air, in fact, played a highly important part, though perhaps not quite so important as the optimistic communiqués of the period suggested. The relay bombing which softened the Mareth Line, the incessant attacks on German concentrations, store dumps, transport and communication lines, all had their effect. The loss to the Axis powers—and particularly to the weaker part of the Axis—was heavy. From March 20 to March 28 over 6,000 prisoners—mainly Italians—were taken by the Eighth Army, together with a huge store of material.

But the second object was not achieved. For over a thousand miles from El Alamein, Rommel had cleverly exploited the advantages of a retreating army and contrived to extricate himself from disaster. Something he owed to the cynical use of his Italian allies as a delaying mechanism to provide for the escape of his chosen German people and something he owed to the good organization and discipline of the Afrika Korps. However that may be, the Axis forces had so far succeeded in escaping annihilation, and at Mareth they did so again. That is the sober fact of the great Battle of South Tunisia. Despite all that the air could do on the limited roads of his withdrawal, Messe's army surged northwards at tremendous speed, while in his rear forces of varying strength stood for a little to make good the necessary time. They did not stand at Gabes town— General Freyberg was knocking at its gates ; nor did they stand in the Gabes gap—there was no time to make that exiguous position strong enough—but beyond Gabes was a long, dry gully down to the sea, the Wadi Akarit.

North and west of the Gabes area the Americans had attacked from Gafsa. That attack was in fact a second left hook. This also had a double object. Its first was, if possible, to threaten the coastal road in the rear of the southern battle ; but, if the mountain positions proved too strong, it could still serve a valuable purpose by diverting troops from the southern battle to reinforce the mountain garrisons.

The attack was delayed at its onset by rain. Rain had been expected in the first phase of the Tunisian campaign; but this was rain in the desert, the worst rain the area had known for six years, a single day of torrential downpour. None the less, the thrust went forward. The Americans, supported by French detachments, recaptured Gafsa; then raced through the gap and secured the hills immediately beyond the town above the village of El Guetar. There the force divided, and one column swept along the old road of the Station Sened thrust to Maknassy and the other pounded at the main Gafsa–Gabes highway. They were held. The Allies discovered then that the Germans had long planned their resistance in this area. At the strategic points were strong and well-sited concrete pillboxes. The fighting was gallant in the extreme and the losses heavy, but progress, once the Americans had broken past El Guetar, was slow and painful. Nevertheless, it drew powerful tank forces from the desperately pressed Axis army of the south, and was a notable contribution to the general battle.

General Montgomery paused for a little to reorganize in the Gabes area. On April 6 the Eighth Army attacked **Capture of Wadi Akarit** the Wadi Akarit. So powerful was Messe's rearguard here that it was thought by many that the main Axis army had been brought to a stand again. But Wadi Akarit was essentially a delaying action which utilized a powerful natural position. The wadi itself, steep, difficult to cross and easy to defend, runs down to the sea. It was strengthened by two hills, Djebel Tebaga Fatnassa on the left and Djebel Er Rumana on the right, north of the actual wadi.

The attack opened in the small hours with a massed barrage of 500 guns—that method of softening which had been so brilliantly developed in the desert. At 4 a.m. the infantry went in. In a magnificent assault the 51st (Highland) Division carried the two 500-foot hills, the Cameron and the Seaforth Highlanders going in with the bayonet under the very skirts of the barrage. Within an hour of the firing of the last shell the heights had surrendered, and through the defile between the hills the armour smashed out on to the open plain. The enemy realized that our hold on the hills was only light, and they put in heavy counter-attacks. At one time the Seaforth Highlanders could muster only 40 fighting men but, calling on clerks, kitchen staff and orderlies to man Bren guns, they held

on until the Black Watch came in to the rescue.

And as that Axis counter-attack failed, the fate of the vast coastal plain of Tunisia was sealed. Between the Wadi Akarit and the mountains of Zaghouan there was no holding ground for an army. Sfax with its port, El Djem, Sousse, Kairouan (the Holy City of Africa), with a thousand villages and a score of lesser towns up to Enfidaville, were virtually surrendered in that hour. South Tunisia was lost to the enemy in two sharp battles, and with it were lost 17,500 prisoners, almost as many killed and wounded, and a vast quantity of tanks, guns, stores, and munitions of war.

ATTACK BY THE EIGHTH ARMY ON THE WADI AKARIT

General Montgomery's attack on the enemy line at Wadi Akarit opened at dawn on April 6, 1943, under cover of a violent barrage by 500 guns. A breach was made in the centre of the Axis front through which strong British tank and mobile forces advanced, taking 6,000 prisoners and over-running the whole of the wadi. The Fourth Indian Division, on the extreme left flank, fought with particular gallantry, climbing a high massif in the dark and wiping out the German garrison without a shot being fired. Above, guns and lorried infantry move forward to attack. Below, observing results of New Zealand gunners' fire on enemy positions, in support of the Fourth Indian Division. *Photos : Indian Official*

Historic Documents CCLXVI—CCLXVIII

TEHERAN & CAIRO: FAR EASTERN PROBLEMS

The first personal meeting between Stalin, Roosevelt and Churchill at Teheran in November 1943 decided the strategy of the European war for 1944; while the conference held in the same month in Cairo between Chiang Kai-shek, Roosevelt and Churchill was conclusive evidence of the importance attached to the war against Japan by Great Britain and U.S.A. India's contribution to the campaigns in the Mediterranean, her difficulties, and her post-war prospects were the themes of Lord Wavell's first public speech as Viceroy.

DECLARATION OF TEHERAN, SIGNED BY ROOSEVELT, STALIN AND CHURCHILL ON DECEMBER 1, 1943.

WE, the President of the United States of America, the Prime Minister of Great Britain, and the Premier of the Soviet Union, have met these four days past in the capital of our ally Iran, and have shaped and confirmed our common policy. We expressed our determination that our nations shall work together in war and in the peace that will follow.

As to war, our military staffs have joined in our round-table discussions and we have concerted our plans for the destruction of the German forces. We have reached complete agreement as to the scope and timing of the operations which will be undertaken from the East, West and South. The common understanding which we have here reached guarantees that victory will be ours.

And as to peace, we are sure that our concord will make it an enduring peace. We recognize fully the supreme responsibility resting upon us and all the United Nations to make a peace that will command the good will of the overwhelming masses of the peoples of the world and banish the scourge and terror of war for many generations.

With our diplomatic advisers we have surveyed the problems of the future. We shall seek the co-operation and the active participation of all nations, large and small, whose people in heart and mind are dedicated, as are our own peoples, to the elimination of tyranny and slavery, oppression and intolerance. We will welcome them as they may choose to come into a world family of democratic nations.

No power on earth can prevent our destroying the German armies by land, their U-boats by sea, and their war plants from the air. Our attacks will be relentless and increasing.

From these friendly conferences we look with confidence to the day when all peoples of the world may live free lives, untouched by tyranny and according to their varying desires and their own consciences.

We came here with hope and determination. We leave here friends in fact, in spirit, and in purpose.

OFFICIAL ANNOUNCEMENT ON ANGLO-SINO-AMERICAN COLLABORATION ISSUED IN CAIRO, DECEMBER 1, 1943.

PRESIDENT ROOSEVELT, Generalissimo Chiang Kai-shek, and the Prime Minister, Mr. Churchill, together with their respective military and diplomatic advisers, have completed a conference in North Africa. The following general statement has been issued:

The several military missions have agreed upon future military operations against Japan.

The three great Allies expressed their resolve to bring unrelenting pressure against their brutal enemies by sea land, and air. This pressure is already rising.

The three great Allies are fighting this war to restrain and punish the aggression of Japan. They covet no gain for themselves and have no thought of territorial expansion.

It is their purpose that Japan shall be stripped of all the islands in the Pacific which she has seized or occupied since the beginning of the first world war in 1914, and that all the territories that Japan has stolen from the Chinese, such as Manchuria, Formosa, and the Pescadores, shall be restored to the Republic of China.

Japan will also be expelled from all other territories which she has taken by violence and greed.

The aforesaid three Great Powers, mindful of the enslavement of the people of Korea, are determined that in due course Korea shall become free and independent.

With these objectives in view the three Allies, in harmony with those of the United Nations at war with Japan, will continue to persevere in the serious and prolonged operations necessary to procure the unconditional surrender of Japan.

LORD WAVELL SPEAKS TO THE ASSOCIATED CHAMBERS OF COMMERCE IN CALCUTTA ON INDIA'S WAR EFFORT AND POST-WAR PLANS, DECEMBER 20, 1943.

I SHOULD like to begin my first public speech as Viceroy by acknowledging again the services rendered to me in the Middle East during the early part of the war, not only by Indian troops but by Indian industry, which supplied so many of our pressing needs. . . . Indian help saved the Middle East at a critical time . . . .

We have every reason for sober confidence in a victorious outcome of the war in Europe in the not too distant future. . . . But the end of the war in the West is no more than the beginning of the war in the East on a scale required to bring about the defeat and unconditional surrender of Japan. . . . The war effort and preparations we have already made have placed severe strains upon our national economy and we must take steps to make this stable to support the strains of the next year.

The food problem must be our first concern. . . . The first thing to get clear about food is that it is not a provincial problem; it is an all-India, and even a world problem. . . If by administrative negligence we are compelled to ask for more help from abroad than we really need, we are expecting other countries, whose people are already rationed, and whose prices are properly controlled, to deny themselves unnecessarily. . . . It is our plain duty to set up an efficient food administration. . . . Key points in our plan are full rationing in the larger towns and control of prices. . . . It is said by some that urban rationing is unnecessary and impossible in India. This is nonsense. It is very necessary and quite possible. . .

In Bengal, the aid given by the Army coupled with the prospects of a bountiful *aman* harvest have eased the position perceptibly. But there are no grounds for complacency. We still have to fight lack of confidence and greed, and to see that administrative action is adequate for the future. The Army cannot remain indefinitely to do the work of the civil administration. Bengal has the sympathy of the world at present, but this will not continue unless it is obvious that she is making every effort to help herself. . . .

The years after the war are going to be of immense import to India's future. . . . The Government has in hand the preparation of plans to take advantage of India's opportunities in as great a measure as possible. In this the Government and industry must work very closely hand in hand. . . . Development must be on an Indian basis and by Indian methods. But India will require assistance and advice at first to help her to realize the great possibilities that are hers. . . .

It seems to me that one of the first necessities is to develop power schemes throughout India to provide the driving force for industries. In some instances it may be possible to combine this with irrigation schemes for agriculture, the improvement of which by all possible means must be our principal aim. . . . The development of industry and the improvement of agriculture must go hand in hand in order to provide for India's growing population and to raise the standard of living. . . .

I have said nothing of the constitutional or political problems of India, not because they are not constantly in my mind. . . . but because I do not believe that I can make their solution any easier by talking about them just at present. For the time being I concentrate on the job of work we have to do. The winning of the war, the organization of the economic home front, and the preparations for peace. . . . If we can co-operate now in the achievement of the great administrative aims which should be common to all parties when the country is in peril, we shall do much to produce conditions in which the solution of the political deadlock will be possible. . . .

Chapter 266

THE MENACE OF WAR RECEDES FROM THE MIDDLE EAST

The record of affairs in the Middle East, continued here by Mr. Kenneth Williams from Chapter 246, remained on the whole a troubled one throughout 1943. There was, however, a marked tendency for opinion to veer towards the Allied cause. The holding in Egypt and Persia of conferences between the leaders of the major Allied states together with the diplomatic activity with Turkey threw Middle Eastern affairs into special prominence that year

DURING the year 1943 the menace of war, though not its consequences, appeared to the Middle East to grow increasingly remote. The result was that, convinced that Germany could not win the war, most of the lands in this region manoeuvred, to a varying extent, to take what advantages were possible from being on the winning side and to safeguard their post-war position. The chief concern of the Arabic-speaking countries related to the possibility of achieving Arab unity; that of Turkey, to how she could best conserve her neutrality and secure her position when peace came; and that of Persia, to mitigating the effects on her economy of the requirements of two of the belligerents, Britain and Russia.

The attitude of Egypt, where were the offices of the Minister of State (Mr. R. G. Casey) responsible for co-ordinating the economic output of all the Middle Eastern territories, was extremely important.

EGYPT

Under the guidance of Nahas Pasha, the Prime Minister and leader of the Wafdist party, Egyptians did not waver in their collaborative effort. But it must be confessed that, as the Axis armies were being surely pushed out of Africa, Egyptian interest in the war tended to become academic. With the fall of Tripoli, Egyptians felt that the threat of war to the Nile Valley was definitely removed, and that it was therefore safe to ventilate domestic problems. Here, a feature of the situation was the tension existing between the Government and the Palace.

This tension must have been one of the constant preoccupations of the British Ambassador, Sir Miles Lampson, who, raised to the peerage, took the title of Lord Killearn. It speaks much for his tact and experience that nothing untoward occurred during the year, and this despite the attacks made by the Opposition, who attempted to gain the ear of the King on the ground that the British were interfering in the internal affairs of Egypt.

Widespread excitement was caused by the publication of the " Black Book," written by a former Minister of

Finance, Makram Ebeid Pasha. This contained charges of corruption and nepotism against the Prime Minister, and thousands of copies were circulated. In April the Opposition tried to make capital out of the accusations, and petitioned the King to dismiss the Government. For a time this affair excluded all other interests. But Nahas Pasha professed himself ready to go to the country on this issue. Such a course, however, did not prove necessary. He met the charges in Parliament, where he demanded a vote of confidence. This, after full debate, he obtained unanimously, all but two of the Opposition withdrawing after it had been decided not to allow Makram Pasha more than three days of the Chamber's time in which to elaborate his charges. It was after this vote that the King withdrew the reservations he seems to have cherished about his Government's project of establishing diplomatic relations with Soviet Russia.

The normal prorogation of Parliament for the summer did not end political interest, which was renewed by talks on Arab unity, begun as a result of

initial conversations between the Prime Minister of Iraq, Nuri Pasha, and the Egyptian Prime Minister from July 31 to August 6. Into this project Nahas Pasha threw himself with some enthusiasm, inviting all the Arab States to send separately delegates to Egypt to discuss ways and means with him. Such representatives did arrive, and within a few months Nahas Pasha was possessed of the views of the Lebanon, Syria, Transjordan, Iraq, Saudi Arabia, and the Yemen. Palestine alone did not send a recognized delegate, the explanation being that all her real leaders were interned. These discussions continued for several months, but by the end of the year nothing concrete had been published. It became evident that though all the Arab States paid homage to the ideal of unity, there was considerable difference of view as to methods of attaining federation.

Facilities for Allied (particularly American) air traffic through the Cairo area were increased sixfold by the opening in October 1943 of a great new airfield constructed in its essentials in 58 days from August 3. It included

EMERGENCY SHIPBUILDING IN EGYPT

Local labour was used at Alexandria to construct from imported materials this special type of small naval lighter needed for transport in the area. Made entirely of wood and canvas, these lighters were capable of carrying up to 200 tons of cargo.
Photo, British Official : Crown Copyright

some 70 buildings, and 6,500 feet of runways. The Heliopolis airfield, on which the Allies had previously been dependent, was small. Working to its maximum capacity by day, it could not be used at night on account of dangerous obstructions, and the immense increase in military air traffic made the construction of the new airfield essential.

But 1943 was not to end without giving Egyptians other matters for discussion. On December 1 it was

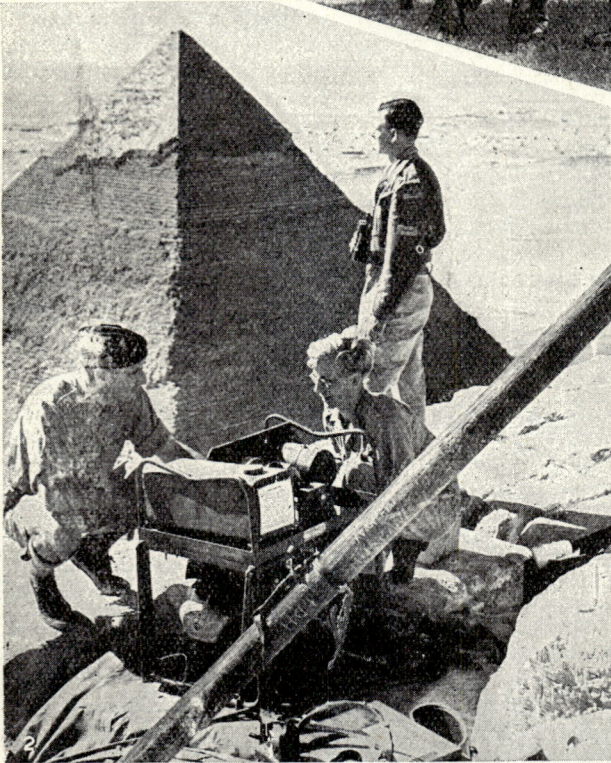

CONFERENCE IN CAIRO

Generalissimo Chiang Kai-shek for the first time came into personal contact with the leaders of Great Britain and the U.S.A. at the conference on Allied strategy against Japan, held in Cairo from November 22–26, 1943. 1. The Generalissimo with Mr. Roosevelt and Mr. Churchill at Mena House. 2. R.A.F. radio observation post on the Great Pyramid, part of the conference security precautions. 3. Chiang Kai-shek and his wife, accompanied by Sir Robert Greg, K.C.M.G., leaving the Ibn Tolun Mosque during a brief tour they made of the city of Cairo.

announced in Cairo that President Roosevelt, Generalissimo Chiang Kai-shek and Mr. Churchill, with military and diplomatic advisers, had completed a conference in North Africa. Actually, the conference began near Cairo on November 22 and ended on November 26. Its resolution, to wage war in the Far East so as to make Japan disgorge not only all the territories she had seized since the attack on Pearl Harbor, but also the lands she had conquered or occupied during the past 50 years, was of world importance ; but Egypt was considerably less interested in the Far Eastern war than in the possibility of Turkey's entering the war against Germany. (See Hist. Doct. CCLXVII, p. 2636.) Speculation in the latter direction was provided by another conference in Cairo on Dec. 4, 5 and 6. This was between President Roosevelt, Mr. Churchill and President Inonu of Turkey. These talks, the result of an invitation to the Turkish President by the U.S.A., British and Soviet Governments, were a sequel to a previous meeting in Cairo between Mr. Eden and the Turkish Foreign Minister, M. Menemenjoglou. At the end, this communiqué was issued:

" Presidents Roosevelt and Inonu and Prime Minister Churchill reviewed the general political situation and examined at length the policy to be followed, taking into account the joint and several interests of the three countries. The study of all problems in a spirit of understanding and loyalty showed that the closest unity existed between the United States of America, Turkey, and Great Britain in their attitude to the world situation. The conversations in Cairo have consequently been most useful and most fruitful for the future of the relations between the four countries concerned. The identity of interest and of views of the great American and British democracies with those of the Soviet Union, as also the traditional relations of friendship existing between these Powers and Turkey, have been reaffirmed throughout the proceedings of the Cairo Conference."

This was interpreted by many to mean that Turkey meant to join the United Nations, but she was still not in the war by the end of **TURKEY** the year. There was little, indeed, in the previous 12 months to suggest that she would depart from her neutrality, though more than one attempt was made to induce the Turks more actively to realize their alliance with Britain. On January 10 a Turkish Production Mission arrived in London; but far more important, politically, was the visit which Mr. Churchill, on the recommendation of President Roosevelt, paid to the Turkish President and Prime Minister in Adana on January 30 and 31. Mr. Churchill went to Turkey at his own request after the Casablanca Conference, and the ostensible object of his journey was to reinforce Turkey's defensive security. The Turkish statesmen were immensely gratified, and the British Prime Minister had a great personal success: but the enthusiasm was followed by a more circumspect attitude.

Speaking on February 20 M. Sarajoglou reaffirmed Turkey's resolve to maintain neutrality and the wish to continue in close and amicable relations with Germany, the U.S.A., and Russia, while friendship with and trust of Britain, he said, were indestructible. Four days later the President said that Turkey would do everything not to get involved in war. It was very clear that neither certain influential Turks nor the ordinary man in the street were ready to participate. Turkish reservations about becoming belligerent were not modified even by the final eclipse of the Axis in North Africa. By the middle of the year it appeared that the

BRITISH GUEST OF THE TURKISH GOVERNMENT
Following the conference at Casablanca in January 1943, Mr. Churchill flew to Turkey at the invitation of President Inonu, who received him at Adana. Host and guest are here seen in conference. The provision of more materials and equipment for the reinforcement of Turkey's defences was the chief subject discussed. Below, a convoy of jeeps and other war vehicles passes an old monastery on the journey from Egypt to Turkey via Syria.
Photos, British Official : Crown Copyright

2 x ²

TRANSJORDAN FRONTIER FORCE CAVALRY

One of the last horse regiments in the British Army, the Transjordan Frontier Force Cavalry Regiment, included Arabs, Circassians, Druses, Armenians and Jews, and was led partly by cavalry officers seconded from British Regiments, and partly by local officers. Mounted in the main on Arab horses, it was furnished with modern arms and equipment. Its chief duty was to patrol the Turco-Syrian border to prevent smuggling and the illegal passage of persons. Here a squadron is encamped at Hambouchi on the Utakia.

Photo, British Official : Crown Copyright

most powerful consideration in Turkish counsels was that, when the time came for a peace settlement, the strength of the Turkish Army should be at its peak.

For a time, indeed, the Turks seemed more than ever determined to adhere strictly to neutrality. Nationalist tendencies hardened, and the "Tax on Wealth" was persisted in in face of Allied representations that it discriminated unfairly against foreign minorities. Over Russian criticism that Turkey was not playing the part of a real ally of Britain, the Turks showed resentment ; and the policy of neutrality remained unchanged after the capitulation of Italy.

Turkish Neutrality

By the autumn the enthusiasm for Britain engendered by Mr. Churchill's visit had largely cooled, and an attempt had to be made to rekindle it. Mr. Eden, on his way back from Moscow, conferred in Cairo on November 5 and 6 with the Turkish Foreign Minister (reputedly the arch apostle of neutrality), and it was announced that there had been an exchange of views in the light of the Moscow Conference, and that conversa-

tions were " conducted in the spirit of friendship and alliance which binds the two countries."

The cautious policy adopted by the Turkish Foreign Minister, together with that of the President in subsequent talks (referred to in page 2638) with President Roosevelt and Mr. Churchill, was confirmed by the People's Party. The Turks, it seemed, were " not biting "—and it was particularly unfortunate that, as if to strengthen and confirm their fears of German might and vengeance, Leros should be lost about this time and Samos have to be evacuated.

In Palestine the High Commissioner (Sir H. A. MacMichael) had made a broadcast appeal, on New Year's Eve, for moderation and good will ; but its effect was only partial. For while the Arabs of Palestine were content largely to leave the defence of their local cause in the hands of Arabs outside Palestine (their own leaders having been mostly deported) the Zionists showed intense anxiety over the future and, in some quarters, a resolve to take the law into their own hands. The Jews, convinced

of an Allied victory, were now mainly engaged in helping as many Jews as possible to escape to Palestine from Nazi-dominated lands ; yet, among the more moderate elements, the existence of " Hagana "—an illegal force of Jews trained on commando-like lines— created misgivings.

The activities of Zionists, both within and without Palestine, caused much perturbation among Arabs, also within and without Palestine ;

but opposition to the **PALESTINE** British Government came from Zionist extremists, who would be content with nothing less than the conversion of the whole of Palestine into a Jewish State. Reacting to a Government communiqué on March 23, which contained proposals for post-war development and reconstruction, they urged non-co-operation. More than that, they were suspected of large-scale thefts of arms and ammunition from British military establishments. They desired, moreover, to do their own recruiting of Jewish volunteers for service with the Allies, and when the Government tried to stop intimidation they showed the greatest resentment. For a few months, indeed, the Zionists closed their recruiting offices.

Matters reached a climax over the trial in Jerusalem on August 11, when two British soldiers were sentenced to 15 years' imprisonment each for

TROUBLE IN THE LEBANON

Disturbances in the Lebanon, described in page 2644, provided one of the major crises of the Middle East during 1943. 1. General Catroux, representative of the French Committee of National Liberation, arrives at Beirut. 2. Mr. R. G. Casey, British Minister of State in the Middle East, with Maj.-Gen. Sir Edward Spears, British Minister to Syria, at Beirut. 3. Bechara el Khoury, President of the Lebanon Republic, released by the French authorities, inspects a guard of honour at the opening of the Chekka–Beirut road, built by R.E.s in a hundred days. With him is Lt.-Gen. W. G. Holmes, G.O.C. 9th Army. 4. Two riflemen reading a copy of 'Ninth Army News,' printed by the Beirut 'Eastern Times' during the crisis. 5. French patrol in a Beirut street.

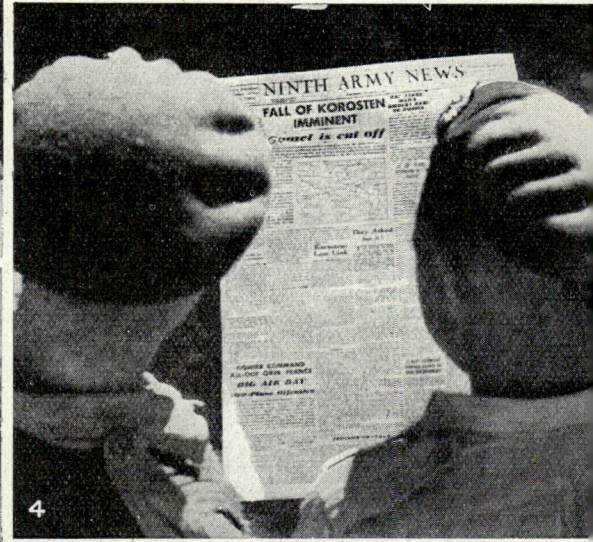

WITH THE TENTH ARMY IN PERSIA

At the Tough Tactics School at Kermanshah, trainees go through a mountain climbing exercise as part of their course, which included organized games, leadership training, unarmed combat, mountain climbing and long distance running and walking. Below, Lt.-General Sir Henry Pownall, K.B.E., C.B., D.S.O., M.C. (centre) arrives to take up his appointment as C.-in-C. Persia-Iraq Command (Tenth Army), announced in March 1943.   *Photos, British Official*

helping to smuggle arms and ammunition to Jews in Palestine. The officer defending them asserted that the Jewish Agency was involved: to which the Agency reacted promptly, calling it a "slanderous and anti-Semitic attack." Later in the year

the notorious Stern gang manifested fresh signs of activity, and two Jewish civilians were sentenced to seven and 10 years' imprisonment respectively for possessing firearms and ammunition. On October 26 Mr. Ben Gurion, the veteran Palestine Jewish leader, re-

signed from the Jewish Agency Executive, owing—it was said—to differences with Dr. Weizmann, head of the Zionist Movement. Dr. Weizmann was credited with favouring partition in Palestine, whereas Mr. Ben Gurion was reputed to want the whole of Palestine as a Jewish State. Tension between the ultra-political Zionists and the Government was maintained until the close of the year, and when, on November 16, the police searched a Jewish settlement in the Vale of Sharon for Polish deserters and illegal arms, there were serious incidents at Tel Aviv.

Of all the Middle East States in 1943, Transjordan was easily the most tranquil. The Emir Abdullah and his statesmen were keenly interested in the discussions on Arab unity, and at one time hoped **TRANS-JORDAN** to have a conference on the project in Amman, their capital. But in September the Emir sent his Prime Minister to Egypt to discuss the issue with the Egyptian Prime Minister, and it is believed that the chief topics investigated were the project of having Syria, the Lebanon, Transjordan and Palestine under a single monarchy, and the possibility of closer union between Egypt and Transjordan.

By contrast, Syria and the Lebanon had a year ending in tumultuous excitement, not only because they were very vocal in expressing their views on Arab unity, but also because, owing to mishandling by the French, events occurred which gave to that feeling of solidarity a new force and significance.

On March 18 General Catroux proclaimed the restoration of the free Constitution of the Lebanon, and a decree was promulgated providing for a general election to be held within three months. Dr. Ayoub Tabet was appointed head of the Lebanese State; and the French hoped that Hashim Atassi would become President of Syria.

In June M. Helleu succeeded General Catroux as French Delegate General in the Levant, and stated that he was resolved to help preserve the independence of the **SYRIA** peoples of Syria "within the framework of friendship with France." But the French, apparently, were not certain of that friendship. The elections were postponed. This procrastination was of considerable embarrassment to the British, still responsible for the military situation in Syria. When at last elections were held, a sweeping victory was obtained by the Nationalists in Syria; and even in the Lebanon, where the French were suspected of trying to "arrange"

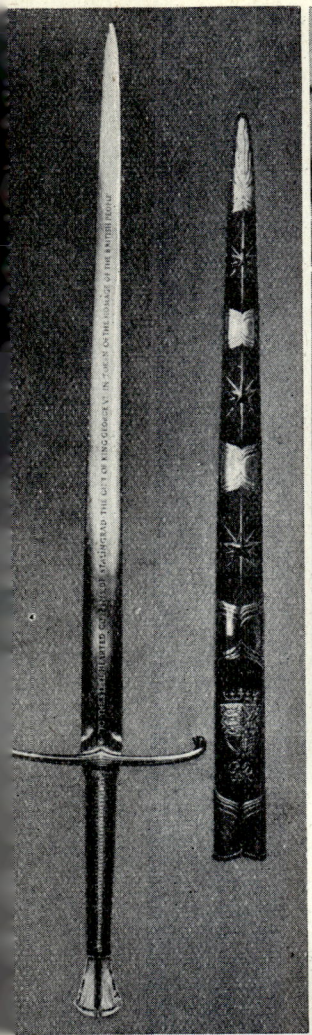

MARSHAL STALIN RECEIVES THE STALINGRAD SWORD

'To mark the profound admiration felt by myself and the peoples of the British Empire, I have given commands for the preparation of a Sword of Honour, which it will give me great pleasure to present to the city of Stalingrad,' said H.M. The King in a message to President Kalinin on February 21, 1943. Mr. Churchill took the sword (left) with him to the Teheran Conference in December, and presented it in person to Marshal Stalin, here seen kissing the scabbard. Below, President Roosevelt and Marshal Stalin with Mr. Churchill at the dinner given at the British Legation at Teheran for the Premier's 69th birthday on November 30, 1943. *Photos, British Official; "The Times"*

ALLIED HELP FOR THE SOVIET UNION

Three British officers and a British civilian (the head of the U.K. Commercial Corporation in Persia), two Russian and two American officers under the chairmanship of a Russian general discuss the kind of supplies needed by Russia, and how to get them through, at the Red Army Headquarters at Teheran. Below, war equipment from America and Great Britain being loaded on to a train bound for the U.S.S.R. frontier, via Persia.

Photos, British Official: Crown Copyright

from Algiers on Nov. 16. His timely advent was reassuring. After studying the position, General Catroux decided that M. Helleu had blundered, and that the arrested men must be freed and reinstated. M. Helleu was recalled to Algiers and replaced by M. Chataigneau.

By the end of the year the Lebanese Arabs, who had been supported throughout their crisis with significant unanimity by all Arabic-speaking States, including Egypt, felt that they had won their case : nor did they omit to thank the British for the part played in vindicating their rights.

Persia (Iran) had another troubled year in 1943, starting with a wheat crisis in Teheran in January. On February 13 the Prime Minister failed to obtain a vote of con- **PERSIA** fidence in the Mejlis, and resigned. He was succeeded by M. Ali Soheily who, four days later, announced a four-point programme consisting of collaboration with Britain, the U.S.A. and Russia ; procuring food supplies on a long-term basis ; reduction in the cost of living and stabilization of prices ; and progress in agriculture, public health and education. On this programme he received a vote of confidence by 89 out of 99 votes.

For the shortage of food, Persians

matters, several anti-French candidates outside Beirut were elected.

In Syria, Shukri Quwatli, leader of the Nationalist *bloc*, was elected President on August 17, and a strongly Nationalist Cabinet was formed under Saadullah Sabri. In the Lebanon, on September 21, after the elections, Bishara al Khuri was made President.

Now the stage was set for the securing by both Syria and the Lebanon of *de facto* independence. On October 11 the Lebanese Prime Minister said that the claim of complete independence by his country was based on the Atlantic Charter and on recognition by the Allies. He announced that the Constitution was to be amended by excluding non-Lebanese authorities from the exercise of any power. This was not at all to the liking of the French Committee of Liberation in Algiers, which declared that it would not recognize any such amending action unless it were taken with the consent of the French representative in Beirut.

Deadlock was complete. The Lebanese, unflurried by French objections, went their way. On November 11 M. Helleu ordered the arrest of the Lebanese President, of the Premier, and of the Cabinet, and dissolved Parliament by decree. He also imposed a curfew in Beirut. Uproar was immediate. There were clashes between

French soldiers and native demonstrators, and casualties were numerous. At once the British authorities protested against French precipitancy. Mr. Casey (British Minister of State in the Middle East) flew from Cairo to Beirut to investigate on the spot. After a few days of utmost disorder, which spread rapidly from Beirut, General Catroux arrived

principally blamed Britain. It happened that supplies were more plentiful in those areas occupied by the Russians, and Britain was accused of being responsible for the shortage of transport. The old allegation was revived that the U.K.C.C. had commandeered lorries for conveying goods to Russia, so that the Persians could not have even what food was available. For a time, indeed, anxiety over the bread situation took the form of criticism of Britain which grew more and more violent. Not even the activities of the "Tudeh" party, the advanced Leftists of Persian politics who were most active in the Russian zone, turned the public's eye from economics to politics.

It was increasingly obvious that, unless wide powers were given to the American Financial Adviser, Dr. Millspaugh, Persian economy could not be straightened. The Prime Minister introduced a Bill to confer on the Adviser large powers, but for several weeks the Mejlis would not hear of it. Meanwhile, the scurrilous anti-British press campaign continued, with the Government apparently unable either to control it or to induce the Mejlis to permit such financial and economic action as would negative the charges. At last, however, on May 4, the Mejlis reluctantly accorded special powers to Dr. Millspaugh.

The food situation then slightly improved, and less dissatisfaction was expressed with the Allies and with the Persian Government. But criticism was not withheld for long. In June Dr. Millspaugh sponsored a new Income Tax bill, drawn up on the British model. While the bill was supported by the

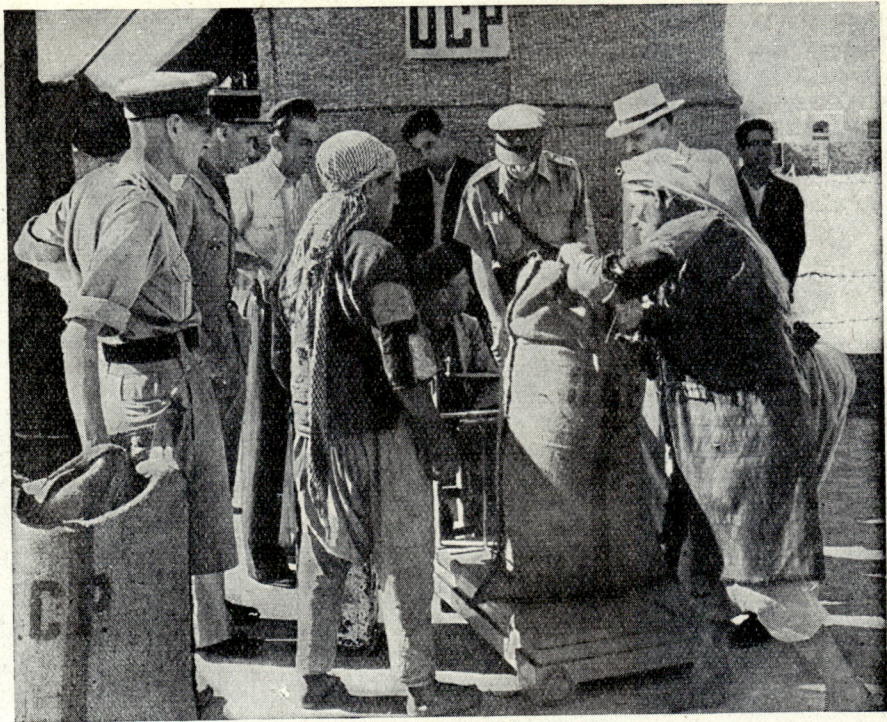

BREAD FOR CIVILIAN AND SOLDIER IN THE MIDDLE EAST

Weighing sacks of grain brought in to the local O.C.P. (Office des Céréales Panifiables—office of cereals for bread-making) set up by the British, French, and local authorities in Syria and the Lebanon to buy grain from the farmers and distribute it to the people, in order to relieve distress caused by maldistribution of cereals after hostilities ceased in the area in 1941. Below, a mountain of flour brought into a Middle East port from Australia for the feeding of Allied troops. *Photos, British Official : Crown Copyright ; Associated Press*

Persian Left Wing, it was bitterly attacked by those papers representing vested interests. But Dr. Millspaugh was in grim earnest. He foresaw possible bankruptcy unless Persians made a radical attack on economic problems.

No Middle Eastern State, however, had shown during the war any lasting interest in the recasting of its national economy ; and already some Persians, as an offset to such recasting, were playing with the idea of Persia's joining the United Nations—not because Persians generally intended to do more for the Allied war effort but because membership of such a body might produce immediate advantages.

It was during such a period of un-certainty that Germany succeeded in sending some agents to Persia by air, and on August 22 the Government offered a large reward for the seizing of any Germans living in the country without permission. In the following month, several arrests were made, including some Persians suspected of complicity with the enemy. Yet even the danger of internal disorders was insufficient to persuade the Mejlis to pass Dr. Millspaugh's Income Tax bill, and the American expert actually handed in his resignation on October 14. His departure would have been disastrous. After strong advice from outside, including that of the Shah, the Mejlis passed the bill and Dr. Millspaugh withdrew his resignation.

German Agents in Persia

Before the end of the year, however, Persians were to have an experience wholly to their liking. This was provided by the Teheran Conference. On November 26, Marshal Stalin, M. Molotov, and Marshal Voroshilov arrived in Teheran, where the utmost precautions for security had been taken. They were followed the next day by Mr. Churchill and President Roosevelt. The leaders of the three great nations at war with Germany, together with their Service and civilian advisers, conferred for four days—November 28 to December 1. Though many Persians knew the secret of the meeting, not a word was allowed to leak out of the country until the conditions of security had been met. But Persians could and did show all the hospitality they were allowed, and it was a typical comment on a meeting after the conference that in the gathering " there were no Persians, no British, no Russians and no Americans—for all were Persians, all were British, all were Russians, and all were Americans."

The findings of the conference, in so far as they concerned Europe, will be found in Historic Document No. CCLXVI, page 2636; here it must be recorded that immense satisfaction was felt by Persians over the Declaration on Iran, in which the three statesmen said:

" The three Governments realize that the war has caused special economic difficulties for Iran, and they are agreed that they will continue to make available to the Government of Iran such economic assistance as may be possible. . . . The Governments of the U.S.A., the U.S.S.R., and the U.K. are at one with the Government of Iran in their desire for the maintenance of the independence, sovereignty and territorial integrity of Iran. They count upon the participation of Iran, together with all other peace-loving nations, in the establishment of international peace, security, and prosperity after the war, in accordance with the principles of the Atlantic Charter, to which all four Governments have continued to subscribe."

Persians were flattered by the choice of their country for the long-awaited meeting between Stalin, Churchill and Roosevelt, but they were really heartened by the Declaration on Iran.

Iraq began the year with an action for which her Prime Minister, Nuri Pasha, had long been ready. On January 16 the Government announced that "in view of the hostile attitude taken by Axis Powers towards Iraq for a long period, their continued subversive activities through their agents, their hostile broadcasts, their unceasing efforts to promote disunity inside the country, their broadcast insults to the Royal Family calculated to undermine the loyalty of the Iraqi people, and their encouragement to rebels who had tried to overthrow the Constitution," Iraq considered herself at war with Germany, Italy and Japan.

The announcement, which was duly acknowledged by Mr. Churchill, created more satisfaction than excitement and enthusiasm in Iraq, where it was emphasized that adherence to the United Nations implied no further war effort than had already been involved for Iraq under the Anglo-Iraqi Alliance. By some Middle Eastern States, Iraq's action was even taken amiss, the theory being that Iraq wanted to usurp the

AMERICAN MILITARY MISSION TO THE KING OF ARABIA
Maj.-General Ralph Royce, commanding the U.S. Armed Forces in the Middle East, in December 1943 headed an American military mission to King Ibn Saud of Arabia, with whom he is here seen in conversation at his palace at Jedda, some 40 miles from Mecca. Seated on the floor is Lieut. William Kalliff, who acted as interpreter.   *Photo, U.S. Official*

leadership of the Arab world. The Iraq Government offered Iraqi troops for service outside Iraq, but it was decided that they could best be utilized on lines of communication within Iraq.

This done, the Iraqi Government concentrated on the problem of attaining Arab unity, and all through the year efforts in this direction went on. By midsummer this campaign, furthered to some extent by alarm over the activities of Zionists in America, achieved considerable momentum. Nuri Pasha visited the Levant States in July and went on to discuss Arab unity with the Egyptian Prime Minister. His aim was to try first to secure agreement on a " United Syria " to include independent Governments of Syria, the Lebanon, Transjordan and Palestine, and he postulated in this scheme a Jewish enclave in Palestine and a Lebanon reduced to its former limited frontiers.

A pleasing success was obtained by the first visit, in November, of the Regent of Iraq to England. The Emir Abdullillah arrived back in Baghdad on December 12.

Saudi Arabia had a quiet year. While manifesting some circumspection on the question of Arab unity—or, rather, on the means of securing it—Ibn Saud proved that he was not a whit behind other Arabs on the Zionist issue. In an interview granted to an American journal in April he denied that the

Jews had any justification for claiming possession of Palestine. Americans displayed unwonted interest in Saudi Arabia. Mr. Kirk, U.S.A. Minister in Egypt, visited Riyadh in May and told Ibn Saud of the decision to apply Lend-Lease to Saudi Arabia. In the following month the Arab King was visited by General Hurley, personal representative of President Roosevelt in the Middle East, and shortly afterwards the President invited Ibn Saud, or his sons, to visit America. The invitation was accepted, and later in the year the Emirs Faisal and Khalid went to the United States for the first time in their lives. On their way home they stopped in Britain for a time, arriving here on November 17.

Ibn Saud had other American visitors during the year. In August President Roosevelt (who had already been approached by Ibn Saud with a request to find other places than Palestine for oppressed Jewry) sent Colonel Hoskins to discuss a possible settlement of the Palestine problem. Then in December an American Military Mission under General Royce, commanding American forces in the Middle East, arrived in Jedda. The General left behind several technical experts to investigate the possible development of the country and to examine the question of supplying Ibn Saud with arms.

ACTION ON GUADALCANAL

These spirited paintings, by Lieut. Dwight Shepler of the U.S. Navy, an artist who served on Guadalcanal during the fierce fighting of 1942-43, give a vivid impression of the country and the bitter struggle that took place there, described in Chapter 250. Above, 'Action on the River' shows Marines crossing singly a sluggish river, the Japanese enemy invisible but menacing in the dense tropical forest beyond. Right, 'Bombardment— Guadalcanal,' painted during the 'first anniversary hate shoot' put down on December 7, 1942 (one year after Pearl Harbor) by Marine artillerymen using 155-mm. Army howitzers. Every piece of artillery on the island fired from dusk to dawn.

BRITISH AND AMERICAN BOMBER AIRCRAFT

FOLLOWING page 2266 appeared direct colour photographs of four outstanding types of British and American fighter aircraft. Here are three contemporary bombers. Left, North American Mitchell B-25, an all-metal American monoplane named after a noted U.S. military pilot. Used by the U.S. Army as a medium bombardment machine, by the R.A.F. as a medium bomber, it carries a crew of five and has two Wright Double Row Cyclone air-cooled, radial motors, and a maximum speed of 308 m.p.h. at 13,000 feet. Service ceiling of the B-25 is 25,400 ft., and range at an operating speed of 243 m.p.h. 2,650 miles. Its tricycle undercarriage is backwards-retracting, the wheels completely covered when fully retracted. This aircraft has a span of 67 ft. 6¾ ins., length 54 ft. 13/16 ins. ; and armament, three ·30 and four ·50 calibre machine-guns. Bombers of this type took part in Maj.-Gen. Doolittle's raid on Tokyo on April 18, 1942. (See illus., page 2126.)

Below, Boeing Fortress II, popularly known as the Flying Fortress, an American all-metal machine used by the U.S. Army for heavy bombardment, by Coastal Command of the R.A.F. for anti-submarine patrol work. It carries a crew of nine, has four Wright Double Row Cyclone motors, and a maximum speed of 305 m.p.h. at 20,000 feet. Its service ceiling is approximately 40,000 ft., span 103 ft. 9⅜ ins., and length 73 ft. 9⅝ ins. The forwards-retracting undercarriage main wheels are partially exposed when fully retracted. The armament of the B-17G type Fortress consists of thirteen ·50 calibre machine-guns. (See illus., page 2516.)

Below, left, the De Havilland Mosquito, a British, two-seat, reconnaissance bomber of all wooden construction with a backwards-retracting undercarriage, the wheels of which are completely enclosed when fully retracted. It has two Rolls-Royce, liquid-cooled, Vee motors, and a speed not far short of 400 m.p.h. The Mosquito's span is 54 ft. 2 ins., its length 40 ft. 9½ ins. ; its armament may be a battery of four 20-mm. shell guns and four ·303 machine-guns, and a light bomb load is carried within the fuselage. Owing to its speed it requires no fighter escort. It was first mentioned in the news when four Mosquitoes made a daylight raid on Gestapo headquarters at Oslo on September 25, 1942. (See illus., page 2176.)

BADGES OF BRITAIN'S HOME FRONT FIGHTERS

1. Women's Land Army : two years' service merit badge. 2. Merchant Navy, Civil Defence, Police, National Fire Service, and other uniformed civilians : badge awarded for brave conduct commendations. 3. Civil Defence : armlet worn by those responsible for investigating reports of unexploded bombs. 4. Civil Defence : badge worn by qualified instructor. 5. Hospital Service : badge issued to all staff (except doctors and nurses) serving a minimum of 96 hours a month. 6. Civil Defence : service badge, and, 7, that worn by Incident Officers. 8. Civil Defence : Ambulance Driver and shoulder flash. 9. Badge worn by workers in Royal Ordnance factories. 10. Boy Scouts war service armlet. 11. National Fire Service : cap badge. 12. Civil Defence : Post Warden and shoulder flash.

Chapter 267

LORD WAVELL GOES TO INDIA AS VICEROY

*During 1943 Lord Wavell's appointment as Viceroy, and the famine in Bengal,
overshadowed the political situation in India which, though no simpler, was
quieter than it had been in the preceding year (described in Chapter 223).
India's war effort continued at a high level, relative to her resources ; and
her peoples increased their splendid contribution in personnel to the Allied
fighting forces*

EARLY in 1943 political controversies in India became overshadowed by anxiety over the economic situation. The detention of Congress Party leaders and the effective measures taken to suppress the disturbances of the autumn of 1942 had brought about an outward lull in political activities, although under the surface there lurked a sense of disappointment.

Defeatist views, which were admitted to have played a large part in the decisions of the Congress Party and its sympathizers, had been discounted by the signs of successful Russian resistance to the German attack. The conference at Casablanca was regarded in India as a portent of Axis discomfiture, especially as it was followed by the prompt visit to India of Sir John Dill. And General Arnold, who had seen Marshal Chiang Kai-shek at Chungking and then in Delhi, acquainted Sir Archibald Wavell, Commander-in-Chief India, with the plans for the United Nations' action against Japan.

This accord and the falling off in enemy air activity over eastern India, increased the confidence of the Indian people. The economic problem had, however, become so much a matter of concern that it took a prominent place in the discussions of the National Defence Council's eighth session in the third week in January. The lack of popular interest in politics was shown by the placid passing of "Independence Day" (January 26).

Mr. Gandhi by his threat of a fast endeavoured to frighten the Government into releasing him unconditionally. But the Government refused to be deflected. They could not be responsible for the effects of a fast on his health, nor prevent him from trying it. Mr. Gandhi had intimated that he proposed to fast " according to capacity" and wished to " survive the ordeal."

This did not greatly reassure that section of the Indian public which is traditionally susceptible to emotional apprehension. Indeed, three members of the Viceroy's Council (Cabinet) who had been parties to Mr. Gandhi's arrest, felt impelled to resign and made no

INDIAN ARMY FIELD AMBULANCE
The Fourth Indian Division played a conspicuous part in the fighting in Tunisia, helping to pierce the Mareth Line in March 1943, capturing Wadi Akarit positions on April 5, occupying Sfax on April 10, and taking part in the final break through to Tunis and Bizerta (during which General von Arnim surrendered to a colonel of Gurkhas). This Field Ambulance of the Indian Army Medical Corps (created in 1943) is carrying to safety a member of a Gurkha battalion wounded in the Eighth Army's attack on the Mareth Line.
Photo, British Official : Crown Copyright

secret of the reasons. They were Sir Hormusji Mody, Mr. M. S. Aney and Mr. Nalini Sarkar.

Their portfolios of Supply, Indians Oversea, and Commerce were eventually accepted by Sir Ramaswami Mudaliar, Dr. N. B. Khare (formerly the first Congress Party Premier in the Central Provinces), and Sir Muhhamad Azizul Huque respectively.

Mention of these appointments makes it convenient to explain that the Government of India is the Executive Council of the Viceroy. It consists of the Viceroy as President, the Commander-in-Chief as Extraordinary Member (with the portfolio of War), and 13 other Members, of whom all except four are Indians.

This Council is in effect a Cabinet, responsible to the British Parliament through the Secretary of State for India. The term " Member "—the capital letter is important—connotes a rank and authority better understood by the word " Minister " in other countries. The Viceroy has—within certain well-defined limits—the power of overriding his Council's decisions, which otherwise go by majority vote. This power of the Viceroy has not been used, at any rate since the enlargement of the Council in 1941.

In the Provinces of British India, according to the Constitution of 1935, the Governors govern by and with the advice of Indian Ministers chosen from, and responsible to, elected Indian Provincial Legislatures —the total electorate in the 11 provinces amounting to 35,000,000 voters. Here, the term " Minister " has replaced that of " Member." Until November 1939 all the 11 provinces had ministerial autonomous governments which had come into power in 1937 as the result of the first elections under the Constitution of 1935.

The decision of the Congress Party to withdraw its supporters from the eight provinces where they had formed Ministries broke this uniformity. Later, in two provinces alternative ministries were formed so that in 1943 the following were still autonomously governed provinces : Assam, Bengal, North-West Frontier Province, Orissa, Punjab and Sind (comprising a total population of about 110 millions) ; while emergency governments (the Governors acting with Advisers) were operating under the Constitution in the remaining five provinces : Bihar, Bombay, Central Provinces, Madras, United Provinces (about 180 millions).

It should be recalled that the decision of the Congress Party " High Command " or Central Executive was pressed on the Provincial Ministries of its political complexion against the will of some of the Ministers concerned.

In 1943 the sense of dissatisfaction over the breakdown of the negotiations with Sir Stafford Cripps in the preceding year, and the virtual extinction of the influence of the Con-

Growth of the Muslim League

gress Party leaders by the consequences of their own actions in August 1942, stimulated heart-searching among the rank and file. The danger of permitting to a Party executive extra-mural authority over the elected members of Legislatures was becoming more clearly appreciated. This was sharply underlined by the strides made by Mr. M. A. Jinnah in organizing the solidarity of Muslim political strength against the Congress Party itself. By the end of the year the Muslim League had become a powerful instrument in Mr. Jinnah's hands, and was threatening the Muslim-Hindu-Sikh coalition in the Punjab, where Provincial Autonomy had proved to be workable in Indian hands and sectional differences had been adjusted in a spirit of compromise and good will.

The successful expansion of India's military and industrial effort for the prosecution of the war, against Germany in the West and—in ever-increasing force —against Japan in the East, indicated the lack of nationalist enthusiasm of the mass of the people, and showed how far the Congress Party and, in a less degree, the Muslim League had failed to grasp the realities of the situation. Mr. Gandhi's theatrical fast was a characteristic bid for re-entry into the limelight, but the firmness of the Government convinced Mr. Gandhi that he had failed. On March 3 the fast ended.

Nevertheless, the personal prestige enjoyed by Mr. Gandhi moved even those among his supporters who deplored his fatal leadership in 1942 to urge some action by the Government to remove the " deadlock," and so enable the Congress Party to re-enter political life in the full sense of the term. This view received support from sympathizers in Great Britain and America.

In April Lord Linlithgow refused permission for five Hindu politicians (including Mr. Rajagopalachariar, the former Prime Minister of Madras who had broken with Mr. Gandhi over the Cripps proposals) to interview Mr. Gandhi in internment. The Viceroy could not accept the contention that a genuine national government could be formed on the basis of such an interview, for the essential preliminary was agreement between the parties, communities and interests to which the excessive claims of the Congress Party had been an obstacle. The other parties approved the Viceroy's attitude.

Under the auspices of the newly created Food Department of the Central Government, the second All-India Food Conference was held in Delhi at the end of February. The year had opened with good prospects for all grains

except rice, which had been badly affected by cyclones and floods. It was estimated that in wheat production there would be a surplus of 1,000,000 tons. But in parts of India, rice is the staple food-grain, and the cyclone's destruction of standing crops and stores of rice in rice-producing Bengal created an unpromising situation.

The Chief Minister of Bengal (then Mr. Fazlul Huq) told the Conference that Bengal could feed itself so long as it was not asked to accept responsibility for supplying food to the All-India pool. This calculation turned out to be inaccurate. The Minister's position indeed was precarious. By the end of March he had resigned, and his place was taken by Kwaja Sir Nazimuddin, a member of the Muslim League who succeeded in forming a coalition Ministry on which fell the burden of handling an increasingly grave economic situation.

By May the gravity of the crisis was apparent to the Government of India, but measures constitutionally within

MEN OF THE WORLD'S LARGEST VOLUNTEER ARMY

Of the 2,000,000 volunteers who made up the Indian Army in 1943, nearly half a million had seen service overseas. They did splendid work throughout the campaigns in Africa, and went on to further battles in Sicily and Italy. Like other armies, that of India has undergone mechanization. Here men of the Indian Armoured Corps are receiving instruction in camouflage with the help of miniature trucks, and a heap of stones to represent a hillside. Top, a new recruit visits his native village for the first time as a soldier.

Photos, Indian Official

THE VICEROY SEES FOR HIMSELF

Immediately after his assumption of the Viceroyalty on October 20, 1943, Lord Wavell visited Calcutta and the famine-stricken district of Midnapore in order to see for himself what was happening. He is seen here at a Rotary Club Free Kitchen in Calcutta with Lady Wavell, Mr. E. M. Jenkins (his private secretary), Sir Thomas Rutherford (acting Governor of Bengal), and Mr. J. K. Briswas, chairman of the Rotary Club Relief Committee. His announcement that the Army would help in the distribution of food was promptly given effect : right, an army truck being loaded with grain. Below, distributing clothing to sufferers in a shelter for the destitute.

Photos, British Official : Crown Copyright ; Keystone ; Topical Press

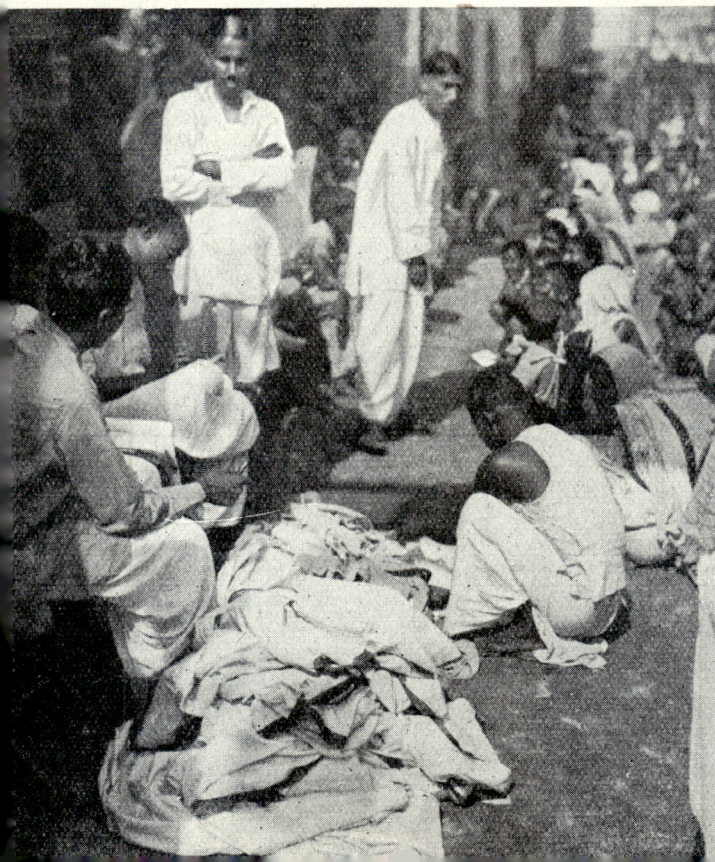

2649

ALL-INDIA MUSLIM LEAGUE CONVENTION

The 30th session of the All-India Muslim League was held at New Delhi from April 24–26, 1943, under the presidency of Mr. Jinnah, re-elected to that office on March 7. In his presidential address, he emphatically reiterated the League's demand for Pakistan—that is, an independent Muslim state in India—a demand endorsed by the convention, which also strongly condemned the anti-Indian legislation in South Africa, and urged the government to frame food policies in consultation with representatives of the people. *Photo, Keystone*

the competence of the Central Government were ineffective in mitigating Bengal's difficulties. The Governments of Bombay and Madras, as well as the Indian-ruled States of Travancore and Cochin, were also confronted by a serious scarcity of rice, but by control and rationing they averted a breakdown.

Looking at the food problem in India as a whole, Sir Azizul Huque, when Food Minister, told the Central Legislature in August: " the consumption needs of India had been calculated on the basis of an average adult diet of one lb. of food-grains per diem," which gave a total of $50\frac{1}{2}$ million tons, in addition to $4\frac{1}{2}$ million tons seed requirements—55 million tons in all. Normal production could be taken at 50/51 million tons.

Recognizing the special difficulties in Bengal—its population of 60 millions with a density of 3,000 persons per square mile in some of its eastern rural areas and its proximity to enemy-occupied territory—the Central Government hoped that its plan for drawing on

more fortunate provinces for the supply of grain to Bengal would operate successfully. In point of fact, only about a quarter of the figure proposed reached Bengal in the first half of 1943.

The law courts treated offenders against the food laws so lightly that confidence fell. The householders in towns took to stocking food against future needs. To sum up, a primitive economy was strained to breaking-point by the complex weight of the vicissitudes of war, the inexperience of a recently set up autonomous ministerial government, the lack of a firmly based civic consciousness, and the diffidence of the Central Government (which was loth to expose itself to the charge of precipitate interference with the functions of an Indian-manned Ministry).

As these factors exercised their cumulative and baneful influence, the evil was worsened by the tongue of rumour —such as, for example, caused the influx into Calcutta of 2,000,000 people from the rural districts in search of allegedly

large quantities of food. Taking the shortage of the Bengal harvest as about 15 per cent, there might have been hardship but certainly not disaster if an even distribution could have been made throughout the province. But the cultivators' retention of grain in the apprehension created by the cyclone passed on the shortage to the towns where it reached, for the urban population, the dimensions of 40/50 per cent. On top of this, the perversity of the speculator and the weaknesses in the Government proved calamitous.

In October Lord Linlithgow's term of office—the longest ever borne by any Viceroy—ended, and Lord Wavell, who had been Commander-in-Chief when the year began, took his place (*see* illus., page 2596). By that time the mortality from famine in Bengal had attracted world attention.

The decision of the Government to break with precedent and appoint an eminent soldier as Viceroy was generally applauded. This did not prevent criticism from those to whom the tradition, thus ignored, was precious. Even they seemed to be

Lord Wavell Appointed Viceroy

prepared to recognize the overriding claims of the situation and, more importantly, the special appeal which, as Commander-in-Chief in India, and as a leader of men in Africa, Lord Wavell had inspired. His personality in short had struck the imagination of Indians, in politics as well as in the administration.

On his assumption of the Viceroyalty (October 20), Lord Wavell promptly showed his sense of the urgency of the famine position in Bengal. Within four days he was in Calcutta, and after a personal visit to the stricken district of Midnapore, he announced that the Army had been asked to help in relief of the people of Bengal. General Auchinleck, who succeeded Lord Wavell as Commander-in-Chief, at once set military assistance in motion. Emergency measures thus taken were directed toward the relief of sufferers—disease taking a heavy toll of an underfed population—and toward the improvement of methods of distribution. Lord Wavell further showed his appreciation of the paramount call of the Bengal famine by making concentration on that problem the ground for not addressing the two houses of the Central Legislature when they met in November.

Indeed, realizing that when the immediate problem of relief had been solved, there remained the highly important task of ensuring due provision against a recurrence of disaster, Lord Wavell proceeded to make a quick tour of the whole of India. He intended thereby to enlist such co-operation from the Provincial Governments that the unhappy events of 1943 would not be repeated. As it was, his personal intervention brought about an agreement which had hitherto been lacking.

Not until the early part of 1944 was the Government of Bengal able to issue figures showing that the total deaths **Bengal : Vital** from all causes in the **Statistics** province during 1943 **for 1943** amounted to 1,873,749, which exceeded the normal average of the previous five years by 688,846. Deaths from cholera were 214,175, or 160,909 above the average, and from malaria 674,330 or 285,792 above the average—the prevalence of both diseases being undoubtedly accentuated by the food shortage, and the movement of people from rural districts into the towns in search of food. These official figures, while not completely comprehensive, for the normal defects of the recording agencies would be enhanced by the dislocation attendant on the disaster, effectively contradicted some unofficial estimates made in token surveys on a "sample" basis, which give the figure of deaths at ·006 of the population.

The picture of India's war effort must not get out of focus because this poignant tragedy of human disaster has demanded—and deserved—close attention. In a sense, the famine illustrated the greatness of India's contribution to the strength of the United Nations, if only because it showed how heavy had been the strain of the conflict on what is after

AMERICANS IN INDIA

Left : American troops arriving in India for service against the Japanese on the Burmese and Chinese fronts. During 1943 many thousands of Americans received in India the preliminary training required for jungle fighting. They also learned to use the elephant for transport in the Naga Hills near the Burma border (above), where they built a number of bases with the aid of native workers.

Photos, Pictorial Press ; Keystone

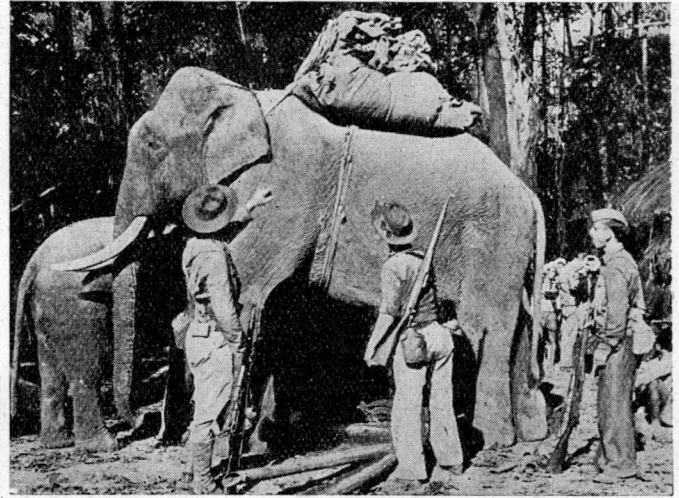

all a country of primitive economy.

The actual operations in which Indian, British, American and Chinese forces were engaged against the Japanese in Burma are described in Chapter 270. In support of those operations, the Com- **India's War** mander-in-Chief India **Contributions** had the rôle of supplying Vice-Admiral Lord Louis Mountbatten, Supreme Allied Commander of the South-East Asia Command (created in August 1943, with headquarters at Delhi), with the tools for the job, whether by the provision of man-power from the Army in India, or by the intensified mobilization of supplies of all kinds under the leadership of the Government of India.

The achievements of the Fourth and Fifth Indian Divisions in Africa were a source of intense pride to the people of India. (*See* illus., page 2647.)

The expansion of the Indian Army, which had reached the high total strength of 2,000,000—the largest volunteer force in the world—and the ever-increasing momentum of industrial mobilization, afforded practical proof of the country's general support of the war. In June part of the price was

ESTABLISHING NEW AIRFIELDS IN INDIA

During the war the aeroplane became familiar in many parts of India where the natives had never seen a railway train, but the bullock, patient draught animal of centuries, remained a common object—even on airfields. Right, Air Chief Marshal Sir Richard Peirse, K.C.B., D.S.O., A.F.C., Air Officer Commanding-in-Chief, India (appointed A.O. C.-in-C. S.-E. Asia Command, December 1943) talking to Air Vice-Marshal T. M. Williams, A.O. Commanding Bengal, during a tour of Bengal in the summer of 1943. Below, Indian women labourers helping to construct an airfield for American aircraft.

Photos, British Official: Keystone

revealed in the publication of India's total casualties in the field for the first three years of war: 101,979, of whom 3,286 were killed, 9,168 wounded, 3,236 prisoners, and 86,289 missing.

By the end of the year Lord Wavell's ascendancy was in fair way to being established, and corrective measures taken by the Central Government had effected an improvement in the general situation in India. Rising prices had been checked by monetary regulations and by the control of commodities.

The Government's determination to make control effective restored public confidence. India could not emulate the results achieved in highly organized countries, but her Government, moving slowly perhaps, could claim that its efforts should be judged in the light of the experience of other countries similarly situated, at a comparable stage of development, and also exposed to the varying fortunes of a global war. The Government, indeed, set itself to handle the affairs of a country peculiarly susceptible to rumour and panic, by striving to restore a sense of balance without which action designed to counteract panic would fail in remedial effect.

India's lessened apprehensions about the outcome of the war were exemplified in December, when the sharpest air raid the Japanese had yet inflicted on Calcutta caused nothing like the excitement and dislocation which had followed the raids of the previous year.

The Japanese employment of Subhas Chandra Bose, ex-Mayor of Calcutta, ex-President of the Congress Party, and ex-I.C.S., as the mouthpiece of their propaganda and the leader of their so-called "Indian Army of Invasion" made little impression. Perhaps his native Bengal, as the province in the forefront of the battle, was little disposed to listen to the protestations of one whom it knew so well. Certainly, the anxieties caused by the Japanese advance seemed to be tempered by the conviction that the enemy could not be formidable if he placed any reliance, or depended to any extent, on Subhas Chandra's military leadership.

The war effort for which India is responsible had in 1943 reached a high pitch in quality and quantity, bearing in mind the resources available. There **Burden of** was no thought of slack-**India's** ening or denying com-**War Effort** mitments entered into towards the United Nations. But a substantial increase in the demands on India's skilled man-power and materials would impose a severe additional burden on her economy. This the Government made clear, introducing safeguards calculated to preserve India's economic stability so that the welfare of her people and her consequent utility as a base of operations would not be imperilled.

The task of handling the great increase of military stores in India owing to the arrivals of guns, ammunition, tanks, lorries and equipment of all kinds from the United Kingdom, U.S.A., Canada and Australia posed difficult problems, towards the solution of which good

tion. Improvement in the conditions of service for Indian troops was effected. The welfare of the Indian soldier has long been looked after by the network of Soldiers' District Boards co-ordinated by a Central Board at General Headquarters. This work was strengthened by the appointment of civil liaison officers to ensure the well-being of the serviceman's family, and also of discharged or disabled servicemen.

Four years of war inevitably caused a partial interruption of social and cultural relations between India and the outside world, particularly Great Britain. Incidental to the establishment of the South-East Asia Command, there was much going to and fro of Service officers of the British and American forces, and missions on their way to China passed through India. But the flow of cultural relationships was checked. The exigencies of the famine, it is true, brought out to India important experts from the Ministry of Food, whose advice and guidance

proved invaluable. It was perceived, however, that interchange of opinion in other fields would be valuable. To this end, the visit to India of Professor A. V. Hill, M.P., was of first importance. Professor Hill's eminence in science as Secretary of the Royal Society, of which there are six Indian Fellows, gave distinction to his acceptance of the invitation to advise the Government of India on matters of scientific research in industry.

Lord Wavell ended a public speech in Calcutta (important extracts from which will be found in Historic Document No. CCLXVIII, page 2636) with words that may fittingly end this Chapter: "As head of the Government, and an old and sincere friend of India, I will do my best during my term of office to guide India on her path to a better future. It is no easy path, there are no short cuts, but I do believe in the future greatness that lies ahead if we can work together to the solution of our problems."

MEN AND WOMEN OF INDIA TAKE TO THE AIR

A radiologist doctor and Sepoy nurses belonging to an airborne unit of the Indian Army Medical Corps directing the unloading of X-ray equipment from a Bisley bomber. Left, personnel of the Indian Air Force, Royal Air Force, and Women's Auxiliary Corps (India) at work in the plotting-room of a radiolocation station. Below, men of a Gurkha regiment begin their training as parachutists at a centre in North-west India.

progress was made during the year. There were more British troops in India than at any time in her history. In addition, the American forces and India's own expanded army, Air Force (which reached its 10th birthday in April), and Royal Indian Navy, further taxed the resources of the administra-

Diary of the War

JANUARY and FEBRUARY, 1943

January 1, 1943. Velike Luki fell to the Red Army ; Elista, capital of Kalmuck Soviet Republic, reoccupied by Russians.

January 2. Chinese troops recaptured Chienshan and Taihu on Anhwei-Hupeh border (China). Buna Mission (New Guinea) captured by the Allies.

January 3. Mozdok recaptured by Russians. U.S. heavy bombers attacked U-boat base at St. Nazaire by day. Macheng (E. Hupeh, China) captured by Japanese. Flying Fortresses raided Rabaul for fifth time in eight days.

January 4. Russians recaptured Chernyshkovsky and Chernyshkov station.

January 5. Nalchik recaptured by Russians ; Kalmuck Republic cleared of the enemy. Formation of American Fifth Army in Tunisia under Lt.-Gen. Mark W. Clark announced. Nine ships aggregating 50,000 tons sunk in Rabaul harbour by U.S. bombers.

January 6-9. Action against Japanese convoy : three transports sunk, three others probably sunk, 85 Japanese pianes destroyed, another 29 probably destroyed.

January 9. Essen heavily bombed by night, many 4,000 lb. bombs being dropped.

January 11. Naples attacked by day by Africa-based American bombers.

January 12. General Leclerc's Fighting French forces from the Chad completed the conquest of the Fezzan.

January 13. U.S. Fortresses (three lost) attacked Lille by day ; heavy attack on the Ruhr (eighth in 11 nights) by R.A.F. Hard fighting near Rathedaung (Burma).

January 14. Bomber Command heavily attacked by night the enemy U-boat base at Lorient.

January 14-24. President Roosevelt and Mr. Churchill and their Chiefs of Staff met at Casablanca, N. Africa, for the " unconditional surrender " conference.

January 15. Another R.A.F. night attack on Lorient. Eighth Army launched an offensive, successful at all points, on enemy positions near Buerat (Tripolitania).

January 16. In the Stalingrad factory area, enemy dislodged from another 26 strong-points. Berlin bombed at night by strong force of British four-engined bombers ; one plane lost. Sanananda Point (New Guinea) stormed by Australians.

January 16-17. Five Japanese ships, totalling 25,000 tons, sunk or severely damaged in air raid on Rabaul.

January 17. Powerful new offensive launched south of Voronezh by Soviet forces ; Millerovo recaptured. Strong R.A.F. formations dropped great weight of bombs on Berlin, including 8,000 lb. bombs and thousands of incendiaries ; 22 bombers lost. London had first night raid since May 1941 ; 10 raiders shot down by tremendous barrage. Anglo-Indian forces occupied Kyauktaw (Burma).

January 17-19. Allied destroyer force sank 13 enemy vessels in Central Mediterranean without damage or casualties.

January 18. Siege of Leningrad raised. U.S. forces on Guadalcanal captured ridge dominating Henderson airfield.

January 20. Ostrogorsk, 50 miles south of Voronezh, recaptured by Russians. Forty-two children and six teachers killed in day raid on London ; 11 enemy planes destroyed.

January 21. Voroshilovsk recaptured by Russian Caucasian Army. Homs and Tahuna (Tripolitania) occupied by Eighth Army.

January 22. Salsk recaptured by Russian tank forces.

January 23. Eighth Army enters Tripoli. Armavir in the Caucasus recaptured by Russians. Brest and Lorient U-boat bases bombed by day by U.S. Fortresses. Ground fighting in Papua ceased.

January 23-24. Successful combined operations raid by British forces on Lervik, Norway.

January 25. Russians cleared Voronezh of enemy. Advanced units of General Leclerc's Fighting French forces joined Eighth Army.

January 27. Siege of Stalingrad raised. Americans attacked Germany for first time in day raid on Wilhelmshaven. " Saturation " night raid by R.A.F. on Duesseldorf.

January 29. Armoured cars of Eighth Army crossed the Tripolitania-Tunisia border.

January 29-February 4. Air-sea action in the Solomons : two Japanese destroyers, one corvette, two supply ships sunk, four destroyers probably sunk, six destroyers, one corvette and two cargo ships damaged, 61 aircraft destroyed ; American losses : one cruiser, one destroyer, three M.T.B.s and 22 aircraft.

January 30. Mr. Churchill visited President Inonu of Turkey at Adana. Maikop and Tikhoretsk in the Caucasus recaptured by Soviet forces. R.A.F. raided Berlin twice (first daytime raids) causing postponement by an hour of Goering broadcast, and interrupting Goëbbels' broadcast of Hitler's proclamation on 10th anniversary of Nazi regime. Germans occupied Faid Pass (Tunisia).

January 31. Complete annihilation of German Sixth Army (originally 330,000 strong) at Stalingrad reported. Eighth Army occupied Zuara, last port in Tripolitania.

February 2. Last centre of resistance in Stalingrad area crushed ; battle of Stalingrad concluded. " Saturation " night attack by R.A.F. on Cologne ; factories used for building U-boats heavily bombed.

February 3. Kupiansk and Krasny-Liman in the Ukraine recaptured by Russians.

February 4. Day raid on the Ruhr by American Flying Fortresses—25 enemy aircraft destroyed ; severe night attack on Turin by R.A.F.

February 6. Announcement of creation of North African Operational Theatre under the command of Lieut.-General Eisenhower. Air victory over Wau (New Guinea) : 37 Allied fighters destroyed 26 of 71 enemy planes and severely damaged another 15.

February 7. Azov recaptured by Soviet troops. U.S. troops on Guadalcanal reached Titi.

February 8. Kursk recaptured by Russians.

February 9. Byelgorod recaptured by Soviet troops.

February 10. Bitter fighting in suburbs of Rostov. Whole of Guadalcanal reported in American hands.

February 11. Lozovaya (Ukraine) reoccupied by Russians. Heavy concentrated night attack by R.A.F. en Wilhelmshaven : main ammunition depot destroyed.

February 12. Russians stormed Krasnodar, capital of the Kuban.

February 13. Novocherkassk, Don Cossack capital, recaptured by Russians. Two concentrated night attacks on Lorient.

February 14. Rostov recaptured for second time by Red Army ; Voroshilovgrad also recaptured. Heavy night attacks on Cologne and Milan. Sidi Bou Sid (Tunisia) captured by Germans. Rabaul (New Britain), Munda (Solomons), and Kiska (Aleutians) bombed by U.S. aircraft.

February 15. Gafsa evacuated by Americans ; Ben Gardane occupied by Eighth Army (Tunisia).

February 16. Kharkov, capital of the Ukraine, recaptured by Red Army : held by the enemy since October 29, 1941.

February 17. Germans captured Sbeitla, Kasserine, and Feriana (Tunisia).

February 18. Zalegosch captured by Red Army. Eighth Army occupied Foum Tatahouine (Tunisia).

February 20. Krasnograd and Pavlograd recaptured by Red Army. Eighth Army occupied Medenine (Tunisia).

February 21. Enemy attack towards Thala (Tunisia) held by British.

February 22. Night commando raid without loss by seaborne British troops on Myebon (Burma).

February 23. Sumi recaptured by Red Army.

February 25. R.A.F. heavily bombed Nuremberg at night. British and American units reoccupied Kasserine Pass ; Eighth Army penetrated to the line of the Wadi Zigzau (Tunisia).

February 26. U.S. bombers made heavy daylight attack on Wilhelmshaven ; heavy night attack by R.A.F. on Cologne. U.S. Fortresses made three-hour attack on Wewak (New Guinea).

February 27. Kasserine reoccupied by Americans (Tunisia).

February 28. Violent tank battles in Donetz basin. Very heavy night attack on St. Nazaire U-boat base.

Chapter 268

ALLIED AIR POWER GAINS THE UPPER HAND

During 1943 new machines and new weapons increased the range, powers of attack and defensibility of Allied aircraft; and the changeover from defensive to offensive gave the Allies opportunities for developing new ways of using their growing air power. Captain Norman Macmillan here reviews events in the fighting zones; in a later Chapter he will describe the intensive and mounting assault on Germany's war production prior to the invasion of France in 1944

DURING 1943 the major executive development in the employment of air power was the greater recognition accorded to the division of air forces into strategical and tactical commands, each equally able to operate separately as a complete air force, or to combine under a supreme commander, responsible not for their tactical control, but for the direction of all air operations in a complete theatre of war.

The first real organization of the overriding control of two air forces, one strategical and the other tactical, came after Air Chief Marshal Sir Arthur Tedder assumed command in the Middle East. Air Vice-Marshal Sir Arthur Coningham commanded No. 1 Tactical Air Force (as it was later called) working with the Eighth Army, and Air Vice-Marshal Sir Leonard Slatter commanded the East Mediterranean Strategical Air Force.

On January 9, 1943, the appointment was announced of Major-General Carl Spaatz, who had commanded the 8th U.S. Army Air Force in Britain, as C.-in-C. Allied Air Forces in North Africa (*see* illus., p. 2519). On Jan. 15 Air Chief Marshal Sir Sholto Douglas reached Cairo as C.-in-C. R.A.F. Middle East. Executive control of air power was further expanded following the advance of the Eighth Army from Tripolitania into Tunisia, which began on January 29, 1943, when armoured cars of the advance guard crossed the border. On February 11 Mr. Churchill announced the appointment of Air Chief Marshal Tedder to control all **Air Force** air forces in the Medi-**Appointments** terranean and the Middle East. The air forces attached to the British First and Eighth Armies, the American Army in Algeria and Tunisia, and the aircraft based on Malta, all came under Tedder's immediate control.

Air Vice-Marshal Sir Arthur Coningham assumed tactical command in north-west Africa under General Spaatz, who was responsible to Tedder for the direction of air operations there. On February 23 the appointment was announced of Air Vice-Marshal Harry Broadhurst, pre-war stunt flier of R.A.F. Hendon displays, to command the Western Desert Allied Air Forces. These air commanders, under General Eisenhower, were responsible for the final stages of the Allied victory in North Africa.

The original small strategical air force that had been commanded by Slatter was now a far larger force, able to play an important part in preparing the way for the tactical air force operating in close support of the army. Indeed, the strategical air force became the spearhead of all three Services by attacking ports, airfields, shipping, railways, factories and other targets hundreds of miles distant from the actual fighting zone, and so strangulating enemy power to wage war.

The old idea of air co-operation with the army, represented by the pre-war No. 22 Army Co-operation Group of Fighter Command which proceeded to France in 1939 with the Air Component of the British Expeditionary Force, was dead. In its place had arisen the tactical air force developed by Tedder, Coningham and General Montgomery. But it was not so much in its com-position—for the air component had possessed a few medium bombers allocated from Bomber Command and some fighters transferred from Fighter Command—as in the employment of the force, that the inno-vation lay. And to be **Tactical** historically accurate, **Air Force** even this was scarcely **Developed** new, for it was but an improvement on the close blitz tactics used by the Luftwaffe when working with the German army in western Europe in 1940. The innovation lay, not in the exploitation of close-support air power, but in the application over and above that of the distant support of the strategical air force—something the Germans had not done, for their whole air force was subordinated to the army.

The strategic application of air power requires a different kind of Intelligence branch from that demanded for tactical close support. The latter conforms to army field requirements, and much can be achieved by army recon-naissance units and air reconnaissance. The former demands a different kind

MEDITERRANEAN AIR CHIEFS MEET AT TARANTO
Air Vice-Marshal (acting Air Marshal) Sir Arthur Coningham, commanding No. 1 Tactical Air Force, Air Vice-Marshal Harry Broadhurst, A.O.C. Desert Allied Air Forces, and Air Chief Marshal Sir Arthur Tedder, A.O.C.-in-C. Mediterranean and Middle East from February 1943, watching R.A.F. fighters circling over Taranto airfield after the surrender of Italy in the autumn of 1943. *Photo, British Official: Crown Copyright*

PLOTTING THE AIR BATTLE OF THE SEAS

Members of the W.A.A.F. whose duty it was to plot the Air Battle of the Seas on a huge map 30 ft. high by 30 ft. wide at Coastal Command Operations Headquarters wore a safety harness attached to a wire working on friction pulleys so that they could move about the map quickly enough to keep up with the rapid changes. In the foreground: Air Vice-Marshal A. Durston, Senior Air Staff Officer, Air Marshal Sir John C. Slessor, C.-in-C. Coastal Command, and Capt. D. V. Peyton Ward, Senior Naval Staff Officer.

Photo, Topical

fighting Services and the munitions, man-power, and communication ancillary services from preventable strain. It is a weapon which blunts the enemy's sword before it can be brought into use. And the modern strategical air force is so flexible that it can be quickly deflected to assist the tactical air force to deliver a stronger close-support air attack.

This conception of the employment of air forces was fully developed in 1943, was later applied in the South-East Asia Command, and served as the model for the organization of the United Kingdom invasion air forces for 1944.

The aircraft based in the United Kingdom during 1943 were flown by personnel of almost all the Allies. Principal among them were the R.A.F. and U.S.A.A.F. Commands. During the year Bomber Command and Fighter Command expanded; Coastal Command, having received priorities in earlier years to play its vital part in surmounting the peril of the submarine war, required less of the nation's flow of air war material. Towards the close of the year Bomber Command was receiving the maximum priorities, and increasing its strength relative to other Commands at home and overseas—and the weight of attack against the European fortress grew even greater.

Coastal Command

Air Vice-Marshal Sir John Slessor took over Coastal Command from Sir Philip Joubert on February 4. Coastal Command harassed enemy shipping off the Dutch and Norwegian coasts, sinking at least 18 merchant vessels during the year, and damaging more than 20, together with many of their escort

of knowledge, that of the intentions of the enemy supreme command in regard to men, material, labour and transport services on the home fronts, and lines of communication, and a shrewd estimation of that command's intentions regarding the reinforcement of any particular front.

The object of such a strategical air force is to save all branches of one's

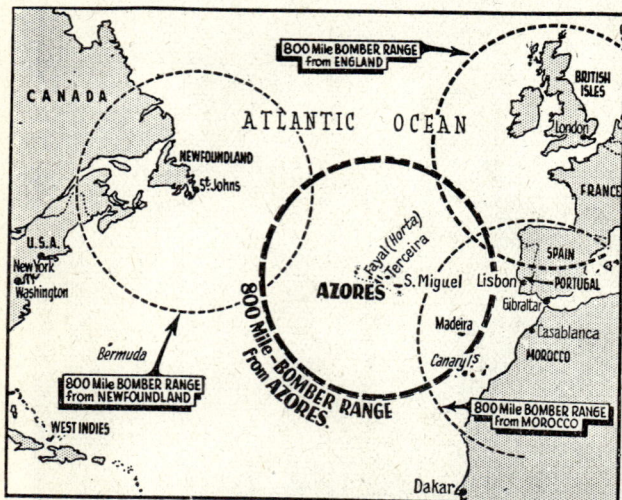

COASTAL COMMAND IN THE AZORES

From October 12, 1943, naval, military, and air units (including the R.A.F. Regiment), under the command of Air Vice-Marshal G. R. Bromet, C.B., C.B.E., D.S.O., were responsible for the Azores offensive which within a fortnight resulted in the killing of a U-boat by a R.A.F. Fortress. Right, drums of petrol for Allied aircraft based on the Azores.

In 1943, rocket bombs were added to the formidable armoury of the Allied air forces. Typhoons, Hurricanes, Beaufighters and Swordfish were equipped for their use. Here two of its eight rocket bombs can be seen flying ahead of a Beaufighter of R.A.F. Coastal Command, which has fired them in an attack on enemy shipping.

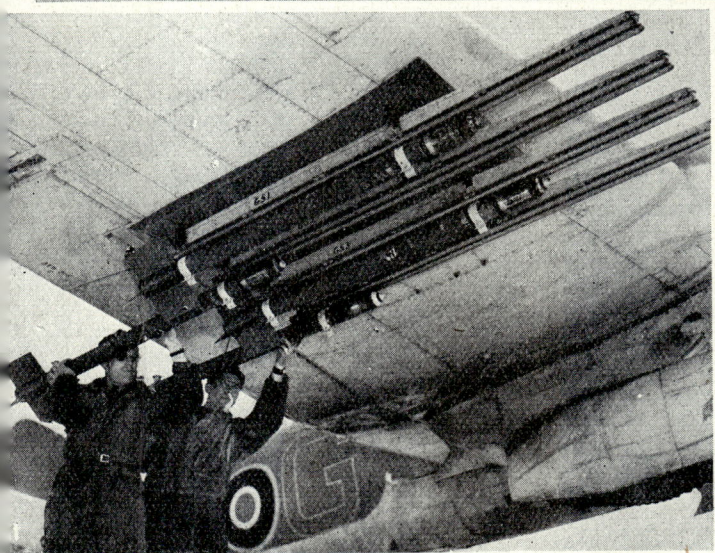

NEW ARMS AND CRAFT FOR ALLIED AIR FORCES

1. Loading rocket bombs into the guide rails beneath the wing of a Beaufighter. Four rockets fit under each wing ; they can be fired in pairs (as in 2), or in a salvo of eight (see page 2659). 3. Preparing a Mustang P-51 long range fighter for a mission : an armourer loads one of its eight ·50 calibre machine-guns while its 1,500 h.p. Rolls-Royce Merlin engine is examined. The Mustang has a combat radius of 450 miles, a speed of 400 m.p.h., and can fly at an altitude of 35,000 ft. 4. British Hawker Typhoon intruder-bomber in flight, its two 500-lb. bombs in position ; it has an armament of four 20-mm. cannon or twelve ·303 machine-guns, and is also adapted for rockets. 5. Clipped wing Mark XII Spitfire, fitted with a Rolls-Royce Griffon engine—23 per cent greater in cylinder capacity than the Rolls-Royce Merlin.

Flt.-Sergt. A. L. AARON
He won the V.C. for devotion to duty 'seldom equalled and never surpassed' when, though fatally wounded in an attack on Turin on August 12, 1943, he directed his aircraft safely to Bône aerodrome in North Africa. He was in the R.A.F.V.R.(see page 2661).

Flying-Officer L. A. TRIGG
Posthumously awarded the V.C for outstanding service in anti-U-boat duties, F/O. Trigg, R.N.Z.A.F., was the first pilot on anti-submarine patrol to receive the award. An account of his Liberator's last fight with a U-boat in August 1943 is given in page 2661.

Photos. " Daily Mirror " ; New Zealand Govt.

vessels. Its anti-submarine organization included squadrons of the R.A.F., U.S. Army and Navy, Australian, Canadian and New Zealand Air Forces, and Czech, Norwegian and Polish units. More than 30 million miles were flown by the Command in 1943 in over 40,000 sorties—more than 760 miles per sortie, and more than 100 sorties a day. During 1943 more U-boats were destroyed by Coastal Command than during the whole of the period from September 1939 to the end of 1942.

The Command's power over the Atlantic was greatly increased after the agreement with Portugal whereby from October 12, 1943, Allied aircraft were based in the Azores. By the close of the year, operating from the United Kingdom, the Azores, Gibraltar and Iceland, Coastal Command succeeded, in co-operation with the R.C.A.F. in Newfoundland and patrols from the U.S.A., in covering the whole of the North Atlantic by shore-based aircraft—a development due in part to the introduction of long-range Liberator aircraft.

Allied Bases in the Azores

To the defeat of the U-boats, operating sometimes in echelons of up to 30, five-sixths of the Command's mileage was devoted. This phase of the anti-submarine war developed into a real battle, for submarine tactics changed from skulking along under water into surface cruising, employing powerful anti-aircraft batteries for protection against aircraft.

The U-boat pack method of convoy attack rose to its height in 1943. From April 29 to May 6 submarines estimated at 25 in number attacked a west-bound Atlantic convoy by day and night. Four U-boats were destroyed and six probably destroyed. During ten days in May Coastal Command sank five U-boats, one west and one south of Iceland, one in northern waters, and two in the Bay of Biscay approaches. As the year wore on submarines were sunk faster than they could be replaced and manned by the enemy.

Fighter Command

Fighter Command organization was modified on June 13, 1943, when the Army Co-operation Command, merged into a tactical air force designed to work with the army in the field, was contained within the framework of Fighter Command under Air Marshal Sir Trafford Leigh-Mallory (*see* illus., p. 2405). Squadrons of medium bombers thus came under the control of the Air Officer commanding Fighter Command, and increasing numbers of fighter bombers were adapted from purely fighter squadrons. This was part of the logical process of the change from the defensive to the offensive, for the bomb is still the principal offensive weapon in the air, whereas the fighter *qua* fighter is mainly a defensive machine. Nevertheless, the development of the cannon-gun and the use of the half-inch machine-gun had made fighters potent attackers of small water-borne craft, and railway and road transport vehicles. Fighter Command began a systematic attack on the German-controlled railway system in western Europe by employing cannon-firing fighters to shoot up locomotives. These attacks had a growing effect on the European railway system, forcing the Germans to use more and more road transport, which they could ill afford to divert from the Russian front.

The Typhoon fighter-bomber with four cannon-guns, the Mustang (*see* illus., p. 2657 and following p. 2266) with its eight machine-guns, the clipped-

R.A.F. DROPS 1,500 TONS ON PEENEMUNDE RESEARCH STATION
In moonlight on August 17-18, 1943, the R.A.F. carried out one of their most concentrated and effective long-range precision attacks of the war. At Peenemunde, on the shores of the Baltic in Pomerania, was a big German aircraft and radiolocation research station—the flying bomb, launched against London and the south of England in June 1944, and the long-range rocket were being perfected there. The attack destroyed 40 huts, 50 others were gutted. Gen. von Chamier-Glisenski and a number of other German scientists were killed.

winged Spitfire Vb and XII (the latter with Rolls-Royce Griffon engine, reinforced the Hurricane fighter-bomber for low level attack, while the Mosquito fighter-bomber introduced another deadly high-speed twin-engined aircraft into the Beaufighter's role. (*See* illus. following page 2646.)

In June 1943 rocket bombs, officially called unrotating projectiles, were introduced into the attack on Europe, and Hurricanes, Typhoons, Beaufighters and Swordfish were all equipped with them. Essentially weapons for low and close attack, rocket bombs were used mainly in attacking the smaller classes of vessels, but German army headquarters buildings, radar stations and railways were also singled out for this form of attack. Small ship draught is too shallow for ordinary torpedo attack, but the rocket soon proved superior to the skip-bomb or cannon-gun form of attack against them. Four rockets are carried under each wing; they can be fired in pairs, one from each wing, or in one salvo of eight. Their cordite propellant is electrically ignited by a small platinum fuse wire when the pilot presses the small firing button. Their discharge shock is taken by the air and the aircraft does not feel the recoil as it does when firing the cannon-gun. The rockets are aimed by sighting with the ordinary gunsight, but allowance has to be made for the slightly more curved drop of the rocket compared with the higher velocity shell or bullet.

Swarming into the western European skies like gnats, all these aircraft harried the Dutch, Belgian and French coasts and hinterland, stinging the whole enemy system of defence and communication. And during 1943 Fighter Command sorties rose to over a thousand a day, a scale of attack at least twice as heavy as that of the Luftwaffe during the Battle of Britain.

Bomber Command

Bomber Command entered 1943 with an increased number of four-engined heavy bombers and a highly trained Pathfinder Force able to reach any target in any weather by night and mark it out with flares of distinctive colours. It became possible to concentrate large forces of four-engined bombers upon urban areas. The force of more than a thousand bombers which attacked Cologne on May 30, 1942, took 90 minutes to drop some 1,400 tons; towards the end of 1943 forces of a thousand bombers were dropping as much as 2,300 tons in 30 minutes.

The attack upon industrial Germany

R.A.F. ATTACKS DAMS IN THE RUHR VALLEY

Among the most striking of the feats performed by Bomber Command during 1943 was the breaching of the Moehne and Eder dams on May 17 by a specially trained squadron led by Wing-Commander G. P. Gibson (right), who gained the V.C. for his leadership in this exploit (see page 2660). Above: The Moehne dam before the assault and, below, after the attacking Lancasters had done their work: note how the water level above the dam has fallen, and the walls of the reservoir below it have been swept away by the force of escaping waters.

Photos, British Official; " New York Times "

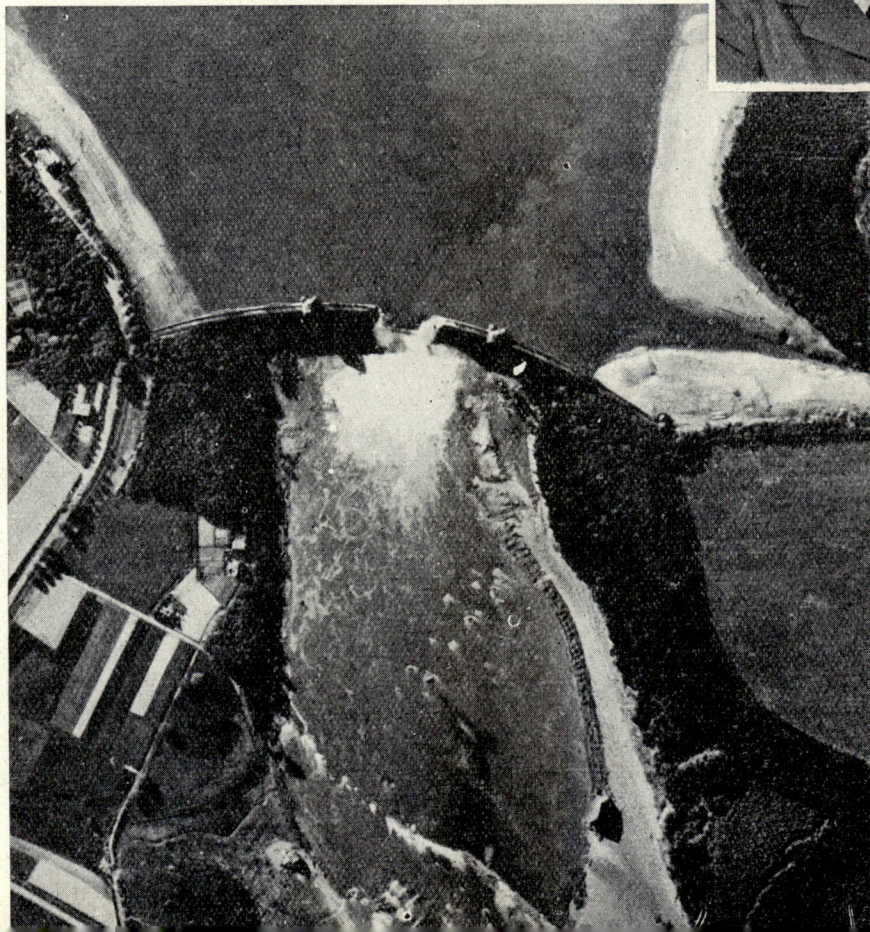

—including the daylight work of the U.S. Army Eighth Air Force, which made its first attack on Germany when it bombed Wilhelmshaven on January 27, 1943—will be dealt with in a later Chapter, but a brief reference must be made to it here. During 1943 nine of Germany's 21 major industrial cities with over 250,000 population were so seriously devastated that they were forced to consume more than they could produce. A number of lesser cities—such as Kassel and Munchen-Rheydt with populations of 216,000 and 200,000—were reduced to the same condition. Hamburg was attacked with great intensity from July 24 to August 3; in this period 11,000 tons of bombs were dropped on this second largest city in Germany. Its air and ground defences were overcome by the shock, and its port, its shipbuilding and its industries were knocked out.

These attacks produced a shortage of German guns, tanks, aircraft and ammunition, and were a very useful strategic collaboration with the offensive of the Red Army. Aircraft were withdrawn from Russia and the Mediterranean to defend Germany, and before the winter of 1943–44 it was estimated that 50 per cent of Germany's day, and 85 per cent of her night, fighter strength was concentrated in western Europe.

Mine-laying was carried out regularly and attacks were made upon the U-boat bases of Lorient and St. Nazaire, upon North Italian industry and railways, and upon communications between France and Italy. Mosquito bombers made many daylight attacks on selected targets, including the special one on January 30 when six Mosquitoes raided Berlin just as Reichsmarshal Hermann Goering was due to broadcast from the Air Ministry (Reichsluftfahrtministerium) in Berlin in celebration of the 10th anniversary of Hitler's accession to power; Goering's speech was delayed for about an hour.

No. 617 Squadron was specially formed under the command of Wing-Commander G. P. Gibson, D.S.O. and Bar, D.F.C. and Bar, to train secretly for an attack on the Moehne, Eder and Sorpe dams supplying water to German industry, canals, and hydro-electric generator stations. Gibson had completed three tours of duty, two as a night bomber pilot, and one as a night fighter pilot, and had flown more than 170 sorties involving over 600 hours of operational flying. The attack on the dams had to be made from a hundred feet or less above the water level. Bright moonlight was shining on the morning of

May 17, 1943, when 19 Lancaster bombers carrying special mines began the attacks. Gibson made the initial attack on the Moehne dam from a height of a few feet. A flight-lieutenant following in another Lancaster saw a spout of water rise to 300 feet. A second Lancaster attacked with the same determination, but still there was no sign of a breach. A third bomber attacked and there was a huge explosion against the dam. The fourth Lancaster's explosives broke the dam and a terrific flood of water burst through its centre. Light anti-aircraft defences were

Air Attack on Ruhr Dams

sited in the wall of the dam itself, and after dropping his load Gibson flew up and down the dam to attract the fire away from those who followed him, while his own gunners replied to and partially silenced the German fire. The Moehne dam breached, he led his forces to the Eder dam, which was likewise broken. The Sorpe dam, with its thicker wall of concrete, was not breached. From the first dam 134, and from the second 202, million tons of water broke away to swamp great areas of land, flood factories, railways, power stations and towns. Kassel was inundated. It was a brilliant strategical stroke, a surprise thrust at German industry, superimposed upon the normal method of bomber attack on Germany and western Europe.

Wing-Commander Gibson brought 11 Lancasters home, and for his great determination, high valour and leader-

FLYING FORTRESSES BOMB LORIENT U-BOAT BASE IN FRANCE

Lorient, port in Brittany from which U-boats issued to harry and destroy Allied shipping in the Atlantic, was the target of a number of attacks by U.S. Army Eighth Air Force during 1943. This photograph, taken from another Fortress, shows the target area enveloped in smoke and two Fortresses leaving after dropping their bombs during an attack on March 6, 1943.

Photo, British Official : Crown Copyright

ship was awarded the Victoria Cross—
one of four gazetted to Bomber Command pilots during 1943. A second, awarded to Flt.-Sergeant R. H. Middleton of the Royal Australian Air Force and No. 149 Squadron Bomber Command, was gained in an attack on the Fiat works at Turin in the night of November 28, 1942 (*see* illus., page 2517). A third, gained in another attack on Turin in the night of August 12, 1943, was won by the captain of a Stirling bomber, acting Flt.-Sergeant A. L. Aaron, D.F.M., R.A.F.V.R., No. 218 (Gold Coast) Squadron, a former A.T.C. cadet, for devotion to duty "seldom equalled and never surpassed." Over Turin three of the four engines were hit, the front and rear gun turrets put out of action, the navigator killed, and other members of the crew wounded. A bullet broke Aaron's jaw and tore away part of his face; he was wounded in the lung and his right arm made useless. He fell forward over the controls. The bomber

V.C.s Won by Bomber Command dived several thousand feet. The flight-engineer got it under control at 3,000 feet. Unable to speak, Aaron signed to his bomb-aimer to take over and set course for North Africa. Aaron was assisted to the rear of the aircraft and given morphia. He rallied and insisted on returning to the controls. He was lifted into his seat and had his feet placed in position. Twice he attempted to take control but was too weak, but he continued to help by writing directions with his left hand. They reached Bône and landed after four attempts made under Aaron's direction. Nine hours later Aaron died from exhaustion.

The fourth Bomber Command V.C. won in 1943 and awarded to Flight-Lieut. W. Reid, will be dealt with in the Chapter on the attack on German industry.

Another Victoria Cross—the 16th air Victoria Cross of the war—was awarded on November 3 to Flying-Officer L. A. Trigg, D.F.C., R.N.Z.A.F., of Houhora, New Zealand, No. 200 Squadron, for outstanding service on convoy escort and anti-U-boat duties, in which he had made 46 operational sorties. This was the first V.C. awarded to a pilot engaged on anti-submarine patrol. In the previous August, after an eight hours' search over the Atlantic, Trigg's Liberator sighted a surfaced U-boat and dived to attack. The Liberator, hit repeatedly by the submarine's A.A. guns, burst into flames. It was a critical moment. By continuing to dive, the Liberator presented a no-deflection target to deadly and accurate gunfire with flames simul-

AIR OPERATIONS IN TUNISIA

During the campaign in Tunisia, Arabs helped the R.A.F. in work on the airfields : here is a bomb train manned by these native workers on its way to a dump. Top, men of an R.A.F. mobile parachute packing unit retrieving a parachute during exercises : their job was to follow up parachute operations, salvage the parachutes, and repack them ready for the next jump.   *Photo, British Official*

BOMBS ON MARETH LINE

The Western Desert Air Force began its assault on the Mareth Line in Tunisia on March 19, 1943, just ahead of the Eighth Army's attack. Relay bombing against German concentrations was an important element in weakening the Axis defence. This light bomber of the South African Air Force is coming in to bomb a large enemy barracks near Mareth village.

Operations in Africa

The year 1943 opened with the Eighth Army at Buerat, 240 miles east of Tripoli, with the Western Desert Air Force smashing at the enemy, weakening still further his air and surface forces. The Luftwaffe scarcely interfered with the Eighth Army, so effective was its fighter cover. General Montgomery evaluated air power thus : " You must win the air battle before you fight the land or sea battle." And he said : " . . . from Alamein through Tunisia, Sicily and Italy you will find that we never fought a land battle until the air battle was won." By January 14, 1943, Rommel was in full retreat from Buerat with the Desert Air Force pounding his transport columns, panzer units, infantry and bases. Tripoli was occupied on January 23, less than three months after the opening of the El Alamein battle. A fortnight later the last enemy soldier was swept out of the Italian African Empire, and fighting in North Africa then concentrated in the French territory of Tunisia. There the Eighth Army formed part of the 18th Army Group, with its strategy controlled from Algiers and not from Cairo.

One important gain of the Allied advance in Libya was the relief of Malta on November 26, 1942. In 1943 Malta was able to hit back hard and became an advanced air base for intruders and bombers, which specialized in destroying trains and rolling stock in Sicily and Italy, in sinking supply ships, and in striking against Tunisia and Sardinia.

In mid-February the Germans were thrusting heavily against the American troops in Tunisia and forcing them back with superior air and ground forces—for the 300 first-line aircraft possessed by the Axis in Tunisia, when concentrated, could give them local air superiority, due to the Allies' lack of forward fighter airfields. The Americans were forced back through the Kasserine Pass. Then the air forces under Tedder's control were swiftly concentrated. For six days from February 19 they lashed the enemy troop concentration. Air aid for the Allied Army reached a scale not seen in Africa since the Battle of El Alamein. The enemy retreat began.

Shortly afterwards the air forces under Tedder were divided into a strategical and a tactical force, and the new conception of the use of air power was applied to provide immediate tactical aid to the surface forces in the field, with the simultaneous strategic disruption of distant enemy supplies intended for the battle zone, and the softening of the enemy zones into which it was planned that the Allied armies should advance.

Reorganization of Allied Air Forces

Preceded and accompanied by fighter bomber attacks from Malta against Sicily, heavy bomber attacks against the ports of Bizerta, La Goulette, Tunis and Susa, air blows at enemy airfields

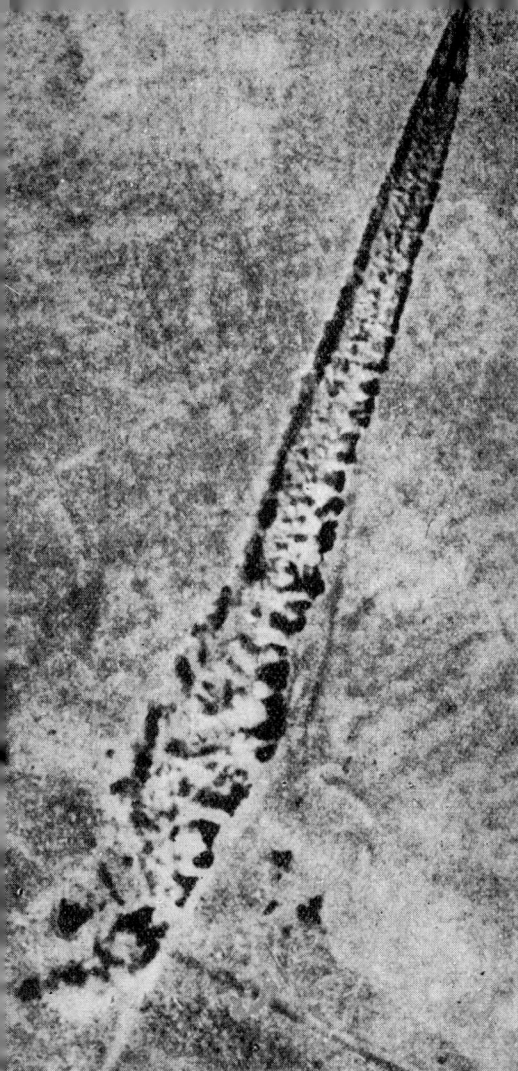

ENEMY GLIDER TAKES OFF

Until his airfields were captured by the advancing Allied armies, the enemy made considerable use of gliders during the North African campaign. Here is a DFS-230 glider, in tow behind a Junkers 87, taking off from a desert landing ground.
Photo, British Official

taneously increasing in the aircraft and diminishing the chances of survival. Trigg could have landed in the sea, but he maintained his course and skimmed 50 feet above the U-boat. A.A. fire entered the open bomb doors of the Liberator, whose bombs fell on and around the U-boat and exploded with devastating effect. The doomed Liberator flew on a short distance before diving into the sea. The stricken U-boat sank within 20 minutes, and some of her crew were later picked up in a rubber dinghy that had broken loose from the Liberator. The air crew —Flying-Officers J. Townsend of Stroud, Glos., and Marinovitch of Auckland, N.Z. ; Pilot-Officer G. Goodwin of B.C., Canada ; Flt.-Sergts. A. R. Bonnich of Hendon, London, and A. Bennett, L. Frost, and T. Soper, all of New Zealand —perished with Trigg.

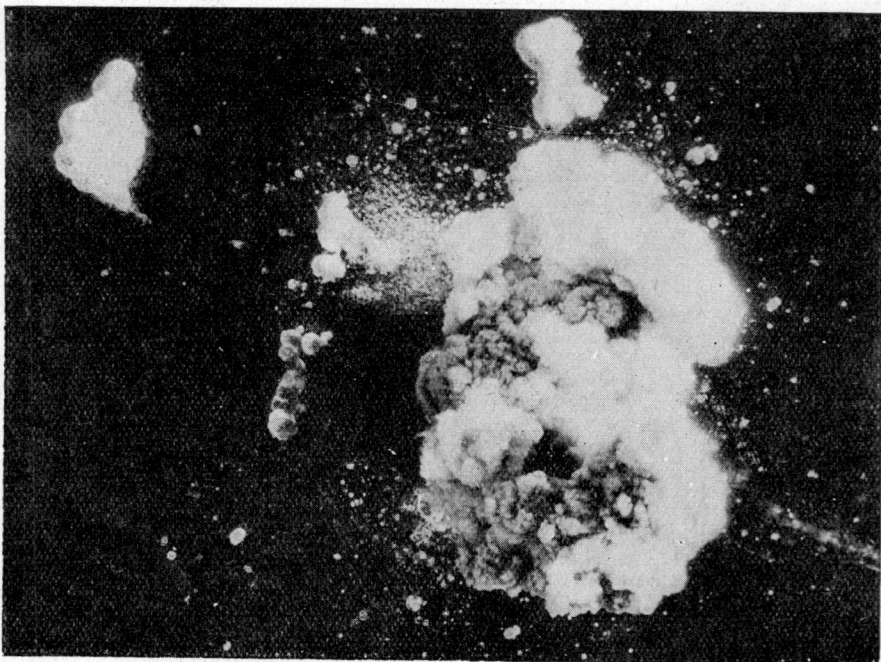

AXIS SEA SUPPLY ROUTES BLASTED FROM THE AIR

Sea convoys bringing much-needed supplies across the Sicilian narrows to the Axis armies in Tunisia were attacked from the air as mercilessly as were the enemy's air convoys (see page 2664). Smoke and flames spread over the sea as Allied bombs take effect on one of 17 Axis ships sunk or damaged by Fortresses off Bizerta on April 16, 1943. This ship was blown to pieces ; none of her crew survived.
Photo, U.S. Official

ALLIED CHIEFS IN THE WAR AGAINST JAPAN

Field-Marshal Sir Archibald Wavell, British Commander-in-Chief India (later Viscount Wavell, and Viceroy) with Lt.-Gen. Joseph Stilwell, commanding U.S. forces in China, Burma and India, followed by Lt.-Gen. Brehon B. Somerville, commanding Services of Supply of the U.S. Army; Field-Marshal Sir John Dill, chief of the British Joint Staff Mission to the U.S., and Lt.-Gen. Henry H. Arnold, Commander of the U.S. Army Air Forces, leaving the Imperial Secretariat building in New Delhi during the conferences on strategy for the war against Japan held in February 1943, immediately after the 'unconditional surrender' conference at Casablanca.

DEVASTATING ATTACKS BY ALLIED AIR FORCES IN TUNISIAN CAMPAIGN

Hangars at El Aouina airfield, near Tunis (above), wrecked by Allied bombing. Below : Part of an Axis air convoy of 35 Junkers-52 transports, 31 of which were shot down in the Sicilian narrows by Mitchells and Lightnings of the North-West African Air Force on April 22, 1943. In this remarkable action photograph, the wing of one American plane, just pulling away after attack, is seen on the right, while another roars overhead. Cannon-gun fire throws up heavy splashes all round the Axis transport just above the water to the left of the photograph.

Photos, British Official : Crown Copyright ; Associated Press

AMERICAN AIR POWER IN THE SOUTH-WEST PACIFIC

These Corsair fighters, on a Bougainville Island airfield, escorted American bombers in a heavy raid on Rabaul on
November 5, 1943—the ninth major raid on that port since October 11.   U.S. Army parachutists were used extensively
in the S.W. Pacific zone for the first time, during the operations which led to the capture of Lae (see Chapter 276).
Boston bombers laid a smoke screen ; then the transport planes came in (below), and the parachute troops jumped,
under cover of the smoke, from a lower altitude than they had attempted to use before in battle.

Photos, U.S. Official : Associated Press

U.S. LIBERATORS BOMB RUMANIAN OILFIELDS

On August 1, 1943, the U.S.A. Ninth A.F. attacked Ploesti, the Rumanian oil centre, whose output of high-grade spirit was of immense importance to the Germans.   In one minute 177 Liberators, led by Brig.-Gen. Ent, dropped 270 tons of bombs on the wells and refineries from roof-top level, and several of the largest refining installations were put out of action for months.   The 2,000 airmen who took part practised for weeks on an exact model of Ploesti constructed in the Libyan desert.

Photos, U.S. Air Force

in Tunisia and Sicily, at sea and air convoys crossing the Sicilian narrows, at targets in southern Italy, including railways outside Rome, the Allied advance in Tunisia began at the end of February. Losing heavily in shipping, the Axis tried to run reinforcements and supplies into Tunisia by air. Their air transports and gliders were roughly handled : for instance, on April 10, 40 German air transports and 13 fighters and bombers were shot down over the Sicilian narrows ; next day 31 enemy transport planes were destroyed over the sea ; on April 18 about 100 Junkers-52 transport planes were intercepted off Cape Bon ; for the loss of nine Allied aircraft, at least 51 were shot down, with 23 of their escorting fighters, in what Allied pilots described as a " massacre." The Messerschmitt-323 air transport— a six-engined wooden " packing case " —came into use during the closing phase of the North African operations. It fared no better than the older Junkers-52 : on April 22, 31 of these power glider-transports (some carrying personnel, the majority petrol) were shot down, together with 11 of their escort, for a loss of four Allied planes.

How different was this from the time when Acting Wing-Commander H. G. Malcolm of No. 18 Squadron, R.A.F., won the only air Victoria Cross awarded during the North Africa campaign— the 13th won in the air during the Second Great War—by the attack he led on an enemy fighter airfield near Cheuigui on December 4, 1942 (see illus., page 2517).

Axis organization in North Africa crumpled under the withering on-slaught of Allied air power striking simultaneously and continuously at tactical and strategical targets. On May 7 the First Army entered Tunis, and the U.S. Second Corps entered Bizerta. The First Army continued to advance. The naval and air blockade of the Cape Bon peninsula increased until, on May 12, 1944, General von Arnim, com-manding the Axis forces in North Africa (for Rommel had earlier been wounded by a bomb burst and had returned to Europe) was captured near Marie du Zit. Next day all remaining Axis forces surrendered. General Mont-gomery's strategy had been followed : the air battle had been won first.

Mediterranean Operations

On May 9 Messina, Palermo and the island of Pantelleria were bombed by day and night. The air bombardment of Pantelleria continued with only an occasional day's respite, and frequently with the accompaniment of naval bombardment, until June 11 when the island surrendered unconditionally—

GIANT GERMAN TRANSPORT AIRCRAFT

Nicknamed ' packing case ' by Allied airmen, the Messerschmitt-323, a high-wing, six-engined transport with a span of 181 ft. and a length of 93 ft., was introduced for carrying troops and material in later stages of the Tunisian campaign and also in Italy. Above, Me.-323 being attacked by a Marauder; it was compelled to crash-land off Cape Corse, Corsica. Below, in use as an air ambulance. *Photo, British Official ; Keystone*

the first time in history that an air force had compelled the capitulation of a strongly fortified enemy territory before land forces had gone in. After the fall of Pantelleria, Lampedusa island, bombed for the first time on May 23, was attacked in force from the air and bombarded from the sea until it surrendered next day at 5.30 p.m.

The way was now clear for an Allied assault across the Mediterranean via the " bridge " of Sicily. Steadily, air preparation to this end went on, with aircraft operating from Cyrenaica, Tunisia, Algeria, Malta and the United Kingdom in a concerted scheme.

On July 9, U.S. bombers attacked Taormina, destroying the Axis head-

quarters in Sicily and wrecking the neighbouring telegraphic centre. In the night of July 9–10 heavy Allied air attacks preceded landings by U.S. glider-borne troops and British para-chute troops, sent ahead to seize bridges and other important focal points upon which the main seaborne forces, landing on the Sicilian beaches in the dawn of July 10, could converge.

Air attacks on the mainland of Italy increased in violence after the landings in Sicily. On July 12 Bomber Com-mand heavily attacked Turin. On July 17 more than 500 bombers from North African bases attacked Naples. Two days later military objectives in Rome and its vicinity were attacked

PANTELLERIA BOMBED INTO SURRENDER

For a month after the close of the Tunisian campaign, the Italian island of Pantelleria was heavily bombed with scarcely a day's respite (left), until it surrendered unconditionally on June 11, 1943. Above, the airfield with entrances to underground hangars in background. Below, white cross displayed as signal of surrender, and the nose of the first Hurricane to land.

for the first time by heavy and medium bombers of the Mediterranean Air Command. "Shuttle" bombing began on the night of July 15–16 when Bomber Command Lancasters bombed transformer stations in North Italy, flew on to North Africa, and returned in the night of July 24–25, bombing Leghorn port on the way.

In the areas where fighting was proceeding the power of the Allied air attack battered down enemy defences and kept enemy forces under cover while the surface troops of the Allies advanced. There was a hold up in the plain before Catania. But air power smashed resistance and the Allied troops got through. Captured airfields were littered with the remains of bombed and burned-out aircraft. Specialized units advanced with the army to create forward airfields for the close-support squadrons out of sand and rock. In several instances an entire fighter-bomber wing was flown to advanced landing-fields complete with bombs, fuel, ammunition, spares and ground-crews, and was operating against the enemy within an hour of arrival. The air cover was so complete that it came to be called "Tedder's carpet." Allied aircraft also guarded the seaborne convoys.

The R.A.F. Regiment, founded early in 1942 to take over the defence of the aerodromes of Great Britain, saw service overseas during 1943, fighting on the invasion beaches, guarding forward airfields, and later landing in the Dodecanese islands. Landings were made on Cos, Leros and Samos with R.A.F. fighters operating from a poor airfield on Cos. But it was found impossible

AIR WAR IN SICILY

1. Loading a 'jeep' on to a British glider ready for transport to Sicily : the glider-nose could be raised as shown to give free entry to the fuselage of the craft. 2. British and American parachute troops were landed in Sicily during the night of July 9-10, 1943, prior to the landings from the sea early on July 10. Here are American parachutists on their way. 3. Flying Fortress attacking Axis military installations at Messina shortly before the Sicilian campaign ended on August 17. 4. Refuelling an American fighter in Sicily with petrol brought ashore by one of the amphibious DUKW trucks, nicknamed 'ducks' by the Allied troops.

Photos, British Official : Crown Copyright ; Planet News ; "New York Times" Photos

ALLIES OCCUPY ITALIAN AIRFIELDS

1. Seafire preparing to land on the aircraft carrier H.M.S. 'Hunter' during the operations off Salerno, which began with an Allied landing on September 9, 1943. 2. Men of the R.A.F. examining bombs abandoned near a wrecked train at the airfield of Taranto, occupied without opposition on September 9. 3. Army levelling machine, under the nose of a Spitfire, clearing Reggio airfield after its capture by the Allies on September 3. 4. R.A.F. fighters preparing to operate from an airfield near Naples.

Photos, British Official ; Crown Copyright

to maintain adequate air coverage, and the islands were lost in October and November. (An account of operations in the Dodecanese is given in a later Chapter.)

By August 12, 1,691 enemy aircraft had been shot down or captured in Sicily, where resistance ceased on August 17. The full air attack was then turned against the Italian mainland. On September 3 British and Canadian troops of the Eighth Army landed at Reggio on the Italian mainland under cover of a strong naval force, and of Spitfires flying from Sicilian airfields ; and on the same day Italy surrendered unconditionally to air power with the immediate threat of the Army behind it. On September 9, British and U.S. troops of the Fifth Army landed at Salerno, 200 miles from the nearest Allied airfields and almost outside range of shore-based fighter cover.

By using long-range fighters it was possible to keep about 50 fighters constantly over the beaches. Short-range fighter cover was provided by

Air Cover at Salerno Seafires from the small aircraft carriers " Attacker," " Battler," " Hunter," " Stalker " and " Unicorn," escorted close inshore by light cruisers and destroyers, and from the large aircraft carriers " Illustrious " and " Formidable " in deep water, covered by the battleships " Nelson " and " Rodney." But the crash rate during the operation of these ship fighters was very high, and this considerable seaborne air fleet flew only about one-seventh of the number of sorties flown by the R.A.F., despite the short range afforded by floating aerodromes.

The landing was successful, and when Field-Marshal Kesselring, commanding the Germans in southern Italy, moved up heavy reinforcements, including tanks, and for a time the issue was in doubt, Tedder turned the combined weight of his tactical and strategic forces on to the battle zone. At the height of the battle almost 2,500 sorties were flown during the 24 hours, and 1,400 tons of bombs were dropped on the German forces on the battlefields and their immediate communications. The key communication town for the Germans, through which the main roads passed, was flattened, and all vehicular traffic, including tanks, ceased before the tumbled masonry that blocked the way.

That air action decided the issue. The Fifth Army entered Naples on October 1, with the support of air cover from behind the Eighth Army, which took Foggia with its 13 airfields on September 27. These airfields

PRIMITIVE LABOUR CONSTRUCTS CHINESE AIRFIELDS
300,000 Chinese labourers, using traditional methods of work, helped to build airfields for the use of Allied aircraft in their struggle against the Japanese. Here is a crowd of workers, trundling primitive hand carts or carrying baskets, moving small, specially shaped stones which they laid by hand as foundations for runways. A Liberator bomber has already landed on a completed runway of this airfield under construction.
Photo, Keystone

enabled the strategic air offensive also to be directed against enemy-controlled industries in south Germany, Austria, Hungary and Rumania, and brought the oilfields of Ploesti (first attacked by Liberator bombers of U.S.A. 9th Air Force from the Middle East on August 1) within a range of some 600 miles. (*See* illus., page 2666.)

When 1943 ended, the Eighth Army was north of the Moro river and the Fifth Army north of the Volturno river, but all air and ground operations had been slowed down by the vicious Italian winter weather.

South-East Asia Command

There was no significant change in the situation in the Burma area. A South-East Asia Command to conduct operations against Japan, based on New Delhi in India, was set up on August 25 with Vice-Admiral Lord Louis Mountbatten as Supreme Allied Commander, S.E. Asia. In the following December Lord Louis issued an order uniting all British and American units into one Allied air force under the command of Air Chief Marshal Sir Richard Peirse. (*See* illus., page 2652.) Air operations over Burma increased as more squadrons became available, and experience made flying possible during the monsoon season, when it had formerly been considered out of the question.

Close air support was given to the army on the Arakan and Chindwin fronts, and supplies for isolated forces—

such as the Wingate expedition—were maintained by air, either dropped by parachute or, in some cases, carried by transport aircraft which landed on crudely prepared runways. Strategic bombing of ports, shipping and communications increased, as far afield as Bangkok. (*See* Chapter 270.)

R.A.F., Dominion and Indian squadrons were reinforced by the U.S. Army 10th Air Force with headquarters at Delhi. The transport air service between India and China grew. An extensive network of military air transport services linked Delhi, Bombay, Ceylon and Calcutta. India was strengthened for its role as major air base for the war to the east of the Bay of Bengal. (*See* Chapter 270.)

Pacific Zone

The year opened with American troops established in Guadalcanal in the Solomons with shore-based aircraft in operation. In New Guinea the fight for Salamaua and Lae was beginning. The tactics of the Allies throughout this zone were to wrest from the enemy a chain of airfields that would give them air superiority over an area dominating Japanese communications, so that Japanese forces on separate islands could be cut off, bombed, and reduced to ineffectiveness against amphibious assault by Allied troops. Longer-term strategy was to squeeze the periphery of the Japanese outposts, and dent it in one place after another, each dent leading to fresh weaknesses,

AIR AID FOR WINGATE'S CHINDITS

The remarkable exploits of Brigadier O. C. Wingate's Chindits in the wild jungle country of Central Burma during 1943 (see Chapter 270) would have been impossible without the assistance this specially trained force received from the air. Sick and wounded were evacuated by air transport (above), and supplies were dropped by parachute (below). The groups into which the expedition separated maintained contact with India and one another by radio.

Photos, Associated Press ; Keystone

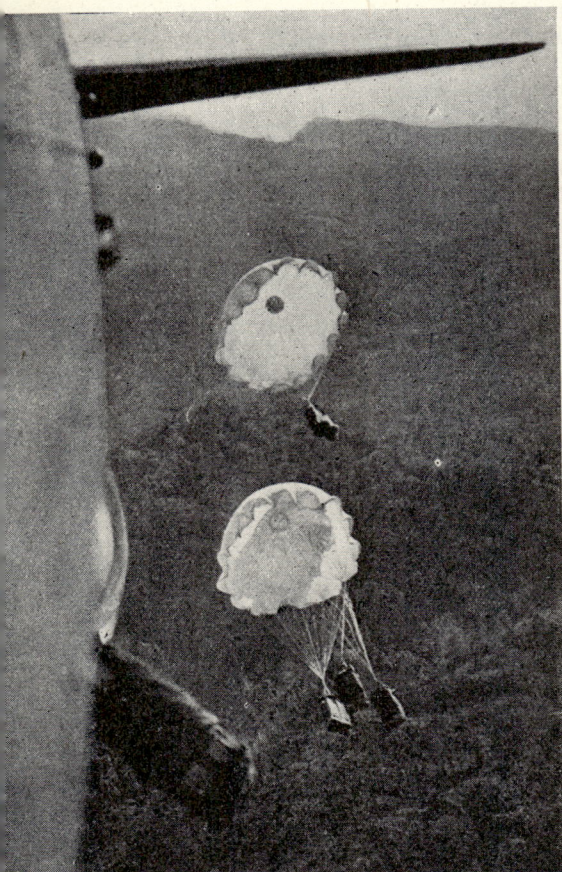

At dawn on March 23, U.S. heavy bombers attacked more than 250 Japanese aircraft grounded at Rabaul aerodromes and caused great destruction without loss to themselves. A similar attack on Rabaul on October 12 destroyed 100 and damaged 51 Japanese aircraft on the ground ; 26 were shot down and heavy shipping loss was inflicted ; on October 18, 60 aircraft were destroyed and more shipping damaged ; on October 23, 24 and 25, 181 aircraft were destroyed on the ground and in combat, with 45 probables, for the loss of only five Allied machines. On November 2 nearly every ship in Rabaul harbour was sunk or hit by air attack and the Japanese lost 85 aircraft in combat during the operation, for the loss of 19 Allied planes ; between November 3 and 5 in the area around Rabaul and Kavieng (New Ireland) two Japanese cruisers were sunk, many warships and merchant vessels damaged and 29 aircraft shot down ; 10 U.S. aircraft were lost. On November 11, in the last big 1943 air attack on Rabaul, a Japanese cruiser and two destroyers were sunk, many other warships severely damaged, and 88 aircraft destroyed ; the Allies lost 17 aircraft.

These powerful air blows at the best harbourage in that area coincided with the marshalling of Japanese forces for counter-attacks against the Allied drive. Time and again enemy concentrations were shattered before they could strike. Continual attrition began to tell on the resources even of so powerful and long-prepared an enemy.

Operations in New Guinea

The end of ground operations in Papua was announced on January 24 ; but the Allied advance in New Guinea went on. On February 6, in air combats over Wau, 21 Japanese fighters and five bombers were shot down without loss. On May 26 and 31 Lae received its two heaviest air attacks from the Allies. By then weather was steadily worsening for air operations in the islands north of Australia.

On June 30, Allied forces landed at Nassau Bay near Salamaua. On July 15, Australian and U.S. forces occupied Mubo. On August 17 and 18 the Japanese base at Wewak was attacked by air and 215 enemy aircraft destroyed. Seven days later enemy shipping at Hansa Bay suffered great damage. Wewak aerodrome was frequently attacked during August : on the 29th, 24 aircraft were shot down and at least 12 destroyed on the ground. The enemy headquarters at Madang was left in ruins and much other damage was done

in accordance with a scheme which would open the way to sea contact with China, so that a bomber force could be maintained on the Chinese mainland to operate against Japan proper.

Heavy and repeated bombing attacks were made on shipping and installations at Rabaul, most important Japanese marine base in the zone. There, on January 5, U.S. heavy bombers sank nine ships totalling 50,000 tons. Next day a convoy left Rabaul for Lae. Although it had an air escort that never fell below 100, it was subjected to almost constant air attack during its four days' passage. The enemy lost 85 aircraft for certain, with 29 probably destroyed and 19 damaged ; three ships were sunk, and three more seriously damaged. Allied losses were light. On January 16, U.S. heavy bombers sank or severely damaged five vessels at Rabaul. The Battle of the Bismarck Sea, fought between March 2 and 4, when a Japanese force of 10 warships and 12 transport vessels heading from Rabaul for the north coast of Guinea was wiped out by Allied aircraft, is described in page 2602. In addition to her naval losses, Japan lost 55 aircraft ; the Allies lost one bomber and three fighters.

AIR OPERATIONS IN NEW GUINEA

Unloading under heavy Japanese air attack 25-pounder guns flown to Wau aerodrome in U.S. transport planes (February 6, 1943). Left, Japanese freighter in Wewak harbour straddled by bombs from an American bomber during one of many Allied air raids on this base during 1943. Below, Liberator bomber over Salamaua photographed from another aircraft during an attack on the Japanese-occupied town shortly before its capture by Australians on September 14, 1943. (See Chapter 276.)

Photos, British Official: Crown Copyright; Australian Official;
Associated Press; "New York Times" Photos

Flt.-Lt. W. E. NEWTON, V.C.

For doing 'all that a man could do to prevent his crew from falling into enemy hands,' this pilot was post-humously awarded the V.C. During his 52nd operational sortie in the New Guinea zone on March 17, 1943, his aircraft caught fire. He kept it under control and brought it down on the sea as far as possible from Japanese positions. Two members of the crew got away, but not Flt.-Lt. Newton.

MUNDA AIRFIELD: BEFORE AND AFTER ITS CAPTURE

Munda, in New Georgia—one of the Solomon Islands—was taken by the Americans on August 6, 1943, after seven weeks of bitter fighting. Below, U.S. marines inspect the wreckage of a Japanese bomber found on the airfield there. Above, the same airfield after the Americans had widened, lengthened, and improved it, with Grumman Avengers in the foreground, and Hellcats beyond.

Photos, "New York Times" Photos; B.I.P.P.A.

by an air attack on September 1. Salamaua airfield was captured by the Australians on September 13, Salamaua itself on the 14th, and Lae on the 16th. On September 22 an Australian force landed behind the Japanese at Finschhafen, capturing the airfield on the 24th. In these operations Australian troops often moved as airborne forces. Wewak took another air attack on September 27, when 50 aircraft were destroyed on the ground, 14 in the air, seven ships were sunk, and others damaged. On October 2 Finschhafen itself was captured. On November 13 there was a heavy Allied air attack on the Alexishafen-Madang area of New Guinea, and four days later an Australian assault began on Sattelberg, supported by R.A.A.F. Vengeance dive-bombers. Sattelberg fell on November 26, and Wareo on December 8. The Australian advance in the Huon Peninsula was continuing at the end of 1943.

For operations in New Guinea, where

he lost his life, Flight-Lieut. W. E. Newton of No. 22 Squadron, R.A.A.F., was awarded one of the seven V.C.s gazetted during 1943, after serving in New Guinea from May 1942 until March 1943, and completing 52 operational sorties. His story illustrates the difficulties of air operations in that country. Leading an attack on March 16, 1943, he dived through intense and accurate shell-fire and his aircraft was hit repeatedly. Nevertheless, he held his course and bombed his target from a low level, destroying many buildings and dumps, including two 40,000-gallon fuel installations. With his aircraft crippled, fuselage and wing sections torn, petrol tanks pierced, main planes and engines seriously damaged and one main tire flat, he managed to fly back to base and land successfully. Next day he returned to the same locality to attack a more difficult target—a single building. He flew through a barrage of fire, scored a hit on the building, and at

the same moment his aircraft burst into flames. He maintained control, turned his aircraft away and flew along the tropical, shark-infested coast, keeping in the air as long as he could, to take his crew as far as possible from the enemy positions. (The Japanese are not noted for their kindness to captured airmen.) Then with great skill he brought his blazing aircraft down on to the water. Two of the crew extricated themselves and swam ashore, but Newton perished with his machine. (*See illus.*, p. 2673.)

Meanwhile, things progressed well in the Solomon Islands. The Japanese evacuated Guadalcanal on February 9. In an air battle over that island on June 16, U.S. aircraft shot down 77 Japanese aircraft against six of their own; 17 other enemy aircraft fell to ship and shore batteries. On June 30, when U.S. forces landed on Rendova Island, 121 Japanese aircraft attacking the shipping were shot down for the loss of 17 U.S. aircraft. One transport was sunk. Next day the Americans captured Viru harbour on New Georgia. Three days later 21 enemy bombers and fighters were shot down over Rendova. More than 200 U.S. aircraft attacked Japanese shipping in northern Solomons anchorages on July 17 and sank one light cruiser, two destroyers, a submarine chaser, and three other vessels, and destroyed 49 enemy aircraft with a loss of six of their own. During the night of July 19–20 a Japanese convoy northwest of New Georgia was attacked by air; a light cruiser and two destroyers were sunk and other craft were damaged, forcing the enemy to abandon his attempt to supply his garrisons in the northern Solomons. U.S. troops occupied Munda airfield on New Georgia on August 6, after seven weeks of bitter fighting. By August 28 all organized enemy resistance on New Georgia ceased.

Then came the next "island-hops." On October 11 Kahili aerodrome on Bougainville Island was heavily attacked and 12 Japanese aircraft were destroyed in combat. During October 16–17, in combined air operations over the Solomons and New Guinea, 104 Japanese aircraft were destroyed in combat, and many more on the ground. On October 27, U.S. and New Zealand troops landed on the Treasury Islands, Mono and Stirling, and next day American parachute troops landed without opposition on Choiseul Island. On November 1, U.S. troops landed on Bougainville Island, most northerly of the Solomons (*see* page 2607).

These advances were not made without air opposition. In a heavy air attack

Air Battles over the Solomons

on Allied shipping in Oro Bay, Papua, on March 28 the Japanese lost 25 aircraft and did small damage. U.S. naval forces were attacked by air near Guadalcanal on April 7 and one destroyer, one tanker, and one R.N.Z.N. corvette were sunk ; the enemy lost 39 of the 98 aircraft employed ; seven Allied planes were lost. On April 12 Port Moresby was attacked by over 100 Japanese aircraft, which were driven off with the loss of 37 destroyed or badly crippled. Darwin, in Australia, was attacked on May 2, June 20, 28 and 30, and July 6, with forces of up to 28 bombers escorted by a maximum of 30 fighters. They were intercepted each time and suffered losses at least twice as heavy as the defenders. Nothing the enemy did could stem the power of the Allies in the air or stop their advances on the surface.

In strategic air attacks on April 2, 3 and 4 off Kavieng, New Ireland, every ship in an enemy force of seven warships and five other vessels was destroyed or badly damaged. In

Allies Bomb Surabaya

that month, too, an attack was made against the Japanese airfield at Kendari (Celebes) in the Netherlands East Indies. During April also Admiral Yamamoto, planner of the Pearl Harbour attack, was killed "while directing operations from a military aeroplane." On June 23, U.S. bombers (one lost) made a 2,000-mile round trip from Australia to attack Macassar in the Celebes. On July 22, Australian-based Liberators attacked Surabaya in Java —a flight of 2,400 miles. On August 13 the oil centre of Balikpapan in eastern Borneo was attacked, in the largest land-based raid made up to that date in the Pacific, involving a flight of 2,500 miles from Australia.

BOMBING-UP IN THE ALEUTIANS

From August 1943 the Aleutian Islands served as a base for Allied air attacks on Japanese shipping and installations in the North Pacific. Here an ordnance crew at an Aleutian outpost is fixing bombs to the wings of one of the U.S. Navy PBY flying boats which regularly patrolled the waters off Alaska. *Photo, Pictorial Press*

PARACHUTE TROOPS OF THE SOVIET ARMY

Soviet Russia was training parachute jumpers as an arm of offence before the Second Great War began, and used them in operations against Finland towards the end of 1939. Here, Red Army parachutists are checking their equipment as they prepare to board transport planes to carry out a large scale attack on the Eastern Front. *Photo, Associated Press*

On December 13 Allied air forces attacked Gasmata, New Britain, where U.S. forces landed two days later. Heavy Allied air attacks on Japanese airfields at Cape Gloucester followed, and by the end of the year they were in Allied hands.

In the North Pacific, following air attacks, U.S. troops occupied Amchitka in the Aleutian Islands in January—Adak had been occupied some little time before. In May several landings were made with air support on Attu, where after severe fighting the Japanese were overcome before the end of May (see illus., page 2602).

On the night of September 18–19, carrier-borne air forces of the U.S. Pacific Fleet attacked Japanese bases on Nauru, Tarawa, Makin and Abemama, in the Gilbert Islands. On October 5 and 6, U.S. naval and air forces attacked the Wake Island group, caused much damage, and destroyed 61 enemy aircraft.

1943 saw the Japanese expelled from Papua, the New Georgia Group, and the Aleutians, and facing expulsion from the Solomons. The threat to Australia and to Alaska had been lifted. In all these operations air power had played a most important part ; photographing, reconnoitring, preventing counter-attacks, breaking up enemy resistance, clearing the seaways, fetching and carrying troops and supplies, and giving Red Cross aid.

Russian Front

The Russian air war was dominated throughout 1943 by ground operations. The Red Air Force, tied to the needs of the Red Army for close air support, had less opportunity than other Allied air forces to bomb strategically ; but targets in East Prussia were attacked. Over the Russian battlefields thousands of German aircraft were destroyed. The bombing (and shelling) of Leningrad was eased after the defeat of the German investing forces on January 18. At the other end of the long front, Stalingrad was captured on February 2, despite the efforts of the weakened Luftwaffe to support the beleaguered garrison. By the end of 1943, despite German counter-attacks, the Red Army was west of Leningrad, Vitebsk, Kiev, and the Dnieper river bend, an advance partly accounted for by Red air superiority in the field, due in good measure to the deadly blows against German industry delivered by Allied air power based on Britain.

Chapter 269

STALINGRAD RELIEVED: THE SOVIET ADVANCE

The second phase in the momentous 1942–1943 winter campaign in Russia —including the relief of Stalingrad, the withdrawal of the enemy from the Caucasus, and the launching of a new Russian Don offensive—is here described by our Military Editor, Maj.-Gen. Sir Charles Gwynn. The first phase, up to the encirclement of Von Paulus's army outside Stalingrad, was the subject of Chapter 252. The third phase is dealt with in Chapter 272

ALTHOUGH it was widely recognized that the German summer offensive of 1942 had led the High Command into an unsound strategical situation involving the continuance of operations into winter, yet military opinion all the world over was astonished when the rapid encirclement of Von Paulus's 6th Army, the success of the Middle Don offensive and the defeat of Von Hoth's rescue attempt from Kotelnikovo (described in Chapter

it was thought that any prolonged pause would give the enemy time to consolidate defensive positions and to bring up reserves.

Before following the course of the winter campaign and the strategical methods by which the Russian High Command overcame the difficulties confronting them, it may be well to recall the situation in the first week of 1943 on the sections of the front which were to become involved in its development.

salient, with its eastern bastions of Gzhatsk and Rzhev, constituted a threat to Moscow that could not be ignored, connected as it was with a possible offensive base provided by the hedgehog centres of Briansk and Orel.

In the previous summer Russian pressure on this part of the front had been maintained, perhaps mainly with the object of preventing the Germans from transferring reserves from it to support their southern offensive. In particular Rzhev had been strongly assaulted, and by the late autumn it was almost completely isolated and under close attack. The protection afforded by rivers and marshy surroundings made it, however, exceptionally defensible, and, standing on the Moscow–Riga railway, it to some extent nullified the importance of the Russian wedge, which in the previous winter had, to the north of that line, almost reached Veliki Luki, threatening to interrupt direct railway communications between the northern and central German armies. During the autumn the Russians, by-passing Rzhev, had gained possession of most of the railway connecting it with Veliki Luki. Rzhev, however, blocked railway communication with Moscow. Heavy fighting went on, but the situation remained obscure, even after the capture of Veliki Luki on January 1 was claimed ; and it was not to be clarified till some months later. About Briansk and Orel the Russians had also engaged in offensive operations, but apparently on no great scale.

Rzhev Isolated

CAPTURED GERMAN GUNS AT VELIKI LUKI

Veliki Luki, one of the strongest and most important German 'hedgehog' bastions on the Central Russian front (see map, p. 2715), fell to the advancing Red Army, after severe fighting, on January 1, 1943 : it had been in enemy hands for 16 months. Some of the heavy guns captured with Veliki Luki are here being hauled away from the town by tractor to be made serviceable for use against their former owners.

Photo, Planet News

252) proved that the Red Army had acquired sufficient offensive power to seize the opportunity. Military opinion, however, failed to realize the extent of Russian recovery or to foresee the great achievements of the winter campaign that was to follow. Professional opinion held that the great initial victories could not be fully exploited under winter conditions by armies that, as they advanced, were bound to leave railway communications far behind ; and it was thought that they must lose their momentum and be brought to a standstill through difficulties of supply. One hundred miles was looked on as about the extreme range of rapid offensive action, and

Russia's Great Recovery

In the north Leningrad was still closely invested and depended on the precarious route across the ice of Lake Ladoga for supplies. Its situation was not as desperate as in the previous winter, but efforts by Govorov's army from within and Meretskov's from without to join hands had so far failed to break through the German line on the Volkov River or to recapture the key fortress of Schluesselburg at the southwest corner of Lake Ladoga. In the Lake Ilmen area Novgorod, Staraya Russa (which had so narrowly escaped capture the previous winter) and, farther to the south-east, Demyansk remained strongly held enemy hedgehog centres.

In the centre of the front the Vyasma

Farther to the east and south heavy fighting without any great change in the situation had gone on at Voronezh ever since the Germans gained a precarious footing across the Don at this point in the early phase of their summer offensive. South of the town they still held the right bank of the Don for over 100 miles and therefore still blocked the Voronezh–Rostov railway, which the Russian Middle Don offensive of December 16 had reached between Katemerovka and Millerovo. Thus this important railway for the time being was of little use to either side. Millerovo, though almost completely surrounded was strongly defended by the Germans and the railway connecting it with Voroshilovgrad, across the Donetz, remained open. For a time it looked as if the Russian offensive had been brought to a standstill at this point, and that the Germans were clinging precariously to Millerovo in hopes that it would prove a pivot for an ultimate major counter-stroke to rescue Von Paulus. Over-sanguine expectations excited by the amazingly rapid success and progress of the Middle Don offensive were, therefore, somewhat damped.

Finally, the position on the Caucasus front should be considered. It was recorded in Chapter 245 how, on November 19, the very day the Stalingrad counter-offensive opened, the Russians had by a powerful counter-attack

defeated the German attempt to capture Ordzhonikidze in the Terek valley. Thereafter the news from Stalingrad must have had an immense effect on the Caucasus operations. It seems probable that some at least of the divisions with which Von Hoth attempted to relieve the 6th Army were drawn from reserves on the Caucasus front, and this may have decided the Germans to accept the Ordzhonikidze defeat and to retire to Nalchick. But it was not until Von Hoth's rescue operations had failed and the Russian Middle Don offensive of December 16 was carrying all before it that the situation of the 17th Army in the Caucasus became by the end of the year extremely serious. Up till then, though they had been compelled to abandon the offensive, the Germans may have hoped to stand during the

winter on the Terek at Mozdok and on the Kuma River in the Mineralnye-Georgievsk area. If that was their intention it must soon have become evident that a much more drastic withdrawal would be necessary; for with Von Hoth's force in full retreat towards the Sal and Manych rivers and the Middle Don offensive showing no signs of losing its momentum, the communications of the 17th Army were obviously threatened; and even the bottle-neck at Rostov through which they ran might ultimately be in danger. Moreover, the Russians in the Terek Valley were now on the offensive and by December 24 were attacking Nalchick violently.

The exact date on which the German retreat began cannot yet be definitely ascertained, nor how far this date was determined by the vigour of the Russian offensive, but it is evident that the retreat, though rapid, was carried out in reasonably good order covered by skilful rearguard actions. German strategy may often have been at fault, but German staffs never lacked executive ability. In this case their task was simplified by the possession of a first-class railway

German Retreat on the Don

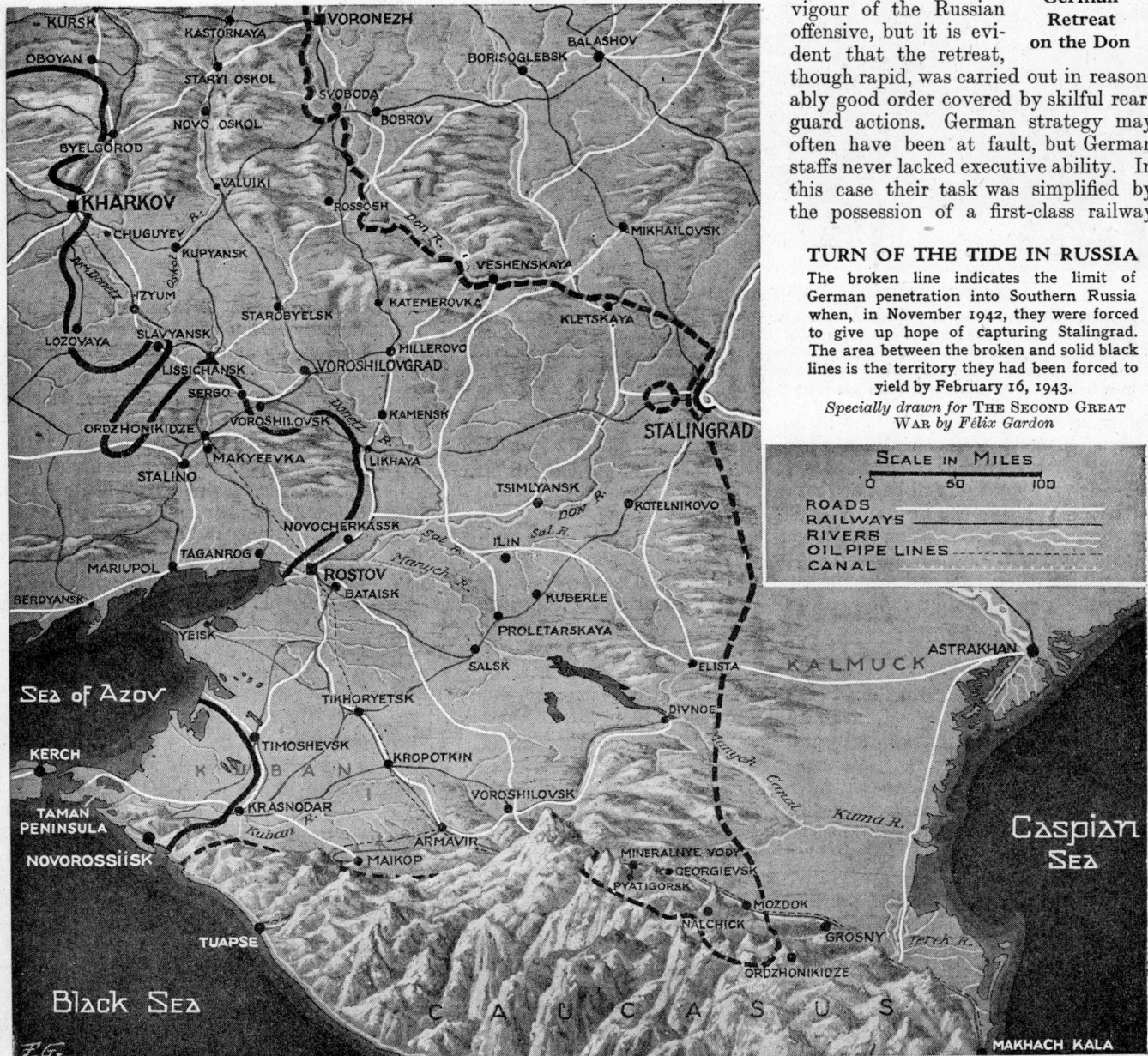

TURN OF THE TIDE IN RUSSIA
The broken line indicates the limit of German penetration into Southern Russia when, in November 1942, they were forced to give up hope of capturing Stalingrad. The area between the broken and solid black lines is the territory they had been forced to yield by February 16, 1943.

Specially drawn for THE SECOND GREAT WAR *by Félix Gardon*

FREEING THE CAUCASUS FROM THE GERMANS

1. Men of the Red Army in a street of Mineralnye Vody, recaptured on January 11, 1943, with a number of other towns in the spa district by Lt.-Gen. Maslennikov, victor of Kalinin. 2. A Circassian Sergeant of the Guards hoists the Red Flag in Mozdok on January 3, the day of the city's liberation: it had been held by the Germans since August 27, 1942. 3. Automatic riflemen fighting in Pyatigorsk, another spa town freed on January 11. *Photos, Planet News*

following their obvious line of retreat, and of a good road on which their abundant mechanized transport could move freely since snowfall had not been sufficiently heavy to cause serious obstruction. The Russian pursuit, on the other hand, in addition to being delayed by rearguards and demolitions, increasingly felt the lack of railways the farther it progressed; and when forced to leave the road by demolitions was hampered by snow. The Germans had therefore every chance of exploiting the elusiveness of modern armies conferred by fast-moving mechanical transport, which has time and again been illustrated in this war when armies found themselves in difficulties and had room to retreat. Only by encirclement or by the necessity of defending some vital point can they be brought to decisive action or even be compelled to hold rearguard positions stubbornly. The first definite signs that the Germans were in retreat were given when, on January 3, the Russians captured Mozdok and on the following day Nalchick. Even then it seemed possible that the enemy would stand on the Kuma, but

the capture of Georgievsk on January 7 and Mineralnye Vody four days later—after some heavy fighting—proved that a much longer retreat was contemplated. About the same time it was known that the German force at Elista, of which nothing had been heard since the siege of Stalingrad began, was also in retreat pursued by Kalmuck Cossack cavalry. It was, in fact, this cavalry advancing with amazing speed that seemed for a time to have a chance of outflanking the retreating columns and of bringing them to decisive action.

By the middle of January it was evident that the Germans had finally abandoned all hopes of ever resuming their offensive towards the Grozny and Baku oilfields, but it seemed hardly believable that they would give up the rich prizes of the Maikop oilfields and the Kuban granary. It was generally expected that they would stand to cover them on the line of the Manych River and on the upper Kuban in the area east of Armavir, where the rivers and the railway communications facilitate defence. At the northern end of that line Von Hoth's force, which had

retreated from Kotelnikovo hotly pursued by Malinovsky, was showing signs of recovery and Malinovsky was handicapped by the fact that Von Paulus's army at Stalingrad partially blocked his main line of communication; moreover, he could hardly expect to be strongly reinforced while the investment of the German 6th Army made heavy demands on Russian resources.

In the centre and south of the line it seemed scarcely possible that the Russian Caucasus armies, which had been so heavily engaged and so long separated from main centres of munitions production, could have great offensive potentiality. Although, therefore, the Germans had suffered disastrous defeat, it appeared probable that they might escape its worst consequences and at least be able to retain possession of a substantial part of Northern Caucasia and of the whole of the Donetz Basin. With Rostov and the crossings of the Donetz in their hands, an eventual resumption of their offensive in the summer might also be contemplated, particularly in view of the probability that Russian resources and offensive power might be exhausted before then.

However, just when it seemed probable that the Germans might be

Situation in the Caucasus

able to stabilize their front if they could check the pursuit in the Caucasus, the Russians gave proof that their initial success was no flash in the pan.

On January 16 a new offensive was opened on a wide front across the Don south of Voronezh, which had the same rapid success achieved a month earlier on the Middle Don. It extended as far north as Svoboda, where the Voronezh–Rostov railway crosses the river, and resulted in the immediate clearance of the German block on that railway. Moreover, linking up with the previous offensive, it threatened a second railway of great importance to the Germans for lateral communication which runs from the Donetz Basin up the Oskol valley, through Valuiki and other large centres, to Moscow, crossing the Voronezh–Kursk railway at Kastornaya. This new offensive, which recalled Foch's strategy in 1918 of opening an offensive on a new sector when the momentum of previous blows began to diminish, not only inflicted heavy punishment but made fresh demands on German reserves. About the same date Millerovo was captured and the original Middle Don offensive resumed its advance southwards, reaching the Donetz River where the railways to Rostov and to Stalingrad cross it.

New Russian Offensive

These successes began seriously to threaten German-occupied Rostov and the line of communications of the whole of the army in Caucasia which ran through the town. Moreover, the demands they made on the limited number of German reserves militated against the reinforcement of Von Hoth's troops, still under heavy pressure on the Manych front.

In face of these new developments the German High Command appear to have dropped any intention they may have had of standing at Armavir to protect the Maikop oilfields. The retreat continued, and on January 23 Armavir was captured by the Russians. Meantime, Malinovsky had driven Von Hoth across the Manych, capturing Salsk on January 22, where the Stalingrad–Novorossiisk railway branches to Rostov. Von Hoth, therefore, was faced with the double task of covering the approaches to Rostov and of checking a drive by Malinovsky along the Novorossiisk railway towards Tikhoryetsk where it crosses the Rostov–Baku line. At that point there was obviously a chance of intercepting the retreating Army of the Caucasus, and something in the nature of a race towards it developed.

At this stage Von Paulus's refusal to surrender, though he must have lost all hope of rescue, undoubtedly had an important influence on the situation since it to some extent limited the strength of Malinovsky's force; and the main body of the Caucasus Army succeeded in passing Tikhoryetsk before the town was captured by the Russians on January 30.

Nevertheless, the loss of Armavir had cut the main communications of the Germans in the Maikop area, and of the force that had been operating towards Tuapse. Pursued by the Russians who, from Tuapse, had launched a counter-offensive, this wing of the Caucasus Army had now to retreat towards Krasnodar through difficult country served by indifferent roads and without railway communications. In consequence, the Maikop oilfields were recovered before the Germans had succeeded in bringing them again into production. Strenuous efforts had been made to restore them, but they had

RELIEF COMES TO LENINGRAD

The siege of Leningrad, which lasted 16 months, was raised on January 18, 1943, when, after a fortnight's heavy fighting, troops of the Volkov and Leningrad fronts joined forces. 1. Soviet infantry dislodging the enemy from a Workers' Settlement near Leningrad. 2. Russian half-track armoured cars arrive in Schluesselburg, recaptured in the advance on Leningrad. 3. The forces of Gen. Govorov and Gen. Meretskov make contact at last.   *Photos, Planet News*

VICTORS AND VANQUISHED AT STALINGRAD

On January 31, 1943, Field-Marshal von Paulus (seen above, under interrogation) and his entire staff were captured at German Headquarters in a building nearly in the centre of Stalingrad. The defence of the city, which had been the focus of bitter fighting for 23 weeks, was conducted from a dugout, seen in the top photograph where (left to right) Major-General H. Krylov, Army Chief of Staff, Lieut.-General V. Chuykov, Commander of the 62nd Army, Lieut.-General K. Gurov, member of the Army Military Council, and Major-General A. Rodimtsev, Hero of the Soviet Union, Commander of the 13th Guards Division, are in conference. *Photos, Pictorial Press*

been thoroughly scorched and local partisans played an active part in interfering with restoration work. The failure to capture Tuapse was another example of wasted effort, and its retention intact by the Russians left the Black Sea Fleet a much-needed base. The German retreat to Krasnodar was successfully accomplished, and no doubt provided a considerable reinforcement to the force operating at Novorossiisk. To anticipate events : although the combined groups became isolated from the main army retreating towards Rostov, and Krasnodar after hard fighting was recaptured by the Russians in the middle of February, yet the Germans were to put up a prolonged resistance in the highly defensible country where the broad swift-flowing lower reaches of the Kuban separate the western spurs of the Caucasus from the marshes of the Taman peninsula. For months this pocket remained the only remnant of territory overrun by the German summer offensive of 1942 that still remained in enemy hands, and though steadily reduced in size, it was not finally cleared until the coming Russian summer offensive had left it far in rear.

Other events now began to succeed each other—or to synchronize—with confusing rapidity over an ever-widening front as the Russian offensive swept on in full flood. Having successfully passed the danger point at Tikhoryetsk, the German main Caucasus Army made all speed to reach the bottle-neck at Rostov and the adjacent minor ports on the Sea of Azov, by which it might escape ; and a bridgehead was formed about Bataisk, opposite Rostov, and at Yeisk on the Azov coast.

German Retreat from the Caucasus

Meanwhile, the Germans had suffered fresh disastrous reverses. In the north, by a combined offensive which opened on January 12, Govorov and Meretskov on January 18 joined hands, opening a

narrow lane to Leningrad and capturing the fortress of Schluesselburg. This had little effect on the great events in the south, but it meant much to beleaguered Leningrad, and was a reminder to the Germans that they could not safely transfer reserves from this front to the southern theatres.

Then, on January 25, Zhukov launched yet another offensive of the Foch pattern on the Don front. Overwhelming the German pocket at Voronezh the army commanded by Golikov drove across the river, along the

Hungarian Contingent Shattered

Kursk railway, with a speed exceeding even that of the previous Don offensives. It shattered the opposing Hungarian contingent and the German divisions which had been mixed with it in an effort to ensure that a pivot, to which both sides attached great importance and for which they had fought for months, should be held at all costs. For the Russians Voronezh had great sentimental value ; it was a symbol of determination to yield no further ground almost in the same category as Stalingrad. But apart from that there were great strategic objects to be gained by a decisive victory at this point. The capture of Voronezh finally cleared the last obstruction on the Moscow–Rostov railway running through Voronezh ; it opened the way for an advance along the railway from Voronezh to Kursk and thence in due course to Kiev. Kursk, the great hedgehog German centre which had resisted all attacks in the previous winter, and which had been the starting point of the principal German offensive in the summer, was obviously now the objective, and advance towards it was rapid. On January 28 Kastornaya (where the Moscow–Kharkov railway crossed the Kursk line) was captured, thus clearing the way for through communication between Moscow and Valuiki, reached a

NEW WEAPONS USED ON THE STALINGRAD FRONT

Russian multi-barrelled rocket-projectors in operation during the Battle of Stalingrad : the men of the Soviet Army nicknamed these weapons 'Katushas.' Top, German six-barrelled mobile mortar, used for projecting either high explosive or smoke bombs. It was an effective weapon, notable for the simplicity of its action which involved no heavy barrel or complicated firing mechanism. Below, Stalingrad streets silent again on February 1, 1943 : one centre of enemy resistance, crushed next day, alone remained. The only other Germans still there were Von Paulus and his staff, discussing terms of surrender, and the wounded being evacuated by Soviet stretcher bearers (right).

Photos, Planet News ; Pictorial News

BATTERED REMAINS OF VORONEZH

Voronezh, whose western suburbs had been in enemy hands since the great German offensive into Soviet territory in the summer of 1942, was finally cleared of the enemy on January 25, 1943. Its recapture removed the last obstruction on the railway between Moscow and Rostov, and opened the way for an advance along the railway from Voronezh to Kursk, and thence in due course to the city of Kiev. *Photo, "The Times"*

week earlier by the second middle Don offensive.

By now the whole front established by the German summer offensive had been broken and was crumbling at an ever-increasing rate. At Stalingrad on January 8 Von Paulus had refused a summons to surrender, possibly less in obedience to Hitler's exhortations than because he realized that he could still exercise some influence on the general situation. His refusal had, however, been followed by an intensification of the Russian attack designed to liberate the investing army for employment elsewhere. Fierce fighting followed, during which the Germans were split into a number of groups, and pounded unmercifully by Soviet artillery at shorter and shorter range. It was a gallant stand, but on February 2 Von Paulus, giving way to the representations of his subordinate commanders, decided to yield in order to avoid further bloodshed. No one can criticize him for his decision, nor his troops who had been sacrificed by the folly and obstinacy of Hitler. Not that that in any way detracted from the amazing achievement of the Red Army and its brilliant leaders. With Von Paulus (now promoted Field-Marshal), 24 generals became prisoners of war; and 190,000 of lower rank had been slaughtered or taken prisoner in the final stand, the remnants of the army of 330,000 which Hitler had promised would establish Germany on the Volga for all time. Never before had German arms experienced such complete and devastating disaster.

But the final scene at Stalingrad was soon relegated to its place in History as all attention became concentrated on the progress of the great wave of the Russian offensive. On the right it overwhelmed Kursk after slight resistance on February 8.

Russian Wave Sweeps on

Farther south it swept forward, crossing the Oskol River, clearing the railway which ran parallel to it, capturing the important centre of Kupyansk and establishing a crossing over the Middle Donetz during the first week of February. Then after a short pause it swept west across the Upper Donetz, taking the hedgehog centre of Byelgorod on February 9, and securing other towns on the railways radiating from Kharkov, which was now clearly threatened. Farther south still the

MEN OF THE COSSACK GUARDS

In the Caucasus, the horse still played a part as a mount during the Second Great War : accounts of fighting there are studded with references to the use of (horse-mounted) Cossack Cavalry in conjunction with tanks and infantry. Advancing with amazing speed in spite of ceaseless rain, sleet and snow, they contributed substantially to the clearing of the enemy from the Northern Caucasus during the early part of 1943. *Photo, Pictorial Press*

AIR POWER PAVED THE WAY FOR ALLIED VICTORY IN ITALY

Heavy day and night air attacks on the railway system of Southern Italy played an important part in the preparations for the Allied invasion of the peninsula, even before the fall of Sicily on August 17, 1943; and grew in intensity between that date and the first Allied landings in Calabria on September 3. Here is a train, laden with aircraft sorely needed by the Germans, in a wrecked railway marshalling yard near Naples. *Photo, British Official: Crown Copyright*

THE REBIRTH OF STALINGRAD

On February 2, 1943, the Soviet Government announced, 'Today the historic battle before Stalingrad has been concluded with the final victory of our forces.' That tremendous battle left the city in ruins, but its inhabitants soon began to return and, with the indomitable courage and faith displayed throughout the war by the citizens of the U.S.S.R., took an oath at this great gathering to reconstruct their city.

Photo, Pictorial Press

'N.W. OF STALINGRAD THE RED ARMY RECAPTURED A NUMBER OF VILLAGES . . .'

The defence and relief of Stalingrad during the winter of 1942-3 is an event that will find a place in history for centuries to come. But the gradual release from the invader of the villages to the north, south, and west of the great city, though it will not be so recorded, was an occasion for profound thanksgiving and rejoicing to the dwellers in them. Here is a group of survivors from families occupying a collective farm to the north-west of Stalingrad talking with men of the Russian advance troops who had liberated their area.

Photo, Planet News

RUSSIAN DON OFFENSIVE

Automatic riflemen advance under cover of a tank to the attack on Kursk (between Orel and Kharkov), recaptured on February 8, 1943 : it had been held by the enemy since November 1941. Right, Russian armour in Byelgorod (50 miles north-east of Kharkov) after its recapture on February 9. Bottom right, General Golikov (head of the Soviet Military Mission to Britain in 1941) commanded the Soviet Army which crossed the frozen Don on December 20, 1942, and thrust southwards. A month later his army overwhelmed the German pocket at Voronezh.

Russians had reached the line of the Lower Donetz by the third week in January, but then met with stiffer German resistance ; moreover, pockets of resistance had to be dealt with within the Don Bend on the Stalingrad railway. It was not, therefore, till the first week of February that the whole line of the Middle and Lower Donetz was reached and a determined attempt to cross it into the Donetz Basin could be made.

Meanwhile, on the left bank of the Lower Don the German Caucasus Army was still holding its bridge-head at Bataisk.

Russian Offensive on the Don

But it was apparent that the Donetz Basin was now becoming a dangerous salient, and when, on February 6, the bridge-head at Bataisk was taken and the Russians about the same time crossed the Middle Donetz in the neighbourhood of Izyum and Lissichansk, the situation became even more critical. The Russian attack now developed in full violence both on the Lower Donetz and Don and, whether the Germans had begun a deliberate withdrawal or not, both rivers were soon crossed. In quick succession between February 12 and 14 the important towns of Voroshilovgrad,

Likhaya and Novocherkassk west of the rivers were taken, and Rostov having been outflanked by crossings above and below, the city was itself captured on February 14.

With the exception of the Kuban pocket, the Red Armies had by now recaptured nearly all the territory that had been overrun in the summer, and had inflicted disastrous losses of men and material on the Germans and their satellite allies, of which latter only a remnant of the Rumanian contingent retained any military value.

This then may be taken as the end of the second phase of the amazing Russian winter counter-offensive of 1942–43, and it only remained to be seen whether the Germans would suffer even more catastrophic defeats. They had withdrawn their Caucasus Army with undoubted

skill, and the German soldier had shown that he had retained his fighting qualities and that his morale remained high, in spite of the fact that his reputation for invincibility had been sacrificed by the mistakes of the High Command. The situation was still fluid, but the Russians had proved that this time hedgehog defences would not prevent disaster.

TRANSPORT PROBLEMS IN BURMA

1. To get supplies to the men engaged in the Burma campaign, roads had to be pushed through the forest in very difficult, unknown, mountainous country. Coolies and mules helped to make preliminary tracks; bulldozers and other road-making machines followed them. Here are troops and supply mules using one of the resulting roads. 2. Men of the Royal Indian A.S.C. on a newly made jungle track. 3. Supplies for the Chinese fighting in Burma struggling along the Ledo road while it was under construction. It was completed as far as the Hukawng Valley by the end of 1943.

Chapter 270

TESTING JAPANESE DEFENCES IN BURMA

When the British retired from Burma in May 1942, as described in Chapter 206, and for many months after, they were too fully occupied with military affairs in Europe and North Africa to be able to give more than defensive attention to the Indo-Burmese frontier. But 1943 saw the opening of Allied offensive operations in Burma—small in scale, these were designed to probe Japanese defences and pave the way for the weightier attacks that were to follow

WHEN 1943 began, the European War had precedence in the strategy of the United Nations. The importance of the Far Eastern conflict was not ignored. Indeed, public opinion in the United States of America, New Zealand and Australia stressed it. Burma, lying roughly at the northern end of the perimeter of Japan's advance stretching through Siam, Malaya, the Netherlands Indies to the Solomons, was additionally vital to the potential offensive in the Far East because of its contiguity to China on the east and India on the west.

Map-reading strategists imagined that invasion of Burma by land would readily solve the problem of China's isolation. In reality the topographical difficulties put such a plan out of the bounds of practical execution. Until command of the sea had been fully restored to the United Nations in the Bay of Bengal, it was impossible to strike at the Japanese in Lower Burma. To a land invasion from the north-west and north-east, the north-to-south trend of Burma's road, river and railway communications presented an almost insuperable obstacle. Moreover, the terrain both on the Indian and the Chinese borders was mountainous, jungly, and devoid of any but lateral roadways—and they were mere tracks unsuited to military transport.

The exigencies of war in the European zone severely limited shipping available for the transport of supplies to India and

Limited Allied Shipping Facilities
for the support of combined operations. The United Nations had perforce to rely for the time being on the relentless pressure exerted by General MacArthur on the southern end of the enemy perimeter in the Far East while Admiral Chester Nimitz slowly but remorselessly and with ever-growing strength swept the Pacific Ocean to the west. To ease China's position, air communications developed a new traffic of supplies " over the hump," and the construction of a new road from Assam through Ledo was undertaken. (*See* map, page 2692.)

So the High Command in India— first under Field-Marshal Sir Archibald Wavell, and on his transfer to the Vice-regal dignity under General Auchinleck, and then under Admiral Lord Louis Mountbatten as Commander-in-Chief of the South-East Asia Command—had to adjust strategy to the realities of the situation. The primary objective was to hold the Japanese forces in Burma so that the danger of air or land attack on India was reduced to a minimum. For the rest, it was necessary to ensure the thorough training of British, Indian, African and, later, American troops (*see* illus., page 2651) gradually marshalled in India for entry into Burma by the north-west passages from the former country. In China, General Joseph Stilwell, in command of Chinese and American forces, was similarly preparing for an invasion from the north-east.

The plan was to drive the Japanese out of the north of Burma and so clear the way for restoring communications with China. Before this could be attempted the building up of forces in China and India had to be achieved, and operations during 1943, therefore, were mainly carried out by the Royal Air Force, Indian Air Force and American Air Force based on India, with valuable co-operation from the American Air Force based on Chungking. The only land campaign was that designed to shake the Japanese occupation of Akyab, in Arakan. In addition there was a spectacular and useful diversion on land by the officially named Long Range Penetration Group, under Brigadier Orde Charles Wingate, D.S.O.

Considerable expansion of airfields and training establishments in India gave splendid support to the Allied airmen. Air supremacy was quickly secured. Although the natural strength of the Japanese positions in Arakan prevented any loosening of the enemy's grip on strong points in that western coastal strip of Burma, the Royal Air Force and the

Allies Secure Air Supremacy

SIKH SNIPERS IN THE JUNGLE OF ARAKAN

In the early months of 1943 the British made a drive into Arakan, the strip of country lying along the west coast of Burma, with the object of capturing the port of Akyab. The expedition failed, but much experience was gained and considerable losses were inflicted on the enemy.

Photo, Indian Official

AIR ASSAULT ON JAPANESE BASES IN BURMA

Gangaw in the Myittha valley, an advance Japanese base in Burma, was one of the objectives bombed on December 22, 1942, by R.A.F. Blenheims, here seen flying low over the village. Left, a striking photograph of incendiary bombs falling towards the Burmese village of Ngazaunghpet during an attack on enemy positions in the Taung-daung district in February 1943.

Photos, British Official

U.S.A. 10th A.F. roamed far afield over Burma and, eventually, Malaya and Siam. Rangoon was frequently attacked and for weeks at a time was virtually closed to Japanese shipping.

The story of this air offensive cannot be properly told without some description of prevailing weather conditions. The development of India's meteorological services since air transport became important has been noteworthy. The **Effects of Weather Conditions** needs of war impelled intensified expansion of facilities for giving airmen information of vital moment to them. The monsoon rains, beginning in Burma somewhere in May and lasting till October, were regarded 20 years ago as an unconquerable hindrance to air transport in the peak months of July and August. But in the monsoon period of 1943 British and American airmen overcame those difficulties as a matter of course.

Apart from torrential rains flooding the airfields, often reducing visibility to zero, the monsoon causes gigantic banks of current-ridden clouds and generates electrical storms which throw instruments out of gear. Its floods change the aspect of the ground below and eliminate landmarks. The meteorological services so enhanced their efficiency that Allied pilots were able to have accurate forecasts for targets even 800 to 1,000 miles away.

The R.A.F. devoted their activities mainly to dive-bombing, medium and light bombing, and machine-gunning of communications, especially road, rail and river traffic. **Concerted Allied Air Offensive** Enemy barracks, troop positions, hutments and tents, oil installations and storage came under these persistent attacks, in which the Indian Air Force played a gallant part. The U.S.A. 10th A.F. directed a heavy and medium bomber offensive against such strategic points as bridges, railway yards and docks. In their tactics "skip-bombing" ("skipping" delayed action bombs to give the bomber time to get away) most effectively blew up bridges, blocked lines and exploded ammunition dumps.

This concerted air offensive prevented the Japanese from exploiting Burma to the full as a base for offensive operations. Their loss of air supremacy forced them to remove their bomber squadrons from forward airfields. Frequently their railway communications from north to south were cut. The air stranglehold on Rangoon made it impossible for them to develop a seaborne attack in that port without coming under the notice of the lynx-eyed watchers in the air. Their trans-

LETTERS HOME FROM THE JUNGLE
Men of the Lancashire Fusiliers fought with distinction, courage and cheerfulness in the difficult jungle warfare in Burma, where they had not only to counter the wiles of an enemy more experienced in this type of fighting, but also to withstand climatic conditions and insect pests peculiarly trying to Europeans in country of a hard and unfamiliar character.
Photo, Indian Official

port difficulties were aggravated to a point which made daylight travel by road, river or rail out of the question.

In July alone they lost 650 rivercraft and 300 goods wagons, while in the four months from May to August inclusive, Beaufighters and Hurricanes by themselves destroyed 1,620 sampans (invaluable oar-propelled canoes), 43 steamers or barges, 683 other craft, 45 locomotives, 510 wagons, 125 transport vehicles, and 18 factories. These records vividly illustrate the startling change in the position as compared with the tragic days of the 1942 retreat when Japanese superiority in the air was unchallenged.

The provision of supplies by air to troops operating in the field and to friendly tribesmen carrying on "partisan" activities was another side of the airmen's work. In January 190 tons of supplies were dropped by air; in July the total for the month rose to 760 tons. Even in the unfavourable month of August supplies from the air were dropped on 27 days.

Operations on land beginning to take shape in Burma when 1943 opened had limited objectives: training the troops in jungle warfare, initiating new methods of handling mobile forces without maintaining outside lines of communication, inflicting as heavy casualties as possible on the enemy. The drive into Arakan, the strip of territory on the west coast of Burma—shut off from the interior by the Mayu Hills—was intended to bring about the recovery of Akyab. British and Indian troops crossed the Burma frontier through Cox's Bazaar some time in the middle of December 1942. Buthidaung was captured and the attacking forces reached Rathedaung, which was strongly held by the enemy. The Japanese had at first withdrawn in the belief that the forces against them were stronger than they really were. At one time British-Indian forces were within 15 miles of Akyab. Then the enemy, strongly reinforced, staged fierce counter-attacks, outflanked our advanced forces, and compelled them to retire. Lacking adequate sea-craft and too small in numbers to meet the strengthened enemy forces, the expedition, fighting fiercely, gradually withdrew to the Indian border. (See map and illus., page 2223.)

Abortive British Drive into Arakan

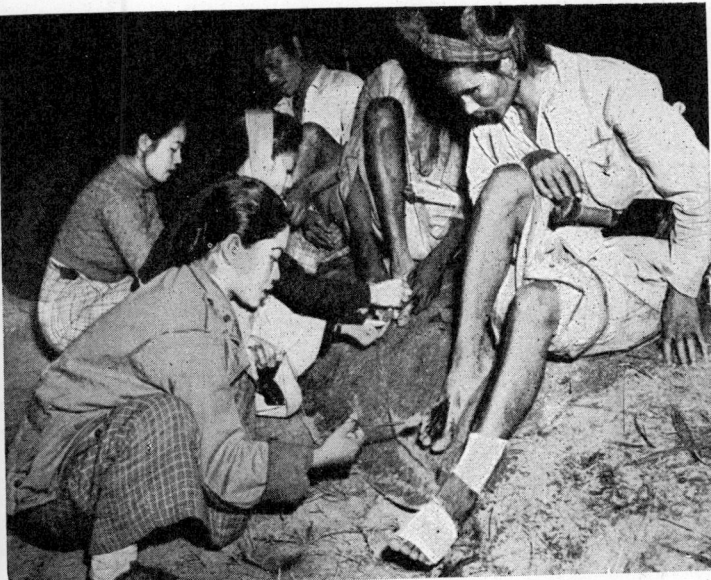

FIRST AID BY BURMESE NURSES
Scouts back from patrol in the Burmese jungle were frequently in need of skilled attention for minor injuries. Leech bites were a common trouble. British, American and Chinese shared the dangers and annoyances of these patrols with Chins and Kachins native to the country. Here, Burmese nurses are giving first aid for foot injuries to Kachin scouts just back from a mission.
Photo, Keystone

BATTLE AREA IN BURMA, 1943

Some idea of the difficulties of launching a campaign into Burma from India can be gathered from this map. Except along the coast, the two countries are separated by difficult, forest-clad mountains through which runs no railway or navigable river. Penetration can be made only by road or air—and the necessary highways and airfields had to be built in the course of campaigning as part of military operations.

Specially drawn for THE SECOND GREAT WAR *by Harrop*

movements. Mules and oxen carried the radio sets on the march. Other mules carried mortars, guns and ammunition. Heavier supplies were carried by the elephants. Each column had its quota of Burmese officers and men, without whom, said Brigadier Wingate on his return to India, the operations would have been impossible. They had mule-borne loud-speakers for addressing the villagers, who were told of the growing strength of the United Nations and the certainty of deliverance from Japan. Mules also carried duplicating machines which produced secret sheets distributed to the Burmans.

The Chindits were not appealing to unreceptive ears. Among the tribesmen of the border hills of Burma were British troops who had never left Burma, but had been re-equipped and returned to the jungle—veteran fighters, fearless and steeped in jungle lore. Their leadership of the Chin hill men was a stimulus to the Chins who, as irregular fighters, have magnificent qualities. So, too, have the Kachins, and both have long served in the Indian Army, proving their worth in many a campaign of the last war. Ever since the British retreat, these Chins and Kachins, under either British or their own leadership, had waged war against the Japanese, and modern arms had been supplied to them from the air. Typical of their spirit was the exploit of a Chin lad of 16 who led a party of 15 men to attack

Wingate and His Chindits

COMMANDER OF THE 14TH ARMY

Lt.-General W. J. Slim, C.B.E., D.S.O., M.C., appointed in January 1943 to command the 14th Army serving in Burma, commanded a brigade of the Fifth Indian Division in Eritrea, where he was wounded, and fought in Burma under General Alexander.

Photo, British Official

As Lord Wavell afterwards told an American audience in accepting responsibility for this failure, the withdrawal was due to an underestimation of the size of the force required for the capture of Akyab. Yet the operations had their value in the lessons taught, and in the heavy toll taken of enemy strength: Japanese casualties were estimated to have been 4,000, about half of them killed. British and Indian casualties, announced on April 25 when the force had been withdrawn, were 3,514, of whom only 392 (171 British) were killed.

Heavy Enemy Casualties in Arakan

More important, and in its special way more successful, was the campaign of the Long Range Penetration Group, who took the name of Chindits—after the fabulous griffins guarding Burmese temples—and penetrated into enemy territory as far as the Shan States. Brigadier Orde Wingate, their commander, had already emerged in Palestine and later in Abyssinia as a genius of guerilla warfare, and had been specially selected for this new task by Field-Marshal Wavell. He chose mixed detachments of Gurkhas and British troops for the expedition. The latter were all aged between 28 and 35—mostly married men from the North of England. Wingate trained them in jungle warfare, river crossing and long forced marches, until they were moulded into shock troops ready for anything. Mule transport had to be used as well as elephants. Wingate's abilities found no difficulty in training British or Gurkha soldiers as muleteers. He recruited Burmese mahouts (elephant drivers) to train them in handling elephants. The columns which crossed the Chindwin River on February 16 were self-contained. Each had R.A.F. officers and N.C.O.s attached to it with radio sets for co-operating with aircraft which dropped supplies, bombed enemy targets and reported news of enemy

THE CHINDITS AND THEIR LEADER

1. 'Chief Chindit' Brigadier Orde Charles Wingate, D.S.O. (right), explaining his plans just before the Chindits marched into Burma. Some account of their exploits is given in the opposite page. 2. A signal section of the R.A.F. attached to one of the Chindit columns establishes contact with base by radio. 3. Elephants as well as mules were used for transport, and both British and Gurkha soldiers were trained by Burmese mahouts to manage the great beasts. 4. Field-Marshal Sir Archibald Wavell inspects the Chindits before they start. He specially selected Wingate to lead the Long Range Penetration Group—nicknamed 'Chindits'—in their campaign behind the enemy lines in Burma.

WITH THE CHINDITS IN BURMA

Fresh rations and other supplies were dropped by parachute into jungle clearings for Wingate's Chindits. 1. A tin being filled with a ten-day ration: it included biscuits, dates, cheese, sugar, salt, tea, matches, chocolate, powdered milk and cigarettes. 2. 'Plane land here now': signal spelt out with parachutes used to drop supplies by men waiting for the landing. Sick and wounded were evacuated by plane. 3. One group of the Chindits fording a river in enemy-occupied Burma.

Photos, Indian Official; Planet News

a Japanese transport column of 100 men. They put the column to flight, killing 15 of the enemy by shotgun or grenade and wounding many more. A Chin village schoolmaster with five companions ambushed 40 Japanese whose surprise was so complete that they put up no defence at all. The various frontier tribesmen, with little military backing, had indeed made it possible for many square miles of north Burma territory to be denied to the enemy. Their determination, rising out of the first torpor prevalent after the British retreat, had grown in daring and ingenuity. With the opportunity of getting again into touch with British forces they asked for arms.

So, in penetrating into enemy country, the Chindits knew that the jungle was

GENERAL STILWELL AND HIS CHINESE TROOPS
Lt.-General Joseph W. Stilwell built up a Chinese army in India to fight in Burma. Here he is addressing a body of Chinese troops in training. Left, Chinese scouts under Gen. Stilwell's command advancing with fixed bayonets through the jungle in the Naga Hills. Head-and-shoulder hoods and puttees to the knee protect them against the noxious insects of the forests.
Photos, Planet News ; Keystone

not entirely unfriendly. They had to swim rivers and plod along narrow, perilous jungle tracks. Their rations were supplemented by mule soup (only one mule returned with them to India), horse liver, python steak, roast elephant and banana leaves. Their columns began to reach the railway joining Mandalay to Myitkina early in March and their attacks on that line—they cut it in 75 places and destroyed four bridges—lasted until the middle of the month. Instead of moving back as the Japanese expected, the Chindits then went farther south to within striking distance of main enemy bases. This had the desired effect of provoking a large concentration of enemy forces ; on which the Chindits, according to their training code, dissolved into thin air—or, to put it technically, carried out a dispersal—and had returned in small groups to their starting point by May 20.

The exploits of the Chindits had a value much beyond the important

losses which they inflicted on the enemy. To begin with, they exploded the notion of Japanese superiority in jungle warfare. Fantastic stories of Malaya and the Burma retreat had created a picture of an almost supernatural uncanniness in the enemy which, never accepted by British or Indian troops, had yet been naïvely sponsored by bewildered commentators in armchairs at home and abroad. In the South-West Pacific MacArthur's men had already pricked the bubble. In Burma Wingate repeated the process. His verdict was : " Although incapable of the sombre and humourless self-immolation of the Japanese, the British soldier can nevertheless beat him on his own chosen ground, provided he gives scope to his greater intellectual powers and stronger, saner character."

Wingate shrewdly summed up the results of Japanese occupation of Burma when he added that the Chindits' success derived in large measure from

the general feeling that the United Nations were " fighting for something that means more than the severe and macabre ideals of the Axis." That was why he was able to say, " To the Burmese, and in especial to the brave and devoted Burma Rifles who went with us, must belong the main credit for what success we enjoyed."

That achievement was bound to have immense influence on the course of larger and wider-planned operations for the recovery of Burma when the time came. Ruthless exploitation and untiring propaganda characterized the Japanese occupation. Its four aims were to win Burmese co-operation ; to destroy British influence ; to persuade the Burmans that the British would never return ; to bring Burma within the so-called " Co-Prosperity " sphere. On August 1, 1943, an announcement of the granting of independence to Burma had undoubted influence in reconciling some Burmese, especially the politically minded urban classes. But they were in a minority. The usually carefree country-folk were not troubled by the circumstance that the puppet Burmese Cabinet had with its " independence " to co-operate on the basis of " sharing life and death with Japan."

Aims of the Japanese in Burma

The gradual spread of economic distress testified to the immediate futility of Burma's dubious partnership in Japanese co-prosperity. The advantages of military success—and Japanese propaganda did not fail to stress the failure of the Arakan campaign as well as the departure of the Chindits—were offset by economic stringency. The idea of rooting out British influence faded before the practical need of maintaining British law and procedure. But above all the Japanese —as in Manchuria, Formosa and Korea—could not shake off their conception of themselves as a "super-race." Cajolery of the powerful Buddhist hierarchy by religious broadcasts and donations did not find support in the day-to-day occasions of the army of occupation. The stabling of horses in pagodas, building latrines in shrines, ill-treating monks and violating the sanctity of monasteries, and outrages committed against the population generally, gave the Burmese a lurid slant on Japan's idea of independence.

Japan's Idea of Independence

The campaigns of the spring of 1943, followed by the sustained air operations through the monsoon period, cleared the way for a concerted renewal of the direct attack on Japan's Burma bases in the autumn. The surrender of Italy in September greatly eased the naval commitments of the United Nations in Europe, thus making it possible to reinforce the Royal Navy's strength in Eastern waters, although obviously the impending invasion of Europe still made the shipping situation difficult. From the north of the Burma frontier to the southern point in Arakan the positions of the United Nations and the Japanese dovetailed along a front of about a thousand miles.

The Japanese had long been preparing a so-called Indian Army of Liberation under the nominal command of the renegade Subhas Chandra Bose. It was believed to be ranged with Japanese units preparing to invade India. Facing them were British, Indians, Chinese, West Africans, Kachins and Chins. The South-East Asia Command came into being in August 1943 under Vice-Admiral Lord Louis Mountbatten, with headquarters in New Delhi (moved in 1944 to Kandy, Ceylon). The 14th Army under Lieut.-Gen. W. J. Slim, C.B.E., D.S.O.,

Havildar GAJA GHALE
Gained the 7th V.C. awarded to men of the Indian Army. Under his leadership, a platoon of young soldiers stormed and took in fierce hand-to-hand fighting Basha East Hill, a well-entrenched Japanese key position in the Chin Hills, on April 25, 1943. Though wounded by a hand grenade in the arm, chest and leg, Ghale led his men forward along a bare ridge swept by machine-gun, artillery and mortar fire.

Havildar PARKASH SINGH
Received the V.C. for his 'high courage and initiative' on two occasions: on January 6, 1943, he saved two gun crews whose carriers had been put out of action and their ammunition exhausted; on January 19 he rescued a carrier carrying its own and another crew; then drove out again, and towed to safety another carrier containing two wounded men, all under heavy fire, on his own initiative.

M.C., was the force chiefly responsible for the defence of India against Japanese invasion from Burma, and for penetrating to link up with Lt.-General Stilwell's American and Chinese forces which, moving in through the Naga Hills, began to make their way up the Hukawng Valley.

Events were thus developing towards the end of the year. But the problem of Burma's rescue from Japanese hands could not be solved by land and air action alone. Until the United Nations could release the full weight of their sea-power and launch combined operations against Lower Burma, it was not possible to aim at more than the establishment of a link with harassed China and the maintenance of a loosely knit front against possible Japanese attacks on India.

Combined Operations Required

Meanwhile, in order to be ready for ultimate re-entry into Burma, the Government of Burma, with headquarters at Simla, proceeded with its task which in February 1943 had been outlined by Mr. Amery as designed (1) to establish an organization to meet the requirements of the military authorities in the operations for the recovery of the country and afford the fullest co-operation in hastening the defeat of the Japanese; (2) to formulate plans for reconstruction and return to normality after the eviction of the Japanese; (3) to study and make proposals for future policy administration.

SUPREME ALLIED COMMANDER VISITS THE BURMA FRONT

Vice-Admiral Lord Louis Mountbatten was appointed Supreme Allied Commander of the South-East Asia Command in August 1943; he was promoted Admiral in September. Towards the end of the year he visited the Burma front, where he inspected officers and men of the Navy, Army and Air Force, and British nurses. He is here seen driving a jeep in the Arakan forward area.
Photo, British Official

Chapter 271

CHINA ENTERS HER SEVENTH YEAR OF WAR

On the seventh day of the seventh month of 1943, China passed into her seventh year of war. Growing stringency of economic conditions ; successful defensive operations on all fronts against the Japanese ; expanding and encouraging contacts, at home and abroad, with her Allies : these are the salient features of Mr. Peter Hume's record of China's continued heroic resistance to the aggressor during 1943. The events of 1942 were set down in Chapter 230

IN 1943 China found herself increasingly pressed by the rigours of the almost total blockade which the Japanese were able to impose after the Allied withdrawal from Burma in May 1942. At the same time 1943 was a year in which China's international position and stature were greatly enhanced by the action of her major Allies, who in

CHINA'S CHIEF OF STAFF
General Ho Ying-chin, Chief of Staff of the Military Council of China and China's Minister of War, took part in the discussions on Allied war plans held in Chungking and in New Delhi immediately after the ' unconditional surrender ' conference at Casablanca Jan. 14–24, 1943. *Photo, Pictorial Press*

other sectors of the Far Eastern and Pacific battle zones were already beginning to go over to the offensive and were able to make it clear to the Chinese people that the expulsion of the enemy from China's soil was a major aim of Allied strategy. The new feeling of moral integration with the general Allied cause after years of bitter and lonely struggle was a vital factor in maintaining the always sturdy morale of the Chinese fighting men and civilians under the increasing stress of a newly acute physical isolation.

Particularly significant in this connexion was the signature on January 11 of new treaties between China and Britain in Chungking and between

China and the United States in Washington. The actual signature of the treaties was in fact only the culmination of a movement on the part of the Western democracies, initiated by Sir Austen Chamberlain in 1926, towards according the Chinese Republic that measure of full sovereignty denied to the corrupt and decadent Manchu dynasty by force of Western arms in the 19th century. The final negotiations which led to the new treaties were opened following an Anglo-American declaration of intent on October 9, 1942 (*see* page 2295). Nevertheless, the impact on the Chinese people of the news that treaties of such importance had actually been signed, thus ending a century of what they rightly or wrongly had come to regard as "national humiliation," was of the first importance in strengthening China's relation with her Allies.

Of more immediately military significance than this long-delayed political step was the visit paid to Chungking by Field-Marshal Sir John Dill and Lt.-General Henry H. Arnold as

representatives respectively of Mr. Churchill and President Roosevelt immediately after the meeting of the British and American leaders at Casablanca in late January. Disappointment in Chungking that a Chinese representative had not attended the Casablanca Conference was largely dissipated by the arrival of these two high officers to confer with Generalissimo Chiang Kai-shek on the decisions reached. A series of conferences in Chungking was followed by the visit to India of General Ho Ying-chin, Chinese Minister of War and Chief of General Staff, and Lt.-General Yu Ta-wei, head of the Ordnance Department of the Chinese Army. These officers, together with Field-Marshal Dill, General Arnold and General Somerville, Chief of the U.S. Army Services of Supply (who had also been at Casablanca) engaged in discussions with Field-Marshal Sir Archibald Wavell, then C.-in-C. India, on questions of joint operations against Japan and of developing the India–China supply line (*see* illus., page 2663). Subsequently Generals Ho and Yu visited

ALLIED MILITARY CHIEFS IN CHUNGKING
Field-Marshal Sir John Dill (representing Mr. Churchill), Brig-Gen. Claire Chennault, Commander of the American Air Task Force in China, Lt.-Gen. Henry H. Arnold (representing President Roosevelt), Lt.-Gen. J. W. Stilwell (American Chief of Staff to Generalissimo Chiang Kai-shek), and Brig.-Gen. Clayton Bissel, commanding U.S.A. 10th Air Force (India), inspecting P.-40 Tomahawk single-seater fighters during the Allied military talks at Chungking.

CHINA APPEALS TO CANADA'S PARLIAMENT
During her tour of America in 1943, Mme. Chiang Kai-shek addressed a joint assembly of Canada's House of Commons and Senate in the Parliament building at Ottawa. She was the first woman, not a member of Parliament, to be accorded this privilege. In the course of her speech she said : ' Through your welding successfully two peoples into one strong and harmonious nation, the world has much to learn in universal brotherhood.'

camps in Eastern India, where a substantial force of Chinese soldiers, some of them veterans of the first Burma campaign and others flown to India in transport aircraft from the Chinese fronts, was in training under United States officers. General Ho expressed satisfaction with the modern weapons being supplied to these troops and their progress in learning the use of them.

Another visit, of great political importance, was that paid by Mme. Chiang Kai-shek to the United States. Mme. Chiang reached the U.S.A. in November 1942, but immediately entered hospital for medical treatment necessitated by a war injury suffered in Shanghai in 1937. On her recovery in February, the Generalissimo's talented wife undertook a series of speaking engagements in the major cities of the United States. She addressed both the U.S. Senate and the House of Representatives in Washington, and wherever she spoke in the ensuing months she paid tribute to the war effort of the United States, Britain, and the Soviet Union, and expressed appreciation of the importance of these countries' struggle against Germany. Nevertheless, she also stressed the disparity of the material resources made available by the Allies for the war against Ger-

many and for that against Japan, which China considered she was fighting almost alone and with bare hands, while in fact Japan was as great a menace to all the United Nations as was Germany. The deep impression made on the American people by her personality was reflected in a substantial swing of public opinion against the accepted Allied strategy of first concentrating the main forces against Germany while limiting the scale of operations in the Far East. This swing was especially encouraged and sustained by the formerly Isolationist Press, where the slogan " Beat Japan first " was much used as an anti-Roosevelt and anti-British weapon. Identification by certain elements of their views with Mme. Chiang's led to some deterioration in Sino-British relations, and it was proposed that Mme. Chiang should visit Britain to correct this inadvertent impression.

Renewed ill-health made such a visit impossible ; but in July Dr. T. V. Soong, Chinese Minister for Foreign Affairs, paid an official visit to London as guest of the British Government. **Dr. Soong, in Britain** In the words of a communiqué issued after his departure : " During his stay he had a number of informal conversations with the Prime Minister, the Secretary of State for Foreign Affairs, other Ministers of the Crown and high British military, naval and air authorities. An extraordinary meeting of the Pacific Council was convoked under the chairmanship of the Prime Minister at which the strategical situation in the Far East was reviewed. In the course of these meetings, which were held in a most cordial atmosphere, views were exchanged on many aspects of the war both in the East and in the West. Post-war issues also came under discussion. There was complete agreement on the need for the rigorous prosecution of the war until the utter defeat of Germany and Japan has been achieved and for the organization of measures thereafter to secure a stable world peace."

Dr. Soong stayed in Britain for three weeks, and during that time was able to meet the British Press, to which he frankly explained the difficulties of China's position, and to broadcast to the British people. On both occasions he stressed China's debt to Russia for her freely given assistance up to the time Germany attacked her, the extent and significance of his country's six-year resistance to Japan, and her hopes for post-war co-operation with Britain and the other democratic nations.

Immediately after leaving Britain, Dr. Soong attended another conference

CHINA HOLDS SALWEEN ATTACKS

1. A typical stretch of the upper Salween River, scene of fierce fighting during 1943. The Burma Road, some 80 miles inside Yunnan province, crosses the Salween by the Haitung Bridge which, after being in Japanese hands, was retaken by the Chinese, supported by U.S. fighters, in November 1943. 2. Chinese machine-gunners in a nest overlooking the Salween River. 3. Chinese wounded in the Salween battles being tended by nurses and orderlies just behind the lines. *Photos, Planet News*

IN THE 'RICE BOWL' OF CHINA

In their attempt to conquer Hunan, China's 'rice-bowl,' the Japanese reached Changteh, its chief centre, which they took on December 3, 1943, after a 15 days' bloody siege—fewer than 300 of the Chinese 57th Division defending the city survived. But, helped by U.S. Mitchells, and despite further heavy losses, the Chinese recaptured it on December 9 and continued to drive forward. The city was reduced to ashes. 1. Civilians return to ruined Yiyang in northern Hunan. 2. Chinese officers plan the re-taking of Changteh. 3. A street in Changteh after its recapture.

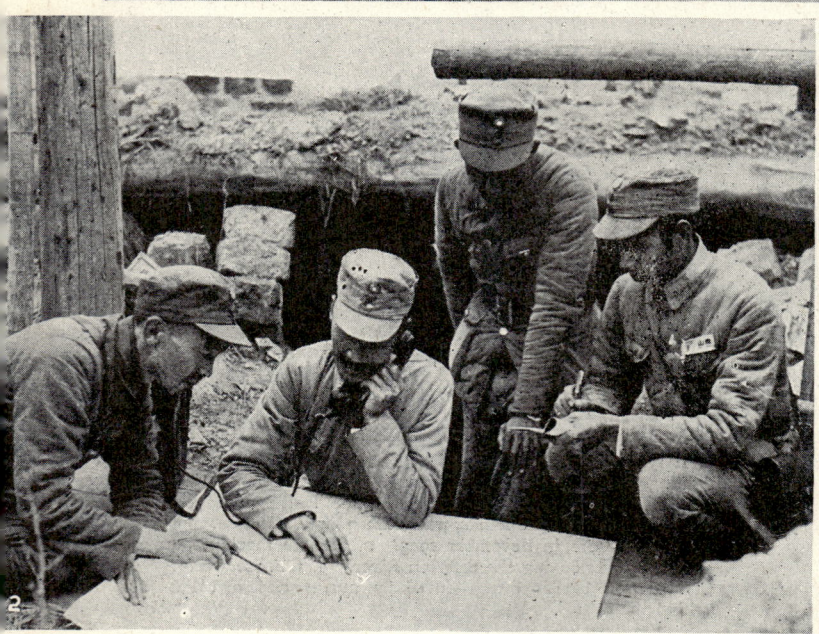

of the utmost importance to the United Nations—that at Quebec, where for the first time a Chinese representative was present with the United States President and the British Prime Minister for talks which, in the words of the communiqué issued after the conference, " turned very largely upon the war against Japan and the bringing of effective aid to China "—a declaration that helped to dispel many half-felt doubts in China about the determination of the western Allies to pursue the Pacific War while that in Europe remained undecided.

A positive and immediate result of this conference at Quebec was the organization of the South-East Asia Command under Vice-Admiral Lord Louis Mountbatten (promoted Admiral a few weeks later). Creation of this Command to fill the gap in the front against Japan between the South-West Pacific zone, under General MacArthur, and the continental Asiatic zone, under Generalissimo Chiang Kai-shek, was enthusiastically received in Chungking, and Admiral Mountbatten found a warm welcome among the Chinese people when he visited Generalissimo Chiang shortly after his appointment was announced.

In this way the stage was set for the adhesion of the Chinese government to the declaration of policy on waging the war and organizing the peace made at the October Conference of the Foreign Ministers of Great Britain, U.S.A., and U.S.S.R. in Moscow (*see* page 2709); and for General Chiang Kai-shek's participations in discussions held at Cairo between him, President Roosevelt and Mr. Winston Churchill in November. In Moscow, where discussions turned primarily on the affairs of Europe, China was not represented throughout the meetings, but it was a development of particular significance, in view of the Soviet Union's continuing neutrality in the war against Japan, that the Chinese ambassador in Moscow was invited to sign with Molotov, Eden and Hull the most far-reaching of the declarations in which the conference resulted : that dealing with the creation of machinery for ensuring post-war security.

China Confers Abroad

Apart from the vital strategic planning for joint prosecution of the war against Japan in which high officers of all Services from Britain, China and the United States were engaged during the conference at Cairo, this meeting was especially notable for the long-term political declaration in which it resulted (*see* Historic Document No. 267,

AMERICAN PLANES IN CHINA'S BATTLE

American aircraft did valuable service for China in her battle with the Japanese, and Chinese workers helped to keep them in the air. Above, a repair hangar at one U.S. air station in China where skilled Chinese are overhauling and repairing fighters so that they can resume action. Below, Chinese workers, watched by their fellows, unload boxes of ·50 calibre machine-gun ammunition for the use of the U.S. Army 14th Air Force serving in China.

OVER THE HIMALAYAN 'HUMP'

Transport planes carried goods, military and civil leaders, and technicians over the Himalayas to China, deprived after the cutting of the Burma Road of all surface contact with her Allies. The windows of these aircraft were fitted with plugs (above) which could be removed in case of attack, leaving apertures through which tommy-guns could be fired. On the 'hump' route, the planes travelled so high that oxygen masks were essential (below).

Photos, Keystone; Associated Press

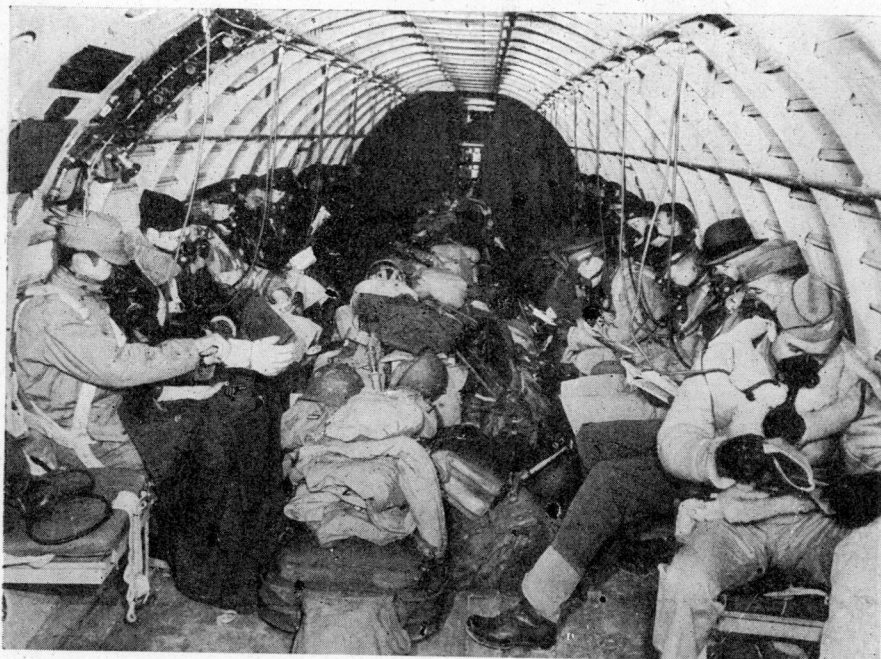

page 2636). This joint declaration embodied views on which all Chinese had always had the strongest feelings, but on which they had had some doubts as to whether full support in what they considered their legitimate claims could be secured from China's allies, and in particular from Britain. The association of Mr. Churchill with the Cairo declaration for this reason greatly helped in clearing old fears and suspicions from China's international outlook.

Vitally important as these meetings and evidences of Allied solidarity were, they have to be set against a less satisfactory picture of the condition of the Chinese Army and people as a result of six years of continuous war on their own soil; and of the Japanese blockade. Lightly felt at first, this became intense during 1943. The very numerous Chinese Army suffered from a desperate shortage of arms and equipment, especially of the heavier kind, and from a state

very near to immobility, since neither transport vehicles nor the fuel on which to run them were available in any quantity. Such limitations made it possible for the Chinese to take little offensive action to clear their territory, and meant in addition that even active defensive fighting imposed a severe strain on the country's sparse resources for the needs of modern mechanical war. Nevertheless, during the year, the Chinese staved off several determined attempts to force them out of the war.

In February the Japanese announced that they now proposed to take " all conceivable measures to crush Chungking " and simultaneously launched offensives in Central, South-East and South-West China. After a month of hard fighting all they could claim was the occupation of Kwangchowwan (a small coastal area in Kwangtung Province, which had been leased by China to France since 1898 and which Vichy complaisance now permitted China's enemy to seize without opposition), and certain local but important advances in the middle Yangtze sector west of Hankow. Japanese attacks across the Salween River from Burma into Yunnan Province and northward from Canton up the Canton–Hankow railway were both thrown back.

The middle Yangtze advances provided, however, a valuable springboard from which the next major Japanese offensive of the year was launched in May. Once again the Japanese spoke of inflicting total defeat on China and of advancing on Chungking. They moved westward in considerable strength (the Chinese estimated that they employed about 120,000 men) into the mountains which here guard the approaches to West China, and at first made considerable progress. But before the offensive was three weeks old the Chinese, employing tactics tested in many a similar campaign, swooped from the flanking hills to which they had retired on the enemy columns advancing up the valley roads and cut them into small segments which faced retreat or annihilation. Many of the Japanese, minus their transport and heavier equipment, got back to the starting line of their offensive, where fortified positions enabled them to blunt the impetus of the Chinese counter-assault. Many more, though, did not get back, and the toll of the retreat was greatly increased by the support given to the Chinese ground troops, on a larger scale than ever before, by American aircraft reinforcing the meagre striking power of the Chinese Air Force in repeated attacks against

Japanese Advance on Chungking

THE CHIEF CHINDIT HOLDS COUNCIL

Of all the exploits which the Second Great War produced, none exceeded in skill, daring and interest that conducted in the spring of 1943 by Brigadier Orde Charles Wingate and his ' Chindits ' (see page 2692). Trained under his experienced guidance, they penetrated in small groups far behind the Japanese lines in Burma, doing an amount of damage greatly in excess of their apparent strength. Here is the leader of this chosen band talking to a few of his men at an outpost on the Burma-Assam border.

Photo, Keystone

LAYING FOUNDATIONS FOR A NEW ROAD TO CHINA

After the Japanese cut the Burma Road, a limited quantity of supplies and a restricted number of technicians still reached China from India by the airway 'over the hump' of the Himalayas. But a new surface route was essential if anything like an adequate amount of war material was to reach China's hard-pressed armies ; and in December 1942 work started on the Ledo Road, planned to run from Ledo in Assam (India) across northern Burma through Myitkina to join the Burma Road just across the Chinese border. Here Chinese forces under American direction are laying foundations for the first part of the new road in Assam.   *Photo, Keystone*

TEMPLE BELL GIVES AIR RAID ALARM

Japan began to raid Chinese cities from the air in 1937, and the Chinese authorities had to improvize alarm signals. Among them was this old temple bell: it gave the alert to the little city of Yiyang, twice bombed during the battle in 1943 for Changteh, in Hunan province—China's 'rice bowl'—described in page 2707. Civilians returning to Yiyang after the tide of war had temporarily retreated from their home are shown in page 2700.

CHINESE TROOPS IN YUNNAN

Fighting on the Salween River in the Burma-China border area went on with varying fortune during 1943; but at the end of the year the Japanese —invading Yunnan Province from Burma — had been thrown back west of the river. Above, Chinese reserve troops moving along the Burma Road in Yunnan to relieve men on the Salween front. Left, Sappers mining a section of the road threatened by the Japanese advance. (See also illus., page 2699; and map, page 2692.)

Photos, Planet News

INDUSTRIALIZATION COMES TO CHINA

Although nearly half a century had elapsed since Chinese resistance to western penetration broke down, when the Japanese invasion began in 1937, China had developed no heavy industries in the interval. After she was cut off from the sea by Japanese advances, she was forced in circumstances of the utmost difficulty to set up her own armament plants—or go down. Here, molten metal is poured into moulds at one of China's improvized iron foundries.

the vulnerable retreating enemy columns. Japanese casualties were estimated by the Chinese High Command at 40,000, though some foreign observers would considerably reduce this figure.

There was no further major movement on the 2,500-mile China front until the beginning of November, when the Japanese launched another offensive

Japanese Offensive in Yangtze Area in the middle Yangtze area—the scene of their summer defeat—but with a different objective. This time they pushed to the south instead of to the west, capturing and holding for a week the important communications centre of Changteh, which is also in the heart of China's richest rice-producing area. The successes of the campaign, which were undeniably important, were also short lived. Once again the Chinese harried the flanks and rear of the columns pushing through their territory; once again they and the United States Army 14th Air Force inflicted heavy damage on a disorganized retreating force whose supply lines had been attenuated into nothingness; once again the Japanese found themselves after a few weeks of costly campaigning back behind the fortifications from which they had set out.

Thus the Chinese in the field had a year of defensive success. The time for a general onslaught against the occupier of their lands was not yet; the building up of sufficient strength in terms of modern warfare for such a great military enterprise had to await the unachieved reopening of a land- or

sea-link between non-industrial China and her arms-producing Allies. Nevertheless, the balance of campaigning was not unfavourable, except insofar as Japan's material losses were more easily replaceable than China's. Nor does the brief story of these few battles give the full account of the fighting involved in China's maintenance of her dual military role: holding her front and pinpricking her enemy. According to the annual report of General Ho Ying-chin, Minister of War, 5,427 major or minor engagements were fought during 1943 between elements of the Chinese Army and of the 39 divisions Japan is stated in the same report to have maintained during the year in China itself, and in the neighbouring territories of Burma, Siam and Indo-China. In these engagements 160,000 Japanese are claimed to have been killed or wounded, while Chinese losses, though considerable, were less.

The *venues* of these sporadic engagements, many of them no more than trench raids or armed patrols, were scattered up and down the front from the Mongolian border in the north to the immediate neighbourhood of Shanghai on the east coast and Yunnan in the far south-west. Only in the last of these sectors, that on the Burma border, can it be said that the year's fighting was of more than tactical significance. Here the Japanese through the year

launched a number of spoiling attacks, evidently in apprehensive anticipation of future joint Allied action from India and Yunnan to clear northern Burma and reopen China's land supply route. At what point the enemy first learnt of General Stilwell's road-building advance from Ledo in north-east Assam (India) is not clear; only in November was any hint of such a move released to the Allied Press. It is also unlikely that the Japanese had learnt before the end of 1943 of the extent to which General Stilwell's "Y" Force was being built up on the east bank of the Salween for an eventual co-ordinated attack into northern Burma in support of the Ledo Road advance.

Nevertheless, the Japanese throughout the year showed acute anxiety about this sector. In the first five months of the year they launched four attacks against the detached Chinese forces which had been operating west of the Salween since the fall of Burma, and in October, as the monsoon ended, an offensive even wider in scope than those which had preceded it was aimed at the sealing-off of all possible ferry points through which the Chinese could attack Burma across the turbulent Salween. None of these operations achieved more than temporary success, and by the

Operations in the Salween Area

GENERALISSIMO AND WAR ORPHAN

China entered on her seventh year of war on July 7, 1943 ; yet here is her leader, Generalissimo Chiang Kai-shek, still able to smile broadly as he talks to a young war orphan at a reception he held in Chungking, the wartime capital of Free China, on July 21, 1943. The Chinese Government had a special concern for the care of China's thousands of war orphans.

Photo, Keystone

end of the year the Chinese were again in possession of several useful springboards for the assault which awaited only the development to a predetermined stage of the offensive from India. In addition Chinese troops continued to be active west of the Salween, paving the way for future larger scale action.

Domestically, the year 1943 was for China one of great and growing economic difficulty and of increasing political war-strain, but one of noteworthy constitutional development. In the economic field, the inflation initiated by early Japanese successes in 1937–38 and checked by international action of the democracies during the subsequent period of growing support of China, was again getting out of hand. Prime cause of this dangerous development was the completion of the Japanese blockade of China by the occupation of Hongkong and Burma and the resultant disappearance from the market of manufactured consumer goods which non-industrial China had always imported. Contributory factors were a disastrous famine in Honan Province in the north-east, which directly affected some 10,000,000 people ; the traditional tendency of the Chinese merchant in difficult times to hoard goods against better days ; and the presence in China of increasing numbers of United States servicemen possessed of plenty of U.S. dollars which were eagerly snapped up by the unscrupulous at rates out of all relation to the official exchange.

Price control measures were applied

Growing Economic Difficulties

by the Government in January, but were successful only in part and in limited city areas. That there was not general starvation was due solely to the nature of Chinese economy, in which the peasants, who form more than 80 per cent of the population, live on their own produce without being vitally concerned with money, and to the Government's system of collecting taxes in kind from the food producer and distributing the accumulated rice or grain on a ration basis at regulated prices to civil servants, teachers, students and other elements of the urban population which are not self-supporting, as well as to the army. This system, which has so far kept China going, can be disturbed only by serious crop failure in some given area, since transport is lacking to convey food in any great quantity from one area to another. This was the case in Honan in the spring and in Kwangtung, in South-East China, in the autumn. Although, ironically, the harvest in China taken as a whole was extremely good, both these areas suffered severely from local failures, and the war situation prevented either large-scale introduction of emergency food supplies or efficient evacuation from the affected districts, both of which are in the front-line zone.

Developments in China's internal political structure during the year included an important change in the status of the President of the Republic. After the death of President Lin Sen on July 31 after 11 years in office, Generalissimo Chiang Kai-shek was elected to succeed him, and at the same time the Central Executive Committee of the Kuomintang (National People's Party), China's supreme political authority, authorized a substantial redrafting of the law governing the functions of the President. Hitherto these had been of a mainly formal character, analogous to those performed by Presidents of France under the Third Republic, and it was specifically laid down that the President as such had no executive authority in the conduct of military or foreign affairs. Under the amended law Chiang Kai-shek, the new President, became *ex*

Chiang Kai-shek Elected President

FAMINE REFUGEES FROM HONAN PROVINCE

Bad harvests in two districts added famine to the difficulties, dangers and privations of the Chinese people during 1943. Honan Province, near China's north-east front line, was one of the worst affected areas : the Provincial Governor stated that millions would die before the next harvest unless help reached them. Here is a train loaded with refugees. Many huddled on the slippery roofs or jammed between the cars fell from such trains as they moved.

officio Commander-in-Chief of the land, sea, and air forces of the Republic, and was empowered to take supreme charge of its foreign relations, thus making his position somewhat akin to that of the President of the United States.

Of greater direct significance than this development was the declaration by the Kuomintang Central Executive Committee after a meeting in September **Term Set to** that constitutional **Kuomintang's** government by demo-**Authority** cratically elected representatives of the people would be introduced into China within one year of the termination of hostilities with Japan. By this declaration the Kuomintang set a precise term to its own authority, which it derived from its leadership of the Chinese Revolution under its founder, Sun Yat-sen, and which it exercised absolutely as arbiter of the country's destiny during the period of " political tutelage " envisaged before his death by Dr. Sun as the necessary prelude to the full enjoyment of democracy by the politically untrained Chinese people.

As witness to the sincerity of this declaration, the Kuomintang ordered the establishment of a preparatory committee to create machinery for the convening at the appropriate time of a National Conference to draft a constitution for China and to put it into effect. On this committee all parties in the state were represented. Two of the committee members were leaders of the Chinese Communist Party, which in 1943 controlled, militarily and politically, a part of Shensi province in North-West China, and whose continued opposition to the Kuomintang had increased during the year as an inevitable consequence of war's stresses and long drawn-out hard-

AIR RAID ALERT IN A CHINESE TOWN

Chinese civilians walking along the banks of a canal to take shelter in the near-by hills after an air raid alarm has been sounded to warn them of the approach of Japanese aircraft. China's power of resistance in the air was much strengthened by the help of the U.S.A. 14th A.F., formed in March 1943 to replace the China Air Task Force, under the same commander, Brig.-Gen. Claire Chennault, also Chief of Staff of the Chinese air force under Generalissimo Chiang Kai-shek.

ships. This opposition came at times to the pitch of local armed conflicts, although the Communist Party in 1937 had pledged the armed forces owing allegiance to it to serve under the orders of the Kuomintang-dominated National Government, and although the Party was allowed to maintain liaison officers and even a newspaper propagating its views in Chungking. Accusations and counter-accusations were exchanged between the protagonists throughout the period under review and both points of view were extensively canvassed abroad. Appointment of Communist representatives to the Constitutional Committee, combined with the categorical statement by the Kuomintang Executive that once constitutional government could be introduced all parties would have equal rights and status, did something to ease

the tension, but at the year's end this basic political difficulty was still engaging attention among China's allies.

Despite these many difficulties, China made considerable progress in planning reconstruction of the country, a movement which she put second only to resistance to Japan. Although material **China's** hardship and isolation **Improving** made 1943 perhaps the **Prospects** most difficult of the years during which she had resisted her enemy, the promise of the future as seen both in the successes of the United Nations on other fronts and in her own improved and heightened relations with her Allies, gave an immediate prospect of some alleviation. Although severely restricted by transport difficulties, Lease-Lend supplies from the United States were coming in in a trickle that promised before long to be a flood. The formation in February of the U.S. Army 14th Air Force on Chinese soil and the steady strengthening of that force throughout the year was valuable not only for the immediate assistance received by hard-pressed Chinese troops on the battle-fronts, but as earnest of a coming attack upon Japan. The beginning of the Ledo Road and the progress made by General Stilwell's Chinese and American forces into Upper Burma made no immediate difference to the situation, but provided positive hope for the year to come. During the year China had not lost ground militarily, had progressed politically though under stress, had maintained herself economically, and had drawn closer to the Allies who could succour her and with whom she was waiting to join in the final offensive against Japan.

THE MOSCOW DECLARATION OF NOVEMBER 1943

DECLARATION SIGNED BY THE FOREIGN SECRETARIES OF THE UNITED KINGDOM, THE UNITED STATES, AND THE U.S.S.R., AND THE CHINESE AMBASSADOR IN MOSCOW, AND PUBLISHED ON NOVEMBER 1, 1943.

THE Governments of the United States, the United Kingdom, the U.S.S.R., and China : united in their determination, in accordance with the declaration by the United Nations of January 1, 1942, and subsequent declarations, to continue hostilities against those Axis Powers with which they respectively are at war until such Powers have laid down their arms on the basis of unconditional surrender ; conscious of their responsibility to secure the liberation of themselves and the peoples allied to them from the menace of aggression ; recognizing the necessity of ensuring rapid and orderly transit from war to peace and of establishing and maintaining international peace and security with the least diversion of this world's human and economic resources for armaments ; jointly declare :

1. That their united action, pledged for the prosecution of the war against their respective enemies, will be continued for the organization and maintenance of peace and security ;

2. That those of them at war with a common enemy will act together in all matters relating to the surrender and disarmament of that enemy ;

3. That they will take all measures deemed by them to be necessary to provide against any violation of the terms imposed on the enemy ;

4. That they recognize the necessity of establishing at the earliest practicable date a general international organization, based on the principle of the sovereign equality of all peace-loving States and open to membership by all such States, large or small, for the maintenance of international peace and security ;

5. That for the purpose of maintaining international peace and security pending the re-establishment of law and order and the inauguration of a system of general security they will consult with each other, and, as occasion requires, with other members of the United Nations, with a view to joint action on behalf of the community of nations ;

6. That after the termination of hostilities they will not employ their military forces within the territories of other States except for the purposes envisaged in this declaration and after joint consultation ; and

7. That they will confer and co-operate with one another and with other members of the United Nations to bring about a practicable general agreement with respect to the regulation of armaments in the post-war period.

Diary of the War

MARCH and APRIL, 1943

March 1, 1943. Marshal Timoshenko liberated 900 sq. miles S. and S.E. of Lake Ilmen, including Demyansk. R.A.F. dropped great weight of bombs on Berlin in 30-minute raid ; city without gas, light or water next day. Allies reoccupied Sbeitla and Feriana (Tunisia).

March 1–5. Battle of the Bismarck Sea (New Guinea) : 22 Japanese vessels all sunk by Allied aircraft.

March 3. Rzhev recaptured by Red Army. R.A.F. bomb Knaben molybdenum mines (Norway). Hamburg heavily raided by R.A.F.

March 4. Daylight attack by U.S. Fortresses on Hamm and Rotterdam.

March 5. Heavy concentrated R.A.F. night attack on Essen ; 14 bombers lost. Mareth Line (Tunisia) pounded for 90 minutes by heaviest barrage since El Alamein.

March 6. Gzhatsk recaptured by Soviet troops. Heavy daylight attack by Fortresses and Liberators on Lorient and Brest (France). Eighth Army withstood six heavy assaults by Afrika Korps.

March 8. Rennes and Rouen bombed by day ; at night hundreds of R.A.F. bombers (seven lost) bombed Nuremberg.

March 9. Red Army retreated under heavy pressure to north bank of Donetz, evacuating Lozovaya and other recently recaptured towns. Over 500 tons of bombs dropped on Munich by R.A.F. (11 aircraft lost).

March 10. Byely recaptured by Red Army. Establishment of U.S.A. 14th A.F. (in place of China Air Task Force) announced in Chungking.

March 11. R.A.F. bombed Stuttgart.

March 12. Soviet forces recaptured Vyazma ; Soviet withdrawal from west of Kharkov. Rouen bombed by day ; very heavy concentrated night attack on Essen. Daylight attack on greater London by 24 F.W.-190s.

March 13. Japanese convoy of eight ships in Huon Gulf attacked : two destroyed, three others hit.

March 14. Light forces of the Royal Norwegian Navy penetrated into Floroe harbour (90 miles north of Bergen) and sank two supply ships.

March 15. Kharkov evacuated by Russians. Heavy fighting in Rathedaung area (Burma). Japanese flung back in disorder in Hupeh Province (China). Darwin (Australia) bombed by 24 Zeros. U.S. aircraft made six heavy raids on Kiska (Aleutians).

March 16. Three heavy raids by U.S. aircraft on Kiska. British light coastal forces torpedoed two large supply ships off Terschelling (Holland).

March 18. American bombers attacked Vegesack U-boat yards (15 miles N.W. of Bremen). U.S. heavy bombers based on N. Africa attacked Naples by day and night.

March 20. Field-Marshal Wavell visited Arakan front (Burma).

March 20–21. Full scale assault launched on Mareth Line (Tunisia) by General Montgomery.

March 21. Red Army evacuated Byelgorod ; recaptured Petrovskoye and 14 other localities in the Kuban. Sened and Bou Hamra captured by Americans (Tunisia).

March 22. Durovo recaptured by Red Army, which also repulsed German attempts to cross Upper Donetz. Eighth Army drove bridgehead into Mareth Line ; British armoured column sweeping west of Matmata Hills (Tunisia).

March 23. Bitter and bloody fighting on Mareth Line. 250 Japanese aircraft in Rabaul area (New Britain) heavily bombed.

March 25. Heavy fighting continued in Mareth Line. U.S. Liberators dropped great weight of 2,000-lb. bombs on Rabaul ; made four raids on Kiska.

March 26. R.A.F. attacked Duisburg (Ruhr).

March 27. Heaviest R.A.F. attack to date on Berlin : 900 tons of bombs dropped.

March 28. First train ran from Moscow to Veliki Luki since 1941. Eighth Army occupied Mareth Line and captured Mareth, Toujane and Matmata. Strong R.A.F. attack on St. Nazaire (France).

March 29. Berlin heavily bombed by strong British force (21 lost). Gabes and El Hamma occupied by Eighth Army (Tunisia).

March 30. Metouia and Oudref occupied by Eighth Army ; Sedjenane by First (Tunisia).

March 31. U.S.A.A.F. bombed Rotterdam. R.A.F. attacked enemy oil installations at Bhamo (Burma).

April 2. U.S. planes bombed Kiska eight times and also raided Attu (Aleutians).

April 3. 900 tons of bombs dropped on Essen by Bomber Command. Allied planes sank two Japanese cruisers and left destroyer sinking off Kavieng (New Ireland).

April 4. Heavy concentrated day attack by U.S. Fortresses on Renault works near Paris ; at night Kiel had heaviest raid to date. Heavy 15-minute daylight attack on Naples dockyards by U.S.A.A.F. based on N. Africa. Kavieng (New Ireland) and Lae (New Guinea) heavily bombed by Allied planes.

April 5. Eighteen Ju.-52 transport planes, six Stukas and seven fighters shot down off Tunisia coast ; enemy destroyer blown up, three supply ships left ablaze off Cape Bon ; over 200 Axis planes destroyed in 24 hours against Allied loss of 12.

April 6. Eighth Army took Wadi Akarit line.

April 7. Eighth Army linked up with Second American Corps (Tunisia). British withdrew 13 miles in Mayu Peninsula (Burma). U.S. fighters shot down 39 out of 98 Japanese aircraft (for the loss of seven) attacking Allied shipping at Guadalcanal ; three Allied ships sunk.

April 10. Soviet planes bombed Koenigsberg. Eighth Army entered Sfax (Tunisia) ; 40 Ju.-52 transport planes and 13 others shot down over Sicilian Narrows.

April 11. First Army captured Kairouan (Tunisia) ; in Sicilian Narrows, 31 Ju.-52 transport planes shot down (making 92 in three days). Twenty-three out of 45 Japanese planes attacking Allied shipping in Oro Bay (New Guinea) shot down. U.S.A.A.F. made four raids on Kiska.

April 12. Thirty-seven out of 105 Japanese planes shot down in violent air battles over Port Moresby (New Guinea).

April 13. Home-based bombers made 1,500 miles round flight to bomb Spezia (Italy). Kiska bombed 10 times by U.S.A.A.F.

April 14. Heavy night attack by Russian bombers on Danzig and Koenigsberg. Heavy 45-minute attack by R.A.F. on Stuttgart. Thirty out of 75–100 Japanese aircraft attacking Milne Bay (New Guinea) shot down. Kiska raided eight times by U.S.A.A.F.

April 15. Creation of single Mediterranean Air Command under Air Chief Marshal Sir Arthur Tedder announced. Naples heavily bombed at night by R.A.F.

April 15–16. Four ships sunk out of nine in Japanese convoy heading for Wewak (New Guinea).

April 16. Over 600 heavy bombers of R.A.F. made night raid on Skoda works at Pilsen (1,800 miles round flight) and Mannheim-Ludwigshaven. U.S. aircraft made 10 attacks on Kiska.

April 17. Strong day attack by U.S. Fortresses on Focke-Wulfe factory at Bremen. Palermo heavily bombed by U.S. aircraft based on N. Africa.

April 18. Strong force of home-based bombers attacked Spezia (Italy). At least 51 Ju.-52s (out of 100) and 23 fighters shot down off Cape Bon ; Allies lost nine aircraft. Nine raids on Kiska by U.S.A.A.F. ; Attu also attacked.

April 20. Tilsit bombed by Russians ; Stettin, Rostock and Berlin by R.A.F. Enfidaville captured by Eighth Army (Tunisia).

April 21. Takrouma stormed by Eighth Army (Tunisia). Large force of U.S. bombers attacked Nauru, 780 miles N.E. of Guadalcanal.

April 22. Thirty-one Me.-323 glider transports and 11 Axis fighters shot down over Gulf of Tunis.

April 23. First Army engaged in bitter fighting between Bou Arada and Medjez-el-Bab.

April 26. R.A.F. dropped 1,300 tons of bombs on Duisburg (Ruhr). Enemy driven from last foothold on Longstop Hill (Tunisia). Soviet Government breaks with Polish Government in London. Kiska bombed 11 times by U.S.A.A.F., twice by R.C.A.F.

April 30. R.A.F. made heavy (55th) raid on Essen, bringing total weight of bombs dropped on city to 10,000 tons.

Chapter 272

RED ARMY TRAINING BEGINS TO TELL

Continuing his account of the great Russian winter offensive of 1942–43 from Chapter 269, Major-General Sir Charles Gwynn here records its final phase. It ended with an enemy counter-offensive which succeeded in driving the Soviet forces from a number of towns in the Ukraine that they had just recaptured and pushing them back to the east bank of the Donetz. The lull that followed was used by both sides to prepare for the struggle in the coming summer

It will be recalled that by the middle of February the Russians had recaptured Kursk, crossed the Upper, Middle and Lower Donetz and the Lower Don. They were threatening Kharkov and had recaptured Rostov and other important towns in the Donetz Basin.

During the winter offensive, Russian communiqués, for reasons of policy, barred personal publicity for commanders until they had proved themselves in battle. Stalin himself exercised supreme direction, and under him General (later Marshal) Gregory K. Zhukov, vice-commissar of national defence, co-ordinated operations on the various fronts which, with their commanders, were as follows : the North-west front under Timoshenko, with Govorov and Meretskov as his subordinate commanders inside and outside Leningrad respectively ; the Central front under Sokolovsky ; the Voronezh front under Golikov ; **Russian Commanders** and the South-west front under Vatutin, with Rokossovsky, at least up to Von Paulus's surrender, commanding on the Don and Malinovsky driving towards Rostov, with whose capture he is credited. In the Caucasus Maslennikov apparently led the offensive from the Mozdok valley, for he is credited with the capture of Mineralnye Vody. Communiqués in general spoke only of Soviet or Red Army troops achieving successes, and orders of the day (few in number at this period) are addressed to the troops and not to their commanders by name, except in the case of lower formations specially mentioned. It is interesting to note that among the latter, the troops which captured Kursk were commanded by Chernyakhovsky, later to become a familiar name. Boundaries between fronts were not clearly defined ; thus we were only told that troops of the Voronezh front recaptured Kharkov and that Vatutin's troops were operating across the Middle and Lower Donetz.

It might well have seemed that the troops which had crossed the Upper and Middle Don would concentrate on the recapture of the great historic city of Kharkov. That was certainly one of the objectives to be aimed at, but there was another and greater strategic prize to be won which claimed precedence. The German armies which had retreated from the Caucasus, and the troops from the Don which had attempted to hold the line of the Lower Donetz, were now cooped up in the salient formed by the Donetz Basin ; and their communication with the west depended largely on the three main railways which run back to the bridges over the Dnieper at Kiev, Kremenchug, Dnepropetrovsk and Zaporozhe. If these lines could be cut, the Germans in the Donetz Basin would be threatened with disaster as great as that of Stalingrad if they did not retreat to the Dnieper before it was too late. Already as early as the first week of February the capture of Izyum and Lissichansk on the Middle Donetz was a threat to the railways to Poltava. But a deeper thrust from the base thus provided would be required to reach the more southerly and more vitally important railways. The thrust, moreover, would have to be rapid or the Germans would have time either to strengthen their flank defences or to elude encirclement by retreat. The danger of such a manoeuvre becoming in its turn exposed to counter-attack in flank was also obvious, especially if the Germans had strong forces in the Kharkov area. For it would have a rapidly lengthening line of communications and might outrun supporting infantry forces. The Russians were, however, in no mood to lose an opportunity by refusing to take risks. While continuing their advance towards Kharkov, threatening to outflank it from the north, they rapidly exploited their Middle Don bridgeheads, driving south-westwards with strong armoured formations. In quick succession they captured a number of important towns on the Poltava railway, notably Lozovaya, Barvenko and Kramatorskaya which had figured largely in Timoshenko's forestalling counter-offensive of the previous spring. Between the two last-named places the German garrison of Slavyansk held out for some time, and the Russian drive, which on February 12 captured Krasnoarmeisk on the Dnepropetrovsk line, was on a

AFTER THE ANNIHILATION OF THE GERMAN SIXTH ARMY

Inhabitants of liberated Novo-Alexeyevskoe search for their belongings among the ruins of their snow-covered village, one of many liberated when German resistance in the Stalingrad area ceased on February 2, 1943. 'Throughout the Soviet territory they have seized, the Hitlerite occupationists have further tightened their sanguinary regime of massacres, punitive expeditions, burning of villages, deportation of hundreds of thousands of peaceful residents to slavery in Germany,' said a Soviet statement issued in December 1942.   *Photo, Planet News*

Kharkov itself was evidently weakly held, as proved by the progress of the Russian encircling attack. The Germans appear to have made a belated attempt to rush in reserve divisions to hold the city ; but when the Russians closed in on it these were used only as a rear-guard to cover its evacuation ; and on February 16 the Red Army was in possession. That in itself was a signal triumph, but strategically the surge forward of the Russians between Kharkov and Kursk appeared likely to produce results of even greater importance, since it seemed possible that it would develop into a still wider turning movement than that which immediately threatened the Donetz

ROSTOV-ON-DON RETAKEN

Lost and recaptured in November 1941, when Berlin stated that Germany would, by the use of dive-bombers and artillery, turn the city into a 'smoking pile of débris covering tens of thousands of Russian dead '; lost again in July 1942, Rostov was finally liberated on February 14, 1943, by the Cossack Guards Division. Here a captain of the Cossack Guards, S. Burmensky, formerly vice-chairman of the Rostov City Soviet, addresses his fellow citizens. Right, inhabitants return to the battered city.

narrow front and soon had to deal with strong German counter-attacks.

By that time, however, this attack from the north had made the position of the Germans in the Donetz Basin increasingly serious, and after the fall of Rostov on February 14 they decided to withdraw to the line they had held after the Russians had recaptured Rostov the previous winter. This strongly fortified line ran from its southern bastion at Taganrog on the Sea of Azov, up the Mius River to the highly industrialized area around Stalino. The Russians from the east pressed hard on the retreating Germans ; but with the close network of railways and numerous towns containing substantially built, easily defended industrial establishments to facilitate withdrawal, the enemy had no great difficulty in checking pursuit. Moreover, as they reached a shorter and highly defensible line they had opportunities for reorganization and were able to withdraw troops into reserve to meet the threat from the north.

Meantime the German situation on the Kharkov and Kursk fronts was no better, and it was evident that not only had their forward positions been shattered, but that they had few reserves with which to stabilize the situation.

Germans Fall Back from Rostov

Basin, and might lead to a complete separation of the German armies of the centre from those of the south.

During the third week of February the Russian offensive continued to make progress. North-west of Kharkov the important railway junctions at Sumi and Sievsk, west of Kursk, had been captured, in spite of increasing German resistance, while to the north of Kursk progress had been made towards Orel which, though strongly held, was becoming a pronounced salient. In the Donetz Basin by the end of the week the Germans were back on their winter line between Taganrog and the Middle Donetz in the neighbourhood of Lissichansk; but though

KHARKOV CHANGES HANDS
Russian anti-aircraft battery set up in the capital of the Ukraine, after its recapture by Col.-Gen. Golikov's forces on February 16, 1943. Left, S.S. troops fighting in the streets of Kharkov on March 30. Third largest city of the U.S.S.R., Kharkov was captured by the Germans on October 29, 1941. After the Russians recaptured it they were forced by massed tank attacks to evacuate it again on March 15. It was finally liberated in August.

still heavily attacked from the east they showed no signs of retiring farther and were continuing to counter-attack in considerable strength between Lissichansk and Krasnoarmeisk, in the neighbourhood of which place fighting was especially fierce.

Farther to the west, however, the Russian drive towards the Dnieper had made rapid progress and on a broader front. Pivoting on its left at Krasnoarmeisk, it had cleared up the German pocket at Slavyansk on February 17 and, driving south-west from Lozovaya in the centre, **Limit of Southern Offensive** its leading troops had reached Pavlograd, 30 miles short of Dnepropetrovsk, while on its right the capture of Krasnograd, February 20, constituted a threat to Poltava. The situation of the Germans in the Donbas, with only one main line of railway left for supply or for retreat, had clearly become increasingly critical. Signs of retreat were therefore expected, for it seemed unbelievable that the Germans would court another Stalingrad.

But the line reached by the Russians on February 22 was to prove the high watermark of the southern offensive. As they approached the Dnieper fresh German forces were encountered and fierce fighting occurred which rapidly developed into powerful counter-attacks, bringing to a halt the Russian

SOVIET TROOPS IN DEMYANSK

On March 1, 1943, Marshal Timoshenko recaptured 900 square miles of territory south and south-east of Lake Ilmen, including the town of Demyansk, which had been held by the enemy since September 1941. The operation took eight days of heavy fighting, in which the Red Army killed 8,000 and captured 3,000 of the German 16th Army.

Photo, U.S.S.R. Official

mechanized columns now far ahead of their supporting main bodies.

At this stage the Russian climate turned traitor. The unusually mild winter, which had so far spared the Germans the sufferings of the year before and greatly facilitated their retreat, was suddenly succeeded by an abnormally early spring thaw, which rapidly turned the ground to mud. Without railway communications the Russians began at once to encounter desperate difficulties in maintaining supplies. This might not have been so serious if they had still had to meet only weak and disorganized troops, but it was soon apparent that they were now faced by a fresh and powerful German force which had, moreover, the advantages of intact railway communications.

Where had this new force come from? Clearly not from other sections of the front, which not only had their own serious preoccupations but had certainly already contributed all the reserves they could spare to buttress the southern front. To find the answer, it is necessary to look back to the early months when the implications of the Stalingrad disaster were realized. Hitler's immediate reaction was to proclaim the instant mobilization of all Germany's man-power resources. This may at first have been with the intention of renewing the offensive in Russia in the summer, but it also enabled the General Staff, as the situation in Russia continued to deteriorate, to withdraw divisions from central reserves and occupied countries and dispatch them to the east, knowing that they could probably be replaced before any serious crisis developed in the west. About 12 divisions (including 4 Panzer divisions) were, it is believed, sent and they appear to have been concentrated on the Dnieper, possibly without Russian knowledge.

The Russians were now in a critical position on this front, fo not only had a powerful attack from the west to be met, but the counter-attacks on the Lissichansk-Krasnoarmeisk front grew stronger as the possibility of exploiting the opportunity became apparent. For some days the situation was obscure, but in the first week of March it became clear that the Russians were in retreat. German claims to have gained a great victory and to have made large captures gave the first indication that the Russians might have met with a disaster, but it was not till the end of the week that Russian admission of the loss of Lozovaya, and of a number of other towns recently captured, showed clearly that retreat on a strategic scale was in progress. It was realized, too, that retreat under the conditions of weather reported must be extremely difficult, especially as the German counter-offensive had been delivered by fresh troops with new equipment against an army to some extent exhausted, and with vehicles notably in need of extensive overhaul. Moreover, the possession of intact railways in their rear was likely to enable the Germans to maintain the impetus of pursuit.

It was soon clear that the Russians would have little chance of rallying until the line of the Donetz was reached, and by March 12 fighting round Kharkov was reported, indicating the breadth of front affected. On March 15 Moscow admitted withdrawal from Kharkov, a desperate blow to Russian sentiment but a proof that the higher Command would not allow sentiment to overrule strategic necessity. Their intentions were indicated by the claim that the line of the Donetz was held firmly. From subsequent information it is clear that the Russian retreat, though it involved hard fighting and heavy losses,

Russians Withdraw from Kharkov

RUSSIAN SKI-TROOPS ON A NIGHT MARCH

Troops of the Russian Army proved themselves in 1942-43 as much better adapted to winter fighting than the Germans as they had done in 1941-42. They wore uniforms heavily quilted with sheepskin, and were supplied with salves and grease specially prepared to relieve frostbite. They also had greater mobility because they could use any kind of sledge that might be available, and they were also, many of them, trained to run on skis.

Photo, Planet News

SCHLUESSELBURG

ENINGRAD

Miles

0   25   50   75   100

Roads
Railways
Rivers
Oil Pipe Line

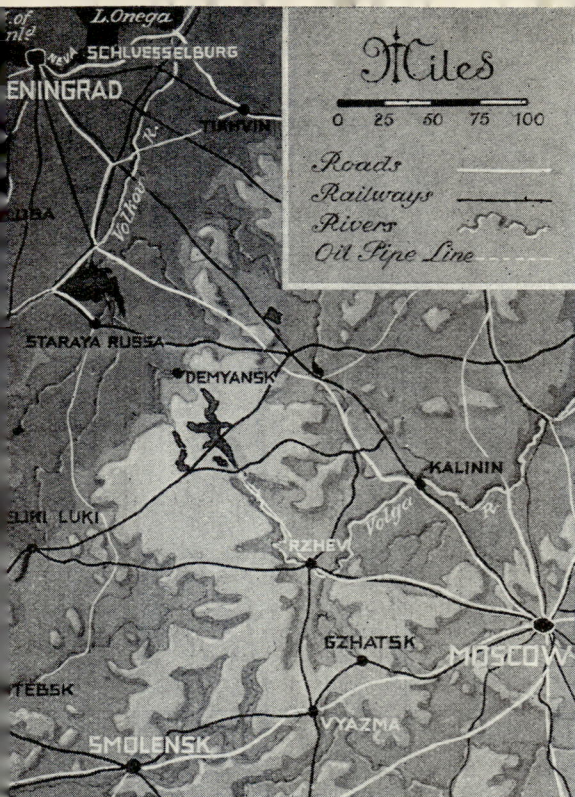

heads also resisted all attacks successfully except at Byelgorod, which the Germans captured on March 21. Farther north the Russian salient west of Kursk was maintained, except for a short withdrawal from Sumi at its apex.

The end of March may be taken to mark the end of the major Russian winter offensive and of the German counter-offensive. It proved to be the beginning of a long lull in Russia, which was to continue well on into the summer.

The Russian offensive had not, however, been confined exclusively to the southern front, and other important operations should also be recorded. In the north a corridor to Leningrad was opened by Govorov's and Meretskov's armies in the first half of January 1943 (*see* page 2680, and illus., page 2679). Subsequent attempts to widen the corridor and to dislodge the Germans from their strong positions on the Volkov failed to accomplish much beyond preventing transfer of reserves to the southern front. On March 1, however, Demyansk, the hedgehog town to the south-east of Staraya Russa, was captured—an important success, since it placed the latter centre in a more exposed salient, thus further necessitating the retention of supporting reserves. In the centre about the same date, Russian attacks on Rzhev, and between Rzhev and Veliki Luki, where the situation had since the beginning of the year been obscure, were intensified; and on March 3 Rzhev, held by the enemy for 18 months, was at last recaptured, although part of the garrison appears to have escaped after heavy rearguard fighting.

The fall of Rzhev and the Russian offensive south of the Moscow–Veliki Luki railway, which was likely to

was in fact carried out with great skill; and that a strong rallying position had been established on the Donetz, including a number of bridgeheads on the right bank of the river. Disaster had therefore been escaped.

Two circumstances contributed to the escape. The drive towards the Dnieper had to a great extent been carried out as a blitzkrieg by mechanized troops with which supporting forces had been unable to keep pace. The latter, therefore, had shorter distances to cover in retreat and were able to establish a rallying line on the Donetz. Moreover, with the thaw, ice on the Donetz had begun to break up, making the river a much more defensible line. The retention by the Russians of bridgeheads across the river was a bold policy, since they would be exposed to concentrated attack, and retreat from them would obviously be difficult. So long as they could be held, however, with artillery support from the left bank reducing the danger of flank attacks, the bridgeheads limited the frontages on which the Germans might attempt to force a crossing. Ultimately, of course, the bridgeheads might also provide sally-ports for a renewal of the offensive.

With the Russians back on the Middle Donetz and on the upper reaches of the river as far north as Byelgorod, the German pursuit was brought to a standstill, and though up till the end of March and even later, many attempts were made to cross the river, they met with no success. The Russian bridge-

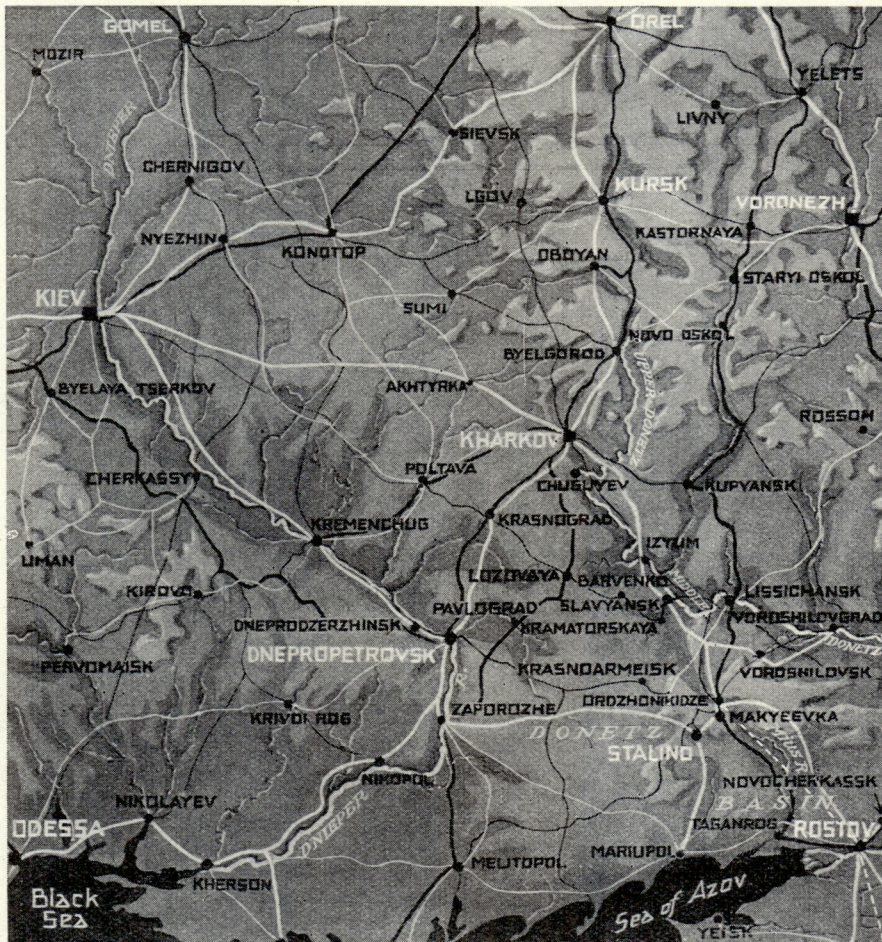

Red Army Rallies on the Donetz

RUSSIAN WINTER OFFENSIVE, 1942–43: FINAL PHASE

The map above covers the battleground around Rostov and the Donetz Basin; here the fighting swept westwards and then back again, leaving the main Russian forces on the east bank of the river, but with firmly held bridgeheads across it; that at the top of the page is of the Leningrad and Moscow fronts, where the recapture of Gzhatsk, Vyazma and Rzhev finally relieved the threat to Moscow, and the capture of Schluesselburg gave Leningrad access by land to the interior once more. *Specially drawn for* THE SECOND GREAT WAR *by Félix Gardon*

THE SHATTERED TOWN OF GZHATSK

Gzhatsk, a strong German 'hedgehog' on the Central Russian front 120 miles west of Moscow and 50 miles south-east of Rzhev, was recaptured on March 6, 1943, following heavy fighting, by a frontal assault after Soviet ski troops had cut the town off from the rear. Some 50 villages in the locality were recaptured at the same time, as well as Osuga railway station 55 miles north of Vyazma.   *Photo, Pictorial Press*

acquire greater strength by the opening of direct railway communication with Moscow, placed the whole Vyazma salient in a highly critical position. Whether the Germans had already decided to withdraw from the salient in order to shorten their front may be questionable, but now they were left with no option if they were to escape the risk of another first-class disaster. The Russian offensive began in consequence to make rapid progress. Gzhatsk, the south-eastern bastion of the salient, was captured on March 6, the garrison again escaping under cover of rearguards. Vyazma itself was now threatened with encirclement from north, west, and south-west, and the Germans had to abandon it also in a similar manner on March 12. The Russians continued their pursuit until they reached the great fortified zone surrounding Smolensk; but after they had captured some of its outer defences fighting died down into minor local engagements. The main object of the offensive had, however, been achieved: the Vyazma salient, so long a menace to Moscow, had been eliminated.

The state of the ground forbad, for the time being, operations on a scale

Enemy Salient at Vyazma Eliminated to break through the German central front in which Smolensk formed the principal stronghold. The elimination of the Vyazma salient nevertheless constituted a major Russian success, for it not only removed a threat to Moscow, but provided a starting line for a new offensive which could now be well served by railway communications. Moreover, it meant another blow to German prestige, and demonstrated to the world that in spite of the success of their counter-stroke in the Ukraine the Germans had not recovered from previous disasters and had developed a

Stalingrad complex. Their retreat had saved them from disaster, but it had involved the sacrifice of quantities of material and the waste of all the labour they had expended with the intention of making the salient an invulnerable springboard for attack on Moscow. By the end of March the great spring lull had extended to this front also, and only in the Kuban were operations continued on any extensive scale.

To close this Chapter it may be worth while to review the achievements of the winter offensive. The disastrous defeats inflicted on the Germans at Stalingrad and in the Don offensive, involving huge losses of men and material and the recapture of immense areas of valuable territory, speak for themselves. What was perhaps even more important, the winter offensive had secured the initiative for the Russians, and, despite their reverse on the Donetz, it was of a strength which seemed to guarantee that they would retain the initiative in the summer. The recovery of lateral communication between Moscow and the southern front immensely facilitated the development of further offensives; moreover, serious breaches had been made in the German defensive positions and in the lateral railways connecting them, notably in the Kursk area.

Russians Secure the Initiative

All views previously held about the quality and characteristics of the Red Army had to be recast. Stalingrad had proved that the Russian soldier was as stubborn as ever in defence and capable of taking terrible punishment. The counter-offensive of the previous

REFRESHMENTS FOR MEN OF THE RED ARMY

Women of the village of Zelenichino, one of the many 'inhabited places' in the neighbourhood of Rzhev taken by the Red Army during the early days of March 1943, came out to give refreshments to their liberators. This district had been in enemy hands for 18 months, and its recapture removed the last menace of the long drawn-out German threat to Moscow.
Photo, Pictorial Press

REBUILDING LIFE IN VYAZMA

Deliberate destruction of the work of years—first by the Russians in the execution of their 'scorched earth' policy, and then by the retreating Germans—coupled with shelling and bombing in the course of operations left many towns and cities in the battle zones of the U.S.S.R. mere heaps of rubble. These photographs of Vyazma, recaptured on March 12, 1943, give an idea of the desolation to which its citizens returned—and of the courage and resource with which they set about rebuilding life there. 1. Men of the Red Army take down the sign indicating the German Commandant's office. 2. Women and old men clear the debris from the ruined municipal baths. 3. At Vyazma station, unloading tractors sent by collective farmers of Novosibirsk in Siberia.

Photos, Pictorial Press

winter had also shown that within limitations he was a formidable opponent under winter conditions to which he was accustomed. But the failure of that counter-offensive to break through well-organized German defences had encouraged the belief that even in winter the Red Army's offensive power was limited and unlikely to achieve far-reaching success. Belief that the Russians in general lacked organizing and administrative capacity was also still widely held, and in modern warfare such capacity was more than ever called for. The success of the German summer offensive seemed to confirm these beliefs and to prove that in summer superior German training and organizing capacity would always assert itself.

The success of the initial counter-offensive at Stalingrad, greatly as it astonished the world, was taken at first to prove the amazing power of recovery conferred by Russia's **Russian Skill Develops** man-power resources and the safe locations of her war industries. It was, however, a short-range offensive and did not severely test Russian reputed weaknesses. As the offensive spread and retained its momentum under most unfavourable conditions, it became clear that administrative and organizing capacity of a high order was being displayed, and that Russian troops were showing in offensive operations skill both in large scale and minor tactical manœuvres which could result only from admirable training. Not only was the higher direction of the strategy of the offensive supremely

MEN WHO GUARDED RUSSIA'S NORTHERN COASTS
The northern coastal areas of Russia have no made roads, and in winter the men who guarded those snowy wastes moved on skis, like the naval unit here, and obtained their supplies by dog or reindeer sledge. Sometimes horses were available in the summer, but more often supplies then had to be carried by the men themselves on their own backs.
Photo, Pictorial Press

good—the timing of successive operations being especially remarkable—but the higher subordinate commanders conducting operations had shown drive and initiative of a standard far exceeding mere competence.

There was nothing to show that the success of the offensive had been due solely to superior ability to operate under winter conditions which had in fact, owing to the exceptional mildness of the winter, given few advantages to

the Russians to compensate for those the Germans had in railway communications. There was no reason to assume, therefore, that in the summer the Germans would display again a superior offensive power.

How far the Germans realized the growing offensive power of the Russians or allowed themselves to admit that in the coming summer they would have to meet a Russian Army of a very different **Growing Power of Red Army** standard of efficiency from the one they had originally encountered, seems doubtful. The disasters of the winter had caused great alarm and had certainly shaken their belief in the invulnerability of their hedgehog centres and defensive organization. But the success of their March counter-offensive may have restored faith in their offensive genius, and had led them to believe that all would be well in the summer when it could be fully exploited. When the crisis had passed they gave no sign that they intended to strengthen their defensive position by shortening their front. Rather, by clinging to the Kuban and the Donetz Basin, from which they could probably have withdrawn without much interference during the spring thaw, and by continuing their fruitless attacks to secure footholds across the Middle and Upper Donetz, they indicated an intention of taking the offensive again. The summer campaign promised, therefore, to open with a struggle between Titans for offensive mastery.

WEATHER HINDERS BOTH ARMIES IN THE CAUCASUS
The mud resulting from the rains of the prolonged spring thaw of 1943 held up Russian offensive operations—but it also played havoc with the transport of the retreating Germans. This German mobile gun and tracked lorry are hopelessly bogged in a Caucasus roadway. Floods later added to the difficulties of the campaign in the Kuban.　　　*Photo, Keystone*

Chapter 273

DEFIANCE OF GERMAN RULE IN EUROPE

The history of Occupied Norway, Denmark, Holland, Belgium, Czechoslovakia, Poland, Yugoslavia and Greece continued, during 1943, to be one of ruthless domination by the enemy, of deportations and terrorization, of humiliation, degradation, and massacre on a scale Europe had never before experienced. Yet—it was also the immortal story of peoples fighting and dying for freedom, of peoples who did not give in to the oppressor. The history of these gallant countries during 1942 will be found in Chapters 218 and 259

ALL the " New Order " instruments of policy in force in 1942—anti-Semitism, the principle of " collective responsibility," the wholesale plundering of economic resources, the requisitioning and transportation of food supplies to Germany, the imposition of slave conditions on all labour, the exploitation of racial differences—were even more ruthlessly carried out in Occupied Europe during 1943 than before—and just as steadfastly resisted.

The German policy of anti-Semitism needs no explanation here, but it is worth noting that the number of Jews said to have perished in Axis-controlled Europe already numbered 2,000,000 by December 1942, with a further 5,000,000 in danger of extermination, and there is little doubt that the massacre of Jews reached appalling new levels during 1943.

In food matters German policy never wavered. The Germans came first always. Consequently many peoples suffered from serious malnutrition, particularly the Norwegians, the Dutch, the Belgians and the Greeks.

The acute shortage of man-power in Germany brought in its train serious repercussions in the occupied countries, centring round the " total mobilization of man-power " order of February 1943, which, broadly speaking, affected all men aged 18–55 and women 21–40. This decree applied with ever-increasing stringency the principles of compulsion of the Sauckel decree of August 1942. It was resisted and evaded with a bitterness born of desperation, especially in Norway where it was announced—ironically ?—as a measure " to save Norway from Bolshevism."

Labour so conscripted was used mainly on extensive military fortifications under the aegis of the Todt Organization. It was **NORWAY** politically useful, too, being made an excuse to round up and send to labour camps all Norwegians—among them intellectuals, politicians and former economic leaders —considered potentially dangerous by Quisling and his followers.

The order also caused the closing of many industrial undertakings, business life was sadly disrupted, and life made very insecure for the masses. Skilled workers and politically dangerous people alike were sent to Germany where, at the end of 1943, according to an estimate by the exiled Norwegian Government, 6,000 Norwegian political prisoners were in detention in addition to 2,500 at the notorious Grini camp. Yet how successfully the Norwegians evaded this order may be judged from the fact that only some 10,000 out of 300,000 affected by the decree had been mobilized by the end of the year.

One effect of these evasions was the passing in April of several new measures designed to tighten up the entire German and Quisling administrations. Under these measures all branches of the German civil and military administration were subject to the unrestricted authority of the Gestapo ; conferences of the German authorities were forbidden unless attended by S.S. representatives ; and the Gestapo instead of the Army was made responsible for dealing with all acts committed against the Wehrmacht.

On March 10, 1943, Quisling appealed for volunteers for service on the Eastern front in the newly constituted " S.S. Panzer Regiment Norwegen " which had replaced the old Norwegian Volunteer Legion. But the response was meagre, only 3,000 (60 per cent members of Quisling's party, the Nasjonal Samling) having joined by May 27.

Trouble in Quisling's Party

Fearful of the repercussions of the ever-increasing tide of resistance, coupled with dissension within the ranks of his own party, Quisling on August 10, 1943, passed a decree creating special courts with powers of summary jurisdiction, without appeal, to deal with espionage, sabotage and " co-operation with Germany's enemies." This was followed two days later by a proclamation by which members of the Norwegian Police, the Germanic S.S. Norway, the Leader's bodyguard,

FUNERAL MARCH OF THE RADIO SETS

In August 1941 the Germans ordered the surrender of all radio sets in the coastal areas of Norway —an order extended in September to Oslo. These inhabitants of a small village in Hardanger decided to make a mock funeral of the occasion. The radio sets were placed in a horse-drawn cart, on which rode a violinist playing mourning music in traditional Norwegian style ; behind followed the villagers in procession—hardly, however, with funereal expressions.
Photo, Norwegian Official

MASS ARREST OF OSLO UNIVERSITY STUDENTS

A fire broke out in Oslo University on November 28, 1943, in circumstances which make it probable that it was caused by the Germans who, however, used it as a pretext for arresting students to the number of 1,200 as well as their professors. The photograph shows Gestapo cars outside Oslo University while members of the German police force are rounding up their victims inside. Some students managed to escape to Sweden.

Photo, Keystone

and the Hird were made part of the armed forces of the Reich.

Then, on September 4, according to the "Norsk Tidend," Quisling faced a crisis brought about by the demand of 110 rebels in his own party that he should accept their resignations and suppress the Nasjonal Samling. Though both demands were refused, the trouble remained.

Militarily the Germans were obsessed with the fear of an Allied invasion, a fear which became acute in August 1943 when the German C.-in-C. in Norway, Gen. von Falkenhorst, issued a proclamation that Hitler had withdrawn his "Magnanimous Order" of May 1940, under which most Norwegian officers had been set free. By October 30 nearly 1,000 officers had been sent to detention in two camps in Wartheland.

Arrest of Norwegian Officers

Sabotage during the year was extensive, the most impressive being the destruction of the "heavy water" equipment at the Norsk Hydro Works at Ryukan (Norway's largest industrial plant) in February, and of the smelting works at Eydebahn on November 21.

Indicative of the extent to which resistance had permeated the everyday lives of the Norwegian people was Quisling's failure to enrol Norwegian children between 10–18 into the Nasjonal Samling's Youth Service. According to the Norwegian Government in London, only 1,000 out of 400,000 theoretically affected had joined by April 30, 1943.

This successful resistance was of course in large part due to the continued active antagonism of both teachers and parents, despite counter-measures, to all German attempts to Nazify the children.

One such counter-measure was the appointment in April 1943 of Prof. Adolf Hoel, a Norwegian Nazi, as Rector of Oslo University. This caused such grave dissatisfaction that over 1,600 students and 67 professors and teachers were arrested for "subversive activities" during November. While most of the students were imprisoned for a time, nearly 300 were deported to Germany. Of the teachers, 40 were subsequently released and 27 sent to the Stavern camp near Larvik.

The Church, too, played a noble part in 1943, its Provisional Church Council, *inter alia*, protesting vigorously against the mobilization decree of February 22 on the grounds that work on military fortifications constituted "German military service," and was therefore a violation of the Hague Convention.

Food conditions worsened considerably, especially during the winters of 1942–43 and 1943–44, owing to the large-scale requisitioning of foodstuffs. The black market flourished, fantastic prices being charged for everyday necessities. Malnutrition, resulting in a 70 per cent increase in sickness, especially diphtheria and tuberculosis, assumed incalculable dimensions, Norway's fate being like that of Greece.

Conditions of life were less difficult in Denmark — Germany's "model Nazi state." Yet the evidence of the Germans' failure to convert the Danes, in spite of especial and gentle treatment, was easily perceptible in the number of **DENMARK** sabotage operations carried out against the oppressors in 1943. Foundries, factories, power stations, workshops, military installations, railways—every type of industrial undertaking was represented in the list of those destroyed or damaged during the year; outstanding examples being the destruction of the main electric power station of the "Riffel Syndikatet" in Copenhagen (the largest small-arms factory in Scandinavia) and of the Ford repair works at Aarhus, one of the largest in North Europe, both in May.

The intensification of sabotage compelled the German C.-in-C. of Denmark, Gen. von Hannecken, in April to threaten collective fines, taking of hostages and the death penalty.

This policy, however, brought him into conflict with Dr. Werner Best, the German Minister in Copenhagen, who subsequently became in effect a Reich Commissioner. Dr. Best, who favoured the method of persuasion and appeal, was said to occupy a peculiar position in Denmark, being mainly responsible for the fall from German favour of the Danish Nazi Party under Fritz Clausen and the holding of the Danish general elections in March. These left the Germans in no doubt as to the wishes of the people, nearly 2,000,000 voting for democracy and a mere 68,000 for dictatorship. That the collaborationist Scavenius (the Danish Premier) retained office was merely an unavoidable detail.

DEUTSCHER SOLDAT!

DIE schimpfliche Zunahme der Fälle, in denen Mannschaften und sogar Offiziere der mir unterstellten Einheiten und Dienststellen sich ihrer Wehrverpflichtung durch Übertritt auf schwedisches Gebiet entzogen haben. In diesem kritischen Augenblick höchster Bereitschaft kommt es auf jeden Einzelnen an.

Der Militärbefehlshaber
für die besetzten norwegischen Gebiete
(gez.) von Falkenhorst
Generaloberst.

Oslo, 2. 6. 1943.

APPEAL TO DESERTERS

Part of a poster (said by the Germans to be a forgery) which appeared throughout Norway in June 1943. Signed by Von Falkenhorst, C.-in-C. of the Nazi occupation forces, it began : ' The shameful increase of cases in which men and even officers of the units and services under my command have violated their military duty by crossing the Swedish frontier '—which suggests not only that desertion was far from uncommon but that deserters could get away.

Photo, " News-Chronicle "

SPITSBERGEN FRONT

On September 7, 1941, it was announced that an unopposed Allied landing had recently been made on Spitsbergen, the coal mines there destroyed, and the miners and their families brought to Britain (see illus., pages 1889 and 1905). A garrison of about 100, engaged mainly on meteorological duties, was left behind. Two years later, on September 1, 1943 (see Chapter 284), a large German force including the 'Tirpitz' and the 'Scharnhorst' arrived off Spitsbergen, shelled Barentsburg for 1½ hours, and landed there and at Longyear. 1. Smoke rising from Barentsburg at 3 a.m. shortly after the German bombardments began. 2. One of the Norwegian defenders of Spitsbergen. 3. German grenadiers assembled ready to re-embark. The map shows the position of Spitsbergen relative to Norway.

despite a proclamation by King Christian on August 21 on the dangers awaiting a continuance of such disorder. On August 27 Dr. Best returned from Berlin and presented an ultimatum, which was promptly rejected. The climax was reached two days later when, with the backing of some 40,000 newly arrived German troops and further reinforcements by sea, Gen. von Hannecken took over complete control, declared a state of emergency and martial law throughout the country, and issued a proclamation which, among other things, ordered all officials to obey German commands, prohibited meetings, demonstrations and strikes, imposed a curfew, and introduced the death penalty for sabotage. On the same day (August 29) many

DANISH SABOTAGE

This photograph, reproduced from the 'Sydvenska Dagbladet,' shows the Forum Hall, Copenhagen, after it had been damaged by an explosion on August 24, 1943. It had been requisitioned as quarters for the German troops brought in to put down sabotage and rioting.

Despite several appeals for order by prominent people, among them King Christian, by August tension had reached such a pitch that the German garrisons had to be reinforced, and strong demands were made by the German authorities for jurisdictional powers over saboteurs and the imposition of the death penalty. These demands were unanimously refused by the Danish Government on August 9.

With fresh outbreaks of sabotage, including the disruption of railways and public utilities, occurring almost daily in all the large cities, the strain increased

COPENHAGEN RIOTS

Policemen running down a street following a riot in which one policeman and two civilians were wounded. Left, two minesweepers resting on the bottom of Copenhagen naval base ; they were scuttled by Danish sailors when the Germans attempted to seize them during the disturbances in August, 1943.

Danish officers were arrested and numerous prominent citizens, both Christian and Jewish, taken as hostages. King Christian and Queen Alexandrine were confined to the Sorgenfri (Carefree) Palace outside Copenhagen, under German guard.

This new German aggression was not accomplished without some bitter fighting in which ammunition dumps, naval and military installations were blown up. Eight Danish warships escaped to Sweden, and twenty others, unable to escape, were scuttled by their crews. Political repercussions took the form

2722

H.M. KING HAAKON VII OF NORWAY

Invited to become King of Norway on the repeal of its union with Sweden in 1905, Prince Carl of Denmark ascended the throne as Haakon VII. His peace-loving country was ill-prepared to meet the German onslaught of 1940, and after being hunted from one refuge to another, King Haakon and his government came to Britain in June. Speaking in London in 1943, he said that while on the home front the entire Norwegian people were resisting the enemy, on the outer front Norway had on active service a small but efficient army, a navy of 60 units, 1,000 merchant ships, and an air force of several squadrons.   *From the portrait by Cowan Dobson*

R.A.F. AIR-SEA RESCUE LAUNCHES; THE FISH QUAY BEYOND　　　Stephen Bone

PARACHUTE DROP　　　Henry Carr

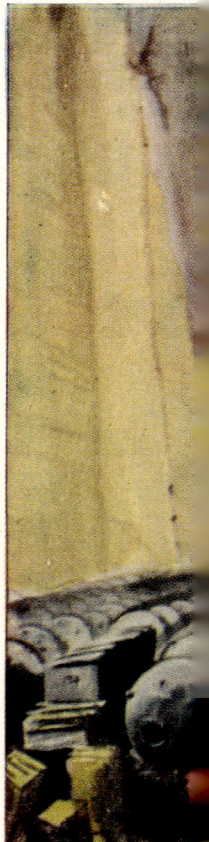

MINES IN MELILL

Exhibited at the National Galle

BASUTOS DEAL WITH OVERFLOW MAIL ON THE CAUSEWAY, VALETTA   Leslie Cole

WOOLWICH ARSENAL, 1943   Robert Austin

Y   John Worsley

SEAWOMEN OF B.O.A.C.

British Overseas Airways employed a number of 'women seamen' at the little fishing town which was the Corporation's wartime base. They worked on the launches used to service the four-engined flying-boats coming in from West Africa, Lisbon and America. These launches required skilful and delicate handling, especially in bad weather, to get them safely alongside the easily damaged aircraft. The women, whose ages ranged from twenty-three to thirty-eight, were promoted coxswain and placed in charge of a launch after they had successfully completed a three-months training in Morse, semaphore, and lamp signalling, compass work, and general seamanship. Duties of women seamen included embarking and disembarking passengers, handling the launch while stevedores loaded and unloaded mail and freight, washing down and scrubbing decks, painting, and splicing ropes. Above, a B.O.A.C. coxswain signalling to the shore from the flying-boat 'Berwick.' Left, coxswains leaving the 'Berwick' after mooring her.

Direct colour photographs by "Illustrated"

of the resignation of the Scavenius government and the assumption by Gen. von Hannecken of full legislative, judicial and executive powers.

Although conditions in September were calmer, the end of the month saw a wholesale round-up of Jews; 3,000 escaped to Sweden, but 1,600 were seized and transported to Germany, notwithstanding Swedish and even Finnish protests.

With the dissolution of the Danish Police Force on October 5 and the arrival in Copenhagen of 1,500 more Gestapo agents, conditions deteriorated still further, a "state of emergency" was proclaimed in the city, and its citizens were fined 5,000,000 kroner for sabotage and the killing of three Germans.

November 22 was a significant day in Danish history, marking the carrying out of the first two executions of Danes for sabotage. Following a threat by the German Minister on December 4 that he would adopt a policy of "pitiless severity, including the death penalty" until order was restored, it was revealed by Danish sources in Sweden that some 300 acts of sabotage were committed in Denmark in November alone.

While the Danes had had special treatment because of Nazi ambitions to make their country a "showroom" of

THE NETHER-LANDS Nazi life and culture, it was the Nazi belief that the Dutch, being a "Germanic" race, should not be treated as a conquered people but as one likely to be specially susceptible to National Socialism.

This policy, responsibility for carrying out which was vested in Anton Mussert, as leader of the N.S.B. (Nationaal-Socialistische Beweging—the Dutch Nazi party), was further implemented during 1943 by various decrees. The first, issued on January 30 by Seyss-Inquart, the Reich-Commissioner, declared that the N.S.B. "would be the carrier of the political will of the Dutch people," and required all German officials to consult with Mussert on important administrative measures. To himself he reserved the right to make final decisions. Simultaneously he announced the creation of a "Dutch Nazi State Political Secretariat," through which the N.S.B. could make proposals on government matters. This new body was set up by Mussert the following day with 18 delegates—three of whom had been assassinated by June 3. Prof. Gerbrandy, Premier of the Netherlands Government in London, broadcast an appeal on February 4 to his fellow countrymen to resist these decrees and Mussert's State Administration.

The resultant wave of resistance brought a decree by Hitler on February 22 investing Seyss-Inquart with all the power and authority necessary to effect the total mobilization of Dutch man-power and Dutch capital in Holland for the German war effort, including the use of the death sentence for sabotage. Another decree, issued on March 17, enacted the large-scale closing down of trade and industrial undertakings not essential to the war.

The vast effort to secure labour vital to Germany by deportation met with

NAZI DEFENCES IN THE HAGUE

A mile and a half inside the 'West Wall' along the coast of Holland, the Nazis constructed a second line of defences consisting of a 65-foot anti-tank ditch and a belt from which all buildings and trees had been removed to give the guns in emplacements built along it an unobstructed range to the coast. Here is a site in The Hague from which public buildings and flats had been cleared. In the foreground is part of the anti-tank ditch. *Photo, Associated Press*

stiff resistance. By the end of May 70,000 people were in hiding (by the end of 1943, 300,000), but thousands, including students, were deported to Germany, protests by the ecclesiastical authorities in mid-February and again in May having no effect.

German fear of intellectual circles was manifested, as in Norway, by their treatment of university students—in a statement on February 15, referring to the mass arrests of students, Mussert said that a purge of all universities was necessary to prevent sabotage. In March many of the students were released, but at the same time a decree

was issued by Seyss-Inquart limiting the number of students by fixing a "numerus clausus," introducing obligatory labour service, and demanding that all students should sign a declaration of loyalty. Eighty-five per cent refused to sign; consequently thousands of students went into hiding and university life came to a standstill.

These troubles, combined with the German consciousness of growing Allied strength, led to a precautionary order by Gen. Christiansen, the German C.-in-C. in Holland, on April 29, in which all members of the former Dutch Army, about 400,000–500,000 men, were ordered to report for subsequent internment. Encouraged by a broadcast from the exiled Netherlands Government in London, the men concerned instantly stopped work and went underground. Factories and shops closed, transport stopped, and there was chaos. Martial law, already imposed in four provinces, was extended to the whole country. New, far-reaching measures were passed, including a ban on the employment of students, an extension of the age limit to men aged 18–35 for compulsory work in Germany, and the imposition of the death sentence for taking part in strikes and demonstrations.

On May 4 work was resumed, but not before the Dutch patriots had seen that "the dress rehearsal for invasion had taken place and shown a remarkable solidarity." Conditions remaining unsettled, a state of emergency was proclaimed by Seyss-Inquart on May 9, but lifted six days later with the issuing of a decree confiscating wireless sets.

An appeal to the Dutch people by Prof. Gerbrandy on May 19 to stand fast was followed next day by a threatening broadcast by Seyss-Inquart in which he attempted to justify recent Nazi measures and the numerous executions. These, almost of daily occurrence, did not affect the killing of Germans and Dutch Nazis by patriots, which reached such a degree that Mussert was compelled on September 16 to appeal to the people to help him to fight "this ever-increasing lawlessness."

Anti-Semitic measures during the year included a German order in June to all Jewish husbands of Aryan Dutch women to choose between sterilization (strongly protested against by all nine Dutch churches) and deportation; and the expulsion of all the 150,000 Jews living in Holland, according to a statement by Mussert on December 4.

As in other occupied countries, the food shortage was acute; in June Dutch physicians stated in a letter to Seyss-Inquart that many people would die of starvation unless their food rations were supplemented. Germany's answer was

CHURCH BELLS REQUISITIONED

In Belgium the Germans requisitioned even the bells from the churches. These bells, cast in 1874 at the Manlius foundry in Dinant, are lying in the cemetery of the church in Liége from which they were removed : the management of the Cockerill Works at Hoboken having refused to melt them down.

UNDERGROUND EDITION OF 'LE SOIR'

On November 9, owing to an air raid on Brussels, the transport of German-controlled newspapers (including the Nazified 'Le Soir') was delayed. Belgian patriots took advantage of this to distribute to the kiosks copies of an underground edition (here is the front page), looking like the real thing, but containing clever parodies of German communiqués, witty attacks on collaborationists, and straight articles.

the deportation of hundreds of Dutch doctors to concentration camps "for protesting about the treatment of civilians," and a threat by Seyss-Inquart in October to export all food supplies to Germany unless sabotage and terrorism ceased.

Across the frontier in Belgium the Germans hoped that, by exploiting the differences between French and **BELGIUM** Flemish speaking Belgians, and by encouraging Flemish nationalists, they might eventually Germanize the whole country. This expectation, owing to the fine work of the underground movement and to sabotage, did not materialize. Indeed, sabotage in Belgium reached such proportions in 1943 as to constitute Germany's biggest problem in that country, a problem met with the usual decrees and counter-measures. One such, issued on January 15, imposed the death penalty on all people possessing unlicensed weapons and all harbouring "terrorists." Four days later this measure was implemented in Brussels by the carrying out of mass executions as reprisals for a number of assassinations and "acts of terrorism and sabotage." By the end of May the Germans were arresting 4,000 Belgian patriots a month, and putting a number to death before the firing squad. Even the Germans admitted that in the first four months of the year 188 cases of violence against collaborators had been reported.

A feature of vital significance in Belgian life was the remarkably large number — about

200—of underground newspapers produced and distributed by patriots. On one occasion under cover of an air raid warning, an underground replica of "Le Soir" was successfully substituted for the Nazified official publication. The following condensed extracts from the underground press show the composition and activities of the underground movement:

"The Belgian Partisans are a self-contained organization, unconnected with any party or group, but uniting all Belgians of whatever politics or creed—Communists, Catholics, Socialists, Liberals, Independents—who have taken up arms against the occupying enemy. . . ."

"A summary of our activity is eloquent of the proportions it has already attained: during the past four months alone (January–April) in guerilla actions against Fascist formations, 34 Hitlerites have been killed; in isolated attacks, 79 traitors have been shot dead . . . 12 Gestapo men have been killed . . . more than 250 German soldiers killed in train derailments. Twenty-two goods trains have been derailed and 30 locomotives, 232 wagons, 33 lorries, and large quantities of supplies destroyed. . . . Eight canal locks and two bridges have been successfully dynamited . . . and 80 attacks carried out against factories and enemy supply depots. . . ."

The German labour shortage inevitably reacted unfavourably on the Belgian people. A decree of January 1 enforced military conscription in the Eupen-

Conscription of Belgian Man-power

Malmédy - St. Vith district—ceded to Belgium by Germany under the Treaty of Versailles, and reincorporated in the Reich after the Nazi conquest of Belgium. A decree in March modified the "total conscription of man-power" order of February to conscription for forced labour of all men aged 18–50 and women 25–30, all under 22 being deported to Germany. Much of this labour was used on new fortifications along the river Meuse and in the Namur province, evidence of the German fear of invasion from the West, which became acute in October when all able-bodied men in coastal districts were arrested and deported.

By February 1943 about half a million Belgians had been deported to Germany alone. To "encourage" the people to obey their "mobilization of labour" orders, Hitler let it be known on June 5 that he was "contemplating the release of the first 20,000 Belgian prisoners-of-war, and raising their status to an equal level with free Belgian workers in Germany, if the population satisfied the German demands in regard to labour service."

Czech patriots continued their courageous resistance despite the execution of 132 of their number by the Germans in the first six weeks of 1943. In a

POLAND DEFIANT IN MISERY

Inside the Warsaw ghetto: for his leadership in the 'battle' there (see p. 2727), Michæl Klepfisz, a Jew, was posthumously awarded the Silver Medal of the Order of Virtuti Militari (Polish equivalent of the V.C.)—the first such award for resistance inside Poland. Top, the words 'Poland will win' painted on a wall of the Vistula embankment in Warsaw. Below, Polish boys and girls building a road in Germany under the supervision of German soldiers.

Photo, Keystone; Associated Press; Planet News

NAZI MIGHT AGAINST YUGOSLAV GUERILLAS

Left, the Germans re-enter Split : General Tito's Partisans captured the town on September 14, 1943, and with Italian help held it against savage dive-bombing and fierce ground attacks by much superior German forces until September 29. Right, Germans belonging to a special corps of Partisan hunters about to break into a house in search of Montenegrin members of Tito's forces.

stimulating broadcast from London on February 13, Dr. Benes, President of Czechoslovakia, reviewed the war situation and, pointing to the steady exhaustion of the material, economic and moral forces of Germany and Italy, said "This is not the end, but it is already more than the beginning of the end. . . ."

CZECHO-SLOVAKIA

Threatening that " if Benes continues to incite the Czech population from England a correspondingly large number of destructive Czech intellectuals will be sent to concentration camps," the German-controlled Prague radio announced that several Czech intellectuals belonging to Benes's former circle had been sent to a concentration camp as a " reprisal " for the President's speech.

On February 26 it was announced in Prague that " total mobilization " was being extended to Bohemia-Moravia. In a proclamation referring to this, Hacha, the puppet President of the Protectorate, referred to Czechoslovakia's return— " after a short, mock independence "— to the protection of the Reich. " The destiny of the Reich," he said, " has become our own destiny. Every ounce of energy here will be mobilized for total war."

German exploitation of Czech resources continued during 1943, notable examples being Hacha's order for the confiscation of all the property of the Christian Science Movement (reported on April 21) and the imposition of a new tax—" a special war contribution " —on all Czechs exempted from military service, made known on April 26.

On August 24 Baron von Neurath, the Reich Protector of Bohemia and Moravia, was replaced by Dr. Frick, formerly the Minister of the Interior in Germany. In the puppet State of Slovakia, Dr. Tiso, the President, was summoned to Hitler's G.H.Q. on April 23 for talks with the Fuehrer. At this meeting Tiso promised that Slovakia would, alongside the Tripartite Powers, " mobilize her entire strength for final victory."

Meanwhile, sabotage, riots, resistance in all forms, and pro-Allied activities continued to be a source of real embarrassment to the occupying forces. Reprisals continued, 57

Reprisals for Czech Sabotage

people being executed during April alone for " treasonable activities." Between May 1942 and May 1943, 1,935 Czechs, including 120 women, were executed, not counting the massacres at Lidice and Lezaky. Executions continued for the rest of the year, and on October 29, 519 Czechs were sentenced to death for " acts of terror and sabotage " at a court-martial at Olmuetz, N. Moravia.

According to an announcement on July 23 by Dr. Ripka, Minister of State in the exiled Czechoslovak Government,

WANTED, DEAD OR ALIVE

Advertisement published in the Belgrade Nazi-controlled paper 'Novo Vreme' for July 21, 1943, offering rewards of 100,000 German reichsmarks (i.e. gold marks) for the capture, dead or alive, of (left) General Draja Mihailovitch, leader of the Chetniks and at the time Minister of War in the exiled Yugoslav Government, and (right) General Tito, leader of the Partisans (in November appointed commander of the Yugoslav People's Army of Liberation with the rank of Marshal).

between March 1939 and the middle of May 1943, 50,000 Czechs had been executed or tortured to death, many without trial, while 200,000 had been sent to German concentration camps, and 500,000 others to forced labour in Germany and elsewhere. These figures did not include the tens of thousands of Czechoslovak Jews who had been killed, imprisoned or deported.

Yet even the miseries of the Czechs pale before those suffered by the Poles. Numbers of instances of German ruthlessness and terror in Poland were reported in the **POLAND** press and by the Polish Government in London during 1943. Among them the following may be cited :

The villages of Kniacodowice and Szaulicze in the Bialystok district were razed to the ground and all the inhabitants shot for the killing of two German police and the wounding of several others.

To create a 70-mile German-inhabited defence belt in the Lublin province, the Germans carried out a wholesale massacre and deportations, affecting some 1,000,000 people. Men and women under fifty and children were deported to unspecified destinations ; all over fifty died in gas chambers or by mass shootings, or were sent to a concentration camp.

On October 13–14, 1943, began a series of " manhunts " all over Poland by the Gestapo, S.S. men and youths of the " Hitler-. jugend." Thousands of people were seized, and by the end of October more than 200 hostages and 100 members of the intelligentsia had been executed. The Gestapo issued an order that all documentary evidence relating to persons who had died after torture should be burned. Similar man-hunts occurred in December, involving the deaths of more than 1,500 people.

Between April 19–28 the Warsaw Ghetto was " liquidated." Using tanks, bombers and artillery against men, women and children, whose only weapons were their fists and a few machine-guns and rifles (smuggled in by the Polish underground movement),

the German army and S.S. troops massacred 26,000 people, the survivors, some 14,000, being deported. About 300 Germans were killed, and about 1,000 wounded. Other ghettos, including that of Cracow, suffered similarly.

Dr. Ignacy Schwarzbart, of the Polish National Council, stated in London on November 22, 1943 : " To-day, after four years of planned extermination, about 2,500,000 to 3,000,000 Jews have

MARSHAL TITO AT HIS HEADQUARTERS
Following a convention of the Anti-Fascist Council of Yugoslavia on November 30, 1943, General Tito was appointed C.-in-C. of the People's Army of Liberation with the rank of Marshal ; a few weeks later he was accepted as a full Allied Commander. He is seen here addressing colleagues at his headquarters.
Photo, " New York Times " Photos

been killed by the Germans in Poland alone. Only a few hundred thousand Jews are believed to be still alive in Poland."

And yet sabotage and resistance continued successfully during the year, under the direction of an underground " Directorate of Civilian Resistance," which gave orders to the whole nation. Disclosing this in a statement in London

on April 21, 1943, Prof. Kot, Polish Minister of Information, said that during a single month it had destroyed or damaged 100 locomotives, derailed 17 trains, rendered seven oil wells useless, attacked 18 military vehicles and killed 300 Germans.

Its secret wireless station " Swit " transmitted news from Poland, announced the decisions of the Directorate and maintained touch with the exiled Government, in which work it was helped by the numerous clandestine papers.

Death sentences were passed and carried out by the Directorate on well over 100 notorious German and Gestapo officials during January–June. These included Gen. William Krüger, the " Secretary of State for Security " and Himmler's right-hand man in Poland, who was served with the notification of his death sentence ; Col. Richard Gassler, S.S. Chief in Cracow ; and Kurt Hoffman, the organizer of large-scale slave-labour man-hunts in Warsaw.

During July–December the Polish Underground Army, said to comprise 250,000 men in special detachments, apart from reserve units of a greater numerical **Poles Execute Germans** strength, had 81 clashes with the German occupation forces. Eighteen high German officials and 1,163 Gestapo agents were executed during the same period.

Dr. Frank, the German Governor-General of Poland, issued a proclamation to the Polish population on February 3, 1943, inviting them to inscribe their names on the so-called " Volksliste " by March 13, thereby " showing their German character." Reports from Poland declared this measure, designed to trap Poles into the German Army, to have been a dismal failure.

An event of hopeful significance, announced by M. Jan Kwapinski, Polish Deputy-Premier, on September 6, was the setting up in Poland of a " shadow cabinet." Comprising representatives of the four main political parties (Socialists, Christian Democrats, Peasant and National parties) it was headed by a delegate of the Polish Government in London.

Political unity was unfortunately lacking in Yugoslavia, where the unhappy divergencies between **YUGOSLAVIA** the Chetniks under Gen. Mihailovitch supported by the exiled Yugoslav Government, and the Partisans led by Gen. Tito continued during 1943, thereby adding to the complexities of the political and military position.

The fundamental differences between the two forces, the reasons for which lie rooted in the racial and national problems of the Yugoslav State, may be summarized under three headings :

1. In the field of military technique, the Chetniks were guided by British strategy and had as their main aim the preparation of the groundwork for a general mobilization to coincide with an Allied invasion of the Balkans. The Partisans, however, irrespective of external considerations, believed in a policy of ruthless guerilla sabotage.

2. Politically, the Partisans, because of their connexions with, and support from, Moscow, were considered more " left " than the Chetniks. Certainly they were known to be opposed to the unitary monarchy of pre-war days and consequent Serb dominance. On the other hand, the Chetniks were in favour of the Karageorgevitch dynasty and the restoration of King Peter, and of the reconstitution of the pre-war Triune Monarchy.

3. Racially, the Chetniks, between 80,000–150,000 strong, were predominantly Serb, whereas the Partisans were representative of all Yugoslav racial groups— Croats, Serbs, Montenegrins, Slovenes and Bosnians. A Slovene and prominent Yugoslav Liberal, Dr. Ivan Ribar, was head of the Partisans' Political Committee.

During 1943 these internal differences resulted in the continuation of a state of " political warfare " between Soviet Russia and General Mihailovitch (leader of the Chetniks, and Minister of War in the exiled Yugoslav Government), and between the Partisans and the Chetniks.

In April 1943 the unification of the Yugoslav forces of resistance seemed probable with the declaration by Mihailovitch that " a national committee of some of the most prominent men in the country has been engaged in clearing up all the faults of the old regime and preventing their recurrence "; appealing for unity, he promised a democratic post-war Yugoslavia. Then, following negotiations between Tito and Mihailovitch in August, it was reported that an agreement had been reached on military aims. Subsequent events, however, dulled the hopes born of these negotiations. British representatives of Middle East Command were serving with the forces of both Tito and Mihailovitch.

These inherent difficulties were naturally exploited to the full by the occupying forces, but especially by the separatist, enemy-sponsored regimes of Pavelitch in Zagreb and Neditch in Belgrade. The "Ustachi" Government in Zagreb pointed **Yugoslav Quarrels Exploited** to the Tito-Mihailovitch crisis as a symbol of the futility of resistance, while Dr. Neditch, in a speech at Kragujevac on August 29, attempted to increase the traditional racial differences of the Croats and Serbs by saying that "we Serbs made every sacrifice, including our name and flag and 1,000,000 graves," and accusing the other races of Yugoslavia of treachery.

On November 8 Gen. Sir Henry Maitland Wilson, C.-in-C. Middle East, broadcast a warning that disloyal Chetniks who persisted in helping the Germans would be regarded as traitors to their own people, and enemies of the United Nations.

ALLIED HELP FOR THE PARTISANS

Allied aircraft made a number of raids on German-occupied ports and towns in Yugoslavia. Here, U.S. Mitchells are attacking Dubrovnik on November 28, 1943. Bombs straddled military storehouses and hit a merchant vessel in dock. On the same day shipping and harbour installations at Zara and Sibenik were also bombed by Allied planes. *Photo, U.S. Official*

Then, on December 4, the Free Yugoslav radio announced that at a convention held on November 30 at Jajce, Bosnia, by the Anti-Fascist Council (a body comprising representatives of all sections supporting Tito), the following decisions had been made :

1. To transform the Anti-Fascist Council into the supreme legislative and executive organ for Yugoslavia.

2. To create a National Liberation Committee to act as a Provisional Government of Yugoslavia.

GERMAN POLICE IN A GREEK MARKET

Living became more and more difficult in Greece during 1943. It was estimated that two million people were homeless, and prices of food, footwear and other necessaries rose fantastically. Conditions were not helped by the ubiquitous presence of German field police—here seen exercising control over trade in the market of a Greek town.

Photo, Associated Press

To Gen. Tito fell the honour of becoming President of the National Liberation Committee and also C.-in-C. of the People's Army of Liberation, with the rank of Marshal.

To this the Yugoslav Government replied, denouncing and repudiating in no uncertain terms Tito's formation of a provisional government. A week later it was announced

Tito Forms Provisional Government

by the Free Yugoslav radio that a constitution of a federal character, based on democratic principles and containing the fullest guarantees of the right of national minorities, had been drafted for Yugoslavia.

The confused position in Yugoslavia led to a decision by Moscow, announced on December 15, to follow Britain's lead and dispatch a Soviet Military Mission to Yugoslavia to make its own investigations into conditions in that country.

The crisis reached its climax on December 22 when, simultaneously with an announcement from Cairo that recent talks between Partisan leaders and British fighting forces would bring about greater intensification of aid to the forces of Marshal Tito, who was at the same time raised to the status of a full Allied commander, the Free Yugoslav radio announced the repudiation of the Yugoslav Government as a result of a meeting of the Anti-Fascist Council. This repudiation was given in a proclamation of 12 points, the first seven of which summed up the charges

2729

and accusations made to date against the Yugoslav Government. The remaining points clarified the new decisions, one being to forbid King Peter to return to his country until after its full liberation. The Yugoslav Government, replying the next day, said that notwithstanding this proclamation it would continue to fight with the Allies.

In the military sphere the fighting against the enemy, greatly assisted by the Italian collapse in September 1943, continued intermittently throughout the year, being governed mainly by three major German offensives.

The first, occurring in May 1943, was launched from Bihac and thrust simultaneously towards the Dalmatian coast and Banjaluka, one of Tito's strongholds. While Tito held the enemy securely at Banjaluka, his Dalmatian forces had to withdraw southwards.

The second enemy offensive, in June, made by seven German and four Italian divisions, assisted by Croat-Fascist and Bulgarian troops, was launched against the patriot fastnesses of Montenegro. Having almost encircled the

Enemy Offensive in Montenegro

Partisans, who were being helped by the Chetniks, the Italo-German army failed to gain a decisive victory when the combined Yugoslav forces successfully cut their way out, though with the loss of much vital equipment.

Then, on December 7, the third German offensive was launched, this time in the former Sanjak of, Novi Pazar, Bosnia and Croatia. Despite initial losses of territory and towns by the patriots, the latter counter-attacked with offensive actions in the Herzegovina and Montenegro provinces, and after much bitter fighting had regained the initiative in practically all sections at the close of the year.

R.A.F ATTACK AN OCCUPIED PORT

Beaufighters of the R.A.F. over Preveza, an Axis seaplane base in Epirus on the west coast of Greece. The flying-boat in the foreground is an Italian Z-501, a bombing and reconnaissance machine built for coastal work—particularly important to Italy with her exceptionally long coastline. Although this aircraft was becoming obsolete in 1943, it had achieved more than one world distance record before the war.

Photo, British Official

ANTI-INVASION PREPARATIONS IN CRETE

The Germans, who occupied Crete in May 1941 (see page 1749), evidently regarded an Allied attempt at invasion there as likely, for they did a great deal to strengthen the island's fortifications, sowed the neighbouring waters with mines, and set up barbed wire defences round the coast. Here an iron framework is being laid down as core for the ferro-concrete platform of a new gun emplacement. In the background is an A.A. gun.

Photo, Associated Press

Unfortunately, as in Yugoslavia, the fine work of the Greek guerilla forces was undermined by differing conceptions of military, political and post-war structure which, aggravated by skilful enemy propaganda and the Allies' recognition of Italian co-belligerency, led to much internecine strife, particularly in October 1943.

GREECE

On October 18, however, negotiations were reported to have taken place in Cairo between the Tsouderos (exiled) Government and six guerilla leaders from Greece. The leaders' demands for Cabinet representation could not be granted, a factor which contributed to the continuation of civil war between the E.D.E.S. (Democratic Liberation Army) and the E.L.A.S. (Popular Army of Liberation). Many appeals were broadcast for unity, principally by Gen. Sir Henry Maitland Wilson (October 22), King George of the Hellenes and M. Tsouderos, the Greek Premier (October 28, the third anniversary of the Italian attack on Greece, and again on December 21), and M. Sophocles Venizelos, Minister for Marine (December). In his appeal on October 28, M. Tsouderos included a 10-point definition of post-war Greece.

As elsewhere, the Greeks strenuously resisted Hitler's declaration on the "total mobilization of man-power," and despite German threats and promises, the enlistment of Greeks for the Reich met with relatively little success.

Hundreds of people were forced underground, many joining the Greek guerilla forces. These, temporarily reconciled in May into one body called the "Bands of Greece," intensified their attacks and sabotage in spite of vigorous German and Italian counter-measures, which included the inevitable reprisals, e.g. 100 Greeks being executed for every German killed, and 50 for every German wounded.

Early in May, following the killing of 60 Italians in an armed clash at Kalabaka on April 29, the German Command issued an ultimatum demanding the cessation of guerilla attacks by May 20. This was treated with contempt, and attacks were continued, the E.L.A.S. under Col. Sarafis being particularly active in Western Macedonia, Thessaly and Roumali, while Col. Zervas commanding the E.D.E.S. operated in the mountainous area stretching from the Albanian frontier to the Gulf of Corinth.

German reprisals assumed the proportion of atrocities; it was reported on January 16, 1943, that at Kalavrika in the Northern Peloponnese all male inhabitants of the village had been assembled and machine-gunned, over 1,000 dying. Then an attempt was made, partly successful, to burn all the women and children to death in the school-house. The famous historic monasteries of Megaspilaion and Aghia Lavra were despoiled of their treasures and then utterly destroyed by fire.

Anti-Semitism, too, was rife; in May it was reported that of the 55,000 Jews in Salonika, 50,000 had been deported to Poland in conditions of the most inhuman cruelty and all trace lost of them.

An estimate of the distress prevailing in Greece during 1943 was given in a statement on February 8, 1944, by M. Sibarounes, the former Director-General of the Greek Ministry of Finance. He said :

"Although Allied help through the Red Cross has, during 1942–43, improved the appalling situation, inflation and the decrease in agricultural production has brought about a new deterioration, and Greece is suffering from famine. . . . Out of a total population of 8,000,000, over 1,000,000 are believed to be in a pre-tuberculous state, and 2,000,000 are suffering from chronic malaria. The excess of births over deaths in the Athens-Piraeus area in 1939 was 5,369—in 1942 deaths exceeded births by 30,351."

He went on to say that there was an acute housing crisis and that some 2,000,000 people were homeless.

An Ankara report gave 1,600 as the number of villages completely destroyed by the Germans and Italians. This destruction of productive centres was one of the main factors contributing to the phenomenal rise in the cost of living—an egg costing 10,000 drachmas and a pair of shoes 2,000,000 drachmas. The extent of inflation can be gauged when it is added that before the war 545 drachmas went to the pound sterling.

SITE OF KANDANOS

Many villages in Greece and Crete were wiped out in reprisal for the killing of German soldiers. Their sites were marked by signposts such as this which says, 'As a reprisal for the bestial murder of one platoon of parachutists and a half platoon of pioneers by armed men and women in ambush, Kandanos has been destroyed.'

Photo, Greek Official

Chapter 274

THE EXILED GOVERNMENTS IN 1943

Norway, the Netherlands, Belgium, Czechoslovakia, Poland, Yugoslavia and Greece continued in 1943 to be represented in the councils of the United Nations by their exiled Governments, though as hope of liberation mounted, events at home—particularly in Yugoslavia and Greece—increasingly influenced the actions of ministers abroad. Denmark, her Government helpless at home, still proclaimed her democratic spirit abroad through certain of her exiled citizens

THE extent of Britain's aid to her Continental Allies became known with the publication by H.M. Government on November 12, 1943, of a White Paper giving details of arrangements. These varied according to the

DESTROYER FOR NORWAY
Captain Storeheill points to the badge of 'Stord,' a British-built destroyer taken over by the Norwegian Navy to replace 'Eskdale,' sunk in 1943. 'Stord' helped sink the 'Scharnhorst' (see Chapter 284) and took part in the Allied invasion of Normandy.

Allies' needs and their resources: Norway, Holland, Belgium and Yugoslavia paying for all they received, while certain other Allies were supplied under credits. The bulk of military supplies, however, were made available free,

returnable after the war only if they still existed and were still needed by Britain. In accordance with this principle, the armed forces of Greece and Czechoslovakia were supplied free, and similar offers had been made to Poland and Yugoslavia.

Quisling's appeal on March 10, 1943, for volunteers for service on the Eastern front, in which he invoked the aid of the Norwegian Constitution, drew from the Norwegian Government strong protests against this threat to mobilize Norwegians for service with the German army, on the grounds that since Germany had long acknowledged a state of war between the two countries it constituted a serious breach of international law.

NORWAY

In her relations with Sweden, 1943 proved a particularly happy year for Norway. Although there was no doubt as to where Sweden's sympathy lay, the Norwegian Government in London remained unrecognized until early June, when Baron Beck-Früs, the Swedish Minister to Portugal, arrived in London to become the accredited Swedish Minister to the Norwegian Government. Then, on December 17, Mr. Jens Bull, Norwegian Chargé d'Affaires in Stockholm since October 1940, presented letters of credence to King Gustav,

the Swedish Monarch. This act, automatically constituting full recognition of the Norwegian Government, was the culmination of a year which had seen the friendship of the two countries, so vital for the difficult post-war period, growing apace. Outspoken expressions of sympathy for the Norwegian people in the fight against oppression, coupled with strong condemnations of the Quisling regime and of the barbarity of the German rule in Norway, characterized the Swedish people's attitude towards Norway. This was doubly important in view of the fact that the Swedish Government was compelled by geographic, economic and political reasons to restrain the sympathetic impulses of its people. Secondly, the chief obstacle to sincere relations was cleared away by the Swedish cancellation in August of her agreement with Germany for the transit across Sweden of German troops going on leave from or returning to Norway. Mr. Trygve Lie, the Norwegian Foreign Minister, on August 5 expressed his Government's pleasure at this action.

On February 17 King Haakon, referring to his country's contribution to the war effort, said in a speech at the Mansion House, London, that the Royal Norwegian Navy comprised about 60 units on active service, that the

NORWEGIANS IN ICELAND
Norwegian airmen (transferred during 1943 to Britain) and Norwegian units (some members of which had landed when their small boats were driven by stormy seas beyond Scotland in their flight from occupied Norway in 1940) both served in Iceland, which was linked with Denmark until it declared its independence in 1941. Left, Norwegian troops in an Iceland village. Right, a Northrop seaplane coming in to its Icelandic station after a convoy patrol.

LEADER OF THE FREE DANES

Mr. John Christmas Moeller, former Conservative leader in Denmark, who escaped after the German occupation of his country and as chairman of the Danish Council in London became a leader of the Free Danish movement. *Photo, Keystone*

Norwegian Air Force, built up at " Little Norway " in Canada, had several squadrons in action, and that a small but efficient Norwegian Army was stationed in Scotland. " It is the policy of my Government," he said, " that the ties between Britain and Norway, strengthened so much during these days of war, shall not be lessened when victory is won."

Some details of the achievements of the Royal Norwegian Air Force were given on April 9, 1944 (fourth anniversary of the invasion of Norway), when the Norwegian Government announced that from April 1940 to April 1944 the Norwegian Air Force had destroyed 162 enemy planes, probably destroyed 38, and damaged 117, while Norwegian air personnel had gained 219 Norwegian decorations and 70 others. A Norwegian fighter squadron was the top-scorer of all squadrons in Britain in 1943, destroying more enemy planes than any other and having the smallest losses.

Denmark was in the peculiar position of an " occupied " country having a democratic government and a monarchy whose word was still **DENMARK** law; and though the crisis in Danish affairs in August 1943, when Gen. von Hannecken, the German C.-in-C., seized power and King Christian and his queen were confined to their summer palace outside Copenhagen under German guard, changed the situation a good deal, to the end of 1943 enslaved Denmark was represented abroad chiefly by the Danish Council in London (*see* Chapter 220). Mr. Christmas Moeller, its president, had broadcast to his countrymen on March

21 calling on them to make the general elections (to be held in Denmark on March 23) a resounding defeat for Germany by voting either for the Government Coalition or only for the " Dansk Samling." The results—98 per cent voting for democracy—reflected the democratic spirit of the people, though this did not affect the composition or policy of the Scavenius Government. Following the August crisis in Copenhagen, Mr. Moeller made an important press statement in London on August 29: " Three years of injustice and brutality," he said, " have finally resulted in revolt against the German tyrants. . . ." Indicating that the Danish Council did not intend to set up a government outside Denmark, he added, " if the head of the State had been outside the frontiers the position would have been quite clear."

On September 2 the Danish Legation in Stockholm announced that, the Germans having deprived King Christian and his Government of any possibility of functioning, the Minister and his staff considered themselves free to represent Danish interests in Sweden independently of the Foreign Office in Copenhagen—a lead followed on September 7 by the Danish Legation in Dublin.

During 1943 a special Danish naval unit was formed within the Royal Navy; 5,000 Danish officers and men were serving on Danish ships for the United Nations, and about 1,000 more had volunteered for the armed forces.

An event of small importance internationally but one which drew the eager attention of Dutch peoples everywhere was the birth in Ottawa, Canada, of a third child to Princess Juliana and Prince Bernhard of the Netherlands, on January 19, 1943. A boy was hoped for—a girl arrived, to be christened Princess Margriet Francisca. In 400 years only

15 male children have been born to the Orange Stadtholders and Kings of Holland. Any child born on Canadian territory automatically becomes a Canadian citizen, but a Royal Canadian decree passed on December 26, 1942, had made the Princess's birthplace temporarily extraterritorial.

The problem of how to combat Hitler's compulsory labour decree and the implied threats of the newly constituted "State Political Secretariat " under Mussert, set up on February 1, 1943, **THE NETHERLANDS** by Seyss-Inquart's orders, occupied a major place in the deliberations of the Dutch Government in London. Attacking Mussert's administration on the grounds that it lacked legal foundation, Prof. Gerbrandy, the Netherlands Premier, in a broadcast to the Dutch people on February 4 called on the whole population, especially civil servants, to resist. " Hitler," he said, " wants to use this organization of traitors, hoping it will enable him to postpone inevitable defeat. . . ." In a broadcast on April 24 Queen Wilhelmina voiced " a flaming protest against the slave drive now going on all over

WITH THE ROYAL NETHERLANDS NAVY

Prof. Gerbrandy, Premier of the exiled Netherlands Government, after handing over the frigate ' Johan Maurits ' to its commander, talks to Leading Seaman Jan Booy, a survivor of the Dutch destroyer 'Isaac Sweers' (see pp. 1896, 2190, 2393, and illus., p. 2188), serving in ' Johan Maurits.' Below, the Dutch submarine O-19 as she reached Britain after three years of service in the Far East. A big minelaying submarine built for use in the East Indies, she reached Colombo after escaping from Singapore and Surabaya.

DUTCHMEN FLY WITH THE R.A.F.

Bombing up American-built Mitchell bombers flown by a squadron of the Royal Dutch Naval Air Service during 1943, their fourth year on operational duties with the R.A.F. They made many successful attacks on enemy targets in occupied Europe, including their homeland. Left, Commander E. Bakker, commanding officer of the squadron, wearing the ribbon of the Dutch Flying Cross. *Photos, Planet News*

our country." Referring to post-war structure, she said that at first a government would be needed to rule with a firm hand—careful, however, to avoid anything even distantly resembling dictatorship. On May 19 Dr. Gerbrandy made yet another appeal to the people of Holland to stand fast and to retain their strength for the day of liberation.

In a further broadcast on September 2 Queen Wilhelmina told the Dutch people that a state of siege—" to provide for the cleansing and revival of civil authority," and for " the removal of all undesirable elements . . ."—would be imposed in Holland as soon as it was liberated, a decree to this effect being duly signed. A Government Commissioner for the repatriation of Dutch nationals abroad, and a Netherlands representative on the United Nations War Crimes Commission were appointed during October.

Plans for the Return to Holland

The war contribution of the Netherlands Government in 1943 was made principally through her navy and air force. The fine achievements of the Royal Netherlands Navy, comprising in 1943 some 63 warships with 6,580 personnel, included active engagements in the Mediterranean (Sicily and Salerno landings included), the English Channel, the Caribbean and the S.W. Pacific, and on convoy duties ; 35,000 tons of enemy shipping were sunk by Dutch submarines. The Dutch naval and army air arms between them operated from Britain, Ceylon, Australia and South Africa.

The agreement announced by Britain, the United States and China on December 1 at Cairo (*see* Historic Document CCLXVII, page 2636), to the effect that Japan would be expelled from all the territory she had taken by force, was warmly approved by the Netherlands Government, with its huge interests in Japanese-occupied territory.

A monetary agreement—important not only in itself, but even more as evidence of the intention of the signatories to collaborate economically after the war—was signed on October 21 by the Netherlands, Belgian and Luxemburg Governments. The agreement had the warm approval of the United States and Great Britain. In a preamble, it defined its purpose as the desire of the three Governments " to stabilize the monetary relations and facilitate the mechanism of payments between the Belgo-Luxemburg Economic Union and the Netherlands, including their overseas territories or mandates."

Other gestures of international friendship made by the exiled Belgian Government included recognition of the French Committee for National Liberation on August 25, and the signing on October 20 of a treaty in Chungking whereby Belgium relinquished not only territorial jurisdiction in China and all special rights in the international settlements at Shanghai and Amoy, but also rights under the final protocol of Pekin and all rights relating to coastal trade and inland navigation.

The Belgian Government was particularly fortunate in being able to augment its help to the Allied war effort in the military sphere by supplying raw materials from the Belgian Congo. This vast territory, said by the Belgian Minister of Colonies on January 5, 1943, to be working at maximum capacity, contributed some 160,000 tons of copper, 21,000 tons of tin, and 6,000–7,000 tons of rubber per year to the Allied pool of war materials. The United States made an agreement with the Belgian Government on February 18 whereby, in exchange for supplies received under Lease-Lend,

BELGIUM

BELGIAN COMMANDOS

Two members of a Belgian Commando unit undergoing training in North Africa. They wore British battle-dress, and the equipment they are demonstrating—a six-foot rope—was used to assist them in climbing trees and walls or crossing rivers.

Photo, U.S. Official

Belgium undertook to furnish the U.S. with essential raw materials.

Belgian shipping, totalling 400,000 tons at the time of the German invasion, had been much depleted, and on June 16 the Belgian Government announced its decision to buy four new ships (three from Britain, one from the U.S.) to replace some of these losses. Twenty-five per cent of Belgian sailors, it may be added, had been lost since May 1940.

Belgian airmen, whose number in 1943 was much in excess of those in service at the time of the German **Belgian** invasion of 1940, were **War** to be found in almost **Contribution** every Command of the Royal Air Force, and had acquitted themselves with distinction. The Belgian Navy, with some seven ships and 350 personnel in mid-May 1943, rendered invaluable assistance to the Royal Navy, by which it was administered.

The Belgian Government protested on January 27 and September 22 against the brutal mass deportations of Belgians to Germany, which, according to the report of the Belgian Committee on Repatriation, published on December 29, 1943, had by that date reached the 600,000 figure—500,000 workers, 70,000 prisoners-of-war, 10,000–15,000 children, and some 6,000 civil prisoners. On July 26 it denounced strongly the tortures inflicted on Belgians in the prisons, and at the same time appeals were made to Belgian patriots, "from the highest official to the humblest navvy," to sabotage the Nazi war effort, especially by attacks

on railways and canals. Equally strong was the Belgian Government's protest of September 20 against the German treatment of Jews and recent mass arrests of Jews in Belgium. Saying that the racial ordinances promulgated and applied by the occupation authorities were unconstitutional and contrary to Belgian law, it reaffirmed that all anti-Jewish measures imposed by Germany would be held null and void when Belgium was free.

An indication of the Belgian Government's future policy was given by the Belgian Premier, M. Pierlot, in a broadcast on Belgian Independence Day, July 21. Describing in some detail the counterfeit legislation which had been responsible for the mutilation of his country's administration, M. Pierlot forecast the transference of his Government to liberated Belgium. This Government's duties, he said, would comprise the co-ordination of food supply services with the assistance of existing agencies; the immediate enforcement of decrees aimed at the cleansing of the public administration, the expulsion of traitors and the reinstatement of lawful officials; and the formation of a new Government with extended powers, incorporating in its administration men who had stayed in Belgium during the enemy's occupation.

A declaration issued by the Czechoslovak Government at a meeting held on February 19, 1943, defined as persons to be included among war criminals and traitors not only the Nazi Government in Germany, but also German officials of all kinds in Czechoslovakia — administrative, judi

CZECHOSLOVAK AIR ACE
Ft.-Lt. K. Kuttelwascher, D.F.C. and bar, famous as a 'night intruder' pilot with the R.A.F., received the Czechoslovak War Cross for the fifth time on July 30, 1943.
From the drawing by Eric Kennington; Crown Copyright

cial, police and military, the Gestapo, the S.S. and S.A.—as well as local traitors. In a broadcast to the Czech people on April 25, Dr. Benes, President of Czechoslovakia, disclosed that Dr. Tiso and his Premier **CZECHO-** Tuka (of the puppet **SLOVAKIA** Slovak State) had on several occasions attempted to establish contact with official Czechoslovak representatives in various countries in order to make excuses for their treachery in 1938. Declaring that Czechoslovakia was once again united, he concluded: "We are preparing a new democratic Republic which will again be the best and most progressive Central European State after the war."

Militarily, Czechoslovakia's war contribution came chiefly from her small but finely trained Air Force which, from the Battle of Britain to October 1943, destroyed 173 enemy planes with 181 probables, and took part in over 1,000 operational bombing flights over Germany, Italy and occupied countries. A Czechoslovak airman, Flt.-Lt. Karel Kuttelwascher, D.F.C. and bar, won the distinction of being one of the foremost "night intruder" pilots.

Czech units were in training in the Middle East and a Czech brigade saw service on the Russian front.

Dr. Benes visited Washington on May 12 for conversations with President Roosevelt. On May 13 he addressed separately the U.S. Senate and the House of Representatives, pledging the reconstitution of Czechoslovakia after

SOVIET-CZECHOSLOVAK FRIENDSHIP
Mikail Kalinin, President of the Presidium of the Supreme Soviet of the U.S.S.R., shaking hands with Eduard Benes, President of the Czechoslovak Republic, after signing the Soviet-Czechoslovak treaty of friendship, mutual assistance, and post-war co-operation in Moscow on December 12, 1943. Standing are Marshals Klementy Voroshilov and Joseph Stalin.
Photo, Pictorial Press

POLAND'S PREMIER

M. Stanislaw Mikolajczyk, who formed a new Polish Government on July 14, 1943, following the death of General Sikorski, stated that his Government would base its policy on the principles laid down by the General.
Photo, Y. Karsh

victory as an enlightened Central European democracy. Later Dr. Benes visited Ottawa, where he addressed the Canadian Parliament, returning to Washington on June 7 for talks with Roosevelt and Churchill. On June 11 he arrived back in Britain, having reached complete accord with the two great leaders on matters concerning his country and her interests, as well as on questions of European policy and the international organization of security.

Then, on December 12, Dr. Benes (who had arrived in Moscow on December 10), on behalf of Czechoslovakia, Marshal Stalin and President Kalinin, on behalf of the U.S.S.R., signed a 20-year treaty of friendship, mutual assistance and post-war collaboration, which, in Dr. Benes's words, was "the consummation of Czechoslovakia's striving for more than 20 years, pursuing the aim of protecting our people and State from German Imperialism. . . ."

A protocol to the treaty left the way open for Poland's adherence at some future date if she so desired. This agreement was warmly welcomed in London and Washington.

Although no official statement was made by the Polish Government regarding the invitation of Czechoslovakia and Russia to Poland to **POLAND** join their mutual aid pact, the semi-official "Dzennik Polski" stated in an article on December 17 that, while Poland regarded the development of friendly relations with the U.S.S.R. as of fundamental importance, the principles re-

ferred to in the agreement defined the relations between two States only, and suggested the addition of five other points important to Poland. The Polish Government's desire to reach a settlement with her neighbours was indicated by Count Raczynski, the Foreign Minister, in a statement to the Polish National Council on May 25, 1943, while on June 8 the Council adopted a resolution declaring that it was in the interests of both Poland and Czechoslovakia to reach an agreement on a basis of the closest co-operation, which would repair mistakes committed by both countries.

Up to April 12, 1943, the difficulties causing tension between Poland and the Soviet Union can be summed up thus :—

1. The question of Poland's post-war frontiers, and Soviet complaints regarding the attitude of the Polish press in Britain and America to this question.
2. The forcible conferment of Soviet citizenship on Poles in the U.S.S.R.
3. The question of the relief and removal from Russia of Poles still in that country, especially those destitute.
4. Polish resentment at the recent execution of two Polish Socialists in Russia for alleged espionage.

Then came the allegations of April 12 by the Germans that in the Katyn region near Smolensk they had found the mass graves of 10,000 Polish officers murdered by the Soviet political police in late 1939 —the nature of the soil being such that the bodies, said the Germans, had mummified and were identifiable from documents found in their pockets. These allegations were instantly described by the Soviet Union as "vile fabrications." Nevertheless, on April 16 the Polish Cabinet announced that it had asked the International Red Cross to investigate the matter—a request also made by the German Red Cross. Failing a similar request from Moscow the I.R.C. refused to undertake the inquiry. A number of statements were issued by both sides, and tension increased until on April 25 the Soviet Government severed relations with the Polish Government.

On May 3, Polish National Day, M. Raczkiewicz, the Polish President, broadcast to Poland, defending the Polish Government as "a Government formed according to our constitution, a Government whose legality never has been, and cannot be, questioned by any of the United or neutral nations. . . ."

No statement, however, could change the fundamental weaknesses of the Polish Government, whose legal status was based on the re- **New Coalition** actionary Constitution **Government** of 1935, which had **Formed** abolished all the democratic provisions of the 1921 Constitution. When a new Coalition Government was later formed under M. Mikolajczyk, composed almost entirely of members of the Opposition who had strenuously fought against the adoption of the 1935 Constitution, and who now lacked the courage to renounce this Constitution, these weaknesses were increased.

On May 4 Gen. Sikorski, the Polish Premier and C.-in-C., broadcast a mes-

GENERAL SIKORSKI IN THE MIDDLE EAST

This photo of (left to right) M. Tadeusz Romer, former Polish Ambassador to Moscow, General Sikorski, Polish Premier and C.-in-C., Lieut.-General Anders, C.-in-C. Polish Army, Middle East, and Maj.-Gen. Klimecki, Chief of Staff of the Polish Army, was taken during Sikorski's visit to the Middle East. On July 4, 1943, during the return journey, his plane crashed near Gibraltar, killing him, General Klimecki, Col. Victor Cazalet, M.P. (British liaison officer to the Polish Forces), and others.
Photo, Keystone

POLISH GUNNERS WITH THE EIGHTH ARMY

Polish gunners in action with a 25-pounder in the mountains of central Italy during the winter of 1943–44. The Polish Second Corps, under Lt.-Gen. Wladyslaw Anders, had undergone intensive training in the Middle East before it arrived in Italy, where it did splendid service with the Eighth Army, both in and behind the fighting line. Polish sappers helped to clear roads deep in snow for troops and transport to go through. *Photo, British Official*

sage to his countrymen in which, among other things, he indicated the hopes of his Government that Russia would soon initiate a move to solve current Soviet-Polish problems—a hope not strengthened when M. Vyshinsky, Deputy Commissar for Foreign Affairs, stated in Moscow on May 6 that the Polish Government, under the influence of the pro-Hitlerites within it and within the Polish press, had provoked the Soviet suspension of diplomatic relations. This and other allegations were refuted by Count Raczynski, the Polish Foreign Minister, in a statement on May 7.

Then, on July 4, came the news of the death of Poland's brilliant 63-year-old soldier statesman, Gen. Wladyslaw

Death of General Sikorski

Sikorski, in an air crash near Gibraltar. This tragedy, described in messages of sympathy and tributes to the General's great qualities as a very deep loss to the Allies, was the culmination of a tour of the Middle East, during which the General reviewed Polish troops there, had important talks with Gen. Sir Henry Maitland Wilson and King George of the Hellenes, and, at a press conference in Cairo on July 2, declared that it was imperative that East Prussia and Danzig should come under Polish control after the war.

On July 14 a new Polish Government was formed, though not without difficulties, with M. Stanislaw Mikolajczyk as Prime Minister, M. Tadeusz Romer,

Foreign Minister, and M. Kot as Minister of Information (a post he had held since May 19). Gen. Kasimierz Sosnkowski, who was second-in-command to Marshal Smigly-Rydz in 1939, was appointed by the President as C.-in-C. of the Polish armed forces. Two days later (July 16) M. Mikolajczyk stated that his Government would base its policy on the principles laid down by General Sikorski. In internal policy it would be guided by the wishes of the Polish people; in foreign policy it would loyally collaborate with the United Nations. It also fully subscribed to the idea of a federation of East-Central European nations. A fuller statement of policy which the Prime Minister made on July 27 was unanimously approved by the Polish National Council.

Poland's military contribution to the end of 1943 (excluding the Polish and French campaigns) was impressive, particularly in the air where, from October 30, 1940, to January 1, 1944, the Polish Air Force in Britain, the third largest in this country, destroyed 610 German planes with 163 probables; damaged 210; made 703 operational flights and 6,350 sorties, dropping over $14\frac{1}{2}$ million lb. of H.E.; engaged upon 151 mine-laying operations in enemy waters; probably destroyed six U-boats and damaged seven in the Battle of the Atlantic, and ferried over 1,000 planes across Africa to the Middle East and beyond. Its pilots had been awarded 158 British awards, including four

D.S.O.s. The Polish Navy, one-third larger at the end of 1943 than at September 1, 1939, up to November 28 (the 25th anniversary of its formation), had sunk three enemy destroyers, probably eight submarines, one auxiliary cruiser, several minesweepers, and 35 other ships.

The Polish Ministry of National Defence, reviewing the achievements of the army up to August 5, 1943, stated that total casualties on all fronts since September 1, 1939, amounted to 902,095. Since the Battle of France, a highly trained and fully equipped army of 80,000 men had been assembled in the Middle East under Lt.-Gen. Wladyslaw Anders, while a smaller army, comprising strong tank, artillery, infantry and parachute units, and 4,000 Polish A.T.S., was established in Britain.

The many reorganizations and changes in the Yugoslav Cabinet in London during 1943 were an indication of underlying uneasiness. On January 2 a **YUGOSLAVIA** new Cabinet (of 10 instead of 16 members) was appointed representative of all political parties, with Dr. Slobodan Yovanovitch as Premier, Minister of the Interior, and acting Foreign Minister, and Gen. Mihailovitch as War Minister. It was unhappily soon torn by dissensions, the main cause of this political disunity being possibly traceable to the Government's failure to define its attitude as to whether post-war Yugoslavia should be constituted as a federation, as desired by Croats and other minorities, or continue on the old unitary basis in which the Serbs were predominant.

On June 17 this Cabinet resigned. After several unsuccessful attempts, M. Milos Trifunovitch, as Premier and Minister of the Interior, formed a Cabinet of 14 on June 26, with M. Milan Grol as Foreign Minister and Gen. Mihailovitch as War Minister; the new Cabinet, while still representing all parties, numbered 10 Serbs to two Croats and two Slovenes. It decided to transfer the Government from London to Cairo, but before departure tried (and failed) to reach agreement on the post-war structure of the Yugoslav State. It resigned in its turn, and King Peter appointed a new Government of eight members composed almost entirely of civil servants, headed by Dr. Puritch as Prime Minister, Foreign Minister and Acting War Minister, with Gen. Mihailovitch still as War Minister. This new Government, however, also failed to reach agreement on post-war Yugoslavia; and Dr. Puritch emphasized in a broadcast to the Yugoslav peoples on August 20 that his administration was a temporary working Government and " would not deal with questions of internal politics, which are, as King Peter has declared, the inseparable life of the people themselves in the country and which they will in agreement with our democratic King determine and settle for themselves." King Peter and his Government arrived in Cairo on September 29.

Following the acceptance of Italy as a co-belligerent in the war against Germany, Dr. Ivan Tchok, speaking for the Yugoslav Government on October 18, demanded the incorporation of Trieste into post-war Yugoslavia on the grounds that its entire hinterland was ethnographically Yugoslav and its Italian population " artificial."

A Royal decree of November 23 abrogated the " Law for the Protection of the State," which, introduced by King Alexander in 1928 to strengthen his authoritarian regime, gave the Government almost unlimited powers against the Opposition and had been used with great severity. " This step," said the official Yugoslav announcement, " has laid a solid foundation for the unhampered and free expression of the will of the broad masses with regard to the future organization of a democratic Yugoslavia."

Meanwhile, the differences between the Chetniks and the Partisans in Yugoslavia (see Chapter 273) resulted in political warfare between the exiled Yugoslav Government in Cairo and the Partisans, who used the Free Yugoslav radio as their mouthpiece. Charges and accusations, met with countercharges, were bandied to and fro. Marshal Tito formed a Government on December 4, repudiated next day by the exiled Government, which also itself was repudiated on December 22 by the Anti-Fascist National Council, the political body representative of all sections supporting Tito. Appeals for unity, of which there were many, had no effect.

Lack of unity, not only among the patriots fighting the enemy in Greece but also among themselves, was one of the problems facing **GREECE** the exiled Greek Government during 1943. On January 21, 1943, the Greek Cabinet issued an announcement in London outlining its post-war plans for a National Government ; a programme repeated on July 4 by King George of the Hellenes in a broadcast to his people, in which he said that on the Greek Government's arrival in liberated Greece the members would resign and free general elections would be held within six months of the cessation of hostilities ; from these elections would arise a new Government fully repre-

sentative of all Greek associations and currents of opinion.

On March 16 King George and M. Tsouderos, the Greek Premier, arrived in Cairo to settle disturbances among the Greek armed forces in the Middle East. The same day, as a result of conversations among Greeks representing every political party and the armed forces, including Partisans still fighting in Greece, and the consequent resignation of five members, the Cabinet was reshuffled, though without affecting the position of M. Tsouderos. The new Government was centred in Cairo.

The fall of Fascism in Italy was naturally hailed as a joyous event by the Greek Government, who were fully consulted regarding armistice terms and whose representative had been present at the signing of the Armistice at Gen. Eisenhower's H.Q. Nevertheless, it viewed with understandable concern the acceptance of Italian co-belligerency, M. Tsouderos making a long statement on the matter on October 15. " . . . If, henceforth, in this policy of co-belligerency," he said, " questions concerning the political and administrative life of our country are not touched, and Greece is not denied the priority to which she is entitled, I am certain that we Greeks will continue to fight for the common victory without criticism."

A fine gesture designed to promote unity, especially among the Greek patriots who were then unfortunately intent on liquidating one another, was made by King George in a letter to M. Tsouderos on November 8. He said that when the time came he would again consult the Government regarding the question of his return to liberated Greece, this being interpreted as a

YUGOSLAV BOMBER UNIT IN U.S.A.

President Roosevelt taking part in the dedication at Washington of four Liberator bombers, to be flown by a newly formed Yugoslav unit, 40 strong, of the U.S. Army Air Forces. He said, 'May these planes fulfil their mission . . . to drop bombs on our common enemy . . . to deliver to your compatriots much-needed supplies.' Below, King Peter accepts the Liberators. Behind him is Maj.-Gen. Ralph Royce, commanding U.S. Forces, Middle East.

cession to the demand of some sections of the Greek populace for a plebiscite on the question of monarchy to precede the King's return to Greece.

On December 14 M. Tsouderos outlined his Government's programme for post-war Greece and the vital matter of the stabilization of the Balkans, thus : (1) preparations for King George's return ; (2) a coalition of exiled parties and those still remaining in Greece in the period immediately following liberation ; (3) development of a Balkan Union ; (4) economic security of the Balkans ; (5) final welding of Greece's internal unity.

Meanwhile, internecine warfare continued among the Greek patriots. Direct appeals for unity made by M. Tsouderos and King George on October 28 and on December 21 had little effect ; the message broadcast by M. Sophocles Venizeles (Minister for Marine) in early December—" the pur-

GREEKS IN TRAINING

Greek units, formed of men who escaped when Axis forces overran Greece and of Greeks who rallied from all over the world to their country's call, saw service in the campaigns of the Western Desert. Here, a detachment undergoing special training with armoured cars learns about maintenance of radio equipment.

SHE CAME HOME STERN FOREMOST

The Greek destroyer 'Adrias' (formerly the British destroyer 'Border') entering Alexandria harbour. Her bows were blown away during operations off Leros. H.M.S. 'Hurworth,' about to take off her crew, struck a mine and sank. 'Adrias' became the rescuer, and made port stern first, carrying 'Hurworth' survivors, on St. Nicholas Day (Dec. 6), 1943. Five of her crew received the highest Greek award for gallantry. Below, a Greek sailing ship turned minesweeper.

suit of political ends while the struggle for liberty is proceeding, and claims to monopolize the national struggle, cannot be permitted "—was no more effective.

Another source of grave trouble was the systematic efforts of the Bulgarians to denationalize the Greek territory under their occupation, some 15,000 Greeks having been massacred up to March 25, 1943, in Thrace and Macedonia. Speaking in the House of Commons on March 24, Mr. Richard Law, Under-Secretary of the Foreign Office, said, " H.M. Government regard as null and void any legislation or other acts by the Bulgarian Government aimed at Bulgarizing the Greek territory they covet. . . ." The Greek Government announced on Greek Independence Day (March 25) that they would pay pensions to the families of all those killed since the enemy occupation, the rate being the same as that for families of Greek soldiers killed in action.

Of the war contribution of exiled Greeks, the major part was borne by the Royal Hellenic Navy, comprising in mid-May 1943 some 33 ships with 5,450 personnel (later enlarged by the transfer of five small warships from the Royal Navy), which rendered excellent service in the Mediterranean and Aegean Seas ; while in the air valuable assistance was given in the Mediterranean area by the Royal Hellenic Air Force of one fighter and one bomber squadron.

WITH THE ROYAL NETHERLANDS FORCES OVERSEAS

Germany overran the Netherlands in 1940 ; Japan swept through the Netherlands East Indies in 1942. But Surinam (Dutch Guiana) and Curaçao, as well as some of the smaller East Indian islands, remained free. Above, Dutch-manned coastal batteries at Curaçao, where big installations refine crude oil from Venezuela for the use of the United Nations. Curaçao has a well-armed and well-trained militia, but owing to the importance of her oil refineries and her port facilities, she accepted Allied military aid for the duration of the war. Below, Royal Netherlands Indies troops on active service during 1943 in one of the islands not occupied by the Japanese in their 1942 advance.

U-BOAT HUNTERS OF THE ROYAL NAVY

Aircraft carriers, specially built and also converted from peace-time merchant ships, played a great part in the Royal Navy's battle against U-boats. Their aircraft closed the Atlantic gap, and gave protection to vessels too far from port for land-based aeroplanes to guard them. (See Chapter 275.) Above, H.M. escort carrier 'Battler,' a 'pocket' carrier built for anti-U-boat work. Below, H.M.S. 'Archer,' a converted merchant ship as seen from a Swordfish taking off from her flight deck. *Photos, British Official ; Planet News*

DEATH DIVE OF A U-BOAT

The conning-tower of this enemy submarine was sighted 12 miles away by a R.A.A.F. Sunderland of Coastal Command at six minutes before noon. The Sunderland closed, dived under the U-boat's fire, put her guns out of action, then straddled her with depth charges. As the flying-boat made a steep turn to come in again to the attack, it took this photograph showing the submarine's stern under water. Before the aircraft could finish a third turn, the submarine's bows rose sharply and she sank. The action was over thirty seconds after noon. *Photo, British Official*

GOING IN TO ATTACK FINSCH HAFEN

Australian troops nearing the beach upon which they disembarked on 22 September, 1943, under cover of U.S. warships and aircraft, to attack Finsch Hafen, 70 miles from Lae. Beach-heads were quickly secured, Japanese opposition—apart from snipers—being negligible. The landings were effected without the loss of a ship or a man, but as the warships were withdrawing, they were attacked by some 30 Japanese bombers and 40 Zeros. U.S. fighters shot down 40 enemy planes (with five probables) for the loss of three machines (one pilot safe). No ship suffered damage.

Chapter 275

CRUSHING DEFEAT OF THE U-BOAT

The history of the Merchant Service in 1943 was very different from that of 1942 (see Chapter 242). In July of that year enemy sinkings reached their highest since 1939. But the turn of the year marked the turn in this phase of the war: not only was Allied shipbuilding outstripping Allied losses, but losses were decreasing—until in the first half of September no allied ships were lost anywhere by U-boat action, a record for this war and the last

THE U-boat was defeated in 1943. That year saw the culmination of over three-and-half years' constant, bitter struggle, a struggle against as great a threat to Britain as the threat of invasion in 1940; after the defeat of the Luftwaffe in the Battle of Britain, the U-boat represented the enemy's one hope of victory over the Western Powers. "The defeat of the U-boat and the improvement of the margin of shipbuilding resources are the prelude to all aggressive operations." Those words of Mr. Churchill were quoted in Chapter 242; they may be repeated to give the measure of achievement at sea in 1943. A more gradual affair than the victories on land or in the air, or in a naval engagement, it passed largely unhailed, and its significance tended to be overlooked at the time. But it shaped the events of the whole of the Anglo-American war effort.

How was the defeat of the U-boat accomplished? No single feature of this complex and diversified form of warfare was responsible for the success; it was the combination of invention, strategy, experience, training, diplomacy and sheer strength. New weapons and new tactics were used. Naval and air crews, and merchant ships' gunners, became more and more efficient in defence and attack. New bases were gained. But, above all, the strength of convoy protection was greatly increased, and most significantly increased in the air. The convoy system, indeed, was finally vindicated.

As recorded in Chapter 242, the German submarine campaign reached its peak in the second half of 1942. Though the Allied losses were noticeably reduced in December of that year and the first two months of 1943, they were still at a dangerous level. The balance of losses and gains was now on the right side; the merchant fleets were at last increasing month by month. But too many ships were carrying their cargoes and sometimes their crews—to the bottom of the oceans.

Allied Losses Continue to be Too High

"It is a horrible thing," Mr. Churchill declared, "to plan ahead in cold blood on the basis of losing hundreds of thousands of tons a month, even if you can show a favourable balance at the end of a year. The waste of precious cargoes, the destruction of so many noble ships, the loss of heroic crews all combine to constitute a repulsive and sombre panorama. We cannot possibly rest content with losses on this scale, even though they are outweighed by new building, even if they are not for that reason mortal in character."

In January the Canadian Chief of Naval Staff, Vice-Admiral Percy W. Nelles, gave the warning: "We have reason to believe German submarine strength is increasing." He put the gain at something more than 10 a month. "We are still far from winning the war against the submarine," the New York

FRESH WATER FROM THE SEA
Lt. J. H. G. Goodfellow, R.N.V.R. (left), invented a still, for use in lifeboats or on board ship if drinking water ran out, which produced fresh water from the sea in a few moments. It worked on paraffin, solid fuel, or wood. The inventor here demonstrates it to Admiral Sir Martin Dunbar-Naysmith, V.C. *Photo, Keystone*

Times declared, adding that "our losses in this battle, in fact, imperil what we have managed to gain in every other battle." Another leading American newspaper wrote: "The submarine defence is just about holding the enemy at the present time; it is not yet fighting a winning battle." In London an International Seamen's Conference called for greater protection by shore-based and ship-based aircraft, more effective grouping of fast and slow convoys, and a "vigorous offensive action against the submarine menace at sea and on land, in particular by bombardment . . . of the naval bases of submarines . . . and the industrial establishments concerned with the building and repairing of submarines."

On both sides of the Atlantic the authorities were pressed to reveal the extent of the losses suffered. Under the title, Peril at Sea, the London Economist described the submarine war as "the one successful offensive which Hitler is still waging." The principle of convoy protection, it was noted, was defence. "With the aid of radio detection and sufficient aircraft, it may be possible to turn defence into attack far more than has yet been done. . . . The only sure means of winning this struggle is to bring the German underwater navy to battle and to destroy it." The words were prophetic: within a few months the U-boats were brought to battle and badly mauled, if not destroyed.

'Peril at Sea'

Already, by the beginning of 1943, the U-boat weapon had been blunted, the rate of killings had been steadily lowered. The steady diminution in the destruction wrought by the U-boats was referred to by Mr. Churchill in reviewing the war situation in the House of Commons on February 11, 1943. In the first year of the war, each operational U-boat that was at work, he stated, accounted for an average of 19 ships; in the second year for an average of 12, and in the third year for an average of 7½.

In January Admiral Karl Doenitz, formerly in charge of the U-boat fleets, became Commander-in-Chief of the German Navy, and this appointment

CARRIER ESCORT FOR AN ALLIED CONVOY

H.M.S. 'Avenger' and H.M.S. 'Biter' in stormy weather, fighters ranged on their pitching flight-decks. They were two of 38 auxiliary carriers of about 10,000 tons transferred for convoy escort duty from the U.S. Navy to the Royal Navy under Lease-Lend. 'Avenger,' a converted merchantman, was lost during the landing operations in French North Africa in November 1942. Aircraft of 'Biter' played a big part in a bitter Atlantic convoy battle in May 1943.

was regarded as the signal of a renewed offensive. " The day will come when I shall offer Churchill a first-rate submarine war," Doenitz declared, threatening at the same time to " smash the British supply sea line with a new submarine weapon." Captain Wolfgang Lueth, U-boat ace, said that Germany had " an important invention " which would be put into all U-boats " and enable them to resume their fight against Allied shipping."

But Allied losses were reduced in January and February. The following month, however, they again rose sharply —though they did not reach the very high totals of the spring and summer of 1942, during which year the monthly figure had been some 600,000 tons gross. March losses, it was stated, were substantially exceeded by new construction; but at this time new ships were being constructed in United Nations' shipyards at a rate of about 1,100,000 tons gross a month. The Germans claimed that 851,600 tons of Allied shipping was sunk in March. April saw some improvement in the situation; the guarded official description was that " sinkings were low compared with March." German claims dropped to 415,000 tons.

Heavy Sinkings in March

The turn of the tide came in May 1943—and it was marked principally by success in offence rather than defence. In a special statement made in the House of Commons on June 2, the First Lord of the Admiralty revealed that the number of U-boats destroyed in May had probably exceeded the number brought into service. " Certainly May is the best month of the war for kills so far," Mr. A. V. Alexander declared. He went on to disclose how

the curve of U-boat destruction had been rising steadily. During the previous 12 months, he said, the kills had exceeded those for the whole of the war up to then, while in the last half of that period the destruction rate had been increased by 25 per cent. Mr. Alexander added the warning that setbacks and periods of heavy loss might still be encountered. " The enemy are bound to make great efforts to alter the present situation."

Similar warnings against over-optimism were made in the United States. But it was the Prime Minister, Mr. Churchill, who tentatively and prophetically gave the turn of events its historical perspective. In the House of Commons on June 8 he confirmed that " in May, for the first time, our killings of U-boats substantially outnumbered the U-boat output "—30 submarines had been destroyed. " That," he added, " may be a fateful milestone." And it was.

On July 10 a statement was issued simultaneously from Downing Street and the White House which revealed that the losses of Allied and neutral merchant ships from submarine attacks in June were the lowest since America entered the war in December 1941, and that losses at sea from all forms of enemy action were the lowest since the war began (the best record of any former month for which official figures were issued was under 100,000 tons gross sunk in March 1940).

This was the first of the reports on the war at sea to be issued thereafter on the 10th of each month under the authority of the Prime Minister and Mr. Roosevelt. Apart from specially authorized announcements " or duly censored accounts of particular incidents or actions," these statements, it was

announced, were to be the only ones to be made on behalf of the British and American Governments. The purpose was to avoid conflicting or unauthorized reports—official, semi-official and unofficial—being issued on both sides of the Atlantic about the anti-U-boat war and the methods and devices employed in it. " The enemy, by piecing together portions of these statements," it was pointed out, " may glean more information than is desirable about these affairs." So far as the general picture was concerned, however, the public was in this way given the first opportunity to follow the course of the war at sea with the aid of regular, official reports since publication of the figures of shipping losses was suspended by the British Admiralty in the summer of 1941.

The new situation at sea was soon reflected in the marine insurance market. Early in June a new " schedule " of war risk rates on cargo was issued in London which showed more numerous, more widespread and perhaps larger reductions in rates than any previous schedules for a very long time. The most striking feature was to be found in the case of voyages through the Mediterranean. For three years such voyages had been excluded from the schedule altogether. By the end of May 1943 the Germans and Italians had been thrown out of North Africa. The Italian island of Pantelleria, devastated from the air and on the verge of surrender, had already been rendered harmless. The Mediterranean had been reopened as a route for " commercial traffic." Voyages to Aden and the Red Sea reappeared in the schedules of insurance against war risks at a rate of 10 per cent via the Mediterranean; for corresponding destinations via the Cape of Good Hope the rate was 15 per cent. " Allied shipping now moves almost unmolested from one end of the Mediter-

Reduction in War Risk Rates

ranean to the other," the U.S. War Secretary declared. War risk insurance rates on other routes were also reduced, while it was notable that United Kingdom east coast ports reappeared in the schedules for overseas voyages on a par with west and south coast ports : " E-boat Alley " had become as safe for Allied shipping as the Bristol Channel. Underwriters, as always, were conducting their business not on hopes or anticipations, nor on the more optimistic assurances of high officials ; it was results—improved claims experience—which had justified the amendments.

A combination of developments enabled the Allies to surmount the submarine menace. Early in the year it was revealed that for some months the highest priority had been given to the construction of convoy escort craft. To some extent the new policy impinged on the mercantile shipbuilding programmes in Britain, and to a lesser extent in the United States and Canada, the theory being that a ship saved was better than a ship built. The corvettes, which had been built in considerable numbers for convoy duties, were gradually superseded in the construction programme by new, faster and better-armed vessels known as frigates (see Chapter 284).

Then gradually there came into service what was perhaps an even more effective weapon—aircraft carriers for

Aircraft Carriers on Convoy Duty convoy service. The new vessels, built in large numbers in the United States, had been dovetailed into the highly organized shipbuilding programme by utilizing merchant ship hulls still in the construction stage. Their success had already been proved by earlier conversions. But now the building of escort carriers, or " Woolworth " carriers, as

they were called, was tackled in earnest. These vessels carried a number of fighter, spotting and torpedo planes, and they soon proved their worth in defence as well as attack. At this time increased patrols of shore-based V.L.R. (very long range) aircraft, operating from both sides of the Atlantic, had forced the U-boat packs to concentrate their attacks in the middle of the Atlantic, outside the bombers' range ; they had already been driven from their once " happy hunting ground " on the United States Atlantic seaboard and the Caribbean (see Chapter 214). In May the German radio spokesman, Vice-Admiral Luetzow, explaining the reduced success of the U-boats, said : " It is true that aircraft based on the coasts of both sides of the Atlantic cover a large part of the ocean, *but there is still a large gap which they cannot reach.*" The escort carriers helped to cover that gap.

Britain's Coastal Command was also steadily extending the range of its convoy protection, operating sometimes 1,000 miles from base (see page 2658). It was not until the end of July, however, that a new and significant stage was reached when a long-range Liberator on an operational sortie from Newfoundland, was diverted in mid-ocean and ordered to land at a Coastal Command station in Northern Ireland. " The Atlantic Gap " had virtually disappeared.

And all the time surface protection was also being increased. It became possible for units to detach themselves from a convoy to continue fighting U-boats while the convoy proceeded with still adequate protection. Before,

submarines had often escaped because screening warships could not be spared to carry home their attacks without exposing the convoy to even greater dangers through inadequate protection than those it already suffered.

Little, of course, was revealed of achievements in the field of scientific invention. But in February it was disclosed that new methods of detecting U-boats on the surface at night or in fog were in use, and that these instruments were particularly valuable to anti-submarine aircraft.

Six months later some details were published of a secret weapon described as a powerful searchlight carried by Coastal Command aircraft known as the **Leigh Light** Leigh Light Squadrons. **Squadrons** The searchlight could throw on the water a beam many millions of candle-power in strength. It was at night that the submarines surfaced for charging their batteries, as well as for cruising to the operational areas in mid-Atlantic. The new weapon was described as " the keystone of the success in the air offensive against U-boats in the Atlantic, where a high percentage of attacks to sightings has been achieved in darkness." The searchlight was developed by Wing-Commander H. de V. Leigh, O.B.E., D.F.C. The offensive against the submarine was being carried out day and night.

Earlier in the year references were made to " a new type of anti-submarine device " in use by the U.S. Navy which was " more effective than the standard depth charges." It could be used in conjunction with depth charges to

COASTAL COMMAND ON ANTI-SUBMARINE PATROL

A Liberator of Coastal Command in flight above a tanker bringing oil to Britain, keeping watch for U-boats, and ready to attack at any sign of the enemy. During 1943 Coastal Command flew over 40,000 sorties (more than 100 a day) on anti-submarine and convoy escort duty, sinking more U-boats in that one year than in the whole period September 1939 to the end of 1942.

Photo, British Official

provide a " double-barrelled barrage." Early in May it was announced from Washington that five U-boats had been sunk in the Atlantic while they were attacking a west-bound convoy. "One of them was sunk," it was added, " by a new weapon, the nature of which is a closely guarded secret." In July a German-controlled French paper stated that the Reich had temporarily ceased its undersea offensive. The British, it was explained, had recently used a " new submarine mine " which was particularly efficacious. " Whether dropped by a destroyer or aeroplane it finds its mark to very great depths." The U-boats, it was added, had been recalled and would be equipped with " special devices to permit them to resume their work with increased power."

It was not enough to provide more weapons of defence and attack, to employ new devices and tactics. The effective use of each depended on

Anti-U-Boat Campaign by Allies

achieving the greatest measure of co-opera-tion, on the one hand, between naval staffs on both sides of the Atlantic and, on the other, between the sea and air forces involved in the battle. On March 16 it was announced that a conference of American, British and Canadian officers had recently been held in Washington under the chair-manship of Admiral Ernest J. King, Commander-in-Chief of the United States Fleet—" one of a series of Allied conferences which have been and will continue to be held, in order that all phases of the anti-U-boat cam-paign can be kept constantly under review, that information and views can be exchanged and that anti-U-boat measures can be adjusted to best advan-tage." It was added that complete agreement was reached on the policy to be pursued in the protection of Allied shipping in the Atlantic and in the best methods of employing the Allied escort vessels, anti-submarine craft and aircraft in defeating the U-boat menace. Naval and air staffs of each country were represented.

The policy of integrating offensive and defensive activities in the Atlantic was carried a stage further at the end of May. It was announced from Ottawa that Canada and Britain had assumed complete charge of trade convoys from north-western Atlantic ports to the United Kingdom. The United States retained strategic re-sponsibility for the western Atlantic and for escort operations not related to British trade convoys and Canadian local traffic. The degree of co-operation

ANTI-U-BOAT CHIEF
Speaking at Weston-super-Mare on Novem-ber 6, 1943, Mr. A. V. Alexander, First Lord of the Admiralty, disclosed that Capt. C. P. Clarke, of Somerset (above), was the man who for two years had directed the success-ful Allied operations against U-boats.
Photo, G.P.U.

achieved between the air and sea forces, a powerful factor in the success, was described by Sir Archibald Sinclair, Secretary of State for Air :

The Battle of the Atlantic is not a series of single combats between the U-boat and the aircraft or the warship, but is made up of prolonged engagements over thousands of miles of sea, in which the work of the surface forces is at every stage integrated with the work of aircraft. The aircraft

C.-IN-C., GERMAN NAVY
Admiral Karl Doenitz, here addressing U-boat crews while on a tour of inspection as head of the German submarine service, became C.-in-C. of the German Navy in January 1943. A U-boat commander in the 1914-18 war, he invented the ' wolf-pack ' U-boat tactics.

and the escort vessel are nicely comple-mentary ; the escort vessel carries a bigger punch, and can track down a U-boat, once detected, even though submerged, but the range of vision of the escort vessel is limited ; the aircraft is less certain of its kill but has, of course, an immensely greater range of vision and a better chance of surprising the enemy. A convoy may be assailed along the whole route across the ocean, first by U-boats and then by bombers and, at every stage, the work of the air and escort vessels on the surface is interlocked. Never has there been a happier period of relations between the Royal Navy and the Royal Air Force than in the past year.

It was not until November 1943 that the name of one of the chief figures behind the anti-U-boat campaign was revealed. Captain C. P. Clarke, who at the age of 45 had for two years been Director of Operations against the enemy U-boats, was credited by Mr. A. V. Alexander with " an important share in the great success we have hewn out of the massive danger which confronted us."

The offensive spirit which marked operations at sea had its prelude in the increasingly heavy air raids on German submarine bases, shipyards and engine works from the beginning of the year. Including the activities of Coastal

Offensive Operations by Sea and Air

Command at sea, the U-boat war represented the chief preoccupation of the R.A.F., while the United States Army Air Force joined in with day-light attacks on bases and building yards at Lorient and Bordeaux, St. Nazaire and elsewhere. The heaviest attack yet delivered against the main base early in February was the eighth which Lorient had received in less than a month and the 56th since the summer of 1940. Within a week an-other 1,000-ton raid had been launched, followed by a further powerful attack three days later (*see* illus., page 2660).

Before the close of the year one more vital influence joined in the " combination of developments " which pronounced the doom of Germany's submarine effort. On October 12 the Prime Minister announced that, under the terms of a treaty dating back to 1373, the Portuguese Government had agreed to grant Britain facilities in the Azores which would " enable better protection to be given to merchant shipping in the Atlantic." This drama-tic development made doubly sure the assurance of success. For the first time a vast area in mid-Atlantic, at one point reaching as far south as the Tropic of Cancer, was brought within range of bomber patrols. Some voyages were cut by many hundreds of miles, the equivalent of more ships. An alter-native was provided to the Icelandic

SUPPLYING U-BOATS AT SEA

In order to keep their U-boat packs at sea, the Germans used big supply submarines to take fuel, victuals and ammunition to submarines preying on Allied shipping. 1. A pipeline, brought across from the supply submarine by rubber dinghy, is drawn aboard the U-boat to refuel her tanks. 2. Dinghy plying between supply vessel and ocean-going U-boat on the high seas. 3. Bringing torpedoes aboard : they have been floated across from the supply ship.

Photos, Planet News ; Associated Press

route for the convoys, with its natural hazards for ships in the winter months and severities for the crews. The tasks of the Allied naval squadrons were eased ; for the U-boats the hazards were multiplied. (*See also* Chapter 268.)

On Oct. 11 it was disclosed that the " Tirpitz," most powerful battleship in the German fleet, had been torpedoed and seriously damaged in a daring attack by British midget submarines (*see* Chapter 284) ; a most dangerous threat to the Atlantic convoys had been lifted. A month previously the Italian Fleet had anchored under the guns of Malta. The whole situation at sea had changed.

We have seen something of the larger factors which gained success at sea—

the development of new weapons and new tactics, the perfection of organization, the effort to close the " Atlantic gap." In the narrower perspective of the actual battles at sea the offensive spirit was again the distinguishing feature. " There are so many U-boats employed now," the Prime Minister said early in June, " that it is almost impossible not to run into one or other of these great screens of U-boats which are spread out, and therefore you have to fight your way through. But there is no reason why we should regret that. On the contrary, it is around the convoys that the U-boats can best be destroyed." The Germans were still relying on the " wolf-pack " system of attack.

At the beginning of the year few large convoys crossed the Atlantic without running into a U-boat pack. Some only of the great battles which developed were described at the time. The U-boats generally shadowed the convoy in the daytime, looking for stragglers, and attacked fiercely at nights or under cover of bad weather. In May came the announcement of four U-boats sunk—there were six " probables "—in the course of one convoy battle, the largest and longest up to that time. A brief action described by one of the officers of a corvette was typical of the fight :—

We had dropped a full load on one U-boat, then almost instantaneously saw torpedoes coming at us from another one. Seven were fired altogether. She submerged and we ran over her, then almost fell over another one immediately afterwards. They both cleared off and we went round to the first one, again preparing to ram. She had been blown up to the top and was turning in a circle, presumably to avoid us. Her crew were climbing over her, yelling to each other and to us and chucking rafts in the water. One chap had made up his mind to have a last pop at us and was clambering over the fore end to get at the 4-in. gun. We gave him the works at about 100 yards.

By now we were doing the tightest turns—all but bending ourselves in two to keep inside the Jerry's turning circle. But it was all up with him. His periscope was smashed and his bows began to go up. Men were swimming about waving torches. In the middle of all this we got another contact and when we came back the submarine had sunk.

Off and on over a period of eight days more than 30 determined attacks were delivered by the U-boats. The convoy suffered some damage, it was stated, but the majority of the merchantmen reached port in safety. In a 10-day period about this time Coastal Command bombers on patrol sank for certain five U-boats, one near Iceland, two in the Bay of Biscay, the others along the western approaches.

An official Admiralty and Air Ministry communiqué described how, later in May, combined forces of escort ships and aircraft of the Royal Navy and of aircraft of Coastal Command " successfully defended valuable Atlantic convoys against one of the fiercest and most sustained offensives ever mounted by U-boats." The battle ranged over hundreds of miles and extended intermittently throughout five days and five nights. Two U-boats were destroyed, three probably destroyed and others damaged. So effective was the anti-submarine offensive on this occasion that most of the engagements were fought many miles from the convoys and 97 per cent of the ships reached harbour without having been molested. Aircraft of the Fleet Air Arm from the carrier H.M.S. " Biter " first spotted the U-boats. They attacked and they led destroyers and corvettes to other U-boats spotted from the air.

The following month it was possible to report that " complete shore to shore air cover, provided by carrier-borne aircraft working in co-operation with land-based aircraft," had assured the passage of another valuable convoy across the Atlantic " without interference from powerful forces of U-boats." A few weeks later it was revealed that a force of between 25 and 30 U-boats, concentrated in a North Atlantic shipping lane, had been subjected to such relentless assaults by surface ships and aircraft that the enemy was denied the opportunity to launch even one attack against a large east-bound convoy.

In the three months May, June and July more than 90 German submarines were destroyed. The July statement issued by Mr. Roosevelt and Mr. Churchill revealed that " the steady flow of transatlantic supplies on the greatest scale **Transatlantic Flow Unmolested** has continued unmolested, and such sinkings as have taken place in distant areas have had but an insignificant effect on the conduct of the war by the Allies." The Allies' conduct of the war in July included the invasion of Sicily. For that operation and subsequent reinforcements, over 2,500 vessels were gathered together. Troop transports, supply ships and landing craft proceeded through the Atlantic and Mediterranean waters with scarcely any interference from U-boats. The official statement revealed that only about 80,000 tons of the huge armada were sunk. Altogether, July was " probably our most successful month ": imports were high, shipping losses moderate, and U-boat sinkings heavy.

In August the shipping losses continued to decrease ; Admiral Luetzow confessed that the " Allies have the upper hand." There were fewer U-boats operating—but the official statement was able to claim the astonishing record that more U-boats had been sunk than merchant ships. For four months up to September 18, Mr. Churchill revealed on Sept. 21, no merchant vessel was sunk by enemy action in the North Atlantic.

The submarine offensive was resumed in mid-September. The official statement for that month, however, recorded that the average merchant ship losses from all causes in September and August together made the best record of the war. On September 21 Mr. Churchill also stated that the net tonnage gain since the beginning of the year, allowing for losses from all causes, including marine risks, exceeded 6,000,000 tons. The failure of the

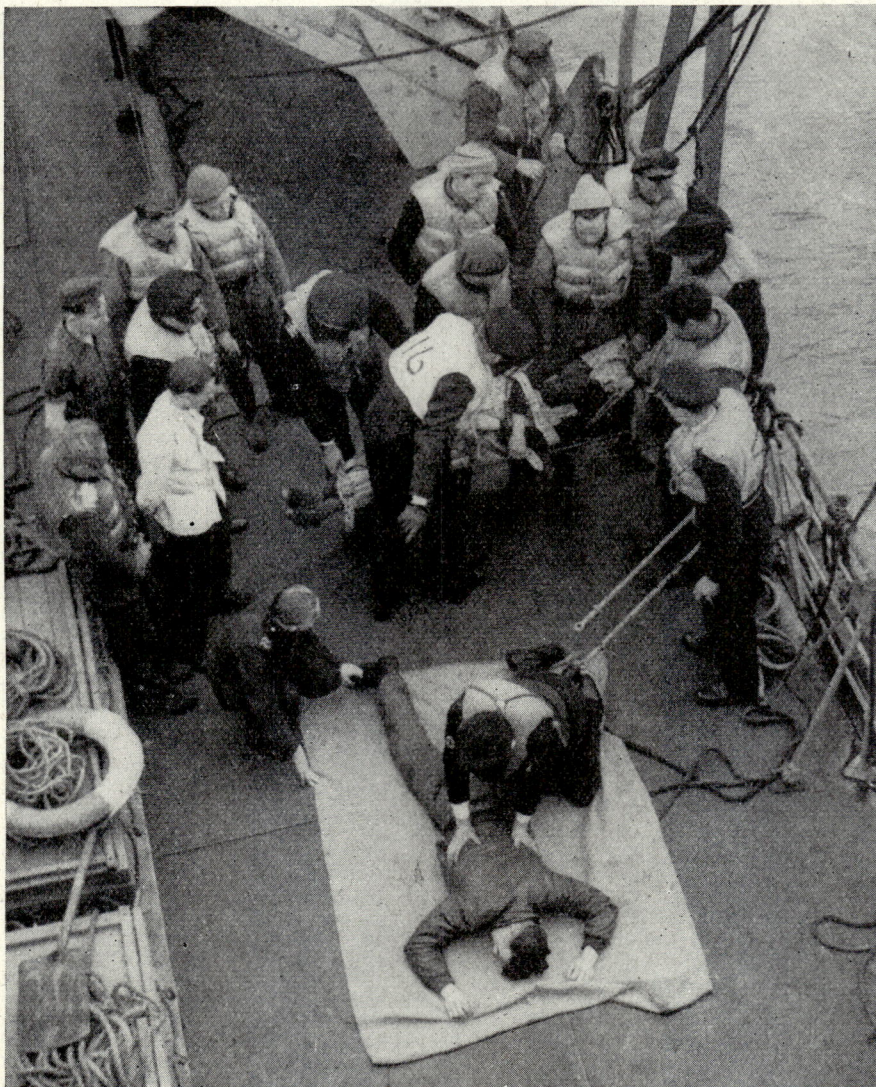

ON BOARD A CONVOY RESCUE SHIP

Cargo boats transformed into rescue ships, whose job it was to save seamen cast adrift by enemy action, accompanied convoys across the Atlantic. Equipped with a hospital and operating theatre and manned by merchant marines, a R.N.V.R. doctor, and medical orderlies, these ships saved hundreds of lives. A stretcher case is brought aboard ; while a medical orderly applies artificial respiration to another man already rescued from drowning.

LAST MOMENTS WITH THE U-BOATS

Over 150 German submarines were sunk between May and October 1943. 1. A U-boat, brought to the surface by depth charges from H.M. corvette 'Starwort' and other ships. Her crew has lined up ready to dive overboard as their vessel begins to sink stern first. 2. Another, one of six destroyed by aircraft of Coastal Command, photographed by one of the attacking planes flying at low level a few seconds before she sank. 3. Bows of a third vessel sinking in the Bay of Biscay after an attack with depth charges by a Halifax of Coastal Command. 4. A ring of oil on the surface where an Australian Sunderland flying-boat sank yet another U-boat—one of five 'kills' in 10 days.

SHIPS IN CONVOY

During the first fortnight of September 1943 not one Allied ship was sunk by a U-boat—a period without precedent in this war or the last, said Mr. Churchill ; and during the whole year U-boats destroyed only 40 per cent of the merchant tonnage they sank in 1942. Surface ships and aircraft, both shore-based and carrier-borne, combined to produce this result. Top, a cruiser keeps constant watch over an Atlantic convoy. Centre, enemy aircraft in the Bay of Biscay bomb a convoy at sunset. U-boats joined in the attack, but both planes and submarines were driven off without loss. Left, American 'Liberty' ships unloading in a North African port ; the ensigns of two British destroyers can be seen in the foreground.

Photos, British Official ; Fox

SALVAGE OPERATIONS IN THE RED SEA

This huge floating dry dock, sunk by the Italians in Massawa harbour before the British occupied Eritrea in April 1941, was salvaged and restored to service by American workmen under the direction of Capt. Edward Ellsberg, U.S. Navy salvage expert. The Axis freighter alongside was one of a number reclaimed from the Red Sea and put into service again for the United Nations.

Photo, Pictorial Press

renewed "offensive" was demonstrated by the fact that the tonnage losses from all causes in October were the second lowest of any month of the war. In the three months from the beginning of August about 60 U-boats were destroyed—a larger number than the merchant ships sunk by U-boat action.

The October statement, however, disclosed that the Germans had introduced new U-boat weapons and new tactics. One of the new weapons was a bomb in the form of a rocket-assisted glider which was released from a considerable height and guided to its target by the parent aircraft. It could be used, however, only against ships operating near the enemy coastline. Another new weapon spoken of was an acoustic torpedo which, directed by the propeller vibrations of the ship attacked, was said to slant upwards to strike the vessel in the stern.

But at the close of the year there had been no marked change in the favourable turn of events which began in the spring. Although, **U-Boats More Cautious** on the whole, the U-boats had become more cautious, they made further efforts to interrupt the vast flow of supplies across the Atlantic. On one occasion submarine packs attempting to attack three Atlantic convoys over a period of about a week were driven off with the loss of six U-boats before any of the attacks had developed. Communiqués issued early in December told a similar story. During a series of engagements over a wide area, lasting two days and two nights, five U-boats were destroyed and three damaged, preventing a serious assault on two valuable convoys; 99

per cent of the ships escorted reached port in safety.

Several attempts were made by the enemy during the year to run the blockade of the European coastline. The sinking of a large German vessel in the Atlantic was announced at the beginning of January. The armed merchant ship "Silvaplana" (4,793 tons), with a cargo of rubber and tin from the Far East, was intercepted in April by H.M.S. "Adventure" about 200 miles off Cape Finisterre and scuttled herself. The crew and more than 100 German Navy men were taken prisoner.

A similar end to the motor vessel "Regensburg" (8,068 tons) was announced at the same time. Also bound from the Far East, she was intercepted by H.M.S. "Glasgow" between Greenland and Iceland. Most of her crew were drowned. The "Glasgow" was also involved in a spirited action which centred round the attempt of another blockade runner to make the French coast. She was a fast, modern ship of about 5,000 tons. A Sunderland flying boat spotted her making for a port in the Bay of Biscay. This was on December 27. The cruisers "Glasgow" and "Enterprise" were detailed to intercept. But later the same day the blockade runner was attacked by aircraft, set on fire and eventually sunk. The next morning 11 German destroyers were seen making for the scene of the action, presumably to keep a rendezvous with the merchant ship. The British cruisers made contact in the early afternoon and a running fight developed in which the destroyers fled for their bases. Three were sunk.

The sinking of two medium-sized United States passenger and cargo ships early in February with heavy loss of life was announced **Sinking of 'Empress of Canada'** by the U.S. Navy Department. The vessels were torpedoed in the North Atlantic within a few days of each other. More than 850 people, mostly Service personnel, were killed or drowned.

Many months later it was learned that the Canadian Pacific passenger

'DEMS' UNDERGO INSTRUCTION

'Dems'—gunners of Defensively Equipped Merchant Ships—were taught how to tackle E-boats and low-level air attacks with the .303 Lewis gun. Here is a group, including men who had been in action, at a training establishment in the south of England. The targets, a model E-boat and aircraft, were illuminated; the gun fired tracer.

Photo, Central Press

3 A 2

liner "Empress of Canada," of 21,500 tons, was sunk by an Italian submarine off the West Coast of Africa in March. She was carrying troops, naval personnel, Italian prisoners and refugees. There were about 800 survivors. The submarine waited until the last man had left the ship before opening fire, but 400 died before rescue ships arrived.

In May the Japanese torpedoed and sank the hospital ship "Centaur." It was before dawn and the "Centaur"

BLOCKADE-RUNNER'S END

On December 27, 1943, a Sunderland flying-boat reported a blockade-runner, a fast modern ship of about 5,000 tons, apparently inward bound for a French west coast port. Aircraft on patrol were diverted to the area, the cruisers 'Glasgow' and 'Enterprise' prepared to intercept, and bombers of Coastal Command were dispatched. A Liberator from a Czechoslovak squadron hit the blockade-runner, her stern burst into flame, explosions followed, and she sank, enveloped in fire and smoke (below).

SHE SCUTTLED HERSELF

Spotted some 200 miles off Cape Finisterre on April 10, 1943, and ordered to stop by H.M.S. 'Adventure,' the German armed ship 'Silvaplana' (4,793 tons) was scuttled and abandoned by her crew. She was attempting to run the blockade with a cargo of rubber and tin from the Far East. Above, some of 'Adventure's' crew watch the end of the scuttled ship.

was fully illuminated, clearly marked with a Red Cross on either side of the hull and funnel and on the poop. The vessel was 40 miles east of Brisbane, Australia, and was sailing unescorted. Visibility was good. Of more than 300 people on board, 268 lost their lives.

Throughout 1943 the supply line to Northern Russia was maintained against hazards of weather and attacks of the enemy such as were described in Chapter 242. A huge flow of supplies went by ship into the Mediterranean— vessels totalling over 22,500,000 tons gross entered the ports of North Africa in the year to November 8. In the Far East merchant ships supported the mounting offensive which began to drive out the Japanese from their far-flung Pacific outposts. The American shipbuilding effort reached its peak, more than doubling the 1942 figure with an output of 19,000,000 tons deadweight. But the Battle of the Atlantic overshadowed all else in the war at sea. It was of the great convoy battles that the First Lord of the Admiralty said : "When the last U-boat is safe at the bottom of the sea or in our ports, and we are able to look back over the vast panorama of the whole war, these actions may well be seen worthy to be counted among the decisive maritime actions of history."

Chapter 276

THE HUON GULF CAMPAIGN IN NEW GUINEA

Slowly but surely the Japanese were driven back in New Guinea during 1943. This second phase in the Allied operations designed to eject the enemy from New Guinea and the neighbouring island of New Britain, resulted in the reduction of his bases at Salamaua, Lae and Finsch Hafen, and the clearance of the country around the Huon Gulf. In this Chapter, Miss L. E. Cheesman describes the arduous but successful fighting which followed the fall of Buna and Gona recorded in Chapter 249

THE ejection by Australian and American forces of the Japanese from the coastal area around Buna and Gona, which was completed in January 1943, concluded the first phase of the Allied operations which were intended eventually to clear the invaders from the whole island of New Guinea. By the last week of January not an enemy soldier remained in the Territory of Papua. But the Japanese still held strong bases at Salamaua and

AUSTRALIAN COMMANDER

Brigadier S. G. Savige, D.S.O., M.C., E.D., commanded the Third Australian Division in New Guinea subsequent to April 23, 1943, and planned the campaign which gradually drove the Japanese from their outposts in the Salamaua area in the spring of that year.

Lae on the Huon Gulf in Mandated Territory, and also controlled the Vitiaz Strait between the mainland of New Guinea and New Britain. The second stage in the campaign, which continued throughout most of 1943, had as its object the elimination of the enemy from this area.

Outside their main bases the Japanese had many strongly held local positions. Owing to the nature of the country, forest alternating with swamp, such posts on mountains difficult of access and on densely wooded hills were seldom vulnerable to air attack. Their supply lines were equally difficult

to attack, and when once Japanese barges carrying reinforcements had safely reached the coast the troops could quickly disperse in the bush, thus avoiding concentrations.

So the fighting, which was carried out continuously until the early autumn, devolved upon Australian troops specially trained for the work. It was jungle warfare, not spectacular but particularly strenuous, the object being not only to locate and destroy enemy fortified positions, but to clear each area in turn in preparation for the main onslaughts on the bases. The devastating precision of the blows that followed was in great part due to the dogged courage and endurance of the Australian troops who prepared the way.

A violent battle for Wau took place in January. Wau town, with its large airfield, was the seat of the administrative headquarters of the Morobe goldfields. It has a lovely situation at 3,000 ft. above sea level at the southern end of the Bulolo Valley, on the flank of Kuper Range which rises

steeply to the north. The airfield has a landing ground 1,100 yards long with the upper end inclined 300 ft. Several trails (named after gold mines) radiate from Wau, of which two leading to Salamaua via Mubo are in general use— the shorter is 34 miles long: but it should be noted that the only accurate measurement of these trails is by track hours. By air the distance between Wau and Salamaua is 26 miles.

This important inland airfield remained in Australian hands as a potential base from which to recover the coastal area. It was defended in the early **Defence of** days of the Japanese **Wau Airfield** invasion by the New Guinea Volunteer Rifles (formed of resident miners and colonists of the Mandated Territory). This small force was augmented by Australian Independent Companies (Commandos) and was then known as the Kanga Force. Vigilant patrols were maintained in surrounding districts, for the Allies realized that a strong force of Japanese

WAU AIRSTRIP FROM THE AIR

This view of Wau airstrip, taken during the Japanese attempt to capture it in January 1943, clearly shows the unusual nature of this valuable landing-ground: the upper end of the 1,100-yard strip is some 300 feet higher than the lower. It was one of the chief bases for the Allied advance towards Salamaua and Lae, and was the scene of one of the decisive battles of the campaign, described above. *Photo, Australian Official*

GUNS BY AIR SAVED WAU AIRFIELD

The Australian troops guarding Wau airfield were at a minimum when the Japanese launched a strong attack on January 30, 1943. But the arrival by air of 25-pounder guns of the 2/1st Australian Field Regiment turned the scale. 1. Men of the 17th Australian Brigade leaving their transport planes on Wau airfield: they went straight into action against the Japanese, who were within rifle shot. 2. Under snipers' fire, gunners assembled their 25-pounders, just unloaded from the transport planes. 3. A 25-pounder in action at Wau. 4. Refreshment for the gunners after the repulse of the Japanese. *Photos, Australian Official*

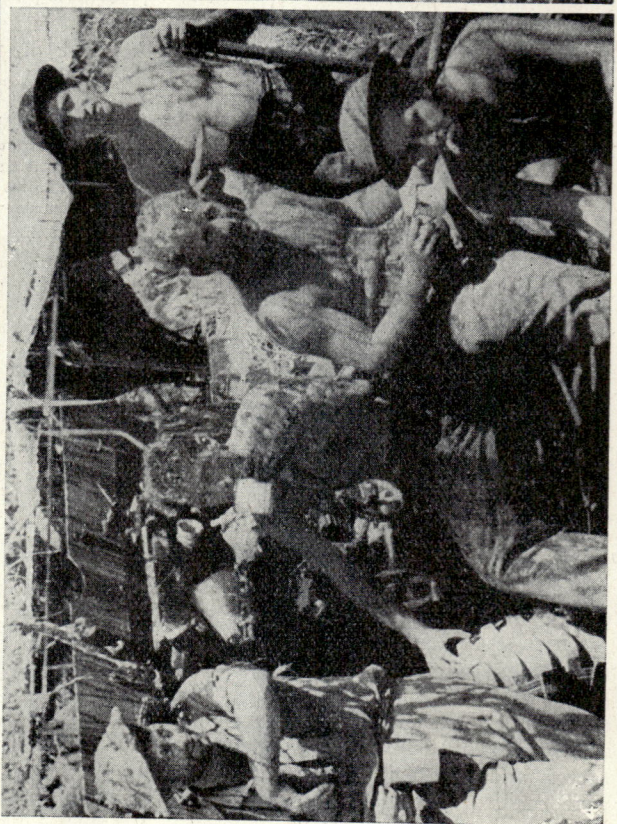

GUNFIRE FROM WAU'S DEFENDERS

Shells from Allied 25-pounders bursting among Japanese positions a stone's throw from the air-field at Wau. Below, Captain W. Sherlock, who commanded 'A' company, 2/6 Battalion, in their heroic defence of Wandumi ridge, which held up the Japanese attack just long enough to allow reinforcements to reach Wau by air from Port Moresby. Those reinforcements turned the scale. Capt. Sherlock and many of his men were killed. *Photos, Australian Official*

was based on Mubo and sooner or later an attack on Wau might be expected from that direction.

The Japanese outpost of Mubo, 16 miles from Salamaua, was twice raided from Wau at the end of 1942, and again in January 1943 a severe raid was carried out. This was after Japanese assault troops had been landed at Lae, despite the destruction of most of their barges by the Allied air force. It became evident that an attack on Wau was imminent, so the Kanga Force was reinforced from Fort Moresby by an Australian infantry brigade, and Brigadier M. J. Moten took over the command. Further reinforcements were detailed, but their arrival was delayed.

Meanwhile, the Japanese attacked in force by a route from Mubo which had fallen into disuse. Although that manoeuvre enabled them to advance to the Wandumi area near Bulolo River before they were detected, this initial advantage was nullified by their having to reopen overgrown parts of the track. The delay thus caused proved of immense importance to the Wau garrison. On January 27 a patrol force under Captain Sherlock (part of 'A' Co., 2/6

Battn.) made the first contact with the Japanese advance troops, and gallantly held them for 48 hours until a relief party arrived. A delaying action was then fought farther up the river with Maj. Muir (Brigade) and Maj. Duffy (2/5 Battn.) in command, until an enemy force of many hundreds succeeded in infiltrating the deep valley of Wau. During the wet and misty night of January 28–29, one strong enemy group came within half a mile of the airfield, but was exterminated. Early in the morning the weather, which had held up reinforcements at Port Moresby, suddenly cleared : at 9 a.m. the drone of aero-engines was heard, and transport planes made a perfect landing. More troops of the A.I.F. disembarked and went straight into the battle ; 57 landings were made that day. Next morning troops of an Australian field regiment were flown in with 25-pounder guns. These, assembled under continual sniper fire as fast as they were unloaded, went into action immediately, and, aided

by Beaufighters manned by Australians, began systematically to blast the Japanese off the surrounding ridges.

The enemy lost very heavily, few returning to the coast. Captured orders revealed that the attacks on Wau had been planned to take place on the 27th instead of the 30th January. Wau had certainly been saved by the delaying actions fought by small Australian forces, particularly that under Captain Sherlock, who, unfortunately, was killed.

Far from being discouraged by their defeats at Buna and Wau, the Japanese persisted in their offensive strategy, and now redoubled their efforts to increase their hold on New Guinea. At the beginning of March a large convoy of Japanese reinforcements in the Bismarck Sea was wiped out by Allied bombers (*see page* 2602). Subsequently, while the Allies were clearing sites formerly occupied by Japanese on the Mambare River in Papua, they discovered preparations for a strong base with gun positions and pillboxes, a hospital, and installations for a large force. It was concluded that this had been the destination of the ill-fated convoy. On April 14 the enemy raided Milne Bay airfield in force.

Japanese Continue their Offensive

THE CAMPAIGN IN NEW GUINEA

The Japanese were cleared from the Papua area of New Guinea by January 16, 1943, and then the Allies began to advance north and west in the direction of Madang and Wewak. This map indicates the strategic importance of Vitiaz Strait and the development of the whole 1943 Allied campaign in New Guinea. This Chapter describes that part of it which took place in the area shown enclosed in a rectangle, an enlarged map of which is opposite.

Allied aircraft available were barely adequate for defence purposes and quite insufficient for taking the offensive.

Mr. Forde and Dr. H. Evatt, Minister of the Army and Minister of External Affairs respectively in the Australian Government, added their voices to his. General Sir Thomas Blamey, touring operational bases in North Australia, warned troops to be on their guard against sudden Japanese attack; and stated that in his opinion even five per cent of American and British output of war material made effective in the South-West Pacific would give the Allies victory in that area. At the end of April Maj.-Gen. George Kenney (C.-in-C. Allied Air Forces in S.W. Pacific) and Maj.-Gen. R. Sutherland went on a special mission to the United States to ask for increased support.

The Allies did not relax their air attacks on all vulnerable points, convoys and troop concentrations, and airfields, not only in all parts of occupied New Guinea but in the Netherlands Indies as well. Estimated Japanese losses for 12 months up to April 1943 showed very serious shipping losses, and 3,000 aircraft destroyed, which was the annual total produced by Japanese factories. Yet greater Allied strength was needed both for reconnaissance and to deal more vigorous blows at the enemy. General MacArthur, C.-in.-C., S.W. Pacific, issued grave warnings that the enemy had great forces assembled within striking distance of Australia, that so long as the Japanese controlled the sea

lanes to Australia the Allies could not pass over to the offensive; Allied defences ought to consist primarily of land-based air forces defended by ground troops, and these could not be established without greatly augmented supplies and especially an amphibious force. He declared that the loss or winning of the battle of the South-West Pacific depended upon a proper application of the air-ground team, that if the Allies lost command of the air, no naval forces could save them, and that the

During the following months the Japanese were gradually driven from their outposts in the Salamaua area by Australian ground forces operating from Wau, under the command of Brigadier Savige, who planned this part of the campaign. Salamaua town occupies an area on the isthmus of Salamaua Peninsula and extends south-east on to the mainland. It is the port of the Bulolo goldfields, and before the Japanese invasion there were daily air and motor-boat services to and from Lae. North of the town, between the Peninsula and Kela Point, is a sheltered inlet, Samoa (formerly Salamaua) Harbour (see map opposite). On the mainland are forested hills, the sharp spurs and hogbacks of which the enemy had utilized to form outer defence works for the town and harbour. Covered with kunai grass or high forest, these blind positions could not well be seen from the air. It was the task of the

Allied Advance On Salamaua

ADVANCE ON MUBO AND SALAMAUA

Left, manhandling a piece of artillery across a creek near Nassau Bay, where American forces landed on June 30, 1943, despite strong opposition. Australian troops from the interior contacted them on July 2, and the combined force advanced on Mubo, which they captured on the 15th. Right, Australians and Americans who fought from Nassau Bay to Mubo gaze at Salamaua, still to be conquered.

Photos, Sport & General

Australian artillery and commando troops to win one position after another, often with bitter fighting, and to clear the ground of foxholes, pillboxes and traps until they commanded the entire area. The strain of such bush warfare in this nerve-racking country is intense. Brigadier Savige later described the conditions as the most difficult of any experienced in New Guinea, not excepting those of the Owen Stanley Range. Transport problems were solved by a system of supply by air and, so that the men should not be overtaxed, front line troops were sent back periodically for 48 hours' rest in special camps.

On May 9 the Allies occupied Bobdubi village, on Francisco River near Salamaua, captured the ridge above and held it successfully against counter-attacks. Bobdubi Ridge controls the main trail to Salamaua where it turns south from Francisco River towards Komiatum. On June 30, U.S. troops landed in Nassau Bay, 11 miles south of Salamaua. They encountered strong opposition but consolidated their position after inflicting heavy casualties on the enemy. They also occupied Trobriand and Woodlark Islands, between New Guinea and the Solomons, without opposition. A few days later General MacArthur arrived in New Guinea to direct operations in person. Mubo, overlooking the harbour of Salamaua, was surrounded and occupied by Australian and U.S. troops, in spite of strong resistance, on July 15. One force was then sent eastward to meet American units advancing up the coast from Nassau Bay. On 16th–18th a severe battle for Tambu Mt. took place, a small force of the A.I.F. dislodging 1,000 entrenched Japanese,

U.S. Landing in Nassau Bay

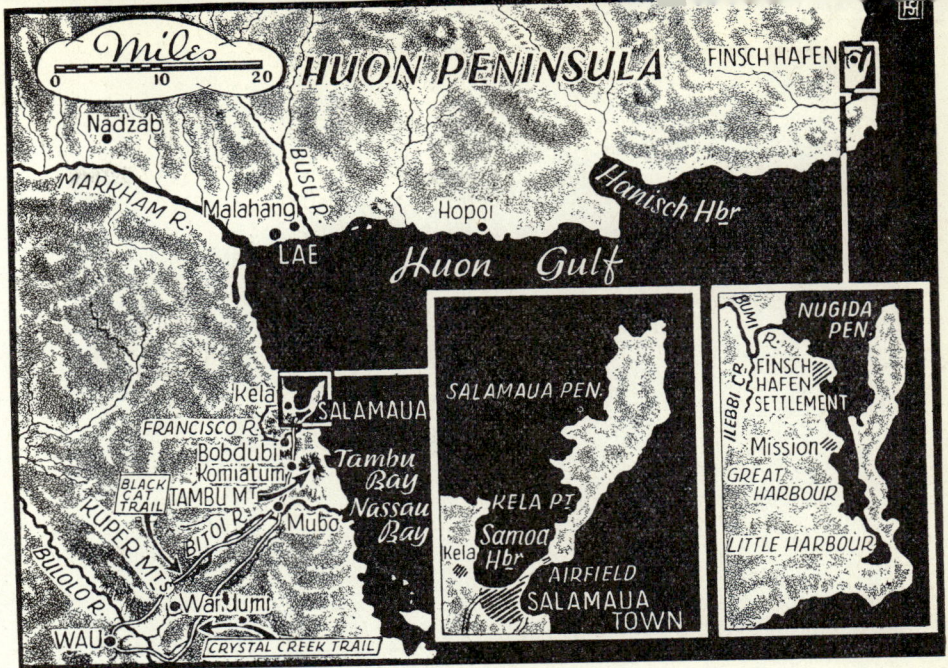

THE BATTLES OF HUON GULF

This map shows the tricky mountainous country in which the campaign of Huon Gulf was fought. Added to the difficulties that can be deduced from the map were others which a map cannot indicate—the tropical climate, with its inevitable accompaniment of insect pests, and alternating dense forest and swamp crossed by only the most primitive tracks.

Specially drawn for THE SECOND GREAT WAR *by Harrop*

killing something like a half of them. The enemy light artillery was markedly inefficient, and the battle ended in a rout, the Japanese abandoning much equipment and even throwing away their rifles. By August 9 the Australians had captured Kela Ridge (1,200 ft. above Salamaua airfield).

The Allied attack on Lae, the largest amphibious operation carried out up to this time in the South-West Pacific, began at dawn on September 4 with a naval bombardment by American warships. Under cover of a smoke-screen and protected by warships, troops of the Australian Field Division (veterans

of the Middle East fighting) were landed in large American transport barges at Hopoi on the coast east of Lae, while Australian and U.S. pilots maintained absolute air supremacy. Within three-quarters of an hour full equipment was on shore with the troops—jeeps and bulldozers, caterpillar tractors, anti-aircraft guns, and heavy artillery. On the first day an advance of eight to ten miles was made. The Commander-in-Chief directed operations from a destroyer; with him were General Sir Thomas Blamey, commanding ground forces, Maj.-Gen. George Kenney (U.S. air force), and Admiral A. S. Carpender (U.S. Commander of Naval Operations). The Australian artillery was under the command of Lt. John N. Pearson, aged 22 years. The enemy was quite unprepared. By the time the Japanese

FIERCE FIGHTING FOR MOUNT TAMBU

Left, an American and an Australian at a heavy machine-gun post 60 yards from Japanese positions on Mt. Tambu. Right, one of the guns of an American battery firing at targets on Mt. Tambu and the Komiatum track. These guns were carried in parts of 100 to 250 lb. weight each over the precipitous Lobabia ridge from Nassau Bay, the gradient frequently being almost 1 in 1.

Photos, Paul Popper; Sport & General

DESCENT ON THE MARKHAM VALLEY

A rain of American parachutists—the first to go into action in the Pacific area—dropped on September 5, 1943, in the Markham Valley, west of Lae, to prevent the escape of the 20,000 Japanese troops there from the Australians landed east of the town. The smoke screen in the background conceals the manoeuvre from the Japanese across the river. Right, General MacArthur watches the hazardous operation from an American bomber. (See also illus., p. 2665.)

batteries at Lae opened fire, the first barges had landed troops and were returning empty. The batteries were soon silenced by the naval guns.

Next day U.S. parachute troops were dropped in the Markham Valley, on the left river bank. After leaving the high mountain chain where it has its source, Markham River flows for the greater part of its course through a wide plain with large mangrove swamps. The banks are low and muddy, and the bed impeded by mud islets covered in mangroves. But beyond the mouth the valley widens out into a fertile plain which has been under cultivation by Lutheran missionaries, who also constructed many air strips there and in the upper valley. The U.S. parachute troops cut off Japanese forces higher up the valley, seized the western approaches to Lae, and joined up with Australian forces who had marched 55 miles through the jungle in five days.

On September 6 other U.S. parachute troops, dropped near Lae, approached the Busu River, which flows into the Gulf of Huon four miles east of Lae; while troops of the A.I.F., fighting through dense jungle country, captured Nadzab, a Japanese air base 20 miles west of Lae.

During the attack on an enemy position at Nadzab, on the morning of September 13, Private Richard Kelliher won the thirteenth Victoria Cross awarded to Australians in the war.

His platoon came under heavy fire from a concealed enemy machine-gun post 50 yards away. Five of them were killed and three wounded, and it was found impossible to advance without further losses. In the face of these casualties, Private Kelliher suddenly, on his own initiative and without orders, dashed towards the post and hurled two grenades at it, killing some of the enemy, but not all. Noting this, he then returned to his section, seized a Bren gun, again dashed forward to within 30 yards of the post, and with accurate fire completely silenced it.

Returning from his already gallant action, Private Kelliher next requested permission to go forward and rescue his wounded section leader. This he successfully accomplished, though under heavy rifle fire from another position. Private Kelliher, by these actions, acted as an inspiration to everyone in his platoon, and not only enabled the advance to continue but also saved his section leader's life. His most conspicuous bravery and extreme devotion to duty in the face of heavy enemy fire resulted in the capture of this strong enemy position.

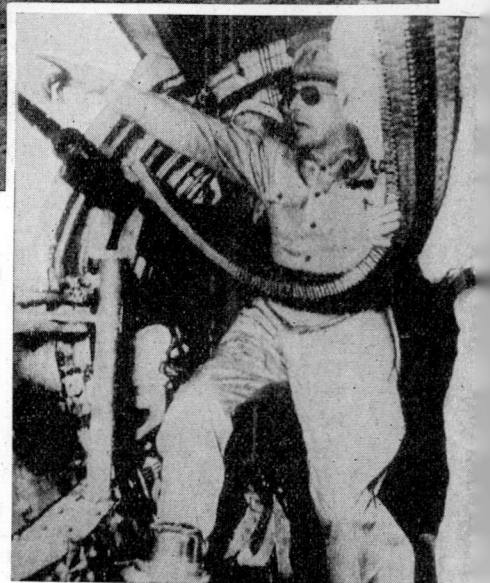

From Nadzab strong reinforcements of the A.I.F., flown in by transport plane, fanned out towards Lae. On September 10 the Allies made a successful crossing of the Busu by boat and pontoon bridge. Japanese resistance in the Lae-Salamaua district was local, their forces not being concentrated. Large areas of *kunai* grass were

THE BROTHERHOOD OF MAN

War produced no more striking example of man's brotherhood than that which developed between Australian troops and the frizzy-haired natives of New Guinea. Here, a native helps an Australian wounded in the fierce fighting for Mt. Tambu in mid-July 1943. Mt. Tambu, six miles from Salamaua, had been turned into a strong network of defences by the enemy. A handful of Australians captured it, killing some 500 out of 1,000 Japanese, and held it for three days and nights against 17 determined counter-attacks until the arrival of fresh Allied troops.

3A 3

VICTORY PARADE IN TUNIS
Pipers of the 51st Highland Division—part of that great Eighth Army which, under Montgomery's leadership, had helped so mightily to hit Rommel ' for six ' right out of Africa—in the Victory Parade through Tunis on May 20, 1943. All the Allied commanders were present, and Generals Eisenhower, Alexander, Anderson and Giraud took the salute at the march past. Mr. Macmillan, British Minister, and Mr. Murphy, U.S. Minister, represented civil affairs.   *Photo, British Official*

TRAINLOAD OF HAPPY ITALIAN PRISONERS

Some of the 252,300 Axis prisoners taken in Tunisia entrained for Tunis on their way to a more permanent camp from temporary compounds at Grombalia. The total Axis casualties from November 8, 1942, when the Allied landings in French North Africa began, until the clearing of all enemy forces from North Africa were about 300,000, more than half of them Germans. Total enemy losses in N. and E. Africa (killed, wounded, prisoners) were not far short of a million. The Germans remained resentful of capture; the Italians for the most part were pleased to be out of the fighting.

Photo, British Official

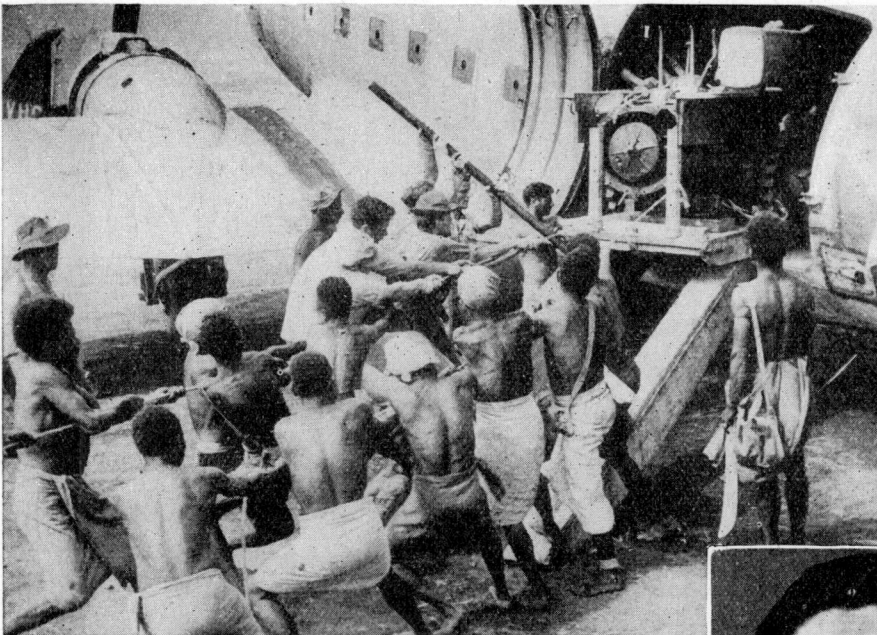

SUPPLIES CAME IN TO NADZAB BY AIR

Equipment for the drive on Lae being unloaded at Nadzab by black men and white working shoulder to shoulder after the capture of this airfield by Australian troops who fought through the jungle to reach it. The story of how Private Richard Kelliher (right) won the V.C. at Nadzab is told in page 2758 : he was photographed while convalescing from malaria. Born in Ballybeggan, Co. Kerry, he migrated to Australia in 1929. *Photo, Sport & General*

was struck at Finsch Hafen, on the south-east coast of Huon Peninsula, where two amphibious landings were made on September 22, the first, six miles north of Finsch Hafen, the second, 32 miles (by water) to the south-west at Hanisch Harbour. (*See* map, page 2757.)

The harbour of Finsch Hafen lies between the mainland and the Nugida Peninsula, which is about six miles long and one mile across at the widest part. The airfield is farther north on the left bank of Bumi River. The coasts are mainly densely wooded, rocky cliffs ; there are few beaches favourable for landing operations. Inland are series of low hills with patches of high forest, thickets of bamboo and *kunai* grass. The whole area had been leased to the Lutheran Mission since the time when the Territory was a German Protectorate. Coconut has been planted on a large scale. Good roads of coral rock intersect the plantations and follow the coast to the jetty, and these were of considerable advantage to the Allies.

The terrain, moreover, did not present so many engineering problems as that of the Lae landings ; but it made very

combed for the enemy, but none was found, though some sharp fighting took place as outposts were disclosed. The main routes by which the Japanese could withdraw from their bases were covered, and some who escaped in small parties to the surrounding hills were rounded up later, the force in the upper valley of the Markham being taken prisoner.

An Australian militia unit swam the flooded Francisco River to capture Salamaua airfield on September 13. Salamaua itself, almost destroyed by **Fall of Salamaua and Lae** Allied bombing, was taken next day. The enemy fled into the jungle, abandoning hundreds of dead and much equipment, including artillery. Lae fell two days later, the Japanese fleeing as at Salamaua. No escape by sea had been possible as the American navy and Allied air force had entire command of the Gulf of Huon. There was no sign of enemy naval activity during this period, although it had been expected that barges would attempt to slip along the coast at night to rescue remnants of the scattered Japanese forces.

The Allies had now won three good airfields from which to attack the Japanese positions farther up the coast : the large airfield of Lae, that of Malahang, less than two miles away, and Hopoi airfield, 25 miles east of Lae.

In a short time these were made serviceable.

The next blow

BOMB-RAVAGED SALAMAUA

Allied bombing devastated the Salamaua peninsula. The truck depot, boat landings and main Japanese headquarters were completely destroyed. It was captured on September 14, 1943, when the enemy fled into the jungle abandoning hundreds of their dead and much equipment, including artillery. Lae, the only remaining strong Japanese base in the area, was taken two days later. *Photo, Planet News*

DELIVER URGENTLY
BLOOD FOR TRANSFUSION

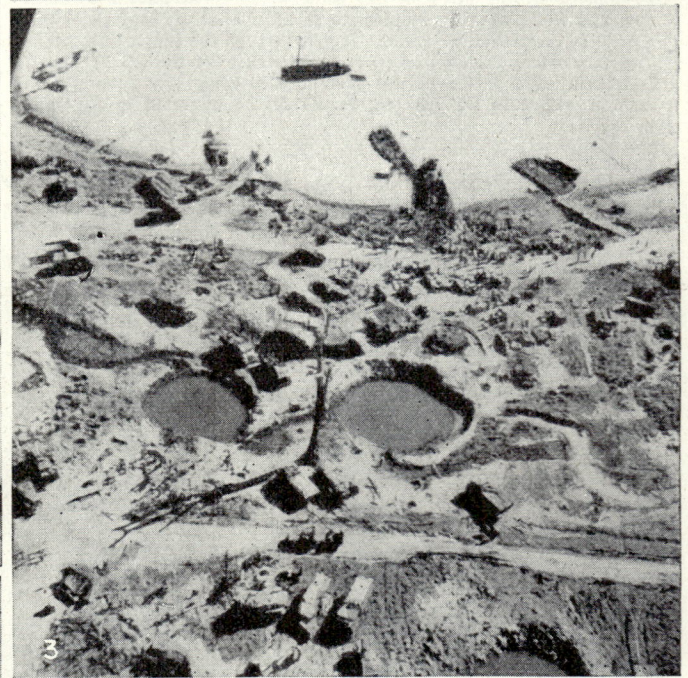

ASSAULT ON LAE

The Allied attack on Lae began at dawn on September 4, 1943, with the landing of forces and full equipment at Hopoi, an operation at which the Australian Boomerang fighter plane, a high-altitude interceptor, went into action for the first time. The landing was followed by the dropping of parachute troops inland. Lae fell on the 16th. 1. Bulldozers manned by Allied soldiers break a way for an assault on Lae; artillery followed. 2. Blood for transfusion to the wounded being brought ashore from a landing barge by natives. 3. The waterfront at Lae after attention from American bombers and Australian artillery. 4. Australian troops march into Lae through country devastated by land and air bombardment.

Photos, Associated Press; Planet News; "New York Times" Photos; Keystone

MATILDA TANKS IN THE FINSCH HAFEN AREA
Arrival of a Matilda tank to support the Australian Imperial Forces in their struggle against the Japanese at Finsch Hafen. Below, a group of Matildas carries out manoeuvres preparatory to going into action to familiarize the drivers with the kind of country in which they had to fight.

without the amphibious force and airborne landings this thorough uprooting of the Japanese from their strongly fortified positions would have been impossible in that time.

As at Lae, American bulldozers and jeeps played an important **Reasons for Allied Success** part. American engineers disembarked with the first troops to prepare tracks laid with wire mesh for the heavy landing craft which were navigated and manned by Americans. American transport planes were also used throughout. After the landing operations Australian engineers and pioneer troops took over the responsibility of all further communications inland, making subsidiary roads and bridges.

The offensive had developed according to plan, and the Allies now commanded the Huon Gulf and the Vitiaz Strait. They had forced the enemy to abandon that part of his strategy which had depended upon this area, and his defence system based on Rabaul had been breached. The Allies were in a position to concentrate upon their main objective : the re-occupation of the important island of New Britain.

BOMBS ON WEWAK
Parachute bombs falling among heavily camouflaged Japanese planes during an Allied raid in the Wewak area. The campaign in New Guinea was the first time these bombs were used extensively : they kept Japanese troops and pack trains off the trails, frequently preventing the enemy from procuring supplies of food and water.

exacting demands upon the fighting troops.

Australian infantry belonging to the Ninth Division of El Alamein fame were landed at dawn and at once engaged by Japanese marines. A sharp fight followed but the enemy was routed by bayonet charges, and retired to a prepared position in a mission plantation south of Bumi River. The Allied beach-head was held in spite of counter-attacks. While some troops kept the enemy engaged at the river mouth, part of the force was deployed to cross higher up, thereby gaining high ground overlooking Finsch Hafen. The airfield was captured by September 24. Two days later the Australians had crossed

the Bumi and some troops were east of Ilebbi Creek and half a mile from Finsch Hafen. In the meantime, the southern force had advanced up the coast from Hanisch Harbour and the Japanese garrison and marines found themselves trapped. Small parties fled into the surrounding bush, but their efforts to reach the shore were frustrated and after 11 days' stubborn fighting the Finsch Hafen area was cleared.

Allied artillery again proved superior to that of the Japanese. Concentrated fire from 25-pounder guns demolished the bunkers and pillboxes which made up the Japanese defences, and the attacks from the rear of their positions had a speedy demoralizing effect, but

Chapter 277

THE AXIS 'HIT FOR SIX' OUT OF AFRICA

*The advance of the Eighth Army to Wadi Akarit was covered in Chapter 265 ;
the operations of the First Army with the U.S. forces up to the battle for the
Kasserine Pass were described in Chapter 264. In this Chapter Mr. A. D. Divine
brings the North African campaigns to their climax with the junction of the
Allied armies from east and west and their final successful assault on Tunis*

FIFTEEN miles to the eastward of El Guetar, beyond the bloody strong-point of "Hot Corner," a patrol of the Eighth Army, racing northward, met on April 7, 1943, the reconnaissance of the American Second Corps thrusting down the dusty Gabes road towards the sea. The junction of the armies of the east and west, so long and so ardently desired, was accomplished.

This was the physical junction. There had been contact before up through the desert backways by Tozeur, but this was the strategic reunion. It was the outward and visible sign of what had already taken place in the command. Mr. Churchill had announced on February 11 in the House of Commons that the allied command

had been re-arranged. Eisenhower, at Algiers, remained generalissimo of the whole theatre of operations. Sir Harold Alexander, coming past the Eighth Army by air, took over the fighting command with absolute authority over the British First Army, the Americans, the French, and the Eighth. With him came Air Chief Marshal Tedder to direct all air operations, with Air Vice-Marshal Coningham as his deputy. Admiral of the Fleet Sir Andrew Cunningham remained as Commander-in-Chief of naval operations. The combined forces were to be known as the 18th Army Group.

There was an apparent simplification of the general problem. The speed of the lightning Axis retreat across the Tunisian plain meant that in a very

short and foreseeable time General Alexander would have to fight on one front only. It was obvious now that the Axis commanders had decided upon holding what came to be known as "the Tunis box." This was an area which began at Enfidaville on the coast of the Gulf of Hammamet and ran in a demi-lune roughly through Pont du Fahs, Medjez-el-Bab, the hills beyond Beja and Sedjenane (*see* map, page 2772).

It was not what the enemy had hoped to hold. In the south the line was determined automatically by the hills of the Zaghouan massif. That was as planned. It is probable that the Axis holdings beyond Pont du Fahs in the eastern dorsale were considered sufficient for their purpose, but it was in the centre of the line that their greatest weakness was apparent ; and it was this centre that had been so gallantly captured by the thin force of the First Army in the initial rush for Tunis ; it was this area that had been so gallantly held

Weakness of Enemy Centre

ANGLO-AMERICAN MEETING IN TUNISIA

On April 7, 1943, at a point 15 miles east of El Guetar, a patrol of the British Eighth Army, racing northward, met reconnaissance units of the U.S. Second Corps of the First Army advancing towards Gabes. Here is the scene as the two forces clambered from their vehicles and ran joyfully towards one another to celebrate this first contact between the men who had come through from El Alamein and those who had made the landings in French North Africa.

Photo, British Newsreels

by them through the bitter reverses and the intolerable weather of the Tunisian winter.

It is within the bounds of possibility that the gallantry of the 155th Field Battery at Sidi Nsir and the heroic defence of Hunt's Gap were the determining factors in the swiftness of the collapse of the "Tunis box" (*see* page 2624). Beyond that, to the north again, Sedjenane, captured by Colonel Witzig and his parachute troops, probably represented the limits of enemy ambition. The Axis forces, in the thrust that ended at Hunt's Gap, had hoped to drive the Allies back to and beyond Beja. If the Allies had had to launch the attack on Tunis from the valley of the Kroumirie, it might have cost six months and 50,000 men.

By April 13 the scurry—it can scarcely be called a campaign—of South Tunisia was over. But before it ended there

End of South Tunisia Campaign

took place one of the most remarkable assaults in all that history of battle. As the enemy streamed north up the coast road through Sousse and the inner road through Kairouan, the Allies made a desperate last attempt to cut them off. Pichon was overwhelmed, but beyond Pichon lay the little Fondouk Pass, heavily covered by mines and strongly held by the enemy. To cut off Messe it was necessary to smash a way through. To smash a way through, the hills on either side had first to be captured. The Welsh Guards captured the northern hill; an American attack on the southern hill failed. The one essential was time. Regardless of loss, the tanks of the Sixth Armoured

ARMOUR OF THE EIGHTH MEETS THE FIRST

Here is the crew of an Eighth Army armoured car greeting men of the First Army when the two armies joined up on April 11, 1943, some 20 miles from Fondouk, between Kairouan and Sbiba. Below, troops of the French forces from the Chad, commanded by General Jacques Philippe LeClerc, which entered Tunisia with the Eighth Army, drive through Kairouan, holy city of North African Muslims, on April 12, 1943, the day after it fell to patrols of the First Army.

THE 'DESERT RATS'

Sign of the veteran Desert Rats, a British motorized brigade that won fame by its unequalled exploits in desert warfare. It included at different times the Rifle Brigade, K.R.R.C., R.H.A., R.A.S.C., R.E., R.A.M.C., Light A.A., 11th Hussars, K.D.G.s and S.A.A.C.; and armoured car regiments co-operated with it.

Division were ordered to smash their way across the minefield. Thirty Sherman tanks were lost in clearing the passage, but a gap was made and through it the rest of the armour streamed. The delay, however, had been fatal—the Allies were too late at Kairouan, though on April 10, 18 out of 30 German tanks were knocked out outside the city. At 11.50 on April 11 a battalion of the 12th Lancers met scout cars of the Derbyshire Yeomanry south of Kairouan, and the British armies were joined. But Messe had reached the mountain "box" of North Tunisia, and effected the junction with the forces under Von

Arnim, who now assumed command of all Axis forces in Africa.

At once General Alexander began to regroup his armies for the final victory. The Americans in the south had now no enemy to face. In a masterly lateral movement, masterfully handled, he swung them across the rear of the First Army to the north. With them he placed a formerly dissident French group, the Corps d'Afrique, composed of Spanish refugees, adventurers of all sorts, and De Gaullists, strengthened with Moroccan Goum. The junction with the First Army was in the initial stages approximately at Beja. From there the First

Lt.-Col. H. R. B. FOOTE
(Royal Tank Regiment)
He was awarded the V.C. for outstanding courage and leadership during the Libyan retreat in May–June, 1942 (see Chapter 224). By his initiative on June 6 he prevented the encirclement of two Allied divisions, and on June 13 delayed enemy tanks while the Guards Brigade was withdrawn from Knightsbridge.

Maj. J. R. M. ANDERSON
(Argyll and Sutherlands)
He reorganized his unit in the assault on Longstop, April 23, 1943, after the battalion commander had been killed and all other company commanders were among the heavy casualties. With only four other officers and less than 40 other ranks left, he captured the ridge. He was awarded the V.C.

Lt. W. A. S. CLARKE
(Loyal Regiment)
He received the V.C. for conspicuous gallantry in the attack on Guiriat El Atach, April 23, 1943. Wounded and the sole remaining officer of his company, he gathered a platoon and under cover of their fire silenced three machine-gun posts single-handed. He was killed advancing again to clear two sniper-posts.

Army held the line eastward until the French took over from them on the eastern dorsale. The Eighth Army took on from the French a little to the west of Djebibina.

General Alexander's plan was to make his major thrust in the centre along one of the two major avenues—the Medjez–Tunis or the Pont du Fahs–Tunis road—and General Anderson and the First Army were entrusted with the assault. The function of the Eighth Army was to hold, both by small-scale attacks and by the weight of its prestige, the greatest possible concentration of German troops in the south. The armour of the Eighth Army was to be swung up to the Bou Arada area to reinforce the Sixth Armoured Division.

This was the landward ring. There were others. The Axis armies of Africa were beleaguered. On the sea the navy was completing the superb work it had begun in the first days of the movement of the invasion armies. Between Cape Blanc and Marittimo, destroyers of the " L " class maintained an almost nightly patrol reinforced, when necessary, by the cruisers of Force Q. In the shallow water the inshore squadrons became with every day of the succeeding weeks more daring. From patrols that took them as far as Cape Blanc and the approaches to Bizerta on the north and to Cape Bon on the eastern coast, they passed to impudent raids in the Gulf of Tunis itself. Seaborne supply was cut down

to a desperate thing of Sebel ferries and fast mosquito craft.

The enemy took to the air—or, rather, they trebled their effort in the air—to make good the deficiencies of the sea. And in the air they were broken utterly. Mareth had begun the last phase of the collapse of the Luftwaffe in Africa.

Axis Utterly Broken in the Air

The progression was swift, bloody and disastrous. In a little the Axis planes were beaten almost out of the sky. Men in the fighting areas scarcely looked up when aircraft passed overhead. Men in transport on the roads hardly bothered to scan the air.

On April 5, over 200 enemy aircraft were destroyed, some fifty of them (including 18 Ju-52 transports) in the air. On April 18, 58 Dornier transport aircraft, carrying petrol and reinforcements of men, were shot down. On this and the next day 95 enemy aircraft were destroyed. On April 24 a strongly escorted group of 20 of the six-engined power gliders approaching the coast were pounced on by South African aircraft of the Western Desert Air Force and blotted out of the sky, together with 10 of their escorting fighters.

The navy had made the night passage of the Sicilian Narrows very near to suicide. The air, combining with the older Service, made the daylight run impossible. The Axis was ringed. Reinforcement was virtually at an end. Escape was virtually denied. The stage was set for disaster.

BRITISH REGIMENTS WHICH FOUGHT IN TUNISIA : Nov. 1942—May 1943.

First Army

Argyll and Sutherland Highlanders.
Bedfordshire and Hertfordshire Regiment.
Black Watch.
Coldstream Guards.
Derbyshire Yeomanry.
Duke of Cornwall's Light Infantry.
Duke of Wellington's Regiment (West Riding).
Durham Light Infantry.
East Surrey Regiment.
Gordon Highlanders.
Grenadier Guards.
Hampshire Regiment.
10th Hussars.
Irish Guards.
King's Own Yorkshire Light Infantry.
King's Royal Rifle Corps.
King's Shropshire Light Infantry.
Lancashire Fusiliers.
16/5th Lancers.
17/21st Lancers.
Leicestershire Regiment.
Lincolnshire Regiment.
London Irish Rifles (18th London Regiment).
Lothian and Border Yeomanry.
Loyal Regiment (North Lancashire).

Northamptonshire Regiment.
North Irish Horse.
North Staffordshire Regiment.
Queen's Bays (2nd Dragoon Guards).
Queen's Own Royal West Kents.
9th Queen's Royal Lancers.
Rifle Brigade.
Royal East Kent Regiment (Buffs).
Royal Fusiliers (City of London Regiment).
Royal Inniskilling Fusiliers.
Royal Irish Fusiliers.
Scots Guards.
Sherwood Foresters (Nottinghamshire and Derbyshire Regiment).
Welsh Guards.
York and Lancaster Regiment.
Units of Royal Armoured Corps.
Units of Royal Tank Regiment.
All ancillary arms.

Eighth Army

Argyll and Sutherland Highlanders.
Black Watch.
Cameron Highlanders.
Cheshire Regiment.
Coldstream Guards.
County of London Yeomanry.
Durham Light Infantry.
East Yorkshire Regiment.

Essex Regiment.
Gordon Highlanders.
Green Howards (Alexandra, Princess of Wales's Own Yorkshire Regiment).
Grenadier Guards.
11th Hussars.
1st King's Dragoon Guards.
King's Royal Rifle Corps.
Middlesex Regiment.
Nottinghamshire Yeomanry.
Oxfordshire and Buckinghamshire Light Infantry.
Queen's Royal Regiment (West Surrey).
Rifle Brigade.
1st Royal Dragoons.
Royal East Kent Regiment (Buffs).
Royal Fusiliers (City of London Regiment).
12th Royal Lancers.
Royal Northumberland Fusiliers.
Royal Sussex Regiment.
Scots Guards.
Seaforth Highlanders.
Staffordshire Yeomanry.
Units of Royal Armoured Corps.
Units of Royal Tank Regiment.
All ancillary arms.

Lce.-Cpl. J. P. KENEALLY
(Irish Guards)
Twice during the assault on the Bou, on April 28 and 30, 1943, he dashed forward single-handed with a Bren gun against a company of the enemy forming up to attack. On both occasions he broke up the attack—an achievement that can seldom have been equalled. It won him the V.C. *From the painting by Henry Carr, Crown Copyright*

The date of the final thrust to Tunis is usually given as May 6. It would be preferable to date it as far back as March 28, for on that date the Allies began a small offensive up the Sedjenane valley to recover from Colonel Witzig and his parachutists the ground they had won the previous month. It was the first of the necessary preparatory moves to clear the road to Tunis. By it, pressure on the flank above Beja was relieved. It was successful. The

MONTGOMERY IN SOUSSE

The Eighth Army occupied Sousse, third port of Tunisia, on April 12, 1943. When General Montgomery drove through the city on April 16, to be received by the civic and military authorities, he was given a great welcome by the people. Left, British troops of the Eighth searching for snipers in a deserted street of Enfidaville, captured on April 20 after very fierce fighting.

second began 10 days later, on April 7. It was planned to recapture the 10 peaks above Oued Zarga which dominated the triangle of roads between Beja, Mateur, and Medjez-el-Bab.

The Battle of the Ten Peaks is one of the masterpieces of the whole Tunisian campaign. It was almost the greatest achievement of that ill-appreciated body, the British First Army. At 4 o'clock on the morning of April 7, the battle began with a mass bombardment from 12 miles of guns along the Beja–Medjez road. Ten minutes later the infantry went in. Churchill tanks followed them at first light. For

VICTORY FOR THE FIRST ARMY IN TUNISIA

Bren carriers moving along the top of ' Recce ' Ridge during the large-scale attack by British troops and tanks which resulted in the capture of Toukabeur on April 8, 1943. Right, a Nazi flag left behind in captured Chaouach. Below, following the capture of Chaouach on April 9, and guided by air reconnaissance, First Army artillery laid a barrage on a high ridge north-west of Heidous, while infantry and tanks crept up to a point half a mile to the west. (See map, page 2773.)

Photos, British Official

the first time in this warfare of the "Djebels," tanks were thrown straight up steep mountain sides. The enemy had not believed this possible. There were few anti-tank guns throughout the area, and against the armour of the Churchills the heavy machine-guns were useless. Across slit trenches and weapon pits the tanks rumbled and groaned, and what the tanks flushed the infantry finished off. By the afternoon the first hill positions had been taken, and where Axis forces had been, Allied artillery was sited now.

The enemy threw in what was left of their air strength in a desperate attempt to retrieve the position, but the attempt was useless. By the second day of the attack, the Allies had five of the 10 hills and were eight miles into the Axis front, and the enemy were withdrawing from Hunt's Gap. It was a superb stroke in which artillery, tanks, infantry, supply and engineers were co-ordinated as they had never before been co-ordinated in mountain warfare.

On the night of April 13, as Messe reached the prepared line of Enfidaville, the battle for the second five hills began.

Djebel el Ang Captured   Almost at once the Lancashire Fusiliers took the Djebel el Ang, the commanding point of the whole massif. The 78th Division, the veterans of Tunisia, had made possible the first steps of the final victory.

It is necessary to make a comparison between November and April. In November of 1942 the "Tunis box" was held by a few battalions of parachutists and airborne troops hastily gathered together, by mortars and heavy machine-guns, backed with the first elements of the 10th Panzer Division. In April of 1943 it was held by a quarter of a million Germans and Italians strongly entrenched, with the preparations of six months behind them, in well-sited hill positions. To back them they had what remained of Rommel's and Von Arnim's armour, and the massive artillery support of two seasoned armies. They had had time to mine every gully and pass in the hills, every road and lane along the front from Enfidaville to Cap Serrat. That was the "box" that General Alexander had to open.

In the east the Eighth Army had come to a stop against the hills. General Montgomery had no open flank to exploit. His frontal attacks succeeded locally, and failed to make any deep impression on the German defences. From him General Alexander took three divisions, the Fourth Indian and the

2771

LAST BATTLE OF LONGSTOP RIDGE

Infantry of the First Army resting under a ridge above Kelbine after they had at last, on April 26, 1942, taken Djebel Ahmera, known as Longstop Ridge, which saw such bitter fighting in December 1942 (see page 2614). Top, Longstop Ridge, still in enemy hands: this formidable natural fortress had been turned by the Axis into one of the most powerful strong points in Tunisia. Below, stretcher bearers moving up behind the troops making the final assault. East Surreys shared the honours of the battle with the Argylls. *Photos, British Official*

First and Seventh Armoured, and brought them round behind the line to support General Anderson and the First Army.

There is an admirable rhythm in the design of his attack. It began on the night of the 19th with a small assault on the Eighth Army sector designed to keep occupied the disproportionate Axis strength that had been attracted by the prestige of the Eighth. The enemy, anticipating that the main attack would take place somewhere in the centre, tried to disrupt it twenty-four hours before the first phase was due to start. But they attacked in the wrong place. At 11 o'clock on the night of the 20th they attacked "Banana Ridge," immediately east of Medjez, with three battalions of infantry and 70 tanks, 40 from the north and 30 from the south. But the Allies were strong in the area in preparation for attack : the Axis assault was battered to pieces. Thirty-four tanks were knocked out and 400 prisoners taken, and the assault of the Sixth Armoured Division on the Bou Arada sector was in no wise delayed.

FROM MARETH TO THE OUTSKIRTS OF TUNIS

This map illustrates the prelude to the final stage in the North African campaign which started from El Alamein in the East, and Casablanca in the West. It covers the operations of General Alexander's armies from the end of March until April 19, 1943. The main enemy line then ran approximately as shown by the heavy shaded band from Cape Serrat to Enfidaville.

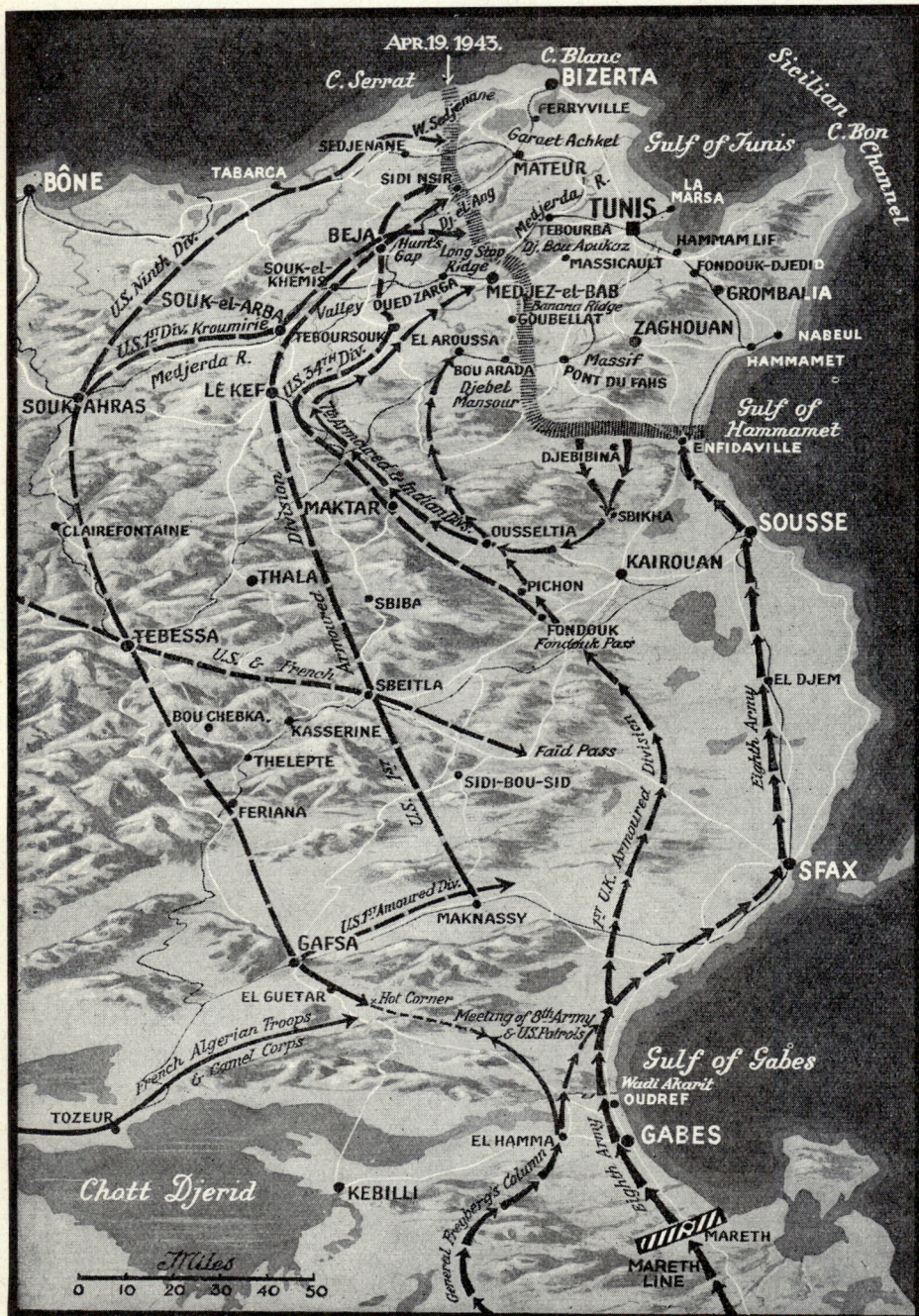

Special Order of the Day

HEADQUARTERS
18th ARMY GROUP
21st April, 1943

SOLDIERS OF THE ALLIES

1. Two months ago, when the Germans and Italians were attacking us, I told you that if you held firm, final victory was assured.

2. You did your duty and now you are about to reap its full reward.

3. We have reached the last phase of this campaign. We have grouped our victorious Armies and are going to drive the enemy into the sea.

   We have got them just where we want them—with their backs to the wall.

4. This final battle will be fierce, bitter and long, and will demand all the skill, strength and endurance of each one of us.

   But you have proved yourselves the masters of the battlefield, and therefore you will win this last great battle which will give us the whole of North Africa.

5. The eyes of the world are on you—and the hopes of all at home.

FORWARD THEN, TO VICTORY

H. R. Alexander

General,
Commander, 18th Army Group

BATTLE FOR TUNIS

General Sir Harold Alexander's Special Order of the Day to the Allied armies in North Africa before the final phase of the war in Tunisia. Tunis fell on May 6, armoured elements of the First Army entering the city at 3.40 p.m. after an advance of 23 miles in 36 hours against stiff resistance.

At 2 a.m. on April 22 the Bou Arada attack began. It was designed partially as an experiment to test the strength of the Axis holding (Bou Arada–Pont du Fahs was a good approach to Tunis) and partially to clear the right flank of the Medjez–Massicault main road to the capital. It did not break through, though it caused the enemy heavy losses in an indeterminate struggle amongst the little isolated hills that dotted the plain ; but it served its secondary purpose.

The left flank of the Medjez-el-Bab road was dominated by the old and brutal bastion of Longstop Ridge. The Allies attacked that on April 23. It took three days to capture Longstop—three of the **Capture of Longstop** hardest days' fighting in the whole history of Tunisia—and it was captured in the end by the Argylls and the East Surreys. Major Jack Anderson, leading the Argylls in the final charge, earned a magnificent V.C.

In the north there was another offensive. On the extreme seaward flank the Goum and the Corps d'Afrique had cut through the terrible scrub country of the coastal hills, and when Longstop fell they were six miles from the Garaet Achkel, the outermost of the two great lakes of Bizerta. Between

Map labels (as shown on the map):

MAIN AXIS DEFENCE LINE Apr. 19
C. Blanc
BIZERTA
C. Serrat
L. Bizerta
Garaet Achkel
Gulf of Tunis
C. Bon
SEDJENANE
MATEUR
PROTVILLE
Dj. Tahent
SIDI NSIR
Dj. el Ang
TEBOURBA
DJEDEIDA
TUNIS
LA GOULETTE
MENZEL HEURR
Dj. Bou Aoukaz
Long Stop Ridge
HEIDOUS
FRENDJ
MASSICAULT
Line intended for final Axis stand
HAMMAM LIF
SOLIMAN
Hunt's Gap
BEJA
CHAOUACH
MEDJEZ el BAB
Banana Ridge
OUDNA
GROMBALIA
TOURABEUR
OUED ZARGA
GOUBELLAT
DEPIENNE
NABEUL
TEBOURSOUK
ZAGHOUAN
HAMMAMET
EL AROUSSA
PONT DU FAHS
BOU ARADA
Gulf of Hammamet
ENFIDAVILLE
MAIN AXIS DEFENCE LINE Apr. 19. 1943
ROBAA
DJEBIBINA
Miles 0 10 20 30

AXIS OBLITERATED IN NORTH AFRICA

Dispositions of Allied and Axis forces during the final assault on the 'defence' box around Tunis—last action of the long-drawn-out North African operations. Allied troop movements before April 19, 1943, are shown by white arrows, and the direction of Allied attacks immediately after that date by solid black arrows. Allied encircling operations after the fall of Tunis are shown by broken black arrows. Numbers and letters (see list on right) show positions of units.

Maps based on information from official sources and specially drawn by Félix Gardon

Allied Forces

1 French
2 U.S. 9th Div.
3 U.S. 34th Div.
4 U.S. 1st Armoured Div.
5 U.S. 1st Div.
6 78th U.K. Div.
7 1st U.K. Div.
8 4th Indian Div.
9 7th U.K. Armoured Div.
10 6th U.K. Armoured Div.
11 4th U.K. Div.
12 1st and 6th U.K. Armoured Div.
13 46th U.K. Div.
14 French
15 French
16 7th U.K. Armoured Div.
17 French
18 4th Indian Div.
19 51st Highland Div.
20 French
21 2nd N.Z. Div. and Armoured Bgde.
22 50th U.K. Div.

Axis Forces

A Italian Marines
B Manteufel Group
C Part of 334th Div.
D 999th Div.
E Part of 334th Div. and Armour
F Hermann Goering Div.
G 10th Panzer Div.
H Superga Div.
I Remains of 21st Panzer Div.
J Remains of 15th Panzer Div.
K Remains of Trieste Div.
L Remains of Pistoia Div.
M Remains of Young Fascists Div.
N Centauro Div.
O 164th Light Div.
P 90th Light Div.

them and the First Army the Americans had gone forward superbly. It was vicious mountain country; limestone ridges, like the comb of an angry cockerel, stood out of the steep shoulders of the hills. It was a place of knife edges and jagged cliffs. But along the last ridges of the Sedjenane valley and up into the hills beyond Sidi Nsir they thrust and, thrusting, broke the perimeter of the north. At Hill 609, Djebel Tahent, they smashed the main Axis defence line and opened the road to Mateur. For days the fighting for 609 went on. On April 30, four days after Longstop had been taken, Sherman tanks, emulating the Churchills of the "Ten Peaks," reached the summit and looked out across the diminishing hills.

On April 25, following the beginnings of the American attack, the French of the Djebel Mansour region, south-west of Pont du Fahs, attacked in the last of the preparatory series. The first phase of the main attack was over and its principal objectives were secure. Right, left, and centre General Alexander had attacked, and by the timing of his thrusts had prevented massing of enemy reserves at the threatened points.

There remained the final blow, and against it one strong-point stood out—the companion hill to Longstop across the valley of the Mejerda River, the Djebel Bou Aoukaz. This was the last bastion of a line threatened already in the north and in the south. The Allies took Bou Aoukaz. This attack began

almost as soon as Longstop Ridge had been taken. It was under Bou Aoukaz that the American Combat Command "B" had met with disaster in the early days of December 1942. It was the

LAST LAP IN THE NORTH AFRICAN CAMPAIGN

1. German 'nebelwerfer,' which projected both smoke and high explosive shells, captured during the advance on Tunis. 2. General Alexander, Deputy C.-in-C., watches the armour closing in on Tunis : after having driven back near Massicault a force of about 60 enemy tanks, a solid wedge of some 400 British tanks moved forward in choking dust clouds towards the city. 3. Transport, troops and armoured vehicles crossing the ford at Djedeida on the way from Medjez-el-Bab. All the way between Medjez and Tunis the First Army had to overcome fierce German counter-attacks, in which the enemy suffered severely.

Photos, British Official

TUNIS IN ALLIED HANDS

Tunis fell on May 7, 1943, the first British units to enter the city being the Derbyshire Yeomanry and the 11th Hussars. During the afternoon, more and more troops streamed in, welcomed rapturously by the French population. But sniping and street fighting continued. 1. Germans surrender to a British tank at Frendj. 2. Men of the Rifle Brigade fire on German snipers in Tunis. 3. A Churchill tank heads a long column of Allied armour and transport that drove through the streets of the city; cheering crowds pelted them with flowers as they went by. *Photos, British Official*

ENTRY INTO BIZERTA
Forward elements of the U.S. Second Corps entered Bizerta from the south at 4.15 p.m. on May 7. They found a dead city, the town and port completely ruined by Allied air bombardment. Here a U.S. patrol crouches under cover of débris while scouts go forward to reconnoitre.

German attack that swamped over these last foothills before the plain that ended the race for Tunis. Bloodily now the Allies had to pay for the weakness of their forces in the early days. Bou Aoukaz was stormed to within 300 yards of the summit, and on that line the Guards Brigade was held. It was still in Axis hands on May 5. Its overwhelming was the first move in the final thunderbolt that fell on Tunis.

In the 12 days between the taking of Longstop Ridge and the final blow, General Alexander massed his forces in the areas behind Medjez and on the

Allied Forces Mass Behind Medjez

borders of the little town, the Ypres of Northern Africa. North of him the Americans had broken through, flooding down the slopes to Mateur and the outskirts of Ferryville. South, the French had moved deep into the mountain tangle of the Zaghouan area. And in the centre General Alexander gathered the Fourth Division and the Fourth Indian Division, the Sixth Armoured Brigade with the 201st Guards Brigade and the Seventh Armoured Division, and elements of the old and well-tried 78th.

The front over which this force was to break was a little over 4,000 yards in width, the shallow valley of the Medjez–Massicault–Tunis road. At 3 a.m.

on May 5, it stormed "the Bou." As the dust of that storming died, the Combined Air Forces went in to the attack. On a lozenge 1,000 yards wide and four miles long they dropped the bombs of 2,000 sorties. And up that carpet of destruction the armour swept. There was still resistance—some of it heavy. The air had not abolished the enemy opposition, but it had diminished it. With the sappers working superbly on the minefields, the armour felt its way down the road to Massicault, and under the red haze of the dust broke out on to the Tunis plain. By nightfall they were 17 miles from the capital, and ahead of them the Derbyshire Yeomanry, with that élan which had been their mark and their pride through the six bitter months, were on the outskirts of the city.

It had been expected that the Axis would hold two inner lines of defence between Medjez and the port. The lines were not held. The skill, the weight and, above all, the demoralizing speed of General Alexander's last attack had shattered the fighting spirit of Von Arnim and his army. At 3.25 on the afternoon of May 7, reconnaissance units of the First Army raced into Tunis. A few minutes later, the Americans reached the centre of Bizerta. The campaign was over.

There remained only the necessary cleansing. Even as Tunis fell, the armour was sweeping on Hammam Lif, roaring through to break the last half-hearted rearguard and shatter Hitler's hopes of a holding position on the Cape Bon peninsula. There was in military theory no reason why that position should not have been held. With a solid barrier of mountains across its isthmus, with its tumbled hinterland, the peninsula was a potential North African Gibraltar, and the Axis forces still had abundant stores. They had *not* fired the last round, *not* used the last gallon of petrol, *not* eaten the last case of rations. But what had happened to them was graver than these things : they had had the will to fight smashed out of them.

General Alexander had freed one continent, Africa ; he had lifted from Southern Asia the fear of invasion from the west; he had made free again an inland sea.

Alexander Frees Africa

Since June 10, 1940, when Mussolini's armies first swept vaingloriously over the empty frontier into the Egyptian desert, the Axis had lost 975,000 men, 7,600 aircraft, 6,200 guns, 2,550 tanks, 70,000 trucks and 624 ships. Another 850 ships are known to have been damaged. Of that tremendous total, no fewer than 163 were ships of war.

And on May 16, when the last cleansing was done, General Sir Harold Alexander sent the following message to the Prime Minister :

Sir,—It is my duty to report that the Tunisian campaign is over. All enemy resistance has ceased. We are masters of the North African shores.

(Signed) H. R. ALEXANDER.

DEFEATED AXIS GENERALS REACH ENGLAND
Colonel-General Baron Sixt von Arnim (left), commander-in-chief in the final battles in Tunisia, and Marshal Giovanni Messe (right), c.-in-c. of Italian forces in North Africa and, after Rommel's retirement, commander of all Axis forces during the Battle of Mareth : photographs taken after their arrival in Britain as prisoners of war on May 17, 1943.
Photos, British Official

Chapter 278

INSIDE THE THIRD REICH AFTER STALINGRAD

Life inside Germany between July 1942 and the end of 1943 is here described by Dr. F. Heymann, formerly of the editorial staff of the 'Frankfurter Zeitung' and foreign editor of 'Bohemia' (Prague). The military successes which had justified confidence in victory came to an end. But cunning propaganda and, as the months passed, sheer suppression kept the German war machine working. For the preceding year in Germany, see Chapter 217

In the summer of 1942 a series of sweeping German offensives in Europe and Africa made most Germans once again believe in the certainty of ultimate, and possibly not very distant, victory. In southern Russia as well as in Libya and Egypt German armies seemed to be as irresistible as ever (*see* Chapters 224 and 227). No wonder that with the successes won and the far greater victories which seemed to be assured, the gloom brought about by the disaster of the preceding winter in Russia disappeared. There were few defeatists left in Germany by July 1942 —though many people welcomed the victories less for their military significance than because they seemed to promise an early end to the war. In August confidence rose that Russia would soon give in. German propaganda did its best to strengthen this belief within and without Germany. In order to split the Allies, rumours were launched that Britain and the U.S.A. intended to replace Stalin by "a more proficient leader." Then, to frighten Russia, Japan was said to be planning an immediate attack upon Siberia.

All these manoeuvres were of no avail, however, and in the course of September German morale dropped slightly owing to the approach of winter without any decisive success having been obtained in the East. All German newspapers had to print long articles emphasizing that preparations for the second winter campaign in Russia had been so thorough that no German soldier would, as in the year before, suffer from cold or lack of shelter. This was small comfort, since it showed that there would be no final victory and no peace in 1942.

By the end of September German propaganda, culminating in Hitler's speech for the new "Winterhilfe" (winter relief work), left no doubt that the great offensive plans of a few months ago had had to be abandoned. Germany had reached all her goals and had occupied all the territories necessary to make herself blockade-proof. She could now go over to the defensive. In his speech, Hitler threatened Britain with retaliation for the air war against Germany. If Churchill and Roosevelt (" military idiots") tried to set foot again in the "fortress of Europe," they could consider themselves lucky if they succeeded in holding out for nine hours, as the forces landed in Dieppe in August had done. Russia, on the other hand, had been bled white by her fearful losses from which she would never be able to recover. By cutting the Volga, the German army had deprived her of her main life line and of nearly all her oil supplies. Stalingrad itself, which was still being assaulted, would also be taken, "worauf Sie sich verlassen koennen" (you can rely on that).

It was one of the last grandiloquent and self-assured speeches in the long series of Hitler's public pronouncements. Sooner than anybody expected events proved him wrong. On October 23 General Montgomery's Eighth Army began its offensive in Egypt; 12 days later he had decisively won the Battle of El Alamein. Rommel, the one German

Events Prove Hitler Wrong

GERMANY'S FUEHRER SPEAKS

Hitler addressing Nazi party members on Nov. 8, 1942, the eve of the anniversary of the 1923 Nazi Putsch. The Allies had that very morning landed in French North Africa. He still boasted, however, that in North Africa 'the enemy moves forward and back, but what matters is the final result, and that you can leave to us.' He also asserted that he had taken Stalingrad. Another phrase ran, 'They will find out in Britain that the German inventive spirit has not been idle, and they will get an answer' (to British air raids) 'which will take their breath away.'

COLLECTION FOR WINTER CLOTHING

This painting by Josef Vietze of Prague, shown in July 1942 at the annual exhibition of German art in the House of German Art in Munich, depicts a young S.S. trooper collecting fur clothing for the use of German soldiers fighting in the snows of the Russian winter.

ganda explained that the invasion of North Africa was one more proof that Churchill and Roosevelt would never dare to invade Europe.

In the meantime new dangers were brewing in the east. The Russian offensive at Stalingrad, begun on November 19, had, by the end of the month, completely encircled the German Sixth Army. The German armies in the Caucasus had to retreat rapidly as they too were in danger of being cut off. All hopes of an early peace vanished. German propaganda, after having pictured Britain as enemy No. 1 of the German people, turned east, depicting the danger threatening "all Europe" from the Bolshevist "Untermenschen" and hinting at

possibilities that an understanding might be reached with the west. In the period preceding Christmas 1942, gloom settled once again over Germany, deepened by the growing strength of British air raids.

To combat this mood and distract attention from happenings at the fronts, war against the "enemy within" was stepped up again. Thousands of helpless Jews, not only from Germany, Austria and the protectorate of Bohemia-Moravia, but also from Norway, France, Holland and Yugoslavia, were sent to the huge concentration camps in Poland which soon became "Vernichtungslager" (extermination camps). Strange as it may seem, these fearful persecutions were continued although—as all neutral observers agree—the masses of the German people, particularly in Berlin, Hamburg and other great cities where they could observe the round up of these unhappy victims, rather resented such measures and in some cases even tried to interfere. The churches also were subjected to continuous persecution. More Roman Catholic abbeys were closed or their possessions confiscated. Hess's successor Martin Bormann, in a solemn declaration to the German people, openly confessed that Nazi philosophy was irreconcilable with Christianity of any description. In place of the old Protestant hymn book, a new hymn book for Protestant congregations was issued which tried to

Renewed War Against 'Enemy Within'

General who, being a hundred per cent Nazi, had been " built up " as a war god by the party propaganda, and who himself had promised the early capture of Alexandria, was fleeing towards the west. It was a nasty surprise for the German public. Official propaganda reacted by declaring that this was only one more of those frequent changes of attack and retreat consequent on the difficulty of safeguarding the long supply lines through the desert. As the retreat went on and Egypt was cleared, Nazi propaganda put all the blame on the Italians, thus for the first time employing an argument which later was used almost regularly to explain defeats in the south.

The Allied landings in French North Africa were a fresh shock. This Allied move came as a complete surprise. The German secret service, so active in Spain and Morocco, had been foxed. When Hitler, on the morning of November 8, arrived in Munich for the anniversary celebration of the Putsch of 1923, he was informed of the landings only just before he had to start his speech at the Bierkeller and thus had no appropriate answer ready. Nazi propa-

WORRIED DICTATORS CONFER

Left to right, Admiral Doenitz, Commander-in-Chief of the German Navy, General Zeitzler, Mussolini, Field-Marshal Keitel, Hitler, and Field-Marshal Goering study war maps during their conference at Salzburg, April 7-10, 1943. 'Complete agreement was achieved about the measures to be taken in all fields,' stated the German communiqué issued on April 11.

A CORNER OF A FOREIGN FIELD THAT IS FOR EVER ENGLAND

The Tunisian grave of Captain the Lord Lyell (left), Scots Guards, who fell during the attack on Djebel Bou Arada. After several days of hard fighting, in which he displayed gallant leadership, his company was on April 27, 1943, stopped by intense fire from an enemy post consisting of an 88-mm. gun and a heavy machine-gun in separate pits. Single-handed except for some covering fire which a lance-corporal was able to give him, he ran forward and silenced both guns before he was killed. The company was then able to advance and take its objective. He was awarded the V.C.

RECONNAISSANCE PATROL IN THE TUNISIAN HILLS

Photo, British Official

While the Allies were consolidating their positions after the capture of Chaouach on April 9, patrols pushed forward into the hills around the village of Heidous, probing the enemy's strength.   On April 25 the German garrison in Heidous was liquidated, and the last slopes of Djebel Tangoucha remaining in enemy hands were stormed by Churchill tanks. Here a First Army patrol, including an artillery officer and two signalmen, is out looking for enemy observation posts. The wireless set carried by the mule bringing up the rear will be used to signal orders to the guns as occasion demands.

REST AND REFRESHMENT FOR THE CONQUERORS OF LONGSTOP

In the early hours of April 22, 1943, after a violent mass barrage of 400 guns, the First Army attacked in the wild mountainous country, pitted with strong enemy defences, between Goubellat and Bou Arada, and also towards Longstop. They stormed the heights of Argoub Hamra (Hill 23), Rahal Mahalla, and Koudait-Sidarka the same day at the point of the bayonet; but it was April 26 before, supported by Churchill tanks, men of the East Surreys and Argylls succeeded in driving the enemy from his last foothold on Longstop Ridge (Djebel Ahmera). (See also illus., page 2771.)

TUNISIAN HARBOURS IN ALLIED HANDS

The important town of Ferryville was cleared by troops of the U.S. Second Corps by 4 p.m. on May 7, 1943. A quarter of an hour later their forward elements entered Bizerta, second port of Tunisia, from the south, while almost simultaneously Moroccan Goumiers reached it from the west. It was found to be a dead city, the town and port ruined by Allied air bombardment. The Germans had sunk eight ships to block the harbour and had blown up the lock gates, but had withdrawn too hurriedly to have time to destroy the electrical and other public services. The Allies set to work to clear the harbour immediately, and soon British and American ships lay at anchor in Bizerta (above). Left, an Axis auxiliary naval vessel, wrecked by Allied bombing, lies on its side in the flooded dry dock at Ferryville. The desolation of the scene testifies to the devastation wrought by Allied bombing.

Photos, British Official

replace all biblical ideas by those of the Nazi creed.

All these measures, aimed at imbuing the whole of the German people with the true Nazi spirit, did little to cheer the masses. The only measure which, to some extent, had that effect was an increase in the meat ration. Goering's announcement that this was no temporary measure but would last throughout the war was generally believed. People thought it a sign that Germany was really blockade-proof.

At the beginning of 1943 things moved quickly from bad to worse. It was impossible to conceal that in the sur-

Goebbels on Stalingrad

render at Stalingrad (*see* Chapter 269) a catastrophe of the first order had over-taken the German Wehrmacht. Hitler, who it had been expected would make a public speech as usual on January 30, the birthday of the Third Reich, was not heard. Goebbels was left to read the Fuehrer's message over the microphone. This was Goebbels's great hour. He knew that the event was sure to cause deep depression. But when there must be gloom, it should be officially shaped and "canalized," so as to be under control. The story had been well prepared : the disaster of Stalingrad was, according to Goebbels, the supreme sacrifice of a German army and its commanders, who had all without exception given their lives to hold the onrush of the "Asiatic hordes" and to enable the German High Command to stabilize the front. It was, absurdly enough, most unwelcome when the news slowly

ARMOURED LOCOMOTIVES FOR THE EASTERN FRONT

By a coincidence, five pilot engines each leading ten new fully-armoured locomotives came together in a German marshalling yard. This concentration of war engines for the eastern front (explains the German description of this photograph) is a 'proof of the fulfilment of the new engine-building programme promoted by the Fuehrer,' and a clear indication of the 'unbroken will to victory of the German armament industry.' *Photo, Keystone*

filtered through to Germany that more than 90,000 men, including Field-Marshal von Paulus, had laid down their arms. When all was over, a great national mourning was organized. No theatrical or other entertainment was given for three days, and there were mourning manifestations of every kind.

At the same time the masses had to be shown that something drastic was being done to redeem the situation. Until then it had been taken for granted that Germany, where the expression "total war" originated, was totally mobilized. Now the discovery was made that this was not the case at all, that

Germany had still vast reserves of unused man- and woman-power whose mobilization would make all the difference. Compulsory registration was ordered for all men between 16 and 65, and for all women between 17 and 45. The idea was to send armament workers to the front and to replace them by the newly conscripted. In general the outcome of this mobilization was far from satisfactory. One of the first measures taken was the closing down of small shops, craftsmen's workshops, catering and entertainment establishments, branches of banks and insurance firms. This was a hard blow to the German middle class, already the chief victim of war conditions. Nearly 1,000 (out of about 2,400) newspapers were closed down, not so much to save labour (as was pretended) as to get rid of all those papers still outside the Nazi party or where the editorial staffs included somewhat lukewarm followers of the party line.

Three months later came another debacle, in Tunisia (*see* Chapter 277). That was much more of a surprise to the German public than Stalingrad. They had, it is true, already learned to respect

Shock of Tunisia Debacle

Montgomery's generalship and the striking power of the British Eighth Army. But they had been told that the other Allied forces in North Africa, particularly American and French, counted for nothing—they had no battle experience and their supplies were constantly destroyed by U-boat attacks on their supply lines. The stubborn resistance offered during

SPECIAL RATION CARDS FOR CHRISTMAS

Cards, left for a child or young person up to 18, right for a worker other than a landworker over 18, issued to German citizens at Christmas 1942. The German description comments : 'While the enemy powers must steadily reduce their food rations, thanks to the brave and victorious German soldiers, the Reich is able to grant all German citizens a considerable special allotment for the Christmas festival '; but the long validity of these cards (14.12.1942 to 31.1.1943) suggests that there may have been some difficulty in meeting them.

the winter of 1942–43 by the forces of Von Arnim and Messe had made people believe that the "African bridge-head" would be held and would make it impossible for the Allies even to contemplate an invasion of Europe from the south. The very suddenness of the final breakdown made it impossible to believe that the Axis armies had "fought to the last man and patrone." All that was left to Goebbels was boldly to announce that Africa had never been of any particular value to the defence of the "Fortress of Europe," whose real bulwark was Sicily, now strongly defended by German and Italian crack troops.

People in general were not quite as depressed by the Tunisian capitulation as they had been by the Stalingrad catastrophe, mainly because there were

HITLER YOUTH IN TRAINING

Physical training camps were established in 1942 by the Hitler Youth organization, in which all youths of 16½ underwent a compulsory three weeks' course before joining the army. Men who had seen service at the front trained the lads, some of whom are here learning direction-finding by means of the prismatic compass.

many fewer killed and many more prisoners among the German casualties, and the next-of-kin of sons or husbands who were prisoners of war in British or American hands were much less afraid for what was going to happen to them than in the case of those held by Russia.

People's minds, moreover, were soon diverted from Tunisia by the sudden announcement of the cutting of the meat ration from 350 to 250 grams per week, a cut not compensated for by a small rise in the bread ration (by 75 g.) and the fat ration (by 12½ g.). This tightening of the belt, though it belied Goering's firm promises of a few months before, was deliberate policy, and it had, in no small measure, the desired effect: people stopped talking of military events; their minds were occupied by the food question.

Meat Ration Cut

The months from February to April witnessed also a sharp increase in the weight of British bombs dropped on Germany. These attacks were much too devastating to allow the German authorities to minimize their effect. Not only the A.R.P. but also the repair organization, which had been effective during 1942, proved to be well nigh helpless in the face of the heavy "saturation raids." After the new raids on Berlin, particularly the raid of March 1, no attempt was made to restore the general façade

MOBILE A.A. GUNS ON THE GERMAN RAILWAYS

The mounting Allied air offensive against Germany was directed against her communications as well as against her industrial towns. Batteries of four guns mounted on rail-chassis were used as mobile defence of the railways. The troops manning them lived in coaches drawn up in the sidings. Crews are here seen undergoing training in handling one of these guns.

'R.A.F. BOMBERS IN GREAT STRENGTH . . .'

A long line of German civilians evacuating an unnamed town in North Germany which had been badly hit by the R.A.F. (Right) Members of a motorized A.R.P. unit of the Luftwaffe in the streets of another unnamed German town the morning after a visit from our heavy bombers. (Below) Berlin blazing after bombing with British phosphorus bombs. 'Although the horror of the actual bombardment is great, the real misery begins when people stand in front of the ruins of their houses,' said a report on Berlin in December 1943. 'Estimates put the number of homeless seeking aid and relief at nearly 3,000,000.'

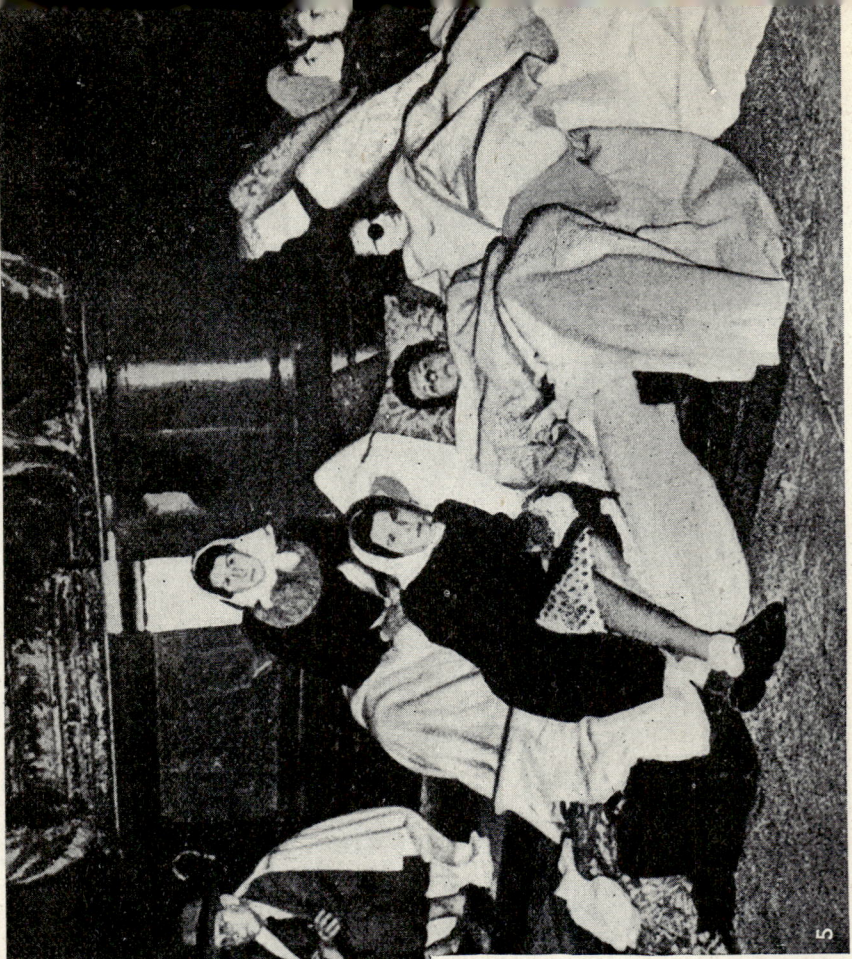

BERLIN UNDER AIR ATTACK

1. Housewives at an emergency field kitchen near the Brandenburger Tor after a heavy R.A.F. raid. 2. Notices chalked up on a wall explaining to friends and relatives how 'To reach Daniels,' and that 'Auer Pilgram and Gottwald all live.' 3. A food lorry in a bomb-wrecked quarter of Berlin : food supply was one of the chief problems of the German capital after the R.A.F. raids. 4. Medal awarded to wounded soldiers, which was given also to civilians wounded on the home front. 5. 'They have lost all—except faith and courage' : homeless Berliners in a public building waiting to be evacuated.

HAMBURG STREET SCENE: AUTUMN 1943

The R.A.F. began bombing Hamburg in 1940, but the number and weight of their attacks were steeply stepped up during 1943. In July they dropped 6,900 tons on the city in less than a week—at that time a battering unparalleled during the war. The docks, industrial and metal-working plants, motor-works and gasworks suffered, damage being especially severe in the industrial districts of St. Georg, Billwarder-Ausschlag, and Grasbrook.

of the capital, and repair was limited to less-damaged houses and factories

In spite of all the setbacks suffered by Germany in the east, in Africa and in the air, the number of Germans who fully realized the plight into which **'The Rommel of the Sea'** Hitler's war had led them was, in the spring of 1943, still limited. There seemed still to be strong reasons for hope. One of them was the Battle of the Atlantic. In January Raeder had been replaced as supreme Commander of the German Navy by Doenitz, who up to that time had commanded the U-boat fleets alone. Doenitz, who had attained flag rank only four years before and was now promoted to the rank of Gross-admiral (Admiral of the Fleet), was intimately connected with the Party. Like Rommel he was studiously " built up " by propaganda—indeed he was sometimes called " the Rommel of the Sea," to imply that he was the very embodiment of the offensive spirit. There was no lack of hints that henceforth the fight against the life lines of Germany's enemies would be conducted with greater vigour than hither-

to, and not by U-boats alone but also by surface forces operating from Norwegian waters and by aircraft. When, in March, Doenitz's spring offensive was at its height special communiqués and radio and press comments made the most of it, to make people believe that the war could be won by the U-boats. As it was impossible for the ordinary citizen to check the correctness of news telling of sea victories (whereas in relation to operations on land he could at least look at the map), such news was, if necessary, invented in order to cheer people up.

The varying lines and twists of German propaganda must be dealt with at some length, since propaganda in Nazi Germany was not only of an importance quite unknown in the history of any other country but actually to a large extent replaced all political life in its proper sense. Still, it would be wrong to assume that the behaviour of the German masses was, and could ever be,

guided by propaganda alone, even by as nimble and cunning a propaganda as that devised by Goebbels and his chief collaborators. As long as events justified at least in some degree confident assurances of victory, the sober or critical voices of sceptics or those in opposition were drowned, and propaganda could do most of the work required to keep up German morale. But the more the course of the war led to the discarding of optimistic views, the more sheer suppression had to be used to keep down currents that might disturb the smooth working of the German war machine. In the second half of 1942 and even more in 1943 the power of the S.S. was steadily increased. Its leader Heinrich Himmler, already the chief of the Gestapo and the whole German police, became Minister of the Interior and thereby head of the whole Civil Service of Germany.

One of the most important fields of influence secured by the S.S. already in

2787

1942 was the Reich Ministry of Justice and the administration of penal law. In August of that year Thierack was appointed Minister of Justice. He had been president of the "Volksgerichtshof," the notorious "people's court" which in reality was a mere party organ whose task it was to judge political "crimes" according to the most arbitrary rules. Thierack was one of Himmler's reliable henchmen, a ruthless S.S.-man, as was also his Permanent Under-Secretary of State Herr Rothenberger, appointed at the same time.

Thierack was given full power to "reform" all existing laws as he (or rather as Himmler and the S.S.) pleased. He closed down a great number of ordinary parochial courts and removed many thousands of judges from office, thereby getting rid in the main of those whose unreserved adherence to the party seemed doubtful. On the other hand he augmented the number of special courts, consisting of juries chosen only among reliable party-members and presided over by S.S. functionaries. They had the right to pass sentences of death or penal servitude without regard to any written law, and there was no appeal against their sentences. These courts got very much busier in 1943, when mass arrests became frequent. The victims were partly workmen who were suspected of having organized opposition groups (in Siemensstadt, the industrial suburb of Berlin, 600 workers were,

Law 'Reformed' out of Existence

according to reliable neutral sources, arrested by the Gestapo at the beginning of 1943), partly intellectuals who, it was thought, might be potential leaders of future opposition movements. In March 1943 two officials of the Foreign Office were executed. Much more of the real background of opposition was revealed when, about the same time, there was a revolt among some of the students at Munich University. Many were arrested, others deprived of their right to continue their studies and sent to the front, while two men supposed to be the leaders, Professor Huber and a student named Hans Scholl, were executed. As the year went on, more such executions followed, some of them given wide publicity. In one fortnight of September 1943 alone, four out of a much greater number of executions were publicly announced and commented on at length in the German press, all the victims being accused of having spread defeatism. Among those executed for this "crime" was a high official in Mecklenburg, Regierungsrat Theodor Korselt.

It was, however, an exception when, within a few days of these events, a higher party official was also put to death for excessive corruption. This was a show trial intended to demonstrate to the masses that Nazi Justice did not tolerate corruption among responsible party officials. In reality it was common knowledge that corruption and venality had become almost a matter of course with a large part of

HIMMLER SEES DAMAGE
The targets attacked by the R.A.F. were not all industrial cities or railways and other communications. Some of them were secret dumps, factories, and research stations placed among woodlands in the country. Himmler, head of the Gestapo, is here inspecting the damage done to one such secret target. *Photo, Associated Press*

Nazi officialdom from top to bottom, the Gestapo by no means excluded. Services of every kind could, and often had to, be bought by bribes. Whereas in previous years money would do a great deal, it was becoming more and more necessary to pay with what was called "Sachwerte," material values, ranging from food "gifts" up to furniture, grand pianos and pictures.

This showed clearly that most people had little confidence in the stability of the Reichsmark, but realized the process of hidden inflation started years before by the economic policy of the Nazis. Money could buy little, shops were empty of all merchandise except the bare necessities of life, everything else was regarded as luxury and could be bought in the black market only for incredible prices. 250 marks (£12 10s.) were paid for one kilogram (two pounds) of coffee, and smokers (whose ration was four cigarettes a day) were prepared to pay sixpence and in some cases even one shilling for a single cigarette.

Lack of Confidence in Reichsmark

From the middle of May until the beginning of July 1943 there was a

NEWLY ARRIVED EVACUEES
The heavy attacks on German towns by the R.A.F. and the U.S.A.A.F. produced almost insuperable difficulties in evacuation. In areas to which large numbers of town inhabitants were drafted, the whole economic organization was upset, with the result that much friction was caused between natives and visitors. Here, a coachload of newly arrived evacuees awaits direction to billets in a 'safe area' town. *Photo, Keystone*

lull in the war on all fronts which gave the German home front some time to recuperate, though the R.A.F.'s attack on the two great dams of the Eder and the Moehne rivers (see page 2660 and illus., page 2659) created havoc in the whole Ruhr district and in the industrial district of Cassel. Their output of war products and (in Cassel) railway engines was greatly impaired by this spectacular success, and it proved very difficult for German propaganda to minimize its effect.

Knowing that the Russians were waiting impatiently for the opening of another front on the Continent, German propaganda used this period for renewed attempts to create mistrust between the Allies. One of these moves had a real and far-reaching success. The Nazis staged the "discovery" of the common grave of some 10,000 officers of the Polish Army, on whose bodies documents were found, "proving" that they had been murdered by the Russians early in 1940. The whole story was another "Reichstag fire," a crime deliberately committed by the Nazis in order to incriminate somebody else. This fact, established beyond any doubt by later investigations, was not then recognized by the Polish Government in London, which asked the International Red Cross to undertake an investigation. But the rest of this sorry story does not belong to German history; it is told in page 2735.

Attempts to Disrupt Allies

In the second week of July the lull in the fighting came to an end. On the 10th the Allied armies landed in Sicily (see Chapter 283), whereupon Nazi propaganda promptly disclaimed having ever thought of Sicily as a stronghold of the Fortress of Europe. Now the great island was nothing but an "unfortified outpost" which belonged rather to Africa than to Europe. Almost simultaneously with the opening of the battle in the south, the East Front sprang to life again. After vast preparations a strong German offensive was started against the Kursk salient (see Chapter 282). Very soon, when its complete failure became apparent, the German High Command claimed that it had been only a "reconnaissance in force," aimed at revealing the Russian offensive plans.

The greatest shock, however, that hit the German home front in the fateful summer of 1943 was the downfall of Mussolini and the surrender of Italy. Even after Badoglio had dissolved the Fascist party, Goebbels tried to persuade the German people that what had happened was only a "change of

government," that Italo-German relations were not influenced by this event and that Italy would stay in the war. When the surrender was announced the effect throughout Germany was enormous. In some circles, Italy's advantage in having a king who could dismiss the Duce was discussed more or less openly. The speed and apparent ease with which the whole intricate fabric of the Fascist state and dictatorship, once a model for Nazi Germany, vanished without any real fight for existence could not fail to impress all Germans. The Nazi leaders took three steps to counteract these dangerous thoughts and impressions. Propagandist talks

DICTATOR AND EX-DICTATOR

Hitler greets Mussolini after the Duce's rescue on September 12, 1943, from imprisonment in an hotel on Gran Sasso, a 9,000-ft. mountain in the Abruzzi, by S.S. men dropped by parachute. The parachutists were followed by Fieseler-Storch aircraft, which landed on a plateau outside the hotel and took off Mussolini and his rescuers.

Photo, Keystone

and articles argued that in Italy the Fascist regime had never been strong enough to eradicate those "plutocratic" elements which, together with the "treacherous dwarf Victor Emanuel," had stabbed in the back and overthrown the Fascist regime. Nothing like that could ever happen in Germany where such elements no longer existed or were much too weak to endanger the "Volksgemeinschaft." The second was a rather theatrical move: the liberation of Mussolini by German S.S. Parachute troops, intended to show the striking power of Germany as well as to allow her to build up the "Italian Fascist Republic" with the Duce at

its head. The third move was mainly military in character, though it had strong political implications as well: it was the occupation of Rome and the greater part of the Italian mainland. Yet this move, and the comparatively slow Allied progress in Italy during the following winter, hardly compensated for the catastrophic worsening of Germany's general situation. It is impossible even to mention all the desperate attempts of Nazi propaganda to deceive or console the German people in the face of the loss of those vast eastern territories on which a little earlier all hopes of a sustained economic war effort had been built. The German armies were now "successfully disengaging" all the time. They were always "retreating according to plan" and "still held the initiative" even when the Dnieper line, which had long been proclaimed as the final line of resistance, was overrun by the Russians.

Actually the masses of the German people at home grew less and less interested in what was going on at the front. They had become more apathetic and weary—and they had their own front: the night attacks by the R.A.F., and now, in addition, day raids by the U.S.A.A.F. This air offensive grew steadily more concentrated, and large scale evacuation, which had already taken millions of people from western Germany, had to be extended to Hamburg, Berlin and other cities. Among the reception areas were regions in western Poland, in Czechoslovakia and, especially, in Austria, which was sometimes called the air raid shelter of the Reich. This great influx of Reich German elements did nothing to soften the attitude of the Austrian people, the majority of whom, former Nazis not wholly excluded, showed their aversion to the intruders in many ways—by strikes and riots, by sabotage in factories where Austrians sometimes made common cause with the masses of foreign slave workers, and last but not least, by many little pinpricks. Thus neutral observers reported that Reich Germans living in Vienna were so consistently shown the wrong direction when asking their way that even policemen sent there from the north relied only on street maps to find their way about.

Increasing Apathy of the People

The profound change in Germany's war situation during the period concerned found a remarkable reflection in the treatment of Allied prisoners of war in German hands. From the beginning of the war it had been German policy to adhere to the Geneva rules and the agreement of 1929 only so long as it

Red Cross representatives tried to give to the British and French prisoners. The main point, however, was that in that first phase there were hardly any German prisoners in Russian hands and that the Nazis felt so sure of their power to turn Russia into a German colony that they regarded and treated the captured **Russians Treated as Slaves** Russian soldiers, as well as the millions of civilians deported to Germany, as just so many slaves who could be ill-treated and exploited up to, and often beyond, the limit of human endurance. Particularly bad and insufficient was the food given to these people, who had none of the invaluable Red Cross parcels without which British and other prisoners of war could never have kept their health for any length of time.

WITH GERMANY'S WAR WORKERS

A girl, formerly a student at the Berlin Academy of Art, in training as an oxy-acetylene welder. Right, the Vienna Philharmonic Orchestra, under the internationally famous conductor Wilhelm Furtwangler, gives a concert in a Berlin arms factory. The Mayor of Berlin was present. It will be noted that this is not a case of 'music while you work': the workers are attending only to the music.

suited their purposes. Polish prisoners had never been treated with any consideration, and after the Battle of France the treatment of British and French prisoners also was harsh. Treatment of British prisoners, however, improved towards the end of 1940, at a time when numbers of Luftwaffe and U-boat personnel were prisoners in British hands. French prisoners in Germany were by far the largest in numbers, and the release of a great part of them, promised to the Vichy Government, was never effected. They were kept in Germany partly to blackmail the French into sending to Germany more skilled industrial workers (most of whom had never been drafted into the army), and partly because this prolonged captivity of a great percentage of young Frenchmen tended to keep the French birth-rate low. Polish and French and, as far as possible, British prisoners were soon made to work on farms.

Their lot was enviable compared with that of the thousands of Russians captured during the first phases of the war in the east. Russia had not been a partner to the Geneva Convention or the agreement of 1929, which made it difficult for her to get anything like the protection which Swiss and Swedish

So little did the Nazis respect the fundamental rules of international law that they were soon using Russian prisoners for armament work. When the building of fortifications was started in the west, Russian prisoners formed a considerable part of the man-power employed for this purpose. In May 1942, when consequent to the huge German losses in the Russian winter war the man-power question grew more acute, an order was issued that of all prisoners of war in Germany, with the exception of the British, one-half should be made to work for armament production.

The basis of this whole policy had always been the fact that the Germans held far more prisoners of war in their

RELIEF FROM THE TEDIUM OF PRISON LIFE

Parcels from home have arrived : British prisoners of war at Camp Oflag IXa smile with happiness during the distribution—a photograph taken and sent home by a prisoner in the camp. Above, one of the combatants knocked through the ropes during a boxing match at another camp. Educational programmes, games, exercises—and parcels from home—kept the British prisoners sane and healthy during their long years of inactivity.

camps than there were German prisoners in Allied camps. The scandalous shackling of British and Canadian prisoners who had been captured at Dieppe in 1942—allegedly a reprisal action—would most likely never have happened had not the balance in the number of prisoners been so much in the favour of Germany. This, however, ceased to be the case in 1943. After the surrender of Germany's African armies, German prisoners in Allied hands at one stroke vastly outnumbered British and American prisoners in Axis hands. Also, after the surrender of Stalingrad and the

losses of the second winter campaign, there were now for the first time huge numbers of Germans in Russian hands.

From then on the treatment of prisoners of war, particularly those of British nationality, underwent a certain change. Until then there had been, on the one hand, "show camps" where prisoners had been allowed " privileges," and these had been given wide publicity in Germany ; and, on the other, " reprisal camps " or camps where prisoners who had tried to escape were subjected to much harsher treatment. Now the standard was somewhat more

unified, and in some camps British prisoners, to their great surprise, found themselves even marched off to the nearest picture house for entertainment. During the winter of 1943–44, Field-Marshal Keitel, in the name of the German High Command, issued a special order which stressed the necessity of treating Russian prisoners of war well. Though some of the worst methods, which had already caused the death of tens of thousands, seem to have been somewhat mitigated, the lot of most of the prisoners from the east was still so hard as to make many of them prefer any other status, however hateful otherwise. Thus, quite a number of Russian, Polish, Yugoslav and other prisoners were pressed into service in the German armed forces, where, of course, they formed very unwilling fighters for the German Fatherland— many of them later surrendered at the first opportunity.

That this experiment was made at all, and made on such a scale, shows clearly the gravest of all problems confronting the German war leaders towards the end of 1943 : lack of man-power. True, besides prisoners of war the number of foreign slave workers —at the beginning of the year some six millions—had, by indiscriminate methods of recruitment, been substantially increased. But this vast and—in the case of defeat—dangerous army of foreign nationals was not sufficient by a long way to fill all the gaps, let alone to free sufficient Germans for the task of defending the long perimeter of the " Fortress of Europe." Thus the end of the year found the German people in complete apathy facing another year of hopeless working and fighting.

Diary of the War

MAY and JUNE 1943

May 1, 1943. U.S. heavy bombers raided St. Nazaire U-boat base. Dover shelled for 75 mins. at night.

May 2. R.A.F. Mosquitoes attacked Thionville after flight of 600 miles (400 over enemy territory) at roof-top height.

May 3. Mateur captured by Allies (Tunisia). U.S. planes attacked Kiska (Aleutians) nine times.

May 4. Krymskaya (Kuban) captured by Red Army. New Japanese offensive S. of Yangtse. Concentrated night attack by R.A.F. on Dortmund.

May 5. Djebel Bou Aoukaz captured by First Army (Tunisia).

May 6. Massicault captured by First Army (Tunisia). Australians occupied Mubo (New Guinea). Five attacks on Kiska and seven on Attu (Aleutians) by U.S. planes. Five U-boats sunk when attacking westbound Atlantic convoy.

May 7. Tunis, Ferryville, Bizerta and Pont du Fahs captured by Allies (Tunisia). Japanese cut Maungdaw–Buthidaung road (Burma). Heavy Allied air raids on Madang, Finsch Hafen and Mubo (New Guinea).

May 8. Tebourba and Djedeida captured (Tunisia). Withdrawal of Allied forces from Buthidaung (Burma).

May 9. Unconditional surrender in N.E. Tunisia.

May 10. Soliman and Grombalia occupied (Tunisia).

May 11. American forces landed on Attu (Aleutians). Mr. Churchill arrived in Washington.

May 11–12. Allies withdrew from Maungdaw (Burma).

May 12. Bomber Command dropped 1,500 tons of bombs by night on Duisburg-Ruhrort. Organized resistance in all Tunisia ceased.

May 13. Last remaining elements in Tunisia surrendered. Pantelleria bombarded from the sea ; heavy air attacks on Naples, Cagliari (Sardinia), Augusta (Sicily) and communications in the toe of Italy. Night attack by R.A.F. on Bochum.

May 14. Velsen (N. Holland), Kiel, Antwerp and Courtrai attacked by day by U.S. Army Eighth Air Force. Civitavecchia (Italy) and Palermo (Sicily) heavily bombed. Australian hospital ship " Centaur " torpedoed and sunk by Japanese; 268 lives lost.

May 17. Moehne and Eder dams (Ruhr area) breached by air attack.

May 18. Pantelleria heavily raided from the air. United Nations Food Conference opened at Hot Springs, Virginia (ended June 3).

May 19. Kiel and Flensburg attacked by U.S. heavy bombers.

May 20. Return to India of Brig. Wingate's Chindits reported.

May 21. Strong day air attacks on Wilhelmshaven and Emden.

May 22. Japanese bombers attack Chittagong (Bengal). Dissolution of Comintern announced from Moscow.

May 23. Bomber Command dropped over 2,000 tons of bombs on Dortmund by night. Three heavy air attacks on Pantelleria in five hours.

May 25. Powerful R.A.F. force bombed Duesseldorf by night.

May 26. Allied air offensive against Sicily, Sardinia and Pantelleria maintained. Lae (New Guinea) heavily bombed by Allied planes.

May 27. First Slovak Motorized Division crossed over to the Red Army. Jena (Thuringia) bombed by Mosquitoes in round flight of over 1,000 miles. British bombers in great strength attacked Essen. Continued Allied air attacks on Sardinia, Sicily and Pantelleria. Ichang–Hankow highway cut by Chinese ; Japanese thrown out of Chihfassu.

May 28. Heavy daylight attack on Leghorn by U.S. Fortresses based in Africa.

May 29. Heavy day attacks on U-boat bases of St. Nazaire and La Pallice. Over 1,500 tons dropped at night by R.A.F. on Wuppertal. Chittagong airfield (Bengal) attacked by Japanese bombers. All organized Japanese resistance on Attu collapsed.

May 30. Frequent German air raids on Leningrad. Daylight raid by 100 U.S. Fortresses on Naples. Chinese counter-offensive launched near Hupeh-Honan border. Dawn attack by Fortresses on Wewak (New Guinea). Talks between De Gaulle and Giraud began (Algiers).

May 31. Pantelleria bombed throughout the day by relays of bombers. Lae attacked by two waves of Liberators (New Guinea). Confirmed in London that French warships in Alexandria joined Allies.

June 1. Allied air offensive against Sardinia, Sicily and Pantelleria maintained. Allied warships bombarded Pantelleria.

June 2. Heavy night air attack on Naples ; Pantelleria bombed by night and day. Germans raided Kursk with 500 planes ; lost 162 (Russia).

June 3. 520 Soviet bombers (one lost) made heavy night attack on Orel. Pantelleria attacked many times from the air and bombarded from the sea. Chinese recaptured Itu and reached west bank of Yangtse. De Gaulle and Giraud reached agreement (Algiers).

June 4. Red Air Force heavily bombed enemy supply centres of Bryansk and Karachev. Sicily, Pantelleria and Italian mainland heavily bombed. Kungan (S. Hupeh) recaptured by Chinese.

June 5. U.S. Fortresses from N.W. Africa attacked Spezia. Pantelleria again attacked from air and sea. Mr. Churchill arrived back in London.

June 6. Night and day air attacks on Pantelleria. Wau aerodrome (New Guinea) dive-bombed by Japanese.

June 7. Pantelleria bombed from dawn to dusk. Composition of French Committee of National Liberation announced.

June 8. Pantelleria bombed and bombarded all day ; leaflets dropped demanding unconditional surrender.

June 9. Main weight of Strategic and Tactical Air Forces against Pantelleria.

June 10. Entire weight of Strategic and Tactical Air Forces thrown against Pantelleria from dawn to dusk, Allied bombers " queuing up " to drop their bombs. Rabaul (New Britain) bombed by five waves of Fortresses and Liberators.

June 11. 200 U.S. Fortresses (eight lost) attacked U-boat base at Wilhelmshaven. At night great force of R.A.F. bombers attacked Duesseldorf. Violent bombing of Pantelleria, which surrendered unconditionally at 11.40 a.m. Chinese forces recaptured Sungtze, S.E. of Ichang.

June 12. At night Bomber Command in great strength attacked Bochum. Lampedusa, heavily bombed and bombarded, surrendered at 5.30 p.m. Day and night air attacks on Sicily.

June 13. Two large formations of U.S. heavy bombers (24 lost) made unescorted attacks on Bremen and Kiel. Sicilian airfields bombed. Allied raid on Rabaul.

June 14. Bomber Command made a heavy night attack on Oberhausen.

June 15. Heavy bomber attacks on Sicilian airfields. Chinese announce recapture of Michitai, S.W. of Shasi. U.S. aircraft bombed Kiska (Aleutians).

June 16. 94 of 120 Japanese planes shot down over Guadalcanal for loss of six American planes (one pilot safe). Naples heavily bombed at night.

June 18. Strong force of U.S. heavy bombers attacked Sardinia and Sicily.

June 19. At night strong force of R.A.F. four-engined bombers attacked Schneider works, Le Creusot. 90-min. dawn air raid on Rabaul (New Britain).

June 20. At night R.A.F. Lancasters made heavy attack on Friedrichshafen. Messina heavily attacked (June 19–20). Japanese lost 24 of 48 aircraft sent to attack Darwin (Australia).

June 21. Over 700 R.A.F. heavies made shattering night attack on Krefeld. Heavy daylight attack by U.S. bombers on Naples. Lightnings shot down 23 out of 36 Zeros in air battles over Lae-Salamaua area (New Guinea).

June 22. Heavy daylight attacks by U.S. bombers on Huels, Antwerp and Rotterdam. Concentrated night attack by R.A.F. on Muelheim.

June 23. Short but sharp raid by 15 enemy planes on Hull. Spezia heavily bombed by same force of Lancasters which hit Friedrichshafen on June 20, on return journey from N. Africa.

June 24. R.A.F. Bombers in great strength raided Elberfeld.

June 25. Heavy night attack by R.A.F. on Bochum and Gelsenkirchen. Day and night attacks on targets in Sicily and Sardinia. U.S. bombers made six attacks on Kiska (Aleutians).

June 26. Lae airfield (New Guinea) heavily bombed by Allies without loss.

June 26–27. Concentrated 15-min. attack by R.A.F. on Naples.

June 28. Heavy attack on St. Nazaire U-boat base by U.S. Fortresses ; night attack in great strength by British heavies on Cologne. Fierce attack on Leghorn by 100 U.S. Fortresses.

June 30. Palermo (Sicily) heavily bombed by U.S. Fortresses. U.S. Marines landed on Rendova (New Georgia) ; 121 Japanese aircraft shot down. American forces landed at Nassau Bay (New Guinea).

Chapter 279

GERMANY'S EUROPEAN ALLIES WAVER

The year 1943 was an ominous one for Germany's satellites: Finland, Hungary, Rumania and Bulgaria. Russia's steady drive westward, the final defeat of the Axis in Africa, and the Allied invasion of Italy showed only too clearly that the chances of Axis victory were fading. Dr. F. Heymann here describes their efforts to disentangle themselves from their alliance with Germany. For the earlier history of the war in these countries, see Chapters 235 and 236

ALREADY in the closing stages of 1942 there could be no doubt that the Finnish people were tired of war. The question whether anything could be won by continuing the fight was answered early in 1943 by the Russian victories in general, and by the relief of Leningrad in particular. After the Russians retook the fortress of Schluesselburg on January 18, every chance of a combined Finno-German victory in northern Russia vanished, and with it the hopes of those who had dreamed of a Greater Finland to which Germany had promised the position of "the leading power in the North." However, there still seemed a chance that by going out of the war Finland might be left in full possession of the Karelian Isthmus which she had ceded to Russia in 1940 (*see* page 746). Many leading politicians hoped that this could be achieved simply by taking up a more passive attitude in the war against Russia.

FINLAND

PREMIER OF FINLAND

Professor Edwin Linkomies, who formed a new coalition government on March 4, 1943, in which all major parties from Conservatives to Social Democrats were represented. Its members included Mr. Vanio Tanner, a leading Social Democrat, who was Minister of Finance, and whose hatred of Russia had unfortunate repercussions for his country.

Photo, Black Star

After the re-election of Mr. Risto Ryti as President (February 15), the new Cabinet formed on March 4 by Professor Edwin Linkomies was again a coalition in which all major parties from Conservatives to Social Democrats were represented. The leading personality among Social Democrats was still Mr. Vanio Tanner, the Minister of Finance, who controlled the strong co-operative organization "Elanto," and was the most powerful man in the Finnish Labour movement. His violent Russophobia made him entirely blind to the fact that by helping Nazi Germany he was betraying everything his party had ever stood for. Much of what happened during the year in relation to the peace issue was due to his sinister influence.

The new Government was soon informed by the State Department in Washington that the United States was prepared to mediate between Finland and Russia. Instead of accepting this offer, the Finns referred the matter to Berlin. Ribbentrop, as was to be expected, forbad any move of the sort, and Finland obediently declined the American offer. Yet the Government seems to have believed that this would in no way affect the American attitude towards Finland, for great surprise was displayed when Washington withdrew the whole staff of the American legation in Helsinki, with the sole exception of the chargé d'affaires. Finnish public opinion, ill-informed about Finland's position in general, was shocked, and criticism of the Government's policy became much more outspoken.

A conference of the Trade Unions Council passed a resolution calling for the utmost effort by the Government to maintain good relations with the United States and Sweden and to preserve the goodwill towards Finland of the Danish and Norwegian peoples, oppressed by Finland's ally Germany. Public opinion was strong enough in these matters to force the Government to make representations to the German Government regarding the treatment of Norwegian students and Danish Jews. Finland, indeed, remained the only one of Germany's vassal states which never agreed to discriminate against its own small Jewish community.

SOVIET-FINNISH FRONT

The 1940 frontier, and the line held by the Finns at the end of 1943, are shown in this map. Although the Soviet capture of Schluesselburg and consequent relief of Leningrad in January 1943, ended Finnish hopes of expansion, Finland continued to evade recognition of the fact. The Russo-Finnish border before 1940 is shown in the map in page 754.

Public discussion on the peace issue continued all through the year. On August 20 a remarkable petition was submitted to President Ryti. It was signed by 33 prominent people from all Government parties except the Conservatives, and urged the President to investigate all possibilities of concluding a separate peace with Russia. That the petition had a strong backing in Parliament was shown in a secret debate on foreign policy in September, and the Government had to give the assurance that everything possible was being done to quit the war. But no steps were taken to fulfil this promise.

One of the reasons given for this passive attitude was that Finland depended on Germany for her food supplies. Actually this dependence was by no means one-sided. Two-thirds of

ENGLISH BOOKS IN FINLAND
However strong anti-Russian feeling may have been in Finland, there was little anti-British or anti-American sentiment—a fact confirmed by this Finnish soldier browsing among English books in a bookshop of his homeland. The Finns, indeed, were very surprised when in 1943 the United States withdrew the staff of the American legation in Helsinki after Finland had refused U.S. mediation in the war with Russia. *Photo, Black Star*

Germany's supplies of nickel, one-fourth of her molybdenum and one-fifth of her copper—all three metals of high military importance—came from Finland, together with huge

Trade With Germany

quantities of timber. On balance, it is true, Finnish imports from Germany, among them about half of her grain supplies, were larger than her exports to Germany, and apart from Italy she was the only Axis state to be a debtor to Germany. But economic dependence on Germany was hardly a valid excuse for not breaking with her, as in the long run it was in the interest of the country to resume her old economic relations with the Western powers. Moreover the United States as well as Sweden had promised to help Finland in case German food deliveries were stopped, and even if it had taken some time to get that help through, there was no immediate danger of any grave scarcity of food as the 1943 harvest was much better than that of the year before had been. Not economic necessity, but the narrow political outlook and shortsightedness of her ruling politicians kept Finland in the war far beyond the end of 1943.

Events inside Hungary in 1943 were in some ways similar to those in Finland. Like the Finns, the Hungarians had realized, even at the beginning of the year, that by allying themselves with Germany they had backed the wrong horse. It was mainly the grave losses, not far from utter annihilation, suffered by the Second Hungarian Army near Voronezh (January–February 1943; *see* page 2681) which effectively cured their ambition to play any further part in the Russian war. As in Finland, there was still some measure of public control left in Hungary, though the "parliamentary regime"

in Budapest was much **HUNGARY** more of a caricature of real democratic government than that in Helsinki. Doubtless Hungary would have liked to break away from the German alliance as much as any of the other satellite states. Yet for geographic, political and, to some extent, economic reasons, it was more difficult for her than for the other vassals of Germany to take this step. She had made enemies of almost all her neighbours—Czechs and Slovaks, Ruthenians and Rumanians, Serbs and Croats. The Germans had an easy access to Hungarian territory from many directions and could always threaten—as they occasionally did—to give Transylvania back to Rumania.

Thus, with their freedom of action limited, the Regent Admiral Horthy and Prime Minister Kallay tried at least to conserve the Hungarian Army and at the same time to win sympathy for Hungary among the great Western nations. Unlike Rumania, Hungary succeeded in recalling most of her armed forces from Russia—only two divisions remained, allegedly to fight partisans behind the front line. At the same time every opportunity was used by Hungarian politicians and journalists to stress that Hungary had really been

REGENT OF HUNGARY AT HITLER'S HEADQUARTERS
Admiral Nicholas Horthy, Regent of Hungary, with Ribbentrop, German Foreign Minister, Keitel, Hitler's Chief of Staff, and Bormann, Deputy Leader of the Nazi Party, during his visit to Hitler's G.H.Q. on the eastern front on April 16-18, 1943. The official German communiqué issued stated, ' The Fuehrer and the Regent expressed their firm determination to continue the war against Bolshevism and its Anglo-American allies unerringly until final victory is won.' Horthy maintained that the words ' Anglo-American allies ' were inserted after he had signed the statement, and refused to agree to this addition. *Photo, Keystone*

forced into the war, that she was a torch-bearer of Western and Latin culture, and that she wanted nothing better than to live in peace—of course keeping all the spoils she had taken from her neighbours.

For the first few months of the year the Government thought that Hungary's case could be strengthened in the eyes of the United Nations by giving **Small Farmers' Party Demands Peace** the democratic opposition in the Diet some opportunity of freely expressing their views. This was used to a considerable extent by the small Social Democratic Party and the Liberal Group led by the Deputy M. Ressay as well as by the much larger "Party of small farmers," some of whose deputies openly asked for peace, social justice and land reform.

Soon, however, Germany tried to stop this "softening up" of Hungary's home front. In April Admiral Horthy was invited to see Hitler at Berchtesgaden. Though he refused to send more divisions to the Eastern front, it was much more difficult to decline some of Germany's political demands. Hitler asked that Hungary's Prime Minister should state, before a plenary session of the Diet, that Hungary was firmly resolved to fight to the end on Germany's side and never to conclude a separate peace. To strengthen the pro-German wing of the Government Hitler proposed that Horthy should give a prominent Cabinet post to M. Imrédy, the former Prime Minister who had always proved to be Nazi-

minded and a hundred per cent supporter of the alliance with Berlin. It is not quite clear whether promises of this kind were made by Horthy in Berchtesgaden. In any case he found, on his return to Budapest, that if the Government went to these lengths it would have difficulty with Parliament, and, in order to free himself, Kallay prorogued Parliament indefinitely.

The double game thus played by the Kallay Government became more difficult when by Mussolini's fall Hungary lost her traditional protector. Until the end, her relations with Italy had been closer than those with Germany, and Hungary, where a professional diplomat, M. Ghyczy, had just been appointed Foreign Minister, did not recall her legation from Italy even after that country's surrender to the Allies. Only German pressure made her recognize the puppet "Fascist Republic" as well.

Some attempts were made to show a more benevolent attitude towards some of the millions of foreign nationals who had come under Hungarian rule between 1938 and 1941. Comparatively best treated were those who had last become Hungarian subjects: the Serbs in the Bačka. The Slovaks had more complaints, which were often voiced in the Bratislava press. Treatment of Rumanians in Transylvania was worse, as attempts were made to prove the Hungarian national character of the country by "Hungarizing" it quickly —one of the reasons which, as well as corresponding Rumanian measures

against Hungarians, led to incessant friction between the two "allies."

Worst of all, however, was the treatment of the people of Subcarpathian Ruthenia, Czechoslovakia's easternmost province "conquered" by Hungary in March 1939. Hungarian military and civil authorities did everything in their power to crush **Brutal Treatment of Ruthenia** the spirit of those people. Hundreds were executed, thousands thrown into the concentration camps of Nyiregyhaza and Garany; but many more thousands went into the mountains and forests to form partisan units. Whereas in Hungary proper the treatment of the Jewish middle class had slightly improved in order to impress the English-speaking Nations —one prominent industrialist, M. Chorin, had even been restored to his seat in the Upper House—the masses of poor Jews in Ruthenia were treated exactly in the same way as those under German rule, tens of thousands of them being deported to Poland.

Economically, Hungary was less affected by the war and by forced exports to Germany than her neighbours in the east and south-east. The bad situation of the smallholders was not, in general, due to the war. One half of the soil belonged to 8,000 people—the greater part of it to only 526 magnates—whereas no less than 4,400,000 peasants had to share the other half. There was some unrest when the Government tried to collect specified amounts of produce, calculated

THIS U.S. BOMBER HIT PLOESTI
An American Liberator forced down in Rumania after the heavy first raid on that centre of Rumanian oil production on August 1, 1943 (see illus., page 2666), was an object of great interest to the Rumanian officials here seen examining it where it drove its nose into the ground as it landed. Some 40 to 50 out of 177 bombers were lost altogether on this occasion, but it was estimated that most of Ploesti's refineries had been put out of action for some time at least.

RUMANIAN GUN CREW IN RUSSIA

The crew of this anti-tank gun near the Black Sea port of Novorossiisk were a small unit among the thousands of men Rumania was compelled to contribute to the armies Germany threw against Russia. Two Rumanian divisions at least were among the forces sacrificed by Germany at Stalingrad, and Rumanian troops fought in the Crimea too. By her defection to the Axis, Rumania gained the doubtful prize of Bessarabia.

Photo, Associated Press

in "Wheat-Units," from every one of them without regard to the actual result of his harvest. Altogether there was little left, towards the end of the year, of the "liberalism" displayed previously, and arrests not only of Communists but also of Social Democrats and other "unreliable elements" did much to lift the "democratic" mask from the face of a dictatorial and semi-Fascist regime.

For some time Marshal Antonescu, Rumania's dictator, had successfully played the strong man. In reality, however, the "Conducator" (a Rumanian translation of

RUMANIA the Italian "Duce" and the German "Fuehrer") had to play a very difficult game to keep himself in power. To a large extent he had to rely on Germany and the German army to maintain his grip on the country ; but at the same time he knew that there was a limit to what he could exact from the Rumanian people without risking an open revolt. Thus he kept trying to play off one side against the other.

But the Germans were equally masters of this game, and they had some tricks ready with which to bring pressure to bear on Antonescu. One was the ultra-fascist "Iron Guard," whose leader, Horia Sima, was still under German protection though a Rumanian court had condemned him, in absence, to hard labour for life.

Early in January 1943, after Antonescu had ventured to block some exports to Germany on account of the huge and ever-mounting German clearing debt, the Germans staged a revolt of the "Iron

Guard" and German troops had to help the Government to restore order in Bukarest, thus making Antonescu much more conscious of his dependence on his masters in Berlin. There is no doubt that the same purpose was served by an interview which Antonescu had with Hitler on January 10. The "Conducator" had tried to persuade Germany that Rumania could not afford to sacrifice an ever-growing part of her army in the fight against Russia. Yet he yielded to German pressure by consenting that those divisions at the front which had lost no more than a quarter of their effectives should once more be filled up by drawing on reserves and new conscripts while the divisions with heavier losses were to be formed into a smaller number of new units. As for maintaining full deliveries of Rumanian produce to Germany, the Minister of National Economy, M. Fintescu, was replaced by M. Dobre, who was a willing tool in the hands of the German Minister, Killinger, and accepted all his demands.

By deciding for complete subservience to Germany, the dictator had to turn more strongly against all those elements which were against his policy, partly out of real democratic conviction and partly because they could not forgive the Antonescu regime for ceding northern Transylvania to Rumania's arch enemy, Hungary. Anti-Government and anti-German demonstrations, disturbances, acts of sabotage, and even occasional fighting, occurred again in parts of southern Transylvania and Wallachia. There was open agitation against sending more troops to Russia. The High

Command thereupon issued an order threatening with severe penalties any public criticism of military and political measures, any listening to enemy broadcasts, and any other hampering of the war effort. As quite a large number of civil servants and other public officials were suspected of "unreliability," a purge was carried out in June, some of the officials being merely dismissed while others were arrested. The persecution of Jews was also stepped up again.

The whole basis of this policy, however, was shaken when, from July onwards, the Russian armies swept forward on the central and southern fronts. The Russian offensive had only just got into its stride when the Government declared that Rumania had no annexationist intentions, that it fought Russia only to preserve the independence and freedom of the Rumanian state, and that the country beyond the Dniester —which in 1941 had been annexed as the province of "Transnistria"—was "only temporarily occupied." When in autumn the Kuban bridge-head, held by German and Rumanian troops, was lost and the Russians gained a foothold in the Crimea, Rumanian officials in "Transnistria" began to quit the country in a sort of panic flight, and with them went the "Governor," M. Alexianu, who for some time had exercised a most arbitrary rule over this part of the Ukraine from his palace in Odessa.

The economic situation deteriorated considerably in 1943. Prices went up steadily : in October 1943 the price of potatoes in Bukarest was three times as high as in 1939, of eggs, onions and maize flour six times, butter seven, milk and cheese eight, wheat flour 10, beef 11, brown bread 14, cloth 16 and shoes 20 times as high as in 1939. The average level of necessities stood about 10 times as high. Wages for skilled industrial workers had in the meantime risen, though not enough to equal the rise in prices. All other salary and wage earners had their standard of living cut down pitiably, and bad distribution made things worse. Though one of Europe's richest agricultural countries, Rumania was forced to introduce three meatless days every week.

Towards the end of the year the fears that had led to the mass flight from "Transnistria" proved to be justified, as the Russians broke the Dnieper line and drew near the frontiers of Bessarabia. This gave a stronger impetus to all the forces opposed to the war, among whom the leading figure was still Julius Maniu, the great leader of the Transylvanian peasantry, whom neither Antonescu nor the Germans had dared to touch (*see* illus., page 2343). Hopes were revived, too, that by breaking away from Germany Rumania might regain the whole of Transylvania. On December 1, the 25th anniversary of the annexation of Transylvania in 1918, great mass demonstrations were held in the capital and all over the country at which resolutions were passed declaring Rumania's right to the whole province.

Bulgaria was, in 1943, the only one of Hitler's vassal states whose armies had not bled on Russian soil. Though proclaiming complete **BULGARIA** solidarity with Germany in her fight to save Europe from Bolshevism, the Bulgarian Government continued to refuse to go to war against Russia, as there could be no doubt that, being strongly Russophil by an overwhelming majority, Bulgarian officers and soldiers would mutiny or desert rather than fight in the East.

Short of open warfare, however, the Government of King Boris and Prime Minister Filoff did everything to help the Germans in the East, first by allowing Bulgaria's ports Varna and Burgas to be used as bases by German Black Sea naval units, and secondly by sending occupation troops into new stretches of Greek and Yugoslav territory, particularly into Serbia, thereby relieving German troops for use against Russia.

Not satisfied with garrisoning the occupied territory of her neighbours, Bulgaria attempted to effect a rapid denationalization of those parts of Thrace, Macedonia and Serbia which, it was hoped by the ruling clique, would become Bulgarian territory after the war. Expulsion of Greeks from parts of Thrace, and attempts to settle Bulgarian peasants in their place, were continued ruthlessly, even after the declaration, on March 24, of the British Government that Britain regarded

STATE VISIT—STATE FUNERAL

King Boris of Bulgaria, first of the Axis satellite rulers to visit Hitler in the spring of 1943, is believed to have met the Fuehrer again in August, when Hitler was reported to have adopted a threatening attitude. The King's sudden death on August 28 following this meeting gave rise to rumours that he had been murdered. Right, Hitler greets King Boris on March 31. Below, the catafalque in which, attended by Marshal Keitel and Admiral Raeder, the body of King Boris was borne to burial in Sofia.   *Photos, Keystone ; Sport & General*

any acts aimed at "Bulgarizing" the occupied territory as null and void and that such acts would have to be undone after the war.

Its ill-gotten gains, however, failed to win popularity for the Filoff Government and the unrest that had started in 1942 increased. Several prominent officials, among them **Growing Unrest** high police officers, were assassinated, and the continued persecution of everyone who opposed the Government (they were always charged with "Bolshevist activity") did nothing to relieve the tension. Opposition grew especially strong in the Army, where groups of officers had long belonged to an organization called Zveno, also known as the "Military League." Though it had Fascist leanings, it was

BULGARIA'S NEW RULERS

According to the constitution of Bulgaria, the King has the right to nominate three persons to serve on the Regency Council; but no will was found after Boris's death, and on September 9 the Sobranje (Grand National Council) approved of Prince Kyril (uncle of the new king), Prof. Bogdan Filoff (Prime Minister) and Gen. Michoff (War Minister) to act as a Regency Council during the king's minority. Here the Regents are being sworn in. Top, the new king, six-year-old Simeon II, with men of the Bulgarian forces. *Photos, Keystone; Sport & General*

at the same time Russophil, and its main representatives never trusted the King and his opportunist policy.

The King's position had never been fully secure. He was probably far from enthusiastic about the alliance with Germany, but he had become the prisoner of the web of political intrigues which he himself had helped to spin. Most of the unquestioned popularity which he had enjoyed with the Bulgarian peasantry in the 30s had gone. Yet despite all his grave mistakes and the

crowning blunder of destroying all chances of understanding between Bulgaria and her neighbours, his was a steadying influence in the turmoil of Bulgarian politics, and the situation became even more chaotic when, on August 28, Boris unexpectedly died.

The circumstances of the King's death remained somewhat mysterious. The official statement described the causes as double pneumonia and cerebral congestion owing to an obstruction of the left artery of the heart, but suspicion

at once arose that the King had been murdered. It is still not quite sure whether he really had visited Hitler's headquarters immediately before, as he was stated to have done. One rumour had it that he was killed by the Germans because it was feared that he intended to break away from the Axis, another version was that he had been the victim of oppositional groups who resented the German rule tolerated, if not established, by Boris.

As Crown Prince Simeon was only six, a Regency had to be set up. Boris had left no will, or at least it was said that no will was found, though according to the constitution he had had the right to nominate three persons to serve on a Regency Council and was believed to have done so. It would have appeared only natural that Boris's widow Joanna, the new King's mother, should belong to this Council. Joanna, however, was a daughter of the King of Italy, and it seems that the Germans opposed her nomination as they feared that the Queen might follow the policy of Italy (who on September 3 concluded an armistice with the Allies). The Council as it was actually nominated seemed to exclude this danger altogether. To it belonged the late King's brother, Prince Kyril, who had always been regarded as being wholly under German influence; the Prime Minister Filoff, whose policy had led the country right into the German camp; and the Minister of War, General Michoff, who belonged to the more Germanophil wing of the Army.

The Regency Council appointed the former Minister of Finance, Dr. Bojiloff, as Prime Minister. His Government showed no intention of deviating from the policy of their predecessors. There was **New Government—Same Policy** one small exception. The persecution of the Jews, which owing to German pressure had been in full progress since May 1943, had proved to be exceedingly unpopular. Sharp protests were launched by the Archbishop of Sofia and the Bishop of Plovdiv at the deportation of thousands of Jews from the occupied territories, and the Government eventually declared that no Jews of Bulgarian nationality were to be deported.

Opposition in Army circles and general unrest again grew stronger towards the end of the year, when a number of bombing raids on the railway yards of Sofia and other targets caused panic in the capital. Many civil servants fled to the country. The Bulgarian people realized that, even by avoiding war with Russia, Bulgaria could not hope to avoid the destruction of the war into which she had been dragged by greedy and irresponsible rulers.

FIELD-MARSHAL THE RT. HON. JAN CHRISTIAAN SMUTS, P.C., C.H., K.C.

Leader against Britain in the South African War of 1899–1902, the great Boer soldier Smuts became reconciled to the conqueror after the Peace of Vereeniging, and fought for Britain in the First Great War of 1914–18. When the Second Great War began he was Prime Minister of South Africa and, despite strong elements of opposition, led the Union to throw in its lot with Great Britain again. His policy was strikingly confirmed by the elections of 1943 (see page 2806). Points from an important speech he made during his second war visit to Britain appear in page 2819.

Direct colour photograph by Pictorial Press

Cyprus

Malta

Palestine

Gibraltar

Aden

Somaliland

Western Samoa

Mauritius

Ceylon

Hong Kong

Seychelles

Fiji

West Pacific Islands

Gilbert and Ellice Islands

Grenada

Straits Settlements

Sarawak

British North Borneo

Brunei

Federated Malay States

·THREE YEARS AGO WE STOOD ALONE. . . . IN THAT DARK,
TERRIFIC AND ALSO GLORIOUS HOUR, WE RECEIVED FROM ALL—

That testing hour of June 1940, referred to by the Prime Minister in the speech from which this quotation is taken,
was a triumphant vindication of the British Empire. Self-governing Dominions and Crown Colonies alike rallied more
firmly to the support of the Mother Country. The coats-of-arms shown in this and the opposite page are of 40
among the Crown Colonies, Protectorates and Mandated Territories of the British Empire. Britain administers—

Northern Rhodesia

Tanganyika

Kenya

Uganda

Nyasaland

Gambia

Nigeria

Southern Rhodesia

Sierra Leone

Gold Coast

Trinidad

Bahamas

Bermuda

Barbados

Leeward Islands

Windward Islands

British Honduras

Jamaica

British Guiana

Falkland Islands

—PARTS OF HIS MAJESTY'S DOMINIONS . . . THE ASSURANCE THAT WE WOULD ALL GO DOWN OR COME THROUGH TOGETHER'

—areas in all the seven seas. Some have belonged to her for centuries: Elizabeth issued a Charter to trade in Gambia in 1588 (though that country was not recognized as British till 1783). Most of the areas represented, however, were acquired during the 19th century. The mandated territories (Palestine, for instance) came under British administration after the First Great War. For the record of the Crown Colonies' part during 1943 see Chapter 281

THE SINKING OF 'SCHARNHORST', DECEMBER 26, 1943

The German battleship 'Scharnhorst,' long a threat to British shipping, was at last sunk on December 26, 1943 (see Chapter 284). Her loss left the German navy with only six heavy units. 'Scharnhorst,' 26,000 tons, was completed in 1939. She had a speed of 27 knots and carried nine 11-in. guns, twelve 5·9-in. guns, and 30 others. She helped to sink H.M. aircraft-carrier 'Glorious' off Narvik in 1940, claimed the sinking of 22 merchantmen in the Atlantic from January to March 1941, lay up in Brest till February 1942, when she escaped through the Straits of Dover with 'Gneisenau' and 'Prinz Eugen.' She joined the main German fleet in Altenfjord in March 1942.

From the painting by Charles Pears, Crown Copyright

Chapter 280

THE DOMINIONS IN THEIR 5th YEAR OF WAR

Though during 1943 the war dominated life in the Dominions as elsewhere, home affairs and political developments, particularly in South Africa and Australia, were of outstanding interest. The following brief review records the chief points in these domestic happenings and describes the amazing production feats and splendid overseas service of these partners in the British Commonwealth. It takes up the story from Chapter 247

THE outstanding public event of the year 1943 in Canada—the series of international consultations held in Quebec during August—was of world importance. Mr. Churchill, accompanied by Lord Leathers and the British Chiefs of Staff, reached Canada on August 10. Next day **CANADA** a joint session of the British and Canadian War Cabinets surveyed " the field of the war " and questions of special interest to the two Governments. Mr. Churchill spent August 12–14 with President Roosevelt at Hyde Park (N.Y.), returning to Quebec on the 15th, where military discussions were going forward between British, U.S., and Canadian services chiefs. On August 17 President Roosevelt, accompanied by Mr. Harry Hopkins, arrived. Next day they were joined by Mr. Eden, Mr. Brendan Bracken, and Sir Alexander Cadogan, Permanent Secretary of the British Foreign Office. Discussions continued.

A Press statement issued by Mr. Bracken on August 19 said, " Our plans are to bomb, burn, and ruthlessly destroy in every way available to us the people responsible for creating this war " ; and the arrival on August 22 of Dr. T. V. Soong, Chinese Foreign Minister (who had just been on an official visit to Britain : *see* page 2698), made it clear that Japan was one of the people whose fate was being settled. The immediate outcome of a meeting on August 23 of Mr. Churchill, President Roosevelt, Dr. Soong, and Mr. Hopkins was the setting up next day of the South East Asia Command.

Mr. Anthony Eden, British Foreign Secretary, visited Ottawa on March 30, after conferring with President Roosevelt in Washington, and discussed with the Prime Minister and the Cabinet shipping, political and economic problems, post-war relief of liberated peoples, and other matters of urgent interest to the British and Canadian Governments. In the course of a speech he made to a joint session of the Commons and Senate, he referred to the achievements of the Canadian forces on land, at sea, and in the air, and to the distinctive part played by the Dominion in the Battle of the Atlantic. He had

some special words, spoken in French, for the French Canadian members on the hope of France's regeneration. The intimate collaboration of Canada in the war policies of Great Britain and the U.S.A. was emphasized when the Prime Minister went to Washington in May to join in the discussions during Mr. Churchill's visit to the President.

General Penaranda, President of Bolivia, arrived in Canada on May 12 for a short official visit at the invitation of the Government : he was the first South American president to visit Canada during his term of office. Another important visitor was Mme. Chiang Kai-shek (*see* illus., page 2698). The Government announced its recognition of the French Committee of National Liberation in August, General George P. Vanier being appointed Canadian representative at Algiers.

The elections held in the Province of Ontario on August 3 resulted in the decisive defeat of the Liberal Government of the province, three ministers losing their seats. The Progressive Conservatives, who had tested the electorate on a provincial scale for the first time since remoulding their policy, headed the poll with 39 seats (out of 90), and formed the new Cabinet.

The Budget, introduced on March 2, provided for the collection of Income Tax on the " pay-as-you -earn " system, follow- **" Pay-as-You- Earn " in Canada** ing discussions of the method in London with British Treasury officials. Canada budgeted for $4,890,000,000 for war expenses in the year ending March 31, 1944, including a contribution to United Nations supplies to the value of $1,000,000,000. (The year before, she had given a similar sum as a free gift to Britain.) Direct taxation raised eight times as much in 1942–43 as in the last full fiscal year before the war.

CANADA BUILDS FOR THE BATTLE OF THE ATLANTIC
From shipbuilding yards at Sorel, Province of Quebec, this corvette, H.M.C.S. ' La Malbaie,' and seven other ships—four minesweepers and three corvettes—were christened at the same ceremonies as they left the slips to be completed and sent out, manned by British and Canadian seamen, to take part in the Battle of the Atlantic. During 1943, 150 cargo and 100 naval vessels were produced in Canadian shipbuilding yards. *Photo, Sport & General*

WAR LEADERS IN QUEBEC

Mr. Winston Churchill, Prime Minister of Britain, inspired one of the wildest displays of enthusiasm ever seen in old Quebec when he rode through the streets in an open car with Mr. Mackenzie King, Prime Minister of Canada, on August 23, 1943, during the Quebec Conference. President Roosevelt, at the end of the conference, visited Ottawa. He is seen (right) addressing a joint session of the Canadian House of Commons and Senate.

Photos, Sport & General; "New York Times" Photos

Canada's war effort in 1943 was as stern as the speech dealing with it which Mr. Mackenzie King delivered at the Canadian Club of Toronto, on April 19, to mark the inauguration of the Dominion's Fourth Victory Loan. By the end of 1943, of Canada's population of 11,000,000, 1,100,000, including more than 260,000 women, were engaged on war work in some form, and Canada had become the fourth largest producer of war supplies among the United Nations. The strength of the Forces was more than 750,000, including over 40,000 women. The Army had increased to more than 470,000 : at the outbreak of war it had numbered only 4,500. Canadians served in Britain, on raids at Spitzbergen and Dieppe, in Newfoundland, Iceland, Hongkong, the West Indies, Bermuda, and in Kiska, one of the Aleutian Islands; while the Canadian First Division took part in the Sicily campaign during July and August, and the landings in Italy. Engineering units built roads in Alaska and Britain, and fortifications in Gibraltar; a Forestry Corps operated in Britain.

Canada's naval strength had increased from 3,600 men and 15 vessels at the outbreak of war to over 74,000 men and more than 700 craft, of which 250 were ocean-going combat ships (destroyers, corvettes, etc.). About 40 per cent of the naval forces engaged in the Battle of the Atlantic were Canadian; her Navy co-operated in the defence of the North Pacific Coast, and took part from the end of 1942 in operations in the Mediterranean.

As to air strength, at the end of 1943 Canada was the fourth greatest air power among the United Nations. Its Air Force had increased from a pre-war total of 4,000 to about 200,000 by November 1943. Squadrons oversea operated under the direction of R.A.F. Bomber Command, Coastal Command, Fighter Command, Allied Expeditionary Air Force, Mediterranean Command, and India Command. The R.C.A.F. also carried out anti-submarine patrols from North American bases. By the end of 1943 the British Commonwealth Air Training Plan, administered by the Canadian Government, which bore half the cost, had turned out more than 86,000 air crew graduates, the majority of whom were Canadians.

Canada's war products were distributed as follows : 30 per cent to Canadian Forces at home and abroad; 48 per cent to the United Kingdom, other Empire countries and Russia; and 22 per cent to the United States and China. Reserve supplies were built up in Canada as part of a strategic plan to meet emergency demands. More than half the motor vehicles used by the British Eighth Army in Africa were manufactured in Canada. Canadian-made vehicles carried the main weight of the Eighth Army advance in Italy.

By December 1943 Canada had produced about 55,000,000 rounds of heavy ammunition and 3,000,000,000 rounds of small-arms ammunition, besides great quantities of aerial bombs, trench mortar bombs, and anti-tank mines. Machine-guns and small-arms production showed a 92 per cent increase over 1942, small-arms ammunition a 30 per cent increase, and guns a 15 per cent increase ; 35,000 army rifles and 6,000 Sten guns were turned out each month. Naval and army gun units, including field, anti-aircraft, tank and anti-tank guns, totalling 80,000, had been produced.

This amazing record was eclipsed by Canada's shipbuilding feats. In 1939 the Dominion had almost no shipbuilding industry. On September 18, 1943, the 620th Canadian-built vessel was launched. Of these 620, 215 were cargo vessels, and 405 were escort and other naval types. During the first three years of the war nearly 10,000 merchant and naval vessels were repaired in Canada. Nine types of aircraft were produced—among them Anson, Cornell, and Norseman trainers, Lancaster, Mosquito, and Hell-Diver service planes, and the Skymaster transport. The first Canadian-built Lancasters and Mosquitoes arrived at a British airfield in the early part of August. Some 10,000 military aircraft had been produced by the end of 1943. Before the war not 40 planes were produced a year.

The war efforts of Canada and the United States were linked through the following committees : Permanent Joint Board on Defence, Materials Co-ordinating Committee, Joint Economic Committee, Joint War Production Committee, Joint Agricultural Committee, and Joint War Aid Committee. Canada was also a member of the Combined Production and Resources Board with the United Kingdom and the United States, and in October 1943 was admitted to full membership on the Combined Food Board with the United Kingdom and the United States. Her food exports were of vital importance to Britain. At the end of 1943 she was sending 10 per cent of Britain's total

Canadians on War Service

Canada's Shipbuilding Feats

FROM VANCOUVER TO SICILY

These three men, all from Vancouver, were among the assault troops of the Canadian First Army who landed on Pachino Peninsula in Sicily on July 10, 1943. Some account of the gallant part the Canadians played in the conquest of the island is given in Chapter 283. Left, memorial to men of this Dominion who fell in Sicily carved by Italian craftsmen from Syracuse white limestone, and erected near the mountain town of Agira, captured by the Canadians in August.

The status of Newfoundland came up for discussion in the Canadian Parliament in July, when the Prime Minister replied to a suggestion that Newfoundland should be invited to enter the Dominion as its 10th province. "Any discussions," he said, "in respect of the possible bringing of Newfoundland into the confederation ought to be initiated on the part of the Newfoundland people rather than by members of this House."

NEWFOUND-LAND

The suggestion had been induced by growing restlessness in Newfoundland over her status : though she remained a Dominion in name, her self-government was in abeyance, her affairs since 1934 having been administered by the Governor, acting on the advice of a

egg supply, 25 per cent of her cheese, 35 per cent of her canned fish, 25 per cent of her wheat, and 60 per cent to 80 per cent of her bacon.

That Canada was thinking in terms of post-war development as well as of wartime effort was evidenced by two things in particular : the position she took on post-war air plans, and the wide interest shown in the Marsh Plan. In the House of Commons Mr. Mackenzie King stated on April 2 that the Government strongly favoured a policy of international collaboration in air transport, and was prepared to take part in international negotiations for that purpose—a policy advocated by Canada's delegation at the Empire Air Conference held in London in October. The Marsh Plan, otherwise "Canada's Beveridge Report," was a national security scheme submitted on March 17 by Dr. Leonard C. Marsh to the newly appointed Parliamentary Committee on Social Insurance. Its aim was to ensure a basic minimum income for every Canadian, irrespective of occupation, sex, or age ; its estimated cost, 225,000,000 dollars a year.

NEWFOUNDLANDERS WITH THE EIGHTH IN ITALY

The 166th (Newfoundland) Army Field Regiment, R.A., after manning heavy coast defences in Norfolk (see illus., page 1182), went into action alongside the French in North Africa on April 1, 1943. They fought through to the end in Tunisia, and, after rest, joined the Eighth Army in Italy. This group of them is waiting to cross the Sangro River. *Photo, British Official*

ITALIAN SUBMARINE PUTS IN AT DURBAN

After the surrender of Italy in September 1943, when the main Italian fleet sailed to Malta, Italian submarines at sea put in to the nearest Allied harbour. Here, the Ammiraglio Cagni, one of the largest submarines in the world, moves to her berth at Durban, South Africa. A black flag, agreed signal of surrender, flies from her periscope. She had been at sea 83 days. Her armament consisted of two 3.9-in. guns, four machine-guns, and fourteen 18-in. torpedo tubes.

Photo, Sport & General

Commission of six (three from Newfoundland and three from the United Kingdom) exclusive of the Governor, and under his chairmanship. This situation had arisen owing to her inability to pay her way.

The use of the island by the U.S. as a naval and military base produced unexampled prosperity, and the Newfoundland Board of Trade, meeting at St. John's on March 8, passed two resolutions, one protesting against the new taxation proposals made by the Commission Government, the second demanding a return to some form of representative government. A petition, backed by many sections of the community, was later sent to the King asking for the appointment of a Royal Commission to inquire into the island's constitutional and financial position.

On May 5 Mr. Attlee announced in the British House of Commons that a parliamentary mission was to pay an informal visit to the island. On December 2 Mr. Emrys Evans, Dominions Under-Secretary, stated that though the British Government wanted self-government to be restored to a self-supporting Newfoundland, if the people expressed a wish for it, such expression could not be given in the abnormal conditions of war. As soon as practicable after the end of the European war, machinery must be provided to enable the Newfoundlanders to express their considered views. This statement was debated on December 15, when Mr. C. G. Ammon, leader of the Goodwill Mission, in proposing a motion (which was agreed to) welcoming the acceptance of the principle of Newfoundland's right to self-government, and urging the

Goodwill Mission to Newfoundland

adoption of necessary steps to give it effect as soon as possible, said that his mission had found no desire to return to the form of government which had been replaced by the Commission, that a minority favoured union with Canada —a wish opposed by the majority— and that a few wished to join the U.S.

By July 1943, of a total of 40,000 male Newfoundlanders between the ages of 20 and 40, more than 10,000 volunteers were serving overseas on land, in the air, and at sea. The 166th Newfoundland Field Regiment R.A. served throughout the Tunisian campaign, and later in Italy. A Forestry Unit with a strength which at one time reached 2,500 men had been working in the U.K. since November 1939. An interest-free loan of $2,500,000 sent to Britain brought the total of such loans made by Newfoundland since the outbreak of war to more than $10,300,000. She also gave $500,000 for the purchase of aircraft for the Newfoundland R.A.F. Squadron.

There was no political truce in Australia, and at the beginning of 1943 the Labour Government could command a majority in the House of Representatives only with the support of the two independent members. On the last day of the old year Mr. Fadden,

AUSTRALIA

SOUTH AFRICAN AMBULANCE UNIT IN TRAINING

South African forces served all through the Allied campaigns in North Africa, and after February 1943 were allowed to serve outside the African continent. The Sixth South African Armoured Division, commanded by Major-General W. H. E. Poole, D.S.O., joined the Allied forces in the Middle East during 1943, first undergoing a period of final training. Here, men of an ambulance unit are practising first aid during the training period. *Photo, British Official*

2802

opposition leader, attacked the Prime Minister, Mr. Curtin, for continuing to refuse to form a Coalition Government. Criticism of the Government continued, and as the opposition held the balance in the Senate, the Government's position was precarious. When a vote of no-confidence moved by Mr. Fadden in June was defeated by one vote only, Mr. Curtin announced that he would advise a dissolution.

The election campaign that followed was characterized by acrimonious charges and counter-charges, and there **Overwhelming Labour Victory** was a record nomination of candidates—70 for the 19 vacancies in the Senate, 345 for the 74 seats in the House of Representatives. The election, held on August 21, gave Labour an overwhelming victory: it gained all 19 seats in the Senate (five of the retiring Senators had belonged to the opposition) and 49 seats in the House of Representatives. Women representatives (two) were elected to Canberra for the first time. Nearly 180 candidates forfeited their deposits.

At the triennial conference of the Australian Labour Party, which opened on December 13, a resolution moved by Mr. Curtin that Australia should collaborate with other peace-loving nations in accordance with the provisions of the Atlantic Charter was adopted unanimously: a step significant as marking

an abandonment by Australian Labour of any tendency towards isolationism.

The Defence Act Amendment Act, (*see* page 2448), passed in February, permitted the use of the Australian militia (previously restricted to service inside Australia) to any territory in the South-west Pacific (defined as lying, west to east, between the 110th and 159th meridians of east longitude, and northward to the Equator) proclaimed by the Governor-General as associated with the defence of Australia. By the middle of November more than 40 per cent of the Australian troops operating in New Guinea (where Australian forces played a decisive part : *see* Chapters 249 and 276) were members of the militia.

By 1943 considerable American forces were based in Australia (*see* page 2446). President Roosevelt announced in October that under reverse Lease-Lend enough beef and veal had been supplied by Australia to meet nearly all the needs of these troops. The amount thus received (and consumed in Australia) was the same as the quantity of beef and veal then being sent by the U.S. to the European theatre of war for the use of troops other than Americans, and these two items therefore cancelled each other out and provided a remarkable saving in transport. The presence of Americans in Australia led to a visit by Mrs. Roosevelt, who arrived in Canberra on September 3. She also inspected American Red Cross facilities.

Private A. S. GURNEY
(Australian Military Forces)
At Tel el Eisa, Egypt, on July 22, 1942, Pte. Gurney's company was held up by intense machine-gun fire, all the officers being killed or wounded. He charged the nearest machine-gun post alone, silenced it, knocked out a second and, though wounded, attacked a third. His single-handed gallantry enabled his company to gain its objective. Pte. Gurney was posthumously awarded the V.C.
Photo, Australian Government

In May and June Dr. Evatt, Minister for External Affairs, paid a second visit to Washington and London, to discuss Pacific problems in relation to world war strategy ; and in August an American War Mission headed by the U.S. Under-Secretary for War visited Australia.

Two appointments made during the year were of special interest : that announced in November of H.R.H. the Duke of Gloucester to succeed Lord Gowrie as Governor-General at the end of his extended **A Royal Governor-General** term ; and that announced in December of Mr. R. G. Casey to be Governor of Bengal—the first Dominions statesman to be elevated to such a post by Britain.

By December 1943 1,181,000 men— or practically half the working male population of Australia—were in direct war work, including the armed forces, which numbered 858,860 men. By September 191,000 women were in direct war work. Men of the A.I.F. had fought in Greece, Crete, Syria, Malaya and Libya. They served in the Middle East from February 1940 to early in 1943. Units of the Royal Australian Navy, in which by December 1943 there were 30,000 men, had served in the Mediterranean, the Indian Ocean, the Persian Gulf, the East Indies, the Pacific and Australian waters. The Royal Australian Air Force by 1943 had increased to 105,000 men. In November 1943,

SOUTHERN RHODESIA REPAIRS AIRCRAFT
A crashed aircraft, reconditioned at a Repair Depot in Southern Rhodesia by R.A.F. craftsmen, receives its top coat of paint, sprayed on by an aircraftsman from England who was a railway coach trimmer in civil life. Shipping difficulties led Southern Rhodesia to develop her iron ore and coal deposits, chromite, tungstic ore and molybdenum resources, and to become a producer instead of an importer of machinery and spares. *Photo, British Official*

STRATEGIC ROAD CONSTRUCTION IN AUSTRALIA

An early stage in the construction of a strategic road through Central Australia. The Allied Works Council, established in February 1942 to see that the requirements of the Chiefs of Staff were carried out, had by the end of 1943 built 5,000 miles of such highways. Docks, aerodromes, munition works, oil storage plants, hospitals, and all other kinds of building and installation required to fulfil war needs were also constructed by the Council. (See also illus., page 2445.)

Photo by courtesy of Australian Allied Works Council

apart from the squadrons in the South-West Pacific area, there were more than 18,000 members of the R.A.A.F. in Britain, the Middle East, India and other theatres of war. In the South-West Pacific area the R.A.A.F. fought against the Japanese in the Carolines, Malaya and the Netherlands East Indies, including Timor and New Guinea, in the Solomon Islands and other Pacific areas.

By December 1943, 47,900 women were enrolled in the Nursing Service; 19,688 in the Australian Women's Army Service; 17,015 in the Australian Women's Auxiliary Air Force, many of whom were serving in New Guinea; and 1,715 in the Women's Royal Australian Naval Service.

The last peace-time Budget was for £A98,000,000; the Budget for the year ending September 30, 1944, was for £A570,000,000. Largely from her own resources, Australia had **Australian-Built Ships** fully armed and equipped her infantry divisions, which were mostly mechanized, and had built up substantial reserves. Her shipyards were also breaking records. At the end of 1943 more than a score of Australian-built corvettes were serving as R.A.N. ships. Two Australian-built Tribal-class destroyers of 1,970 tons were on active service. Australia was also building sloops, patrol boats, mine-sweepers, freighters, assault and landing craft, and other small craft attached to invasion fleets. From the outbreak of war up to November 30, 1943, Australian shipyards repaired and maintained merchant ships totalling 13,815,000 tons (including 3,109,000 tons of American shipping). An equal tonnage of naval

vessels was also repaired, maintained or docked.

A wide variety of war material was turned out at an amazing rate. A complete range of operational aircraft was produced—trainers, fighters, medium bombers, torpedo-carrying bombers and heavy bombers. They included the Beaufort torpedo-bomber, the Boomerang interceptor (first used in the Allied landings at Lae, New Guinea), and the Beaufighter. Deliveries of the Beaufort torpedo-bomber to the end of November 1943 exceeded 500. This development of aircraft production is all the more remarkable when it is realized that before the war Australia had not built even a motor-car. By March 1943 she was producing cruiser tanks, armoured universal carriers and cars. In October 1943 it was decided to abandon the production of Australian cruiser tanks and other armoured vehicles, as the supplies of tanks available far exceeded the demand. In 1943 the production of artillery and ammunition was also reduced, to give place to the demands for engineering stores, such as bridging equipment and electrical fittings. The sulphanilamide which proved so valuable in the New Guinea campaigns was produced in the Commonwealth; intricate surgical instruments, formerly imported, were manufactured there; ether was sent to Russia, surgical catgut and hypodermic syringes to India and New Zealand, and serums to the whole Pacific area.

The general election due in New Zealand in 1941 had been twice postponed for a year; but in 1943 the Prime Minister, Mr. Peter Fraser, expressed his conviction that the time had come

for the country to give its verdict on the Labour administration, which had been eight years in office. Though there were a record number of candidates (291) for the 80 seats in the House of Representatives, the **NEW ZEALAND** election campaign was the quietest ever held in New Zealand. At the election, held on September 25, Labour was returned again, but with 45 seats instead of 49.

"In the interests of the war effort, and in support of the Mother Country," butter was added in October to the foodstuffs already rationed: the allowance was 8 ozs. a week; cream also was made available only on production of a medical certificate—evidence indeed of the all-out war effort of this land of dairy products. Mrs. Roosevelt, whose visit to Australia has already been mentioned, came to New Zealand also in August, to visit American troops (*see* page 2450) and Red Cross installations established there.

More than 189,000 men had, by September 1943, been enrolled in the armed forces—one-fourth of New Zealand's male population; 95,340 had gone overseas, including nearly 6,000 Maoris—among whom was Second-Lieut. Ngarimu who won the V.C. in Tunisia (*see* illus., page 2623). Over 2,000 Maoris had joined the Territorial Force for home service, 10,000 the Home Guard—which attained its maximum strength of 124,000 in mid-1943, and was due to be placed on reserve from January 1,

MRS. ROOSEVELT AT CANBERRA

Australia's Prime Minister, Mr. John Curtin, welcomed Mrs. Roosevelt when she arrived at Canberra on September 3, 1943, during her tour of American troops and Red Cross installations in the Antipodes. She also studied the work being done by the women of Australia and New Zealand.

Photo, "New York Times" Photos

1944. Maoris in essential industries numbered 10,000.

Contingents of New Zealand airmen continued to arrive at British ports. The New Zealand Division under General Sir Bernard Freyberg, V.C., fought right through with the Eighth Army to the end of the Tunisian campaign (*see* map, page 2773). The first party of officers, men, and nurses of the Division reached New Zealand on furlough on July 12, and were received with considerable pride and excitement. Many of the men had fought from Greece to Tunisia. By the end of the year the New Zealand Division was back with the Eighth Army in Italy, where their share in the crossing of the Sangro River earned General Montgomery's congratulation. In the Pacific, New Zealand troops were stationed in New Caledonia, Fiji and Samoa; at Tonga a U.S. naval establishment was under the command of a New Zealand officer; units of the

Royal New Zealand Navy operated with Allied forces around the Solomons, where New Zealand airmen and troops also fought.

Until 1939 New Zealand had little heavy industry. Yet in 1943 construction of war vessels reached the rank of a substantial industry. Shipyards at Auckland, and other ports, constructed ships for coastal trade and minesweepers. Merchant vessels were converted and equipped for defence. Universal and Bren-gun carriers and certain types of tractors were assembled. Factories produced 2-in. and 3-in. mortars, shells, grenades, and aircraft and tank parts. By June 1943 151,613,000 rounds of small-arms ammunition, 1,850,000 hand grenades, 70,000 mortars and mortar bombs, 19,000 anti-tank mines, and thousands of parts of weapons of war had been turned out. From 1939 to May 1943 New Zealand delivered to the services

over one million blouses, over one million pairs of trousers, 400,000 greatcoats, 2,300,000 pairs of boots, and over 500,000 pairs of blankets.

An Act to assist in the settlement of returned soldiers on the land—one of

WITH THE ROYAL AUSTRALIAN NAVY

To meet the needs of Empire shipping, Australia produced under the guidance of men from Clyde- and Tyneside merchant ships, cargo vessels, and naval minesweepers and escort vessels. Right, 'Warramunga,' Australian built Tribal-class destroyer of 1,870 tons, on her trials. Below, Dr. Evatt, Australian Minister of External Affairs, visits 'Shropshire,' 9,830-ton cruiser handed over by Britain to replace 'Canberra,' lost in the Solomons in August 1942.

Photos, Australian Official ; Central Press

a number of points in the Dominion's programme for rehabilitation after the war—came into effect on October 18 : after that date, all sales or leases of land were to be subject to the approval of District Land Committees and a Land Sales Court set up under the Act. The object was to prevent a recurrence of the speculation in land which had adversely affected many returning soldiers after the last war.

Two events during 1943 were pointers to the part South Africa intended to play in world and in empire affairs. The first was the decision taken early in

SOUTH AFRICA February when the House of Assembly (by 75 to 49) and the Senate (by 21 to 6) approved the Prime Minister's motion to permit Union troops (who are all voluntary recruits) to serve outside the African continent. The second was the general election held in July. The campaign had been fought on a single issue—whether the Union should continue or cease active participation in the war—and the result, which gave Field-Marshal Smuts's Government a strength of 107 to 43 (compared with 84 to 66 in the old House) was an outstanding triumph for his policy. The widespread and general support of the Prime Minister was confirmed at the Provincial Council elections held in November : out of a total of 170 seats in the four provinces, the Government won 118.

The trial and condemnation of Robey Liebbrandt, former South African heavy-weight boxing champion, for high treason, marked the end of the attempts by the noisy and truculent elements among the pro-Nazis in South Africa to overthrow the Government by violent means. Condemned to death (a sentence

MEN OF THE TIMOR 'SPARROW' FORCE

Timor Island, part Dutch, part Portuguese, was occupied by the Japanese in February 1942 ; but a force of Australian and native guerillas, led by Capt. Jeff Laidlaw and known as the 'Sparrow' Force, continued to harass the enemy. They succeeded early in 1943 in establishing contact by radio with Darwin, Australia, and thereafter were kept supplied. Here, Capt. Laidlaw (left) shakes hands with two of his N.C.O.s. *Photo, British Newsreels Association*

confirmed on appeal), Liebbrandt was reprieved and the sentence commuted to imprisonment for life : he had not been guilty of sabotage or responsible for the death of any person.

The first conference representing the Labour movement in all Southern Africa, and including representatives of the Union, Southern and Northern Rhodesia, and the Belgian Congo, was held in Johannesburg on July 17–18 under the presidency of Mr. Walter Madeley, Union Minister of Labour and Social Welfare. Problems affecting all the South African states were discussed, and motions adopted on questions of

economic and social security. A flow of selected immigrants after the war was approved ; and it was decided to hold similar conferences annually.

Smuts described the death of the Governor-General, the Rt. Hon. Sir Patrick Duncan, on July 17 as the " grievous loss of a great man." On the recommendation of the Union Government, King George approved the continuance in office as Officer Administering the Union (the official title of the acting governor-general) of Chief Justice N. J. de Wet, on his relinquishing his Chief Justiceship.

In October Field-Marshal Smuts paid a second wartime visit to Britain, breaking his journey at Cairo to address South African and Rhodesian **Field-Marshal** troops there : he warned **Smuts in** them against hoping **Britain** that the war was near-ing its end. In London he was warmly received by the people, took part in the deliberations of the War Cabinet (of which he was a member), and made two notable speeches, one a war commentary at the Guildhall, the other an address to the Empire Parliamentary Association, called " Thoughts on the New World," which caused considerable international controversy, particularly by its references to France (*see* Hist. Docts., p. 2819).

Of the 570,000 white males in South Africa between the ages of 20 and 60, one in three had volunteered for service by June 1943, when the Union Defence Force had a total strength of 169,000 trained white men and women

NEW ZEALAND LAND GIRLS

Girls in New Zealand left town jobs to train for farm work, which there often included spending hours in the saddle looking after sheep : this photograph was taken on a farm of 6,000 acres carrying 5,000 sheep. New Zealand land girls learned also tractor driving, milking, butter-making, and all the other skilled jobs needed on a farm, just as their counterparts in England did.

Photo, New Zealand Official

volunteers. Since the war began 86,000 white South Africans had served in East Africa, the Middle East, and Madagascar, some of them, however, being counted more than once because they served in more than one campaign. Cape Coloured, Indians, Malays, and Natives had been enrolled to a total of 117,000 (of whom 15,000 had been discharged by 1943); 39,000 served outside the Union. At the end of 1943 the South African Army (including the Air Force) numbered over 200,000 trained men; the Air Force itself in June numbered 37,500; while in April 1943 there were 2,400 men serving with the Royal Navy. Volunteers in the women's army and air force services, enrolled to serve anywhere in Africa, were about 20,000. A Women's Auxiliary Naval Service was formed at the end of 1943.

The cost of the war continued to mount, and was to a considerable extent met by heavily increased taxes. For the year 1943–44, defence cost £105,000,000. Mostly from her own factories, South Africa clothed, fed and equipped her own armies. Supplies were also going to others of the United Nations. It was stated at the end of 1943 that war industries, under a revised programme, would concentrate largely on the production of engineering combat equipment, such as pontoon bridges, barges, etc., for certain items of which South Africa would be the only source of supply. Small minesweeping vessels and anti-submarine craft, including fast motor patrol boats, were produced.

From March 1941 to March 1943 6,400 Allied ships were repaired in South African ports. Spare parts for aircraft, tanks, armoured vehicles, and guns had been made and flown north: 2,107,000 spare parts for aircraft and 1,250,000 spare parts for tanks and motor vehicles had been made by Nov. 1943. Approximately 90 types of army motor vehicles were being assembled. To the end of 1943, 5,000 armoured and 32,000 transport vehicles had been produced.

The exigencies of war had tended to foster a spirit of cordiality between the Union and Southern Rhodesia—to such an extent that the **SOUTHERN RHODESIA** latter placed her armed forces under the command of Field-Marshal Smuts, whose efforts were all towards closer co-operation between the Union and the territories adjacent to it. The Southern African Labour conference already referred to was another instance of this trend. Towards the end of July, Smuts, accompanied by Lt.-Gen. Sir Pierre van Ryneveld,

2807

Chief of the Union General Staff, visited Southern Rhodesia, meeting Sir Godfrey Huggins, the Prime Minister, and other leaders, and inspecting defence forces at Salisbury and Buluwayo. In August the Union Ministers of Railways and Harbours and of Commerce and Industries arrived in Southern Rhodesia to discuss questions relating to transport and post-war industry in Southern Africa; and in October the Prime Minister foreshadowed the formation of a Pan-African Council (such as had been advocated in a motion passed by the Southern Rhodesian Parliament in May) to co-ordinate problems of communications, trade, defence, native policy, health and veterinary research common to African countries.

Rigid control of land speculation was introduced in March, in which month also about 1,000 Polish women and children, after three years' wandering in Russia and the Middle East, were settled in two camps in Southern Rhodesia. Buluwayo, once Lobengula's capital, was declared a city on November 4, the 50th anniversary of its occupation by white men.

Of Southern Rhodesia's population, 70,000 are white and 1,383,000 Africans. In 1943 over 8,000 white Southern Rhodesians and nearly 12,000 Africans were serving with the forces. Rhodesian troops, scattered throughout the British Army, served with distinction in the East African and Middle East campaigns, in Italy and in S.E. Asia.

For the year ending March 31, 1944, Southern Rhodesia budgeted for a war expenditure of £5,640,000 out of a total budget of £10,020,000. She also contributed £800,000 a year to the general cost of her Air Training Group.

NEW ZEALANDERS AT WADI MATRATIN, TRIPOLITANIA

In December 1942, New Zealanders, fighting under General Sir Bernard Freyberg, V.C., succeeded in cutting the retreating Afrika Korps in two at Wadi Matratin, some 60 miles west of El Agheila, by advancing 100 miles in three days along a disused track to the south of El Agheila which led through desolate sand dunes and rocky wadis. They struck north again to the coast road along the Wadi Matratin. Enemy troops coming from the east suffered heavy casualties in desperate efforts to break through. *Photo, British Official*

IN MALTA AFTER THE SIEGE WAS RAISED

1. The cathedral of St. John, built in 1573 for the Knights of the Order of St. John of Jerusalem, suffered badly during the siege of Malta, which lasted from June 1940 until May 1943. 2. Valetta celebrates the fall of Tunis. 3. All that remained of 'Faith'—sole survivor of the three Gladiator fighters christened Faith, Hope, and Charity which constituted Malta's entire defence against the Regia Aeronautica in the initial period of Axis bombing (see Chapter 229)—was placed with due ceremony in the armoury of the Palace of the Knights of St. John of Jerusalem at Valetta.   Photos, Wm. Jones, Malta

Chapter 281

FINE RECORD OF OUR COLONIES IN 1943

The widespread units of the British Colonial Empire continued during 1943 to support the Mother Country with men, raw materials and money. Some account of the significance of their contributions to Great Britain and the other Allies is given here by Sir John Shuckburgh, K.C.M.G., C.B., formerly Deputy Under-Secretary of State for the Colonies. The part played by the Colonies in earlier phases of the war is recorded in Chapters 228, 229 and 248

THE year 1943 witnessed a marked change in the general war situation as affecting a large portion of the Colonial Empire. The final expulsion of the Axis from Northern Africa in May 1943, following upon earlier Allied successes in Abyssinia, the reconquest of British Somaliland and the occupation of the Italian Red Sea Colonies, meant not only that British East Africa was removed from the immediate sphere of hostilities, but also that the potential threat to British territory, on both the East and West African coasts, had virtually disappeared. The magnificent part played by African troops in the campaigns of 1941 and 1942 has been described in Chapter 248. The year 1943 saw the end of their activities so far as fighting in Africa was concerned. It is true that West Africa, though its troops were no longer engaged on African battlefields, and though its own borders were no longer exposed to the risk of direct attack, continued for some time to come to play a vital part in the general war strategy of the Allies.

After the defeat of France the region had been gradually transformed into a great strategical highway for air communications and a naval base for the convoying of shipping bound to and from the Cape. To quote the words of Lord Swinton, Minister Resident in West Africa, "the only way to get aircraft quickly to the danger spots in the Middle East was to fly them overland from West Africa to Egypt. . . . During the earlier months of the campaign in North-West Africa practically every aircraft which flew from America to that battlefront came via airfields in the Gambia." Again, the closing of the Mediterranean meant that ships for the Middle East had to make the long voyage round the Cape. The West African ports lay on their direct route, and it fell to West Africa to arrange for their supply, fuelling and protection on the outward journey. Naturally these requirements led to immense activity in all the British West African territories. A great chain of airfields had to be constructed. Public works,

harbours, roads, railways, camps, water supplies and oil installations had to be organized and maintained on a wholly unprecedented scale.

The tension was not immediately relaxed even when the last German

SWAZI WARRIORS BOTH

A Swazi in native warrior dress observes a fellow-countryman in British uniform on sentry duty in North Africa. Some 3,500 men of the British Protectorate of Swaziland joined the Pioneer Corps. First recruited in 1941, they served in North Africa, and many went on to Sicily and Italy with the Allied armies. *Photo, British Official*

soldier had surrendered in Cape Bon peninsula (*see* Chapter 277). Some months had still to elapse before the effective reopening of the Mediterranean Sea route; but once that was accomplished and once the Mediterranean had reverted to something like its normal status as the maritime highway to the East, the situation, so far as West Africa was concerned, underwent a modification. The area lost some of its character as a key-point in strategic communications. This change was a vital one but, as affecting the local war effort, it was a change of direction rather than a relaxation. The utility of West Africa to the Allied cause remained unaffected. Relieved of its more pressing responsibilities in one sphere, it was able to concentrate its utmost efforts in another.

'TOUGH TACTICS' FOR MEN OF THE SUDAN

Men of the Sudanese Defence Force in training in North Africa, where they learned to handle all the weapons used in present-day war, went through a 'tough tactics' battle course, and trained as signalmen, wireless operators and gunners. Legislation enacted in the Sudan in October 1943 establishing Province Councils and Advisory Councils in the six northern provinces was an important step in the association of the Sudanese with the machinery of government.

Photo, British Official

NIGERIA'S CHIEFS CONFER

The Chiefs of Oyo, Benin, Abeokuta, Iuebu, Ondo, and Warri provinces of Nigeria, with their counsellors and interpreters, at a conference summoned by the Nigerian Government in 1943 at Ibadan. Mr. A. G. Grantham, Officer administering the Government, thanked them for what they had done already, and appealed for even better results. (Below) Nigerian labourers at the Pengal Camp Mine, Bauchi Province, Northern Nigeria, removing the overburden concealing the wash containing tin concentrate which lies 15 feet below the ground. *Photos, British Official*

nearly every other territory throughout the Colonial Empire. The needs of the Allied Nations for vital raw materials grew more urgent every month.

Perhaps the most important product of all was rubber. One effect of the Japanese conquest of Malaya and the East Indies was to exclude the Allies from their principal field of pre-war rubber supply. By one means or another, the loss had to be made good; and it was in the first instance to the British Colonies that an appeal for increased production had to be made. The largest remaining source of natural rubber was Ceylon, and immense efforts were made in that Colony to expand local production to the highest possible point. Another potential source of supply was Nigeria, where a great drive for extended production was carried out during the year. It was no easy matter. The rubber had to be collected, not from self-contained and well-organized plantations, but for the most part from trees and plants scattered over thousands of miles of forest. Everywhere, Lord Swinton said, "people are hunting for wild rubber; it is a sort of family treasure hunt."

Rubber was one of the most urgent needs; but it was far from standing alone. There were many other commodities for which the demand had been enormously en-hanced, sometimes as a result of enemy action (as in the case of Malayan tin and rubber), sometimes by the mere force of circumstances inseparable from a world-wide war. Nearly every Colony played its part in developing its resources to meet the constantly increasing demand. Among the Eastern Colonies, Ceylon provided not only rubber, but tea, graphite and copra. Sugar came from Mauritius and the Western Pacific; copra from the Western Pacific and the Seychelles. The British West Indies supplied sugar in large quantities; bauxite (the raw material of aluminium, essential in aircraft manufacture) came from British Guiana; mahogany from British Honduras; and oil from Trinidad.

Raw Materials from the Colonies

With Malaya out of action, the Nigerian tin mines were called upon for redoubled efforts. This colony, also, supplied the mineral columbite (containing tantalum and niobium, found in association with tin ores) which was extensively employed by American plants in the making of special steels for aircraft construction. Formerly regarded as of slight commercial value, its rise to importance for alloying steel led to the opening of many mines in

Emphasis has been laid on the case of West Africa because it was there, more than in any other part of the Colonial Empire (except Malta), that the events of 1943 created a wholly new situation. To put it quite briefly, the West African territories found themselves diverted from the more directly military problems of transport and communications to the less directly military (though almost equally important) problems of the production of raw materials. It was by no means a new role, but it was one that the turn of events greatly accentuated. It was also a role shared by West Africa with

H.M.S. 'SPURWING': NAVAL AIR STATION, SIERRA LEONE

This naval air station on a river of Sierra Leone, West Africa, was cut by the Fleet Air Arm out of the untouched bush. It included a first-class airfield, barracks and all the installations of a large naval establishment, as well as this arm of the river whence the station's amphibious aircraft could take off. Properly equipped shops looked after maintenance and repairs. Aircraft of the station carried out convoy duties, anti-submarine patrols, coastal reconnaissance, and ambulance duties from up-country spots.   *Photo, British Official*

Northern Nigeria. Among other products from West Africa were cocoa, manganese and bauxite from the Gold Coast; groundnuts and palm kernels from Nigeria; iron ore from the Marampa mines in Sierra Leone; and industrial diamonds from Sierra Leone and the Gold Coast. East Africa furnished sisal (for which the loss of Java and the Philippines had created an immensely increased demand), pyrethrum (a valuable insecticide), hides, copra and coconut oil, tea and coffee.

Such a bare list of commodities, with unfamiliar names, does not make inspiring reading. Words like copra, palm kernels and groundnuts may mean

RHODESIANS IN MADAGASCAR

The Northern Rhodesian Regiment, which fought with distinction in British Somaliland and in Abyssinia, then went on guard duty in Ceylon, where their arrival was announced on May 8, 1942, and in Madagascar. Here, members are preparing new defences on Madagascar after its occupation by British and Fighting French troops in Nov. 1942.

Photo, Pictorial Press

little or nothing to the average reader. But everybody is aware that war conditions bring about a serious shortage of oils and fats. Soap and margarine, for example, have to be strictly rationed. What are the raw materials that supply these everyday requirements, and from what part of the world are they obtained? They are, in fact, some of the very commodities that have just been mentioned, and it is on the Colonies in the main that we depend for the maintenance of an adequate supply.

It was to meet this deficiency of oils and fats that special measures were organized by the Resident Minister in West Africa in May 1943 to stimulate oilseed production within the four territories under his control. Of the four, Nigeria offered the most promising field, and it was there that Lord Swinton set on foot his main campaign. He sought and secured the willing co-operation of the Mahomedan Sultans of the Northern Provinces. He was able to report a month later that his action was already producing favourable results, not in Nigeria alone, but also in Sierra Leone and the Gold Coast. Later a scheme was inaugurated for substantial purchases by the West African Produce Control Board which controls, on behalf of the British Government, the purchase of all oil seeds and vegetable oils in West Africa. So it was that the maintenance of Britons' home-front rations owed not a little to their African fellow-subjects.

An interesting statement made by the Prime Minister in the House of Commons on May 10, 1944, dealt with the supplies sent to Soviet Russia from the British **Supplies to Soviet Russia** Empire. Among other items, he mentioned £1,168,000 worth of industrial diamonds, mainly of African production; 81,423 tons of rubber from the Far East and Ceylon (£9,911,000); 8,550 tons of sisal from British East Africa (£194,000); 3,300 tons of graphite from Ceylon (£160,000); 28,050 tons of tin from Malaya and the United Kingdom (£7,774,000). Turning to foodstuffs (the total value of which amounted to over £7,000,000) he included tea from Ceylon; cocoa beans, palm oil and palm kernels from West Africa; coconut oil from Ceylon; pepper and spices from Ceylon and the British West Indies. These figures show that towards the aggregate amount of all the materials supplied to our Ally (valued at over £80,000,000) the Colonial Empire made a substantial contribution. It may fairly claim to have played a part, small no doubt but not wholly negligible, in the brilliant achievements of the Russian Armies throughout the year.

Apart from the drive for increased production of essential materials, immense efforts were made throughout the Colonial Empire to expand the local cultivation of food crops, with a view to making each territory as far as possible self-supporting and so relieving the pressure upon the shipping space required to bring imports from overseas. Even in such an arid region as Aden, the recently established agricultural services succeeded, under conditions of extreme difficulty, in increasing the production of food.

Mauritius had an unfortunate experience: she valiantly planted maize in large tracts of land hitherto under sugar, but a hurricane intervened and the maize crops were almost entirely destroyed. Jamaica took to eating, instead of exporting, her home-grown bananas. Rice presented a problem of special urgency. It was the staple food of many parts of the Empire; but the Japanese conquests in the Far East, and particularly the loss of Burma, brought the available supply to a dangerously low level. To meet the situation and to reduce imports to a minimum, rice cultivation on a largely increased scale was undertaken in East and West Africa, British Guiana and Ceylon. Steps were taken in the West Indies to increase the home-grown supply of corn and tapioca.

Food Problems of the Colonies

The process was assisted by grants from the British Treasury under the Colonial Development and Welfare Act, 1940. For example, a loan of £150,000, free of interest, was made to Jamaica to stimulate the production of food yeast in the colony. A similarly interest-free loan of £10,000 was made to Mauritius for the same purpose. Among other grants sanctioned during the year was one of £15,250 to enable the Gambia Government to intensify its rice production.

These operations had little that was spectacular in their character, and were probably known to a mere handful of people outside those directly concerned. The general public, absorbed in the turmoil and shifting fortunes of a great war, had little time or inclination to acquaint itself with all the thousand-and-one activities that were in progress in every part of the

SUGAR FROM MAURITIUS

Sugar cane arriving at an extraction factory in the island of Mauritius, one of Britain's smallest colonies, which lies in the Indian Ocean, and at one time seemed in imminent danger from the Japanese.

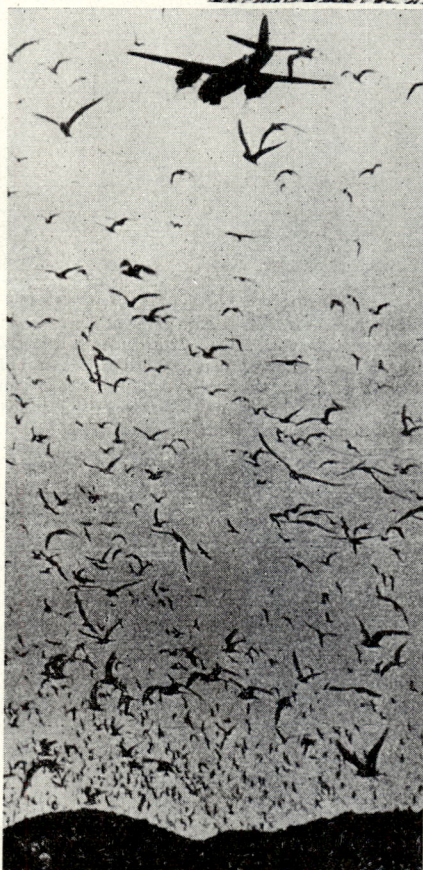

ASCENSION AIR-BASE

Before the war, Ascension Island, in mid-Atlantic between Brazil and Africa, was important as a wireless station relaying messages from all parts of the world. From July 1942 it became a vital base and ferry point for Allied transatlantic aircraft. Left, a U.S. army plane comes in to land through flocks of sooty terns, otherwise wideawake birds.   *Photo, Keystone*

British Empire. But the Colonial effort was nonetheless a great and important one—a real and solid contribution towards the achievement of final victory.

The cessation of hostilities in Africa by no means implied that the African forces of the Crown were no longer needed for defence purposes or employed on active military duties. The East Africa Command remained in being and still had many important military tasks to discharge. East African troops were sent to garrison both Ceylon and Madagascar, the former still in the war zone, and the latter an important outpost in the defence of Africa against possible aggression from the Far East. East and West African contingents were sent to India to reinforce the armies assembling for the onslaught against the Japanese on the Burma frontier. The West Africans soon demonstrated in the Burma theatre that they could fight Japanese as successfully as they fought Italians in Africa. They enhanced their already high reputation in a new sphere of action. The East Africans could be trusted not to fall behind the standard set by their West African comrades.

African Forces of the Crown

A communiqué published on September 8, 1943, recorded that "the largest and best equipped fighting force ever to leave the shores of East Africa has recently arrived in Ceylon and India." Behind that brief notification lay a long story: a story of months of intense training, intricate and efficient planning, collection of immense quantities of stores, and effective co-operation between Europeans, Asiatics and Africans, all of whom had their

AIRFIELD AT ADEN

Aden, British outpost in Southern Arabia, fuelling station and port of call for shipping bound east or west through the Suez Canal, and commanding the entrance to the Red Sea and so to the Canal itself from the east, increased its value in wartime by constructing a new airfield. Camels were used to help in levelling the ground.

Photo, British Official

CEYLON JUNGLE INTO AIRFIELD

The outbreak of war between Japan and the Allies in December 1941 brought Ceylon into the front line, and it became necessary to create airfields in her jungles. Machinery destroyed the vegetation, armies of labourers burned, cleared and levelled the ground, and steam-rollers came to compress the runways. One such airfield was completed and in use in two weeks, in spite of all the difficulties of work in jungle conditions. Life in these jungle airfields was tough and monotonous, with little activity, but under a constant threat. *Photo, Canadian Official*

share in the constitution of the greatest East African force that had ever been assembled. African troops formed by far the greater part of this vast fighting machine. They came from every territory in British East and Central Africa and represented nearly every tribe throughout the region. Many of the men saw the sea for the first time in their lives. They were quick to settle down in their novel environment. One report from Ceylon recorded that the sight of a tame elephant had interested the newly arrived African soldiers beyond anything else in their new experiences. Their one desire was to be photographed, for the edification of their relatives in Africa, riding one of these unaccustomed mounts.

Outside Africa there was much sustained military effort in a variety of directions. In the West Indies a new regular unit known as the South **Local Defence Forces** Caribbean Force was formed in April 1943. Its personnel was recruited from, and stationed in, Barbados, Trinidad, the Windward Islands and British Guiana. A North Caribbean Force was also formed for Jamaica, British Honduras, the Bahamas and the Leeward Islands. Later in the year a scheme for the recruitment of tradesmen and technicians for the ground staff of the R.A.F. was started in the West Indies. It met with a most favourable response. After the close of the year it was decided to employ West Indian and Bermudian troops on service overseas. In Ceylon the local Defence Force continued to grow in numbers and efficiency. The local Naval Volunteer Force was taken over by the Admiralty during the year, and its title changed to the Ceylon R.N.V.R.; its strength was approximately 1,000 of all ranks.

In Mauritius the Territorial Force was reorganized under the name of the Mauritius Regiment and placed under the direct control of the War Office. An Ordinance was enacted enabling the Force, if required, to operate under local law outside the Colony. Recruitment, both for Arabs and Jews, proceeded in Palestine. In Fiji steps were taken to place the personnel and vessels of the Fiji Naval Volunteer Force at the disposal of the Crown for general service with the Royal Navy. The Force, which was renamed the Fiji R.N.V.R., had a strength of about 350 in April 1943. It was mainly engaged in manning local patrol launches and was responsible for the security of ships in the Suva harbour.

In the Pacific region the activities of the Fijian troops (including their Commando units) and of the British Solomon Islands Defence Force demand record. "Scarcely an American has come back from Guadalcanal in the past few months," the Governor of Fiji reported on May 8, 1943, "without bringing fresh stories of the daring and resourcefulness **Native Units in the Pacific** of the Fijians there, who have shown themselves to be more than a match for the Japanese as jungle fighters." They were described by American correspondents as probably the finest jungle fighters in the world. The British Solomon Islands Defence Force, under the inspiring leadership of Lieutenant-Colonel Marchant, British Resident Commissioner in the islands, rendered services just as remarkable within their own particular sphere. This force could claim to be the youngest combatant unit in the British Empire. Its maximum strength never exceeded 400, and it was at no time sufficiently

OFFICERS FOR THE SOUTH CARIBBEAN FORCE

N.C.O.s of the Third Trinidad Battalion who were candidates for commissions being interviewed by the Garrison Commander, Trinidad Battalion, South Caribbean Forces, at area headquarters, Piasco. Units of the South Caribbean Forces saw service overseas after intensive training in jungle warfare, commando, infantry, and artillery work. *Photo, British Official*

FIJI COMMANDOS ON BOUGAINVILLE

Plasma transfusion for a Fijian casualty during the bitter fighting on Bougainville, most northerly of the Solomons. The Japanese captured the island in April 1942. Not until November 1, 1943, did the Allies return, when U.S. Marines made successful landings at Empress Augusta Bay. Fierce fighting for possession of the island was continuing at the turn of the year. It was announced on September 16 that Fiji Commandos were fighting in the Solomons and had also fought on Guadalcanal; they were more than a match for the Japanese as jungle-fighters, being more intelligent and resourceful and having greater powers of endurance. *Photo, New Zealand Official*

disengaged from active operations as to admit of the regular training of new recruits. Nevertheless, the force accounted in all for 350 Japanese killed and 34 taken prisoner. This was accomplished for the loss of seven men killed in action and two taken prisoner.

The newly formed Solomon Islands Labour Corps did good work during the final stages of the Battle of Guadalcanal. While the Americans were driving the Japanese into the sea, units of the Corps carried munition supplies right up to the front line, along tracks exposed to continual shell-fire. Their courage under novel and terrifying conditions earned them the warmest commendation. One particular act of heroism by a Solomon Islander, though it actually took place before the end of 1942, may fitly be recorded here. The hero was Sergeant-Major Vouza, of the British Constabulary in the Solomons. While carrying out a mission on behalf of the American Command, he fell into enemy hands. He was lashed to a tree and subjected to the most savage brutality. In spite of everything he refused to betray his trust or to give the enemy any information. Severely bayoneted about the chest and throat, and left for dead by his tormentors, he nevertheless managed to free himself from his bonds and to make his way back to the American lines with valuable intelligence about enemy dispositions. The American army doctor, who treated him on his return, expressed

Heroic Solomon Islander

amazement that a man could survive such injuries.

In the North African and Sicilian campaigns Colonial Pioneer units from East and West Africa, Mauritius and the Seychelles, as well as transport units from Cyprus and Palestine, played an important part. They brought forward supplies, constructed roads, cleared and reconditioned occupied ports. Their work, often carried out under enemy fire and usually in circumstances of great difficulty, gained little publicity; but it earned the highest of all compliments — the warm gratitude of the troops whom they served.

To Malta the year brought a dramatic change of fortune. September 10, 1943, was a red letter day in the history of the island. It was on that day that the Italian Fleet, or what remained of it, steamed into Maltese waters to place itself at the disposal of the British Naval Command. "It was something," wrote The Times correspondent, "seen but once in a generation. Not since the German Fleet steamed into Scapa Flow at the end of the last war has the world seen the like of this event. The line of ships stretched along the Mediterranean's dark blue surface for a distance of five miles." There were scenes of wild rejoicing in Malta. Few parts of the Empire suffered more savagely than Malta during the second and third years of the war. The stubborn heroism of the Maltese people during the prolonged agony of intensive bombardment from the air had excited the admiration of all free peoples in every part of the world. Now at last the grim ordeal was over. No longer a beleaguered fortress, Malta could take her place as a jumping-off ground for Allied attacks upon the Hitlerite forces in Europe.

The direct financial assistance rendered by the Colonial Empire in meeting the expenses of the war was substantial. Apart from contributions to the cost of local defence services, its peoples had, by April 1943, contributed over £23,000,000 in gifts and nearly £7,000,000 in loans to the Government of the United Kingdom. There were, in addition, a number of local loans raised by Colonial Governments, the proceeds of which were spent on local defence or loaned free of interest to the United Kingdom. In some cases gifts were made in kind. The small South Atlantic island of Tristan da Cunha contributed a whole year's wool clip. The sale of War Savings Certificates in Trinidad reached a new weekly record early in 1943 with purchases of over £8,400 worth of Certificates.

The position was aptly summarized by the Prime Minister in a speech delivered on June 30, 1943. "Three years ago," he said, ". . . against the triumphant might of Hitler . . . we stood alone. Then, surely, was the moment for the Empire to break up, for each of its widely dispersed communities to seek safety on the winning side. . . . But what happened? . . . In that dark, terrific and also glorious hour, we received from all parts of His Majesty's Dominions, from the greatest to the smallest, from the strongest to the weakest, and from the most modern to the most simple, the assurance that we would all go down or come through together." The British Colonial Empire, whatever the future may have in store for it, could ask for no nobler tribute to its war-time record.

Mr. Churchill's Tribute

SOLOMON ISLAND VOLUNTEER

Sgt.-Maj. Vouza, of the British Constabulary in the Solomons, who gained the George Medal for remarkable courage when captured by the Japanese (see this page). His other medals are Colonial Police Medal, Coronation Medal, and American Silver Star for Valor. *Photo, British Official*

REFUGEES FROM BOMBED BERLIN IN EAST PRUSSIA

Women and children evacuated from heavily bombed Berlin being sorted out for the final stage of their journey to
' safe ' areas in East Prussia. By the end of 1943 several square miles of the city had been ' erased.' Killed were
estimated at twenty to thirty thousand. The bombed-out were put to work clearing debris because, it was explained
officially, idleness represented a great danger to their sanity. Food had to be brought in by lorry, owing to the breakdown of the railways ; and queues running into tens of thousands waited for soup to be ladled into their receptacles
—often old tins or cracked jugs. *Photo, Keystone*

NEW ZEALANDERS IN THE SOLOMON ISLANDS

The fighter revetment at Ondonga, in New Georgia, where New Zealand Warhawks are being serviced. Below, New Zealanders land at Baka Baka on Vella Lavella, also in the New Georgia group of the Solomons, on September 17, 1943. American troops landed on Vella Lavella on August 15 (see illus., page 2606), and gained control of most of it; but only on October 13 did General MacArthur's G.H.Q. announce that enemy resistance had ceased when this New Zealand landing wiped out the last Japanese garrison. *Photos, Royal New Zealand Air Force; Central Press*

THE RETURN TO A VILLAGE FREED BY THE RED ARMY

The recapture of Bryansk was one of the most spectacular of the Russian victories in the summer campaign of 1943. General Rokossovsky crossed the Desna about September 10, and began to outflank Bryansk. Soviet troops, under Lieut.-General Fedyminsky, made a second crossing of the Desna in another skilful outflanking movement through difficult wooded, swampy country hitherto regarded as impassable. This double envelopment forced the Germans to evacuate the city on September 17. Here is a village liberated by the Red Army in its advance on Bryansk. Below, a Russian heavy howitzer in action on this sector.   *Photos, Planet News ; Pictorial Press*

HOW KENYA NATIVES SAVED A BRITISH AIRCRAFT

A hundred and fifty East Africans, natives of the village of Meru, by building this special runway retrieved a R.A.F. plane which had made a forced landing on Mount Kenya. They cut heather, dragged trees to bridge gullies, carried rocks to fill holes, and finally stamped the surface level with their feet. They then hauled the aircraft (seen at far end) to this improvised runway along the road to the left, and cheered loudly as it took off again. *Photo, British Official*

Historic Documents. CCLXIX–CCLXXI

HITLER TO THE NAZIS: SMUTS TO THE WORLD

In the speech quoted below, Hitler mocked at his opponents—"military idiots" as he called them—on a note he was never to reach again : little more than a month later the Allies landed in North Africa ; in under two months the Russians began their offensive at Stalingrad. The appeal made by Mr. Churchill and President Roosevelt to the Italian people bore fruit shortly in Italy's defection from the Axis. Document CCLXXI consists of extracts from an important speech made by Field-Marshal Smuts

SPEECH MADE BY HITLER TO A NAZI PARTY AUDIENCE AT THE SPORTSPALAST IN BERLIN ON SEPTEMBER 30, 1942 :

WHEN Mr. Eden or some other nincompoop declares that they have a belief we cannot talk with them, as their idea of belief seems to be different from ours. We believe we have to beat our enemies until final victory is won. They believe that Dunkirk was one of the greatest victories in the world's history. They believe that an expedition lasting nine hours is an encouraging symptom for a victorious nation. If they believe this, of course we can hardly compare our modest victories with theirs.

What have we to offer ? If we advance 1,000 kilometres it is nothing. It is a veritable failure. . . . If we could cross the Don, thrust to the Volga, attack Stalingrad—and it will be taken, you may be sure of that—then it is nothing. It is nothing if we advance to the Caucasus, occupy the Ukraine and the Donetz Basin. . . .

They say the second front will come. . . . Had I before me a serious opponent I could figure out where the second front would come. But with these military idiots one never knows where they will attack. The maddest enterprise may be launched and—this is the only disagreeable thing—one never knows what next when faced with such lunatics and drunkards. Of course we must prepare everywhere. Let me assure Mr. Churchill that wherever he may choose for his next attack he may consider himself lucky if he remains on land for nine hours. . . .

Our programme for this year was as follows : 1. In all circumstances to hold what it was necessary to hold. . . . 2. We were determined to attack wherever attack was necessary. . . . We had three objectives : 1. To take away the last great Russian wheat territory. 2. To take away the last district of coking coal. 3. To approach the oil district, paralyse it, and at least cut it off. Our offensive then went on to the enemy's great transport artery, the Volga and Stalingrad. You may rest assured that once there no one will get us out of this position.

The German Reich will never capitulate . . . let our enemies wage the war as long as they please. National Socialist Germany will come out of this war with glory and victory.

MESSAGE TO THE ITALIAN PEOPLE FROM MR. ROOSEVELT AND MR. WINSTON CHURCHILL BROADCAST ON JULY 16, 1943 :

AT this moment the combined armed forces of the United States, Great Britain and Canada . . . are carrying the war deep into the territory of your country. This is the direct consequence of the shameful leadership to which you have been subjected by Mussolini and his Fascist regime. . . .

In spite of Italy's great vulnerability to attack by air and sea, your Fascist leaders sent your sons, your ships, your air forces to distant battlefields to aid Germany in her attempt to conquer England, Russia, and the world. . . . Your soldiers have fought not in the interests of Italy, but for Nazi Germany. They have fought courageously, but they have been abandoned by the Germans on the Russian front and on every battlefield in Africa. . . .

The sole hope for Italy's survival lies in honourable capitulation to the overwhelming power of the military forces of the United Nations. If you continue to tolerate the Fascist regime which serves the evil power of the Nazis, you must suffer the consequences of your own choice. We take no satisfaction in invading Italian soil and bringing the tragic devastation of war home to the Italian people. But we are determined to destroy the false leaders and their doctrines which have brought Italy to her present position. . . . The time has now come for you, the Italian people, . . . to decide whether Italians shall die for Mussolini and Hitler—or live for Italy and for civilization.

"THOUGHTS ON THE NEW WORLD," BY FIELD-MARSHAL SMUTS, TO A MEETING OF THE U.K. BRANCH OF THE EMPIRE PARLIAMENTARY ASSOCIATION ON NOVEMBER 25, 1943 :

THERE are two dangers that face us. . . . One is the danger of over-simplification. . . . The other danger is what I may call the danger of following slogans or catchwords, and so missing the real inwardness of the problems before us. . . .

When I look at the sort of problems that we shall have to deal with at the end of this war, . . . I doubt whether . . . we shall ever come to a peace conference at all at the end of this war. We may be faced with questions so vast, so complicated, so difficult and intractable, that we shall have to be satisfied with making a pretty comprehensive Armistice dealing with the general military question of ending the war, and leave the rest of the problems to a long series of conferences, a long process of working out solutions. . . .

Take the danger of following slogans and catchwords. Today we hear a great deal of democracy. We are fighting the battle of democracy. We are fighting for freedom. . . . Our opponents have another set of formulas. They fight for the leadership principle. . . . I would say that in arranging for a new world organization for security, . . . we shall have to provide not only for freedom and democracy, which are essential, but we shall also have to provide for leadership and power. . . . To my mind that can be done much more effectively than in the Covenant of the League of Nations by giving a proper place to the three great Powers that are now at the head of our United Nations. . . . I think it was largely because in the League of Nations we constituted after the last war we did not recognize the importance of leadership and power that everything went wrong in the end. What was everybody's business proved to be nobody's business. . . .

I now come to much more explosive things, for which I hope you will not hold me responsible hereafter. . . . Europe is completely changing. . . . At the end of this war . . . three of the five Great Powers in Europe will have disappeared. France has gone, and if ever she returns it will be a hard and a long upward pull for her to emerge again. . . . We may talk about her as a Great Power, but talking will not help her much. . . . France has gone and will be gone in our day and perhaps for many a day. Italy has completely disappeared, and may never be a Great Power again. Germany will disappear. . . .

We are therefore left with Great Britain and with Russia . . . Russia is the new Colossus on the European continent. What the after-effects of that will be nobody can say. . . . Then outside Europe you have the United States. . . .

Many people look to a union or closer union between the U.S.A. and Great Britain, with her Commonwealth and Empire, as the new path to be followed in the future. I myself am doubtful about that. . . . If you were to pit the British Commonwealth plus the United States against the rest of the world, it would be a very lopsided world. . . . So we come back to where we started—namely, the trinity. . . . But . . . in that trinity you will have two partners of immense power and resources—Russia and America. And you will have this island, the heart of the Empire and of the Commonwealth, weak in her European resources in comparison with the vast resources of the other two. . . . The idea has repeatedly floated before my mind . . . whether Great Britain should not strengthen her European position . . . by working closely together with those smaller democracies in Western Europe which are of our way of thinking. . . . Neutrality is obsolete, is dead. They have learned the lesson that, standing by themselves on the Continent, they are lost. Surely they must feel that their place is with this member of the trinity. . . . We have evolved a system in the Commonwealth which opens the door for developments of this kind. . . .

THE GERMANS ATTACK

After an intense artillery bombardment and heavy bombing by the Luftwaffe, large German tank and infantry forces, with very strong air co-operation, launched a violent offensive at dawn on July 5, 1943, on the 200-mile Orel-Kursk-Byelgorod front. 1. Panzer grenadiers showing a swastika flag and signalling their position to supporting Stukas. 2. German prisoners captured near Kursk. 3. Heavy enemy armour advancing across cornfields near Orel : the Germans used seven panzer divisions in this unsuccessful attack.

Photos, Associated Press ; Pictorial Press

Chapter 282

THE RUSSIANS DRIVE ON TO THE WEST

In Chapter 272, Major-General Sir Charles Gwynn carried the history of the campaigns in Russia up to the end of March 1943, when a lull had fallen on the fighting on all fronts. Here he describes the opening of the summer offensive by the Germans, and the subsequent counter-offensive in overwhelming strength by the Russians, which drove the enemy back beyond the Dnieper in the south, and west of Smolensk in the north

DURING the long lull in the spring and early summer of 1943, both sides were preparing to take the offensive on a maximum scale. The Allies also took the opportunity to concert their strategy more closely : in April a British Military Mission under Lieut.-General Sir G. LeQ. Martel, K.C.B., visited Russia to discuss matters with the Russian General Staff.

The Russians had had heavy casualties, especially during the German counter-offensive which saved the situation for the enemy in the Donbas and temporarily gave him back the initiative. Much reorganization was therefore necessary, and in particular much had to be done to restore to working order the great mileage of recaptured railways.

The Germans similarly needed time for reorganization, for although they had the advantage of an intact railway system, their losses of men and material had been colossal. Whole formations had disappeared, including nearly all the satellite formations ; and these had to be replaced. The total mobilization ordered by Hitler in January 1943 probably gave him sufficient numbers to make good losses ; but to train men and absorb them into their new units required time.

It was evident that when the clash came it would be on the front between Orel and Kharkov. There the Russians still held a deep and broad salient west of Kursk which gave a springboard for an offensive towards Kiev. This threatened to separate the German armies of the centre from those in the south and to cut off the German salient at Orel. In this salient the Russians had massed a great concentration of force. On the other hand, the Germans had at Orel and in their bridge-head across the Upper Donetz at Byelgorod, springboards which threatened the Russian Kursk salient with a pincer attack. Their Orel salient, although of no great width, was immensely strongly fortified and covered a sufficient area to provide room for the deployment of a large force. They would have been in a stronger position if they had, in their spring counter-offensive, secured bridge-heads across the Middle Donetz, east of Kharkov ; the Russian successful defence of this river line proved to be of great importance, all the more because it maintained a threat to the Germans in the Donbas.

In the event, the Germans on July 5 struck first in what was meant to be a blitzkrieg attack directed southwards from Orel and north-eastwards from Byelgorod towards Kursk. Evidently their primary design was to capture that centre and annihilate the whole Russian forces within the salient. On the Orel front they employed seven panzer, two motorized and 11 infantry divisions, and on the Byelgorod front 10 panzer (four being S.S.), one motorized and seven infantry divisions—a very formidable force, but one, owing to its comparatively small infantry component, better calculated to secure rapid limited results than to execute far-reaching operations.

The attacks opened with a hurricane artillery and air bombardment covering an infantry assault, supported by tanks, intended to break through the crust of the Russian positions. But the Russians were fully prepared, with defences organized in great **Kursk Offensive Opens** depth, and with their armour held in readiness for counter-attacks. There developed what was undoubtedly the greatest defensive battle of the war. The Russian infantry held firm, allowing the enemy's armour, in many instances, to pass over them as they lay in their deep trenches, only to emerge, as the tanks passed, ready to meet the German infantry and prevent its giving support to the tanks. Many tanks were knocked out by infantry anti-tank weapons as in passing they exposed their less heavily armoured parts ; those that got through

Army-Gen. NIKOLAI VATUTIN
Led forces advancing from Kursk towards Kharkov at the opening of the Russian summer offensive of 1943. In September he thrust towards Kiev, capturing Sumy on September 2, Romny on September 16. He reached the River Dnieper on September 22.

Col.-Gen. IVAN KONIEV
Awarded the Kutusov Order, First Class, in April 1943, he led the forces advancing towards Kharkov during July and August. Following the capture of Kharkov on August 23, he made a concerted pincer movement with Malinovsky and Tolbukhin towards Kremenchug.

Army-Gen. MARKIYAN POPOV
His forces, operating north of those under Rokossovsky, kept pace with them in their advance after the repulse of the German July offensive. His men helped to free Orel, and then advanced towards Bryansk, which town was actually recaptured by the army under his command.

Army-Gen. K. ROKOSSOVSKY
A Pole by birth, he played an outstanding part in the great Russian summer offensive of 1943, capturing Karachev on August 15, Sievsk at the end of the month, Konotop on Sept. 6, Bakhmach on Sept. 9, Nyezhin on Sept. 15, and then advancing to outflank Bryansk.

Photos, Pictorial Press ; drawing of Rokossovsky by Pavel Malkov

KHARKOV FINALLY LIBERATED

Col.-Gen. Golikov's troops recaptured Kharkov on February 16, 1943, but were forced to evacuate it again on March 15 (see illus., page 2713). A week's stubborn fighting preceded its final recapture on August 23 by forces under General Vatutin, General Malinovsky and Col.-Gen. Koniev. Above, motorized infantry, equipped with anti-tank rifles, moving up to the front are overtaken by the commander's car. Left, a woman soldier of the Red Army regulates traffic at a street crossing in liberated Kharkov. *Photos, Pictorial Press*

suffered heavily from the Russian artillery fire and had still to encounter Russian armour.

On the Orel front the German attack definitely failed and little progress was made, but on the Byelgorod front the Russian positions were penetrated in places to a depth of some 30 miles. There was no retreat, however, and the German panzers never broke right through, the battle developing into a number of furious tank encounters in a country very favourable to mobile tank tactics. This confused mêlée continued until the Germans gradually became exhausted.

But while this battle raged, a Russian offensive started on July 13 against Orel, from north and east. It at once made substantial progress, despite desperate German resistance, in a terrain made highly defensible by permanent fortifications, water obstacles, and woods. The Orel area, with its northern bastion of Bolkhov and eastern bastion of Mtsensk, was a major stronghold in the German defensive system established in the winter of 1941–42, and now further developed as an offensive base, it and its exposed line of communication to the west were defended by additional troops of high quality.

The offensive had been admirably timed, for although the German drive southwards from Orel had been held, it might soon have become dangerous again. As it was, formations, including at least one panzer division, were withdrawn from their offensive force to strengthen the defence. Gradually both in their offensive at Orel and in the defensive battle on the Byelgorod front, the Russians established mastery, and on July 24 Stalin claimed that the German offensive had been defeated. The Orel pincer arm had been broken and Orel itself was in danger, while on the Byelgorod front the Germans were being forced back.

Russian Counter-attack Begins

During the next 10 days, although heavy fighting continued, it became certain that the German offensive had failed and that the enemy had begun to withdraw. It seemed questionable whether he would escape encirclement at Orel although still improbable that he would retreat beyond his starting line at Byelgorod. But on August 5 it became clear that the Russians, having fought a wonderful defensive battle, had won it without exhausting their reserves, and were now in a position to launch their main offensive. On that day Orel and Byelgorod were recaptured and the Russians were in full pursuit towards Bryansk and Kharkov—Popov's and Rokossovsky's armies towards

CAVALRY FORD THE RIVER DON

Taganrog, important Sea of Azov port, was recaptured on August 30, 1943, after two years in enemy hands. A breakthrough by Russian cavalry (a detachment is here fording the Don) and tanks into enemy rear areas isolated the city, whose rail communications with the Donetz had been cut earlier, and forced the Germans to evacuate it. The Ninth (Kuban) Guards Cossack Cavalry Division was among the formations specially mentioned for their part in this operation.

OREL IN SOVIET HANDS AGAIN

A great Russian double victory—the recapture of Orel and of Byelgorod—took place on August 5, 1943. Right, women of Orel—liberated after German occupation since October 1941 —greet men of the Red Army. Left, Soviet soldiers inspect a German tank captured on the Orel-Kursk sector : note the armour plate protecting its tracks. During the German July offensive, many tanks were knocked out by Russian infantry who held their ground in deep trenches and attacked the less heavily armoured parts of the tanks as they passed.

Photos, U.S.S.R. Official ; Associated Press

Bryansk, and those of Vatutin and Koniev towards Kharkov.

Writing later of the Russian summer campaign, and of the work done by the British Military Mission to Russia of April 1943, General Martel said, " Based on our experience in North Africa, we wanted to see the Russians remain on the defensive and let the German panzer divisions become committed to battle. When they were thus committed, and when, as we hoped, they had been repulsed with losses, that would be the time to launch the Russian offensive. The action by the Russians followed exactly on these lines. The German panzers broke themselves on the Kursk salient and the Russians then launched their offensive."

Before following the development of the Russian offensive the aims of the abortive German offensive deserve examination, if only in order to appreciate the magnitude and importance of the Russian victory in this battle of the Kursk salient. Primarily, it was a forestalling offensive designed to disrupt Russian offensive preparations. It was evidently hoped by swift blows delivered mainly with armour to recapture Kursk and to annihilate the strong Russian forces within the salient, which had clearly been concentrated for a projected offensive. If successful it would have been a crippling blow, and it might have been exploited to disrupt again restored Russian communications between Moscow and Rostov—one of the main Russian achievements in the winter.

Battle of the Kursk Salient

It seems improbable, however, that the Germans, unless there had been a complete Russian collapse, would have again attempted a far-reaching offensive, either towards Moscow or the Causasus. After their disastrous losses in the winter and with the possibility of a western front materializing, an entanglement in the east was to be avoided.

The offensive had therefore probably as a secondary object the restoration of the defensive front that had run from Orel through Kursk to the Donbas. This would have shortened the line and tended to make the German position in the Donbas more secure. During the winter crisis, retreat from the Donbas to the Dnieper at one time seemed inevitable, but as the Germans had held on to it, an advance to Kursk was necessary to secure its flank. Essentially, therefore, the German offensive was strategically defensive—designed to disrupt Russian offensive plans and to establish a better defensive front. In

TALES OF THE GERMAN OCCUPATION

On September 8, 1943, forces under General Malinovsky and Col.-Gen. Tolbukhin recaptured Stalino, important industrial city of the Donetz basin—an operation which expelled the Germans from their last stronghold in the Donbas—and pushed on a further 12 miles, freeing a number of other industrial centres. Here, citizens of Stalino talk to officers of the Red Army. *Photo, Planet News*

both these objects it failed decisively owing to the magnificent Russian defence and to the determination of the Russian High Command not to be deterred from their offensive projects, for which reserves were evidently husbanded and not expended in the defensive battle. The Germans, on the other hand, had exhausted their reserves.

On the Orel front in a month the German losses amounted to 120,000 killed, 12,000 prisoners, over 4,500 tanks, and immense quantities of other material, and their Army here was in full retreat towards Bryansk. On the Byelgorod front, the situation developed even more sensationally. Attacked from the north and east, the Germans, who had fallen back to their original position on the Donetz about Byelgorod, were suddenly overwhelmed—probably their panzer divisions had been withdrawn to refit—and the Russians broke through, thrusting at great speed towards Kharkov. Akhtyrka, north-west of Kharkov, was captured on August 11, and the Kharkov–Poltava railway cut, while on the following day Chuguyev, on the Donetz south-east of Kharkov, was taken. By August 16 Kharkov was threatened with encirclement, while, in the north, approach to Karachev brought Bryansk in danger.

At this stage the Russians had greatly widened their Kursk salient, but had as yet made no strong effort at its apex between Sievsk and Sumy. Their main immediate object was to recapture Kharkov, and thus open the way for a thrust towards the communications of the Donbas with the Dnieper. The Germans made a great effort to react

German Losses Near Orel

RUSSIAN THANKS FOR BRITISH CHOCOLATE

A Soviet sniper writes to thank British friends for chocolate sent to him through Mrs. Churchill's Aid to Russia Fund, which supplied small luxuries and comforts to Russia's fighting men and women as well as much valued medical aid. By the end of October 1943 this fund had passed the £4,000,000 mark. It will be noted that this sniper's long-barrelled rifle is fitted with telescopic sights.

Photo, U.S.S.R. Official

to this threat. Between Kharkov and Zmiev, at the Donetz elbow, they fought stubbornly against a Russian outflanking thrust towards Merefa, and about August 16 launched a powerful counter-attack towards Akhtyrka. This counter-stroke had a considerable temporary success, checking the Russian attempt to outflank Kharkov from the west. Certainly the time it gained must have been very valuable if, as is probable, a decision to withdraw from the Donbas to the Dnieper had now been taken. For about a week the situation round Kharkov was confused, and it seemed as if the Russian drive might be held up. But, though checked, it continued to make progress; and on August 18 Zmiev was captured, on August 23 Kharkov itself again fell into Russian hands.

On the same date successful operations were reported farther east in the Izyum and Voroshilovgrad regions. All through the period of the Kursk battle, there had been strong local engagements in these areas maintaining pressure on the head of the German Donbas salient, although nothing in the nature of a general offensive had been attempted. Now, however, major attacks were launched by Malinovsky's Army in the elbow of the Middle and Lower Donetz, and by Tolbukhin's Army on the Rostov front. On August 30 an Order of the Day announced that the latter had broken through the Mius line and by a daring cavalry outflanking thrust had at last captured Taganrog which twice had held up Russian armies. This victory, moreover,

2824

Army-Gen. R. MALINOVSKY
He was responsible for the drive westward through the Donbas towards Stalino (captured September 8) during July and August 1943. The forces under his command then went on to form the eastern arm of the pincer movement towards Kremenchug.

Col.-Gen. F. I. TOLBUKHIN
An Order of the Day of August 30, 1943, announced that his forces had broken through the Mius defences and by a daring cavalry outflanking thrust had at last captured Taganrog, which had twice held up Russian Armies. He went on to capture Mariupol on September 10.

Photos, U.S.S.R. Official ; Pictorial Press

cleared the enemy from the whole of the Province of Rostov.

Meantime there were important events away to the north. On August 15 Rokossovsky captured Karachev and began to close in on Bryansk, while on August 13 a new offensive opened with the capture of Spasdemiansk, between Smolensk and Bryansk, which aimed at severing direct rail communication between these two fortress towns in the neighbourhood of Roslavl. By the end of the month it became clear that Rokossovsky was also threatening to outflank Bryansk on the south when he recaptured Sievsk which had hitherto marked the apex of the Kursk salient.

From the beginning of September onwards the Russians pursued the offensive with two main objects : (a) the destruction of the Germans in the Donbas by a pincer attack delivered from the east by Malinovsky and Tolbukhin, and from the Kharkov region by Koniev's Army ; (b) the separation of the German armies of the south and centre by a thrust towards the Dnieper about Kiev, which would cut all lateral railways connecting them. Essentially a frontal offensive, conducted by Vatutin's and Rokossovsky's Armies, it gave few opportunities for large-scale outflanking manoeuvres, but the terrain contained no strong defensive position until the Dnieper and its tributary, the Desna, were reached. This was definitely a weak sector of the German front ; but it was buttressed on the north by the Bryansk stronghold (itself protected by the

Main Objects of Russian Offensive

SMOLENSK RECAPTURED

Smolensk, most important strategical centre of German resistance, was taken by storm on September 25, 1943. The vast network of its defences, built by the Todt organization, had been claimed by the enemy to be impregnable. 1. Red Army troops enter the city's deserted streets. 2. Smolensk burns as the enemy retreats. 3. Spasdemiansk, hinge of the Smolensk and Bryansk fronts, recaptured on August 13 after three days' fighting. 4. Military policeman directs last German traffic out of Smolensk: note demolition charges.

Desna) and on the south by a strong German force based on Poltava.

In addition to these two major offensives heavy pressure was also maintained by subsidiary offensives north of Bryansk, towards Roslavl and against Smolensk, which would prevent the withdrawal of German reserves from that sensitive sector of the front. The offensive towards Smolensk opened with the capture on August 30 of Yelnya, the scene of Timoshenko's counter-offensive in 1941 which did so much to delay the opening of the great German offensive against Moscow.

The failure of their Kursk offensive, and the loss of Orel, made it necessary for the Germans to withdraw to a shorter front; but until their counter-attack failed to save Kharkov they may still have hoped to hold the Donbas with its valuable products. After that, however, withdrawal from the Donbas to the middle Dnieper became inevitable, and the Russian break-through on the Mius line accelerated the retreat, which had to be carried out under heavy pressure. At Taganrog the Germans suffered heavy losses of men and material, and though some of the defenders succeeded in cutting through the encircling forces, Tolbukhin pursued them vigorously. To cover the withdrawal from the Donbas against Russian drives southwest from Kharkov and the Middle Donetz the best available reserves were concentrated about Poltava and to the east of it. These provided a strong flank guard to the withdrawal from the Donbas and also a link with their armies withdrawing farther north.

The German withdrawal was undoubtedly well co-ordinated and skilfully executed, but it entailed many rearguard actions in which both sides had heavy losses, the Germans in particular having to abandon much equipment. They had, however, always an intact railway system to aid their withdrawal, whereas the Russians must have found it difficult to maintain their ever-lengthening lines of communication. Much of the heaviest fighting took place in the neighbourhood of key railway junctions, which the Germans invariably fought hard to retain as long as possible.

On September 2 Vatutin captured Sumy, bringing his army up in line with Rokossovsky, who had captured Sievsk a few days earlier. His farther advance, however, met with stiff resistance as he approached the Gomel–Kremenchug railway, especially at Romny; the Germans evidently fearing an attempt to cut the communication of their Poltava group with Kremenchug. Rokossovsky, on the other hand, made good progress, capturing in succession the important junctions of Konotop (September 6) and Bakhmach (September 9). By the 15th he had reached Nyezhin west of the Gomel–Cherkassy railway, thus severing all railway communications east of the Dnieper between the German central and southern armies. On his right he had closed in on Bryansk and reached the line of the Desna. During the same period Malinovsky and Tolbukhin were driving steadily westward in the Donbas, the former capturing Stalino

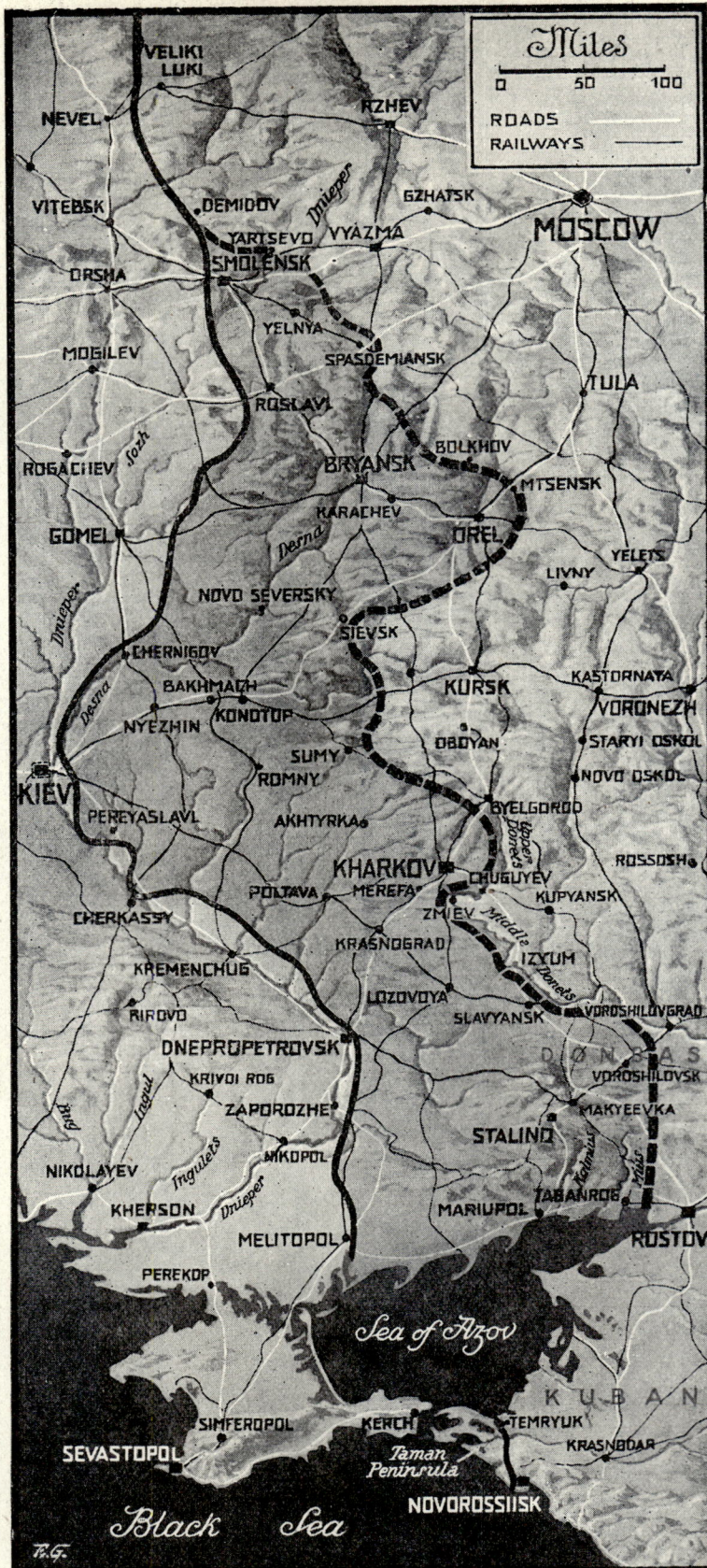

RUSSIAN ADVANCE—SUMMER 1943

When the German offensive against Kursk opened on July 5, 1943, the Russians stood on the broken line to the east. They smashed that fierce assault before the month was out, counter-attacked, and by October 25 had reached the solid black line to the west, having recovered all the shaded territory in their advance. *Specially drawn for* THE SECOND GREAT WAR *by Félix Gardon*

(September 8), coal-mining and metallurgical centre, and the latter Mariupol (September 10) after defeating a German attempt to hold the line of the Kalmius by a landing beyond the river mouth. By September 22 these two armies had closed in on the Dnieper between Dnepropetrovsk and Zaporozhe and on the railway between the latter town and the Crimea. The German retreat on this front had been costly but it had not, as at one time seemed possible, been cut off by the Russian drive from the Kharkov direction. The German Poltava group had fulfilled its purpose well and its own line of retreat towards Kremenchug remained open. It began to be generally believed that the Germans had again made a successful withdrawal and that with the autumn rains approaching the Russians could not hope to achieve much more until the winter, when, however, they would probably find the Germans firmly established on a new defensive front.

But about September 16 a rapid deterioration in the German situation north of Poltava began to threaten their hold on Kiev. About the 10th, Rokos-

Rokossovsky Outflanks Bryansk sovsky gained some bridge-heads across the Desna and a few days later began to outflank Bryansk, although, owing to the very difficult nature of the marshy country, it did not seem probable that he would be able to exploit these successes. German confidence in the security of their position was, however, their undoing; for the Russians attacking over swamps deemed impassable caught the enemy by surprise, and captured his principal strong point on the Desna at Novo Seversky. The line of the Desna thus became untenable and on September 17 the Germans were forced to withdraw from Bryansk. Whether the Germans had intended to halt their withdrawal on the Desna may be doubtful, but they certainly had intended to choose their own time to withdraw from it. Now it became probable that they would be forced to retire to their stronghold at Gomel and the upper Dnieper. At this same period Vatutin was making progress to the south-west, capturing Romny, which the Germans had held stubbornly, and threatening the Kiev–Poltava railway. By September 22 he had crossed this railway and two days later his advanced troops had reached the Dnieper opposite Cherkassy and at Pereyaslavl. By that time, too, Rokossovsky had crossed the lower Desna and had captured the important town of Chernigov after heavy fighting. It was evident that if the Germans had intended to hold a

RED ARMY'S ENTRY INTO YELNYA

On August 30, 1943, the Red Army broke through strong German defences consisting of an intricate system of trenches, barbed wire entanglements, mines, portable steel pillboxes made of armour plate 4¾ ins. thick, and iron and concrete forts, to recapture Yelnya. Scene of Timoshenko's counter-offensive in 1941 (see illus., page 1838), Yelnya, biggest German stronghold guarding Smolensk, lies on the railway between Spasdemiansk and Smolensk, and is the focus of seven roads.

substantial bridge-head across the Dnieper east of Kiev, that had now become impracticable. Moreover, their force at Poltava was now occupying a dangerous salient and, pursued by Koniev, began a rapid retreat to Kremenchug.

By the end of the month the Russians were in close contact with the strongly fortified Melitopol line, which the Germans had constructed to link the Crimea with the Dnieper defences, and had reached the Dnieper nearly all the way from Zaporozhe to the neighbourhood of Gomel, the defences of which were half encircled.

Farther north, Popov to the right of Rokossovsky had kept pace with him, his being the army that actually took Bryansk, and he was now closing in on Gomel from the north-east. Still farther north, Sokolovsky's Roslavl offensive was making progress, outflanking Smolensk on the south; while an Order of the Day revealed that Yeremenko had taken the offensive between Veliki Luki and Smolensk and, on September 19, had taken Yartsevo north-east of the latter. Three days later he also captured Demidov, an outpost of the Smolensk defences. Smolensk had thus become another dangerous salient and on September 25 Sokolovsky, after some heavy rearguard fighting, occupied the town, the Germans withdrawing to Vitebsk and Orsha. On the same day Roslavl was also captured, the Germans withdrawing to the Dnieper about Mogilev and Rogachev.

The Germans had now reached a line on which they must stand, if not through the winter at least until they had reorganized and made good the immense losses of men and material they had **Russians Reach the Dnieper** suffered in retreat. They presumably shared the general opinion that the Russian summer offensive with its immensely lengthened lines of communication had almost exhausted itself, and that with autumn rains approaching no serious attempt would be made to force the formidable Dnieper line, at least until winter. They apparently intended to hold Gomel, and the line of the river Sozh protecting its northern flank, to prevent the Russians from closing up to the upper Dnieper position. Moreover, they showed no intention of abandoning the Crimea, and even still held a small bridge-head across the Kerch Straits, although on September 16 they had finally been driven out of Novorossiisk, the denial of which to the Russians had appeared to be the main object of their stubborn retention of a foothold in the Kuban. Except where Tolbukhin on the Zaporozhe-Azov front was still attacking strongly and in the Taman peninsula where fierce fighting was going on in the marsh lands adjoining the lower reaches of the Kuban, by the beginning of October the summer offensive had ended, and there seemed little prospect of a further offensive until the winter.

WITH THE ALLIED AIR FORCES IN SICILY

The landings on July 10, 1943 were preceded by heavy air bombardment of Sicilian and Italian airfields, parachute and glider-borne troops were landed inland before the seaborne forces were brought in to the beaches, and air bombardment was kept up ahead of the Allied advance. Above, Mitchells of the Tactical Air Force, manned by U.S. crews, make a low-level bombing attack on Sicilian roads. Top right, airborne troops wait at a North African airfield to enter the gliders which carried them to Sicily. Right, R.A.F. Servicing Commandos about to overhaul a Spitfire on the newly captured airfield at Comiso.

Photos, British and U.S. Official

Chapter 283

SICILY FALLS IN THIRTY-EIGHT DAYS

When they invaded Sicily on July 10, 1943, the Allies had prepared for a campaign lasting ninety days. In fact, Messina was in our hands on August 17, and all organized Axis resistance ceased after only thirty-eight days of fighting—some of it among the stiffest the Allies had met up to that date. Moreover, this campaign of record swiftness was carried out in mountainous country that compared in difficulty with the terrain in Tunisia, as this first-hand account by Squadron-Leader Derek Adkins, R.A.F., testifies

AFTER the conquest of North Africa, terminating on May 13 with the surrender of the last remaining enemy elements in Tunisia (*see* Chapter 277), the world waited anxiously for the promised attack on what Mr. Churchill had referred to as " the soft under-belly

IN A PACHINO STREET
Royal Marines who stormed the coastal batteries at Cape Passero pushed inland, and the same day (July 10) captured the town of Pachino (which has a population of 20,000) and the adjacent airfield after overcoming stubborn Italian resistance. Here, a British patrol passes along a Pachino street on the lookout for snipers. *Photo, British Official*

of the Axis." There were even signs of impatience at the delay in following up the North African campaign. In point of fact, the Allied High Command had been busy completing plans for the next phase of the war as agreed at the Casablanca Conference (*see* Chapter 290).

This was the invasion and conquest of Sicily, to be preceded by the reduction of the two islands of Pantelleria and Lampedusa, and to be followed by a land invasion of the Italian mainland, using Sicily as the logical stepping-stone.

The surrender of Pantelleria and Lampedusa (*see* Chapter 268) demonstrated the potentialities of Allied air power and eliminated the risk of enemy interference with the greater tasks that lay ahead from these useful bastions in the Mediterranean.

The Sicilian campaign could have been suitably completed with the capture of Catania on August 5, but the remaining pocket of German resistance in the north-east corner might have proved a serious menace, not only to the Allied occupation of the island but also to the subsequent land invasion of the toe of Italy. For these reasons it was essential to occupy the entire north-eastern tip, including the important port of Messina.

The period of preparation for the invasion began within a few days after the fall of Tunis and continued uninterruptedly until the first week of July. The Royal Navy and Merchant Navy carried troops and supplies safely through the Straits of Gibraltar to Oran, Algiers, Philippeville and Bône. Other ships sailed from Alexandria and found safe anchorage at Sollum, Tobruk, Derna, Benghazi, Tripoli, Sfax, Sousse and Malta, while one convoy of assault landing ships and special cargo craft, carrying the First Canadian Division, completed a 2,000-mile voyage from Great Britain. Allied aircraft not only protected the ships and harbours from air attack; they also kept a constant vigil for enemy submarines.

The Strategic Air Force was responsible for the softening up process which began with constant heavy and medium bomber raids on the eastern aerodromes of **Preliminary 'Softening Up'** Sicily, the vital supply hub of Messina, important rail centres, marshalling yards and other ports through which the island could be reinforced. The same pattern developed as at El Alamein, when Liberators and Wellingtons blasted ports as far away as Benghazi and Palermo. But this time the bombing was by day as well as by night.

Then, in the final preparatory stage, light bombers joined in the attack on aerodromes, installations, communica-

ALLIED COMMANDERS CONFER
General Dwight D. Eisenhower, Allied Commander-in-Chief, Mediterranean Forces (right), and General Sir Harold Alexander, Deputy C.-in-C., at the meeting of Allied war chiefs held in Tunisia on July 25, the day Mussolini resigned from his leadership of the Italian Government. Allied Naval forces were under the command of Admiral of the Fleet Sir Andrew Cunningham, Allied Air Forces under that of Air Chief Marshal Sir Arthur Tedder. *Photo, British Official*

ITALIAN DEAD IN AVOLA

Men of a British patrol passing dead Italian soldiers in Avola, which lies near the south-east corner of Sicily and was captured by British troops pushing north from Cape Passero the day after the invasion began. Other British forces moving inland after the capture of Syracuse met moderate resistance from an Italian division, and much stronger opposition from German troops.

Photo, British Official

the ports of Syracuse and Augusta and the airfield at Pachino. The Americans were to land farther west in the Gulf of Gela and occupy the airfields at Comiso, Biscari, Ponte Olivo and Licata.

Two of the British divisions—the 50th and the 5th—landed in the Gulf of Noto between Cape Passero and Syracuse. The 50th (Northumbrian) was in front of Avola, and the 5th farther north near Cassibile. The 51st (Highland) Division and the First Canadian Division were in the centre to the west, south and north of Cape Passero. British units taking part included the Royal Scots Fusiliers, 14th London Regiment (London Scottish), Highland Light Infantry, the Cameronians (Scottish Rifles), the Welch Regiment and men from the Devon, Dorset and Hampshire Regiments which had seen years of service in Malta.

British Forces Engaged

When the Allies landed in Sicily, enemy strength there was estimated at 12 divisions (about 400,000 men) consisting of five Italian infantry, among them the 4th (Livorno) and 54th (Napoli), five Italian coastal, and two

tions and other special targets. (Flying Fortresses, Mitchells and Wellingtons were used for the sledge-hammer blows ; Bostons, Baltimores and Marauders for the stinging, lightning thrusts. For more spectacular work there were Mosquitoes and Mustangs.) Fighter squadrons of the Desert Air Force were moved in advance to Malta and Pantelleria, and Spitfires swept across the Mediterranean to clear the skies.

The stage was set. Under the supreme command of General Dwight D. Eisenhower the Allies were about to land on European territory in adequate force.

The huge armada of nearly 3,000 vessels of all types was massed with escorts, in readiness for the grand assault. It carried some 12 divisions of British, Canadian and American troops formed into two armies—the Eighth (which included the First Canadian Division under Maj.-Gen. Guy Simonds), under the command of General Sir Bernard Montgomery, and the Seventh, commanded by the American Lieut.-Gen. George S. Patton. As in Tunisia, the general direction of operations by the 15th Army Group, as the attacking forces were known, was in the hands of General Sir Harold Alexander, Deputy C.-in-C., with Admiral Sir Andrew Cunningham as Allied Naval Commander-in-Chief Mediterranean.

The main landings took place at 3 a.m. on July 10 along a 100-mile stretch of

The Allies Land on European Soil

coast in the south-eastern corner of Sicily between Gela and Licata to the west and extending to Cassibile, a few miles south of Syracuse ; by 6 a.m. the success of the landings had been assured. This section of the island was chosen owing to the necessity of having continuous fighter cover over the beaches during the initial stages, and to provide ports and airfields as soon as possible from which to maintain and support the advance.

The British and Canadians were given the task of seizing the east coast southwards to include the whole of the Pachino peninsula, so that an immediate advance could be made on

BRITISH NEWSPAPER IN SICILY

Four days after the Allied landings in Sicily, the first number of Eighth Army News, the front page of which is here reproduced, was printed in Syracuse. Note particularly the appeal to the troops to avoid aggravating the acute shortage of food in Sicily by refraining from buying local supplies. That set the tone for British troops throughout the invasion.

German (the reconstituted Hermann Goering and 15th Panzer Divisions), all under the command of General Guzzoni, who led the Italian invasion of Albania in 1939. During the later stages of the campaign, the 29th Motorized Division —destroyed at Stalingrad and re-formed —appeared; and German parachute troops offered some of the toughest opposition in the course of the fighting.

On the evening before the main assault, detachments of British glider-borne troops (of which the Border Regiment and the South Staffordshire Regiment formed the **Airborne Landings** spearhead) were landed near Syracuse, while American parachutists came down north of Gela. They were to disrupt the enemy's communications and hold key positions until the infantry had established contact with them. (See illus., page 2669.)

It was planned that the landings should take place in the last light of the moon. The airborne troops would thus have the advantage of moonlight to pick out their actual landing areas before darkness set in to conceal their movements. But heavy cross winds buffeted the aircraft, and the gliders arrived half an hour late, making it impossible for the landing areas to be picked out as planned. In spite of the great risks involved, large parties of

MEETING IN CALTAGIRONE

United Kingdom and Canadian soldiers greet one another in the main square of Caltagirone, a town of 38,000 inhabitants, captured on July 16 by the Canadians striking west from Vizzini. Both Caltagirone and Grammichele, taken on the same day by the Canadians, are important railway and road centres, and their capture represented an Allied advance on this sector of some thirty miles.
Photo, British Official

troops and equipment were safely landed, although in the high wind they became scattered and were unable to attack their objectives in full strength. Nevertheless, the enemy's second line of defence was successfully thrown into confusion during the hours immediately preceding the arrival of the assault forces by sea. (It was later revealed that many of the glider pilots, after the strain of flying across 400 miles of land and sea, fought on the ground as infantry for nearly 15 hours.)

The operation differed from the German technique against Crete (see Chapter 159), where troops were landed in a continuous shuttle service without artillery, which was brought up later by transport. In the Sicilian invasion, for the first time in history, a self-contained unit, complete with its own engineers, artillery, ammunition and quartermasters, was committed to battle by air. This was a bold step forward from the former method of dropping small groups of parachutists behind enemy lines to seize or destroy a specific point. It was, in fact, the first time that the Allies had used airborne troops extensively in any operation.

General Montgomery later stated that these operations advanced the progress of the campaign in the Eighth Army sector by a week. But if they were important in the British sector, they were even more so to the American landings near Gela. Here, armoured elements of the Hermann Goering Division struck during the actual land-

ings, but one airborne combat team with light howitzers and other infantry weapons had fortunately landed in the same area and took the brunt of the German attack. They held the Germans all Sunday, July 11, and well into Monday before American warships intervened and reinforcements finally arrived to hold the German threat.

The Allied forces were attacking an island nearly 10,000 square miles in

U.S. TROOPS IN THE SICILIAN CAMPAIGN
Divisions

82nd Airborne	Maj.-Gen. Matthew B. Ridgway
2nd Armoured	Maj.-Gen. Hugh J. Gaffey
1st Infantry ...	Maj.-Gen. Terry de la Mesa Allen
3rd Infantry ...	Maj.-Gen. Lucian K. Truscott, Jr.
9th Infantry ...	Maj.-Gen. Manton S. Eddy
45th Infantry ...	Maj.-Gen. Troy H. Middleton

area with a 600-mile coastline, whose natural defences had been strengthened by countless pillboxes and other fortifications. But the enemy defences and preparations proved to be surprisingly inadequate. The Italian coastal batteries were not heavily defended and many were rushed and captured from unguarded flanks. Even when they realized that a large-scale landing had been made and that more troops were coming in from the sea, the local enemy commanders were unable to organize any concentrated resistance.

Major-General Julio Cesare Gotti Percinari, the commander of the 54th (Napoli) Division, the most important Italian field division, admitted, after capture, that the disorganization of their communications had left them

CANADIAN COMMANDER

Major-General Guy G. Simonds, C.B.E., D.S.O., commanding the First Canadian Division, wades ashore from a landing craft at the invasion of Sicily. After a month's fighting, in which they contributed brilliantly to the Allied campaign, the Canadians were withdrawn from the front line in the first week of August. *Photo, British Official*

PRIMO SOLE BRIDGE ACROSS THE GORNALUNGA

Two hundred British parachutists, dropped on the night of July 14-15, captured Primo Sole bridge and held it for 24 hours against constant shell- and mortar-fire, machine-gunning and air-bombing. Forced to withdraw three hours before the arrival of the Eighth Army, they saved the bridge by removing the enemy's demolition charges. The Durham Light Infantry then took and held the bridge against repeated and violent German tank and infantry attacks.

completely bewildered. He said that the British attack on the east took them by surprise, for they had expected it in the west: there the enemy's main forces had been concentrated in anticipation of an assault from the direction of Tunis.

In the initial stages of the landings, the protection of the Allied beaches was undertaken by short-range fighters from Malta, which flew nearly 1,100 day sorties on July 10. But so limited was enemy air opposition that it was possible to divert the fighters to the role of harrying the Axis armies in the field. After the first landings, for example, beach patrols dwindled to 450 sorties a day, and by July 17 no further such patrols were necessary. An attack by the Luftwaffe on the newly landed forces in any strength might have frustrated the whole invasion.

The Royal Navy's main task, in the execution of which American warships and units of the Royal Indian, Dutch, Polish and Greek fleets rendered valuable aid, was the support of the armies by commanding the sea and disembarking troops and their supplies.

The invasion was maintained by the steady, uninterrupted flow of something like 10,000 tons of supplies and stores daily. British supply services established themselves on the beaches by noon on the first day of the landings, and before dark had constructed roads across the sands to inland dumps. Arms and ammunition, vehicles, machinery and equipment of all kinds, fuel, food and water came ashore in an unending stream and were hurried forward to the fighting troops. In all this work the Pioneer Corps played an essential part.

Among the hundreds of vehicles, tanks and guns accompanying the Allied forces was the amphibious

DUKW—a cross between a launch and a six-wheeled 2½-ton lorry with a boat-shaped and boat-sided body whose name, happily translated into "duck" by the Army, was derived from the factory serial letters: D for the boat, U the lorry body, KW the lorry chassis. It was making its first appearance in the European theatre of war manned by the R.A.S.C. (see illus., page 2669). While these strange-looking craft can sail the seas like a lifeboat or be driven ashore on their six wheels, all other vehicles, tanks and guns had to be waterproofed so that they could go through sea water from the ramps of the landing craft on to the beaches.

By the end of the first day a continuous strip of beach had been consolidated and many coastal towns, including Pachino, were in Allied hands. Eighty-four men of the South Staffordshire Regiment who had landed in gliders to take the Ponte Grande bridge, south of Syracuse, held it for 14 hours in a gallant stand against heavy odds and made it possible for the 5th Division to capture Syracuse by 10 p.m. The port was immediately used to bring up supplies.

Capture of Syracuse

A Spitfire wing that had fought all the way from El Alamein was flown across from Malta to the newly won airfield at Pachino. As more aerodromes were captured in rapid succession, fighter and fighter-bomber and bomber squadrons moved in to provide the maximum close support to the advancing infantry. A constant shuttle service operated by Transport Command carried troops and equipment to the island and returned with Allied casualties. The lessons learned in the long and bitter battles of North Africa were exploited to the full.

NIGHT BARRAGE ON THE PLAIN OF CATANIA

The battle for Catania was the fiercest and most prolonged action of the Sicilian campaign. The Eighth descended to the plain of Catania on July 16, but their advance was delayed by extensive mines and demolitions and by German troops who, despite heavy losses, resisted with bitter stubbornness. The city, shelled, bombed, bombarded from the sea, was taken on August 5. Here, British 25-pounders put up one of their famous night barrages. *Photos, British Official*

THE EIGHTH ENTERS CATANIA

After nearly three weeks of savage fighting, the Eighth Army entered Catania on August 5 at 8.30 a.m. and occupied it without resistance. 1. Looters throwing goods to crowds waiting below: large-scale looting of shops and Italian and German stores occurred after the Eighth Army's entry. The people, who were undernourished, fought desperately not only for food, but for trumpery articles of little or no value. Order was restored by the British military authorities. 2. A street in Catania after its occupation by the Eighth. 3. Flowers and fruit for the invader. 4. The first British patrol penetrates to the centre of the city. *Photos, British Official*

Many of the Sicilian aerodromes had been wrecked by bombing and sabotage (at Pachino the landing ground had been ploughed to a depth of 18 inches, but within 48 hours it was in use again). Harvest fields had to be cleared and Servicing Commandos of the R.A.F. helped the local farm hands to cut and gather the crops. Then the Airfield Construction Group and Pioneers set to work with bulldozers and scrapers to tear up the stubble and level the runways. Supplies were moved up from the beaches, often under attack by low-flying Axis aircraft.

It was not until the Germans entered the picture on July 11 that any properly staged counter-attack was launched by armoured formations of the re-formed Hermann Goering Division which came within 300 yards of Gela. The battle raged for 24 hours with the Germans continuing spasmodic attacks, now against this point, now against that, instead of massing for one determined drive supported by infantry. By midday on the 12th the Americans had won and the Axis force was in retreat. Thereafter the American line was pushed firmly and evenly ahead and up into the hills which form the backbone of Sicily.

German Troops Enter the Picture

The Eighth Army, having secured a firm bridge-head, continued their advance in two directions, northwards

through Augusta, and north-westwards through Palazzola to Vizzini. Farther south, Ragusa was captured, also on the 12th. On the same day, while cruisers and monitors lay outside, a British destroyer and the Greek destroyer H.H.M.S. "Kanaris" entered the port of Augusta, and found that the enemy had evacuated the town. Naval landing parties hoisted the Unión Jack, and an Italian submarine trying to escape was captured by a British minesweeper. Admiral Leonardo Priato, Commandant of the Augusta naval base, and General Achille d'Havet, commander of the Italian 206th (Coastal) Division, were among the 2,000 prisoners taken up to this stage. The Sicilians seemed completely dazed

by the invasion, in much the same way as the French had been by the German blitzkrieg of 1940. Proclamations over the signature of General Alexander, whose appointment as Military Governor was announced on the 17th, were posted in the main square of each city immediately after its capture. These declared that the Allies had invaded Sicily to deliver the people from the Fascist regime and to restore Italy as a free nation. They added that the rule of the Crown of Italy was suspended and the Fascist party dissolved and all its discriminatory decrees and laws annulled. Executive power rested in A.M.G.O.T. (Allied Military Government of Occupied Territory), an organization set up, with Major-General Lord Rennell of Rodd as Chief Civil Affairs Officer, long before the invasion took place. Staffed by British and American officers, A.M.G.O.T. took over the executive government of provinces and towns. As the Prime Minister said in the House of Commons on July 21, the aim of the administration would be " the elimination of the doctrines and practices of Fascism." He added, " It is the earnest hope of H.M. Government that, when delivered from the Fascist regime, the people of Sicily will of their own accord, turn towards liberal and democratic ideas." The civil population everywhere welcomed the arrival of Allied troops, and their manifestations of joy were at times almost embarrassing. Fruit and wine were lavishly bestowed on the invaders, and many of the peasants offered to show where mines had been sown in roads and bridges.

Alexander: Military Governor

The Eighth Army continued on its two lines of advance, northwards towards Catania, and north-westwards in the direction of Vizzini and Enna. Early on July 14 an enemy counter-attack reached Augusta and succeeded in cutting off some troops, but the situation

BRITISH PATROL ENTERS PATERNO

British troops crossed the river Simeto and captured Paterno, an important enemy base on the circular railway running round Mount Etna, on August 5, the day on which Catania fell. They were welcomed by the people with joy and relief. Canadians, pushing on from Regalbuto, were reported within five miles of Adrano, another important enemy base on the Etna circular railway, on the same date. *Photo, British Official*

SUPPLIES FOR THE ALLIES LANDED AT SYRACUSE

Syracuse was captured in the evening of July 10, 1943, by a combined land-air-sea operation in which glider-borne troops played an important part. Apart from some German resistance in the streets, there was little opposition, and the excellent port and harbour facilities, with safe anchorage for many ships of large displacement, were found undamaged. Allied minesweepers soon cleared the mines. Here, tons of equipment are stacked on the beach after unloading. Below, Bren gun carriers haul anti-tank guns inland shortly after the Sicilian landings.

Photos, British Official

3 c³

BRITIS

ME
This impr
was asser
in April 19
(2) ' Nel:
' Formida
submarine
(6) boom
(7) M.L.
Tribal cla
bows only
(10) crui
class destr
are units
vessels v
carrying
for the i
Pioneers
the coast
of Allied
North

P

MIGHT

EAN

H.M. ships
rs Harbour
1) 'Rodney,'
raft carrier
'Dido,' (5)
'Maidstone,'
'Leonian,'
Vienna,' (8)
'Ashanti'—
s destroyers,
(11) Hunt
Among them
illa of naval
the ships
lies to Sicily
10. Left,
ashore on
procession
leaving a
r Sicily.
ficial

ACTION IN THE FOOTHILLS OF MOUNT ETNA

British gunners shelling from a position among lava-rocks in the foothills of Mount Etna, the great volcano visible in the background of this photograph. Even before the fall of Catania (August 5), the capture by the Allies of Centuripe threatened the main Axis defence line in Sicily, which was based on Mount Etna. The capture of Bronte on August 7 cut the line in two, and the fall of Randazzo (August 13), key to the whole Axis position in Sicily, led to a rapid German retreat into the north-east corner of the island.

Photo, British Official

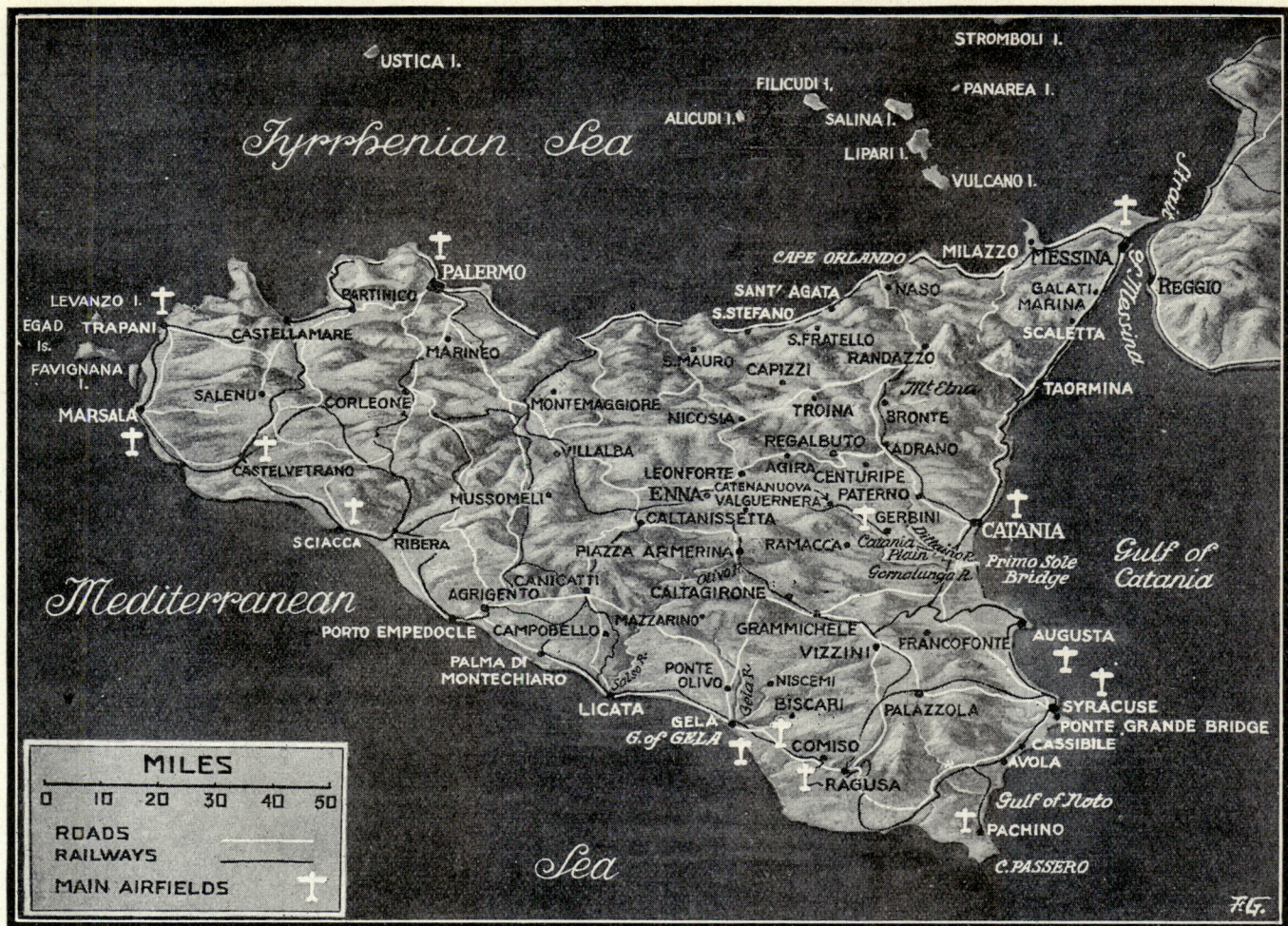

Tyrrhenian Sea

USTICA I. • STROMBOLI I.

FILICUDI I. PANAREA I.
ALICUDI I. SALINA I.
LIPARI I.
VULCANO I.

LEVANZO I.
EGAD TRAPANI
Is.
FAVIGNANA I.

CAPE ORLANDO MILAZZO MESSINA
SANT' AGATA NASO GALATI REGGIO
PARTINICO PALERMO S.STEFANO MARINA
CASTELLAMARE MARINEO S.FRATELLO SCALETTA
S.MAURO CAPIZZI RANDAZZO TAORMINA
MARSALA SALENU CORLEONE MONTEMAGGIORE NICOSIA TROINA Mt Etna
CASTELVETRANO VILLALBA REGALBUTO BRONTE
MUSSOMELI LEONFORTE AGIRA CENTURIPE ADRANO
ENNA CATENANUOVA PATERNO
SCIACCA RIBERA VALGUERNERA GERBINI CATANIA Gulf of
CALTANISSETTA Catania Plain Catania
PIAZZA ARMERINA RAMACCA Dittaino Primo Sole
CANICATTI Olivo R. Gornalunga R. Bridge
Mediterranean AGRIGENTO CALTAGIRONE
PORTO EMPEDOCLE CAMPOBELLO GRAMMICHELE
PALMA DI Salso R. MAZZARINO VIZZINI FRANCOFONTE AUGUSTA
MONTECHIARO PONTE NISCEMI
OLIVO SYRACUSE
LICATA Gela R. BISCARI PALAZZOLA PONTE GRANDE BRIDGE
GELA CASSIBILE
G. of GELA COMISO AVOLA
RAGUSA Gulf of Noto
PACHINO
Sea C. PASSERO

F.G.

MILES
0 10 20 30 40 50
ROADS
RAILWAYS
MAIN AIRFIELDS ✠

'IMPREGNABLE BASTION' OF THE EUROPEAN FORTRESS

When the Allies landed in Sicily on July 10, 1943, they were engaged in large-scale fighting on the soil of western Europe for the first time since June 1940. The first 'impregnable bastion' of Hitler's Fortress of Europe had been penetrated. The campaign went much better than the plan: instead of taking 90 days, as anticipated, the Allies cleared Sicily of the enemy in 38 days

Specially drawn for THE SECOND GREAT WAR *by Félix Gardon*

was quickly restored. Nevertheless, it delayed the capture of Vizzini which, after changing hands five times, was finally taken on the 15th. At Francofonte German parachutists, fighting as infantry, compelled the attacking British forces to accept proportionate casualties for the first time in Sicily.

It was not, however, until the second week of the campaign that the Eighth Army encountered the main enemy forces. Resistance stiffened everywhere, especially near Catania, where the fighting became very fierce.

On the night of July 14–15 less than 200 British parachute troops were dropped seven miles south of Catania and seized intact the im-

Battle of Primo Sole Bridge

portant 400-ft. long bridge (Ponte di Primo Sole) over the Gornalunga river. They removed the demolition charges and took up defensive positions. Throughout the day of July 15 they were continuously attacked by greatly superior forces and were finally forced to withdraw after they had run out of ammunition. Relieving forces reached the bridge during the night and, after many heavy counter-attacks had been repulsed, it was again in Allied

hands by the following morning. However, the enemy made good use of the respite thus gained, and hundreds of transport vehicles and tanks poured into the Catania plain. A quarter of the island had been liberated, and prisoners numbered 25,000.

At this stage the 50th and 5th Divisions were brought to a temporary standstill north of the Primo Sole bridge. On their left the 51st Division was pushing against strong German resistance, but managed to form two more bridge-heads over the Gornalunga, north of Ramacca. The Canadians were still advancing on the extreme left of the Eighth Army against fierce opposition by the (re-formed) 15th Panzer Division, and places changed hands several times. After capturing Grammichele and Caltagirone on the 16th, and with American help Piazza Armerina on the 18th, they entered Valguernera by the 19th. Though delayed by demolitions and mortar fire, Americans pressing on from

Caltanissetta and the Canadians from Valguernera captured Enna in a joint attack on July 20. The Canadians went on to take Leonforte after bitter fighting on July 28.

On the west flank the American Seventh Army had made rapid progress. Opposition had been slight, except for short fierce local engagements, and at no point did they meet such determined or prolonged resistance as that encountered by the Eighth Army. They captured Niscemi, Canicatti, Campobello, and Palma di Montechiaro on July 15, and, after fighting their way northwards through hilly country, made contact with the Canadians near Enna. Caltanissetta fell to them on July 18. After a naval bombardment and 24 hours' confused fighting, the Americans captured Agrigento on the 16th. Next day, U.S. Rangers took Porto Empedocle. The possession of these coastal towns facilitated the landing of supplies and reinforcements. The Seventh Army then

AMERICAN 7th ARMY TROOPS IN SICILY

An American heavy artillery unit moving its 155-mm. gun along a winding mountain road recently repaired by a U.S. Engineer detachment. One of these guns hurled the first Allied shell on to the Italian mainland from a position near Messina. Left, General Sir Harold Alexander, Deputy C.-in-C. Allied Forces, and Lieut.-Gen. George S. Patton, commanding General, American forces, hold a consultation at a Sicilian airfield. Below, U.S. troops passing through the main street of a little town on their way to Palermo. The citizens shout 'Viva America' and 'Viva Inghilterra.'   *Photos, U.S. Official ; Keystone*

OPERATIONS AROUND ENNA

Left, enemy troops who have surrendered to the Eighth leave the wrecked building on the outskirts of Enna which they have been using as a strong-point. Right, temporary Battn. H.Q. of the Carlton and York Regiment from which part of the Canadian attack on German positions near Enna was directed. Enna itself, focal point of all Sicilian road and rail communications, fell to a joint U.S.-Canadian attack on July 20. *Photos, British and Canadian Official*

pushed forward rapidly through the west of the island. They entered Castelvetrano (with one of the best airfields in Sicily) and a number of other places on July 21, Palermo on the 22nd. Marsala fell to them on the 23rd, Trapani on the 24th. The Allies now possessed more airfields and, in Palermo the capital, a most valuable port.

All Sicily except the north-east corner was in Allied hands; over 70,000 prisoners had been taken, 50,000 of them by the Americans. The number of pris-

Little Resistance from Italians oners captured in the first three weeks of the campaign was not surprising. Italian resistance was almost non-existent, and there were many indications that a number of the Italian soldiers actually welcomed the invasion. At Caltanissetta, for example, large quantities of civil and military stores were found intact, although orders had been received for their destruction. The booty included 14 steam locomotives and 100 railway wagons in good condition. The Italian soldier thought in terms of his vineyard rather than of the Italian Empire. Most of those who did put up a fight were inspired either by German pressure or by the few fanatical Fascists who still had faith in the slogan that was everywhere on the walls—" Viva il Duce." There were only three armoured Italian battalions, able to muster some 150 tanks, many of them the archaic Fiat B-3000, which was designed in 1918 and then known as the " breakthrough " tank : the Italians referred to it more aptly as the " breakdown " tank. The main reason for the failure of Italian armoured fight-

ing vehicles in Sicily was lack of petrol and the low morale of their crews after months of tinkering with obsolete equipment. Broken tracks, broken springs, blistering engines, apart from casualties in action, made them useless.

CANADIAN TROOPS IN SICILY
1st Canadian Division
(Maj.-Gen. Guy Simonds, C.B.E., D.S.O.)
Units

Alberta Regiment	Nova Scotia Regiment
Canadian Recce Regiment	Ontario Regiment
11th, 12th and 14th Canadian Tank Regiments	Princess Patricia's Canadian Light Infantry
Carlton and York Regiment	Royal Canadian Regiment
Edmonton Regiment	Royal 22nd Regiment
French Canadian Regiment	Saskatoon Light Infantry
Hastings and Prince Edward Regiment	Seaforth Highlanders of Canada
48th Highlanders of Canada	Vancouver Regiment
New Brunswick Regiment	West Nova Scotia Regt.
	Winnipeg Regiment

By July 20 the Eighth Army's line ran from the bridge-head at Ponte di Primo Sole westwards along the railway to Enna. It soon became evident that the Germans intended to form their main defensive position on a line running from Catania north-westwards to the coast through Troina, a small town on a rocky summit west of Mount Etna.

In the following week Allied pressure against these Axis positions, which covered the Messina peninsula, increased, and by August 1 the tempo had risen to such a pitch that the final assault may be said to have started. Activity on the Eighth Army's eastern sector had been limited in the main to offensive

patrols and considerable exchange of artillery and mortar fire. Inland, some progress was made—the Americans captured Nicosia on July 29, and by the 31st an appreciable bridge-head had been secured over the Dittaino river. The Canadians took Regalbuto on August 2 in fierce hand-to-hand fighting, and on the same day the newly arrived British 78th Division (veterans of Longstop and Bou Aoukaz in Tunisia) stormed the mountain stronghold of Centuripe. Catenanuova was also secured. Agira, captured by the Canadians on July 29 and lost again, was firmly in Canadian hands on August 3. (The 78th Division took over the front held by the Canadians when the latter were withdrawn from Sicily about this time.)

There were now indications that this Allied pressure against the central sector was forcing the enemy to make preparations for a general withdrawal and Eighth Army patrols probing the area a mile

Enemy Prepares for Withdrawal

north of our own positions on the Catania plain on August 3 failed to make contact with the enemy. At the same time it was observed that ammunition dumps in Catania and on the Gerbini landing grounds were being destroyed.

Meanwhile, the Americans were meeting very stiff resistance from the German 29th and the Italian 26th Divisions near Troina and on the difficult northern

CANADIAN TANKS IN REGALBUTO

Regalbuto, a strong and heavily defended mountain fortress, fell to the Canadians after severe hand-to-hand fighting on August 2—the day on which the 78th Division captured Centuripe. Smashed by R.A.F. bombing and British and Canadian shelling, Regalbuto was more completely destroyed than any other town in Sicily. Bitter fighting on the whole Sicilian front marked this phase of the campaigns. *Photo, Associated Press*

coastal road. The country is here superbly beautiful, but appalling for offensive warfare. All the valleys run north and south, and mountain rocks overlook the narrow strip of road. Water from the springs and rivers cascades down deep furrows into the turquoise-blue sea. The Americans had to move from west to east, across the grain of the hills and across the many ridges and ravines. It was country more difficult

than any in Tunisia, with ample cover for the enemy in olive groves, among the cypresses and behind thick stone walls. They took Capizzi on August 1, then San Stefano on the 2nd, and after a five-day battle of intense bitterness

Troina fell to the U.S. First Division on August 6. Farther north the Goums (French Moroccan troops) worked their way through the mountains towards San Fratello.

On July 30 the islands of Favignana, Levanzo and Marettimo, forming the Egadi group off the west coast of Sicily, surrendered unconditionally. On August 5 a U.S. combined naval and military force occupied the island of Ustica, some 40 miles north-west of Palermo. The garrison consisted of about 100 Italian soldiers and sailors, who were taken prisoner; the Germans had left on July 11.

Although progress appeared slow once the general offensive had started, the main object was achieved. The enemy's line south of Mount Etna was split and his lateral communications cut. He **Enemy's Line South of Etna is Cut** probably intended to create a new defensive line from Troina to Catania through Adrano; but this plan was upset by the capture of Centuripe.

The enemy had to withdraw from Catania, which was entered by the Eighth Army on August 5; but a strong rearguard and extensive demolitions made further advance slow. In the central sector also road blocks, mines and other obstacles had to be dealt with before progress could be made against equally determined German rearguards. After extremely heavy fighting, the Canadians captured Adrano on August 7, and this success was exploited by a continuous advance, carried out by " leap-frogging "

THE 78th DIVISION TAKE CENTURIPE

The British 78th Division, veterans of Tunisia, replaced the Canadian units withdrawn from the line in Sicily in the early days of August 1943. They scored their first spectacular success in Sicily when they stormed the natural fortress-town of Centuripe (nicknamed ' Cherry Ripe ') on August 2. Left, Royal Inniskilling Fusiliers look down on the ' Grimm's fairy tale place perched on a crag ' which they helped to capture. Right, stretcher-bearers bring in a casualty.

FALL OF MESSINA

Early in the morning of August 17, 1943, U.S. troops entered Messina from the west. They were joined at 10 a.m. by British units from the south : the Sicilian campaign was over. 1. General Eisenhower, Allied C.-in-C., and General Montgomery, C.-in-C. Eighth Army, inspect the Italian mainland from Messina. During this visit to Montgomery's headquarters, General Eisenhower invested him with the highest order America can bestow on a soldier of another nation—that of Commander of the Legion of Merit. 2. Men of the East Yorks Regiment, first British infantry to enter Messina, gaze across at the mainland from a gun emplacement in the harbour. 3. An American reconnaissance unit searches a Messina street for snipers. 4. The waterfront of Messina when it fell.

BRITISH AND AMERICANS MEET NEAR RANDAZZO

Randazzo, vital point in the enemy's defence line based on Mount Etna, was defended with desperation by the Germans against concentric attacks by the British Eighth and U.S. Seventh Armies. It fell on August 13, the British 78th Division entering it shortly after the American Ninth. Before they abandoned this key to their entire Sicilian position, the Germans set many mines and booby-traps and fired the town.

they captured Milazzo on August 15. The whole of Mount Etna was in Allied hands by the 14th. The Eighth Army, on the eastern cliff road, occupied Taormina on the 15th, and were then held up by a demolished bridge. But next day a daring Commando landing was made farther up the coast at Scaletta, only eight miles south of Messina. Simultaneously an amphibious group from the American Seventh Army landed beyond Milazzo, also about eight miles from Messina, and it became a race between the two armies. The Americans won : advanced U.S. forces reached the outskirts of Messina by 8 p.m. on August 16. By 10 a.m. the following morning British Commandos and units of the Fourth Armoured Brigade joined them, and organized resistance ceased.

Mount Etna in Allied Hands

The Sicilian campaign had lasted 38 days, whereas the Allied High Command had prepared for a 90-days' campaign. The number of prisoners reached approximately 200,000, nearly all Italians, of whom some 70,000 (mostly Sicilians) were allowed to return home.

German losses in killed and wounded were not less than 23,000 ; similar losses by the Italians were between 7,000 and 8,000. British and American casualties were comparatively light, the Eighth Army suffering 11,835 and the Seventh Army 7,500. (Up till August 4, when

battalions of infantry, on Bronte, which fell during the night.

In the northern coastal sector, on the night of August 7–8, an infantry battalion of the Seventh Army made an unopposed landing in the enemy's rear some five miles east of Sant' Agata. They met an enemy motorized column moving west and a sharp engagement followed in which 1,500 prisoners were taken. They then took San Fratello and Sant' Agata, both on the 8th. Next day the Seventh made contact with the Eighth northwest of Bronte. The advance continued up the coast towards Cape Orlando. On the night of August 10–11, U.S. forces landed north of the Cape and struck inland towards Naso. By this time the Germans were showing signs of exhaustion. They were not short of supplies, however, but of reserves.

After the capture of Bronte on August 8 the left wing of the Eighth Army swung round the western **Fall of** slopes of Mount Etna, **Randazzo** leaving Randazzo, lying almost central on the enemy's lateral communications across the Messina peninsula, as the next and most important objective. The Germans strained every nerve to hold the town, but it fell on August 13 after fierce fighting. Its capture set a time limit to the campaign and was the signal for a speed-up of the enemy's withdrawal. The Axis forces were cornered. A general evacuation across the Messina Straits followed. Bombers kept up almost incessant day and night attacks on the coastal roads leading to Messina, on the barges and ferries in the Straits, and on landing beaches and towns on

the Italian mainland. The small craft, however, were not easy targets and the concentration of flak was described as " one of the greatest ever assembled on any battlefield." The enemy thus succeeded in withdrawing some 45,000 of his remaining 70,000 troops.

Meanwhile, German demolitions and mines failed to check the Seventh Army's advance along the north coast, where

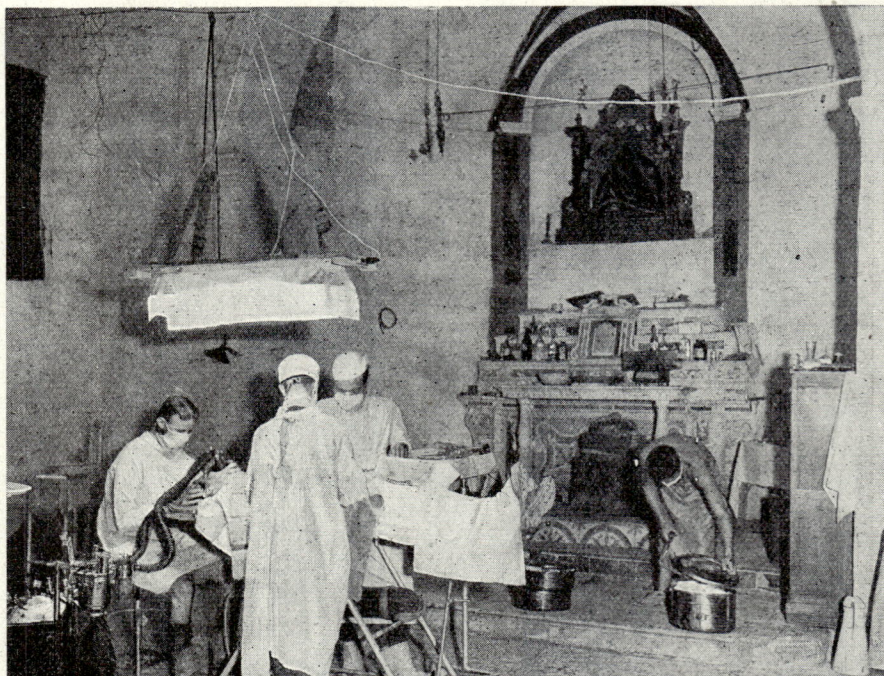

EMERGENCY OPERATION IN A MONASTERY CHAPEL

The chapel of La Casella Monastery, built in 1624, served as theatre for emergency operations during the fighting round Catania. Medical supplies and bandages were placed on the altar ; lighting was supplied by a portable apparatus. After treatment at this casualty station, wounded men were taken to a near-by airfield for evacuation by air to base hospitals. In its first 36 hours 17 abdominal operations were performed at this C.C.S. *Photo, British Official*

they were withdrawn from the line, the First Canadian Division lost 135 officers and 1,760 other ranks—395 killed, 1,200 wounded, and 300 missing.)

Between July 1 and August 17 the Axis lost 1,691 aircraft, of which 591 were destroyed in the air and over 1,000 destroyed or captured on the ground. Allied losses totalled 274 aircraft. From July 3, when the softening-up process began, more than 33,000 sorties were flown—27,000 by fighters and fighter-bombers, and many more than 5,000 by light and medium bombers.

Up to August 10 the enemy had lost 260 tanks and 502 guns, either destroyed or captured ; Allied figures were 103 tanks and 251 guns, including those sunk during the landings.

Allied merchant shipping losses totalled 85,000 tons, while over 300 Axis vessels were sunk or damaged. The Royal Navy lost two submarines, H.M.S. " Saracen " and H.M.S. " Parthian," three motor-torpedo-boats and one gunboat. The United States destroyer " Maddox " was sunk by air attack on July 10, and the U.S. minesweeper " Sentinel " was lost on July 11.

The part played by the medical services in the campaign was a notable one. Apart from battle casualties, the Casualty Clearing Stations worked stren-

Part Played by Medical Services uously to cope with the large number of cases of malaria—often, the majority of the patients. The Royal Air Force and United States Army Air Force were responsible for the evacuation by air of nearly all battle casualties. From July 6 to August 14 a total of 14,898 patients, wounded or sick, were flown from Sicily to the North African coast and from forward hospitals on the African mainland to base hospitals in Egypt or Algeria. Mobile Field Hospitals of the Royal Air Force, each equipped with an operating theatre, an X-ray section, and a small clinical laboratory, and having among their staff members of Princess Mary's R.A.F. Nursing Service, had a dual role to play. Like the army's Casualty Clearing Stations they provided emergency surgery and treatment in the field, while in addition they had the important task of holding, selecting and preparing cases for evacuation by air.

The work of the Sub-Commission for Monuments, Fine Arts and Archives needs a passing reference. Not the least important of its tasks was the protection of war-damaged buildings and arranging essential repairs to monuments, works of art, libraries and archives. In Palermo, for example, only minor patching was required to

safeguard the 17th century stucco reliefs of New Testament history and of the battle of Lepanto in the Oratory of Santa Zita, and those other masterpieces by the same artist, Serpotta, which enrich the Oratory of San Lorenzo.

General Montgomery described the campaign as " very well planned, very well executed and very cleanly finished off," and in a congratulatory message to General Eisenhower, H.M. The King referred to " the ordered progress of the campaign by sea, by land and by air." In point of fact, it can be regarded as the prototype of air-supported amphibian operations. The strength and

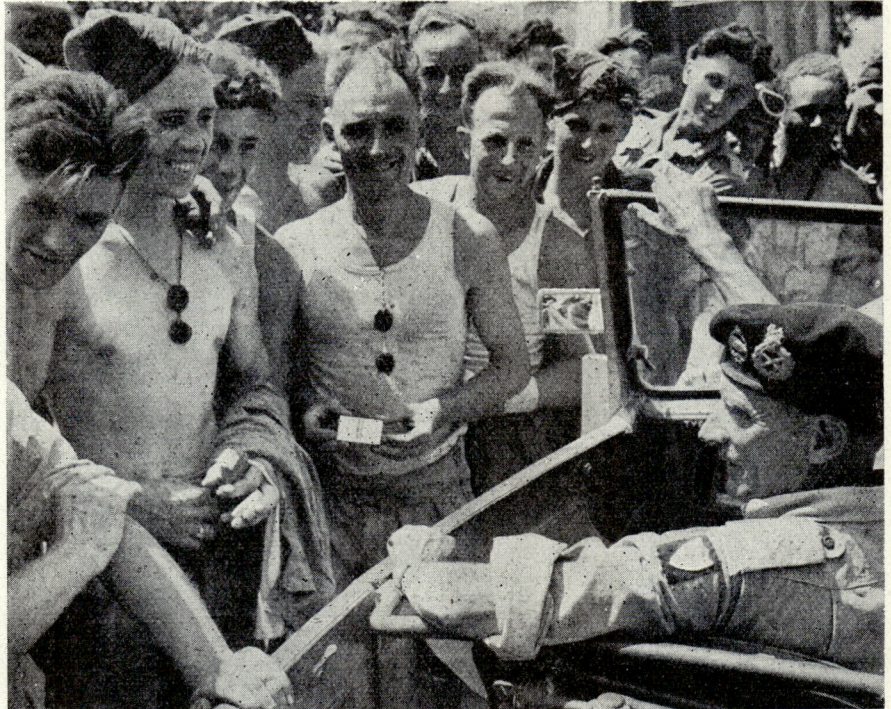

COMMANDER-IN-CHIEF WITH THE SAPPERS

General Montgomery, driving near the front in Sicily, came on a group of Royal Engineers working on the road and stopped to chat with them. Throughout the campaign, sappers played an immensely important part in the Allies' progress. Locating and digging up often thickly sown enemy mines, making new roads and repairing old ones damaged by Allied bombing and enemy demolitions, improvising bridges—these were among their vital duties, all of which were frequently carried out under fire. *Photo, British Official*

direction of the first assault took the enemy by surprise, particularly and most satisfactorily the German element. Leadership and fighting qualities of the two Allied armies never allowed the Axis to recover from that surprise, and the initiative remained in Allied hands throughout the campaign. After the Italian collapse in the coastal belt, the Germans were never given the chance to concentrate a formidable force at any given point and, though they brought in reinforcements by air and sea, they were never able to form a mobile reserve.

The master plan was based on the increased striking power and flexibility of Air Marshal Sir Arthur Coningham's

seasoned First Tactical Air Force, consisting of squadrons of the Royal Air Force, Royal Australian Air Force, South African and United States air forces. Such opposition as the Axis air forces offered at first rapidly collapsed, and the decline of the Luftwaffe was a noticeable feature of the campaign. After July 13 Allied fighters roamed the skies at will, almost completely unchallenged, and on the 15th nearly 200 Spitfire sorties were flown during the day without a single German or Italian aircraft being seen. As the assault forces went ashore the air cover and air offensive moved with them in complete co-ordination. Never before had an army attacked with such complementary air power. At the same time, the Royal Navy and United States Navy kept the sea lanes open and gave direct support to the two armies by continual bombardment of enemy coastal positions.

With Sicily in their hands, the Allies had gained three things. First, a springboard for the invasion of Italy ; second, naval advantages from its ports ; and third, a useful base for bombing Italian industrial centres and airfields. Politically, the conquest of Sicily revealed Italian impotence and accelerated the elimination of Italy from the war.

SURRENDER OF THE ITALIAN FLEET

1. Italian personnel line the deck of the battleship 'Giulio Cesare' as she approaches Malta. 2. H.M.S. 'Valiant' leads in the Italian fleet, consisting of two battleships, five cruisers, and four destroyers. 3. The Grand Harbour, Valetta: in the foreground, 'Eugenio di Savoia,' then 'Andrea Doria,' 'Caio Duilio,' 'Raimondo Montecuccoli,' and (left) 'Luigi Cadorna.' 4. Commodore R. M. Dick, Admiral Cunningham's Chief of Staff, receives Admiral Romeo Oliva as he steps ashore on Sept. 10, 1943, to tender his surrender.

Chapter 284

ALLIED NAVIES DEFEAT GERMANY AT SEA

Allied strength in the western seas increased steadily during 1943. Italy's surrender freed the Mediterranean from the threat of her fleet, and considerably reduced the strain on both Allied naval and merchant shipping. The curbing of the submarine menace is described in Chapter 275 ; here some of the outstanding exploits carried out against larger units of the Axis fleets are detailed. Naval operations for the same period in the Pacific are covered in Chapter 263

IN the western theatres, the naval war in 1943 started with the Allied fleets steadily increasing their superiority and their grip on major problems ; but in the area of greatest news interest—the Western Mediterranean—progress on land was disappointingly slow and automatically slowed down naval operations. But for the men engaged in them there was plenty of excitement as well as hard work, and there was no relaxation of pressure.

In one operation in January against enemy shipping in Palermo—revealed only 15 months later when decorations were announced for men taking part in it—the new Italian cruiser "Ulpic Traiano," completing for service, was sunk and the 8,500-ton transport "Viminale" so severely damaged that she had to be towed away for repair and was sunk in transit. This feat was carried out by two "human torpedoes" —craft of approximately the same size and shape as ordinary torpedoes, driven by electric batteries and manned by a crew of two wearing diving-suits and sitting astride the body. Completely silent, and navigated at night at "periscope depth" (the "periscope" being the commander's head), they were very nearly invisible. The "human torpedo" was manoeuvred at slow speeds towards its target, under which it dived. There, the crew detached a charge (similar to the warhead of a torpedo, and forming the nose of their craft), fixed it to the bottom of the enemy ship, set a time fuse, and navigated their now headless craft clear of the target area before the charge detonated.

At sea, submarines, surface ships and aircraft constantly attacked the stream of enemy supply ships —as the U-boats and Luftwaffe attacked ours—but the Allied results were much more satisfactory, and it soon became very difficult to persuade Italian seamen to sail. The operations of the Italian Navy became more and more half-hearted —although it is difficult to estimate the extent to which Italian inactivity was due to lack of oil, of which the Germans, mistrusting their allies,

Submarines in the Mediterranean

kept them very short. Their battle squadrons were prudently kept in harbour, and their cruisers were seen comparatively seldom. In April an American air raid on Maddalena sank the cruiser "Trieste" and damaged the "Gorizia." Destroyers and light coastal craft, many of the latter German-manned, were the most active and suffered severe losses ; while several Italian submarines surrendered tamely.

The capture of Tunis and Bizerta on May 7 virtually ended the North African campaign, although the last Axis forces did not surrender until the 13th. General von Arnim had made every effort to evacuate the German forces, the Italians being largely left to take their chance, but many Axis transport planes were shot down (*see* page 2667) and a large number of their surface vessels sunk.

Then began "island-hopping" towards the mainland of Italy. Pantelleria and Lampedusa were bombed and shelled into surrender (*see* page 2667), and on July 10 the Allies invaded Sicily

THE HUMAN TORPEDO

First used by the Royal Navy in January 1943 to attack shipping in Palermo Harbour, the human torpedo was a craft much the size and shape of an ordinary torpedo. The front of it was a charge which was fixed to the bottom of the craft attacked ; a time fuse was set, and the crew then steered the now headless ' torpedo ' out of the danger zone. Left, the control panel.

Photos, British Official ; Associated Press

under naval cover. According to President Roosevelt, 3,000 ships of all kinds were engaged in the Sicilian operations, and they suffered very small loss : the British Navy lost two submarines, three motor torpedo-boats and one motor gunboat. The defenders were rapidly driven into the north-east

NAVAL GUNS BOMBARD ITALY AND SICILY

H.M.S. 'Roberts,' one of the British monitors, specially designed to attack land objectives, which played a great part in Allied drives in the Mediterranean. She was first mentioned for the assistance she gave during the landings in Italy on September 3, 1943. Top, a British battleship firing at Catania on July 17, 1943. Operating at a range of from 15,000 to 11,000 yards, she sent in tons of shells while destroyers engaged shore batteries at closer range (see Chap. 283).

Photos, British Official

corner of the island, where many of their number were prevented from getting away by light coastal forces controlling the Straits of Messina (*see* Chapter 283).

Then came the invasion of Italy (*see* Chapter 286), carried out with the same naval co-operation, land positions being bombarded by heavy and light guns which covered the landing of troops and assisted them as long as they were within range. In these operations the existence of the new monitors "Roberts" and "Abercrombie," armed with 15-inch guns, was revealed, while the similar guns of "Warspite" and "Valiant," and the 16-inch guns of "Nelson" and "Rodney" also did

magnificent work and, apart from the material damage they inflicted, had an important effect on enemy morale. H.M. battleships "King George V" and "Howe," with aircraft carriers and many smaller vessels, joined the Fleet for the operations on the Italian coast.

Italy's unconditional surrender took effect on September 8. It seems to have been welcome to the Navy, always suspect by the Fascist Party, and most of the officers and ratings begged to be allowed to fight alongside the Allies. On the 10th the battleships "Italia" (formerly "Littorio"—renamed after Mussolini's fall) and "Vittorio Veneto" reached Malta with five cruisers and small craft from Spezia and the battle-

ships "Caio Duilio" and "Andrea Doria" with two cruisers from Taranto. Admiral Cunningham, with General Eisenhower as his guest, watched their arrival from a destroyer, while the veteran "Warspite," with "Valiant," had the honour of leading them in. Within 24 hours a hundred warships and 150,000 tons of merchant shipping was in Allied hands, and others, especially submarines, trickled through later.

On September 9 German aircraft, apparently using the newly introduced glider bomb with wireless control, fiercely attacked the Italian fleet in the Straits of Bonifacio while on its way from Spezia to Malta, and got direct hits on the flagship "Roma." A colossal explosion amidships broke her back, confirming the British naval opinion that the scantlings of the Italian capital ships were far too light. She went down with the greater part of her crew, including Admiral Bagliria, the Italian C.-in-C.

The uncompleted battleship "Impero" fell into German hands at Trieste and was used for propaganda although she was of doubtful utility; at Fiume the Germans seized the damaged battleship "Cavour," some cruisers, destroyers and submarines, and they took possession of the damaged cruisers "Gorizia" and "Bolzano."

The Allied forces were also gradually joined by ships of the Fighting French Fleet; early in January the authorities

'ROMA' SINKS

Left, bows and stern of the Italian flagship 'Roma,' bombed while sailing with the Italian fleet from Spezia to Malta. The vessel was hit by radio-controlled glider-bombs of the type illustrated below : this particular specimen was found near Paris after the liberation of France.

Photos, British Official

in North Africa had pledged the ships outside German control to co-operate. Most of them were very badly in need of reconditioning, and several, including the battleship "Richelieu," were sent to the United States for that purpose. As the work was completed they joined the Allied fleets, the men being tremendously keen, but requiring a good deal of training in the use of new weapons. Enthusiasm to join the Fighting French Navy led to difficulties by denuding French merchant ships of men. The ships immobilized at Alexandria since June 1940 voluntarily joined the Allies in May, badly in need of shipyard attention. By the end of the year the "Richelieu" and many others were on active service again, and Fighting French ships had been reported in several theatres of war.

The determined resistance of the Germans in Italy, and the slow progress of the northward advance, gave the Navy a great deal of work guarding lines of communication, covering new landings and bombarding enemy defences in coastal areas. Most of the last, on both coasts, was done by the 6-inch and 4·7-inch guns of cruisers and destroyers, which proved most effective. The Allies practically controlled the sea outside the range of the coastal batteries and aerodromes, but there were many exciting fights between Axis and Allied light coastal forces. The one unfortunate German success happened during the night of December 2–3 when a surprise low-level attack at dawn by 30–40 bombers on the Allied base of Bari sank 17 supply ships, and caused about 1,000 casualties. Though some of the vessels were empty, and others had discharged part of their cargoes, still the Eighth Army suffered in the matter of supplies for two or three days as a result of this raid.

The disappearance of the Italian "fleet in being" and the reopening of the Mediterranean route had immense indirect results—Germany **Mediterranean** estimated that the sub- **Route** stitution of the direct **Reopened** sea voyage for the long passage round the Cape was worth approximately 2,000,000 tons of merchant shipping to the Allies, while many capital ships were released for service in the Pacific : by November already Berlin reported British ships from the Mediterranean fighting at Bougainville.

The overwhelming by the Germans of the Italians on Cos and other islands of the eastern Mediterranean made it possible for the enemy to continue to use the Dardanelles and to withdraw from the Black Sea ships which had been supplying his armies there—for the end of his rule in that area was obvious. The Russian armies were steadily advancing west, retaking port after port. In February Moscow reported

AMMUNITION FOR RUSSIA'S BLACK SEA FLEET

A torpedo being taken aboard a submarine of the Soviet Black Sea Fleet. With Allied control of the Mediterranean re-established, and the Russians steadily advancing westward on land, retaking one port after another on the Black Sea, the situation of Axis shipping in that ocean became more and more precarious. Axis forces attempting to escape from the Caucasus and the Crimea by sea suffered heavily from attacks by the Red Navy.

Photo, U.S.S.R. Official

that the battleship " Paris Kommuna " had reached the Black Sea from the Baltic via the Cape, and her big guns gave magnificent backing to the light cruisers, destroyers, submarines and light coastal craft which formed the bulk of the Russian fleet. The Germans could respond only with constant air attacks, for their floating material was entirely overwhelmed. The Russians recaptured the naval base of Novorossiisk on September 16 and restored it as quickly as possible.

In the Baltic the Russian surface forces were still held in Kronstadt and Leningrad through the enemy's

Operations in the Baltic
possession of both sides of the Gulf of Finland, and the intensive mining operations which were maintained. Their Naval Air Force, however, carried out incessant attacks which harried both Germans and Finns, and a certain number of submarines slipped through. On the Northern front the Russians

were hampered by the cutting in some places of the White Sea–Baltic Canal, so that little support could be sent to their White Sea Squadron. Nevertheless, submarines, and aircraft supplied largely from Britain, were very active, and there were constant reports of enemy transports and supply ships sunk.

The vital necessity of keeping open the northern route to Russia called for constant vigilance from the Royal Navy —the action in Arctic waters which began on December 31, 1942 (and for his part in which Captain R. St. V. Sherbroke, D.S.O., won the V.C.), has already been described in page 2397. The enemy kept strong naval forces in Norwegian waters for the dual purpose of cutting the northern supply route and forcing the British to retain heavy metal at home. In the second purpose they were successful ; but, although they moved their main strength north from Trondhjem to Alten Fjord in April, convoys were generally too well guarded to invite naval attack. The Russian

NAVAL BOMBARDMENT—
The first landings in the Salerno area were successfully effected at 1.15 a.m. on September 9, 1943. They were carried out by a very great force of amphibious craft which sailed from many African ports under the protection of Allied Naval forces commanded by Vice-Admiral Henry K.—

Navy took a big part in protecting ships in the Barents Sea, where their submarines, light coastal forces and aircraft sank a large number of German and Finnish supply ships. Some losses there were, however, particularly from attack by aircraft, and the Honours Lists gave an inkling of the work of ships' crews.

The German battleship " Tirpitz," lying in Alten Fjord, was a constant threat to shipping in Northern waters. On September 22 a number of "midget" submarines of the "X" class, which had been built and tested in the greatest

'Tirpitz' Attacked by 'Midgets'

secrecy, were detailed to attack her. They were carried to within striking distance of the fjord and then left to their own devices. They were true submarines in miniature (quite distinct from the " human torpedoes " used at Palermo), about 40 feet long and manned by three officers and one engine-room rating, all volunteers. They had no conning tower, and the officer on watch on deck when they surfaced had to strap himself to the periscope.

Their target on this first occasion of their use was moored behind net defences in a corner of the fjord very difficult of access (*see* map opposite), and to reach her the little ships had to pass through a big minefield and then up a 50-mile channel guarded by listening posts, guns and nets. Nevertheless, they got through and scored several hits which rendered the " Tirpitz " unfit for battle. That started an inferno of fire, and three of the " midgets " were lost. When full

THE ROYAL NAVY HAS FRIGATES AGAIN
A new type of escort ship, named the frigate, was used on the North Atlantic sea lanes during 1943. Designed as a result of convoy experience, frigates were of several classes. They carried more men than a corvette, were more heavily armed, and had newer and better equipment for U-boat hunting. Here, a frigate of the Royal Canadian Navy plunges through an Atlantic swell in the teeth of a gale.
Photo, Royal Canadian Navy

2850

—Hewitt, U.S.N. A constant stream of reinforcements was landed, Allied warships offshore giving support. Here, British warships are bombarding enemy positions ashore as fighting proceeds on the beaches of Salerno Bay. Their heavy guns engaged German armour with 'good success.'

reports reached Britain, the captains of two who were taken prisoner—Lieut. Basil C. G. Place, D.S.C., R.N., and Lieut. Donald Cameron, R.N.R.—were awarded the V.C. for their gallantry in the attack and for the measures they took for the safety of their crews when they scuttled their boats—X-6 and X-7 —to prevent their falling into enemy hands. The third captain, Lieut. H. Henty-Creer, R.N.V.R., a 23-year-old film producer, with three other R.N.V.R. officers and two engine-room ratings were posthumously mentioned in dispatches for gallantry in August 1944.

On Boxing Day the battleship "Scharnhorst," from Alten Fjord, under Rear-Admiral Bey, attempted to intercept a convoy to North Russia. A cruiser squadron under the command of Vice-Admiral R. L. Burnett, C.B., O.B.E., D.S.O.— "Belfast" (Capt. F. R. Parham, R.N.), "Norfolk" (Capt. D. K. Bain, R.N.) and "Sheffield" (Capt. C. T. Addis, R.N.)—was screening ahead of the convoy, which was protected by destroyers, while to the westward Admiral Sir Bruce Fraser had his flagship "Duke of York" (Capt. the Hon. G. H. E. Russell, C.B.E. R.N.), with the cruiser H.M.S. "Jamaica" (Capt. J. Hughes Hallett, D.S.O., R.N.) and four destroyers. "Norfolk" made contact S.E. of Bear Island at 9.30 a.m., in bitter cold with a heavy sea running, and passed on the information while she opened fire and scored two hits. The "Scharnhorst"

'Scharnhorst' Attacks Convoy

2851

turned north-east and soon outstripped the cruisers, which took position between her and the convoy to intercept the expected attack. This came at 1 o'clock. A half-hour action started, in which "Norfolk" was struck by an 11-inch shell which started a fire: the engine-room crew had to work in respirators, but her speed never slackened.

The "Scharnhorst" turned towards the Norwegian coast, exactly carrying out one of the plans which had been carefully rehearsed by the Home Fleet. "Duke of York" and her escort made contact just before 4.30, opening fire at 12,000 yards by the light of star shells fired by "Belfast," and the enemy replied ten minutes later. Fires broke out on board the "Scharnhorst," and Admiral Fraser, fearing she would escape by her high speed, risked submarine attack on his flagship and sent in his destroyer screen—the British "Savage" (Cdr. M. D. C. Meyrick, R.N.), "Saumarez" (Lt.-Cdr. E. N. Walmsley, R.N.), and "Scorpion" (Lt.-Cdr. W. S. Clouston, R.N.), and

the Norwegian ship "Stord" (see illus., page 2731)—to torpedo her. They attacked her, two on either side, and scored three hits, pulling her speed down to a few knots. Then another destroyer force, comprising H.M.S. "Musketeer" (Cdr. R. L. Fisher, D.S.O., O.B.E., R.N.), H.M.S. "Matchless" (Lieut. W. D. Shaw, R.N.), H.M.S. "Opportune" (Cdr. J. Lee-Barber, D.S.O., R.N.), and H.M.S. "Virago" (Lt.-Cdr. A. J. R. White, R.N.), came up and inflicted further damage, enabling the "Duke of York" to close in. Blazing in several places from the "Duke of York's" 14-inch guns and with great patches of her sides red hot, the big German took a heavy list, and at 7.45 the cruiser "Jamaica" sank her by torpedo some 60 miles N.E. of North Cape. Thirty-six survivors of her complement of about 1,400 were rescued. "Norfolk" and "Saumarez" suffered minor damage and some casualties. The convoy proceeded untouched.

Sinking of 'Scharnhorst'

'RICHELIEU' RESUMES ACTIVE SERVICE

After the invasion of North Africa, more and more units of the French Navy which had been dismantled and laid up after the Franco-German armistice of 1940 joined the forces of the United Nations. Among them was the 35,000-ton battleship 'Richelieu,' here riding at anchor at an east coast port of the United States where she was refitted after crossing the Atlantic from Dakar. Her return to active service was announced on November 19, 1943.   *Pho'o, Pictorial Press*

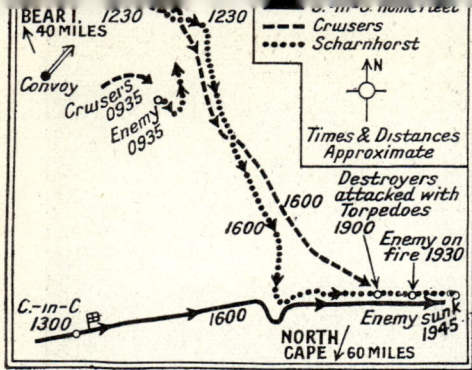

'SCHARNHORST' CHASE

Diagram illustrating the chase and sinking of the German battleship 'Scharnhorst' on December 26, 1943, by units of the Home Fleet under the C.-in-C., Sir Bruce Fraser. Times and distances are approximate. Carried out far within the Arctic Circle, these operations took place entirely in the dark.

From the official Admiralty chart

By the beginning of 1943 light coastal forces in home waters had acquired the initiative, and they improved their position steadily. Their repeated attacks on German patrol and destroyer formations under the guns of the occupied coasts became a great strain on the enemy's nerves, and on a number of occasions enemy boats fired into one another for some time after ours had withdrawn. Most of the coastal actions took place at night, and the special training of the British in operations in the dark, coupled with particularly careful and well-rehearsed co-ordination between the various types of ships in all circumstances, showed excellent results. Co-operation with larger units was also excellent. On October 24, for instance, a force of 30 E-boats attacking a convoy off the coast of East Anglia was driven off, four being sunk and seven damaged, by light coastal forces backed by two old destroyers and one of the Hunt class.

Some of these small craft were manned by Norwegians who were more than delighted when ordered to co-operate with British forces, sometimes including commando units, off their own coast. A number of enemy supply ships were sunk and many casualties caused in spite of the enemy's elaborate arrangements for calling up aircraft from his numerous shore bases.

In one incident in Norwegian waters early in October, the Home Fleet, including a number of American ships —among them an aircraft carrier—made a raid some 60 miles S.E. of the Lofoten Islands. U.S. naval aircraft scored hits on eight enemy merchant-men of 3,000–8,000 tons (sinking or severely damaging them), a 1,200-ton ore-vessel, and a landing barge. Only two enemy planes, both shot down, were met; and no enemy naval forces.

Naturally, there were failures, too. In September a German naval force, including the "Tirpitz" and the "Scharnhorst," attacked Barentsburg in Spitzbergen (*see* illus., page 2721). Six of the Norwegian garrison of 100 were killed, and a number taken prisoner. The remainder reorganized the defences after the enemy's with-drawal. And on October 23 H.M. cruiser "Charybdis" was sunk, and the destroyer "Limbourne" so badly dam-aged that she had to be sunk, in an action against light naval forces off the Sept Islands, Brittany.

A very large part of the time of the Navy in home waters was devoted to the escort of merchant shipping and the destruction of enemy submarines which were still very dangerous, even though the de-fence had secured the upper hand—a position maintained and improved only by constant pressure and the unceasing evolution of new ideas.

Operations in Home Waters

One of these last was the formation of special Escort Groups. They generally consisted of fast sloops, frequently accompanying the convoys but free to leave them and carry on the hunt wherever it might take them. The captains in these groups developed a fine technique and perfect team work, carried out in close co-operation with aircraft. The Second Escort Group, under Captain F. J. Walker, C.B., D.S.O.,

SUBMARINE EXPLOITS

The crew of H.M. Submarine 'Safari' which up to September 1943 had made fourteen successful war patrols—four under Lieut. Richard Barklie Lakin, D.S.O., D.S.C., R.N. (centre), ten under Commander Ben Bryant, D.S.O. and Double Bar, D.S.C., R.N. (above, left). She had sunk at least 40 Axis supply ships totalling more than 50,000 tons. Left, H.M. Submarine 'Taku,' forced more than once to lie submerged for hours while depth charges were raining round her, was known as the 'Elusive Taku.'

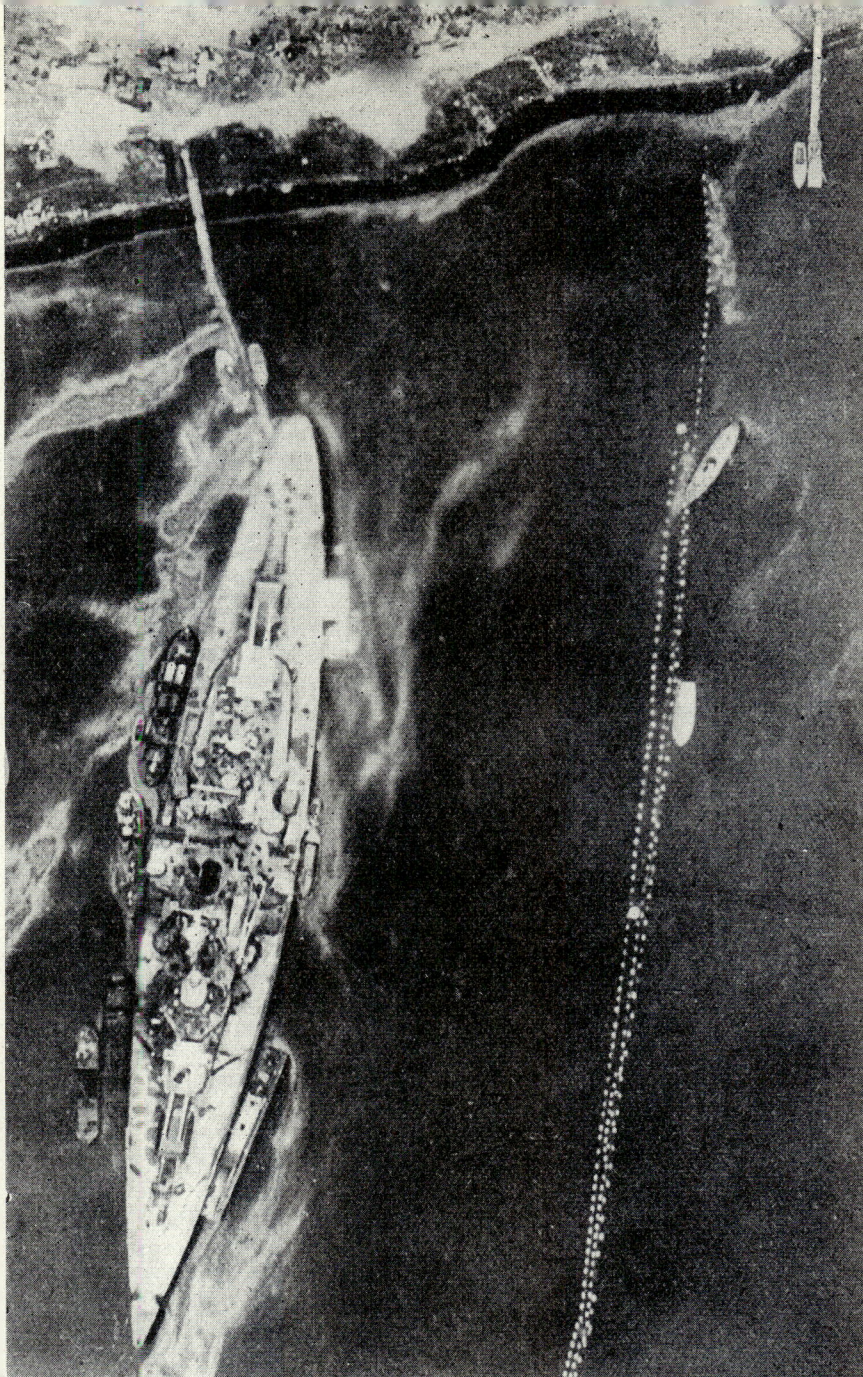

Lt. B. C. G. PLACE.   Lt. DONALD CAMERON

Commanding officers of H.M. Midget Submarines X-6 and X-7 which helped to carry out the attack on 'Tirpitz' in September 1943, they were awarded the V.C. for their 'courage, endurance, and utter contempt of danger' in their part of the enterprise. They were both taken prisoner, but they scuttled their ships first to prevent them from falling into enemy hands. Other members of the crews were appointed to the Distinguished Service Order.

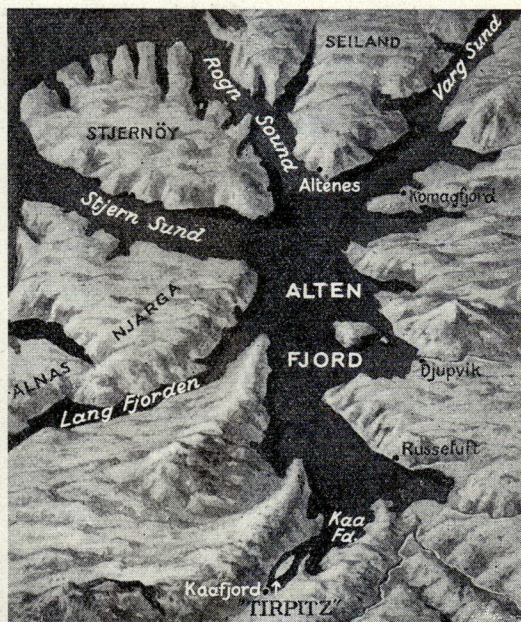

'TIRPITZ' AT BAY

The German battleship 'Tirpitz' as she lay in Alten Fjord was a constant threat to Allied shipping in northern waters and a number of attacks were made on her. None was more daring than that carried out on September 22, 1943, by new secret 'midget' submarines of the Royal Navy. An account of the action appears in the opposite page. Above, 'Tirpitz' at her moorings in Kaafjord photographed by a R.A.F. aircraft of the Photo Reconnaissance Unit under the direction of Coastal Command. Right, midget submarine proceeding at speed on the surface. The map shows the position of 'Tirpitz' in Alten Fjord.

Photos, British Official; Associated Press; Keystone; Topical Press

'WALKER'S CIRCUS' IN ACTION

Capt. F. J. Walker, C.B., D.S.O., R.N. (commanding the astoundingly successful Second Escort Group in the sloop H.M.S. 'Starling') shouts encouragement to another sloop of his group : 'Go on, Woodpecker, do your stuff, and beat the pants off her.' Above, H.M. sloop ' Magpie ' of the same group ploughs through heavy seas. Below, a U-boat, already abandoned by her crew, sinks for the last time, killed by ' Walker's Circus.' Capt. Walker's death from a heart attack was announced on July 10, 1944. *Photos, British Official*

ferred to Britain in exchange for bases. (*See* pp. 1429 and 1763.)

Carrier-borne aircraft were used against U-boats to an increasing extent, the force of escort carriers, or " baby flat-tops," being steadily increased and effectively closing the previous gap in the Atlantic umbrella. The Canadian and American Navies took a gallant part in these operations, and it is significant that within 24 hours in December the Admiralty attributed the better anti-submarine results to the much larger number of small craft available, and the Germans attributed the U-boat lack of success to the " almost incredible difficulties which they had to surmount."

Except in the Bay of Biscay and off the Spanish and Portuguese coasts, enemy air attacks on shipping fell off during the year ; while surface raiders, although still troublesome, were repeatedly run down and put out of action. The protection of shipping in the Atlantic was greatly simplified after October, when Portugal granted us air and shipping bases in the Azores for anti-submarine work. (*See* page 2658 and map in page 2656.)

The Navy's last remaining major job was to deal with blockade runners carrying raw materials—particularly oil, rubber and tin—to Germany from Japan and Japanese-occupied territories. The whole of their passage was beset with the danger of interception by Allied men-of-war, particularly at its European end. Several intercepted in the Bay of Biscay scuttled themselves. A two-day engagement in the Bay fittingly rounded off the year.

Dealing with Blockade Runners

was the most successful. Consisting of the sister sloops " Starling " (flag), " Wild Goose," " Kite," " Magpie," and " Woodpecker " until she was sunk, it started its career in the summer of 1943, and was soon known in the Fleet as " Walker's Circus."

The hunting fleet in the Atlantic was greatly strengthened by the introduction of a new type of frigate. This included more than one class ; some were enlarged corvettes with greater steaming radius and sufficient size to make them far better gun-platforms, while others were the American destroyer-escorts trans-

Early on December 27 a blockade runner of 5,000 tons was sighted by a Sunderland flying boat 500 miles W.N.W. of Cape Finisterre. The vessel was shadowed, and two 6-inch gun cruisers, " Glasgow " and 24-year-old " Enterprise," prepared to intercept. Other aircraft attacked, a Liberator of a Czech squadron scoring a direct hit which caused a violent explosion, a fire, and more explosions which sank the ship. Early next morning 11 German destroyers were sighted, five of them of the powerful new 2,400-ton Narvik class mounting five 5·9-inch guns, apparently sent to meet the lost blockade runner. " Glasgow " and " Enterprise " went into action. The German force scattered and fled towards France. In a running chase, assisted by aircraft of Coastal Command, the cruisers sank three of the German destroyers, suffering only minor damage themselves and a few casualties on " Glasgow." (*See* illus., page 2752.)

GUNS OF THE ROYAL ARTILLERY IN THE MAIN STREET OF SAN ANTONIO
After the occupation of Catania on **August 5**, the Eighth Army pushed inland round the south and western slopes of Mount Etna and northwards along the coast road leading to Taormina and, eventually, to Messina. Here, 25-pounders of the Royal Artillery are being moved through San Antonio, some eight miles north of Catania. Acireale, two miles farther on, was captured on August 8 ; Taormina, where British **troops** received a great welcome from the people, on the 15th.
Photo, British Official

THEY SANK THE 'SCHARNHORST'

The British force which sank 'Scharnhorst' on December 26, 1943, was disposed in two formations. One, under the immediate command of the C.-in-C. Home Fleet, Admiral Sir Bruce Fraser, K.C.B., K.B.E. (right), flying his flag in the battleship H.M.S. 'Duke of York' (below) was covering the convoy at a distance. With him was the cruiser H.M.S. 'Jamaica' (above) and four destroyers. The second formation of three cruisers was under the command of Vice-Admiral Burnett, C.B., O.B.E., D.S.O. (left). The action is described in page 2851.

FIFTH ARMY AT SALERNO

Not until December 28, 1943, did Allied G.H.Q. announce that the Fifth Army at the time of the Salerno landings comprised only two British and one American divisions, and that the issue at one time 'hung on a thread.' The British were driven from Battipaglia, German tanks almost split the Fifth Army in two, and at one time Allied warships were firing on enemy tanks trying to storm the beaches. On September 13, a British armoured division (held in reserve) was thrown in, and an American airborne division, dropped on the beaches, went straight into action as infantry. On September 14 every available Allied aircraft was flung in, and the Germans began to retreat. Above, British troops move up the Salerno beach from a landing craft. Right, infantry take cover behind blazing and derelict German Mark IV tanks on the roadside near Salerno.

3 D

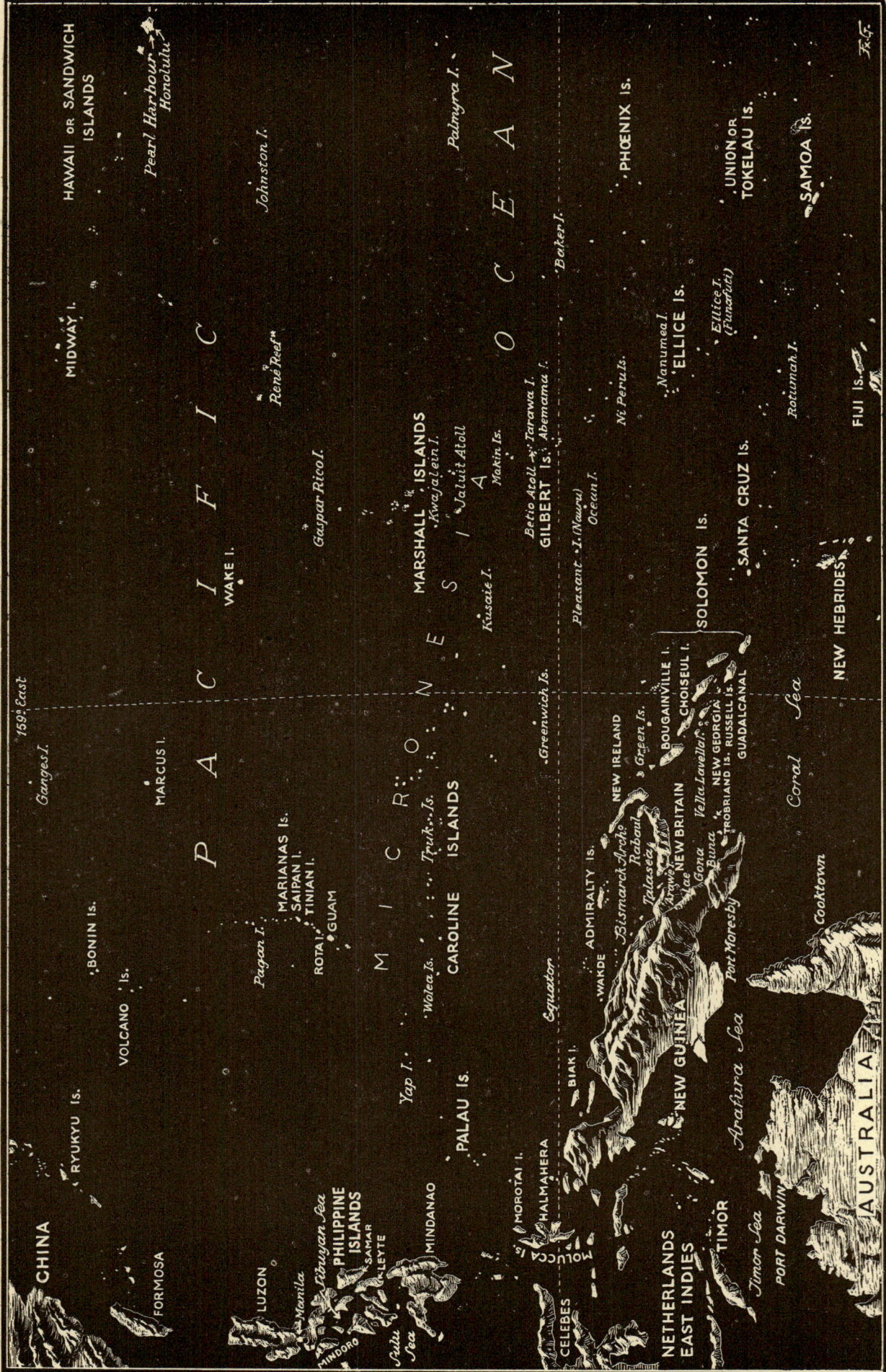

VAST BATTLEFIELD OF THE SOUTH AND WESTERN PACIFIC

The immensity of this Far Eastern theatre of war may be gauged by the distance from Manila to Honolulu—4,835 miles. Progressive seizure by the Allies of Japanese-held islands began with the clearing of Guadalcanal and the expulsion of the enemy from the Buna-Gona area of New Guinea in February 1943; by the end of the year the Gilberts, most of the Solomons and all S.E. New Guinea were in Allied hands. Dividing line between Gen. MacArthur's S.W. Pacific Command and Adm. Halsey's S. Pacific Command was the 159th meridian East longitude. Detail maps of New Georgia and Bougainville are given on pages 2883 and 2887.

Specially drawn for THE SECOND GREAT WAR *by Félix Gardon*

REVOLUTION IN ITALY: MUSSOLINI FALLS

Italy was the first of the Axis partners and satellites to surrender, and this Chapter tells of the rapidly changing internal conditions which led up to the overthrow of Fascism and the signing of an armistice between Italy and the Allies. It is contributed by Ruggero Orlando, an Italian journalist who, brought up under Fascism, became a convinced anti-Fascist, and had to leave the country. He was, however, in a position to follow events in his native land. For a record of events on the Italian home front in 1942, see Chapter 234

THE year 1943 was perhaps as momentous for twentieth-century Italy as 1848 was for Italy of the nineteenth. In 1848 the Liberal spirit which had long lived underground and was nourished in the hearts of selected individuals and groups, burst into the open and possessed the whole people. A poet called 1848 " a year of portents " : a nation awoke from slavery, alined herself with, and contributed to, the new trends developing in Europe, and, in spite of bitter disappointments, hard defeats, misunderstanding and suspicion from friends, wrote one of the most beautiful pages of world history—the *Risorgimento*. A tide had risen which no human force could stop.

For the Italian people, 1943 meant the ninth year of Fascist war. Since the early preparations for Italian aggression against Ethiopia, the number of people serving in the armed forces had steadily increased, propaganda for country and Empire and against the enemy of the

Ninth Year of Fascist War

day had become steadily more nerve-racking, police repression had become more ferocious, and legal respect for the dignity of the individual had disappeared. Through the Abyssinian campaign and intervention in Spain, the Government of Rome had abandoned all pretence of loyalty to world peace and balanced alliances. In fact, since Mussolini's acquiescence in Hitler's march on Vienna, the average Italian considered Mussolini the first " quisling " of his German ape. A mordant joke was current in Italy : " How well off we were under Mussolini ! "

In 1940 the overwhelming majority of Italians had felt that the war declared by the Duce on Britain and prostrate France was not their war. This feeling was often hardly realized by the men themselves ; but it resulted in a general lack of resistance in the fighting forces. Very few units of the army put up any determined fight ; those who did had either some strong regimental tradition which inspired them or they found themselves in exceptional circumstances which made surrender perilous.

Partly with intention and partly merely from lack of interest in the war, the nation at home grew into one single body of passive resisters and saboteurs ;

'SECRET WEAPONS' PROPAGANDA IN ITALY

This poster, shown all over Italy in the days preceding her surrender, depicts a miniature submarine or oversize torpedo directed by two men in diving suits, described as Italy's latest 'secret weapon.' Designed to penetrate port defences, it was used without much effect against British shipping at Malta and Gibraltar. British 'human torpedoes,' meanwhile, were successfully attacking Italian shipping (see page 2847). *Photo, G.P.U.*

bribery and black-market activities surpassed anything experienced in other European countries. Hitler was compelled to instal his own agents at all key points of Italian administration, had to send his own troops to the Balkans, to Africa and to southern France to do the work he had expected his ally to do.

The economic condition of the Italian people, which had grown from bad to worse ever since Mussolini's rise to power in 1922, had reached the point of general starvation during the Fascist wars. During prolonged periods of this war the rations of Greeks and Poles were larger than those of the Italians.

The corruption of Fascist leaders grew as they saw the abyss yawning in front of their eyes, for by 1943 every one of them had recognized the bankruptcy of the Party, and thought only of saving himself. The most prominent leaders had already brought pressure to bear on Mussolini, urging him to find a way out of the war ; very many thought that it was already lost, and all were convinced that it was impossible to win.

As he had done several times before in moments of crisis, Mussolini withdrew from the limelight and allowed his subordinates to look for a policy. He had already given up all dreams of Mediterranean

Twilight of Mussolini

hegemony, oceanic outlets and conquest of Middle Eastern oil. With the Wehrmacht stopped at Stalingrad and El Alamein, all he wished for was to achieve "non-belligerency," or even neutrality. He reckoned on Hitler's consent ; the Nazis, now forced to take the defensive, could not but regard Italy as a liability. Would it not be better for Germany if she could defend herself on a neutralized Alpine frontier with four divisions, instead of having to occupy the long Italian coastline with 20 or 30 divisions ? The Allies, on the other hand, would be only too glad to exchange the long route round the Cape for the shorter Suez way. To sail 3,121 miles from Britain in order to reach the Middle East instead of having to sail 11,438 miles—was that not an advantage ? Thus, at least, ran the Fascist calculations.

If Fascist diplomacy had been as capable of making peace as it had shown itself of stirring war, the ruling clique would have gained some respite, however temporary, from the menacing pressure exercised on them by the people. The conclusion of an armistice would have appeased the masses for the time being and the ruling clique could have strengthened their crumbling power.

But in January 1943 the " unconditional surrender " announced by

ITALY'S DUCE VISITS GERMANY'S FUEHRER

Hitler and Mussolini met twice during 1943 before the Duce's fall—from April 7-10 at Hitler's G.H.Q., and on July 19 at Verona. Here, during the first meeting, Mussolini (1), with Goering (2) by his side, advances towards Hitler. Others in the group are Joachim von Ribbentrop, German Foreign Minister (3), Giuseppe Bastianini, Italian Under Foreign Secretary (4), Dr. Schmidt, Hitler's interpreter (5), General Vittorio Ambrosio, Chief of Italian General Staff (6), Hans Georg von Mackensen, German Ambassador in Rome (7), Dino Alfieri, Italian Ambassador in Berlin (8). *Photo, New York Times Photos*

President Roosevelt and Mr. Churchill smashed all these plans to dust and ashes. With that peremptory demand thundered from Casablanca, all hopes for an easy and negotiated armistice disappeared. In the same month Palermo was bombed, Tripoli fell amidst the rejoicing of Arabs, Jews and Italians, and General von Paulus surrendered at Stalingrad.

Mussolini openly admitted that the "unconditional surrender" demand was a direct hit. For the first time after many months of silence, on February 1 he made a public speech in which he attacked the "criminal policy" of the United States President and the British Prime Minister.

Fearing that now his subordinates would try to rid themselves of the first and foremost obstacle to any possible renewed attempt at making an armistice —namely, his person—Mussolini dismissed his Commander-in-Chief, Marshal Ugo Cavallero, the army man who was most closely in touch with Fascist circles. The new Commander-in-Chief was General Vittorio Ambrosio; although he was no "political" general he was deeply compromised in the Fascist war through his association with the Serbian General Mihailovitch and his ferocious reprisals against Tito.

A few days later, on February 5, Mussolini dismissed his whole cabinet, getting rid, for the first time in the history of Italian Fascism, of the "old guard." His son-in-law and former Foreign Minister, Count Ciano, was appointed Ambassador to the Vatican. Among other powerful Fascists, Renato Ricci retired into private life. Alessandro Pavolini and Giuseppe Bottai were appeased with editorships.

Even the youthful Aldo Vidussoni, secretary of the Fascist Party, a hero of the Ethiopian and Spanish wars, was sacked. His successor was Carlo Scorza, **New Secretary for Fascist Party** ferocious squad leader of the early days of Fascism, unpopular with his more successful comrades of the ruling clique. Scorza immediately started on a colossal purge in the very ranks of the Party. More than 60,000 people had their party cards—and therewith, in most cases, their livelihood—withdrawn.

The new cabinet was an assembly of nonentities who owed their position to Mussolini, and could more or less be relied on not to intrigue behind his back.

The Rome-Berlin Axis seemed suddenly to revive. On February 24 Ribbentrop came to Rome; on March 15 Admiral Doenitz visited his Italian counterpart, Admiral Riccardi. From April 7 to 10 Mussolini visited Hitler at his headquarters. Nevertheless, Mussolini had not given up all hope of concluding a separate armistice; he merely wanted to show to the United Nations that he was still a powerful ally of Hitler and that they had much to gain in dealing with him.

A very different picture of the solidity of the Axis, however, presented itself to Allied intelligence in Tunisia. It is true that in Tunisia Italian troops did, for once, fight with determination. But they were led by the most anti-German of all Italian generals, Messe. His report on the Mareth battle, the only one in which Italian troops caused the Eighth Army a temporary setback, was fully published on April 15. In it he throws the whole responsibility for the Tunisian defeat upon the Germans who enforced the order to retreat in spite of the favourable position reached by the Italian spearhead. Later it became known that General Messe went about among his troops telling them, "It is time to show those German swine who retreat that we can fight better than they." Certainly these words were not dictated by moral sense or true patriotism, but rather by ambition and military prejudice. It was short-term propaganda ; but for a week it worked (*see* illus., p. 2776).

While from Phalangist Spain the Foreign Minister, Gen. Jordana, was offering his services as a mediator, **Passive Resistance Becomes Active** Mussolini and Scorza tried to take advantage of the last days of fighting in Africa to put on a mask of strength and national unity. But news, leaking out from the Italian underground, gave the lie to this show. It was clear that a process, familiar to all historians of revolutions, was taking place. Within the mass of the people, the feeling of dislike for the regime and its war had turned to action ; unconscious opposition had become conscious, passive resistance had become active and organized.

On March 6, 1943, a general strike broke out in northern Italy. This event will pass into the history of social insurrections as the greatest general strike ever organized up to that date entirely underground. (It was afterwards surpassed by the North Italian strike which broke out in March 1944, and was organized under German occupation.) Properly to assess the far-reaching importance of the strike of 1943, one must remember that the first step modern tyrannies have taken in any country has been the abolition of free Labour organizations. Once Labour organizations had been brought under Fascist control, every precaution was taken to prevent the workers from associating with and trusting each other. Chains of spies, agents provocateurs and thugs were introduced into every factory, every working district, every home. They were disguised as workers, accountants, shopkeepers, so that nobody could say whether the man working on the next bench was a friend or an enemy. The Fascist secret police, the armed Militia, Party ward groups, After-Work organizations, syndicates and shop stewards watched over the daily life of the working class. Suspen-

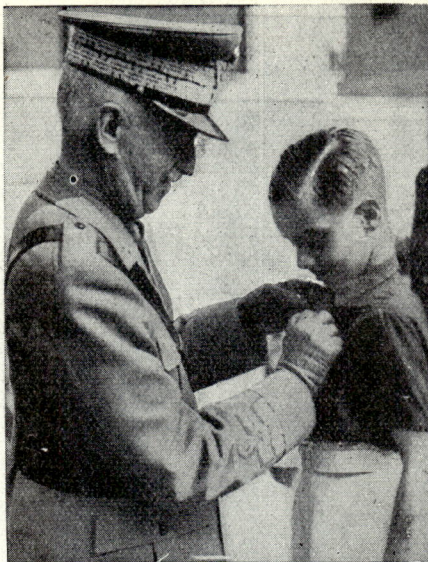

THE YOUNG FASCIST
On the occasion of the Italian Navy Day parade, King Victor Emmanuel pins a decoration to the black shirt of a young member of the Balilla. The abolition of the Fascist youth organizations, and their incorporation into the Ministry of Education, was announced on August 5, 1943.
Photo, New York Times Photos

sion of work by more than three workers in the same factory was punished with many years of jail. The writer of this Chapter was himself witness of a strike near Rome in 1935, enacted by *nine* workers. The armed police of three provinces was mobilized in order to arrest the men responsible and to prevent the strike from spreading to other factories.

Yet, on March 6, 1943, the workers of the FIAT Mirafiori, near Turin, refused to go back to work after lunch, because the promised indemnity for evacuation expenses had not been paid to their families. On March 8 work stopped in

five factories. Two days later 40 workshops in Piedmont were immobilized. In the following days the strike spread and developed into a general strike in the neighbouring region of Lombardy. It suddenly became clear that behind the economic claims of the workers there was a powerful organization of factory committees whose authority was recognized by hundreds of thousands of workers. A complete report on the strikes was circulated underground in Italy and reached anti-Fascist groups in Switzerland. It was broadcast over and over again by the B.B.C. for many days. The official Fascist " Stefani " agency at first denied its authenticity. Finally, however, more than three months later, Mussolini confirmed that " suspension of work " had taken place. Significantly, the speech in which he admitted the strikes was his last speech as a dictator. No dictatorship can last if the masses are able to organize themselves.

Side by side with the factory committees, the underground C.U.P.I. (Committee for the Union of the Italian People) was active. **New Parties Begin to Form** It rallied together anti-Fascist leaders of Catholic, Liberal, Socialist and Communist tendencies. Within the C.U.P.I., closely linked with the anti-Fascists in France and Switzerland, six parties were forming themselves : the Party of Liberal Reconstruction, the Party of Christian Democracy, the Action Party, the Party of Democracy of Labour, the Socialist Party, and the Communist Party. When the Allies landed in Sicily in July, they found branches of the C.U.P.I. everywhere.

After the Axis collapse in Tunisia, antelleria and Lampedusa surrendered.

ROME FLOCKS TO HEAR MUSSOLINI FOR THE LAST TIME
This immense crowd gathered on May 5, 1943, seventh anniversary of the Italian entry into Addis Ababa and two days before Tunis fell to the Allies, to hear Mussolini, their ' loved chief,' proclaim from the balcony of the Palazzo Venezia, ' I feel vibrating in your voices . . . faith in Fascism, and a certainty that the bloody sacrifices of these difficult times will be repaid by victory. . . . Italy must and will return to Africa. . . . God is just. Italy is immortal. We shall win.' It was his last oration from this favourite platform. *Photo, Associated Press*

MILAN BATTERED BY ALLIED BOMBS

On the night of August 15-16, 1943, the R.A.F., making its fourth heavy attack on Milan since August 7, dropped over a hundred 4,000-lb. bombs on the city. Swiss reports said hundreds of thousands of refugees were flocking to the country, and vast crowds were demonstrating for peace in the ruined streets. The city was without gas, water, or electricity. Left, the remains of the famous shopping arcade, Galleria Vittorio Emanuele, near the Cathedral. Right, men clearing bomb damage take their midday meal at a salvaged table.

Some prominent citizens of Pantelleria wrote a letter denouncing Fascism and advocating the greatest help possible by Italians to the destruction of the Nazi-Fascist evil. When the Allies landed in Sicily some units of the Italian Army even went so far as to greet the "invaders" with cheering, and the enthusiasm of the local population—who in many parts had suffered heavily from Allied bombing—reached peaks unequalled since the landing of Garibaldi.

As a result, the Sicilian campaign cost much less in terms of lives, equipment and time than had been estimated by Allied leaders (see Chap. 283). Three German divisions which managed to retreat first to the north-eastern corner of the isle and later to the mainland had to defend themselves alone. If the full meaning of the enthusiasm of Palermo and other cities was misunderstood by some Allied observers (some believed that Sicily was rejoicing to be liberated from Italy!) it was fully and rightly interpreted by the ruling clique in Rome.

Why Sicilians Welcomed the Allies

Hitherto the Fascists had still clung to the hope that once the "invaders" had set foot on Italian home soil a spirit of resistance would awaken in the people. Now this hope was fading. The Fascists went to the length of appealing publicly to the "anti-Fascists" for help—the anti-Fascists, whose existence had never been admitted. Scorza, the ultra-Fascist, sounded the trumpet of national unity and called the nation to resist in the name of King, Flag and Catholic Church, independently of all the "symbols of revolution," meaning, of course, the fasces.

The Directorate of the Fascist Party, instead of publishing the usual flattering communiqués addressed to the genius of the Duce, sent him a list of "recommendations" which were, in fact, a series of criticisms concerning the organization of the war effort. Mussolini answered with the speech made on June 24, and not published until July 5 (another obvious sign of uncertainty), in which he admitted the strikes and promised the severest discipline throughout the country.

The Allies were advancing in Sicily, and a hurriedly arranged meeting between Hitler and Mussolini took place in Verona on July 19. Mussolini asked Hitler for German reinforcements. Hitler is reported to have declared that only if the whole of southern and central Italy were evacuated and a defence line established on the Po would he assist Mussolini. The political implications of such a move, which meant the handing over to the advancing enemy of the greater part of the Italian homeland, were obvious to any Italian, including even Mussolini. Whatever the exact details of the Verona conversations (and the non-committal Axis communiqués were careful not to betray any) it became clear that Hitler would do nothing that promised a successful defence of Italy against the Allied onslaught from without, and the successful defence of Fascism against the revolutionary forces from within.

Hitler Meets Mussolini in Verona

In these circumstances the leading Fascists saw only one way out : to give a non-Fascist leadership to the people. They hoped thus to unite the people under the national flag and make them fight a war for King and country, with the idea that prolonged resistance might make the Allies more amenable to a negotiated armistice, and would at least give the leaders themselves time to reach safety.

On July 24 Dino Grandi moved in the Fascist Grand Council that the King should resume supreme command of the armed forces, held since 1936 by Mussolini. The motion had been discussed and agreed upon by various members of the Grand Council at a private meeting held beforehand in Bottai's home. Mussolini, Scorza, Farinacci and a few other extremists, taken by surprise, opposed the motion violently. Nevertheless, after a debate which lasted all through the night and far into the next day, it was carried by 17 votes (including that of Count Ciano) to nine.

At 10.50 p.m. on July 25 Rome Radio announced that the King had accepted Mussolini's resignation and had called on Marshal Badoglio to **Mussolini's** lead the Government. **Resignation** In fact—as it became known later—Mussolini had been arrested outside the Royal Palace after having threatened the King with the mobilization of the Fascist militia if he were made to resign. Proclamations by the King and Marshal Badoglio followed. The essence of both proclamations was, in Badoglio's own words : The war goes on.

Hardly had the news of Mussolini's fall been made known than in all towns and villages of Italy mass demonstrations were held. Fascist signs were torn down, papers were burnt, old democratic leaders whom the Fascists had silenced appeared on public rostra, young leaders emerged from underground, old and new democratic papers came off the printing presses. The whole country demonstrated for freedom and peace. Despite Badoglio's declaration, the war seemed over.

Badoglio reacted immediately. He declared martial law, assumed direct control of the police forces, including the Fascist militia, again muzzled the press, and forbade all assemblies of more than three persons. At the same time he tried to convince the people that this was no longer a Fascist war by sacking the old cabinet and appointing one of " technical experts."

Despite the severe penalties threatened by Badoglio for any political activity, the six democratic parties, united in the national committee, organized mass demonstrations, backed by mass strikes. In a manifesto, which even the severe censorship could not prevent from getting into the columns of the great Turin daily La Stampa, they put forward the following demands : 1. Liquidation

ROME SUFFERS AIR-RAID DAMAGE

Rome experienced two air raids, on July 19 and on August 13, 1943. Both took place about midday, and had the San Lorenzo and Littorio marshalling yards as their objectives ; the 500-strong forces of U.S. bombers which made the attacks were in both cases led by Major-General James H. Doolittle (who led the first air raid on Tokyo on April 18, 1942). Here, people are removing their belongings from a damaged apartment house after the second raid. Below, the Pope, who visited the bombed areas on August 13, talks to the people who crowded round him, and knelt in prayer in the Piazza San Giovanni.   *Photos, Associated Press ; Planet News*

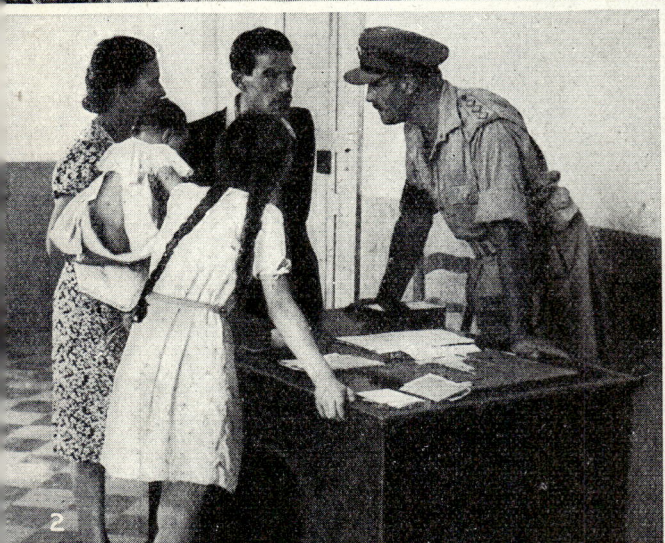

SICILY'S WELCOME TO THE ARMIES OF LIBERATION

When the Allies landed in Sicily, the people met them with an enthusiasm unequalled since the landing of Garibaldi : they regarded the 'invaders' as liberators who would free them from Fascism—and from war. 1. A welcome to the Allies painted on a wall at Misterbianco, near Catania. 2. Capt. R. B. Waters, R.A., advising civilians at his company headquarters. 4. Salvatore Campanelli, lawyer of Milotello, a small town in central Sicily, announces the end of Fascism from the bonnet of a British army vehicle ; the news evidently did not displease a number of his audience. 3. Citizens of Catania cheer as the troops of the Eighth Army move through the town after the enemy. 5. Portrait of the Duce—aptly in pensive mood—defaced by Sicilians.

Photos, British Official

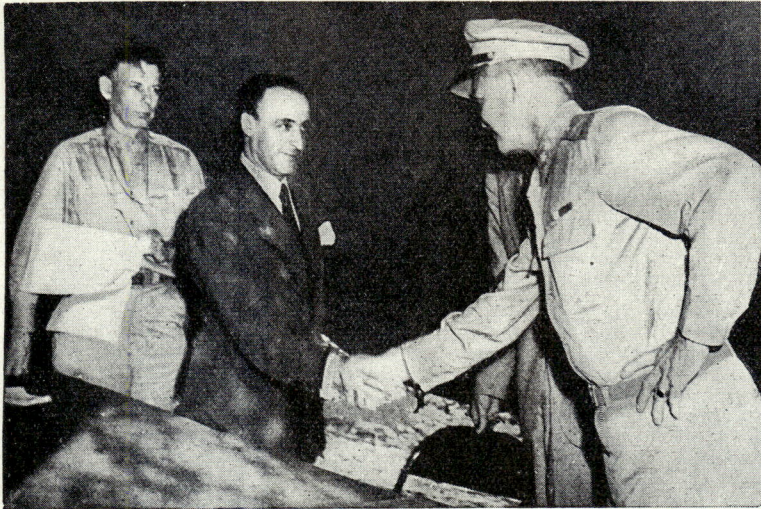

ALLIES SIGN AN ARMISTICE WITH ITALY

After a month's negotiations, carried on in the greatest secrecy by Brig.-Gen. Giuseppe Castellano, representing Marshal Badoglio, and Maj.-Gen. Walter Bedell Smith, of the U.S. Army, and Brig. Kenneth Strong, of the British Army, representing General Eisenhower, an armistice was signed by Gen. Castellano and Gen. Bedell Smith at Syracuse on September 3, 1943. It came into effect on September 8. Left, Gen. Eisenhower shakes hands with Gen. Castellano, behind whom Gen. Bedell Smith holds the terms. Above, Gen. Castella 10 signing : behind him, Brig. Strong, Mr. Montenari of the Italian Foreign Office, Gen. Bedell Smith. *Photos, British Official*

of the Fasces ; 2. Armistice ; 3. Civil liberties ; 4. Release of political prisoners ; 5. Independent judiciary ; 6. Abolition of racial laws ; 7. Representative government.

If the new Government did not want to be swept away like the old dictatorship, it had to give way to these demands. The Party was formally dissolved and Law 2693, giving almost unlimited power to the Fascist Grand Council, repealed. The Senate and the Chamber of Fasces and Corporations were closed down. A commission was set up to expunge from Italy's penal and civil codes purely Fascist laws. Prominent Fascists were arrested and some political prisoners freed. Although all political parties were forbidden, Badoglio appointed men, each of them clearly representative of one of the six officially non-existing parties, as commissioners for the various

Fascist Party Dissolved

PARLEY ON THE ROAD TO ROME

Marshal Badoglio's broadcast of September 8, 1943, stated, 'Italian forces will cease all acts of hostility against the Anglo-American forces. . . . They will, however, oppose attacks of any other forces,' but said nothing of how 'other forces' who did not attack were to be treated. Hence the uncertainty of these Italian guards on a road south of Rome as they surround a car containing German officers making their way to the city shortly after the Italian surrender came into force. *Photo, Keystone*

trade unions, with instructions to bring them back to elective procedure.

Yet, while the people saw that Italy was slowly getting into the path of democracy, they would give no credit to Badoglio because he had not brought about a break with Hitler. To fight on the Nazi side seemed now more illogical than ever. Having witnessed the constant arrival of German reinforcements since Mussolini's fall, they had no illusions as to German reactions to such a break. A manifesto, issued by the joint six-party Committee on August 3 and calling again for an armistice, stated : " It is certain that the Italian people will be united in facing whatever danger may arise as the result of this decision."

Why did Badoglio not sign an armistice immediately he came to power ? Why did he delay, and thus give the Germans time to get an even firmer hold on Italy than they had had in Mussolini's time ? He answered this question himself in an article published in the Corriere, of Salerno, in March 1944. He states that at the time when he took over, 37 Italian divisions were out

of the country. (In a press interview given previously he indicated that Mussolini had scattered 30 divisions all over the Balkans, for fear of keeping too many armed and able-bodied Italians in the country.) Only 12 divisions, ill-armed and without petrol for mobility, were on the Italian mainland. They could not possibly have resisted the Germans. " Meanwhile," the article goes on, " while it was not possible to carry on with the war owing to the lack of means and to the aversion of the people, we had thought to get in touch with the adversary and conclude an armistice."

Apart from the delay which occurred in the armistice discussions between the Allies and the Italian emissaries owing to difficulties of communications, it can be assumed that, at least in the very first days of his Government, Badoglio hoped that the Germans would of their own free will evacuate at least as far as the Po Valley, once they had seen which way things were developing. A soldier himself, he could see little advantage to be gained by the Germans by defending themselves in southern Italy. He had no understanding of the political motives that were undoubtedly the determining factors in Hitler's decision.

Badoglio's Unfounded Hopes

On September 3 the Allies landed on the Italian mainland between Reggio and Catona. The armistice was signed that very day ; but the Italian forces, who offered no resistance and in many instances helped the Allies, did not know it. It was announced only five days later.

FIRST AXIS POWER SURRENDERS UNCONDITIONALLY

The announcement made by General Eisenhower on September 8, 1943, that Italy had
surrendered unconditionally did not mark the end of fighting in that unhappy country.
But it did mean a great easing of Allied problems and an added burden to Germany
when she decided to defend the Italian peninsula. The speech quoted below, in which
Mr. Churchill related the diplomatic moves preceding Italy's surrender, gave more
satisfaction to the Empire than any wartime pronouncement of his had so far done

TERMS OF THE ARMISTICE WITH ITALY, SIGNED SEPTEMBER 3, WHICH CAME INTO EFFECT AT 5.30 P.M. ON SEPTEMBER 8, 1943:

(1) Immediate cessation of all hostile activity by Italian armed forces.

(2) Italy will use its best endeavours to deny to the Germans facilities that might be used against the Allies.

(3) All prisoners or internees of the United Nations immediately to be turned over to the Allied C.-in-C. and none may now, or at any time, be evacuated to Germany.

(4) Immediate transfer of the Italian fleet and Italian aircraft to such points as may be designated by the Allied C.-in-C. with details of disarmament prescribed by him.

(5) Italian merchant shipping may be requisitioned by the Allied C.-in-C. to meet the need of the military and naval programme.

(6) Immediate surrender of Corsica and all Italian territory, both of islands and mainland, to the Allies for use as operational bases and other purposes as they may see fit.

(7) Immediate guarantee of free use by the Allies of all airfields and naval ports in Italian territory, regardless of the rate of evacuation of Italian territory by German forces. These ports and fields to be protected by Italian armed forces until this function is taken over by the Allies.

(8) The immediate withdrawal to Italy of Italian armed forces from all participation in the current war from whatever area wherein they may now be engaged.

(9) Guarantee by the Italian Government that if necessary it will employ all available forces to ensure prompt and exact compliance with all provisions of this armistice.

(10) The C.-in-C. of the Allied Forces reserves to himself the right to take any measures which in his opinion may be necessary for the protection and interests of the Allied Forces for the prosecution of the war, and the Italian Government binds itself to take such administrative or other actions as the C.-in-C. may require, and, in particular, the C.-in-C. will establish Allied Military Government over such parts of Italian territory as he may deem necessary in the military interests of the Allied Nations.

(11) The C.-in-C. Allied Forces will have full right to impose the measures of disarmament, demobilization, and demilitarization.

(12) Other conditions of a political, economic, and financial nature, with which Italy will be bound to comply, will be transmitted at a later date.

(13) The conditions of the present armistice will not be made public without the previous approval of the Allied C.-in-C. The English version will be the official text.

MR. CHURCHILL SPEAKS ON ITALY'S UNCONDITIONAL SURRENDER, IN THE HOUSE OF COMMONS, SEPTEMBER 21, 1943:

ON July 10, British and American armies, on the scale of perhaps 500,000 men, the first wave of whom were carried in upwards of 2,700 ships and landing craft, began their attack upon Sicily, and in a campaign of 38 days the entire island was conquered with loss to the enemy of 165,000 in killed, wounded, and prisoners, or more than four times our Allied losses in the operation. . . . July 25 was a memorable day. Even before we had half completed the conquest of Sicily or had set foot on the Italian mainland, the dictator Mussolini was overthrown and the Fascist regime, which had lasted for 21 years, was cast down and vehemently repudiated by the whole mass of the Italian people. The Badoglio Government came into existence with the intention of making peace in accordance with the will of the nation. They were, however, intruded upon at all points and overlaid by the Germans, and they had the greatest difficulty in maintaining themselves against this hateful pressure. We knew nothing about this new regime. Once Fascism was completely overthrown we were naturally anxious to find some authority with whom we could deal, so as to bring about the unconditional surrender of Italy in the shortest time and with the least possible cost in the blood of our soldiers. It was necessary to wait till the position became more definite. We therefore continued our preparations for the invasion in strength of the mainland of Italy on which we had resolved at the May Conference in Washington.

Presently, some feelers were put out by the new Italian Government through various channels asking for terms and explaining the deadly character of the difficulties in which they were involved. . . . We made the reply that the surrender must be unconditional. On August 15 the Italian envoy, an officer with the rank of general, called upon H.M. Ambassador at Madrid, Sir S. Hoare, with credentials proving that he came with full authority from Marshal Badoglio, and that he came to say that when the Allies landed in Italy the Italian Government were prepared to join them against Germany. . . .

With the approval of the War Cabinet, it was decided that General Eisenhower should send an American and British staff officer to meet the Italian envoy in Lisbon. We at once informed Premier Stalin of what was in progress. On August 19 the meeting in Lisbon took place. The envoy was informed that we could accept only unconditional surrender . . . He replied that the purpose of his visit was to discuss how Italy could join the United Nations in the war against Germany. . . . The British and American officers replied that they were empowered to discuss only unconditional surrender. They were, however, authorized— and this was a decision which we took at Quebec—to add that if at any time, anywhere, in any circumstances, any Italian forces or people were found by our troops to be fighting Germans, we would immediately give them all possible aid.

On August 23 the Italian general departed. . . . On August 31 the Italian envoy returned. He met General Eisenhower's representatives at Syracuse. The Italian Government were willing to accept the terms unconditionally, but they did not see how they could carry them out in the teeth of the heavy German forces gathered near Rome and at many other points throughout the country. . . . We did not doubt the sincerity of the envoy nor of his Government, but we were not able to reveal our military plans for the invasion of Italy, or, as it had now become, the liberation of Italy. The real difficulty was that the Italians were powerless until we landed in strength, and we could not give them the date. We therefore timed the announcement for the moment which we deemed would give us the best military chance and them the best chance of extricating themselves from the German grip. This meant that the Armistice should be accorded only at the moment or just before our main descent.

The terms were signed at Syracuse on the night of September 3. . . . The Soviet Government, having studied the terms, authorized General Eisenhower to sign them in their name. Accordingly, he did so not only on behalf of the United States and Great Britain but on behalf of the Soviet Government and of the United Nations. . . .

Most strenuous efforts were made by all concerned to speed up our onfall. . . . The date which had originally been the 15th was in fact brought forward to the 9th—the night of the 8th and 9th. Thus the whole of this operation . . . was planned as a result of decisions taken before the fall of Mussolini and would have taken place whatever happened to Italy at the earliest possible moment. The Italian surrender was a windfall, but it had nothing to do with the date of harvesting the orchard. The truth is that the Armistice announcement was delayed to fit in with the attack and not the attack to fit in with the announcement. . . .

ITALY: FIRST ALLIED INVASION AREA OF AXIS-OCCUPIED EUROPE

The Allies entered Tunis on May 7, 1943, landed in Sicily on July 10, entered Messina on August 17, and made their first landing on the mainland of Axis-occupied Europe on September 3, near Reggio (see Chapters 277, 283, and 285). For the 1943 revolution in Italy, see Chapter 285. *Specially drawn for* THE SECOND GREAT WAR *by Félix Gardon*

Chapter 286

THE ALLIES LAND IN ITALY & FREE NAPLES

The conquest of Sicily, described in Chapter 283, was completed on August 17, 1943. Little more than a fortnight later, on September 3, an Allied army set foot again on the western mainland of the continent of Europe. The Italians offered slight opposition even before the Armistice with the Allies was announced on September 8; but from Salerno onwards the Germans disputed every Allied advance. This Chapter, contributed by Squadron-Leader Derek Adkins, R.A.F., carries the history of the campaign to the occupation of Naples on October 1

THROUGHOUT the Sicilian campaign (*see* Chapter 283), political and military events in Italy developed rapidly, as recorded in Chapter 285, culminating with Italy's unconditional surrender on September 3.

The end of the Sicilian campaign coincided with the Quebec Conference (August 11–24, *see* Chapter 280), and public opinion, which had perhaps been somewhat spoilt by the initial rapidity of the Allied successes in Sicily, felt that an apparent military opportunity was not being properly exploited. But the strategy of the Allied High Command could not be revealed at the time, owing to political and military considerations, and the announcement of Italy's capitulation was not made until five days after the armistice terms had been signed.

The rapid conquest of Sicily had been a severe shock to the Italians, in spite of the claims, particularly from the German side, that the fighting in and evacuation of Sicily was a great military victory for the Axis powers. On the other hand, Italy's surrender took the Germans by surprise.

In the absence of any government-inspired policy, the initiative of joining the Allied cause was left to individual Italian commanders, but it soon became clear that the majority would be content to play the part of onlookers, although the anti-German hostility of the Italian population was rather more than passive.

From a total of some sixty-two Italian field divisions, nine came over to the Allies, fourteen were disarmed by partisans or deserted to the guerillas

in the Balkans, and the remainder, except for four which continued active collaboration, were disarmed by the Germans and ceased to count as operational formations. Of the twenty to twenty-five Coastal divisions, about half in southern Italy, Corsica and Sardinia co-operated with the Allies. The remainder in German-occupied territory disintegrated, the bulk of the men deserting to their own homes.

The British and American air forces, operating under Air Chief Marshal Sir Arthur Tedder, initiated the Italian campaign immediately after the invasion of Sicily began by attacks of increasing violence **Pre-Invasion Air Attacks** on the Italian communication system, and on industrial targets (*see* pp. 2667 *et seq.* and illus., p. 2683). The bombing of the San Lorenzo marshalling yards at Rome on July 19—the first attack on military objectives in the Italian capital—was just one step in the Allied plan to paralyse the Italian communications system.

That system is a simple one. Its focal point is Naples. From there electric lines branch north to Rome, south to the toe and east to connect with the steam railway on the east coast route. It was clear that if bombs could freeze communications at only three points—Naples, on the west, Benevento in the centre, and Foggia governing the east—the servicing and reinforcement by rail of the armies south of these points would become impossible.

The battle of the marshalling yards began in full strength on August 19. As the invasion date drew near and reinforcements from Germany became more necessary, the attack on communications spread as far as the Brenner. In twenty days following the fall of Messina no fewer than 58 attacks, involving some thousands of sorties, were directed against 29 vital rail centres. The result was that by invasion day rail activity had virtually ceased at Benevento, Aversa, Sulmona, Paola, Pisa, Cancello, Catanzaro, Foggia and Salerno. Elsewhere in marshalling yards, sidings and junctions, at individual river bridges and on carefully chosen

READY TO EMBARK FOR HITLER'S 'FESTUNG EUROPA'

The conquest of Sicily was completed with the entry of the Allies into Messina on August 17, 1943. Just over a fortnight later, on September 3, British and Canadian units of the Eighth Army crossed the Straits of Messina and landed in Calabria, between Reggio and San Giovanni. Here, infantry assault troops stand by on the quayside at Catania ready to embark.

2868

CANADIANS 'TOUCH DOWN' AT REGGIO IN 'DUCKS'

The first landings of the Allies on the Western European mainland were effected at 4.30 a.m. on September 3, 1943, from a huge fleet of invasion barges, 'ducks,' and other amphibious craft under cover of a powerful air umbrella, and following a violent 'softening up' artillery bombardment lasting several days across the straits from Sicily. Canadians landed near Reggio captured the town and its airfield by nightfall.

Photo, British Official

choke points, damage by blast had turned the enemy's transport problem into a military nightmare.

The fact that the land assault on Italy took place on the fourth anniversary of the outbreak of war was purely coincidental. It was in the hands of the same battle-planners who had designed and brought the Sicilian campaign to such a brilliant conclusion (*see* page 2830). At 4.30 a.m. on September 3, under cover of heavy artillery fire and naval bombardment from H.M. battleships, cruisers, destroyers and monitors, British and Canadian troops of the Eighth Army landed on the Calabrian coast of Italy from ports on the east coast of Sicily.

On the right flank a Canadian Infantry Division landed on a one-brigade front at Reggio, where they

Canadians Capture Reggio
quickly captured the town and airfield which was reported fit for fighter aircraft. On the left flank a British Infantry Division landed on a two-brigade front between Gallico Marina and Catona and turned north. Forward troops immediately advanced through San Giovanni. Everywhere resistance was slight and there were no mines or demolitions. The Italian end of the submarine cable was found to be intact.

R.A.F. Servicing Commandos (*see* illus., page 2828) landed with the spearhead of the invading forces, and their work began as soon as Reggio and other airfields had been captured. After clearing away obstructions, repairing the runways or laying out emergency landing strips, maintenance crews were ready to refuel and service aircraft before handing over to the ground crews

proper. Their task corresponded to that of the sappers, engineers and technicians whose job it was to ease the path of the Eighth Army's mechanized units.

Calabria forms a distinct region of Italy, the main features of which are, topographically, its mountainous char-

acter (only about 15 per cent is under 300 feet and some ranges rise to 6,000 feet), the length of the coastline (485 miles or nearly a fifth of the total coastline of continental Italy), combined with a lack of good harbours. Roads are few and, apart from the main Reggio to Naples route, poor. There is a good deal of rough forest and scrub. The surface is generally bad and subject to landslides, while in many parts clayey or shaly soil seriously hampers any possibility of movement. The peninsula is nowhere more than sixty miles across and at

A 'PRIEST' LANDS ON THE SHORES OF ITALY

The 105-mm. self-propelled gun howitzer, christened the 'Priest' by men of the Eighth Army in North Africa (see illus., p. 2555), accompanied them in their invasion of the Italian mainland. These Allied landings met with no opposition in the air and little on the ground. The Italians surrendered after a 'token' resistance while the Germans had already evacuated the toe of Italy.

Photo, British Official

THE BEACHES OF SALERNO

This map shows the scene of the main onfall in the Allied plan for the invasion of Italy. The actual descent had to be undertaken a week earlier than had been intended, owing to the difficulty in keeping Italy's armistice with the Allies secret from the Germans, and the need for Allied support to maintain the new Italian government in its stand against its former partner.

Specially drawn for THE SECOND GREAT WAR *by Félix Gardon*

mander, had concentrated in the Alban and Sabine hills, ready to seize the capital. Warning, however, came from the Italian Government that the Germans were in possession of the airfields, and the plan was never carried out.

The landings began at 1.15 a.m. near the mouth of the river Sele, with American forces to the south and British to the north of the river. The weather was favourable, as appears from the following extracts taken from an account broadcast by Commander Anthony Kimmins on September 15:

. . . As we approached the Italian coast-line, conditions were perfect for the landing. A calm sea, clear sky and good visibility; a half-moon lit up the sea brilliantly . . .

C.-S.-M. P. H. WRIGHT
(Coldstream Guards)

Sergt.-Maj. Wright took charge of his company in the attack on the Pagliarolli hills near Salerno on September 25, 1943, after all the officers had been killed, advanced single-handed up the slopes under heavy mortar and machine-gun fire, and knocked out three German machine-gun posts with hand grenades and the bayonet, thus enabling his company to reach its objective. He was first awarded the D.C.M., but this was later replaced by the V.C.   *Photo, Daily Mirror*

its narrowest point, the isthmus of Catanzaro, it is only 19 miles from sea to sea. In most areas, particularly along the west coast, the mountains descend sharply to the sea, and there are few plains. Rainfall is heavier than elsewhere in Italy, and an average of 50 inches a year is not unusual, while on the west coast it has been as high as 95.

The Calabrians themselves have for many centuries stood outside the main line of European development, and the neglect from which they suffered **The People of Calabria** under the Neapolitans was continued under the Kingdom of Italy. Consequently they harboured a justifiable grudge against the more advanced northerners by whom they considered they were exploited. The country peasants are proud but poor, rather rough but generally hospitable. The standard of living is extremely low. These factors are not merely of historical interest. They had an important bearing on military operations. The local inhabitants were even more cordial and enthusiastic than in Sicily.

After the initial landings disembarkation proceeded quickly and smoothly. During the first three days and nights the R.A.S.C. performed feats of endurance. The loaders handled rations and 25-pounder ammunition for 72 hours non-stop, while the drivers covered 380 miles of overcrowded roads in 48 hours, also without a stop. In one day alone they cleared 600 tons of stores from the beaches.

From Reggio the Canadians advanced in two directions — north - eastwards through San Stefano to Delianuova, which they occupied on September 6, and southwards along the coast road to Bova Marina (8th). At the same time they branched off into the mountains and reached Roccaforte, also on the 6th. Meanwhile the British troops who had landed north of Reggio pushed up the coast, captured Scilla on September 4 and made contact with a Commando force which had been landed at Bagnara. Palmi was taken on the 6th. The first real contact with German troops was made on the fifth day after the invasion, when some units attempted to hold up the advance. Patrols proceeding northwards to Gioia met with some opposition outside the town where the bridge over the river Petrace had been blown up. Italian resistance had been negligible, and 3,000 prisoners were captured in the first few days. When the Italian capitulation was announced on September 8 it had little effect on the operations. The Eighth Army's advance continued to be hampered by demolitions, however.

On September 9 the Fifth Army, under the command of Lieut.-Gen. Mark W. Clark, U.S. Army, landed in the Gulf of Salerno. This was the main Allied descent, which the Eighth Army's attack on Calabria was intended to supplement. It was a hazardous and bold operation, mounted a week ahead of time to exploit the favourable military and political situation created by the armistice: it had been originally planned to land near Naples on September 15, but it was doubtful whether the Badoglio Government, after the signing of the armistice, could hold their position so long without British support. Preparations had also been made to land at the same time an American airborne division in Rome to help the Italians fight off the two German armoured divisions which Kesselring, the German com-

it would set at 1 a.m. and so give the landing craft complete darkness for the final assault. A warm, balmy breeze added the final touch to one of those perfect Mediterranean nights.

As the darkness closed in, the flagship fog-horn boomed out, and all the leading assault ships stopped engines; they drifted quietly on, way being lost. The assault landing craft had been lowered down to sea level packed tight with eager, silent troops. . . . Every one of those men was a great hero. As they approached the beaches, there were the inevitable explosions as mines went up, but soon another more cheering noise—the terrific bombardment from covering warships just before the final touch-down. . . . As the first lots of troops leapt ashore, searching in the darkness for mines and trip-wires, more men poured in from behind. . . . Throughout the remaining hours of

SALERNO LANDINGS

The Allied landings at Salerno, planned for September 15, 1943, and advanced to coincide with the announcement of Italy's surrender, began at 1.15 a.m. on September 9. The assault was made by British and American troops of the Fifth Army. 1. Allied landing craft lays its own smoke screen during the attack. 2. Crowded invasion vessel nearing the beach: bombs from Messerschmitts fell on either side of it shortly after this photograph was taken. 3. Brengun carriers coming ashore from a landing craft near Salerno. 4. Lieut.-Gen. Mark W. Clark, U.S. Army, commanding the Fifth Army, approaches the Salerno beaches.

Photos, British Official; New York Times Photos; Keystone

BRITISH TROOPS ENTER SALERNO

British Commandos landed unopposed west of Salerno on September 9, 1943, and soon entered the town. They were reinforced by other British troops from a beach-head farther south, who completed the capture of the town on September 10. Here is a Bren-gun carrier passing through the bomb damaged streets of Salerno after the Allied occupation. Below, British and German wounded outside an advanced dressing station near Salerno. *Photo. British Official*

darkness, more and more troops and supplies were rushed ashore. As the dawn broke the enemy bombers made a determined effort to sink our ships before it was too late. But long-range Lightnings and Spitfires from Sicily and Fleet Air Arm Seafires from the aircraft carriers were there ready to meet them, and their bombing met with little success.

Just as at Sicily, first light disclosed a staggering picture of shipping. The whole Gulf of Salerno seemed to be packed tight with craft of every kind, while more and more approached from seaward. The beaches were shrouded in smoke. Lines of dust drifted up as tanks and guns rushed to their appointed positions. Then, great columns of dark earth as enemy batteries loosed off at them. Almost immediately the flashes from these guns were surrounded by more shell bursts as cruisers and destroyers took them on. And then again, great columns of water round the ships from the return fire. . . . Through all the fire and counter-fire, streams of landing craft plied to and fro, while our minesweepers cleared the mines. Ships were hit, of course, but considering all things, casualties were light.

On the beaches, men stripped to the waist, heaving and tugging in a wild rush to get everything possible ashore before the inevitable counter-attack. Mortars and shells were bursting around them, but the work went on just the same. On **Getting Troops and Supplies Ashore** a signal from the naval beach master, the next landing craft would come in, lower its doors as it touched down, and almost before it had stopped, troops would be rushing ashore, or heavy vehicles floundering up the wire netting over the soft sand. As they emptied, urgent stretcher cases were rushed on board, and the craft pulled off from the beaches to make room for more. . . .

For some reason, the first real counter-attack did not develop until the sun was well up, and those first few hours made all the difference. As tanks appeared from the woods inland and came down the roads, anti-tank guns were already in position to take them on. . . . Forward observation posts had already been established, so that cruiser and destroyer fire could be directed on to those points where it was most required. . . . La Forey, the famous flotilla leader who has taken part in nearly every engagement throughout the Mediterranean war, there she was, charging in and taking on every battery or tank she could find. Her particular target at one period was a coastal battery considerably stronger than her own broadside. . . . She received a direct hit on the water-line. But almost simultaneously her own shells landed in the battery and knocked it sky-high.

As La Forey steamed out to seaward with a heavy list, a collision mat over the side and her pumps working at full pressure, I thought to myself, "What a glorious end to a grand commission." But not a bit of it. There she was back in the afternoon, a temporary patch over her side and taking on all comers closer than ever inshore. And she was only one of very many on the job.

West of Salerno, British Commandos landed unopposed and entered the town. At Maiori, still farther west, American Rangers pushed inland and blocked the roads leading south through the hills. These subsidiary landings were reinforced by British troops from the south who completed the capture of Salerno on September 10 and began to advance northwards into the hills. Unfortunately their advance was of little use owing to lack of success in the Battipaglia area. Although the Americans had established a firm bridge-head south of the river by September 11, the airfield at Montecorvino, seized by the British on September 9, was still under artillery fire and heavy fighting was in progress against German armoured forces with the right flank of our troops advancing north seriously exposed.

The Germans were quick to appreciate that of all the Allied landings in Italy this was the most dangerous, and with the object of cutting the bridge-head in half the 16th Panzer Division (destroyed at Stalingrad and re-formed), assisted by elements of other divisions, launched vicious counter-attacks. On September 12 the situation became critical and the British were forced to withdraw from Battipaglia after it had changed hands several times, while the Americans withdrew from Altavilla and Albanella following a penetration by the enemy on a two-mile front along the river Sele. Farther north German infiltration had brought Salerno within artillery range and rendered unusable the small harbour which had only just been cleared of mines and booby traps.

Vicious Enemy Counter-attacks

For three days the Fifth Army was hard pressed, but reinforcements, including armour, continued to arrive by sea and air, while the maximum support was given by fighters, fighter-bombers and bombers and by naval bombardment from Allied vessels (*see illus., page 2850*) including the battleships " Valiant " and " Warspite " and the destroyers " Jervis," " Ilex," " Petard," " Pathfinder," " Panther " and " Penn." The cruisers " Aurora " and " Penelope " arrived in the Salerno area on September 14 and the " Sirius " and " Dido " shortly afterwards. (This was the first occasion on which naval units were used to break up enemy tank attacks.) Between September 9 and 14 inclusive, an average of more than 1,000 sorties a day was flown by Royal Air Force and United States Air Force fighters and bombers in the Salerno battle area. In all, Allied aircraft flew a total of over 8,000 sorties, the balance being on targets outside the fighting for the beaches and bridge-head.

By September 15 the position had been consolidated and the German breakthrough held, but only the superb determination of the infantry, coupled with the concentration of all available sea and air effort, averted disaster and turned a momentary German triumph

AXIS C.-IN-C.

Field-Marshal Albert Kesselring is here seen with Lt.-Gen. Heidrich. After the Allied conquest of Sicily, he withdrew the German forces from the extreme south of Italy, but was ready to offer stubborn opposition to the Allies at Salerno. *Photo, Planet News*

into an eventual Allied victory. (General Sickenius, G.O.C. of the 16th Panzer Division, described the fire power and air superiority as " entirely unknown to us from Russia.")

Meanwhile the Eighth Army continued to advance in spite of the ex-

LAYING COMMUNICATIONS

One of the first things army commanders needed if their forces were to co-operate effectively was satisfactory telephone communication. Here the U.S. Army Signal Corps is laying wires into the hills above Salerno. *Photo, P.N.A.*

tremely difficult nature of the country. Their rapid progress had a considerable influence on the Salerno battle by making the enemy pull back his vulnerable left flank, while at least two German divisions—the 29th Panzer Grenadiers and the 26th Panzer—were diverted from the Eighth Army's front. Although roads were blocked by demolitions and craters, there were few mines—a formidable obstacle in Sicily. British troops moved steadily up the west coast and entered Rosarno on September 7. Next day the Canadians gained control of the road from Locri on the east coast to Gioia on the west. On the night of September 7–8 units made an amphibious landing near Vibo Valentia and captured a number of prisoners. Three days later British patrols reached Nicastro; and the Canadians passed through Catanzaro, to enter the port of Crotone, which was found in excellent condition, on the 12th. The tempo of the advance was then stepped up to relieve the Fifth Army at Salerno. By September 13 the British had reached Cosenza, and by the 14th Canadian patrols were in the area east of Spezzano Albanese. The British passed Belvedere on the 14th, Scalea on the 15th.

During this period of favourable conditions following the Italian capitulation the important ports of Taranto and Brindisi were captured intact. A naval force, including battleships and cruisers, entered Taranto harbour on September 9 and landed British troops of the 1st Airborne Division who entered Brindisi two days later with forward patrols operating near Bari. Contact was eventually made with the enemy at Gioia delle Colle, 25 miles northwest of Taranto. Reinforcements arrived, and patrols joined up with the Canadians on September 14 after rescuing 300 British prisoners of war from a camp at Pisticci. The Eighth Army reached Vallo on the 16th, and next day after covering 67 miles in three days their armoured cars made contact with the left flank of the Fifth Army near Agropoli. The enemy began to withdraw his troops from their more southerly positions under cover of rearguard actions and demolitions, at the same time retaining a hold on some of the high ground north of Salerno where the bulk of the enemy forces was concentrated and British troops of the Fifth Army continued to meet strong resistance. Inland, a bridge-head was extended to include Acerno and Contursi, while the Eighth Army pressed forward towards Auletta

Allies Capture Taranto and Brindisi

ALLIES TAKE OVER TARANTO AND BRINDISI

The important naval base of Taranto was captured on September 9, 1943, by British troops landed under cover of the Royal Navy. Within a few hours, Allied warships were using its great harbour, which was in good condition. Two days later the port of Brindisi was secured, also without effective opposition. Left, landing craft loaded with Allied troops entering Taranto harbour. Right, Italian aircraft in the seaplane base at Brindisi. *Photos, British Official*

and Potenza. On the eastern side of Calabria the Canadians kept pace and were themselves in Potenza on September 21, with patrols forward to the north and east.

During the night of September 22–23 British troops on the left flank of the Fifth Army launched an attack north of Salerno. Progress was slow at first,

The Enemy Dislodged from Nocera
but by the 26th the highest points in the passes had been gained and tanks brought up ready to advance into the more open country that lay ahead. The Germans were finally dislodged from the Nocera defiles two days later and the tanks debouched on the left into the area between Nocera and Castellamare di Stabia, while lorried infantry penetrated to a point three miles north. Resistance was stubborn and at times company attacks had to be supported by the entire divisional artillery before enemy strong points could be overcome. On the right flank the Americans quickly followed up the German withdrawals and fought their way steadily northwards. By September 30 they had entered Avellino and made contact with the left

flank of the Eighth Army at Pescopagano. Farther east the Canadians advanced to Canosa and Melfi against little opposition.

On the Adriatic side the arrival of fresh formations through Taranto increased the striking power of the Eighth Army in this sector and mobile patrols crossed the river Ofanto and captured Cerignola on September 26. Foggia was entered on September 27 by armoured units which pushed on to Lucera and San Severo, while infantry reached Manfredonia at the same time to clear the whole of the Gargano peninsula— the spur of Italy. The acquisition of Foggia's network of airfields, together with their satellites, was a matter of great tactical and strategic importance. Not only did they offer immediately enormous advantages in the destruction of Germany's war potential as far as the Italian campaign was concerned but after expansion, for which they

were well sited, they opened up the possibility of sending long-range bombers to strike at Germany's dispersed war industries and factories and then fly on to land in England.

Once the high ground covering the Naples plain had been cleared, General Clark was able to deploy his armour. British tanks were through Pompeii by September 30, and that night the Germans completed the evacuation of Naples. The first Allied nationals to enter the devastated city next morning were four British and American war correspondents in a jeep : they were greeted by a weeping, cheering, hysterical mob. Troops of the Fifth Army arrived at 8 a.m. to receive a similar frantic ovation.

Germans Evacuate Naples

Apart from the inevitable effects of prolonged air bombardment, the city showed abundant signs of spiteful ingenuity exercised by the retreating Germans : the enemy might justifiably have destroyed installations of possible use to the Allies, but not even the cemeteries had been spared. Nor was their destruction finished with their departure : on October 7 a delayed

EIGHTH ARMY ADVANCES ON FOGGIA

Left, one of a series of notice boards erected by the Corps of Military Police on what the Eighth Army christened 'Monty's Highway.' Right, the railway junction at Foggia, wrecked by intensive Allied bombing from the air : the line was found to be strewn with rubble for a distance of three miles when the town with its network of airfields was captured by armoured units of the Eighth Army on September 27, 1943. *Photos, British Official*

YOUNG SICILY 'TAKEN FOR A RIDE' BY THE EIGHTH ARMY

The welcome accorded the Allies by the civilian population throughout the Sicilian campaign was astonishingly enthusiastic, and these gay Sicilian lads, waving from a British tank as it rolls through the main street of Milo, present a typical picture of the smiles that greeted British and American troops everywhere as the Germans withdrew. Milo, on the eastern slopes of Mount Etna, was captured on August 13, 1943, only four days before the conquest of Sicily was completed.

Photo, British Official : Crown Copyright

AMERICAN NAVY AIRCRAFT AND MARINE PARACHUTISTS

The U.S. Navy's combat training plane 'Yellow Peril' (officially Stearman N2S-2) stands in front of Curtiss 'Hell-Divers'—scout and dive-bombers, which each carried two men (radio-gunner and pilot) and were used extensively in the Pacific from carriers and land bases. Bottom left, mobile barrage balloons at Parris Island training centre in South Carolina for all Marines on the east side of the Mississippi : men are seen learning to operate the balloons. Top left, two stages in practice parachute jumping—touching down (right) and spilling out the air (left). Nine men could jump from a transport plane in five seconds. They took 20 to 25 seconds to get rid of their parachutes (which were left behind—see illus., p.2544—but collected later if operations permitted). When jumping, a parachutist carried 40 to 50 lb. in weight, his equipment varying with his mission: the Marine shown (top centre) is carrying a ·45-calibre revolver and a knife, and wearing special boots, a light-weight uniform, and a helmet. Right, a Naval aerial cameraman, in a SN-J naval training plane : he wears a yellow 'Mae West,' and holds a long-focus lens camera employed for reconnaissance.

Direct Colour Photographs by Pictorial Press

CAMPAIGNERS IN SICILY

There were quieter moments even for the British troops who fought in Sicily : here (left) are men of the 78th Infantry Division about to sample the evening brew they have made over a camp fire. Below, two British wounded smile cheerfully as they wait to be evacuated from an advance dressing post. Nearly all Sicilian battle casualties, after preliminary attention at emergency dressing stations, were evacuated by air : up to August 14, 1943, 14,898 sick and wounded were flown to hospitals in North Africa. Mobile Field Hospitals of the R.A.F. provided emergency surgery and treatment in the field and prepared cases for evacuation.

Photos, British Official : Crown Copyright

action mine planted in the basement of the General Post Office exploded, killing a very large number of civilians, including women and children, and on October 10 another bomb concealed in a barracks in the centre of the city went off and killed twenty-five and wounded thirty Allied soldiers. Good progress, however, was soon made in restoring the life of the city. Three Italian submarines were brought in to provide power for the drainage system and to maintain emergency lighting. In common with all other towns in southern Italy, Naples suffered from a shortage of water, owing to the destruction of aqueducts, and the food available was barely adequate to meet the needs of the civilian population.

The capture of Naples marked the end of the first phase of the Italian campaign. Progress had been slower than anticipated, and General Alexander confessed that he was disappointed with the rate of the Allied advance. But nearly a third of Italy had been occupied at a cost of approximately 15,000 casualties, and the campaign was holding down in Italy and the Balkans some thirty-five to forty German divisions which might otherwise have been employed on the Russian front.

The heroism of the British and American troops who went ashore at Salerno to face powerful and prepared defensive positions that gave the enemy an enormous advantage, and the coolheadedness of the Fifth Army's high Command which directed operations under heavy gun-fire are worthy of record. The work of the North-West African Strategic and Tactical Air Forces (see page 2671) and of the Allied navies in the Gulf of Salerno, were both vital to the success of the action. The order of battle on land and sea was so criss-crossed with British and American formations that to establish national identity is almost impossible, but among

the British units which shared some of the fiercest fighting at Salerno were Royal Marines and soldiers of the Commandos, the Cheshires (who also fought as machine-gunners with the Eighth Army), the Queen's Royal Regiment, the Royal Northumberland Fusiliers, the Oxford and Buckinghamshire Light Infantry, the Sherwood Foresters, the Durham Light Infantry, the Hampshire Regiment, and units of the Grenadier, Coldstream and Scots Guards, and the famous 7th Armoured Division. Among the units which, in the words of General Montgomery, were given " the supreme

British Units in South Italy

THE BOOT OF ITALY

The first Allied landings were made on September 3, 1943, by the Eighth Army, crossing the straits of Messina, between Reggio and San Giovanni. New and larger landings were made by the Fifth Army on September 9 on the beaches of Salerno (see detail map in p. 2870), on which day also Eighth Army troops landed and occupied Taranto. Main roads are shown in white, railways in black. Airfields are also marked.

Specially drawn for THE SECOND GREAT WAR *by Félix Cardon*

ALTAVILLA'S MAIN STREET
Very fierce fighting took place in the area round Altavilla, a village in the hills near Salerno, in the middle of September 1943, when for a time the success of the Allied landings at Salerno hung in the balance. Here, inhabitants of Altavilla watch the American invaders after their capture of the village on September 18. *Photo, U.S. Official*

THE R.A.F. IN ANCIENT POMPEII
The modern village of Pompeii was captured by the Eighth Army on September 29, 1943. Here, R.A.F. officers, visiting the remains of the ancient city near by, buried in the eruption of Vesuvius of A.D. 79 and excavated over the last century and a half, look across the theatre towards the volcano. The Germans camped on the site, which was as a consequence bombed by Allied aircraft, fortunately without greatly damaging the antique remains. *Photo, British Official*

honour of being the first troops of all the Allied armies to land on the mainland of the continent of Europe " were the Inniskilling Fusiliers, the Canadian Carlton and York Regiment, the Northamptonshire Regiment, the Royal Scots Fusiliers, the Cameronians, the Green Howards, the King's Own Yorkshire Light Infantry, the York and Lancaster Regiment, and the Cheshire Regiment, these last three also taking part in the Salerno landings.

On September 21 Mr. Churchill described the Battle of Salerno as " the most daring amphibious operation we have yet launched " (*see* Historic Document 273, p. 2866) and in spite of the many hazards the episode ended in " an important and pregnant victory."

Taking into consideration the paucity of suitable ports and the difficulties in providing adequate lines of communication, the maintenance of the Allied forces during the opening phase of the Italian campaign was an achievement of the first order. Up to September 23, 148,000 men of the Fifth Army, with 21,000 vehicles and 70,000 tons of stores, had been transported; while up to the 29th, 127,400 men of the Eighth Army, with 27,580 vehicles and 53,389 tons of stores, had been landed on the beaches and ports in Calabria and the heel of Italy.

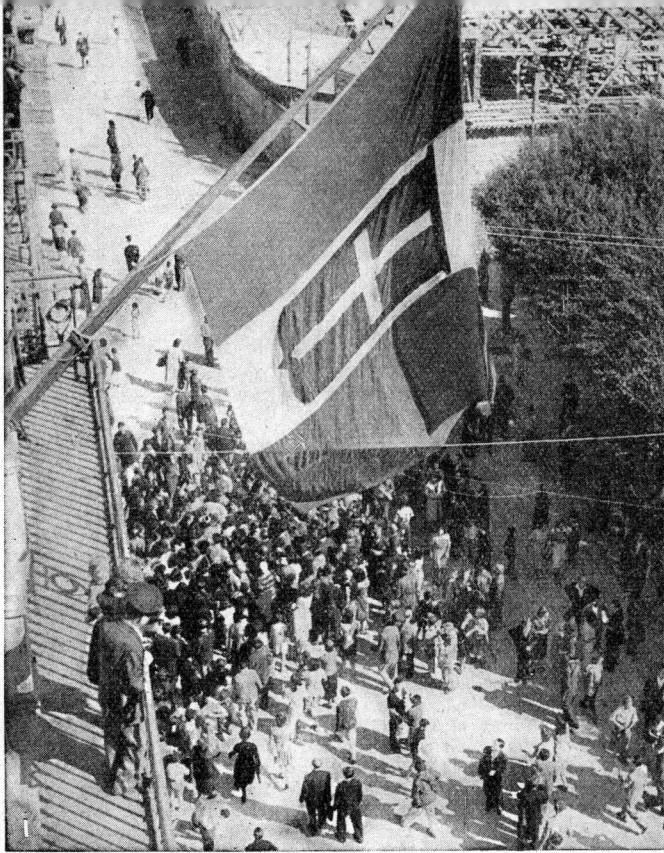

NAPLES DOUBLY LIBERATED

The Fifth Army entered Naples on October 1, 1943, after the five German divisions holding the city had been withdrawn. Their arrival freed the city not only from German occupation, but also from Fascism. 1. Flag of Italy (minus the crown) flies in Naples again without the Fascist flag: scene from the balcony of the municipal buildings as citizens greet British reconnaissance units. 2. A Neapolitan crowd cheering Allied troops on their arrival. 3. American infantry resting on the tramway lines (the Germans had destroyed electricity installations) in a typical Naples street. 4. Troops landing at Naples docks after these had been restored. *Photos, British Official; Keystone*

ALLIES OCCUPY RENDOVA

In the early morning of June 30, 1943, U.S. Marines effected a landing on Rendova, a wooded and mountainous island in the New Georgia group 170 miles north-west of Guadalcanal, and separated from New Georgia Island by a seven-mile strait. By midday the Americans had overcome the not very serious Japanese defence and occupied the whole island, and two hours later their batteries were shelling Munda airfield, important Japanese base on New Georgia, from Rendova. Here, a U.S. Army P-40 flies at tree-top level above a group of Marines scurrying across the beach during the attack on Rendova. Left, U.S. Marines load a 155-mm. gun in a camouflaged emplacement on the island. Below, stores pile up on Rendova beach.

Chapter 287

THE AMERICANS ADVANCE TOWARDS TOKYO

In the Pacific, 1943 saw the beginning of movement westward and northward by the Allies, until at the end of the year they were preparing to attack islands mandated to Japan after the First Great War. Concurrent operations by the Australians in New Guinea were recorded in Chapter 276. Here, Gilbert Cant, an American correspondent who was with the advance patrol that captured Munda airstrip on August 2, describes the far-flung operations —extending from the Aleutians to the Solomons—conducted by our American Allies after the capture of Guadalcanal (see Chapter 250)

To appreciate the situation in the Pacific after the reduction of Guadalcanal (*see* Chapter 250), it is necessary to consult the maps of this longest of all war fronts between pages 2038 and 2039, and on page 2858. Its extreme northern flank was in the Aleutian Islands, where the Japanese held Attu and Kiska.

From the westernmost Aleutians, the area of Japanese domination extended south-south-west to a line between Marcus and Midway Islands, and then swung east in a vast loop embracing Wake Island and all the far-flung archipelagos of Micronesia, with the Marshalls and the captured Gilberts forming the " front." The Ellice Islands, south of the Gilberts, were never attacked by the Japanese, and by the winter of 1942–43 were being developed as an advance Allied base. The enemy had unsinkable aircraft carriers, valuable as observation posts, at Nauru, Ocean and Greenwich Islands. Then the front swung south to the Solomons, where the Japanese were undisturbed in their possession of the northern and central groups, and west to New Guinea, where they were being driven slowly westward to Huon Gulf (*see* Chapter 276). The Netherlands East Indies, dividing the Pacific from the Indian Ocean fronts, were in enemy hands.

The United States Navy took the view that Japan could be defeated most readily by an attack aimed through the myriad islands of the Central Pacific.

Strategy in the Central Pacific
But before such an approach could be hazarded, it was necessary to clear the flanks. And in the early stages, before the United Nations could assemble an overwhelming superiority of force, offensive operations were conditioned and limited by the need for employing a large proportion of the forces in the area for the defence of advanced bases against possible Japanese counter-attack.

This was the broad framework in which the developing Pacific offensive was conceived.

Many hard lessons had been learned in the six-month campaign for Guadal-

canal, and the equipment available for the next operations was not only more plentiful, but superior in design. Most notable of all was the arrival in the South Pacific of the magnificent types of landing craft first used in North Africa, such as LSTs (landing ships, tanks), LCTs (landing craft, tanks) and LCIs (landing craft, infantry). It should be noted, however, that the United States Pacific Fleet under Admiral Chester W. Nimitz was still woefully weak in aircraft carriers, following the loss of four in 1942. Only " Saratoga " was in operation, " Enterprise " being under repair. It was necessary for the former to be reinforced by H.M.S. " Victorious," which served in the South Pacific under Admiral William F. Halsey (*see* illus., p. 2604). The only new carriers available at this time were of the escort type, affectionately known in the American navy as " jeep carriers."

The first tentative step towards Tokyo after the reduction of Guadalcanal (February 10, 1943) was made for the purpose of extending aerial domination farther to the north-west through the Solomon Islands. Fighter planes at this time had a sharply limited range, and from the bloody battleground of Henderson Field they could scarcely reach the Japanese strongholds off southern Bougainville, 300 miles away, and still have enough fuel left for combat in protecting bombers over the target area. An advance of 60 miles, representing a saving of 120 miles on the round trip, meant the addition of about 20 minutes to their flying time. So the last shots on Guadalcanal had barely died away when elements of Marine Corps Raider battalions landed on February 21 on Banika in the Russell Islands. The Japanese had used these islands as a staging point only a few weeks before, and the

U.S. SUPPLIES FOR THE RUSSELL ISLANDS

Banika and Pavuvu, the two principal islets in the Russell Islands, lie 18 miles north-west of Guadalcanal. The Japanese evacuated them before the Allies attempted to land, and they were occupied without opposition by Marine Corps Raider battalions in February 1943. Here, anti-aircraft shells in clips of three and cases of canned goods are stacked up on the shore.

Photo, Associated Press

BATTLE OFF THE ALEUTIANS

On March 26, 1943, a Japanese naval force comprising two heavy and two light cruisers, and six destroyers, and heading towards the Aleutians, was intercepted by American light naval forces and retired after an exchange of fire at long range in which at one moment it looked as though the American cruiser 'Salt Lake City' would fall a victim to the enemy. Here, a U.S. heavy cruiser, shrouded in smoke, bombards distant Japanese warships. *Photo, New York Times Photos*

Marines were prepared for the bitterest kind of combat. But when the medical officers, who had been put ashore first by mistake, began to explore the island's extensive coconut groves, they were unmolested. The Japanese had vanished. The Marines occupied Banika and adjacent Pavuvu without opposition, and the construction of airfields on the former was begun at once.

Although the Japanese had been ousted from the south-eastern Solomons, they were by no means ready to give up the rest of the chain without a struggle. **Allied Attacks on Munda and Vila** They had completed an airport at Munda, on New Georgia Island, 180 miles west-north-west of Henderson Field, and were about to complete another at Vila, on Kolombangara Island, ten miles beyond Munda. At this short range Japanese aircraft could have interfered seriously with the mounting of the coming offensive, so the two bases were continually bombed or bombarded. For three months Munda was bombed on an average once a day. With inconceivable tenacity, the Japanese filled in the craters and persisted in trying to maintain operations from the field. Even bombardment by cruisers or destroyers (as on the nights of January 4–5, March 5–6 and May 12–13) did not put it out of commission for more than a couple of days.

The Japanese were gradually building up their strength not only in the northern Solomons, but also in New Guinea to repel the increasing threat offered by Australian and American

forces under General Douglas MacArthur advancing into Huon Gulf. They had been fortunate when they first occupied Buna and Gona, the principal positions below the Gulf: Allied air forces, then under Lieut.-General George H. Brett, had offered no resistance until the transports had reached their destination and begun to unload. Evidently they counted upon a repetition of this error of judgement, for on March 1, 1943,

C.-IN-C., ALEUTIANS

Vice-Admiral Thomas Cassin Kinkaid, commanding American Naval Forces in the Aleutian area, at his headquarters in Adak. He was responsible for the campaign which restored the Aleutians to Allied control by mid-August 1943. *Photo, U.S. Official*

they sent a dozen troop and cargo transports, with an escort of ten warships, into the Bismarck Sea to reinforce Lae and Salamaua. But this time the air forces, now under Lieut.-General George C. Kenney, met them at sea: in a three-day series of attacks, every Japanese ship was sunk and 15,000 Japanese were destroyed (*see* pages 2602 and 2672). The stage was being set for Allied offensive action all along the southern flank.

But action occurred first in the far north. On the morning of March 26, Rear-Admiral Charles H. McMorris, flying his flag in the light cruiser "Richmond," was patrolling the **Sea Action in the North** Bering Sea between the Komandorski Islands and the Aleutians. He had with him four destroyers and the heavy cruiser "Salt Lake City," one of the most gallant ships in any navy, Captain Bertram J. Rodgers commanding. Shortly after the late northern sunrise, two Japanese transports with destroyer escort were sighted. They turned away to the north, and the American squadron turned to cut off their retreat. But a second Japanese force appeared: two heavy cruisers, two light cruisers, and six destroyers. The Japanese commander disposed himself between the Americans and their Aleutian bases. The unequal battle was joined as Admiral McMorris began to retire.

The enemy's 8-inch shells first straddled "Richmond" to no avail, then "Salt Lake City." The latter, using her ten guns at maximum rate of fire, soon drew blood, touching off an explosion on the Japanese flagship. The enemy's damage control was excellent, and the pursuit continued, with "Salt Lake City" able to fire only half her guns astern. After 45 minutes she was hit, but not badly; after an hour she was hit again; after two and a half hours she was hit twice, and badly. Water reached the boilers, and her captain soon signalled: "My speed zero." The enemy seemed assured of an easy kill. The after-magazines were empty, so shells and powder bags had to be trundled along the open deck for a last stand.

The admiral ordered Commodore Ralph S. Riggs to take three destroyers and deliver a torpedo attack on the Japanese. The suicidal tactics worked. Two hits are believed to have been scored; at any rate, the Japanese began to retire just as "Salt Lake City's" engines came to life. The engagement had lasted three hours and 25 minutes. The extent of damage inflicted on the enemy is not known, but it is certain that the convoy was turned back. Whether the Japanese were bent on reinforcing or evacuating Attu and Kiska, they failed.

This action bore fruit in May, when the recapture of the western Aleutians was begun. Attu was chosen for invasion, rather than Kiska, because it outflanked the latter, was less strongly peninsula of Attu. The plan was for the main U.S. Army force to land at Massacre Bay, on the south shore (*see* illus., p. 2602), and push north for a junction with a diversionary force landing near Holtz Bay. When the two forces were united, the enemy would be hemmed in with his back to

FIGHTING AT ATTU

American forces landed on Attu, westernmost of the Aleutian Islands, on May 11, 1943. Fighting was fierce and bloody, but the campaign was over by June 2. Of the 2,300 Japanese defending the island, only 20 were taken alive. Above, bringing in wounded during the operations on Attu (shown in the map). Below, Americans who went ashore at Massacre Bay return the fire of Japanese snipers concealed in mountain crevices. *Photos, U.S. Navy*

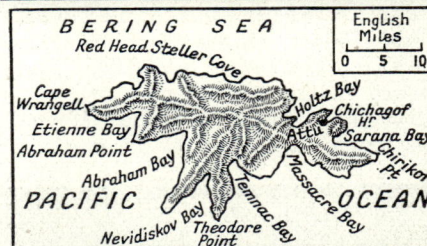

held, and would bring the Kurile Islands, most northerly part of Japan proper, under aerial observation and attack. D-day had been set for May 7, but when the invasion force arrived the area was shrouded in a typical Aleutian fog, and the operation was postponed to the 11th. Even then a further postponement was necessary, from 9.40 a.m. to 3.30 p.m.; but by this time the weather had lifted sufficiently to permit landing boats to leave the transports and head for the beaches.

Vice-Admiral Thomas C. Kinkaid was in command of all North Pacific operations; his deputy for the Attu landing was Rear-Admiral Francis Rockwell, flying his flag in a battleship which had been damaged at Pearl Harbor. The 7th Division, United States Army, supplied the assault force of somewhat more than 12,000 men, and was under the command of Major-General Walter Brown.

The Japanese, estimated to number 2,500, were concentrated on the eastern

the sea. The landings were only lightly opposed, but on D-plus-one the usual determined, suicidal Japanese resistance developed against the southern force moving up Massacre Valley. From the north, Colonel Frank L. Culin made excellent progress; but the junction which it had been expected would occur in 36 hours was long delayed—advance patrols did not meet until May 18.

The week of bitter fighting had produced more casualties than gains, and Admiral Kinkaid relieved General Brown of his command, replacing him with Major-General Eugene Landrum. The latter changed tactics, fighting up the ridges rather than through the valley in which the Americans had been enfiladed. Towards the end he was materially aided by the First Battalion, Fourth Regiment, United States Marines, which captured a height overlooking the Japanese lines. (*See* map.)

New American Tactics in Attu

On June 2 the campaign ended; 400 Americans were dead or missing, 1,135 wounded. The Japanese, under Colonel Yasuyo Yamasaki, had numbered 2,300 (200 less than U.S. intelligence estimates). Only 20 were taken alive; the rest died, many of them in a ceremonial suicide charge. The Japanese never had constructed a satisfactory air base on Attu; American engineers quickly remedied this defect.

The next offensive operation was at the opposite end of the long Pacific battle line. The dividing line between Admiral Halsey's South Pacific Command and General MacArthur's South-

Australian and American forces landed unopposed on the Trobriand and Woodlark Islands, north-east of the eastern tip of New Guinea, on June 30, 1943. Airfields were rapidly developed there to extend the area of fighter-plane coverage for land operations. Landing craft are here seen bearing down on the Woodlarks. *Photo, Australian Government*

west Pacific Command was the 159th meridian East Longitude, running straight through the Solomons chain, just west of the Russell Islands. Consequently, although geography might seem to dictate that the drive up the chain should be based upon Guadalcanal, and executed by South Pacific forces, it was placed under the strategic direction of General MacArthur.

On June 30, United States and Australian troops under General MacArthur moved unopposed into Woodlark and Trobriand Islands, east of New Guinea, and airfields were developed there to extend fighter plane coverage in the same way as this had been achieved in the Solomons by development of the Russells. On June 30 also landings were made at Nassau Bay as a preliminary to the reduction of Salamaua (*see* Chapter 276).

The envelopment of Munda airport, at the south-western tip of New Georgia

Island, was scheduled to begin on June 30. As a preliminary, Segi Point, 40 miles away at the south-eastern tip of the island, was occupied on June 20 by two companies of a U.S. Marine Corps Raider battalion, and construction of an emergency landing strip was begun. During the night of June 27–28 these Raiders were moved by boat to Regi, and entered the jungle to take Viru Harbour from the rear. Viru was scheduled to be taken June 30; the Marines took it on July 1 after a stiff four-hour battle. Meanwhile, army troops and two companies of the Fourth Marine Raider Battalion had landed at Wickham Anchorage, which also was secured on July 1.

The main operation against Munda was begun in the dark of the morning

of June 30 by elements of the 43rd Division, U.S. Army (Major-General John H. Hester commanding). It took the form of a landing on Rendova Island, seven miles from Munda across Blanche Channel—close enough to permit heavy artillery to bear along the projected line of advance up the New Georgia coast. Japanese resistance at Rendova was spirited, but not in great strength, and the only usable part of the island was quickly secured.

Rear-Admiral Richmond Kelly Turner, in command of the campaign, at once began to land a considerable force at Zanana Beach, six miles east of Munda on New Georgia proper (July 5). The assault troops were the 169th and 172nd Regiments of the 43rd Division, and they were quickly reinforced by the 145th Regiment of the 37th Division. The only enemy counteraction came from the air and submarines. Turner's flagship, the transport "Macawley," which had been his flagship also in the Guadalcanal campaign, was torpedoed and later was

PACIFIC LEADERS

From left to right, these United States Commanders in the Pacific during 1943 are: Rear-Admiral Richmond Kelly Turner, director of amphibious operations; Vice-Admiral Raymond S. Spruance, in command of all Central Pacific forces under Admiral Nimitz; Admiral Chester W. Nimitz, C.-in-C., U.S. Pacific Fleet; Brig.-Gen. H. B. Holmes, Jr.; Lt.-Gen. R. C. Richardson, Jr.; Maj.-Gen. Ralph Smith; Maj.-Gen. H. M. Smith, in command of landing forces; Rear-Admiral Charles H. McMorris, commanding in Northern Pacific.

Photo, U.S. Navy

sunk by U.S. forces. There was a savage air attack on the Rendova command post area on July 4, in which the American forces suffered from inadequate dispersal of their positions; but a heavy toll was taken of the attackers—21 out of 54 aircraft—and in successive raids the enemy quickly reached the point where his attacks ceased to pay.

For the first week, advancing slowly as the narrow foot trails along the coastal plain (running partly through jungle and partly through coconut plantations) were widened to accommodate jeeps, the invaders met little opposition. But on July 8 they reached a major Japanese strongpoint at the junction of the Munda and Lambeti trails. After four days it still had not been reduced, so the 169th was left to contain it, and the 172nd pushed ahead, establishing a new beach-head at Laiana on the 13th. This became the principal point of debarkation for the campaign. But at this stage resistance stiffened. The 3rd Battalion of the 103rd Regiment, 43rd Division, was committed. On the 17th a strong counter-attack drove a gap into the American lines, and shortly thereafter two battalions of the 169th had to be withdrawn for rehabilitation, having suffered many casualties, including a high proportion of "war neurosis" cases.

The 148th Regiment of the 37th Division was committed on the 23rd, making a total of three regiments, with **American Units Engaged** some reinforcement, on a front only 1,600 yards long. The 161st, part of the Americal Division but attached to the 37th for this operation, was put in to reduce the stubborn enemy strongpoint at the trail junction.

By this time General Hester had been relieved of command of the 43rd Division, being succeeded by Major-General John R. Hodge. With the committal of the bulk of the 37th Division, Major-General Robert S. Beightler commanding, the ground command fell to Major-General Oscar W. Griswold, commanding the XIV Corps, of which the 43rd and 37th Divisions were components. He enlisted the support of a Marine Corps tank company, whose light tanks, with 37-mm. guns, were of limited value against skilfully prepared Japanese positions.

The slow progress of the campaign was disappointing in view of the careful preparation and the fact that the enemy was outnumbered three or four to one. The principal causes on the American side were: the inexperience of the troops, the poor quality of a limited

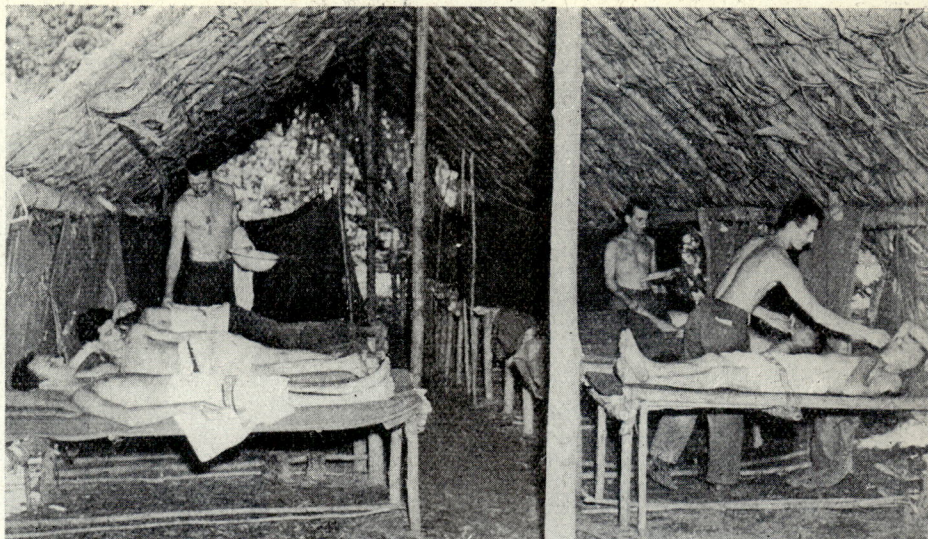

IN NEW GEORGIA

U.S. Marines captured Viru Harbour in New Georgia (see map) on July 1, 1943. One party landed a week before at the south-west tip of the island, the other landed north-west of Viru. They converged on the harbour, trapping its defenders. Here, U.S. casualties wait in a field hospital for evacuation to a base hospital. Below, Viru Harbour seen from the air.   *Photos, Keystone*

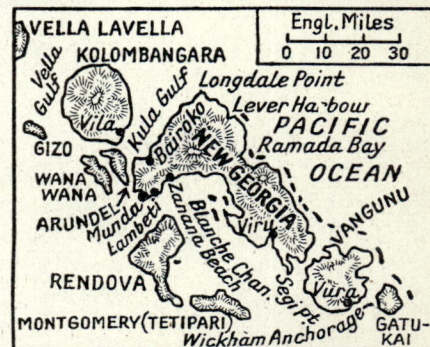

number of officers which prevented the men from giving of their best, and difficulty in communications among the several forces participating (Army

ALLIES IN KISKA

A landing ship, tanks (LST), with other assault craft, approaches the northern shores of Kiska, in the Aleutians: Canadian and U.S. troops landing on August 5, 1943, found the Japanese had evacuated the island. Right, British and United States flags fly side by side over Kiska.

Photo, U.S. Navy

infantry, Marine tanks, Naval support craft, and Air Forces of the three services). On the Japanese side there were two outstanding elements: their unshakable determination to stand or die, which generally developed into a case of stand *and* die, and their elaborate preparation of tough pillboxes, built of nothing but the materials to hand—coconut logs and lumps of coral sandstone, over which dirt had been thrown to permit the jungle vegetation to provide natural camouflage within a few weeks.

July 25 opened with a destroyer bombardment and the heaviest air attack of the campaign: 186 tons of bombs dropped on Munda in an area of less than a square mile. The effect was not at once apparent, but as succeeding days brought fresh air attacks and

ground advances, the benefit developed. Every enemy installation above ground had been wrecked; all his telephone wires were cut; his stores of rice had been scattered in the mud; his troops were dazed by shock. On August 2 an advance patrol reached Munda airstrip; three days later it was officially captured. Within a few days American and New Zealand air forces were using it for the reduction of the next objectives.

Meanwhile, there had been plenty of naval action around New Georgia (*see* page 2603), and a diversionary

campaign on its northern shores by Marine Raiders and Army Rangers under Lieut.-Colonel Harry B. Liversedge, U.S.M.C. These ground forces were bogged down by an unexpectedly large enemy force at Bairoko, but were able to join the Army forces from the south in the final mop-up of New Georgia after Munda was reduced (*see* map, p. 2283).

With the conquest of New Georgia the South Pacific Command was faced with a strategic problem: should it continue "island-hopping," i.e. advancing

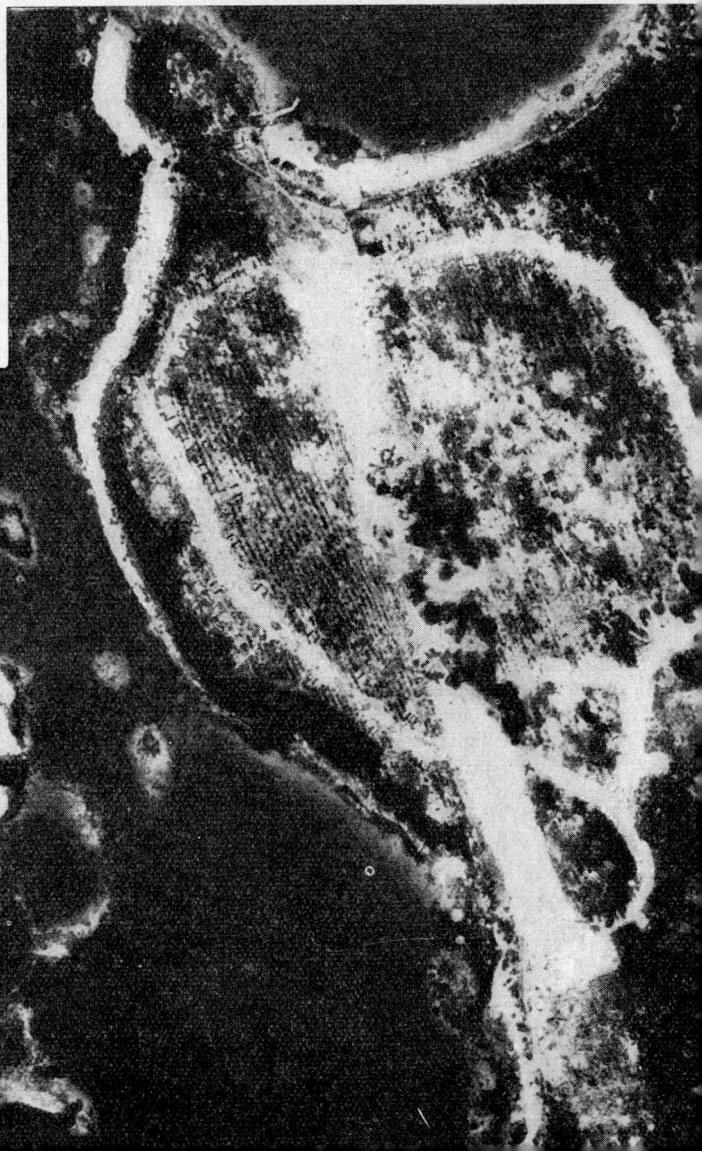

MUNDA AIRFIELD IN ALLIED HANDS

Advanced American patrols reached Munda airstrip in New Georgia Island on August 2, 1943. By August 6, Munda was at last in Allied hands after seven weeks of bitter fighting. It was stormed in the final assault with tanks and flame-throwers which blasted the Japanese out of their positions. 1. Munda airfield after it had been captured by the Allies : a number of wrecked Japanese aircraft can be seen. 2. U.S. Marine Corps torpedo-bombers fly out on a mission to Munda. 3. A Japanese field marker on Munda airfield. 4. Heavy bombs bursting on the landing strip built by the Japanese at Munda, which was repeatedly bombed from the air before the land assault began.

Photos, U.S. Marine Corps ; BIPPA; Keystone

ALLIES SEIZE A FOOTHOLD ON BOUGAINVILLE

1. A landing barge approaches Empress Augusta Bay, Bougainville, on November 1, 1943: the only heads visible are those of the commander, pilot, and A.A. gunners.   2. Men and machines disembarking under fire on Mono (Treasury Islands).   3. U.S. Marine Raiders return to their base, Piva, after a night in foxholes beyond the front line on Bougainville.   4. A Marine Corps bulldozer pushing sand to form a base for a ramp of logs over which jeeps and trucks can roll from the waiting LSTs.   *Photo, U.S. Official*

from one island to the next, or should it adopt "leapfrog" tactics, and take the risk of leaving a strong enemy force in its rear on Kolombangara while proceeding at once to reduce the more thinly held island of Vella Lavella? The bolder course was decided upon, and on August 15 landings were made at Vella Lavella by New Zealand troops, with some U.S. Army and Marine Corps support (*see* illus., p. 2606). Before the island was completely secured (*see* illus., p. 2816) U.S. Army forces went

New Zealand Troops Land on Vella Lavella
ashore on Arundel Island (on August 27), which flanked Kolombangara more closely, and from which the enemy's main positions around Vila could be bombarded. After the Japanese on Kolombangara had been pounded almost into insensibility from land, sea and air, assault troops were put ashore. The result was gratifyingly as expected. Resistance had been largely inhibited, and the Japanese put their major effort into attempts at evacuation which were unsuccessful in the main, thanks to interception of their vessels and barges by U.S. destroyers and PT-boats.

The "leapfrog" pattern, later to be adopted by General MacArthur and magnificently exploited in his New Guinea coastal campaign, and to be used over much greater distances by Admiral Nimitz among the islands of the Central Pacific, had been set.

The landing on Vella Lavella coincided, fortuitously, with the reoccupation of Kiska. For this, an even more elaborate expedition than that for Attu had been prepared, with a reinforced brigade of Canadian troops assigned to fight alongside U.S. Army infantry. But even before the landings, flyers had reported that Kiska appeared to be deserted. Still, no reconnaissance parties were landed to gather information. After heavy preliminary bombardment, the invaders stormed ashore, to find the island empty of Japanese.

The northern flank in the Pacific was now secure. The southern flank saw the Japanese being rolled back in New Guinea (*see* Chapter 276) as well as in the Solomons, where Allied aerial suprem-

acy over the northern islands, from new or captured fields on New Georgia and Vella Lavella, was now established. The campaign for the central Solomons ended on October 5, when the Japanese began evacuating Kolombangara. The enemy was now concentrated on the southern tip of Bougainville (largest of the Solomons) and islands near by, such as Shortland, Ballale, Faisi and Fauro. He also had sizable forces on Buka, north of Bougainville (*see* map opposite).

The problem was how to neutralize this concentration without paying the heavy price which would be exacted by a frontal assault. Fortunately, Bougainville's great size supplied the answer: the enemy could not be strong everywhere, and plans were made to seize a foothold at Empress Augusta Bay, north-west of the island's southern tip, and expand sufficiently to embrace airfields. As a preliminary, the Treasury Islands (Mono and Stirling) were invaded on October 27 by U.S. and New

Zealand troops. On the following day a Marine Corps Parachute Battalion, under Lieut.-Colonel Victor Krulak, landed on Choiseul Island, across "the Slot" from Vella Lavella. Commando parties stormed ashore on the same island. The Japanese were distracted and the main movement toward Empress Augusta Bay was thus much facilitated.

Preparation for the Bougainville offensive had included also the neutralization **Preparing to Attack Bougainville** of Japanese airfields in the vicinity, by daily bombings and occasional bombardments. These enemy air bases were at Ballale, off southern Bougainville ; Kahili and Karu, at the tip of the island ; Kieta, half-way up its east coast ; Bonis, at its northern tip, and one on Buka across the strait. In addition, there had been a devastating inhibitory air attack at Rabaul on October 12 (see page 2672).

The assault force for the Bougainville landing was the First Marine Amphibious Corps, commanded by Lieut.-General Alexander A. Vandegrift, who had directed the conquest of Guadalcanal. The Corps had as its spearhead the 3rd Marine Division under Major-General Allen Hal Turnage, reinforced by the 2nd and 3rd Raider Battalions (Lieut.-Colonel Fred Beans and Lieut.-Colonel Joseph McCaffery, respectively, commanding). The overall commander until the command post could be moved ashore was Rear-Admiral Theodore S. Wilkinson, at whose direction the cruiser task force under Rear-Admiral Merrill carried out inhibitory bombardments of airfields and other installations on Buka and around the eastern and southern coasts of Bougainville.

Only a small proportion of the 25,000 Japanese estimated to be on Bougainville were in the Empress Augusta Bay area, and the northerly beach-head was established on schedule, at 7.30 a.m. on November 1, following a bombardment. Units attacking at Cape Torokina, however, encountered more opposition than had been anticipated, and it was not until late afternoon that they had more than a precarious toehold on the beach.

The plan did not call for conquest of a large area of Bougainville, but only for the establishment of an enclave which would be a running sore in the Japanese flank. Work was early begun by the "Seabees" (the U.S. Navy's Construction Battalion) on airfields. On D-plus-7 the Army's 37th Division began to land. Two days later General Vandegrift turned over the Corps command to Major-General Roy S. Geiger, U.S.M.C., and on D-plus-14 the Americal

2887

Division under Major-General John Hodge began to land. Within a few weeks the Marines had all been relieved by the Army, and the operation was turned over to the XIV Corps under General Griswold. On December 5 the first airstrip near Torokina was put into operation ; two weeks later a larger strip for bombers was in use at Piva, where a third strip was added later.

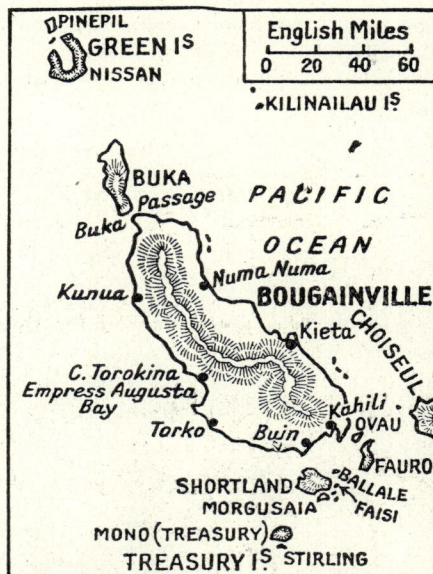

BOUGAINVILLE ISLAND
Map showing the positions attacked and occupied by American forces in 1943. Below, supplies for the U.S. forces on Bougainville arrive. The use in the Pacific of a wider variety of landing craft in larger numbers greatly facilitated the 'island-hopping' campaigns of 1943 with their frequent amphibious operations.
Photo, U.S. Marine Corps

The Japanese reaction was prompt, at first violent, and then tenacious and protracted. As early as noon of November 1 they had a cruiser squadron in the vicinity ; at 2.30 a.m. on the 2nd this force, of four cruisers and eight destroyers, was engaged by Admiral Merrill's force and routed (see page 2606).

After the withdrawal of American troops from Choiseul on November 12, the enemy hurried men back from that island to join the beleaguered, half-starved garrisons on Bougainville. But the great Pacific offensive swirled past the unsung heroes of the Empress Augusta Bay beach-head, and the battle of Bougainville developed into a "forgotten war."

Not until the first week of June 1943 did the first Essex class carrier, laid down before American involvement in the war, reach Pearl Harbor. On September 1, two such carriers and one of the light Independence class attacked Marcus Island, a pin-point of land a thousand miles from Tokyo, and Japanese since 1877. The occasion was notable also in that it provided the début of the Navy's Hellcat (Grumman F6F) fighter plane, which immediately proved itself a worthy successor to the smaller, lighter Wildcat **Work of Carrier-borne Aircraft** (known in Britain as the Martlet). But still more carriers were needed before offensive operations could be extended to the Central Pacific archipelagos, for here there was no Allied air base within fighter plane reach.

Three days after the Japanese

attacked Pearl Harbor they occupied Makin in the Gilbert Islands, a chain of British atolls lying across the Equator, south of the Japanese-mandated Marshalls. In October 1942 American forces under Rear-Admiral Carleton H. Wright moved into the neglected Ellice Islands, south of the Gilberts, and began the development of a base at Funafuti, from which bombing attacks were made against the Gilberts and such isolated enemy outposts as Nauru. " In August, September and October," said Admiral King, " carrier-based air strikes on Marcus, Tarawa, Abemama and Wake

served to soften Japanese installations and keep the enemy guessing as to where our next full-scale attack would be delivered. . . . During October and early November, planes from our bases attacked the Japanese in the Gilberts and also the Marshalls."

Vice-Admiral Raymond A. Spruance was placed in command of all Central Pacific forces under Admiral Nimitz ; Rear-Admiral Turner was given direction of all amphibious operations, and Major-General Holland M. Smith, U.S.M.C., was put in command of landing forces.

THE BATTLE FOR TARAWA ATOLL

Betio Island, in Tarawa Atoll, most strongly held of the Gilberts, was captured by U.S. Marines in a violent three-day battle that began on November 20, 1943. 1. Tarawa from the air. 2. A few of the Japanese prisoners taken at Tarawa being marched away under guard : they were ordered to proceed in a stooping position as a precaution against attempts to escape. 3. Japanese armoured strongpoint on Tarawa knocked out by a direct artillery hit.

Photos, U.S. Marine Corps and U.S. Navy

Three of the Gilbert Islands were in use by the enemy : Makin, which had been raided by Marines from submarines under Lieut.-Colonel Evans F. Carlson in August 1942, and was probably manned only in battalion strength; Tarawa, where the garrison was much stronger, and Abemama. The Tarawa atoll is triangular, its southern side consisting mainly of the island of Betio, two and a half miles long and nowhere more than half a mile wide; its north-eastern face is a series of broken strips of sand and coral; its north-western face is awash, and contains the passes into the lagoon.

It was decided to attack Betio directly from the lagoon side after a heavy preliminary bombardment, instead of " creeping up on it " from the tiny islets on the north-east face of the lagoon. Japanese air power in the entire region had already been virtually eliminated. Dawn of November 20 broke with a thunderous barrage laid down by the great battleships (many of them mounting 16-inch guns), cruisers and destroyers. When the invasion barges started across the treacherous, coral-studded lagoon toward the only practicable beach, the barrage was lifted to permit dive-bombers and

U.S. FLAG FLIES ON MAKIN

On November 20, 1943, the 27th U.S. Infantry Division, commanded by Maj.-Gen. Ralph Smith (see illus., p. 2882), and including the 165th Infantry Regiment (the former 'Fighting 69th' of the First Great War) landed on Makin in the Gilberts. An hour later, the American flag flew from a palm tree, though fighting continued next day.

Photo, U.S. Official

fighters to go in and give close support to the assault forces of the 2nd Marine Division, under Major-General Julian C. Smith, and the 2nd Brigade, under Brigadier-General Merritt Edson. It was anticipated that by this time most of the 3,500 Japanese on the islet would be dead or stunned. But their counter-fire was intense, and the landings had to be postponed, first for 31 minutes, then again for 45 minutes, while more hundreds of tons of shells were poured on to the enemy positions.

The first landings were the costliest in the Pacific War (*see* illus., p. 2605), comparable only with the 1942 raid on Dieppe, and resulted in establishing no more than a narrow, insecure beach-head. Again that day and on the following day, when heavy losses were suffered in

ALLIED ACTIVITY IN ELLICE ISLANDS

American forces moved into the Ellice Islands, which were never occupied by the Japanese, in October 1942 and established an air base at Funafuti. During 1943, Allied activity in the group increased: here, guns, tanks, tractors and trucks are being brought ashore on Nanumea Island.

Photo, U.S. Marine Corps

additional landings, the guardian surface fleet subjected the defenders to a punishing bombardment. But still the issue had to be decided in close-quarter fighting by infantrymen and companies of light and medium tanks. Marine casualties on Tarawa were 1,026 killed and 2,557 wounded—almost exactly the same numbers as the Corps had lost in the six months' campaign for Guadalcanal. The Japanese, in their concrete, coconut-log and coral sandstone positions, had absorbed 2,200 tons of steel and high-explosive in naval bombardment, and 700 tons of bombs.

Clearly, it was not enough. Clearly, it would be advisable in the future to secure preliminary footholds on lightly held islets and advance from them, under counter-battery fire from mortars and field artillery, upon the main objective. How well these lessons were learned was soon to be shown in the Marshall Islands.

But by this time action was in progress along the vast front. General MacArthur was preparing to close a vice on Rabaul, the enemy's main South Pacific base at the northern tip of New Britain Island. The eastern face of the vice was in the making at Bougainville and soon would be completed with the occupation of the Green Islands, farther north. The western face required the occupation of western New Britain. On Boxing Day, while U.S. Army units made a costly diversionary landing at Arawe, the 1st Marine Division (reinforced), now under Major-General William H. Rupertus, which had been lent to General MacArthur for this purpose, landed at Cape Gloucester. The campaign, conducted under appalling conditions up and down jungle-clad ridges over a mud floor, was brief and brilliantly successful. Within a short time the Marines were able to move down the coast to Talasea, and start pushing the Japanese into the north-eastern peninsula of New Britain, where they could be left while Australian and American fighting men drove westward along the coast of New Guinea.

In the South and South-west Pacific, the counter-offensive was in full swing by the last day of 1943, and General MacArthur was free to begin his return to the Philippines. The North Pacific east of the date line had been cleared of the enemy. In the Central Pacific, the last counter-offensive move had been completed with the recapture of the Gilberts, and the stage was set for lifting the curtain on the offensive, pure and simple, through positions held by the Japanese long before the war, toward Tokyo itself.

On Towards Tokyo

Diary of the War

JULY and AUGUST, 1943

July 1, 1943. U.S. Marines captured Viru (New Georgia).

July 1-9. Intensive Allied day and night air bombardment of Sicilian targets.

July 2. Heavy daylight attacks by U.S.A. 9th A.F. on aerodromes in S. Italy. Announced that Greek patriot forces had agreed to act under Allied C.-in-C. Japanese lost 28 planes in two attacks on Rendova Is. (Solomons).

July 3. Night attack in great strength by Bomber Command on industrial districts of Cologne.

July 4. General Sikorski killed in plane crash near Gibraltar. U.S. Fortresses made heavy daylight attacks on Le Mans and Pallice (France).

July 4-5 (night). Successful Allied landing raid on Crete.

July 5. Germans launched violent offensive on Orel-Kursk-Byelgorod front.

July 6. Americans captured Vangunu Is. (New Georgia). Seven Japanese planes (out of 48) shot down in raid on Darwin (Australia). Naval battle in Kula Gulf (New Georgia): 10 Japanese warships sunk or damaged for loss of U.S.S. " Helena."

July 8. Bomber Command dropped 1,000 tons of bombs on Cologne (night). Successful British land raid on Maungdaw (Burma).

July 9. Great tank battles on Orel-Kursk-Byelgorod front (Russia). Very heavy night attack on Gelsenkirchen (Ruhr) by Bomber Command. U.S. Liberators obliterated G.P.O. and Axis Sicilian headquarters in raid on Taormina.

July 9-10 (night). Allied landings in Sicily began.

July 10. Syracuse, Pachino, and other places captured by the Allies (Sicily).

July 12. Red Army launched new offensive N. and E. of Orel. Heavy concentrated night attack by home-based Lancasters on Turin (Italy). Ragusa and August captured by Allies (Sicily). Japanese launched new offensive in Shansi (China).

July 12-13 (night). Second Japanese naval defeat in Kula Gulf (New Georgia).

July 13. R.A.F. in very great strength attacked Aachen by night.

July 14. U.S. Fortresses attacked outskirts of Paris, destroying 45 enemy fighters. Mr. Mikolajczyk appointed Polish Premier.

July 14-15. Primo Sole bridge (Sicily) captured by British. R.A.F. and R.C.A.F. heavily bombed Naples.

July 15. Moonlight attack by R.A.F. on Peugeot works, Montbéliard (France). Mubo (New Guinea) captured by Allies.

July 16. R.A.F. attacked transformer stations near Milan (Italy). Eighth Army captured Lentini and descended to plain of Catania; Caltagirone, Grammichele and Agrigento captured by Allies (Sicily).

July 17. Porto Empedocle captured by Americans (Sicily). Setting up of AMGOT (Allied Military Government of Occupied Territories) in Sicily announced.

July 18. Caltanissetta and Piazza Armerina captured by Allies (Sicily). Chinese High Command announced that Japanese attacks in Shansi had failed.

July 19. Over 500 American bombers made first air attack on Rome. Hitler and Mussolini met at Verona (N. Italy). U.S. Liberators bombed Paramushiro (Kurile Is., Japan).

July 19-20 (night). Japanese naval force (3 warships sunk) driven off by U.S. aircraft in Vella Gulf (Solomons).

July 20. Allies captured Enna (Sicily).

July 22. Palermo, capital of Sicily, captured by U.S. 7th Army. Surabaya (Java) attacked by Australian-based Liberators.

July 23. Americans occupied Marsala.

July 24. Trondheim and Heroya (Norway) bombed by U.S.A. 8th A.F. Hamburg ground defences swamped in heaviest night attack to date by R.A.F. Americans occupied Trapani (Sicily). Fascist Grand Council met (first time since Dec. 7, 1939). Leghorn bombed by R.A.F. Lancasters.

July 25. Strong U.S.A.A.F. day raid on Hamburg; heaviest raid of war on Essen by R.A.F. at night. Termini captured by U.S. 7th Army (Sicily). Mussolini resigned; Badoglio formed government (Italy).

July 26. Fascist Party dissolved (Italy).

July 27. Wake Island (Central Pacific) heavily bombed by U.S. Liberators.

July 28. Leonforte captured by Canadians (Sicily).

July 29. Kiel and Warnemunde bombed by strong formations of U.S. Fortresses. Americans captured Nicosia (Sicily). U.S. bombers attacked Andaman Islands (Bay of Bengal).

August 1. Oil centre of Ploesti (Rumania) attacked by 177 U.S. Liberators from Middle East.

August 2. Heavy night attack on Hamburg by R.A.F.: ninth raid in eight days; 10,000 tons of bombs dropped; 7 square miles devastated. Regalbuto, Gerbini, Centuripe, Catenanuova and San Stefano taken by Allies (Sicily).

August 3. Canadians captured Agira (Sicily).

August 5. Russians recaptured Orel and Byelgorod. Eighth Army captured Catania (Sicily). Munda (New Georgia) captured by Americans after 7 weeks of bitter fighting.

August 6. Troina stormed by U.S. troops after 5 days' hard fighting (Sicily). Three Japanese warships sunk off Vella Lavella (Solomons).

August 7. Night attack by home-based Lancasters on Milan, Turin and Genoa. Adrano, Bronte, and other places captured by Allies (Sicily). R.A.F. Blenheims bombed Maungdaw (Burma).

August 8. R.A.F. Bostons attacked Rennes (France). Eighth Army captured Acireale (Sicily). Shihpu (Chekiang, China) recaptured by Chinese.

August 9. Heavy night attack by Bomber Command on Mannheim and Ludwigshafen. Chinese recaptured Chipuyaotze (W. Suiyuan, China).

August 10. R.A.F. dropped 1,500 tons of bombs by night on Nuremberg; 18 bombers lost. Mr. Churchill arrived in Quebec for inter-Allied conference.

August 12. Gelsenkirchen, Wesseling and Bonn attacked by U.S. bombers. Milan and Turin heavily attacked at night by Bomber Command. Bases in Kurile Is. (Japan) bombed by U.S. Liberators.

August 13. Spasdemiansk recaptured by Soviet troops in continuing advance. Wiener Neustadt, 27 miles S. of Vienna, bombed by U.S. Liberators from N. Africa: first raid on Austria by western Allies. Randazzo captured by Allies (Sicily). Rome raided from air again. Balikpapan (Borneo) raided by Australian-based Liberators.

August 14. Whole of Mt. Etna (Sicily) in Allied hands. Rome declared an open city by Badoglio government.

August 15. Red Army recaptured Karachev. At night R.A.F. Bomber Command dropped over a hundred 4,000-lb. bombs on Milan (fourth raid in nine days). Taormina and Milazzo captured by Allies (Sicily). U.S. Liberators heavily attacked Chatham Is. (Andamans). Americans landed on Vella Lavella (New Georgia group). Kiska (Aleutians) occupied by Canadian and U.S. forces.

August 16. Le Bourget (Paris) attacked in force by U.S. Liberators. Concentrated night attack by Bomber Command on Turin.

August 16-18. 215 Japanese planes (out of 225) on airfields near Wewak (New Guinea) destroyed by U.S.A. 5th A.F. for loss of 6 planes.

August 17. Campaign in Sicily ended with entry of Allies into Messina. U.S. Fortresses made deepest penetration into Continent to date to bomb Schweinfurt on the Main and Regensburg on the Danube, destroying 307 German fighters. Night attack by R.A.F. on Peenemunde. President Roosevelt arrived in Quebec.

August 18. " Round-the-clock " Allied air offensive against targets in Italy began.

August 21. Australian troops took Komiatum by storm (New Guinea).

August 23. Recapture of Kharkov by Red Army. Bomber Command dropped 1,700 tons of bombs on Berlin. Chungking raided by Japanese aircraft for first time in two years.

August 24. Forum Hall, Copenhagen, wrecked by saboteurs. Quebec Conference ends.

August 25. Setting up of South-East Asia Command announced.

August 26. French Committee of National Liberation recognized by British, Canadian, and U.S. Governments.

August 27. Shattering night attack on Nuremburg by Bomber Command. French Committee of National Liberation recognized by U.S.S.R. and China.

August 28. Danish Government refused German ultimatum and resigned. Whole of New Georgia in American hands.

August 30. Taganrog, Yelnya, and many other places recaptured by Russians. New Japanese thrust on Salween front reported (China). Martial law in Denmark.

August 31. Great force of British 4-engined bombers (47 lost) made heavy night attack on Berlin. U.S. Fortresses made heavy 10-minute attack on Pisa.

IN SAVAGELY CONTESTED BATTIPAGLIA, NEAR SALERNO

Battipaglia, midway between Salerno and Agropoli, and a few miles inland, changed hands several times during the days following the landings of the Fifth Army on the beaches of Salerno on September 9, 1943. On September 13, fighting on the whole 25-mile front in an arc round Salerno was exceedingly bitter, particularly in the neighbourhood of Battipaglia. The village was finally captured by the Allies on September 18.

Photo, British Official

INTO BATTLE ON TARAWA IN THE GILBERT ISLANDS

The U.S. Marines fought their bloodiest fight to date when they captured Betio Island, southern side of Tarawa atoll in the Gilberts. In this three-day battle, beginning on November 20, 1943, their losses—1,026 killed and 2,557 wounded—were almost as large as in their reconquest of Guadalcanal, a campaign which lasted from August 1942 to February 1943. Here, members of a squad of U.S. Marines prepare to crawl forward to attack Japanese positions on Betio. Below, Tarawa lagoon when the fighting was over. *Photos, U.S. Official*

ON BATTLE-SCARRED BETIO ISLAND, TARAWA ATOLL

The first landings of U.S. Marines on Betio Island were preceded by an intense bombardment from the sea followed by heavy dive-bombing and fighter attacks from the air. These photographs give an idea of the pounding received by this small island 2½ miles long by half a mile wide. Above, concrete, steel-reinforced building which served as Japanese headquarters on Tarawa and withstood direct hits by artillery fire. Below, a Japanese ammunition dump on Tarawa after a direct hit had been scored by a Marine Corps bomber. (See map, p. 2858.)   *Photos, New York Times*   **3 E**

SOLDIERS OF THE NEW WORLD AMONG REMAINS OF THE ANCIENT

Americans of the Fifth Army move forward over a Roman road past the ruins of a Greek temple at Paestum after Kesselring had withdrawn his troops from the plain of Battipaglia on September 21, 1943. Paestum (the ancient Greek colony of Poseidon) lies on the Gulf of Salerno, some ten miles north of Agropoli. Founded by the Greeks in 600 B.C., it became a Roman colony in 273 B.C. No fighting took place at Paestum in 1943, and its antique remains—three Greek Doric temples, and a Roman temple and amphitheatre—were untouched.

Photo, Keystone

Chapter 288

ATTRITION ON THE JAPANESE HOME FRONT

The beginning of 1943 found Japan in possession of all the riches of Further India, Indo-China, the East Indies, the Philippines, Formosa, and a large section of the Chinese mainland. But her enemies refused to accept her conquests as final, and the year saw the gradual pushing back of her more extended octopus-like tentacles—with depressing and unsteadying effects on the home front here described by Peter Hume, member of the Council of the Royal Central Asian Society. For Japan's history in 1942, see Chapter 231

THE unquestioned bravery of the Japanese soldier, amounting often to a suicidal fanaticism, has given rise to a widespread belief that the whole mass of the Japanese people is so indoctrinated with mystical subservience to the State as to form a perfect, uncomplaining and ever-toiling war machine. That this belief is based on a fallacy was well shown in 1943. The Japanese were in possession of large rich territories on whose distant periphery only comparatively small-scale fighting was going on; they were free from air attack; casualties among their menfolk at the front were not heavy. Yet their leaders found it necessary repeatedly to warn them throughout the year that the situation was "too serious to be described by words" (Tojo in June) and "truly grave" (the Emperor in October), and to appeal constantly for a more determined war effort.

This unsatisfactory attitude of civilian workers was, in fact, directly and unfavourably compared with that of the fighting soldiers by Premier General Tojo

Demands for Greater Home Effort

when he, in August, took the remarkable step of himself appealing to the workers at the great Mitsubishi aircraft factory "for better achievement." He had previously, in his first public speech of the year on January 28, told the people as a whole that while Japan "possesses the world's greatest treasure house and has secured ample resources for waging war on whatever scale it may be," a "real effort" on the part of the population was necessary if these newly gained resources were "to demonstrate their real worth."

During the year there were, indeed, many Japanese victories on paper and on Tokyo Radio, but even to a people so bathed in propaganda, such victories had not the savour of the real thing as the Japanese had been able to savour it in 1941 and 1942.

Announcements such as that of February 9, when the Japanese were told that their troops at Buna and at Guadalcanal had been "transferred after attaining all their objectives in the destruction of enemy forces," might

have worked quite well had it been a fact, as is so often assumed, that the Japanese listened to no voice other than that of their own Government. But there is plentiful evidence that this was not the case. Although the most reliable index of the degree to which the truth was penetrating Japan was lost when the Government at the end of 1942 enforced the closing of all Stock

NEW FOREIGN MINISTER
Mamoru Shigemitsu, Japanese Ambassador in London at the outbreak of war between Japan and the United Nations, in July 1943 replaced Masayuki Tani, former secret agent of the militarists, as Foreign Minister in General Tojo's cabinet. Shigemitsu favoured a more conciliatory policy towards China.
Photo, Associated Press

Exchanges in the country following a series of profound slumps in prices after each unadmitted Allied victory, the magazine "Current Affairs" was frank enough to admit in October 1943 that there had just been a police campaign in which several hundred short-wave radio sets had been seized. "We may be sure," the paper added, "there are several thousand still undiscovered. Enemy reports heard today are spread throughout the country tomorrow."

In conditions of daily living, the position was well summed up by the

Japanese Procurator-General in September, when he said: "The black market is the ruler of our wartime economy. It has spread so as to cover the whole field of the people's living, and is getting worse and worse." At the same time Japanese magazines were indignantly pointing out that shopkeepers had formed the habit of retaining for their personal use or for private barter at least half of the rations allocated to them for distribution to their customers. Restaurants were open for at most a week or ten days in each month, while for the rest of the time the restaurateurs, their families and friends enjoyed the meals they should have sold.

Of the correctness of the obsession that Japan has a divine right to rule the world little doubt had entered the Japanese mind; but during 1943 it became increasingly evident that there were flaws in the belief that her armies could not

Lower Living Standards

be halted in the execution of their holy mission. The people had been repeatedly told that their enemies had been annihilated. Now, instead of a return to the comparative plenty and leisure they had enjoyed before the attack on China, the people found themselves adjured and compelled (as far as was within the power of the Government) to redouble their efforts and to make new sacrifices for the struggle against their "annihilated" enemies. There was no emotional excitement in getting less rice, working longer hours, paying more taxes, and the Government, which had never based its exhortations on logic, found it increasingly difficult to find for them any basis at all which would awaken popular response. For this reason, Japanese propaganda (our only direct source of information from the country) revealed throughout 1943 an astonishing duality. On the one hand the people were never allowed to know factually of the reverses suffered by their forces; on the other they were constantly warned of the grave dangers confronting them if their efforts were not maintained and increased.

At first the emphasis was all on ship-building. An "authority" broadcast on January 10 that "unless an adequate number of vessels are constructed, it will be very difficult to continue the prosecution of the war in a satisfactory manner," and in July Tokyo Radio declared that it was "essential to concentrate on shipbuilding to exploit the conquered areas." This propaganda campaign coincided with a great drive for the construction of wooden, and to a lesser degree concrete, ships to compensate for the losses inflicted by the Allies. But since these losses were never openly admitted, and, indeed, the Minister of Communications in February claimed that the Japanese merchant marine had been kept up to strength by new building, reconditioning and the refloating of sunk Allied ships, it was not easy for the workers to put their hearts into this emergency programme.

Later in the year emphasis was shifted to the production of aircraft, and the people who in January had

Drive for More Aircraft

been told the war would be won when Japan had built 20,000,000 tons of shipping were in October informed (on the authority of an officer of the Naval H.Q. Bureau of Information) that it would be lost if Japan were defeated in the air. To this warning the officer added with unusual frankness that "at the moment the Americans are producing four aeroplanes for every one produced by Japan." In the same month the magazine "Shin Taishi" remarked: "'Is everything really all right?' is the question which is most frequently asked nowadays."

During the year the Government introduced a series of regulations of increasing stringency designed to compel that total mobilization which could not be secured voluntarily. In February yet another Budget for "extraordinary supplementary military expenditure" was introduced. It amounted to 27,000 million Yen (about £1,588 million) and resulted in the seventh consecutive general increase in taxation since 1937.

In March the appointment of seven industrial and commercial magnates as advisers to the Government "to buttress Japan's wartime structure and give further driving force to production" was the opening move in a powerful campaign to concentrate the country's industry. Three months later it was announced that the Cabinet had approved a plan for the "consolidation of productive elements in industry, the expansion of undeveloped industries vital to the prosecution of the war, the improvement and renovation of production technique, the readjustment of labour supply, the rationalization of the transport industry and the reorganization of finance and banking." The effect on war production of this largely conceived plan cannot be definitely assessed, but the hand of the seven commercial magnates firmly guarding the interests of their own vast monopoly organizations can be traced, as can the unrepentant individualism

of the smaller capitalists who were to be concentrated out of existence. The latter were informed that owing to the war situation they would not receive compensation in cash for the requisitioning or closing of their factories and the removal of their machinery. Compensation would be "by book entries and various forms of special loan." A series of conferences took place in June between the Economics Bureau of the Government (which had the responsibility of carrying through the scheme) and the police authorities.

Some criticism of the Government was forthcoming when on September 22 Tojo announced a further important step towards total mobilization on the home front, a key point

24-Hour Working Day Introduced

in which was the introduction of the "24-hour day"—a system under which all war factories and offices were supposed to spin out their available labour supply so as to keep going at full pressure day and night. Even for the Japanese, long accustomed to phenomenal hours, this seems to have been a bit too much and one news-

PREMIER TOJO TOURS THE 'CO-PROSPERITY SPHERE'

General Tojo, Premier of Japan, visited the conquered territories during the spring of 1943. Here, in Burma, he takes the salute at a march past of the 'Indian National Army.' Subhas Chandra Bose, leader of the Indian Independence League formed in Singapore with Japanese backing, is on his left. A 'Provisional Government for Free India' with Bose as political and military head, was set up in Singapore on October 21, 1943. Above, Tojo and Wang Ching-Wei, quisling Chinese president of Nanking, toast one another during the same tour.

Photos, Associated Press; Keystone

Postcard left side:
From:
Name DIXON. H.
Nationality BRITISH.
Rank DRIVER
Camp No. 4 P.O.W. CAMP THAILAND.

PASSED
P.W. 7799

To:
MRS. H. DIXON.
13. H. PEABODY EST.
ROSENDALE ROAD.
S.E. 24. LONDON. ENG.

Postcard right side:
IMPERIAL JAPANESE ARMY
I am interned in No. 4 P.O.W. CAMP THAILAND
My health is excellent.
I am ill in hospital.
I am working for pay.
I am not working
Please see that EVERYTHING is taken care

My love to you HENRY.

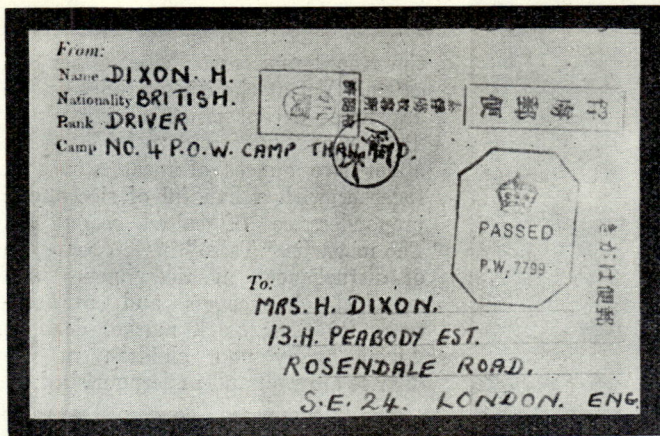

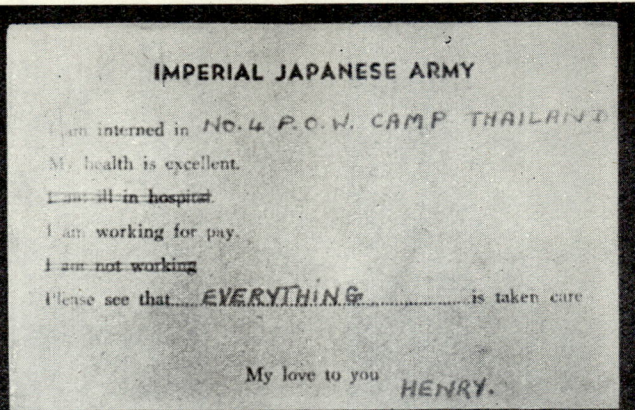

MESSAGE FROM A JAPANESE PRISON CAMP

The address and the message on one of the first batch of postcards to reach Great Britain from prisoners of war in Japanese camps in Siam (Thailand) a year after their capture. In August 1943 an official statement issued in London gave the numbers of British prisoners in Japanese hands as 40,000–50,000 soldiers, sailors and airmen, 20,000 Australians, 2,000 Canadians, 70,000–80,000 members of the Indian Army, and 25,000 civilian internees. *Fox Photos*

paper sharply remarked that the only effect would be to decrease production by reducing the workers to an impossible state of fatigue. Early in the year a standard working day of eleven hours with two rest days a month was fixed for women and children under sixteen, with the additional provision that these hours might be exceeded "during emergencies." In May compulsory direction to war work had been extended to girls of thirteen.

One of the most important concomitants of this drive for labour was the disruption of the educational system on which Japan had prided herself and which had played so large a part in the political indoctrination of the people. In March the newspaper "Asahi" reported that "all the country's technical, primary and middle schools have been converted into useful factories, and the students are helping to turn out army cars and bullet boxes."

This transformation of school buildings into factories, carried out in the first months of 1943, is one of the most startling internal developments of

Schools Become Factories

the year. No detailed account of the methods employed is available, but it appears that these buildings, which owing to the pride taken by the Japanese in their children and their education were generally the best constructed of any in each neighbourhood, were surveyed and that some suitable form of light war industry was introduced into each. In the primary schools, up to the age of twelve some form of educational curriculum was maintained, well interlarded with military drill and construction and assembly of the simpler forms of war material under the guise of "handicrafts." Beyond the age of

twelve all organized education ceased, though a high proportion of pupils might remain in "school factories" pressed to productive work under the guise of technical training. All Arts courses were abandoned, and even theoretical scientific training necessary to provide some sort of a corps of experts was conducted on a shortened syllabus, compressed between yet more pre-military training and munitions production. In addition, many boys were forced to leave school altogether at twelve and go to work sweated hours in previously existing factories. A Japanese newspaper commented: "It had originally been intended to raise the school-leaving age, but owing to the war this has had to be abandoned as boys of twelve or thirteen can play

a very useful part in light industries."

With this drive for industrial labour the Japanese Government was simultaneously confronted with a problem of keeping away from the better-paid industrial jobs the farmers on whose diligence depended the country's precarious self-sufficiency in food. In March it was admitted that a great number of these farmers were putting in only part-time work on the land, growing enough for their own and their families' immediate needs, while the rest of the time they were earning good wages in war factories. This drift from the land may have been responsible in part for the poor rice and wheat harvests gathered during the year, wheat being as much as 21 per cent down on the no-more-than-normal crop of 1942.

Drift from Farm to Town Work

Japan certainly had rice and other cereals enough in the territories she had conquered, but the destruction of

ROYAL VISIT TO THE WOUNDED

The Empress of Japan paid a visit to a Tokyo hospital on December 8, 1943, second anniversary of Pearl Harbor, and is here inspecting men wounded in the most recent Pacific battles. General MacArthur gave the following figures of casualties in the New Guinea campaign up to March 31, 1943 : 2,379 Australians killed or missing, 3,833 wounded ; 2,175 Americans killed or missing, 2,144 wounded ; 38,000 Japanese casualties, nearly all killed. *Photo, Keystone*

JAPANESE PRISONERS
With few exceptions, the garrison of 4,000 Japanese on Tarawa atoll when it was attacked by the Americans on November 20, 1943 (see page 2888) were killed. Here is one of the wounded survivors being marched to captivity by U.S. Marines. Left, Chinese guard with a Japanese prisoner taken in the week's fighting for Changteh (see page 2707).
Photos, Associated Press ; Planet News

Japanese shipping by the Allies prevented this food from reaching Japan : on September 3 it was announced in the United States that 2,539,600 tons of Japanese shipping, more than a third of the estimated pre-war total, had been sent to the bottom since the beginning of the war by American submarines, surface vessels and aircraft. In the same month Tojo declared that absolute self-sufficiency in food must be achieved.

An intensive campaign was launched both to increase food production—by such measures as the ordering of large numbers of students from the age of ten up to assist the autumn wheat sowing—and to persuade people of the virtue of substitute foods, sweet potatoes and pumpkins being the most

heavily advertised. The year's programme called also for the slaughter of the record number of 350,000 head of cattle. Yet at the end of the year the Japanese—except prime producers and distributors—were said to be living on about two ounces of meat a month, together with a handful of rice and a preponderance of salted vegetables. The magazine "Taizo" in October spoke of disturbances in rice queues and attacked shopkeepers and restaurateurs for their black market dealings "while many poor children in the district are wan and undernourished."

The Japanese continued their attempt to weld together the inharmonious elements of their "Co-prosperity Sphere." During the first half of the year General Tojo himself visited many of the conquered territories from Manchuria to Malaya. The "preparation of a new policy" was the advertised purpose of these tours, and lavish promises of independence were made, for instance to the Philippines "if the people are ready to co-operate." At Nanking, seat of the puppet government of occupied China, Tojo came up against a good deal of dissatisfaction on the part of the Japanese-appointed Chinese authorities with the way in which carpet-bagging Japanese, including many officers of the Special Service Branch of the Army, had for six years been enriching themselves at the expense of the supposedly brotherly Chinese. Announcing "a fundamental change in Japanese policy towards China," the Premier ordered these commercially minded gentry to "liquidate activities detrimental to" the interests of the country in which they had so long been unwelcome, greedy and overbearing guests.

A month after Tojo's return from this visit to China the Japanese Cabinet underwent a major reshuffle, of which the most important feature was the appointment as Foreign Minister of Mamoru Shigemitsu, Japanese Ambassador in London at the outbreak of war. He replaced Masayuki Tani (*see* p. 2301). The change was variously interpreted, but a link with the Premier's visit to China may be seen in Shigemitsu's first speech on taking up his appointment. In this he urged the Japanese people "to link themselves closely with the peoples of various countries in East Asia and exert greater efforts in order to gain confidence and respect. In this lies the basic spirit of Japan's new policy to China." Other Cabinet changes effected at the same time were designed primarily to speed the tightening

Tojo Tours 'Co-prosperity Sphere'

up of home policy and control over the Japanese people themselves which was complementary to the new conciliation of Asiatic "allies." Tojo himself took over portfolio of Education from the civilian Kunihiko Hashida, thus taking a further step towards the complete militarization of this branch of Japanese life, while the notoriously repressive General Ando went to the Home Ministry in place of Michio Yuzawa, another civilian. A new Minister of Agriculture and a new President of the Board of Information were also appointed. This last change may be taken as an after-effect of difficulties at the beginning of March, when the Diet proved recalcitrant about passing a revision of the penal code primarily designed to increase the Government's control over free speech. The Bill was eventually passed by the Cabinet over the head of the Diet on the basis, enunciated by Tojo, that "any public opinion which is not worthy for the prosecution of the war should be strictly controlled." In October Tojo installed himself concurrently with his other posts as Minister of Commerce and Industry, a post which gave him control also over the Ministry of Munitions established in November.

Tojo's New Posts

Japan's relations with her European Allies in 1943 were gravely clouded by the fall of Mussolini and Italy's subsequent surrender to the Allies. It was particularly unfortunate that the former event took place little more than a

RAISING A SHIP SUNK IN BATAVIA HARBOUR
Here the Japanese are salvaging a vessel sunk in the harbour at Batavia during their invasion of Java—either by the Dutch to prevent its falling into enemy hands or by Japanese air attack. Batavia, capital and most important town of the Netherlands East Indies, was abandoned by the Dutch on March 6, 1942, in face of an enemy superiority of five to one. The Japanese occupied it next day. (See Chapter 208.) *Photo, Associated Press*

month after Tojo had declared to the Diet : " I firmly believe in the smashing success of Germany, Italy and their Allies because of their already established invulnerable position." Nevertheless the Japanese were not slow to take positive measures when the crash did come in September. Italians throughout East Asia were promptly rounded up—exactly as if Japan had already declared war on their country—and their property sequestered. Although some proved Fascists later regained their liberty, it was not until

the Japanese had liberally helped themselves to any things Italian within their grasp which they coveted. This process was officially designated as "taking all necessary measures in advance" in a statement which denounced the surrender as a violation of the Tripartite Pact. A subsequent joint statement by Germany and Japan announced the continued validity of this pact.

Japan's always delicate relations with Russia pursued a relatively quiet course during the year, though immediately before the German summer offensive in the Kursk salient the Japanese co-operated with their allies so far as to threaten over the radio that "if the Soviet Union gives bases to the United States for attack on Japan, the Kwantung Army (Japan's army of occupation in Manchuria) will deliver blitzkrieg blows." On the other hand in March they renewed for another year the all-important Fisheries Convention with Russia.

Relations with Russia

Neither the major effort to regain the Solomons announced at the beginning of February nor the "all-out effort to crush Chungking" proclaimed by an Army spokesman on the 18th of the same month produced results suitable to a propaganda machine ; and in May another well-heralded offensive in China petered out in inglorious stalemate, while at the end of the same month it had to be announced that the garrison of Attu in the Aleutians "were presumed all to have died on the field of honour" (*see* p. 2881). Attu though a major defeat did, however, mark an

JAPANESE PROPAGANDA IN PEIPING
This poster, put up at a street corner in Peiping in Japanese occupied China, is an attempt to promote hostility towards the West among the city's inhabitants. The inscription reads, ' Away with Anglo-Americans from the great eastern area '—that ' co-prosperity sphere ' which Japan was attempting to co-ordinate.
Photo, Associated Press

attempt on the part of Tokyo propagandists to exert once more their emotional appeal to the people, and was treated in a way somewhat similar to the German orgies of self-immolation which followed Stalingrad.

A month later the old boastful tone had returned. An Army spokesman told of the importance of land bases for aircraft and of how Japan had converted all important bases in **Japan's** south-east Asia into **Costly Losses** impregnable fortresses, and was therefore ready to shoulder heavier pressure from the United States and Britain. Two days later a "military observer" declared that Japan was ready to attack Australia at any moment. Unfortunately this statement coincided with the American attack on Rendova Island, succeeded within the week by those on Vangunu and New Georgia (see p. 2882), and the Japanese found themselves compelled to admit on August 9 that the loss of these islands had "for the time being eliminated the gravest threat to Australia." By September 7 they were speaking of their "costly losses" in New Guinea, to which Tokyo Radio added, "the development of the war situation hereafter warrants absolutely no optimism."

The Navy also was not without its admitted difficulties. Although in September it was "gradually gaining the upper hand" between New Guinea and the Solomons (at a time when the Allies were in fact successively reducing Salamaua, Lae and Finsch Hafen—see Chapter 276), and although in November

GERMANS GO SIGHTSEEING IN SINGAPORE
The enemy garrison at the naval base of Singapore, under the command of the Japanese general Yamashita, included a number of German soldiers, some of whom are here being conducted by Japanese officers on a sight-seeing tour of the area. Singapore, great British naval base of the Far East built at a cost of £60,000,000, fell to the Japanese on February 15, 1942, after a siege of less than a week (see page 2046). *Photo, Planet News*

it sank over the radio 56 Allied warships and damaged 78 more in a battle off Bougainville (see page 2606 and illus., p. 2607), by December 12 Tokyo Radio was summing up the position in these words : "The war situation manifests a grave and serious aspect. The material strength of which the enemy boasts is not to be slighted ; and it is limitless. The Imperial Navy continues to gain victories in separate battles, but it cannot be said that the Navy has the war situation under complete control."

At the same time Tokyo's listeners were told that the Allies had advanced their bases to Bougainville and the Gilbert Islands, that they were closing in on Japan's strategic points, and that they advanced "most persistently."

The Emperor himself told the Diet on December 26 that "the war situation is most serious and Japan must exert her utmost effort to defeat the inordinate ambitions of the enemy." **People Told** Tojo, too, was any- **'War Situation** thing but complacent, **Serious'** saying on December 8 : "Victory cannot be won with folded arms but only when our 100 million people demonstrate their fervent spirit of service by offering their all in their respective operations and their daily life. We must . . . consolidate our position for a protracted war. . . . Only by so doing shall we be able to surmount the present Heaven-ordained trial."

The last word probably rests in the unconscious symbolism of a representative of the rarely vocal Japanese people —a farmer of Fukuoka Prefecture, who in April wrote to the newspaper "Mainichi" expressing his gratitude to the Government for its generous gift of wine to him as a bonus for satisfactory production. But, he added, it is rather towels, sugar, soap, salt and cotton thread that the country people need. As the farmers could have done without free wine, so could the people as a whole in 1943 have done without the heady liquor served them by their propagandists. A little of the cotton thread so bounteously promised in the days of victory would have served them better.

IN A JAPANESE ARMAMENT PLANT
The Allied advance towards Tokyo during 1943 put a strain on Japan's industrial life. In particular there was a drive for more aircraft. Allied airmen reported in June that they were meeting two new fighters and a new bomber ; and in October the Japanese announced that three new types were in action—the Shoki fighter, the Donryu bomber, and the Shitei reconnaissance plane. In October also a Munitions Ministry was created. *Photo, Associated Press*

Chapter 289

VICHY DECLINES AS RESISTANCE GROWS

M. Edmond Vermeil, Professor at the Sorbonne, who here describes the course of events inside France during 1943, has first-hand knowledge of much of what he writes : he lived in hiding in the countryside of south-west France for six months during the winter of 1942–43. He escaped to Great Britain in the summer of 1943. For the history of Metropolitan France during the second half of 1942, see Chapter 258

SCARCELY had the Allies landed in North Africa, in November 1942, when Hitler occupied the whole of France. This time the invader of 1940 went to all lengths, revealing fully to France his true thoughts and intentions—his determination to destroy her as completely as possible, together with the other nations of the European periphery. No doubt Germany was aware that her defeat was inevitable. But she intended, if possible, while there was still time, so to enfeeble Europe as to ensure advantages to herself for the years to come, with a view to a third world war.

The total occupation of France at once produced two complementary results. In 1940 Vichy had believed that Britain's defeat would follow that of France; now, faced with facts and responsibilities which had not then been foreseen, its regime gradually broke down until there came, in December 1942, an extremely grave crisis. On the other hand, as the occupation overran the whole of France, so did the Resistance movement. This had already taken firm root in the former occupied zone, and now it spread with intense and increasing activity throughout the national territory. Before November 1942 the youth of France, to whom their duty to Marshal Pétain had been preached as a religious precept, had been hesitant; now the young people of both sexes, and every class of society, threw themselves into the struggle. The Maquis was born, and as time went on it was organized into a real army of National Liberation, powerfully assisted by the Algiers Committee.

Vichy Begins to Break Down

The months which marked the decline of Vichy can be divided into two periods: before and after Mussolini's resignation. When news of the Allied landings in North Africa came, there was great confusion at Vichy. The Reich declared that it would intervene only at the express request of France. Roosevelt's appeal, by broadcast and leaflet, to the French not to hinder, but rather to assist the Allies, had aroused wide interest; and people were asking whether General Giraud had changed

sides. In the Vichy Cabinet two tendencies came to light : one, represented by Marion, Bonnard and Admiral Platon, in favour of war ; the other, that of Pétain and Laval, more guarded. Moreover, General Weygand refused to take command of the troops in North Africa.

As soon as Darlan was made prisoner by the Americans, Vichy informed the United States that diplomatic relations were severed. It was learned, too, that Giraud had gone over to the Allies. After many hesitations, Pétain gave the order for resistance to the Allies in North Africa (*see* Chaps. 256 and 258). On December 11, 1942, the day after his interview with Marshal von Rundstedt (Commanding German Forces in France, with H.Q. at Montpellier), the Marshal, embittered and discouraged, told Laval that through the latter's fault he, Pétain, had lost the friendship of the Americans and the respect which the Germans had hitherto shown him. German demands were, indeed, growing more and more insistent. Pétain was

set aside, but refused to abdicate. It was Laval who ruled. In December he promised the Germans that he would hand over the Mediterranean merchant fleet to them, create an African Legion, form a new army, and merge the single Party with the militia. In these last days of 1942 Germany tried to set up in face of the Anglo-Saxons a completely Nazified France. And she chose as her agent Laval, under threat of replacing him by Doriot or a gauleiter.

From then on, the men of Vichy were forced to drink to the dregs the cup of their shame. If Laval had full powers, it was only that he might place them the more unreservedly at the service of Germany. He detached from Pétain's Légion des Anciens Combattants the "Service d'Order de la Légion" (S.O.L.)—recruited largely from gangster elements, and regarded as the "militant vanguard" of the Légion. The Germans continued to exercise full control in police matters. And they

Full Powers for Laval

LAVAL MEETS HIS MASTER HITLER

Following the German occupation of the whole of France in November 1942, the Fuehrer received the French Chief of Government Laval at his headquarters on December 19. Count Ciano, Italian Foreign Minister, Marshal Goering, and Ribbentrop, German Foreign Minister (with his back to the camera), were also present. According to the German News Agency, these talks ' indicated the possibility of further collaboration between France and the Axis.'

DESTRUCTION OF OLD MARSEILLES

Beginning on January 24, 1943, the Germans evacuated the 40,000 inhabitants of the Old Port of Marseilles from their homes, preparatory to the destruction of the entire area for defensive reasons. Vichy radio announced next day that ' to safeguard order in Marseilles ' 6,000 persons had been arrested in the process of evacuation. Here, the Cathedral of Ste. Marie-Majeure rises among the ruins of the Old Port. *Photo, Sport & General*

exerted more and more powerful pressure on the Vichy Government. With the Resistance movement starting fierce activity everywhere against the occupying Power, one Darquier de Pellepoix became the instrument of anti-Jewish legislation in France. And after the transfer of the American Embassy to Berlin by the Germans, the men of Vichy declared that the victory of the Americans would mean the triumph of the Front Populaire and of Bolshevism. Roosevelt was declared to be responsible for the "destruction of Europe." That was pure German propaganda.

The S.O.L. was transformed into a French National Militia, recognized as **German Pillage Becomes General** "of public utility": it was expected to achieve "the recovery of France." At the same time German pillage became general. In many of the departments of the former free zone there was soon no meat. Everything was pitilessly requisitioned for the enemy army. The country people found most of their harvests taken from them. In February recruiting of French labour to work for Germany began in the former free zone. One French commune was fined 300,000 francs—for not having prevented the occupation of the factories in 1936. The German authorities proposed, meanwhile, to create at Vichy a Ministry of the Interior, to be placed under Doriot, Déat or Darnand. On March 6 Laval met Gauleiter Sauckel, German Delegate-General for the Mobilization of Labour, at Paris, and agreed to hold a census of

men of 42 years and under; he thought the departure of French workers for Germany would disorganize Resistance.

Thenceforward Vichy was but a sort of island in the middle of France, a Chosen Land of every sort of cowardice. In April poor Pétain set forth his Labour Charter to oppose the Bolshevist menace, and declared that his one aim was the renewal of France. In fact, the country was escaping entirely from his control. Governmental and administrative disorder reached its height. To the "legal" Vichy, comprising the Government and its clientele, the police and the prefectoral body, was opposed the "real" Vichy of officials, the army, the press, and the clergy, while diplomats abroad were resigning because they had no contact either with London or with Washington.

Then began the exodus of the young men, threatened with two years' obligatory service. Taxes were heavier than ever. No effort was made to restrain the black market or set limits to the rise of prices. The deportation of workers brought final ruin to Franco-German relations. The Reich increased its demands, while Laval, getting nothing from it in return, suffered a series of setbacks without precedent. The public was asked to believe that only the Communists were against him. In reality, Pétain and Laval were sinking into slavery, even exhibited their disagreement to the Germans; while the country bore the burden of this lamentable statecraft. In May their whole position was menaced by a sort of

plot in Paris. And at that moment they suffered two hard blows—the dissolution of the Comintern, and the meeting between Giraud and De Gaulle. While Resistance grew stronger, collaboration, torn by a thousand internal quarrels, was going under.

Nor was it at the end of its troubles. On July 25 came Mussolini's resignation. Frossard, former Minister of Information, proposed that the National Assembly should be summoned and the Republic proclaimed anew. Laval, however, imagined that in Italy Badoglio might be replaced by Grandi, and that France must then make some "great" effort, resist German pressure, no longer send workers to the Reich. But it was too late. It was De Gaulle who, at Algiers, prepared the way for the new Republic.

Thenceforward the policy of collaboration seemed definitely condemned. Should the Senate and the Chamber of Deputies be summoned, under Jeanneney and Herriot? **Political Confusion in Vichy** Would Laval get the upper hand of Déat and Doriot? Would Gauleiter Sauckel defer his demand for half a million French workers, or not? What conclusion was to be drawn from the terrible crisis through which Italy was passing? And would it be possible, as Moysset suggested, to constitute an anti-Communist coalition with the Anglo-Saxons? All these were but vain discussions doomed to futility. The evil was beyond remedying by any reconstruction of the Ministry. De Brinon followed Himmler's lead; De Monzie preferred Goering. Thus did the

DORIOT—FRENCH NAZI

Jacques Doriot, leader of the Parti Populaire Français and a notorious collaborator, drives down the Avenue des Champs Elysées in Paris giving the Nazi salute. An unsuccessful attempt was made on his life on October 4, 1943, by a time bomb placed in a cinema at which he was addressing a meeting. *Photo, Planet News*

men of Vichy take joyless part in the great debate between capitalists and Nazis. Their days were numbered. What was the use of repeating endlessly that Germany was a sort of buffer between France and Bolshevism? Nobody any longer believed that.

September was an agitated month, with the problem of the French workers creating countless difficulties between Vichy and the Germans. Calm returned in October. Franco-German talks seemed to have come to a deadlock. The Germans themselves adopted a waiting policy, the result of their military anxieties. Nobody knew whether Laval was going to meet Hitler again. Neither he nor Pétain accepted the offer of peace made by Germany. Among the collaborators there was an epidemic of resignations and desertions.

German Offer of Peace

Towards the middle of November came a very grave crisis. Pétain was prevented from broadcasting to the French. His message was to have been that they were on the eve of civil war, and that a National Assembly was to meet to appeal for unity and to appoint the Marshal's eventual successor —who would certainly not be Laval. The latter, aided and abetted by the Germans, categorically opposed this plan. There was a state of more or less disguised war between the first and the third floors of the Hôtel du Parc. Realizing that he was no longer master in his own house, the Marshal shut himself up in his quarters and refused to see anyone.

GAULEITER FRITZ SAUCKEL

Sauckel, German Delegate-General for the Mobilization of Labour, is here seen (left) during a tour of inspection he made of the Atlantic Wall, talking to the chief of the Todt Organization labour battalions working on the fortifications. His efforts to secure half a million French workers for Germany failed. *Photo, Associated Press*

The crisis continued into December. In point of fact, Pétain had never been prepared to return to any sort of Parliamentary regime. What he wanted was to eliminate Laval. After Laval's disappearance, he would have reinforced his own dictatorship, but he was not sharp enough. Laval played the subtler game, making use of the Germans, who affected to disapprove of this return to a rotten democracy, but would on no account abandon the precious Marshal.

Inevitably the collaborators were panic-stricken in those last weeks of 1943. The year had proved a bad one for Vichy: Germany increasingly hated, Vichy increasingly despised, the Allies victorious in Italy and Russia, thousands of young Frenchmen going over to resistance, the formation of the Maquis, and an Anglo-American landing in France impending. The one certain fact was the German's desperate effort to complete the Nazification of the Vichy Cabinet, to get rid of recalcitrant Ministers, to obtain from a France bled white the material aid demanded by the tragic circumstances.

Growth of Resistance

It is difficult to give in a limited space a true idea of the actual scale and significance of the French Resistance Movement. But it is of more importance to render an exact interpretation of that historic phenomenon than to describe its details. Here, more than anywhere else, it was the spirit that counted, with the heroism that this engendered and fed.

Like the other European nations conquered and occupied by the Reich,

SALVAGING FRENCH WARSHIPS AT TOULON

When the Germans entered Toulon on November 27, 1942, Admiral de Laborde gave the order to scuttle the ships of the French navy which lay there (see p. 2566 and illus., pp. 2400 and 2564). Salvage operations carried out for the Germans by Italian engineers resulted in the raising of some at least of the ships. Frequent Allied air raids, however, interfered with the work, and when Toulon was finally freed in August 1944 the great naval base was found completely destroyed.

Photo, Planet News

France had her resistance movement. But the French case is distinct from the others. For resistance in France was carried on simultaneously against the invader and against the Vichy regime, which was collaborating with the invader. Once again in her history, France was divided into two camps.

In the years preceding the war, France had been like a candle burning at both ends. On the Right the privileged ruling classes, in concert with part of the middle classes, had betrayed the national cause, imagining that the victory of Hitlerism would end the so-called "Communist" peril. On the Left, pacifism and the desire for unduly accelerated social reforms had weakened the good sense and the fighting capacity of the masses. Common to both tendencies was ignorance of the pan-German programme and of the German danger.

Pre-War Political Divisions

When invasion and defeat came, bringing with them so much individual and collective distress, a substantial part of the population, especially in the zone left free by the enemy, turned to the Vichy regime, seeing in Pétain a kind of protector of the conquered and humiliated motherland. This fact, together with his prestige and his ability, accounted for the initial successes scored by the old Marshal. But the nation now came into contact with the Germans, and this contact proved the decisive psychological factor in the formation and development of Resistance.

Resistance began in France very quickly. But the Nazis knew what they

PETROL TRAIN DERAILED BY FRENCH PATRIOTS

All that remained of a train, specially built for carrying aviation spirit, after it had been derailed near Varennes-le-Grand during the night of August 31, 1943, and set on fire. A supply train travelling in the opposite direction was also destroyed. Reports reaching Algiers showed that during this month of August 45 trains (including 15 troop trains) were derailed, 58 locomotives sabotaged, and 45 other acts of sabotage against the railways carried out by French patriots.

papers, its leaflets, and its propaganda. It struck at the enemy at every opportunity. And it was equally active against the partisans of Vichy, against the Marshal's "Legion," his Labour Charter, and his Peasant Corporation. During the winter of 1942-43, the peasants met at night, young and old together, in isolated farmhouses to listen fervently to the French broadcasts from London, with but one common thought, one hope : Liberation—represented by General de Gaulle, by the British-American alliance, by Russia victorious against the German offensive.

Towards the middle of March the Socialists, assembled in congress, proposed the setting up of an Executive Committee of Resistance, embracing all parties : an idea soon carried out in full.

Resistance Identified with Unity

Thenceforward resistance tended to be identified with the union and unity of all French energies. The likeness between the mother-country, completely occupied, and North Africa as it underwent political reconstruction, became more and more evident. Events in Haute-Savoie, where numbers of young Frenchmen—according to some estimates, 70,000—took to the hills in mid-March to avoid calling up by the Germans, opened the eyes both of the German authorities and of the Vichy regime. On March 22 the "Français de Grande Bretagne" organized in London a moving demonstration on the occasion of the thousandth day of

were doing when they established the famous line of demarcation between the "occupied" and the "free" zones. It was in Paris, it was in Brittany, it was in the eastern departments of France that the spirit of resistance began to take a firm hold. People who crossed from the free zone knew at once when they had passed the line. This does not mean, however, that the spirit of resistance did not exist from the outset in the free zone. How many ardent and courageous Frenchmen and Frenchwomen the present writer himself knew in southern France ! These people, of all ages and of every class, came together and began working in the days when Britain was carrying on the struggle alone against Germany. If they did not have the Gestapo actually at their heels, they had to face the Vichy police. Arrests multiplied. The severest sentences, "for anti-national activities," were imposed on patriots.

Undoubtedly the Vichy regime sometimes tried to mitigate this severity and to elude the vigilance of the enemy.

Effects of Persecution of the Jews

But from 1940 to 1942 the French population of the two zones was not deceived ; and at the end of that period Germany's activities against the Jews opened their eyes fully. It mattered little whether the anti-Semitic persecution was carried on by the Gestapo or by the French police. When in September 1942 French men and women saw Jewish families suddenly delivered up to the caprice of the oppressors, split up, mothers losing their children for ever in the space of a few minutes and these children deprived

of their normal civil rights, the French understood. They saw the Jewish tragedy for what it was : the prelude to the tragedy of all France.

That tragedy began with total occupation at the end of 1942. That is why 1943 was the year, the great year, of French Resistance. This grew in intensity during the last months of 1942 and the first quarter of 1943. At this time, Resistance was almost fully equipped. It was intellectual and political, and already military. It had its news-

GRAVE OF BRITISH AIRMEN IN FRANCE

In spite of the watchfulness of the Gestapo and the Vichy police, and of the damage and injury to Frenchmen caused by Allied raids, the graves of Allied airmen shot down over France were tended carefully by the people and covered with flowers. Here is the grave of six British airmen killed when their four-engined Halifax bomber crashed near Annecy. *Photos, U.S. Official*

GERMAN FORTIFICATION OF THE ATLANTIC COAST

Here are some glimpses of the structure and weapons of the 'Atlantic Wall'—built in the main by forced labour under the direction of the Todt Organization—which Hitler boasted was impregnable to Allied attack for the whole length of the Atlantic coast of Europe. 1. One-man revolving fort set up in towns along the French and Belgian seaboard. 2. Marshal von Rundstedt, commanding German Forces in France and the Low Countries, inspects the defence works of the Atlantic Wall. 3. Manoeuvring a heavy, camouflaged gun into position in its concrete emplacement in the coast defences. 4. Constructing fortifications in the heart of the Channel cliffs.

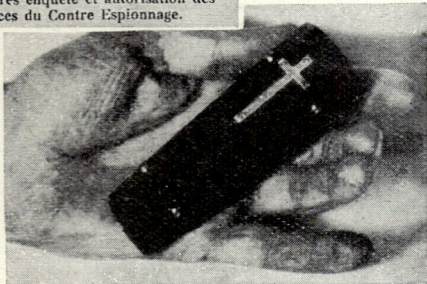

"la lutte du people français pour sa libération" (the struggle of the French people for their liberation). Who does not know that phrase, repeated many times a day by the British Broadcasting Corporation? After referring to the Germans and the obvious representatives of the Vichy regime, Abetz, De Brinon, Henriot, Doriot, Luchaire and others, M. Grenier said:—

"Here is the immense multitude of the others—the sabotaging workers, the clandestine printers, the franc-tireurs and partisans, Flemish, Norman, Breton, Parisian, Burgundian, Alsatian, Savoyard ; the 400,000 in prison ; the weeping multitude of widows and orphans of the 25,000 massacred hostages ; all the renewed valour and courage of many a Joan of Arc, many a Lazare Hoche, France, the true France, pure and immortal ! "

When he reached London in April to join De Gaulle, M. Pierre Viénot (Under-Secretary for Foreign Affairs in **From Passive to Active Resistance** M. Blum's cabinet, 1936–37), speaking from experience of Vichy prisons and of French resistance, said : " Total occupation, increased distress and privation, forced labour and deportations, had transformed *passive* resistance into *active*, *militant* resistance. Irritation, disgust, and discontent had grown to a degree. Cases of disobedience in the administration were increasing. At the same time, in relation to the Allies, the position had been accentuated. The anti-British campaigns launched by Vichy produced no effect. The people built the highest military hopes on the Allies and showed themselves full of

confidence politically . . . *Vichy remained so entirely apart from the mass of the people that the French were exactly as they had been from 1917–18.*"

These words are entirely true and profound. I have seen peasants who had been soldiers in the first great war listening with tears in their eyes to citations broadcast from Algiers recounting the exploits of Frenchmen at the time of the Tunisian campaign. There they heard once more the accents and the spirit of their own war. They had recovered a tradition which they had for a moment feared was dead.

This astonishing struggle had three main elements, especially after the middle of 1943 : (1) the deportations to Germany ; (2) the development of groups of franc-tireurs and of armed patriots ; (3) preparation for a national

PACIFIC DEFIANCE

During the night of November 10-11, 1943, someone in Bourg-en-Bresse erected this bust of the Republic, with the Republican flag and the cross of Lorraine—symbol of De Gaulle's followers—on the pedestal of a statue removed by the Germans for scrap. Next morning the people of the town filed past.

rising, correlated with the eventual opening of the so-called Second Front.

The enemy was out to empty France of all her able-bodied men. Railwaymen went on strike, workers and labourers called up fled, there were mass protests, imposing demonstrations, dramatic incidents. At St. Etienne it took 900 gendarmes to restore order. The youth of the country, formerly hesitant, now gave proof of admirable courage. At this time the students of Paris, themselves menaced with the same fate, wrote the Marshal a magnificent letter, a little belated, perhaps, but revealing the very soul of the nation.

If franc-tireurs are men who keep on with their usual work, the partisans

were full-time franc-tireurs. Living outside the law, they engaged in important operations such as the derailing of trains. From 1943 onward they were organized under a national military committee. Finally, the orders " *de débarquement*," that is the orders issued in readiness for the coming Allied landing, were prepared and perfected during 1943.

In and through the Resistance Council (*Conseil de la Résistance*), formed in March 1943, the French achieved unity, the Council representing some 90 per cent of the population. After many hesitations the masses **Rise of the Resistance Council** of the people were associated with the work of liberation. It remained to organize and arm them. The extraordinary efficiency of the F.F.I. (*Forces Françaises de l'Intérieur*) during the military operations of 1944 proved the excellence of the training.

On August 26, in a moving appeal, the Resistance Council was able to say : " The nation is enduring with daily increasing wrath and impatience its sufferings under German tyranny . . . The Resistance Council, uniting the active movements throughout the land, embracing every tendency of French political thought . . . claims throughout the land the rights and responsibilities of the directing body and of the provisional organ of national sovereignty. . . . *Against the enemy and against treason, the Council, in close community with the French Committee of National Liberation, and faithful to the doctrine of Fighting France, assumes the mission of inspiring, co-ordinating, and directing the struggle of the French people on their own soil.*"

BADGE OF GRATITUDE

This badge, with a chamois on one side, and the phrase 'May the king of the mountain protect you' on the other, was given to people who supplied them with food by the young men hiding in the mountains of Upper Savoy to escape the German labour call-up. During October 1943 bitter fighting developed between these young Frenchmen—numbering tens of thousands—and German troops sent against them.

Chapter 290

HOW FRANCE PREPARED FOR LIBERATION

Professor Edmond Vermeil, who in Chapter 289 related the history of Metropolitan France during 1943, here records what happened in Algiers from November 1942 until the end of the following year. There, the French Committee of National Liberation, set up in June 1943, steadily gained power and prestige as it prepared for the day when France would once more be freed from the enemy. For the history of Fighting France up to the Allied landings in North Africa, see Chapter 220

THE year 1943 was a decisive stage in the evolution of the second great war. France also, thanks to the efforts of the National Committee at Algiers, profited from the tremendous lift of spirit imparted to the Allied forces by success to unite her scattered energies, to join the Allies, and to follow in the wake, as General de Gaulle had predicted in June 1940, of Anglo-American-Russian victory. Thenceforward, it was certain that, if she had lost a battle, she had not lost the war.

Up to November 1942 the policy of Free France had been worked out in London. General de Gaulle had set up there an invaluable nucleus of government which, from the time of the Allied landings in North Africa, secured in that essential part of the French Empire the confirmation and expansion of its first efforts. The French Committee of National Liberation had set itself not only to do its best to look after French interests, but also and above all to prepare the way for French participation in the Allied military effort. The campaigns in Libya, Tunisia, and finally in Italy, offered France the longed-for opportunity. And all this was the prelude to the action which French troops were to carry to success in 1944 on the Mediterranean shores of France herself.

In the history of what may be called Algerian France from November 1942 to December 1943, it is easy to distinguish three essential phases. The **Fighting France in North Africa** first is associated with General Giraud, High Commissioner after the death of Darlan (*see page 2567*). Giraud detached himself with a certain slowness from the influence of Vichy, thus preparing the way for General de Gaulle. De Gaulle arrived at Algiers on May 30 and there, in agreement with Giraud, set up the Committee of National Liberation. On November 3, 1943, with the meeting of the Consultative Assembly—temporary substitute for the parliament of the future—a third period opened in the political development of Fighting France in North Africa.

Nobody regretted Darlan's death. Scarcely had he disappeared when the Imperial Council appointed General Giraud to be High Commissioner of North Africa. This Council included MM. Châtel, Governor-General of Algeria, Boisson, Governor-General of French West Africa, and Noguès, Resident-General of Morocco, and Generals Bergeret and Giraud. The last-named declared that he had but one aim, to liberate North Africa and France. He intended to prepare a powerful army to play its part in national liberation—a hope justified by the defeats suffered by Hitler in Africa and in Russia. At this moment the Giraud period began.

ALLIES SEND FOOD TO NORTH AFRICAN CIVILIANS

Labels like this, in many sizes, and printed in red, white and blue, were attached to the food and other goods sent into North Africa after its liberation. The message, 'Delivered by the United Nations whose fleets rule the waves,' appeared in French and Arabic. The central Arabic character is the equivalent of the Western 'V' sign: on the scroll of it is the phrase, 'Victory for the United Nations is certain,' on the diamond part above, 'God willing.'

Photo, British Official

Minister of the Interior, on January 20, and General Bergeret was transferred to the Higher Economic Council (Conseil Supérieur Economique) created by Giraud in February.

On February 6 General Giraud assumed the title of Civil and Military Commander-in-Chief of French North Africa. A War Committee was set up. Certain modifications were made in the Vichy measures and regulations. The Service d'Ordre de la Légion (*see Chapter 289*) was dissolved. Political prisoners and persons who had assisted the Allied landing were set free. Dismissed officials were reinstated. But these remained piecemeal decisions. And they were badly carried out.

Not until March 14 did Giraud clearly define his position. He delivered a speech setting out his programme in which he repudiated Vichy, Fascism and monarchism, and declared his adherence to the Republic. He annulled the legislation enacted by Vichy since June 1940. He took upon himself, however, to abrogate the Crémieux Act of 1870 (under which native-born Algerian Jews received French citizenship). He protested formally against the German annexation of Alsace-Lorraine. He

Darlan had not disarmed the collaborators—they had even organized subtle resistance to the Allies. No decisive measures had been taken against the Fifth Column of Fascists and Hitlerites. It was this toleration of his that cost him his life. His assassination wrecked the Monarchist and Fascist conspiracy at Algiers, but the atmosphere was still poisoned by Vichy. It was impossible to abolish at one stroke Fascism, still less Hitlerism. They had, indeed, gained astounding power in North Africa. Use was still being made of deeply compromised men. Châtel was replaced as Governor-General of Algeria by Peyrouton, a former Vichy

General Giraud concluded military, economic and financial agreements with the Americans. The United States promised to arm a certain number of French divisions. After their meeting at Casablanca, Giraud and De Gaulle continued to discuss the conditions and the modalities by which union could be achieved. In these discussions General Catroux acted as intermediary, arranging the exchange of notes. On April 14 Giraud addressed to the French National Committee in London a memorandum in which he set out the bases of the future organization. Discussion went on until the end of May. Only a direct conversation was needed to conclude it. Giraud wanted this to take place elsewhere than in Algiers. De Gaulle, on

Results of Casablanca

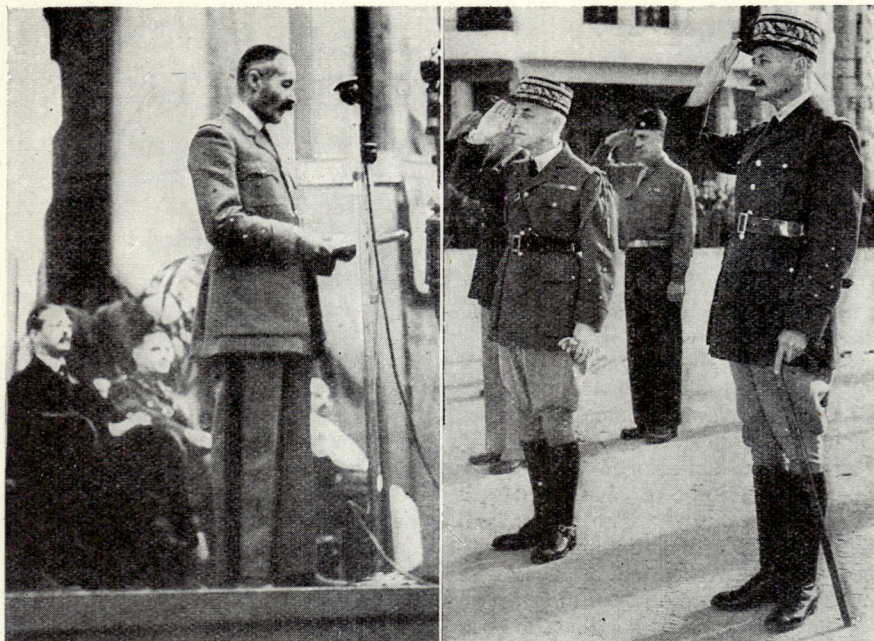

GENERAL GIRAUD TAKES OVER IN NORTH AFRICA

Following the assassination of Admiral Darlan on Christmas Eve, 1942, General Giraud was appointed High Commissioner of French North Africa by the Imperial Council which Darlan had set up. Giraud is seen here, left, delivering the speech of March 14, 1943, in which he set out his programme : behind him sits Mr. Harold Macmillan, British Minister-Resident at Allied G.H.Q. ; right, with General Noguès (then Resident-General for Morocco) at his right, taking the salute at a march past
Photos, British Official ; Planet News

declared above all that he had no personal ambition : he was the servant, not the leader, of the French people. It was for the French to determine later the form of their government.

This new policy could be put into effect only slowly and painfully. Everywhere strange contradictions persisted. General Bergeret still held a military command. Though a special commission was active in emptying the concentration camps and the prisons, those who had interned, persecuted and tortured political prisoners suffered no punishment. And no member of the administrative staff was removed.

On the other hand, while the greater part of the French Empire rallied to the resistance movement, the colonies and their administrators were still divided into two camps. North Africa adhered to General Giraud and the other colonies to General de Gaulle. There were even a Giraud army and a Gaullist army. A dualism that threatened to be fatal to France was thus instituted in North Africa and the Empire. Pro-Fascists and Republicans were beginning silently to range themselves against each other.

Threat of Dualism in the Empire

Union was essential. But it was not to be easily achieved. The first step towards it was taken early in the year.

On January 14 President Roosevelt and Mr. Churchill and their Chiefs of Staff met at Casablanca. Premier Stalin was invited, but was unable to leave Russia ; he was, however, kept fully informed of the military proposals made. The prime object of the meeting was to concert measures which would draw as much of the weight as possible off the Russian armies (then engaged in the Stalingrad counter-offensive—*see* Chapter 269) by engaging the enemy as heavily as possible at the best selected points, and for ten days the combined Staffs surveyed the entire field of war throughout the world. In an interview to pressmen at the end of the conference Mr. Roosevelt emphasized that world peace could come about only by the unconditional surrender of Germany, Italy and Japan ; by this he did not mean the destruction of their populace, but of the German, Japanese and Italian philosophies of fear, hate and subjugation of other peoples, and he suggested that the Casablanca meeting might be called the " Unconditional Surrender Meeting."

During this conference General Giraud was invited to confer with the combined Chiefs of Staffs, and a meeting was arranged between him and General de Gaulle, who came to Casablanca accompanied by General Catroux and Rear-Admiral d'Argenlieu. After close consultation the two leaders issued a joint declaration stating, " We have registered our entire agreement on the end to be achieved, which is : the liberation of France and the triumph of human liberties through the total defeat of the

DARLAN'S LAST PORTRAIT

Admiral Darlan, Minister of Defence in the Vichy Government, who, happening to be in North Africa when the Allies landed in November 1942, assumed responsibility for French interests there, and threw in his lot with the Allies. He made no clearance of Vichy influences, however, and paid with his life for his ' trimming ' policy. This is his last photograph, taken shortly before his assassination on December 24, 1942.

the contrary, was in favour of Algiers. He had his way, and left for Algiers on May 26, accompanied by MM. Massigli, Commissioner for Foreign Affairs, and André Philip, Commissioner for the Interior. It should be mentioned also that on April 18 Giraud and De Gaulle had joined in an important move. They had sent a message to the Secretary General of the League of Nations informing him that France did not consider herself bound by the declaration of the Vichy Government announcing a breach with the League. The months that followed saw the constitution at Algiers of the Committee of National Liberation.

On May 30 General Giraud and General de Gaulle met at Algiers. Two Commissioners from London, M. Monnet and General Georges (the latter had

CORSICA FREED BY THE FRENCH

French troops landing at Ajaccio in Corsica (see map) on the night of September 13–14, 1943, were welcomed by thousands of enthusiastic islanders. The liberation of the island took twenty days, being completed with light losses by the taking of Bastia on October 4. 1. French troops come ashore at Ajaccio and march into the town, already freed by Corsican guerillas. 2. The tricolour flies again from the town hall of Bastia. 3. M. André Philip, Commissioner for Home Affairs in the Committee of National Liberation at Algiers, visits liberated Corsica. 4. A Corsican guerilla armed with a British Sten-gun watches Spitfires, flown by French pilots to a Corsican airfield.

FRENCHMEN RETRAIN FOR MILITARY SERVICE

Thousands of Frenchmen who escaped to North Africa after the Allies gained control there, began at once to retrain for France's new fighting forces. A British sergeant is here instructing some of them in the use of the Bren-gun. By the end of 1943 the French army in North and West Africa totalled 450,000 well-equipped men, of whom 175,000 were Europeans. A year earlier it had numbered only 160,000, with no modern weapons and very short of other equipment.

Photo, British Official

flown from France a week earlier), and General Catroux were also present.

Final agreement was not reached at once. Opinion at Algiers was still confused and feverish. **De Gaulle and Giraud Reach Agreement** There had been various incidents. M. Peyrouton had at last resigned, but under strange conditions: he had informed General de Gaulle before General Giraud, who had appointed him, and he received from the two leaders two different military appointments. A few days later General Catroux became Governor-General of Algeria and M. Helleu took his place as French Delegate General in the Levant. On June 3 union was finally achieved, and the formation of the National Committee of Liberation became possible. It issued an appeal to all Frenchmen without distinction, containing these declarations:

"The Committee directs the French war effort in all its forms and in all places. In consequence it exercises French sovereignty in all territories outside the enemy's power, and it guarantees the management and protection of all French interests throughout the world. . . .

"The Committee will surrender its powers to the French Provisional Government which will be constituted in accordance with the law of the Republic as soon as the liberation of the metropolitan territory of France permits, and at latest when the total liberation of France has been achieved. . . .

"The Committee solemnly undertakes to restore all French liberties, the laws of the Republic, and the Republican regime, by destroying completely the regime of arbitrary and personal power that has been imposed on the country."

The first members of the Committee were Generals Charles de Gaulle and Henri Giraud (Joint Presidents), General Georges Catroux (Muslim Affairs), General Jacques Georges (National Commissioner without Portfolio), M. René Massigli (Foreign Affairs), M. André Philip (Interior), and M. Jean Monnet (Armaments). On June 7 the Committee was completed by the appointment of M. Henri Bonnet (Information), Dr. Jules Abadie (Education and Public Health), M. Maurice Couve de Murville (Finance), M. André Diethelm (Production and Trade), M. René Pleven (Colonies), and M. Adrien Pierre Tixier (Labour and Social Security).

The first steps of this Committee were not easy. There were heated discussions, particularly on the subject of military organization. M. Monnet, M. Massigli and General Catroux intervened several times as mediators between De Gaulle and Giraud. After a fortnight's break the Committee resumed its sittings on June 17, and on June 27 a military committee was appointed to carry out the unification of the military forces. It included De Gaulle, Giraud and the three Chiefs of Staff.

A purge was undertaken in the course of which a number of doubtful or compromised men disappeared from the scene. **Compromised Men Removed** Giraud went to the United States and signed at Washington, with President Roosevelt, an agreement for the arming of 300,000 men. But that did not solve the problem of the reorganization of the army. The Committee decided to inject younger blood into the ranks of the officers; but it did not succeed in settling the delimitation between the civil authority and the military command. Not until August 1 was a new solution produced. A Defence Committee was set up, presided over by De Gaulle, and composed of Generals Giraud and Legentilhomme, together with the Chiefs of Staff of the Army, the Navy and the Air Force. The Committee arranged within itself a suitable division of labours. Giraud was to preside over military debates and De Gaulle over political ones. On both planes decisions were to be arrived at by majority vote.

Two months later, as September passed into October, the military organization was again revised. A War Commissariat took the place of the Committee of National Defence. Its head was General Legentilhomme (*see* illus., p. 1263), Giraud remaining Commander-in-Chief. Fusion of the military forces could now be arranged.

While these changes were taking place, French forces were recovering the island of Corsica. By the time the armistice between the Allies and Italy was signed, 15,000 **Recovery of Corsica** Corsicans had been secretly armed by the Allies. Immediately the news of the armistice became known, these men took up the fight against the Germans, forcing them to withdraw to Bastia and Bonifacio, and there was a popular rising in which Vichy officials were arrested in many towns and villages, and the Mairie and Préfecture at Ajaccio, the capital, were seized. When at midnight on September 13–14, a French naval force consisting of the cruisers "Montcalm" and "Jeanne d'Arc," the light cruisers "Le Fantasque" and "Le Terrible," the destroyers "L'Alcyon," "Le Fortuné," "Basque" and "Tempête," and the

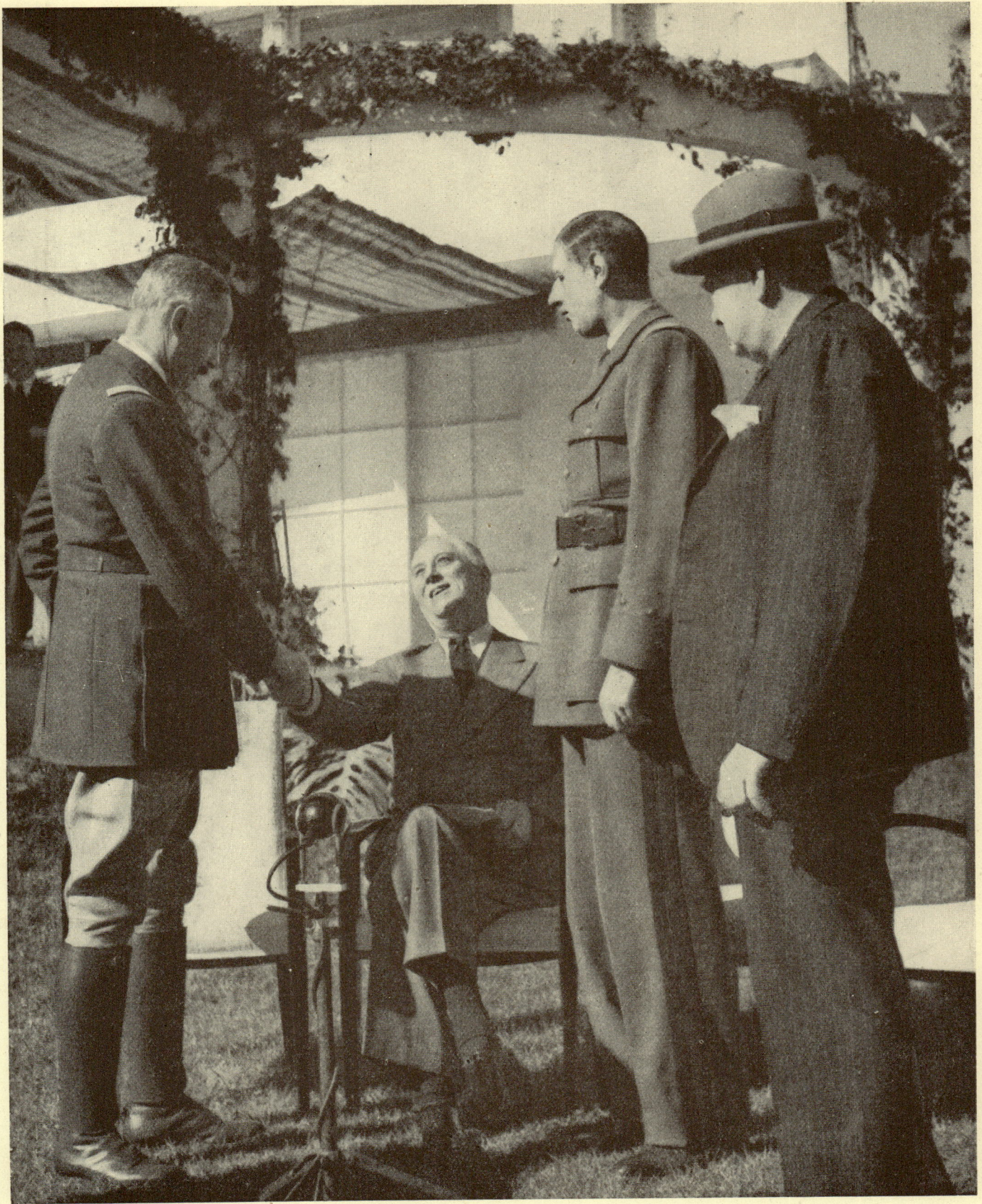

PREMIER, PRESIDENT AND FRENCH LEADERS AT CASABLANCA

The conference between President Roosevelt and Mr. Churchill, Premier of Great Britain, which took place at Casablanca in French Morocco from January 14–26, 1943, resulted in the announcement that unconditional surrender was the only condition on which the Allies would grant peace to the Axis. General Giraud, at that time Commander-in-Chief in French North Africa, and General de Gaulle, leader of the Fighting French with headquarters in London, were both invited to the conference and held their first consultation on unifying the French fighting forces. Here Roosevelt shakes hands with Giraud ; De Gaulle and Churchill stand on the President's left.   *Photo, British Official*

HIS MAJESTY KING GEORGE VI WELCOMED—

H.M. The King, accompanied by Sir Archibald Sinclair, Secretary of State for Air, and Sir James Grigg, Secretary of State for War, and members of his staff, left England by air on the night of June 11, 1943, to visit British and Allied troops in North Africa. He arrived back on June 25, having met the military and civil chiefs directing British, Ameri-

—BY HIS VICTORIOUS TROOPS IN NORTH AFRICA

can, and French operations ; visited a large Army convalescent camp where 3,000 troops
gave him an ovation ; reviewed the Fifth Army under its Commanding General, Lt.-Gen.
Mark W. Clark, and troops of the French North African Army, and paid a short visit to
the gallant island of Malta.

Photo, British Official

MEN OF THE MAQUIS OCCUPY A TOWN IN THE AIN DEPARTMENT

On November 11, 1943, some two hundred men of the Maquis drove sixty miles from their secret camps by devious ways to Oyonnax, a town of some 12,000 inhabitants lying six miles north-east of Nantua. They took over the town. Then they marched past in column of three to the war memorial, where they laid a wreath in the form of the cross of Lorraine—symbol of the Fighting French—inscribed 'From the victors of tomorrow to those of 1914–18.' The Last Post was sounded ; the Marseillaise, forbidden by the Germans, sung ; the police set free ; and the men climbed into their lorries to return to camp. Germans and Vichy police were at Nantua, where an armistice day celebration had been announced. Above, the march past ; below, a lorry crowded with men of the Maquis arrives.

submarines " Casabianca," " Perle," and " Arethusa " arrived at Ajaccio to land French Commandos, it was met by thousands of enthusiastic Frenchmen. The ships returned to North Africa, returning later with Moroccan troops. Units of American Rangers (equivalent to Commandos) were also landed, and many of the 40,000 Italian troops on the island joined the French.

Ajaccio itself was firmly in French hands by September 17, and Bonifacio and Porto Vecchio were occupied on September 23. By the 27th, the enemy hold on Corsica was reduced to a small area in the triangle Bastia-Borgo-Folelli. The French, under the command of General Henri Martin (Chef d'Etat-Major to General Giraud in 1940) continued to advance, though the Germans put up a desperate defence, until on October 4 they entered Bastia. Next day the French High Command announced, " French troops have achieved the liberation of Corsica twenty days after the first landings. Losses were extraordinarily light ; the booty is very large." The enemy on the other hand had suffered considerable losses. Allied warships and air forces had maintained an effective blockade of the island, and German efforts at evacuation by air were intercepted by

long-range aircraft of the N.W.A.A.F. Seven transport planes were shot down on September 23, 19 on the 24th, when several hundred German technicians were drowned. The Germans nevertheless claimed that their evacuation of Corsica was an " organizational and operational masterpiece," effected, said the German High Command, without loss of heavy weapons, guns or tanks.

On August 26 the Governments of Great Britain, the United States and Canada recognized the French Committee " as administering those French overseas territories which acknowledge its authority." Russia went further, and recognized it as " representing the State interests of the French Republic."

Thus constituted, the French Committee of National Liberation could attack the four problems that demanded its attention : (1) to obtain the complete recognition which would enable it to figure in the councils of the United Nations as the governmental representative of France ; (2) to pursue a policy

of purification that would culminate in the winding up of the Vichy regime and the condemnation of Pétain and of his Ministers ; (3) to administer the colonies and protectorates ; and finally (4) to direct the Resistance movement, while making political and material preparations for the return to France.

The Committee soon found that it could not long continue alone to watch over the interests of France. It needed a wider collaboration with France herself, a preliminary Parliamentary representation of the country. This took shape in the Consultative Assembly. From the moment this Assembly was formed and took up its duties French energies, encouraged by the German defeats and by the hope of a speedy liberation of the French mother-country, began steadily to show more unity.

The Consultative Assembly was not elected, simply because it could not be. It was composed of 84 delegates, of whom 52 were chosen by the Resistance movement inside and outside France,

COMMITTEE OF NATIONAL LIBERATION IN SESSION

A meeting of the Committee as formed in Algiers after agreement was reached between Generals de Gaulle and Giraud, who were its Joint Presidents (see p. 2910). Round the table, beginning on the left, the members shown are : M. André Philip (Interior), General Catroux (Muslim Affairs), General de Gaulle, Dr. Jules Abadie (Education and Public Health), M. Jean Monnet (Armaments), M. René Pleven (Colonies), M. André Diethelm (Production and Trade), M. Maurice Couve de Murville (Finance), General Jacques Georges (without portfolio), General Giraud, M. René Massigli (Foreign Affairs).
Photo, Topical Press

FRENCH LEADERS MEET ON FRENCH SOIL
General de Gaulle, leader in London since June 1940 of those Frenchmen and women who continued the fight after France's defeat, reached Algiers on May 30, 1943, and was met by General Giraud, High Commissioner of North Africa and C.-in-C. of French forces there following the Allied invasion. Talks between the two resulted in the formation of the Committee of National Liberation and the consolidation of all French fighting forces. *Photo, British Official*

20 were drawn from among the deputies and senators who had not voted for Vichy in 1940 and 12 from the *Conseils Généraux* (Departmental Councils) throughout the French Empire. For the moment it was invested with strictly limited powers. It had the right only to give advice, and to sit every other month. It was simply consultative.

But this "Rump Parliament" was none the less able to assert itself at once, to proclaim its independence and to display a zealous activity. Starting

Parliamentary Methods Justified

from modest beginnings, the new French parliamentarism was to prove its quality by its own record. This was of capital importance and of incalculable import. For the success of these efforts and discussions put an end to the appalling anti-parliamentary campaign which Germany had so efficiently encouraged in France before the war, and which had justified itself by pointing to transient mistakes that offered no genuine argument against the principle of Republican parliamentarism. At the same time, the Committee of National Liberation saw growing at its side a new force capable of presenting to it under a more organically united form the desires and the true interests of the French nation.

The Committee itself was reorganized to include well-known representatives of the principal French parties. M. Henri

Queuille became a Commissioner of State, M. André Le Troquer Commissioner for War and Aviation, M. Louis Jacquinot Commissioner for the Navy, M. Pierre Mendès-France Commissioner for Finance, M. Henri Fresnay Commissioner for War Prisoners and Deportees. M. Emmanuel d'Astier de Lavigerie replaced M. André Philip as Commissioner for the Interior. M. Philip and General Catroux became Commissioners of State. General Giraud retired from the presidency of the Committee, General de Gaulle remaining sole President while Giraud was to devote himself entirely to his military duties. Various people disappeared from the Committee. The Communists were no longer represented, and the problem of their eventual participation did not arise until 1944, for, in 1943, no agreement was reached between them and De Gaulle. Public declarations had been made on both sides. Both had insisted on their goodwill. But, the Communists having refused the two Commissionerships reserved for them, for the time being negotiations ceased.

The Communists had, moreover, published their programme. They considered that the future Constitution could be adopted only by a Constituent Assembly elected by universal suffrage. They were opposed to the creation of a Presidency of the Republic armed with very strong powers, in which they saw

the beginning of a scarcely disguised dictatorship. Realizing that the evils from which France had suffered had had their source in the weakening of the national sovereignty and in the general corruption of the executive power and the legislative powers, they desired, through universal suffrage, a more effective control over those elected, and by those elected over ministers and high officials. Finally, they wanted great parties honestly based on clear programmes. The Communists also, therefore, wanted to strengthen the stability of the government, but by the reinforcement of national and political consciousness among electors, members of parliament and ministers. Nor did they forget the need for sound representation of the Empire.

During its first session the Consultative Assembly concentrated on the problem of purging the administration and on foreign policy. It was, indeed, at these two points that it could best complement the labours of the National Committee.

Problems Before the Assembly

Its debates, marked by the truest dignity, were from the first full of promise for the future. The Assembly resumed at once the tradition of the great parliamentary debates of the past. It renewed the bond with all that had been best in the Third Republic. Men of the Resistance, such as the University professors Mayoux and Haurion, worked with well-known

LIAISON OFFICER CATROUX
General Catroux, French Delegate-General for the Levant, announced in February 1943 that he would act as Fighting French liaison officer between General de Gaulle and General Giraud. In this capacity he made many journeys between London and Algiers prior to the leaders' agreement. Catroux became Commissioner for Muslim Affairs in the Committee of National Liberation, and Governor-General of Algeria.
Photo, Topical Press

parliamentarians such as M. Vincent-Auriol.

From the outset the Assembly wanted more energy in the purge. It wanted a more open and more effectual break with the Vichy regime, still in such high favour in North Africa. Representatives of Resistance and of unsullied parliamentarism had not crossed the Mediterranean for nothing. From this point of view the Assembly was ungrudging in its support of General de Gaulle, as President of the Committee of National Liberation. In the first debate the General declared that he wanted authority " backed by sufficient strength and continuity to impose on all within

Assembly's Full Support for De Gaulle

FRENCH NORTH AFRICAN TROOPS IN ITALY

General Charles de Gaulle, President of the Committee of National Liberation, talks with a colonel of an Algerian division somewhere in Italy. Left, a typical French Goum, tireless Arab warrior from North Africa, in camp in Italy. These famous fighters and swordsmen of the French colonial forces did magnificent service during 1943 in Tunisia and in Italy. They also helped to free the island of Corsica. *Photos, U.S. Official*

papers of North Africa were made subject to confiscation. Proceedings against Pucheu, Peyrouton, Flandin, Boisson and others were started. The Crémieux Act was renewed on October 21. Liberal measures were adopted in regard to the native population.

At the same time public life blossomed anew in Algiers. The Communist, Socialist and Radical parties were reconstituted locally. " Fighting France" held two congresses. Weekly newspapers started. Protests began, and a struggle started against the military and political censorship.

the country the supreme power of the State, and to pursue abroad aims worthy of France." This required a purge and a programme of foreign policy. The Committee took into account the desires of the Assembly, not only in regard to the purge but also in the Lebanon affair (*see* p. 2642 and illus., p. 2641) and in favour of conciliatory solutions. The Commission d'Epuration, the committee responsible for the purge, was reorganized. The news-

To sum up, from the Darlan-Giraud period to the National Committee, and from the National Committee to the Consultative Assembly, France accomplished in North Africa, in close association with the occupied mother-country and with London, remarkable political progress from which she was to reap the full fruits in 1944, at the moment of liberation.

CO-PRESIDENTS AT ASSEMBLY

Generals Giraud and de Gaulle at the first session of the Provisional Consultative Assembly, made up of 40 members representing resistance inside France, 20 members of the former Senate and Chamber, 12 representing resistance outside France, and 12 representing Departmental Councils, which met at Algiers on November 3, 1943. In the foreground is General Catroux.

THE RUSSIANS FORCE THE MIDDLE DNIEPER

The Red Army's swift, successful forcing of the Dnieper river—one of the largest in Europe—astonished not only the enemy, but the rest of the world as well. The high west bank, well fortified by the Germans, dominates the low marshy east bank, and the Russians swept the Germans back and achieved what appeared to be the impossible by choosing the most unlikely, and therefore lightly defended, places for their initial crossings. 1. Bridge over the Dnieper destroyed in every span by the retreating enemy. 2. The last Germans cross another bridge before blowing it up. 3. Enemy machine-gun post on the strongly fortified west bank. 4. Soviet machine-gunners on the east bank cover their comrades crossing the river in light assault craft.

Photos, G.P.U.; Keystone; Associated Press

Chapter 291

ATTACK AND COUNTER-ATTACK IN RUSSIA

The Red Army's summer offensive of 1943 (described in Chapter 282) came to an end at the beginning of October. But with scarcely a pause, and before the enemy was ready, Soviet forces renewed their attacks with an intensity that carried them forward, despite some setbacks from fierce German counter-attacks, right up to the end of the year. Major-General Sir Charles Gwynn here describes this series of autumn attacks and counter-attacks

THE great Russian summer offensive of 1943 ended when the Soviet forces found themselves confronted by the line of the Dnieper. It seemed improbable that any attempt would be made to cross the river in strength until the winter. But although there was a definite pause of a week or so at the end of September and beginning of October, it soon became evident that the Russians had no intention of remaining inactive, despite the need for work on their lines of communication and on reorganization. The pursuit, however, had ended, and the Germans were standing to fight, so that the campaign took on a new character. Broadly speaking, operations were designed to prepare the way for the winter campaign, but were more ambitious than might have been considered practicable in view of autumn weather and the strength of the German position.

Reference to the map (*see.* p. 2921) would no doubt make it appear a tempting proposition to force a crossing of the Dnieper somewhere between Kiev and Dnepropetrovsk before the Germans had recovered from their retreat, and, striking south-westward towards Odessa, to cut off the enemy within the great bend of the river. That arm-chair strategy takes little account of the residual strength of the enemy, of weather conditions, of the nature of the obstacles presented by the river, or of the immense strain already imposed on Russian communications.

Russian operations were more practical in character and aimed in the first place at eliminating all German bridge-heads east of the river.

Koniev Captures Kremenchug

On September 29 Kremenchug, which was one of the few large towns on the east bank, was captured by Koniev, and next day Rokossovsky crossed the Sozh river, increasing the Soviet stranglehold on Gomel and allowing the front to close on the upper Dnieper towards Mogilev and Rogachev. On October 7, Yeremenko, having taken the offensive on the Veliki Luki front, captured Nevel, thereby at last cutting the great lateral railway between Leningrad and Vitebsk and threatening to outflank the latter

stronghold. This operation marked the end of the pause and the beginning of the autumn campaign all along the front. On the same day it was announced that three bridge-heads had been established across the Dnieper—to the north of Kiev, south of Pereyaslavl, and south-east of Kremenchug. In the Kuban the last of the Germans were being driven out of the Taman peninsula, which was finally cleared on October 9—the Germans losing 20,000 men killed and 3,000 prisoners in the final stages of their seemingly purposeless effort to retain a fraction of their previous year's conquests. Tolbukhin continued to press on the Melitopol line.

The successful establishment of bridge-heads across the Dnieper excited surprise and speculations as to Russian intentions, for the pause had been so short that it seemed impossible that the Russians could be making a serious attempt to force such a formidable obstacle. The river is one of the largest in Europe and its high western bank, strongly fortified by the Germans, dominates the low and marshy east shore. Furthermore, the Germans had

good railway communications and it seemed certain that they could without much difficulty concentrate an overwhelming force for counter-attack long before the Russians could establish a firm footing, much less exploit success.

The Germans may have been over-confident in the strength of the position and, in the first instance, employed local reserves of inadequate strength to counter-attack, to avoid disturbing the dispositions of their main formations and **Russians Achieve Complete Surprise** the processes of re-equipment and reorganization which must have been going on. Only in the neighbourhood of Kiev, where no doubt they had considerable forces, was a determined attempt made to eliminate the Russian bridge-head. But the Russians here and elsewhere had chosen what seemed to be the most unlikely places for a crossing and therefore found them lightly held. Surprise was complete; and guerilla troops on the west bank gave much assistance in consolidating bridge-heads—guiding the regular troops through marshy country.

KREMENCHUG FREED FROM THE GERMANS

On September 29, 1943, after three days' fierce fighting, troops of General Koniev's army, under Generals Zhadov, Mangarov, and Grinov, took by storm Kremenchug, one of the few large towns on the east bank of the Dnieper, and an important railway junction. The victory was saluted in Moscow by 12 salvoes fired from 124 guns. Here, women and children of the freed city talk with Lieut.-Col. Andreiko of the 214th Rifle Division.
Photo, Pictorial Press

GERMAN 'TIGER' TANK IN WHITE RUSSIA

The 'Tiger' (Mark VI) tank made its first appearance in Tunisia (see illus., p. 2620). Here is one on the Nevel front during the autumn of 1943. The 'Tiger' was 11 ft. 8 ins. in width, with tracks 28½ ins. wide—exceptional widths necessary to take the great weight of the tank (variously estimated at 58 to 62 tons), and to counterbalance the length of the 88-mm. gun. In the four months beginning July 5, 1943, the Red Army disabled or destroyed 800 'Tigers,' and captured 204.

Photo, New York Times

The Russians had by now acquired much experience in the crossing of rivers, and they relied less on elaborate equipment and preparation than on

'Impossible' Dnieper Crossings

improvisation and the initiative and courage of the troops. Here is how Colonel Vassiliev of the Red Army, after describing the formidable nature of the Dnieper obstacle and the strength of the German defences, explains the success of one of the crossings : " The Soviet Commander [presumably Vatutin] deliberately chose places where the Germans thought a crossing was out of the question and so had contented themselves with comparatively weak defences. According to all the rules, the area south of Pereyaslavl was unsuitable in the extreme. It was swampy and thoroughly inconvenient. It was just there that the Red Army crossed with the invaluable aid of the local guerillas. The bridge-heads are being enlarged day by day. The Germans are resisting viciously but they have only losses to show for it." And here,

in a condensed form, is a more picturesque account of the crossing north of Kiev, given by a Russian front-line correspondent : " No one could sleep that night waiting by the Dnieper north of Kiev—the moon glittered on the water and the high right bank was clearly visible with its trees and German defence works—then barges, fishing boats, all kinds of craft pushed off from the bank. There were rafts made of old German petrol barrels, planks, lumber and fences. The Germans did not notice a thing till the men were half-way across. Then all their guns thundered into action. The Soviet artillery replied with terrific power, and the men on the boats and rafts opened up with small arms. More and more flotillas pushed off, spreading out so that the enemy could not judge the main points of landing. Savage fighting broke out as the vanguards landed. One enemy garrison surrounded in a small village was resisting furiously, when suddenly machine-gun fire crackled behind them. The Red Army men did not know who their allies were. It

was the guerillas who had been operating on the west bank. Guns were soon brought over on rafts under heavy fire, and when pontoon bridges were thrown across reinforcements poured over faster and faster. The German reserves counter-attacked and the Luftwaffe came into action, but failed to recover ground or to stop the flow of troops across the river. Some units crossed without a pause after long marches."

The crossing at Kremenchug was made in much the same manner. Surprise was no doubt the main factor which contributed to success, but it was psychological rather than tactical surprise, due to the German belief that a crossing could not be attempted without long and elaborate preparations.

Although bridge-heads had been established it was obvious that, even if they could be retained, they would not form bases for large-scale operations until they had been extended and bridges on an adequate scale had been constructed. For a time, therefore, little was heard of what was happening beyond reports of heavy fighting in the Kiev bridge-head. Interest centred on Tolbukhin's attacks on the Melitopol line, and on Zaporozhe, situated on the

Heavy Fighting in Kiev Bridge-head

east bank of the river, where Malinovsky was also attacking. Their efforts achieved remarkable success. On October 13 Tolbukhin gained a foothold in Melitopol and stubborn street fighting began. Next day the railway connexion with the Crimea was cut—this in spite of the fact that the Germans had reinforced that front with three divisions from the Crimea; and by a brilliant tank attack, supported by a great weight of artillery, Malinovsky broke through the powerful defences of Zaporozhe. Exploiting this success rapidly he drove the garrison across the river with heavy losses, many being shot or drowned in a panic attempt to reach the west bank. The anchors of the Melitopol line were thus beginning to drag; but there was still holding ground in the marshy country near the Dnieper and about Melitopol itself; and of this the Germans were making desperate efforts to take advantage.

Then, on October 17, came the astonishing news that Koniev's Army after two days' hard fighting, had broken through the German defences sealing the Kremenchug bridge-head, and had advanced to a depth of 18½ miles

RUSSIAN GUNNERS IN ACTION

'Battles of annihilation' took place for every house in the eleven days of bloody street fighting which preceded the recapture of Melitopol by Soviet troops under General Feodor Tolbukhin on October 23, 1943. In Melitopol the Germans lost their most important strategic position east of the Lower Dnieper. Here is a gun crew which helped in its capture. *Photo, Pictorial Press*

RUSSIAN ADVANCE IN THE AUTUMN OF 1943

The summer offensive of 1943 brought the Red Army to the eastern bank of the Middle Dnieper. With a pause of only a week or two at the end of September, they forced the river at a number of points and continued their advance. The broken line in the map indicates the Russian position at the close of September, the dotted line shows it at the end of the year. *By courtesy of The Times*

on a 28-mile front. Less immediately important, the Russians had also established a bridge-head across the upper Dnieper south of Gomel.

During the following week the Kremenchug thrust continued to make rapid progress, cutting the important lateral railway between Dnepropetrovsk and

Kiev at Pyatikhat. It was clear that this thrust was directed at the great iron mining and railway centre of Krivoi Rog, immensely important to the Germans both for strategical communications and as a source of raw material for war industries. If Krivoi Rog were recaptured, the thrust threatened to outflank the Germans in the Dnieper bend and therefore also those holding the Melitopol line. The Germans naturally reacted violently, for this was a threat that could not be met by passive defence. Reserves were rushed up, and while the Krivoi Rog area was stubbornly defended, a series of powerful counter-attacks were delivered, chiefly to the north-west of the city, against the Russian western flank. The Russians had made an amazingly bold move which seemed almost to invite defeat; but as always they displayed an immense capacity to turn from the offensive to the defensive. They were not to reach Krivoi Rog for many weeks, but they held their gains and, equally important, they had drawn many German reserves to the threatened point and forced them to fight at a time when they were probably greatly needing rest and reorganization.

Meanwhile Tolbukhin was redoubling his pressure on the Melitopol line, and on October 23 an Order of the Day announced the capture of the town. Then on the 25th Malinovsky came into the picture by capturing Dnepropetrovsk. Koniev's left flank had made considerable progress towards the city, thrusting south-east from his Kremenchug salient, but it was not until Malinovsky effected a surprise crossing of the Dnieper in the rear of the Germans opposing Koniev that a rapid capture of the city became possible. The crossing of the river where it was exceptionally wide and elaborately fortified was another astonishing feat and a masterly conception based on admirable co-ordination of effort.

These were shattering blows to the Germans, and the complete disruption of the Melitopol line after the recapture of that city was irretrievable; for although the line formed an integral part of the Dnieper position, it was separated from it by a bridgeless river, denying lateral communication. The German Sixth Army, reconstituted after Stalingrad, had been responsible for this sector, and now it was in full retreat with no easy escape outlet, and with indifferent communications. Tolbukhin's armour and cavalry pursued it relentlessly, driving part of it back against the swamps of the lower Dnieper where some found temporary refuge in the bridge-head the Germans had established opposite Nikopol, and part towards the Dnieper estuary at Kherson where there was an adequate ferry service.

Synchronously Tolbukhin's left swept along the shores of the Siwash swamps at the western end of the Sea of Azov, cutting off the whole of the Crimea and establishing a firm grip of the Perekop isthmus. **Tolbukhin Isolates the Crimea** It was a complete disaster, for the German Sixth Army was for a second time almost annihilated, suffering immense losses of men and material. Only at the bridge-heads of Nikopol and Kherson did the Germans, assisted by marshy surroundings, succeed in making a stand. The isolation of the Crimea was complete and the Russians, by-passing the Kherson bridge-head, were also able to command the entrance to the Dnieper and Bug estuaries with their guns. It seemed possible that the Russians would now attempt the capture of the Crimea, for by November 1 they had penetrated up to the "Tartar Wall," a huge ditch and rampart six miles long and 50 yards deep dug across the Perekop isthmus in the 15th century, and had captured Armyansk. Five days later they effected landings on the Kerch peninsula. Wisely, however, the Russians were satisfied for the time being to have deprived a large enemy

CELEBRATING THE CLEARANCE OF THE KUBAN

On October 9, 1943, the Kuban was finally cleared by Soviet troops under the command of Marshal Timoshenko, who was awarded the Order of Suvorov. The Germans and Rumanians lost over 20,000 killed and 3,000 prisoners in the last stages of the battle. Above, men of the 227th Temryuk Division celebrate the liberation of the Kuban as Moscow fires victory salvoes for the same occasion. Below, German troops and equipment retreating across the Kerch Straits by Siebel ferry, which made 2,000 trips. *Photos, Pictorial Press ; Associated Press*

RAVENS CIRCLE ABOVE THE GOMEL BATTLEFIELD

Autumn rains turned the roads into quagmires during the last weeks of General Rokossovsky's advance on the Germans' 'hedgehog' position of Gomel, which was occupied by the Red Army on November 26, 1943. Gomel, one of the most important industrial centres of White Russia, had been in enemy hands for 27 months. Above, the desolate battlefield after the capture of the city. Below, Major Tsybulsky reads Stalin's Order of the Day announcing the victory.

force of almost all offensive power. To annihilate it might have entailed costly operations without certainty of rapid success; but it could easily be contained without much diversion of troops from the main operations in course of development. It was therefore left to be dealt with at a more convenient moment.

While the Krivoi Rog and Melitopol operations were engaging attention, heavy fighting had continued in the Kiev region, but the situation remained obscure.

Kiev, Capital of Ukraine, Recaptured

The Germans made many counter-attacks, but they had achieved no great success. Possibly the Krivoi Rog battles had limited their available reserves. Then suddenly on November 6, the eve of the twenty-sixth anniversary of the October Revolution, an Order of the Day addressed to General Vatutin announced the capture by storm of Kiev, capital of the Ukraine, following a brilliant outflanking movement from the north—a success of incalculable value in view of the political and strategic importance of the city. Few events could have contributed so greatly to the heightening of Russian morale. Moreover, the capture of this great centre of railway communications opened the way for the development of the winter campaign against the whole German force in the Ukraine.

But Vatutin was not content to wait for winter. He had heavily defeated the Germans opposed to him, and without hesitation he proceeded to exploit his success, not merely in order to enlarge his bridge-head but to strike at German communications, both those connecting Von Manstein's southern armies with the armies north of the Pripet marshes and those leading direct back into Poland. Striking westwards and south-westwards at great speed, he captured Fastov to the south-west, from which direction Von Manstein's counter-attacks were certain first to develop. But having thus secured his left flank with great daring, he continued to push westwards, meeting only feeble opposi-

tion, and on November 13 he captured Zhitomir, 80 miles west of Kiev, thereby cutting the railway running north across the Pripet through Mozyr. Extending his right next day, he captured the railway junction of Korosten (the town itself was captured on the 18th).

By these operations Vatutin had formed a wide and deep salient, containing two main railways leading westwards and well protected on its right by the Pripet marshes. Moreover, the salient might evidently form the base for a further thrust south-westwards towards the Odessa–Lvov railway, the main line of communication between the armies in the Ukraine and Germany.

It was an amazing feat, all the more so because autumn rains had now set in, hampering movements—especially of

the mechanized vehicles on which Vatutin relied both for supplies and striking power. A conspicuous part of the latter, however, was provided by his cavalry. As was to be expected, Von Manstein reacted swiftly, counter-attacking first at Fastov with such reserves as he had immediately available and with troops that had rallied after being driven out of Kiev. These counter-attacks delivered before Vatutin had reached Zhitomir would, if successful, have cut into the base of the salient and might have recovered Kiev; but they were repelled by Vatutin's flank guard. Von Manstein then shifted the weight of his counter-attacks to the west, striking at the head of the salient where he may have hoped to find the Russians disorganized by their rapid advance. Also,

2923

MOBILE ROCKET GUNS

Ten-barrelled, self-propelled rocket guns—
called by the Germans 'Panzer-spitters'—
were used on the Russian front in 1943. They
projected smoke, incendiary, and explosive
bombs simultaneously. Here are some of
these formidable weapons being prepared for
action. Left, loading a self-propelled rocket
gun. *Photos, Keystone; Associated Press*

the railway communications in the
Zhitomir area enabled him rapidly to
assemble his reserves, not only from
the Ukraine but also from Poland. An
assemblage of reserves in that area
provided maximum protection for the
Odessa–Lvov railway.

Von Manstein opened his counter-
attacks from the south-east in the
Zhitomir area before the Russians had
actually captured the town, and there
was heavy fighting. **Von Manstein**
At first the counter- **Counter-**
attacks were held, but **attacks**
Von Manstein was
constantly receiving reinforcements,
especially of Panzer Divisions, and,
extending his front westwards and northwards, compelled the Russians to
evacuate Zhitomir on November 19, and
Korosten on November 30. He never
reached Ovruch, farther north on the
Mozyr line, and thus failed to reopen
lateral communication across the
marshes. In all this period there had
been intense fighting with heavy losses
on both sides, but Vatutin fought a
magnificent defensive battle in which
his artillery took heavy toll of Von
Manstein's Panzer Divisions, compelling
him to pause at intervals for fresh reinforcements and preventing him from
making anything in the nature of a
break-through. Nevertheless, Vatutin
had to give ground, falling back in places
as much as 30 miles.

To the outside world, Vatutin's position appeared very critical as Von

FIRE RAGES IN DISPUTED ZHITOMIR

Fierce battles, described in Moscow as of Stalingrad ferocity, raged in the Kiev salient, where Von Manstein staged a strong counter-offensive in November 1943, launching wave after wave of attacks with massive tank and infantry forces and compelling the Russians, despite heroic resistance, to retreat—in some places up to 30 miles. But withdrawal ceased on December 15, and on Christmas Eve Vatutin took the offensive once more. Zhitomir (above), recaptured by the 1st Ukrainian Army on November 13, and lost again on the 19th, was finally taken by storm on December 31. Below, heavy German self-propelled guns near Berdichev, which town, 30 miles S.S.W. of Zhitomir, was retaken by the Russians on January 5, 1944.   *Photos, Associated Press*

KIEV—CAPITAL OF THE UKRAINE—IN RUSSIAN HANDS AGAIN

On November 6, 1943, troops of the 1st Ukrainian Army, by a swift and bold outflanking attack, carried by assault Kiev, capital of the Ukraine, a most important industrial centre on the right bank of the Dnieper, and a strong focus point of German resistance. 1. The city from the east bank of the river. 2. Tanks and infantry go in to the attack as the Russian assault on Kiev begins. 3. General Vatutin (right) Commander of the 1st Ukrainian Army, with Maj.-Gen. Osetrov, looks over the terrain on the eve of the battle. 4. Russian armour rumbles through Kiev.

Manstein's counter-attacks assumed increasingly the character of a major counter-offensive. It was suggested that Vatutin had been over-bold, and even that the Germans had deliberately lured him into a trap. But the fact that Von Manstein had frequently to pause to regain strength and that the forces that he was employing, though powerful, fell far short of those employed in the Kursk offensive, made it probable that his counter-stroke had essentially a defensive purpose—the elimination of the threat to his main communications. He no doubt hoped to defeat Vatutin heavily, but failure of his counter-attacks at Fastov made it improbable that he would be able to pinch out entirely the threatening Kiev Russian salient. The recapture of Korosten was the last notable success Von Manstein achieved, and although he continued to attack east of Korosten and south-east of Zhitomir, it became evident by the middle of December that his effort had exhausted itself.

While the battle in the Kiev salient was in progress, the Russians in the other sections of the front maintained the

Russians Recapture Gomel

offensive pressure preparatory to the main winter operations. North of the Pripet marshes, Rokossovsky continued his operations for the encirclement of Gomel. In touch with Vatutin's Army on his left, he had gained ground across the Dnieper from the mouth of the Pripet up to and beyond the mouth of the Sozh. The Gomel–Pinsk railway which crosses the Dnieper at Rezhitsa, a strongly fortified hedgehog centre, still, however, remained open. Swinging northward, Rokossovsky attacked Rez-

FIELD-MARSHAL VON MANSTEIN INSPECTS HIS MEN.
Field-Marshal Erich von Manstein, here seen with troops in camouflage smocks on the Cherkassy sector, commanded two German army groups on the Dnieper front in the autumn of 1943. He was responsible for the only serious setback the Russians suffered during their autumn offensive when, on November 17, he struck hard at the Soviet flank in the Zhitomir-Fastov region with 150,000 men and hundreds of tanks (see opposite page). *Photo, Planet News*

hitsa from the west, capturing it on November 18, after three days of fierce assault. Gomel was now almost surrounded, only a narrow avenue of escape for its defenders being left, along the railway to Zhlobin and Bobruisk; but this line ran through difficult marshy country and was well defended, and the greater part of the garrison escaped before the Russians captured Gomel by assault on November 26. Nevertheless, the capture of this great railway centre provided an invaluable advanced base for future operations.

In the Dnieper bend, although heavy fighting continued about Krivoi Rog and thence to the river opposite Zaporozhe, nothing spectacular was achieved, the Germans evidently being determined at all costs to hold a defensive front

covering the Nikopol–Krivoi Rog railway which served the manganese mines of Nikopol, so essential to German war industries.

There can be no doubt, however, that Russian pressure on this front contained German reserve divisions which Von Manstein badly needed for his attacks on the Kiev salient. Koniev was also exert-

Fighting in the Dnieper Bend

ing pressure from the northern flank of his Kremenchug bridge-head, and on December 10 took Znamenka, thus severing direct railway communication between Von Manstein's Krivoi Rog group and his armies farther north. On December 14 Koniev, having previously established a bridge-head down stream of the town, captured the important German stronghold of Cherkassy where the Gomel–Odessa railway crosses the Dnieper.

The autumn offensive had been prolonged by an abnormally mild and wet season to the end of December. The weather had made operations difficult, but much had been accomplished towards preparing the way for the more ambitious winter offensive, and that despite the fact that the Germans possessed good railway communications, while those of the Russians were still to be restored. Ever since April work on restoration had been intensified and a state of emergency had been proclaimed on all Soviet railways with a view to heightening the individual worker's sense of responsibility and discipline. "Pravda" rightly claimed that the railways were the right hand of the Red Army and contributed not a little to its successes by assuring the movement of military supplies to the front line.

GERMAN TRANSPORT TROUBLES IN THE PRIPET MARSHES
Among the treacherous, boggy quagmires of the Pripet marshes, which cover an area of some 10,000 square miles, armoured operations were almost impossible, and all military movement was difficult. But the sandy hills of the district are covered in forest—the haunt of guerillas—and the Germans cut down much timber, both to provide materials for light, horse-operated 'railways' such as that shown, and also to reduce the guerillas' cover. *Photo, Planet News*

Chapter 292

SOVIET RUSSIA BEGINS TO REBUILD

Developments in the U.S.S.R. during 1943 reflected the greater confidence felt by the people, and their nearer vision of victory, after the great battles of the autumn and winter of 1942–43, culminating in the overwhelming German disaster at Stalingrad. This Chapter, like Chapter 253 which described Soviet home affairs in 1942, is contributed by Mr. Andrew Rothstein, correspondent of Tass, the official Soviet news agency

As in 1942, war needs continued to dominate Russia's economic activities in the momentous year 1943. But the liberation of immense areas of Soviet territory from enemy occupation, and the need to resettle its citizens, meant that their domestic needs had to play some part in production programmes. The process of rebuilding the economic life of the Soviet Union had begun.

On March 20 the Government published its agricultural plan for the year, entailing an increase of sixteen million acres tillage compared with 1942 (it was overfulfilled by the year's end). On April 15 an edict of the Supreme Soviet placed the railways under military law. All war industries heavily overfulfilled their year's plan—among them iron by 28 per cent, steel 17 per cent, machine tools 160 per cent.

But the most striking economic achievements were in the sphere of reconstruction of the liberated areas. Soviet individual initiative and civic solidarity found full scope in this immense work. A visitor to ravaged Mozhaisk on January 20 reported that in twelve months since its liberation over 2,000 new houses had been built, with many new schools, a new town theatre, etc. In the Smolensk region (stated a report to the regional Soviet in March) 3,725 houses were built in a year, hundreds of collective dairy and poultry farms organized, paper, motor, glass and clothing factories restarted.

An outstanding feature of similar reports from all over the country was the nation wide collection of gifts in kind for the stricken districts. Thus, Novosibirsk region presented Kharkov with 240 tractors and 236 ploughs; Irkutsk collective farmers contributed 12,000 head of cattle and 180 tons of seed grain to a "fund of fraternal aid," etc. (see illus., page 2717). Particularly lavish was the help that poured into the hero-city of Stalingrad after its liberation—100,000 textbooks from school-children of other towns, carloads of window glass from a Gus-Khrustalny glassworks, millions of roubles' worth of clothes from the great textile centre of Ivanovo, tens of thou-

Gifts in Kind for Stricken Districts

sands of volunteers for building work from all over the U.S.S.R. Factories, mines and steelworks came to life again all over the liberated areas in an astonishingly short time.

An historic decree on August 22 laid down, probably for the first time in history, a precise programme for the rehabilitation of agriculture, housing, education and communal services for a huge area covering ten regions and territories—providing what factories for building materials were to be erected, and where; how many sheep, cows and other livestock were to be brought back from the east to each region; what government departments were to provide equipment, what districts seed-corn, and so on. The report on the fulfilment of this plan by January 1, 1944, showed remarkable results :

	Plan	Fulfilled
Cattle, sheep and horses (head):		
To be returned from the East	5 1,526	630,830
To be purchased (from collective and State farms elsewhere)	200,000	250,613
Poultry for collective farmers (from State farms)	500,000	516,853
Winter crop seed-grain (tons)	55,000	96,324
Repair shops and factories for State machine and tractor depots	440	975
Houses repaired or built	—	326,000
Persons housed (from dugouts and ruins)..	—	1,814,000
Railways : Stations built	122	122
Linesmen's barracks	1,157	1,399
Children : Military and industrial schools	32	32
Reception centres	29	36

AMBASSADOR TO BRITAIN
On July 27, 1943, Moscow announced that M. Ivan Maisky, Soviet Ambassador to Britain since 1932, had been appointed a Vice-Commissar for Foreign Affairs. Five days later M. Feodor Gusev (above), Soviet Minister to Canada since October 1942, was named as Maisky's successor. Aged 39, M. Gusev had made a special study of British institutions. *Photo, Pictorial Press*

As in 1942, an important part in achieving these results fell to voluntary production drives known as Socialist emulation. By these methods a famous artillery works celebrated Red Army Day by producing above its programme enough guns to equip ten regiments and three tank brigades. In March, engineering workers made 20,000 suggestions for technical improvements in production, of which 8,000 were adopted. To celebrate May Day, No. 1 Aircraft Factory produced a second flight of Stormoviks above its programme, and the Baku oilfield turned out 8,000 tons instead of 2,500. In July 1943 a letter to Stalin from 1,502,000 workers of the Sverdlovsk region announced that, in the first half of the year, they had doubled electric power output compared with 1942, doubled iron ore smelted and trebled coal output compared with 1941, and produced ten times as much manganese ore as in the first half of 1940. In November, in view of grave shortage of skilled labour for the liberated areas and for new factories, a national movement began for doing without more skilled workers, while increasing output. Thus, the great Kuznetsk and Magnitogorsk centres of heavy industry undertook (at mass meetings) to produce 130,000 tons of

Socialist Emulation Drives

NEWS OF THE WAR REACHES UZBEKISTAN

The Muslim women of the Uzbek Socialist Soviet Republic (once the land of Tamerlane), unveiled since the coming of the Soviet regime, worked increasingly in the fields as their men were called for war service. Here a group of women field workers listens attentively to the war news read out to them at the dinner hour by their brigade leader.

Photo, Pictorial Press

pig-iron and 30,000 tons of steel in the last quarter of 1943, without asking for more workers ; Tank Factory 183 cancelled its application for 800 more workers ; Aircraft Works 24 did the same in respect of 500 workers, and so on.

Inspiration for a great part of this campaign came from the matchless story of Leningrad's fortitude in conditions of famine, cold, and 24 months' continuous shell-fire. In the icy winter

Leningrad's Matchless Fortitude

of 1941–42, when lighting, central heating and water supply had all been interrupted by German bombardment from Finnish-occupied territory, and water had to be brought from iceholes in the river, the citizen received five ozs. of bread and two glasses of hot water per day. Tens of thousands died. Although skeleton communications over Lake Ladoga were reopened in 1942, the citizens in September were still having to pull wooden houses to pieces to provide the city's fuel for the winter of 1942–43. The curators of the famous Hermitage Museum fell back for heating and light upon a power cable laid from a warship in the river Neva. By March 1943 the bread ration had been increased—20 ozs. for manual workers, 18 ozs. for office workers, and 14 ozs. for

NEW STATION ON MOSCOW'S UNDERGROUND

Pressure by war workers on Moscow's transport led to the extension of the underground railway, a new part of which was opened in the spring of 1943. Here is the first train, decorated with a portrait of Marshal Stalin, at the Stalin Plant station. Building and rebuilding of houses, factories, farms, and installations took place progressively as more and more of Russia was freed from the enemy.

Photo, U.S.S.R. Official

MOSCOW'S GUNS FIRE A VICTORY SALVO FOR KHARKOV

'At midnight tonight Moscow will honour our valiant troops who liberated Orel and Byelgorod by 12 artillery salvoes from 120 guns,' said Marshal Stalin in an Order of the Day broadcast on August 5, 1943. That was the first such salute. A year later 147 had been fired—though after the Kharkov salute of August 23 (shown above) tracer bullets were not used : they had fallen on the enthusiastic crowds, a small section of whom are seen in the bottom picture. Below, inhabitants of Kharkov study the news after liberation. *Photos, U.S.S.R. Official ; Pictorial Press*

members of their families, and little else—but incredibly difficult conditions still prevailed. Worst of all, perhaps, was what the famous Leningrad writer Nikolai Tikhonov called the "tiresome, methodical cruelty" of the German-Finnish bombardment—sometimes at dawn, sometimes midday, sometimes in the evening—trying "to turn the life of every Leningrad citizen into a bloody lottery, so that everyone going to work, or shopping, or to the theatre, should feel that he may never return again, so that fear and death should accompany him at each step and at every moment. . . ."

Nevertheless, the cultural life of the city went on. Exhibitions of paintings ; crowded lectures on the great national poets of the Asiatic republics, Nizami and Navoi ; repairs to wrecked theatres ; Saturday evening dances at workers' clubs in the summer, skating and ice hockey in the winter ; concerts and dramatic performances by the best Soviet artists, who flew in over the German lines—these and similar events showed what sort of people were the people of Leningrad.

Cultural Life Went on in Leningrad

As for the rest of the Soviet Union a mere catalogue must suffice. A Chaikovsky Music Festival in Moscow, and a "Britain at War" Exhibition, opened with the aid of the British Embassy (January) ; book collections all over the U.S.S.R. for Stalingrad, and 1,600,000 contestants in nation-wide ski races (February) ; over 500 scientists, inventors, writers, painters, sculptors, actors, cameramen and musicians awarded Stalin prizes (March) ; 50,000 copies of "Ballads and Songs of the British People" sold out in a few days, and 400,000 paying their last tribute at the bier of Nemirovich-Danchenko, founder of the world-famous Moscow Art Theatre (April) ; yet another branch of the Academy of Sciences opened in a formerly illiterate, backward area—this time Soviet Kirghizia (May) ; the first volume of a scholarly "History of English Literature" in four volumes (July) ; and many more notable occasions showed the variety and continued growth of Soviet culture. Two important changes in the Soviet educational system in 1943 must be recorded —the introduction of military subjects into the school curriculum (January), and the abolition of co-education in secondary schools, to provide greater differentiation in the teaching of boys and girls between the ages of 12 to 18 (October).

To turn to general affairs, the Extraordinary State Commission on German Atrocities published on April 6 the first

WITH GUN AND CAMERA ON THE DNIEPER FRONT

After the infantry, the artillery: here is a Russian field gun being dragged up the steep west bank of the Dnieper after it has been brought across the wide river by raft. The Russians, who used mounted cavalry with success in the Caucasus battles, also, it will be noted, sometimes used horses to haul their guns. Left, machine-gunner and cine-cameraman shelter behind an armoured car as they both cover the retreating Germans following the Russian reconquest of the west bank of the Dnieper in the autumn of 1943.

Photos, Pictorial Press;
Planet News

SOVIET WAR INDUSTRY IN THE URAL MOUNTAINS

When Russia was invaded by Germany in 1941, roughly half her heavy industry lay in the Ukraine. Loss of that area was made good by the rapid intensification of the movement of industry eastward to the Volga, the Urals and Soviet Central Asia, begun with the First Five-Year Plan. New cities and old centres had been growing quickly, and a mass planned evacuation of plant and workers was carried out before the German advance. The Urals became the centre of tank, gun and aircraft production. Above, guns leaving a factory in the Urals for the front. Below, a tank damaged on the battlefield undergoes repair in a Ural workshop.

Photos, Pictorial Press

LENINGRAD UNDER GERMAN BOMBARDMENT

Life went on in Leningrad, besieged for two years and not finally liberated until January 27, 1944, despite daily shelling by the Germans who delivered one of their heaviest bombardments of the city on Christmas Eve, 1943, when they shelled it for seven hours with 170-mm., 210-mm., 240-mm., and 305-mm. guns. Above, boys fishing in the Neva opposite St. Isaac's Cathedral in July 1943. Right, Metropolitan Alexei wearing the medal awarded on October 17 to him and other clergy for their part in the defence of Leningrad. Below, repairing street damage done by German shells.

Photos, U.S.S.R. Official ; Pictorial Press

BRITISH 'ACK-ACK' UNIT SHOWS ITS PACES TO AMERICA

On August 31, 1943, the men of a British anti-aircraft unit marched through New York from Battery Park up Broadway to City Hall. Next day they drilled and carried out a demonstration of various types of anti-aircraft gun at Teaneck Armory, New Jersey, before an audience that included officers of the U.S. Army and Navy, and U.S. government officials. Here they are parading in front of the old City Hall of New York. Mayor La Guardia (in mufti) stands in the centre of the platform between the British and American flags.

Photo, Fox

of a series of horrifying reports of German cruelties, involving the massacre, torturing, starvation and freezing to death of hundreds of thousands of Soviet citizens. Vyazma, Orel, Krasnodar, Kharkov, Rostov and many other important centres were the scenes of these ghastly deeds attested by the evidence of scores of medical witnesses, civic officials and survivors, supported by photographs of "mass graves."

The first trial of war criminals took place in public at Kharkov before a **First Trial of War Criminals** Soviet Military Tribunal on December 15–18. Nine Germans and a Russian traitor were indicted, accused of complicity in the asphyxiation of thousands of Soviet citizens by carbon monoxide gas, in specially equipped "murder vans," mass extermination of old people, women and children, brutal treatment and murder of Soviet war prisoners, and the deliberate destruction of towns and villages. Three Germans and the Russian were in Soviet hands. All four, who were represented by counsel, pleaded guilty. All were found guilty and sentenced to death by hanging, a sentence carried out in the city square of Kharkov on December 19 in the presence of a crowd estimated at 50,000 people.

At the third meeting of the All-Slav Committee held in Moscow on May 9 there were present, for the first time, by the side of leading representatives of Soviet civil, military and ecclesiastical society, the commanders of Polish

MEMORIAL TO THE POLES AT KATYN

In April 1943 the Germans accused the Russians of murdering 10,000 Polish officers at Katyn. A Soviet commission, set up after the freeing of the area, declared on January 26, 1944, that these men, prisoners of war left behind when the Russians retreated in 1941, had been murdered by the method used by the Germans against Soviet citizens in Orel, Voronezh, and elsewhere: namely, a pistol shot in the nape of the neck. Here is the memorial placed by the Russians over the common grave of the unfortunate Polish prisoners.

and Czechoslovak—brother Slav—units fighting on the territory of the U.S.S.R. A Czech officer, Lt. Yarosh, was the first foreign officer to receive (posthumously) the title of Hero of the Soviet Union. The First Polish Kosciusko Division, formed in Russia in May 1943 to fight on the Soviet front, went into action for the first time on the Dnieper front on October 12, and succeeded in forcing the river. It was awarded a series of decorations for valour on

November 15. (*See* illus., p. 2588.)

On May 22, the Executive Committee of the Communist International announced its proposal to the constituent parties that the Communist International should be dissolved; a decision which was ratified by the national sections and put into effect on June 10. Stalin described this step as one which cleared the way for the "future organization of a companionship of nations." **Comintern Dissolved**

A delegation of the British Trades Union Congress, led by Sir Walter Citrine, arrived in Moscow on June 23, and spent a month visiting Soviet factories and holding joint sessions with Soviet trade unionists. One important decision was to foster direct contacts between individual British and Soviet trade unions.

The formation of a Free Germany National Committee, with the object of stimulating a national revolt against Hitler in Germany, by a conference of German war prisoners, anti-Fascist political emigrants, literary men and trade unionists, was announced on July 21, and on September 14; following a conference of German officer-prisoners from five camps, representatives of the Union they set up were admitted to the Free Germany National Committee.

Four grades of rank in the Red Army —Red soldiers, sergeants, officers and generals—were established by new regulations on July 29.

An article published in "Izvestia" on November 18 aroused international

WAR CRIMINALS HANGED AT KHARKOV

The first war criminals to be tried were brought before a Soviet Military Tribunal at Kharkov on December 15, 1943. Nine Germans and a Russian were indicted, of whom three Germans and the Russian were before the court. Found guilty of mass extermination of civilians in gas 'murder vans,' they were condemned to be hanged publicly—a sentence carried out in the city square of Kharkov on December 19. *Photos, Pictorial Press*

AT THE STALIN AUTOMOBILE WORKS IN THE URAL MOUNTAINS

Among the big factories set up in the Urals following the Russian retreat in 1941 was the Stalin Automobile Works. Building of this factory began in the winter of 1941–42 ; production started in 1944.   1. Fitting pistons on the assembly line.   2. Final inspection of trucks before they are dispatched.   3. The Stalin Automobile Works and the beautiful country surrounding them.   Other photographs of wartime industrial development in the Urals will be found in page 2932.   *Photos, Pictorial Press*

SOVIET'S OWN ANTHEM

The adoption of a national anthem by the U.S.S.R. (in place of 'The International,' which had been used by Russia since the Revolution instead of a national song) was announced in Moscow on December 19, 1943. The opening bars of its music are shown here. The first verse runs:

'An indestructible union of free republics
Great Russia has forged for ever.
Long live the Soviet Union, united and mighty,
Formed through the will of its peoples.'

On December 19 Moscow radio announced that "The International" would no longer be the Soviet anthem, as it does not reflect "the basic changes that have taken place in our country as a result of the success of the Soviet system, and does not express the Socialist nature of the Soviet State." A new national anthem, "corresponding in spirit and in word with the Soviet system," came into use on March 15, 1944.

A series of statements by Stalin gave the key to the thoughts and aspirations of the Soviet people during the year. In his Order of the Day on the 25th Anniversary of the Red Army (February 23), Stalin again underlined that, in the absence of a second front in Europe, the Red Army was bearing the whole burden of the war; but pointed out that, while Germany was becoming more exhausted, the Soviet Union was becoming stronger, both in war industry and in the seasoning of its Red Army. In another Order of the Day on May 1 he paid tribute to the Allied victories in North Africa, and the shattering air blows of the R.A.F. and U.S.A.A.F., declaring: "Thus for the first time since the beginning of the war the blow at the enemy from the East, dealt by the Red Army, merged with the blow from the West, dealt by the troops of our Allies, into one joint blow."

After a series of purely military Orders of the Day in the second half of the year, regarding the great Soviet victories which liberated an area of over 130,000 square miles inhabited by

NEW SOVIET STAMP

To celebrate the alliance of the United Kingdom, the United States, and the Union of Soviet Socialist Republics in their fight against Germany, the People's Commissariat of Postal and Electrical Communications of the U.S.S.R. issued a series of postage stamps. Here is the three rouble stamp, which carries the flags of the three Allies and the inscription, 'Hail Victory, Anglo-Soviet-American alliance! Stalin.'

35,000,000 people, Stalin on November 6 summed up the lessons of the war in a speech in which he noted that the Soviet State now had an efficient and rapidly expanding war economy; that successes in industry, transport and agriculture were primarily due to the establishment

interest; it denounced schemes for "federations" in Europe in the immediate post-war period, declaring that the various countries must be allowed to settle down to their new national life before such schemes could be other than harmful.

'FRIENDSHIP OF THE PEOPLES OF THE U.S.S.R.'

This composite painting by T. Gaponenko, O. Odintsov and D. Shmarinov—displayed at an exhibition in the Tretyakov State Gallery in Moscow dedicated to the 'Great Patriotic War'—symbolizes the friendship, strengthened by common suffering and common effort in the war against Germany, that bound together the many and highly various peoples of the Soviet Union. Types of Soviet citizen from north and south, east and west, with a shadowy figure of Lenin on a pedestal watching over all, figure in this allegorical work. *Photos, U.S.S.R. Official*

STALINGRAD RISES AGAIN

When the Battle of Stalingrad ended on February 2, 1943, after 23 weeks of the bitterest fighting known to history, the great new industrial city was a hideous desolation of rubble and ruin. But rebuilding began at once. 1. Women of Stalingrad clearing away wreckage. 2. The west bank of the Volga at Stalingrad, once more alive : the archway marks the limit of retreat of the troops commanded by Lt.-Gen. Chuykov. 3. An invitation to a football match beside a marble tablet commemorating the spot where the last shot in the great siege was fired. 4. Preparing to repair a damaged building.

2 ФЕВРАЛЯ 1943 ГОДА
ЧАСТЯМИ 226 СД В
СОСТАВЕ 66 АРМИИ
СТЗ
БЫЛ ОЧИЩЕН
ОТ НЕМЕЦКИХ ЗАХВАТЧИКОВ

ФУТБОЛЬНЫЙ МАТЧ

of the Soviet system 26 years before; that while Allied unity had been consolidated, the cause of German Fascism was lost and its sanguinary "New Order" was approaching collapse. The liberation of the European peoples, the restoration of their full national sovereignty, the punishment of war criminals and the establishment of a new order in Europe, based on co-operation and mutual confidence of the peoples, and excluding the possibility of fresh German aggression, were, he said, the tasks facing the Allies.

In the diplomatic field, Soviet-Polish relations occupied a prominent place during the first few months of 1943. In 1941 it had become widely known

Soviet-Polish Relations that, at the time of the Stalin-Sikorski declaration in Moscow (December), both sides had felt that it was better not to raise the question of frontiers until the end of the war. The Polish unofficial press in London did not regard itself as bound by this, and in fact discussed the question actively all through 1942. It was not until December of that year, however, that an official Polish body—the State Council—adopted a resolution on the subject. For the first time there followed a Soviet retort—in the shape of an unofficial article by the well-known Ukrainian dramatist and Deputy, Korneichuk, strongly rebutting the Polish claims in respect of territory inhabited by Ukrainians and Byelorussians. Then came a Polish Government declaration (February 25, 1943) that "from the moment of the conclusion of the Polish-Soviet Treaty of July 30, 1941" (by which the Soviet Government recognized that the Soviet-German treaties of 1939 as to territorial changes in Poland had lost their validity; *see* page 1947), it had "maintained the unchangeable attitude that so far as the question of frontiers between Poland and Soviet Russia is concerned, the *status quo* previous to September 1, 1939, is in force." The Tass Agency commented that Ukrainian and Byelorussian peoples had as much right to self-determination as the Poles. Then, on April 12, the Germans published their allegations about the massacre of Polish officers at Katyn, which was followed by a Polish invitation to the International Red Cross to investigate the allegations. This led to the breaking off by Russia of diplomatic relations with the Polish Government (*see* page 2735).

Stalin declared on May 4 that the U.S.S.R. wanted to see a strong and independent Poland after the war, with a Russo-Polish alliance of mutual

CHURCH OF ENGLAND DELEGATION VISITS RUSSIA

On September 15, 1943, Dr. C. F. Garbett, Archbishop of York, arrived in Moscow to convey to the Russian Orthodox Church a message of sympathy (reproduced below) from the Anglican Church to the suffering Soviet peoples. The group above, taken in Moscow, shows (front row, left to right) Metropolitan Alexei of Leningrad (see page 2933); Archbishop of York; Patriarch Sergei; Metropolitan Nicolai of Kiev. *Photos, British and U.S.S.R. Official*

To His Beatitude Sergei,
Metropolitan of Moscow and Kolomna,
Guardian of the Holy Patriarchal Russian Throne

Beloved Brother in Christ

It is with singular joy that we put our hands to this message of greeting, which one of us will have the profound happiness to present to Your Beatitude.

We have watched with deep sympathy the sufferings of the peoples of the Soviet Union in these last two years, and have been inspired by the patriotism and constancy of the Russian Church in faithfulness to the One Lord, our Saviour Jesus Christ. We share with all our countrymen the admiration aroused by the heroic resistance of the Russian people and the Red Army to the attacks of a treacherous aggressor. And we look forward to the time when, the evil forces of Fascism being destroyed, a true peace may be established, rendering possible the fuller realisation of true brotherhood among all nations, and of fellowship in the work of Christ our God among all Christian people.

We are deeply grateful for the loving message from Your Beatitude, in response to which one of us has now come to Moscow to assure the Russian Church and Russian Nation of our unity of heart with them. We are moved to make known to Your Beatitude our great desire to welcome here in London at an early date a delegation of the Holy Russian Church, which, we assume, you will be welcomed with joy and eagerness, if as we trust it can be arranged.

Finally, asking your prayers and the prayers of your people both for ourselves and for our Church of England, we pray that the blessing of Almighty God may rest upon Your Beatitude and upon the Church committed to your care.

We are Your Beatitude's most faithful and loving Brothers in Christ

William   Cantuar: Cyril   Ebor:

8 ix 43

2939

ANGLO-SOVIET-AMERICAN FRIENDSHIP

At the conclusion of the tripartite conference of Foreign Secretaries which met in Moscow from October 19-30, 1943, Mr. Cordell Hull (Secretary of State, U.S.A.), Mr. V. M. Molotov (People's Commissar for Foreign Affairs, U.S.S.R.), and Mr. Anthony Eden (Secretary of State for Foreign Affairs, U.K.) sign the declaration binding their three countries to a joint waging of war against Germany until final victory.

Photo, Associated Press

assistance against the Germans. On May 6, following broadcast references by General Sikorski to the position of Polish citizens in the U.S.S.R. on May 4, M. Vyshinsky, Deputy People's Commissar for Foreign Affairs, supplied the foreign correspondents in Moscow with two statements detailing charges against the Polish Government of refusing to send its troops to the eastern front and of using its charitable organizations on Soviet territory for espionage purposes.

On June 8 the newly formed Union of Polish Patriots in the U.S.S.R. held its first congress. Polish guerillas, Polish deserters from the German army, soldiers of the Polish divisions on Soviet territory, Polish immigrants, etc., were represented, and resolutions envisaging a free, democratic and sovereign post-war Poland, on terms of friendship with the U.S.S.R., were adopted.

Union of Polish Patriots Formed

At the end of July M. Maisky, Soviet Ambassador in Great Britain since 1932, was appointed Deputy People's Commissar for Foreign Affairs; and on August 1 it was announced that his place in London would be taken by M. Gusev, Soviet Minister to Canada. On August 22 M. Litvinov (who already held the post of Deputy People's Commissar for Foreign Affairs) was replaced as Ambassador in Washington by M. Gromyko.

On August 26 the Soviet Government recognized the French Committee of National Liberation at Algiers as "representative of the State interests of the French Republic and leader of all French patriots fighting against the Hitlerite tyranny"; and on December 12, in Moscow, during a visit of President Benes, it concluded a treaty of friendship with the Czechoslovak Government (*see* page 2735 and illus., page 2734).

As a preliminary to the conference held at Teheran in November, and attended by President Stalin, President Roosevelt and Mr. Churchill (*see* page 2645), Mr. Eden (British Foreign Secretary) and Mr. Cordell Hull (U.S. Secretary of State) arrived in Moscow on October 18 for an Anglo-Soviet-American conference which met at the Kremlin under the chairmanship of M. Molotov, People's Commissar for Foreign Affairs, from October 19-30. Declarations were issued stating that: (1) it was essential for the three governments to continue their close wartime collaboration into the period following the end of hostilities; (2) the three governments favoured the restoration of democracy in Italy; (3) it was their purpose to restore independence to Austria; (4) German officers and men and members of the Nazi party connected with atrocities would be charged and punished according to the laws of the countries in which their crimes had been committed. The Chinese Ambassador in Moscow was invited to sign a joint declaration on war-aims and post-war co-operation (*see* pp. 2701 and 2709).

For many, the most unexpected feature in Soviet home affairs was the establishment of friendly relations between the Soviet authorities and the Churches, brought about by the gradual reformation of religious bodies in the U.S.S.R. over a period of years. On January 1 the acting head of the Russian Orthodox Church, Metropolitan Sergei, telegraphed to Stalin that the Church was collecting subscriptions for a "Dmitri Donskoi" tank column, named after the hero-prince who defeated the Mongol invasion at Kulikovo in 1380; by February 23 over six million roubles had been collected. Other religious bodies followed this example. On August 4 Stalin received Metropolitan Sergei and other Church dignitaries and informed them that there would be no objection to the assembly of Bishops they intended to hold in order to elect a Patriarch of Moscow and All Russia and to constitute a Holy Synod; and a week later the Soviet Government formed a special Committee for contact with the Russian Orthodox Church. The Assembly of Bishops (September 12) elected Metropolitan Sergei as their Patriarch—and appointed a Holy Synod (as a supreme Church body, not a State organ as in Tsarist days). Three days later the Archbishop of York arrived in Moscow, for a goodwill visit on behalf of the Church of England. On October 15 Muslims of the five Union Republics of Western and Central Asia—Kazakhstan, Kirgizia, Uzbekistan, Turkmenistan and Tadjikistan—held a congress and elected an Ecclesiastical Administration, situated at Tashkent, with a President-Mufti at its head.

Soviet Recognizes Church

Diary of the War

SEPTEMBER and OCTOBER, 1943

September 1, 1943. Annihilation of German forces at Taganrog announced (U.S.S.R.). U.S.A. 10th A.F. dropped great weight of bombs on Mandalay (Burma). 206 tons dropped on Madang (New Guinea).

September 2. President Roosevelt and Mr. Churchill met in Washington. Entire Kursk province liberated; Sumy, Lisichansk and other places recaptured by Red Army. Bolzano and Trento heavily raided from the air (Italy).

September 3. 8th Army landed on Italian mainland near Reggio. Five Luftwaffe repair bases in France heavily attacked by U.S. Fortresses; R.A.F. Lancasters dropped 1,000 tons of bombs in 20-minute attack on Berlin.

September 4. Voroshilovgrad province entirely freed (U.S.S.R.). 8th Army took Scilla, Baghara and Melito (Italy).

September 4 and 5. Large-scale Australian and U.S. sea and air landings east of Lae (New Guinea).

September 5. At night Bomber Command dropped 1,500 tons of bombs on Mannheim-Ludwigshafen.

September 6. Konotop and many other places recaptured by Red Army. Palmi and Delianuova captured by 8th Army; day and night air attacks on enemy communications and airfields round Naples. Australians captured Nadzab air base (New Guinea).

September 8. Surrender of Italy announced. Stalino recaptured by Red Army. Germans raided Spitzbergen.

September 9. Bakhmach recaptured by Russians. Allied 5th Army landed in Salerno area; Taranto occupied from the sea (Italy).

September 10. Russians captured Mariupol. British captured Salerno; Rome occupied by Germans (Italy).

September 11. Brindisi captured by 8th Army; Italian fleet surrendered at Malta.

September 12. 8th Army captured Crotone (Italy). Paramushiro (Kurile Islands, Japan) raided by U.S. bombers.

September 13. British hospital ship sunk by German bombers off Salerno.

September 13–14 (night). French commandos landed at Ajaccio (Corsica).

September 14. Australians captured Salamaua (New Guinea).

September 15. Nyezhin recaptured by Soviet troops.

September 16. Recapture of Novorossiisk, Lozovaya and many other places by Red Army. Montecorvino captured by 5th Army (Italy). Split reported in Patriot hands (Yugoslavia). Australians captured Lae (New Guinea).

September 17. Bryansk recaptured by Russians. Patrols of 5th and 8th Armies linked near Agropoli (Italy).

September 18. 5th Army captured Battipaglia and Altavilla (Italy). Strong U.S. carrier-borne task forces attacked Nauru Island and the Gilberts.

September 19. Mr. Churchill arrived back in London. Desna river forced; Dukhovschina, Yartsevo and many other places recaptured by Red Army.

September 20. Over 2,500 places, including Velizh, recaptured by Russians.

September 21. Red Army took Chernigov by storm. 8th Army captured Potenza (Italy). Occupation of Aegean islands of Cos, Leros and Samos by British forces officially announced.

September 22. Anapa, Pereyaslavl and other places recaptured by Red Army. Concentrated night attack by British bombers on Hanover (1,500 tons in 30 mins.). British midget submarines attacked "Tirpitz" (Norway).

September 23. Poltava and Unecha recaptured by Soviet forces. At night Mannheim-Ludwigshafen attacked by Bomber Command in great strength. 5th Army opened offensive north of Salerno (Italy). French troops occupied Bonifacio and Porto Vecchio (Corsica).

September 25. Russians recaptured Smolensk and Roslavl.

September 27. Very strong force of U.S. Fortresses attacked Emden and Aurich; at night 1,700 tons of bombs dropped by Bomber Command on Hanover. Foggia captured by 8th Army (Italy).

September 29. Russians recaptured Kremenchug. Heavy R.A.F. night attack on Bochum (Germany). Castellamare, Pompeii and other places captured by 5th Army; Manfredonia by 8th (Italy). Loss of Split to Germans admitted by Yugoslav government.

September 30. Badoglio formed new government (Italy).

October 1. 5th Army entered Naples. Curfew lifted in Malta. Heavy attacks on Munich and Wiener Neustadt by U.S. bombers based on North Africa.

October 2. Lancasters heavily bombed Munich, dropping ten 4,000-lb. bombs per minute from 10.30–10.55 p.m. 5th Army captured Benevento (Italy). Australians captured Finsch Hafen (New Guinea).

October 2–3 (night). 8th Army landing at Termoli (Italy).

October 3. R.A.F. dropped 1,500 tons of bombs on Kassel in 30 mins. Sea and airborne attack by Germans on Cos.

October 4. Heavy daylight attack by Fortresses followed by Lancaster night attack on Frankfurt-am-Main. All Corsica liberated.

October 5 and 6. Raid by U.S. task force (warships and carrier aircraft) on Wake Island (Central Pacific).

October 7. Nevel and Taman captured by Soviet troops; Soviet forces crossed the Middle Dneiper. Heavy night attack by Bomber Command on Stuttgart. 5th Army captured Capua.

October 8. Bremen and Vegesack bombed by day, Hanover and Bremen by night. 5th Army captured Caserta.

October 9. Kuban entirely cleared of the enemy. Day attack by U.S. Bombers on Danzig, Gdynia, and Marienburg. Bitter fighting reported in Trieste.

October 10. U.S.A. 8th A.F. bombed Muenster by day.

October 11. Patriots destroyed all blast furnaces and other installations in Zenica, Central Bosnia. Madras had first air raid (by one Japanese plane).

October 12. Mr. Churchill announced acquisition of bases in Azores. Heavy Allied air attack on Rabaul; 177 Japanese planes destroyed, 3 destroyers, 3 merchantmen, 43 seagoing vessels and 70 harbour craft sunk for loss of 5 Allied planes.

October 12–13 (night). 5th Army launched offensive on Volturno river; new Allied landings north of river.

October 13. Italy declared war on Germany. Whole of New Georgia group in Allied hands.

October 14. Red Army took Zaporozhe by storm; violent street fighting in Melitopol. Heavy daylight attack by U.S. Fortresses on Schweinfurt; 104 German fighters destroyed, 60 Fortresses and 2 U.S. fighters lost.

October 15–17. Japanese lost 127 planes and many probables, Allies 5 with many damaged, in three days of air battles between Wewak (New Guinea) and Buin (Solomons).

October 18. Bomber Command made heavy night attack on Hanover.

October 19. Conference of Foreign Ministers of U.S.S.R., U.K., U.S.A. opens in Moscow. Battle for Volturno river over.

October 20. Heavy day raid by U.S. Fortresses on Dueren; first raid on Leipzig for 3 years by R.A.F. at night. U.S. Mitchells heavily bombed rail junction of Nish (Yugoslavia).

October 21. Destruction of Lyubiya iron mines by Yugoslav partisans reported; enemy attacks near Cetinje repulsed. Admiral Lord Louis Mountbatten left Chungking after 5-day visit.

October 22. Strong British bomber forces dropped 1,500 tons of bombs on Kassel. Allied Liberators dropped 221 tons of bombs on Japanese positions round Sattelberg (New Guinea).

October 23. Melitopol captured by Red Army. 8th Army attacked across Trigno river (Italy). H.M.S. "Charybdis" and "Limbourne" sunk off Ushant by enemy action.

October 23 and 24. Rabaul (New Britain) attacked by nearly 300 Allied planes; 123 Japanese planes destroyed (with 45 probables), Japanese destroyer and 5 coastal vessels sunk for loss of 4 Allied planes.

October 24. Four E-boats sunk, 7 damaged in running fight against force of 30 off East Anglia. Heavy U.S. air-raids on Ebenfurth and Friedburg (Austria).

October 25. Dnepropetrovsk and Dneprozerdshinsk taken by storm by Soviet troops. Heavy air attack on Rabaul; 58 Japanese planes destroyed, 1 Liberator lost (New Britain). 5,495 repatriated prisoners of war arrived at Leith.

October 26. Allied evacuation of Cos announced. 790 prisoners of war arrived at Liverpool.

October 27. Allied landing on Treasury Islands (Solomons).

October 28. Montefalcone captured by 8th Army (Italy). U.S. Parachute troops landed on Choiseul (Solomons).

October 29. Bitter fighting for Krivoi Rog (U.S.S.R.). 5th Army captured Mondragone; Genoa heavily bombed. Allied bombers destroyed 45 Japanese planes at Rabaul (New Britain).

October 31. Russians captured Chaplinka. 5th Army captured Teano (Italy).

Chapter 293

ACTION IN THE DODECANESE: 1943

Possession of Rhodes and the Dodecanese Islands is of great strategic value for all war operations in Eastern Europe. In Italian occupation since 1912, they should have come into Allied hands after Italy's surrender (see Historic Document CCLXXII). But the Italian garrison proved unable or unwilling to hold Rhodes, and though after its loss the Allies put troops and supplies into the Dodecanese, these were not sufficient to keep the Germans out. The course of these operations is outlined here by Francis E. McMurtrie

AFTER Italian resistance ended on September 8, 1943, experience soon proved that Italian troops, in the absence of support, were unable to offer effective resistance to the Germans, who did not take long to recover from the surprise of their ally's defection.

A sphere which it was particularly desirable to bring under Allied influence was the Dodecanese—a name derived from the Greek for "Twelve Islands" which refers to Nizyros, Cos, Casos, Patmos, Charki, Leros, Tilos, Symi, Astropalia (Stampalia), Lipso, Scarpanto and Calimno. The group, predominantly Greek in population, was occupied by Italy during the war with Turkey in 1912. Eight years later it was agreed to cede the islands to Greece, but on Mussolini's advent to power in 1922 this transfer was rescinded.

Rhodes, a larger and more important island to the south-eastward, was the seat of Italian administration in the Aegean. Though there were about 40,000 Italians and only some 9,000 Germans on Rhodes, the Italians surrendered on the instructions of the Fascist military governor, Vice-Admiral Inigo Campioni, after a German dive-bombing attack. It was then realized that energetic action must be taken if the Dodecanese were to be prevented from falling into enemy hands; so small Allied forces were landed on Cos, Leros, and Samos about the middle of September. From an airfield in Cos, an island 28 miles in length, with an area of 115 square miles and a population of 20,000, the R.A.F. proceeded to bomb enemy objectives in Rhodes and Crete with a fair degree of regularity.

The Germans immediately began heavy air attacks on Cos with first line aircraft, and early on the morning of Sunday, October 3, launched a sea and airborne attack. South African pilots who escaped said the Germans carried out a "miniature Crete campaign with gliders, parachute troops, and seaborne forces" after keeping up a "shuttle service" of Stukas and fighters several times daily for some four days, in which they lost some fourteen machines, but succeeded in neutralizing Cos airfield and putting out of action another airfield under construction. To hold Cos against such a determined assault would have required a much stronger force than was available. The British garrison included a battalion of the Durham Light Infantry and units of the R.A.F. Regiment with ground personnel. It had only light A.A. and little air support. The 4,000 Italian troops did nothing.

German Air Attacks on Cos

EASTERN MEDITERRANEAN AND THE DODECANESE

This map shows the position of the Dodecanese Islands (within dotted line), in relation to the mainland of the Middle East. Two of them, Cos and Leros, were the scene of fierce fighting in October and November 1943. Possession of these islands gave their occupier a very considerable measure of control over the passage through the Dardanelles, and so over access to the Black Sea and South Russia. *Specially drawn for the* SECOND GREAT WAR *by Félix Gardon*

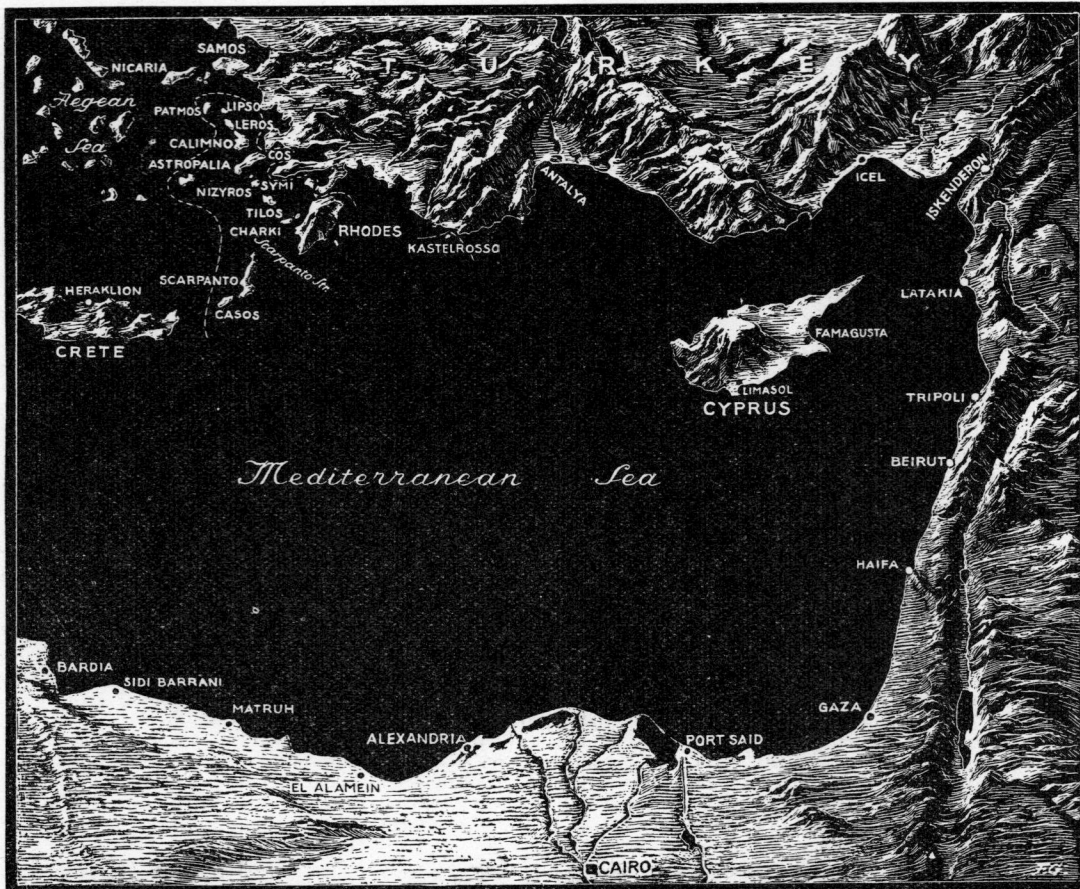

GERMAN ARMOUR IN RHODES

The Italian-owned islands in the Aegean Sea should by the terms of the armistice with Italy have come under Allied control. But 40,000 Italians on Rhodes, savagely dive-bombed from Crete within 30 minutes of the publication of the armistice terms, surrendered on the instructions of their Fascist commander, Vice-Admiral Campioni, to the 9,000 Germans on the island. Here German armoured reconnaissance cars are parked in front of the castle of the Knights of St. John on Rhodes. *Photo, G.P.U.*

naval base, with a small floating dock, and it was on this port that German air attacks were chiefly concentrated. At the same time the R.A.F. made frequent attacks on enemy aerodromes in Crete, Rhodes and Cos.

On October 29 it was reported from Ankara that for two days past heavy air raids had been in progress over Leros. The Germans were employing some 300 aircraft, mostly bombers, based on airfields in Rhodes, Crete and Greece. Early on November 12 **Germans Land on Leros** the Germans succeeded in landing on Leros, and during the two following days established a bridge-head at the north-east corner of the island after sharp fighting. These troops were all landed from the sea with the exception of the first party, which alighted by parachute in the central section of the island. Leros is only about eight miles long, and it is divided into two parts by an isthmus a mile wide, stretching from Alinda Bay to Gurna Bay (see map, p. 2944.) No enemy troops had gained a foothold in the southern part, where the harbour is situated, and fighting was for some time confined to the north.

Continual dive-bombing was the biggest trouble the defenders had to face. R.A.F. attacks on neighbouring aerodromes failed to prevent this, and anti-aircraft guns were not numerous enough to stop it. An eye-witness

The German High Command's communiqué of October 5 stated : "On Sunday all sections of the German armed forces began a landing operation against Cos. Resistance was smashed, and the island was occupied in two days' fighting." On October 11 it was stated in Cairo that except for small isolated pockets of resistance, Cos must be presumed to be in German hands, and on the 26th it was officially announced from Middle East headquarters that "in Cos our remaining land patrols, having completed their task, have been successfully withdrawn."

After the loss of Cos, the Allied Command decided, with full appreciation of the risks involved, to hold Leros and Samos. The Germans followed their capture of Cos by heavy air attacks on Leros, where the British garrison totalling 3,000 comprised units of The Buffs (Royal East Kent Regiment), the Royal West Kent Regiment, the King's Own Royal Regiment, and the Royal Irish Fusiliers ; the Italian troops numbered 6,000. Much smaller than Cos,

with about a quarter of its population, Leros is of greater importance owing to its excellent harbour. This had been equipped by the Italians as a minor

GERMANS LAND ON THE ISLAND OF COS

Small Allied forces were installed on Cos, Leros and Samos after the surrender of Rhodes to the Germans, who almost immediately began to attack them. The enemy claimed that he began to land on Cos on Sunday, October 3, 1943, and completed the conquest of the island in two days. South African pilots who escaped described the German attack as a 'miniature Crete campaign.' The Allies admitted the loss of Cos on October 25. *Photo, Keystone*

BRITISH AND GERMAN COMMANDERS ON LEROS
Brigadier R. A. G. Tilney, who commanded the British forces in Leros and was taken prisoner when the fighting there ceased on November 16, 1943, is here seen (right) with General Mueller, commander of the German forces which captured the island. The enemy claimed that he had taken 3,200 British and 5,350 Italian prisoners, among them 200 British and 350 Italian officers, including the British commander. *Photo, Planet News*

being between 750 and 1,000 men. A supply ship was torpedoed by H.M. submarine " Surf " (Lieut. Douglas Lambert, R.N.).

Air attacks continued day and night for five days, but on the third day the enemy had made no appreciable progress, and Brigadier R. A. G. Tilney, in command of the garrison, signalled that if reinforcements were provided he was confident of holding his positions. By a great effort the reinforcements were sent in destroyers and submarines, which had not, however, space for large numbers of men or considerable quantities of supplies. The Germans were reinforced heavily the same night.

British Reinforcements Sent In

German air and sea bases were on the surrounding islands and within easy reach, whereas the Allies' nearest were in Cyprus and North Africa, 350 to 400 miles away. British warships and supply vessels had to cover a large part of the passage to the Dodecanese in daylight ; and a full moon during the period of operation did not make matters any easier for the defenders.

H.M.S. " Echo " (Lt.-Com. R. N. C. Wyld, R.N.)—now the Greek destroyer "Navarino "—was the last ship to maintain communication with the island. She left at 4.30 on the morning of November 15, at which time the garrison, though hard pressed and very tired, remained full of fight. By 6 p.m. on the following day all organized resistance had been overcome, it being found impossible any longer to withstand the

declared that " the Germans made use of their local air superiority to fling in Stukas with the object of pinning down our troops while the enemy consolidated his hold upon the bridge-head he had managed to establish at a heavy cost. Wave after wave came thundering over, then screamed down upon the defenders. Our A.A. gunners gave them everything they had, and the men of the Italian garrison stood their ground bravely too. Low-flying transport aircraft next appeared and started to drop parachutists with supplies to the enemy's landing parties, which were having all they could do to cling to the foothold they had won. Ships of the German invasion fleet kept circling the island, but appeared reluctant to try their luck again after the battering they received at the first attack."

During the first two days some ground was regained from the enemy in the north-eastern corner of the island. Heavy casualties were inflicted on the Germans—at least 4,000 were drowned—and a number of prisoners were taken ; and the screen of troops which the enemy had thrown across the waist of the island was prevented from extending in either direction. The insufficiency of their air support was the greatest handicap of the garrison, who had to be constantly on the lookout for fresh landings.

Heavy Enemy Casualties

In anticipation of German attacks on Samos, a flatter island less easy to defend, the British troops there were reinforced about this date by picked Greek soldiers of the Sacred Brigade, dropped by parachute.

A correspondent who was on Leros almost to the last, escaping in a British

---

BRITISH UNITS IN COS AND LEROS

Cos
Durham Light Infantry
Units of the R.A.F. Regiment with ground forces and W/T staff and Air-Sea Rescue personnel.

Leros
King's Own Royal Regiment
Royal East Kent Regiment (The Buffs)
Royal West Kent Regiment
Royal Irish Fusiliers

---

destroyer, described how Stukas circled overhead waiting for signals from their troops below to indicate where to bomb. During daylight the noise was terrific, and flying fragments from bomb explosions obliged our soldiers to keep in the shelter of slit trenches. In spite of this, our troops managed to push a temporary wedge through the line of German parachutists holding the mile-wide " waist " already mentioned.

Every night British destroyers and smaller craft would creep into the little harbour, bringing fresh supplies of ammunition, food and an occasional handful of soldiers, and evacuating casualties. More than once German landing craft were intercepted and sunk while trying to run in reinforcements under cover of darkness. In the last 36 hours' fighting a Siebel ferry and three lighters were sunk. All were packed with troops, their total capacity

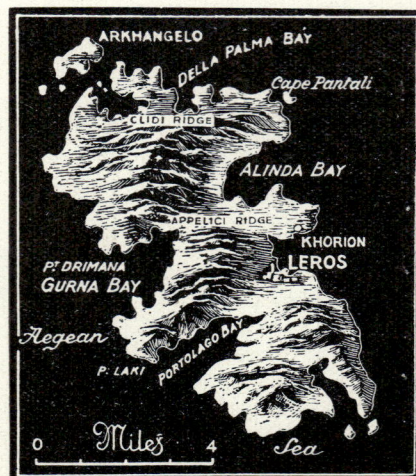

LEROS ISLAND
The land phases of the short, sharp action which resulted in the loss of Leros to the Germans can be clearly followed on this map. The first German landings were made on November 12, 1943, in the central section of the island by parachute troops. Seaborne forces followed, but were for some time contained north of the isthmus between Gurna and Alinda Bays. By 6 p.m. on November 16 the garrison was overwhelmed.

LEROS UNDER AIR BOMBARDMENT BY THE GERMANS

The Germans carried out heavy air attacks on Leros for several days before they landed parachute troops, followed by seaborne forces, on November 12, 1943. Here are bombs exploding about the village of Portolago. Below, British and Italian prisoners taken when Leros surrendered waiting to embark. Some of the 8,550 prisoners taken were left behind to clear up the island after the fierce fighting, but most of them were very soon transferred to prison camps on the mainland.   *Photos. British Official : New York Times*

REFUGEES FROM THE ISLAND OF SAMOS

On November 22, 1943, the British War Office announced that, several days before, all British and Greek and some Italian troops had been evacuated from Samos, together with a large part of the civil population. Here is an evacuated Samos family in a Middle East camp. The father, a cobbler, can fortunately carry on his usual occupation. Below, men of the Greek 'Sacred Brigade' waiting on a Middle East airfield to take off in R.A.F. planes for Samos, where they landed by parachute to reinforce the British garrison. *Photos, British Official*

concentrated enemy air attacks and at the same time hold a defence line against the fresh German troops pouring in.

A special announcement from Hitler's headquarters asserted that 200 British officers and 3,000 other ranks under Brigadier Tilney, together with 350 Italian officers and 5,000 other ranks under Rear-Admiral Luigi Mascherpa, had surrendered. Booty claimed included 16 heavy A.A. guns, 20 of 20 mm. calibre and 80 machine-guns, besides about 120 low-angle guns up to 6-inch calibre. It was also stated with questionable accuracy that " nine destroyers and escort vessels, two patrol craft, two submarines, a gunboat, four merchantmen and several small supply vessels " had been sunk. British and Italian casualties were said to be heavy.

On November 18, in a statement to the Press in Cairo, General Sir Henry Maitland Wilson maintained that the British reinforcement of the Italian garrisons on Cos and Leros had " paid a dividend." He explained that the operations, intended as a diversion, had obliged the Germans to divert substantial land, sea and air forces which they very badly needed elsewhere. They withdrew troops from the Balkans and Crete, and aircraft from France, Denmark and Russia, thus relieving pressure on the Allies elsewhere. German casualties in the attacks on Cos and Leros were equal in killed alone to the total number of British employed, many of whom got back safely. Enemy losses in aircraft and shipping could not be replaced as could similar Allied losses.

On November 19 a German High Command report stated : " In the Aegean Sea light German naval units yesterday made a sortie against the islands of Lipso, Patmos and Nicaria, to the north and north-west of Leros. They forced the Italian garrisons of these islands to lay down their arms, and brought back much booty."

Three days later came the announcement from the German news agency that Samos had capitulated on the morning of November 21. Confirmation came from Cairo 24 hours afterwards, followed almost immediately by a War Office announcement that, " having accomplished their task, all British and Greek and a proportion of the Italian troops have been evacuated without loss from Samos, together with a large portion of the civil population [later given as 4,000–5,000]. This evacuation was carried out several days ago."

Not till nearly the end of November was it disclosed that the landing and maintenance of the British garrisons

Allied Press Statement

LIBERATORS LEAVE A MIDDLE EAST BASE

One of the difficulties of British defence of the Dodecanese Islands was their great distance from Allied airfields. The Germans had airfields in Rhodes and in Greece within easy flying distance, whereas the Allies' nearest bases were in Cyprus and North Africa, 350 to 400 miles away. In spite of this, however, continual air raids on enemy targets in Greece and the islands of the Aegean Sea were carried out by Liberators flown by the R.A.F. from Middle East bases.

on Leros and Samos resulted in the biggest Allied naval operation in the Eastern Mediterranean since Tobruk. For more than a month the Royal Navy carried out long, hazardous runs from Levantine ports into the network of the small Dodecanese islands, where the enemy had definite air superiority. Air bases at Crete and Rhodes lie on either side of the Scarpanto Straits, through which our ships passed in broad daylight. Almost every night destroyers took troops, supplies and ammunition into the Aegean, transferring their cargoes into lighters, caïques and coastal craft off the harbour at Leros. Remaining only long enough to embark wounded, the destroyers then proceeded to patrol around the islands, searching for enemy vessels. An out-standing exploit was the complete destruction of an invasion force off Astropalia by Captain P. W. B. Brooking, in H.M.S. "Sirius," accompanied by another cruiser, H.M.S. "Penelope" (Captain G. D. Balden; see illus., p. 2285), and two destroyers. Motor launches landed troops in the early stages of the campaign. Later motor torpedo-boats, motor gunboats and motor minesweepers took an active part, acting as anti-aircraft defence, anti-invasion patrol and ferries for the Leros garrison.

In his statement in the House of Commons on November 24 on events in the Dodecanese, Mr. Attlee, Deputy Prime Minister, said, "The operation contained superior forces at a critical period of our invasion of Italy, and inflicted serious losses on the enemy," but though from the military point of view the operation may have been worth while, its immediate international political effect was unhappy. In Moscow the loss of Leros was said to have caused "bewilderment and shock." Turkish public opinion was also baffled; it was said openly that the lack of any action against Rhodes at the time of the Italian surrender was a complete enigma. To the average Turk, the Allies seemed to have shown themselves to be lacking in enterprise.

H.M.S. 'SIRIUS,' VICTOR OFF ASTROPALIA

The British defence of the Dodecanese involved the biggest Allied naval operation in the Eastern Mediterranean since the siege of Tobruk. For more than a month, units of the Royal Navy carried out long, hazardous runs from the Levant to the islands. An outstanding exploit was the complete destruction of a German invasion force off Astropalia by H.M.S. 'Sirius,' accompanied by another cruiser, H.M.S. 'Penelope,' and two destroyers.

Photos, British Official ; badge reproduced by permission of the Controller of H.M. Stationery Office

In a message to Congress in September 1943, the President stated that since May 1940 the U.S.A. had produced 123,000 aircraft, 349,000 aeroplane engines, 53,000 tanks, 93,000 pieces of artillery, 9½ million small arms, 1,230,000 trucks and lorries. The country had also built and launched 2,380 fighting ships and auxiliaries and 13,000 landing barges; during the preceding six months more warships had been launched than during the whole of 1942. Above, launch of U.S.S. 'Alaska,' at Camden, New Jersey, on August 15, 1943. Top left, a final polish to plastic glass noses for U.S. and Allied fighter planes. Left, a new 200-acre plant in the eastern U.S. which in its first year produced 117,500 tons of styrene and butadiene, bases of 'buna' rubber.

Chapter 294

AMERICA'S SECOND YEAR AT WAR

Dwindling fear of air raids somewhat reduced American awareness of the war during 1943, and labour unrest increased. There was further friction, too, between whites and negroes. But no sectional difficulties affected the average American's wholehearted support of the war. Mr. Selden Menefee, lecturer in sociology at the National University, Washington, who contributes this Chapter, told of U.S. internal affairs in the second half of 1942 in Chapter 251

THE second full year of war for the United States was a time of settling confidently down to work after the first year of anxiety and tension. No longer was there concern as to the outcome : United Nations victories in North Africa, Russia, the North Atlantic, and the South Pacific removed all doubt on that score.

There was no single military event in 1943 that compared in emotional impact with the invasion of North Africa in November 1942. The defeat of the Axis in Africa was a bit anti-climactic, after the excitement of the initial landings. The Sicilian campaign went off almost too easily. Only after U.S. troops met stiff enemy fire on the Salerno beach-head did Americans become greatly keyed up about the European conflict.

Nor was the war against Japan fraught with the danger it had carried the previous year. Japanese submarines no longer prowled along the West Coast of America ; nor, for that matter, was the Doolittle raid of April 1942 on Tokyo and Japan's home islands repeated by the U.S. air force. The year 1943 was one of "inching along," with MacArthur's forces slashing through the jungles of New Guinea and island-hopping westward from the Solomons against declining Japanese resistance. There was one exception in the Central Pacific area : the bloody battle for Tarawa, in the Gilbert Islands, which aroused new fury against the Japanese. The most dramatic victory over Japan was the reoccupation of Attu and Kiska Islands in the Aleutians by United States forces, but the typical reaction to this news was to heave a sigh of relief and say, "It's about time."

Reaction to Victories Against Japan

America's attitudes toward her Allies became stabilized in 1943, according to the opinion polls. The previous year, the average American's evaluation of Great Britain's contribution to the war had fluctuated with every British victory or defeat. Throughout 1943, however, at least seven out of ten Americans felt that Britain was doing all she could to help win the war. A majority of Americans named Britain as their favourite ally among the "big four,"

although fifty per cent thought there was some truth in the charge that the English have taken "unfair advantage . . . of their colonial possessions "— thinking primarily of India.

Opinion towards Russia continued predominantly favourable. At the close of the year, a clear majority expressed confidence that the Soviet Union could be trusted to co-operate with her allies after the war. Trust in Russia's good faith was greater, oddly enough, among Americans who were above average in economic status than among the poorer strata of the population. More than four-fifths of Americans favoured trying to work with Russia as an equal partner both in war and in peace.

As for political warfare, the Allied

Conferences at Casablanca, Moscow, Cairo and Teheran cleared the air somewhat, although American opinion was still sharply divided on the U.S. policy of supporting Giraud against De Gaulle. The great majority favoured an " unconditional surrender " policy against Germany. Opinion continued to grow for immediate steps toward setting up an international organization to preserve the peace ; three Americans out of four were willing even to support an international police force to achieve this end. Public pressure was largely responsible for Congressional resolutions pledging the United States to co-operate fully with other nations after the war.

There were danger signals, too. The polls showed willingness on the part of

UNRRA AGREEMENT SIGNED AT THE WHITE HOUSE

On November 9, 1943, representatives of 44 nations met at the White House to sign the agreement establishing UNRRA (United Nations Relief and Rehabilitation Association). The first session of the association was held at Atlantic City, New Jersey, from November 10 to December 1. Here the President is talking with Lord Halifax, the British Ambassador, while Mr. Leighton McCarthy prepares to sign on behalf of Canada. Behind Mr. McCarthy stands Mr. George Summerlin, Chief of Protocol, U.S. State Department. *Photo, Keystone*

PRISONERS OF WAR IN A SAWMILL

Inmates from the camp for German prisoners of war at Aliceville, Alabama, are here seen splitting a log into boards under the eye of an armed guard. Their work outside the camp was paid for at the rate of $2.50 a day (about 12s. 6d.) of which they received 80 cents (about 4s.) in canteen credits, the rest going towards the cost of their maintenance. *Photo, Keystone*

economy. In Russia and in Germany, civilian economy almost ceased to exist. But in the U.S. the fabulous war-production job had been so well done in such favourable conditions that economists claimed the American standard was one-sixth higher than in 1939.

Manpower to staff the new factories was a major problem in 1943. In June 1940 almost nine million workers were still unemployed as a result of the depression and of technological improvements.

Increased Employment of Women

Three years later only a million or so were without jobs, and these were mostly in a few isolated mountain areas or were so-called "marginal workers" who had difficulty in holding jobs even in wartime. Meanwhile seven million young men (and women) had entered the armed forces; but the total labour force had declined by only a third of a million, the rest of the deficit being made up by increased employment of young people and of women, many of whom had never worked before. Employment of women jumped from 11,580,000 in June 1940 to 17,780,000 in June 1943.

In addition, some five million workers migrated to the great centres of war industry to fill the manpower vacuum. The New York City metropolitan area, which specialized in light industry not adaptable to war production, lost

Americans to continue rationing and paying high taxes after the war to help build a union of nations aimed at preventing war. But they were unwilling, most of them, to disarm, forgo lend-lease repayments and reparations, or try free trade for the same purpose. Eight Americans out of ten said that the U.S. should play the leading role in world affairs after the war, while only half as many Britons thought that Great Britain should take the lead. This somewhat self-centred American attitude fairly beckoned to such isolationist propagandists as Col. Robert R. McCormick of the "Chicago Tribune," whose specialty was trying to split the United States from her allies.

The pangs of converting America's industry to war production were largely over by 1943. In 1942 President

100,000 Aeroplanes a Year

Roosevelt's goal of 50,000 planes had been achieved; in 1943, 85,000 were turned out, and by the end of the year the production rate stood at 100,000 planes a year. Aircraft plant equipment had been increased forty times over pre-war levels.

In 1943 also, aluminium production capacity had increased sevenfold; machine tools had been produced in three times the volume of the ten pre-war years put together; and shipyards had been expanded to produce at 80 times the pre-war rate, turning out 20 million tons of merchant shipping alone. But these were only items. The great overmastering economic fact of 1943 was

that the U.S. had boosted its 1939 production by a thundering 100 per cent.

Under far greater pressure, Britain had increased her production some 20 per cent, despite air raids and manpower shortages. And the war took 15 per cent from British civilian

AIR RAID ALERT IN NEW YORK CITY

Mayor La Guardia announced the creation of a wardens' service in New York City on June 20, 1941, nearly six months before Japan attacked Pearl Harbor, and though the possibility of air assault on the city remained remote, exercises were held from time to time. Here passengers leave Fifth Avenue buses to take shelter when an alert sounded during the rush home-going hour on August 12, 1943. *Photo, New York Times*

WITH THE BRITISH FORCES IN ITALY

Pack animals, which proved to be an essential part of army equipment in North Africa (see illus., p. 2619), had to be used also in the mountains of Italy in the slogging Allied campaign against dogged German defence. Mule trains carried stores and ammunition to forward areas, and brought the wounded back to safety—in the manner shown here—over trails which no motor vehicle could negotiate and through country where no aircraft could land. Below, the British crew of a 5·5-in. howitzer in action. These photographs were taken during September 1943 when the Salerno battles were in the balance (see Chapter 286)

Photos. British Official   Crown Copyright

GENERAL HENRY H. ARNOLD—CHIEF OF U.S. ARMY AIR FORCES

President Roosevelt created General Arnold full General (then the highest rank in the U.S. army) on March 19, 1943, and on December 15, 1944, he was appointed to the new highest rank, General of the Army. In both steps he was the first airman so honoured. Returning from the Teheran and Cairo conferences in 1943 he visited the Italian front, and there on December 11 he told press correspondents that the Allies were almost ready to begin a 24-hour bombing assault on Germany from North, South, East and West. *Direct colour photograph by Pictorial Press*

ADMIRAL CHESTER WILLIAM NIMITZ—C.-IN-C., U.S. PACIFIC FLEET

Admiral Nimitz was appointed C.-in-C., U.S. Pacific Fleet, in succession to Admiral Kimmel after the Japanese attack on Pearl Harbor on December 8, 1941. In a press statement he made a couple of months later he said, ' This war will keep us busy every moment of the day and night across the vast reaches of the Pacific.' Increasing strength of the Allied navies enabled him to sweep ever farther westward, nearer and nearer to Japanese home waters. His appointment as Admiral of the Fleet, new highest U.S. naval rank, was announced on Dec. 15, 1944.   *Photo, U.S. Official*

INTREPID · LIGHTNING · CHARYBDIS · FIREDRAKE · ECLIPSE
DULVERTON · PAKENHAM · BLEAN · BEVERLEY · PANTHER
PUCKERIDGE · PARTRIDGE · LIMBOURNE · HARVESTER · HURWORTH
TURBULENT · EGRET · TROOPER · REGENT · WELSHMAN
UTMOST · ABDIEL · TIGRIS · SPLENDID · TRAVELLER

'IN GREAT DANGERS WE SEE GREAT COURAGE'

Among the ships of the Royal Navy lost at sea during 1943 were those whose badges are reproduced here. 'Charybdis' was a cruiser. The other ships whose badges appear in the top three rows were destroyers. The rest are of submarines except 'Welshman' and 'Abdiel' (minelayers) and 'Egret' (sloop). (See also pages facing 1811 and 2571.)

From material supplied by H.M. Dockyard, Chatham. By permission of H.M. Stationery Office

U.S. GOVERNMENT TAKES OVER THE RAILWAYS
President Franklin D. Roosevelt's signature on the executive order he signed at the White House
on December 27, 1943, giving notice of the taking possession and operation of the railroads by
the Government. Right, men of the Norfolk Naval Training Station put to work on the railroads to ease the manpower shortage while they wait for drafting to their naval duties.
Photos, New York Times

800,000 people in this tidal wave.
Smaller cities, villages, and the poorer
farm regions supplied the remainder.
The population of the three West Coast
States increased by nearly two million.
San Diego, a naval base and aircraft
manufacturing centre, jumped from
203,000 to 400,000 while Bremerton,
Washington, rose from 15,000 to 75,000
—a five-fold increase from 1940 to 1943.

In some localities the situation
bordered on the fantastic. In New
Britain, Connecticut, a restaurant owner
named Miro Grubisch
Dishwashers: was reported to be
$54 a week paying wages ranging
from $54 a week for
dishwashers to $80 a week, board, and
10 per cent of the profits to the top
member of his staff. He had also taken
over a house for his family and employees to live in, he said, and supplied
his help with three gallons of wine and a
case of beer daily to hold them on his
payroll. "It's a disgrace when dishwashers make more than I do," he
complained.

By the end of the year, however, the
manpower situation was beginning to
clear up in most places. Agitation for a
labour draft had been successfully
resisted by both employers and labour
unions. But the War Manpower
Commission had adopted a modified
form of draft in Detroit and other
"labour stringency areas." This consisted of "freezing" war workers on
the job, requiring clearance by the public

employment offices before workers could
be released to take new jobs, and
assigning new workers to the plants
where they were most needed on a
priority or quota basis. In some places,
too, a system of split (four-hour)
shifts was worked out for housewives,
teachers and others who could not put
in a full day in the factories.

Despite this revolution in America's
way of living, there was a growing
tendency toward complacency in 1943.
This trend has often been exaggerated,
but it did exist. The reasons were
several : the war abroad, and war
production at home, were going well ;
millions of workers were earning good
wages for the first time in more than a
decade ; and the fighting war was

thousands of miles away. As the fear
of air raids dwindled, the feeling of all-
out war gradually faded.

Complacency was most prevalent in
the Middle West, where isolationism
was strongest before the war. But
even in that region
the war could not **War Closest**
be forgotten for very **in Villages**
long. Personal experi-
ence in a 15,000 - mile trip around
the Nation in early 1943 showed that
the war was closest in the smaller
towns and villages, especially in the
South, for there the birth rate is higher
and more young men had gone off to
war. Since everyone knows everyone
else in the villages, almost every family
had a direct personal interest in the war.

One unmistakable sign of complacency was the growth of labour
unrest in 1943. Early in the year,
public attention was focused on the
problem of industrial absenteeism. This
reached a climax when Captain Eddie

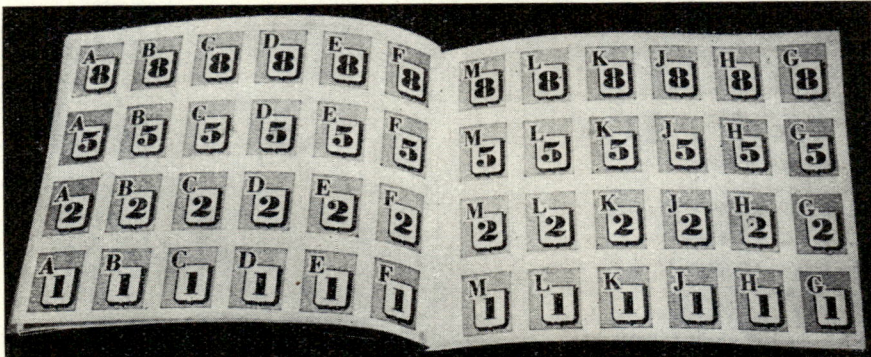

AMERICAN WAR RATION BOOK TWO
Here are two pages in a ration book prepared towards the end of 1942 and issued to the American
public at the beginning of 1943. Half the coupons were blue, and half red. The blue ones were
used for processed and canned foods and came into force on March 1 ; the red ones for meat,
fats, cheese and butter, and came into force on March 29. *Photo, Associated Press*

WARTIME TRAFFIC ON THE ALCAN HIGHWAY

The Alcan Highway, built in six months in 1942 to connect the United States with Alaska, links up a road that already ran from the U.S. to Dawson Creek in British Columbia with Fairbanks in Alaska, via Fort St. John, Fort Nelson, and Whitehorse. It is 1,671 miles long, 24 feet wide, and its construction involved bridging 200 streams. It played an important part in defence and attack against the Japanese in the North Pacific.   *Photos, U.S. Signal Corps*

Rickenbacker, flying ace turned aviation executive, returned from a visit to the south-west Pacific after having been given up for lost in a plane wreck, and scorchingly indicted those workers who neglected their jobs while their sons and brothers were suffering in the fox-holes of the Solomon Islands.

The hysteria subsided, however, when investigation showed that these accusations had been greatly overdrawn. In the shipyard industry, for example, absenteeism averaged only about 10 per cent even in January, the worst month of the year for outdoor work, compared with 18 per cent during the whole of the First Great War. A third of these absences were excusable because of sickness or other good reasons. Unaccustomed prosperity, drunkenness and general shiftlessness among a minority, largely " marginal " workers, accounted for some of the remaining absences. But lack of housing, transport and other community facilities were at least equally important, and in some plants and shipyards, inefficient management also contributed to low morale.

More significant was the wave of strikes which hit the country in mid-1943. The worst blow was the coal strike, or series of strikes, which involved nearly 600,000 workers. This aroused the nation and precipitated the passage by Congress of the Smith-Connally anti-strike act. This ill-considered piece of legislation did nothing to remove the causes of the trouble, and only antagonized the leaders of labour who had faithfully observed their pledge of 1941.

CIVILIAN POPULATION MOVEMENTS, 1940-1943

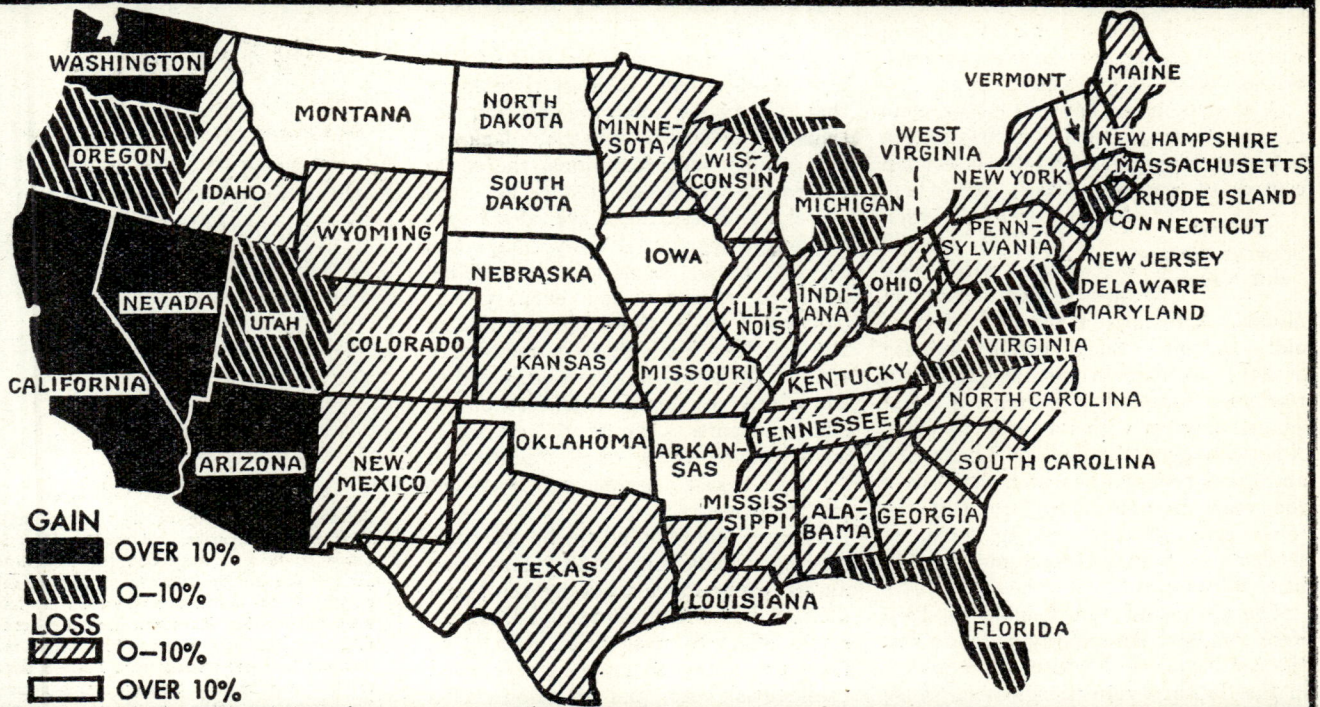

GAIN
OVER 10%
0–10%
LOSS
0–10%
OVER 10%

MAJOR CIVILIAN POPULATION SHIFTS
(APRIL 1940—NOVEMBER 1943)

METROPOLITAN COUNTIES   LOSS

 NEW YORK

 PITTSBURGH

 BOSTON

METROPOLITAN COUNTIES   GAIN

 LOS ANGELES

 SAN FRANCISCO OAKLAND

 WASHINGTON

Each symbol represents 100,000 civilians

The coal miners had been earning a basic wage of $7 a day since 1941, but extensive deductions from their wages by the mine operators, plus rising prices and somewhat sketchy price control, made them feel the necessity of still higher wages. The United Mine Workers' union having been responsible for most of the gains the miners had made over a period of twenty years, its members were almost unanimous in following the union leadership when a strike was called. The situation was complicated by the fact that John L. Lewis, President of the Union, was an isolationist and used the strike as a political weapon against

ROLLING TIDE OF WAR MIGRANTS IN THE U.S.A.
The greatest and most rapid internal migration that the U.S., land of westward trekking, had ever known was caused by war industry. Population shifted not only from rural to urban areas (though there was increased urbanization), but also from districts of light industry to those, old and new, of heavy industry. By November 1943 the shifts between States affected 2,500,000 people. Shifts inside States were estimated at another 2,500,000. *New York Times Magazine*

President Roosevelt and his administration.

After three walk-outs, Lewis extracted concessions which amounted to a violation of the spirit, though not the letter, of the wage stabilization order of April 1942. Meanwhile a rash of strikes had broken out in other industries, where workers also wanted to break through the wage ceiling. In the end, however, the ceiling held.

Coal production broke all records in 1943, with 589 million tons dug, although this was 21 million tons short of the quota. The other strikes were mostly of very short duration, and had even less effect on war production than the miners' walk-outs.

Over the entire year some 1,900,000 workers were involved in 3,750 strikes. The net result was 13,500,000 man-days of strike idleness, of which almost two-thirds resulted from the three coal strikes. But this amounted to only one-twentieth of one per cent of total working time, or only a sixth as much time as was lost in 1939.

A second major home front problem in 1943 was the increase in friction between Negroes and whites in certain centres of war production into which **Friction between Whites and Negroes** Negro labour had flocked. This reached a climax with the bloody race riots in Mobile, Alabama; Beaumont, Texas; and Detroit. Such racial violence is hard to explain to non-American readers, especially during a war against fascism with its racial theories. Americans generally deplore racial strife, and great progress has been made over the years in alleviating it. But the job is not an easy one to solve, as students of South African racial problems will realize.

The causes of the trouble in 1943 were complex. An underlying factor was the tradition of " White supremacy " in the South, where the great majority of the country's 13,000,000 Negroes live. White Southerners fear Negro participation in politics because in some regions the white population is outnumbered by the coloured. Politicians make capital of this fear. The poorer whites jealously guard such social advantages as they have against Negro encroachment because they have little else to cling to. Most of them resent the promotion of Negroes to skilled jobs not only because their racial status is challenged, but also because they fear Negro competition after the war, when jobs may be harder to obtain. What is true in the South is true also in Detroit and other cities which have drawn heavily on the South for their labour supply.

The Negroes, for their part, feel a new independence because they know that plenty of jobs are waiting for them. They resent their lack of opportunity for promotions, the social restrictions hedging them in, and especially the treatment accorded Negro soldiers in segregated army camps and overseas units. Sometimes this feeling leads to rudeness and even violent outbreaks, as in the all-Negro riot in Harlem, New York City, in September 1943. These tensions are aggravated in war centres by competition for housing and transport. The result, especially when fanned by a small minority of " native fascist " propagandists, is not pretty to see.

Congress contributed to the Administration difficulties in 1943 by contesting almost every move made by the President on home front issues. A Congressional effort to raise price ceilings on farm products was stopped only by a presidential veto, and Mr. Roosevelt's price control programme was severely handicapped when Congress cut the funds requested by the Office of Price Administration for hiring investigators. Serious inflation was averted only by a conscientious effort to enforce price ceilings for staple foods and other necessities of life.

The Congress elected in 1942 was, however, not representative of a fair cross-section of the people. The small number of votes—28 million, or little more than half as many as were cast in the 1940 presidential election—explains its trend towards conserva-

★ ★ ★ ★ ★ ★ ★ ★ ★ ★ ★ ★

NOTICE

Government possession and control of the coal mines of this mining company have been terminated by order of the Secretary of the Interior.

Harold L. Ickes
SECRETARY OF THE INTERIOR

★ ★ ★ ★ ★ ★ ★ ★ ★ ★ ★ ★

RETURNED TO OWNER
Following the strike of the United Mine Workers of America, led by Mr. John L. Lewis on May 1, 1943, Congress passed an act empowering the Government to seize and operate plants and mines where strikes had been called. Mr. Roosevelt used this act to take over the coal mines. Pits where the workers had not struck were handed back to their owners and displayed this notice. The strike was settled on November 3, the miners agreeing to work eight instead of seven hours for a wage of $8.50 a day instead of $35 a week (compared with $46.44 in aircraft construction and $60.75 in shipbuilding). *Photo, Keystone*

tism. Those who did not vote were largely soldiers and war workers who would normally be pro-Administration but had not been able to register and cast their ballots.

The opinion polls showed that three-quarters of the American people approved the job their President was doing in 1943. They were critical about some things— notably the way in which Selective Service, rationing, and war **Approval of the President** taxation had been handled. Some of them even accused the Administration of setting up an inefficient, bureaucratic regime. But the balance of sentiment was in Mr. Roosevelt's favour.

The average American did not worry much about Government policies, except when they affected him personally. But he did support the war wholeheartedly. The great majority of industrial workers allotted at least 10 per cent of their salaries for the purchase of war bonds in 1943. Many of them also gave their blood for the wounded overseas. Their wives worked in Red Cross activities by the thousand, and in America's second year of war more than twenty million American families had " victory gardens," which did a great deal to prevent a food shortage and an inflationary rise in prices.

NEGRO A.A. GUNNERS IN HAWAII
In 1943 there were 13,000,000 Negro Americans, most of whom lived in the South and were disfranchised because they were too poor to possess even the small property qualification necessary in a number of States to qualify for a vote. Like other American citizens, they were liable for military service, and segregation in separate army camps and overseas units was an added source of resentment to Negroes. *Photo, U.S. Signal Corps*

Chapter 295

LATIN AMERICA DRAWS CLOSER TO ALLIES

Though Argentina maintained her neutrality throughout 1943, and the revolutions that took place in other South American republics produced governments whose democracy was dubious, the ties between the countries of Latin America and the Allies grew steadily stronger during the year, as did the importance of those countries' contributions to the Allied war programme. Latin American happenings in 1942 were described in Chapter 216

THOUGH fear of fifth column activities in Latin America led to the publication of a number of unwieldy and apparently well-documented volumes on whose jackets lurid swastikas cast black shadows over the South American continent, the melodramatic forecasts of their authors did not materialize during the year 1943, which brought to light no larger proportion of fifth column activities in Latin America than could have been discovered in territories a good deal closer to Washington and London. It would have been surprising if some of the thousands of Germans and Italians established in Latin America had not tried to do at least a little to help their native countries : no less was expected of Britons, Frenchmen and citizens of the United States; but in the main Latin Americans of German or Italian origin showed themselves to be loyal to the country of their adoption, and the vast majority of the people ranged themselves on the side of the Allies.

Axis propaganda bore singularly anaemic fruits : on the whole Latin America proved unresponsive to propaganda, the effect of which seemed to bear an inverse relation to its violence and intensity. But the **Axis Propaganda Unsuccessful** lack of success of Axis propaganda did not make it any more desirable from the point of view of the United Nations and it is not, therefore, surprising that the failure of Argentina and Chile to implement the recommendations of the 1942 Pan-American Conference at Rio de Janeiro caused grave dissatisfaction in Washington and in London. During January and February 1943, Uruguay, Mexico, Peru, Paraguay, Argentina (despite her continued neutrality), Colombia, Brazil, and Chile all announced their adhesion to the United Nations' declaration of January 5, invalidating economic plundering of occupied territories by the enemy. Brazil declared her adherence to the Atlantic Charter and the United Nations' declaration of January 1, 1942, on February 6 ; and Venezuela notified Britain and the United States of her adherence to the Atlantic Charter on February 13.

After flying the Atlantic on his return from Casablanca, President Roosevelt had a conference with President Vargas of Brazil on January 28 on board a U.S. destroyer in Natal harbour. Mr. Roosevelt informed President Vargas of the results of the **BRAZIL** Casablanca conference, and discussed with him Brazil's co-operation in the Allied war programme. The elimination of the possibility of a German-held Dakar was an important result for Brazil of the

Allied landings the previous autumn in North Africa. During 1943 Brazil's own contribution was chiefly in the form of fighting the U-boats in the South Atlantic : on August 22, the first anniversary of her entry into the war, it was stated in Rio that the Brazilian Navy and Air Force (both greatly expanded) were patrolling large areas of the South Atlantic and had sunk to date eight U-boats. The sinking of another U-boat off Rio by a Brazilian aircraft was announced on October 30,

PRESIDENT ROOSEVELT VISITS BRAZIL

On his way back from the Casablanca Conference, President Roosevelt called at Natal, Brazil, where on January 29, 1943, he met President Vargas, told him the results of the Allied meeting, and discussed Brazil's contribution to the war programme of the United Nations. Here the two Presidents are on a tour of inspection of Brazilian army, navy, and air force installations, under the guidance of a Brazilian officer. *Photo. New York Times*

BRAZILIAN EXPEDITIONARY FORCE REVIEWED

During 1943 Brazil equipped and trained a force of 300,000 for overseas service, units of which are here seen marching through São Paulo. Left, General Joao B. Mascarenhas de Moraes, head of the Brazilian Military Mission which arrived in North Africa on December 12, 1943, in conversation somewhere near Naples with Maj.-Gen. J. G. Ord (right) of the U.S. Army : he had just visited the Fifth Army front in Italy.

Photos, Associated Press ; Keystone

on which day also the loss of the Brazilian ship "Campos" (4,553 tons) by U-boat attack on the night of October 23-24 was reported : this brought Brazil's shipping losses by submarine attack to 150,000 tons.

Brazil also proceeded energetically with the training and equipment of an army of 300,000 men for service overseas. The arrival of a Brazilian Military Mission in North Africa to complete preparations prior to the arrival of a Brazilian Expeditionary Force was announced in Algiers on December 12. In the economic field, Brazil increased her output of minerals and of rubber, and steadily developed her own industries—in July the Brazilian Ambassador in England stated that she had 76,000 factories turning out goods for Allied needs. In June she granted Bolivia the use of the port of Santos ; and on August 22 her abandonment of extra-territorial rights in China was announced in both Rio de Janeiro and Chungking.

The Chilean delegation to the Rio conference had been embarrassed by the fact that Chile was on the eve of a presidential election. President Ríos was elected in February **CHILE** 1942. By the end of the year the balance of power in the Pacific had been restored, and on January 20, 1943, a rupture of diplomatic relations with Germany, Italy and Japan was announced. There can be no doubt as to the popularity among the general public of the decision, which was received with acclamation in Santiago. The U.S.-Chilean agreement of March 9 included Chile in the countries to whom the benefits of the Lease-Lend Act were available. Mr. Henry Wallace, Vice-President of the U.S.A., arrived in Chile on March 26 while on a tour of the west coast countries of South America. He addressed the Chilean Congress on March 27, and left on April 4 to visit Bolivia, Peru, Ecuador and Colombia. On May 20, it was announced that Chile had broken off all diplomatic and commercial relations with the Vichy government, Rumania, Hungary and Bulgaria. She took a step towards the economic unification of the South American republics when on August 24 she and Argentina signed a convention providing in principle for a customs union between the two countries which contiguous countries could join if they wished.

Though the majority of people in Argentina were unquestionably favourable to the Allies, they were more concerned **ARGENTINA** with their own material prosperity. Argentinians in the main were busy and prosperous ; their losses in the exporting of grain were more than compensated in the increased exports of meat. But the press was muzzled and could neither lead nor interpret popular feeling. Finally, the radical party, which should have been the rallying point of opposition to the government's policy of neutrality, was broken and disunited, not yet recovered from the heavy blow it had suffered by the death of its leader, Dr. Alvear, on March 23, 1942.

An attempt made by Argentina to show that Britain understood her attitude led the British Foreign Office to issue a statement on the last day of 1942

Military Revolt in Argentina

deploring Argentina's policy of remaining in diplomatic relations with "the enemies of humanity" and leaving no doubt of Britain's complete unanimity of view with the United States of America on this point. But there were many who fully realized the dangerous position of isolation into which Argentina had manoeuvred herself. The supply of arms under Lease-Lend to Chile and Brazil, and their refusal to Argentina caused much alarm, and the first effective opposition to the government of President Castillo came in the form of an armed military revolt on June 4, led at first by General Rawson, who within a matter of hours was joined by General Ramírez, Minister of War in Castillo's government. Next day General Rawson announced the formation of a provisional government

CONVOY ARRIVES AT RIO DE JANEIRO

An Allied convoy, escorted by U.S. Navy Mariner patrol bombers, is here seen entering the harbour of Rio de Janeiro, capital of Brazil. Brazil's own air force and navy played an important part in keeping down enemy submarine activities in South Atlantic waters : between August 22, 1942, when she entered the war, and October 30, 1943, her forces had sunk nine U-boats.
Photo, Keystone

under his presidency. Two days later he resigned, and General Ramírez assumed the presidency and formed a government of military men which was generally recognized by June 14.

The supporters of the new government were of many shades of opinion : some were favourable to the Allies and genuinely desirous that active steps should be taken to bring Argentina into line with her sister nations of America ; others were anxious only to secure Lend-Lease arms for Argentina ; not a few were genuine idealists whose one desire was to bring to an end the political corruption and graft for many years rampant in the republic ; others again had a distinct leaning to fascism.

The new Minister for Foreign Affairs, Vice-Admiral Segundo Storni, was openly sympathetic to the Allies, though his soundness of principle was greater than his ability. On June 11 the government issued a decree (effective from the 16th)

'Corporative Democracy' Develops

forbidding the use of secret codes in international radio-telegraph and radio-telephone messages—a step in the right direction, for unquestionably Axis diplomatic missions were being used as centres of espionage. But this step was not followed up, and before the end of July the American press was reporting that the new government planned to introduce a "corporative democracy." In spite of indignant denials, developments supported this report. A vigorous campaign against communists—a term interpreted in the usual wide fascist way—was started in August, and a number of trade unions were suppressed.

An extraordinary note, dated August 5, from Admiral Storni to Mr. Cordell Hull pleaded for "understanding" of

AXIS RUBBER FOR THE ALLIES

From time to time the sinking was announced of German blockade-runners inward bound from the Far East and laden with precious cargoes of rubber and tin from the Japanese-occupied Indies. Here, fishermen of Fortaleza, Brazil, are salvaging rubber coming in from the sea from some enemy merchant vessel sunk in the South Atlantic by U.S. and Brazilian naval and air patrols.
Photo, Paul Popper

corporative organization was announced in December. At the end of 1943 Argentina's relations with the Allies were anything but satisfactory; nor were there any signs of improvement.

Mr. Henry Wallace travelled from Chile to Bolivia on April 4. On April 6 a special session of the Bolivian cabinet agreed to a declaration of war on the Axis powers, which was made on April 7 by decree of President Enrique Peñaranda, **BOLIVIA** who a month later signed the Atlantic Charter while on a visit to Washington. The creation of a General Bureau for the Co-ordination of Mobilization, to carry out the mobilization of resources decreed when Bolivia declared war on the Axis, was announced early in August. Revolution, headed by leaders of the National Revolutionary Party, broke out in La Paz during the night of December 18–19, and it was announced on December 19 that a new government had been formed under the presidency of Major Gualberto Villaroel. The National Revolutionary Party had had seven members in Congress out of 70. It was a violently nationalistic movement, strongly opposed, however, to "big business," and in particular to the great Bolivian tin mining interests. It had been very critical of the administration following the suppression by government troops of the Catavi tin mine strike in December 1942, in connexion with which Dr. Hans Kempinski, a German, was arrested on charges of promoting subversive activities. The report published in June 1943 by the mission of U.S. labour experts, appointed by the U.S. State Department

CHILE DECLARES FOR THE ALLIES

Chile broke off relations with Germany, Italy, and Japan on January 20, 1943—a step greeted with acclamation in Santiago, the capital, on a wall in which appeared the chalked notice shown here. Top, Mr. Henry Wallace, Vice-President of the United States, reviewing Chilean troops at Arica on March 26 during his tour of the west coast countries of South America.

Photos, Keystone ; Paul Popper

Argentina's position, and for arms to restore her position in relation to her neighbours. Mr. Cordell Hull's reply was sharp in tone as it was blunt in manner. The publication of these letters a month later led to Storni's resignation. He was replaced by General Gilbert, an Axis sympathizer. When, owing to the death of Rear-Admiral Saba Sueyró, the Vice-Presidency had to be filled, Colonel Farrell—a man of the extreme right—was appointed. Colonel Peron, at first Under-Secretary for War and later Director of the National Department of Labour, was another prominent man of the right. General Rawson was forced to accept an appointment as Argentine Ambassador to Brazil.

The suppression of Yiddish papers in October was revoked after a rebuke from President Roosevelt; but the dissolution of a number of Jewish (as well as Masonic) institutions followed. The government's intention to bring workers and employers into a joint

U.S. VICE-PRESIDENT VISITS BOLIVIA

From Chile Mr. Wallace went on to Bolivia. He is seen here in the presidential palace at La Paz, the capital, with General Enrique Peñaranda, President of Bolivia (right), who declared war against the Axis on April 7, 1943. With Mr. Wallace and the President is Mr. Pierre de Lagarde Boal, U.S. Ambassador to Bolivia.

Photo, Associated Press

En memoria del pueblo de la
ce Checoeslovaquia, que la
barie nazi destruyo, pero
continuará viviendo eter
mente en el corazón de to
s que aman la libertad
El pueblo libre de Méxic
erige este monumento.

MEXICO CONDEMNS THE AXIS

1. San Geronimo Asculo changes its name to San Geronimo Lidice in honour of Lidice, Czechoslovakia, destroyed by the Nazis (see p. 2569 and illus., p. 2568). 2. President Roosevelt and President Camacho of Mexico salute their countries' flags at a parade in honour of Roosevelt's visit to Monterrey, Mexico, in April 1943. 3. Notice affixed to shops in Mexico City on December 9 : it announces the closing of the premises as a protest against the mass murder of Jews in Europe. 4. Department store in Mexico City closed as an expression of sympathy with persecuted Jewry.

CERRADO
DE LAS 9 A LAS 10 H.
En señal de protesta contra el
ASESINATO EN MASA DE LOS
ISRAELITAS DE EUROPA
POR LAS HORDAS DE HITLER

LAS FABRICAS UNIVERSALES

NEW ROAD LINKS AMAZON AND PACIFIC

On August 31, 1943, President Prado of Peru opened a new highway linking Callao on the coast with Pucallpa on the Ucayali (a tributary of the Amazon), a river port accessible all the year round to vessels of 3,000 tons displacement. President Prado is here seen (fourth from the right) with some of the men who carried the road over the Blue Cordillera by the pass of Padre Abad, used in 1757 by a missionary named Abad, lost, and rediscovered in 1937. *Photo, Topical Press*

in January 1943 at the request of the Bolivian government to investigate labour conditions and advise on the possibility of increasing output, disclosed that the trouble was based on more fundamental causes than enemy activity: the mission found "tragic conditions" among the workers, 75 per cent of whom were illiterate. Poverty, overcrowding, insanitary housing, child labour, absence of normal safety devices, and a very heavy incidence of occupational diseases—8-9 per cent of the tin miners being permanently incapacitated every year—were among the conditions reported, and the mission recommended assistance from U.S.A. technicians, teachers, sanitary experts, etc., with a view to the betterment of Bolivia's social and economic life.

In a manifesto issued by Villaroel on taking office, he declared that his administration would " promote the welfare of the people, who will never again meet with machine-guns backing the great economic interests," would maintain solidarity with the United Nations, and respect the " good neighbour " policy. A day or two later he pledged Bolivia to export tin to the United States and Britain only. On December 21 all Bolivian legations abroad issued a statement affirming the new government's continued adherence to the United Nations Pact and the Atlantic Charter. The revolution was the first to be directed against the great mining interests which had for many years dominated the political and economic life of the country; but the democratic nature of the new government was so much in doubt that by the end of the year no country except Ecuador had recognized it.

Under an agreement signed in Washington on February 3 by Mr. Litvinov, Russian Ambassador in the U.S.A., and Mr. Turbay, Foreign Minister of Colombia, their two countries entered into diplomatic relations and agreed to appoint Ministers in Moscow and Bogotá. In **COLOMBIA** October a state of siege was declared in Bogotá following clashes between police and striking transport workers in which seven were killed and many injured. The cabinet resigned, and a new administration was formed. The transport strike was called off on October 10, the workers demands were met, and order was restored. The disturbances had been due to a great rise in prices while the workers were still drawing pre-war wages. The salaries of government and municipal employees were raised, an Office of Price Control was created, and commerce and industry were appealed to by the government to raise wages by 20 per cent. Following the sinking of a Colombian steamer by a U-boat on November 27, the government declared a " state of belligerency " with Germany on November 28.

A new highway from Callao and Lima across the Andes to Huanaco and thence across the Montaña to the port of Pucallpa on the Ucayali River was inaugurated by President Prado of Peru on August 31, 1943. This new road was a vital auxiliary of the great Pan-American highway, **PERU** planned to stretch all the way along the west coast of America from Alaska to the south of Chile. It was essential also to the development of Peruvian Amazonia, from which the Allies were able to draw important rubber supplies. Peru intensified her production in other directions too, especially of quinine and flax, to meet Allied needs.

In Uruguay the new President, Dr. Juan José Amezaga, with Dr. Alberto Guani as Vice-President, assumed office on March 1. Dr. Amezaga was the leader of the left wing of the Liberal Party, **URUGUAY** and had polled 402,000 votes against 110,000 cast for his chief opponent, Dr. Alberto de Herrera, leader of the Conservative National Party. Dr. Guani as Foreign Minister in the previous government visited Canada and the U.S.A. at the end of January for economic conversations, during which he met Mr. Litvinov. Under a presidential decree of July 25, Uruguay resumed diplomatic relations with Russia, which had been broken off on December 27, 1935. The breaking off of relations with the Vichy government in France was announced on May 12.

The first exchange of Ministers between Mexico and the U.S.S.R. was announced in Mexico City on December 23, 1942. On December 7 of the same year the Mexican **MEXICO** Ministry of National Defence estimated that under the measure of conscription imposed the previous October the country would have 1,600,000 trained fighting men by the end of 1943. Five thousand recruits were inducted on March 1, and another 5,000 on July 1. By March also 60 centres for pre-military training, where men attended for two hours' training every Sunday, had been established in the Federal District of Mexico City.

Following a tour of U.S. military and naval establishments in the south, President Roosevelt arrived at Monterrey (Mexico) on April 20 for talks on the war situation with President Avila Camacho. The meeting, which took place in Mr. Roosevelt's presidential train, was the first between the heads of these two States for 34 years. On April 21 the two presidents crossed into U.S. territory, parting at Corpus Christi (Texas). They agreed on the setting up of a U.S.-Mexican committee, consisting of two representatives of each country,

2961

to study economic relations between their countries, which had been disturbed by the inability of the U.S.A. (owing to her war production programme) to provide the farm machinery and electrical appliances Mexico urgently needed in return for the metals and other invaluable war materials with which she was supplying the United States. An agreement of May 1 allowed the temporary admission to the U.S.A. of Mexican non-agricultural workers, the first 6,000 of whom were to be employed on maintenance work on railways in the south-west. Up to September 1943, more than 11,000 Mexicans had enlisted in the U.S. armed forces.

The war made only too clear to Latin Americans their dependence upon the Great Powers. Paradoxically, Argentina probably suffered least economically: her meat and other foodstuffs were essential to Britain. The tin of Bolivia, and the oil of Venezuela, Mexico, Colombia and Peru also became indispensable to the Allies as a result of the Japanese conquests. But for long, shortage of shipping hampered even these exports, while the coffee growers of Brazil and Colombia, the tobacco planters of Cuba and many others

REVOLT IN ARGENTINA

On June 4, 1943, a successful military revolt broke out in Buenos Aires against President Castillo of Argentina. It was led by General Arturo Rawson (saluting) and General Pedro Ramirez (in the foreground). Ramirez assumed the presidency on June 14. Below, an omnibus burns in the Plaza de Mayo, near Government House, Buenos Aires, during the June revolt.

Photos, Keystone; Associated Press

suffered severely. Even worse was the position of importers of manufactured goods unable to obtain supplies from Europe and entirely dependent on the United States. Inevitably this situation led to some resentment, and in spite of the "good neighbour" policy, relations between the Latin American countries and the United States were less cordial and friendly than official declarations implied. Still, the year 1943 saw on the whole a steady increase in goodwill towards the Allies in Latin America as continued Allied successes seemed to justify hopes of an Axis defeat in the not very distant future.

Chapter 296

AIR POWER PAVES THE WAY FOR INVASION

Steadily mounting in intensity during 1943, the Allied air assault on German industry was designed to serve a purpose similar to that of a blockade by sea. It was not intended, and never reached the proportions necessary, to defeat Germany by bombing alone, even assuming that to have been possible; but it did increasingly hamper the enemy's production and prepare the ground for the invasion of Western Europe. Captain Norman Macmillan, M.C., A.F.C., who recorded the progress of Allied air strength in other fields during 1943 in Chapter 268, here describes the combined attack by the R.A.F. and U.S.A.A.F. on the enemy's war production up to the spring of 1944

THE British outlook on the employment of a force of strategic bombers was perhaps unique. Continental air forces (including Russian) were designed primarily to co-operate with ground forces. United States bomber forces were intended to wage war over long distances, such as obtain in the Pacific and throughout the Western Hemisphere. The French High Command view was so inflexible that not until June 18, 1940, did the strategic bombers of Bomber Command set out from their East Anglian bases to begin in earnest the execution of the plan for the air blockade of German industry.

From a maximum striking force of about 100 heavy bombers when Portal took command, striking power of Bomber Command under Peirse rose to about 300, and under Harris, before the invasion of Normandy, to about 1,300 aircraft. From less than 100 tons, bomb concentrations increased to 2,500 tons against distant targets, and 5,000 tons against near targets.

Britain produced only 41 four-engined bombers in 1940, the first year of their construction; 498 in 1941; 1,976 in 1942; 4,614 in 1943, and 2,889 in the first half of 1944. It was the rising output of these heavy aircraft—in order of appearance, the Stirling, Halifax, and Lancaster—and their capacity to carry a bomb load of from 16,000 to 18,000 lb. (about four times the load of preceding heavy bombers) that enabled Bomber Command to increase its weight of attack as the old bombers were replaced. For, although 23½ new R.A.F. squadrons were formed in 1942, only the one-half squadron reached Bomber Command, the 23 full squadrons being deflected to Coastal Command for use against the submarine, and to Mediterranean and Eastern theatres of war.

In 1942 the Pathfinder Force was created. Within it were assembled the most expert pilots and navigators,

commanded by the pre-war Imperial Airways pilot D. C. T. Bennett, a tall, slim Australian, who was promoted to the acting rank of Air Vice-Marshal on December 6, 1943, the first "civilian" member of the R.A.F. to reach that rank. The duty of Pathfinder pilots, who wore a special badge on the flap of their left breast pocket, was to find the

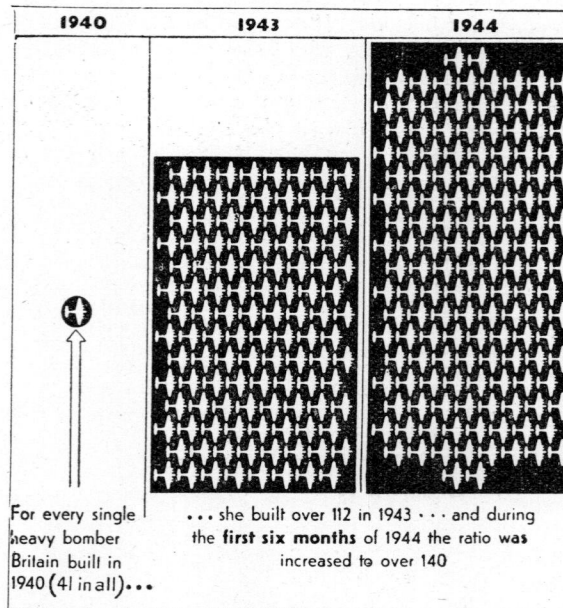

For every single heavy bomber Britain built in 1940 (41 in all)... ...she built over 112 in 1943 ... and during the **first six months** of 1944 the ratio was increased to over 140

BRITISH BOMBER PRODUCTION
Issued by the Ministry of Information

target and identify it with pyrotechnic flares of distinctive colours (varied from one attack to another as a code is changed) so that the bomb-aimers of the main force were required only to drop their bombs within the flare-lit area.

A force of about 300 bombers made the first experiment in area bombing against Lubeck. The target was the old city, almost enclosed within a three-quarters bend of the river, which there forms a natural boundary marker. Severe damage was done within Alten Lubeck, and from photographs it was possible to assess the effectiveness of this form of attack upon a built-up area (*see illus.*, p. 2118).

Then the experimental thousand-bomber attacks were planned to demonstrate what could be done by concentrated bombing against large targets. From its first-line units Bomber Command could not place 1,000 bombers into the task force. Aircraft were therefore drawn from the Operational Training Units (which had been created to train new air crews instead of training them within first-line squadrons) and from Coastal Command. In the night following May 30, 1942, the first such attack was made by 1,130 bombers against Cologne (*see illus.*, p. 2131). It lasted 90 minutes; 1,500 tons of bombs were dropped; 44 aircraft were lost. Two more experimental plus-1,000 bomber attacks were made in June 1942 against Essen and Bremen.

The Photographic Development Unit flying Spitfires with long-range tanks instead of armament had grown into Photographic Reconnaisance Units, and air photographs of the damage inflicted by the mass attack on Cologne showed that great devastation was wrought by the concentration of bombs. This result was no doubt one basis for the decision to allocate more manpower to the production of heavy bombers.

These first experimental plus-1,000 bomber attacks were succeeded by a period of preparation for the later mass attacks by forces equipped mainly with four-engined bombers.

While lesser scale attacks continued, new devices and methods were evolved to suit the new technique. One was the Mark XIV Bomb Sight, first issued to the Pathfinder Force in August 1942 and subsequently to all aircraft in Bomber Command and to U.S. medium bombers under the classification T.1 Sight. Earlier British bomb sights required a level platform to ensure accuracy; bombers using them had to fly straight towards their targets at a level height without banking their wings. When the pilots could not weave to counter the effects of shell-bursts, weather and interceptors, because it disturbed the accuracy of the sighting, their bombers were easier prey for anti-aircraft gunners and night fighters. Because it was not affected by banking, the new sight facilitated mass bombing, for instead of repeated aiming runs, a single run up to the target usually sufficed.

Teleradar was developed for blind navigation. The returning impulses of electrical emissions from the aircraft echoing from objects on the ground or sea are picked up by an instrument

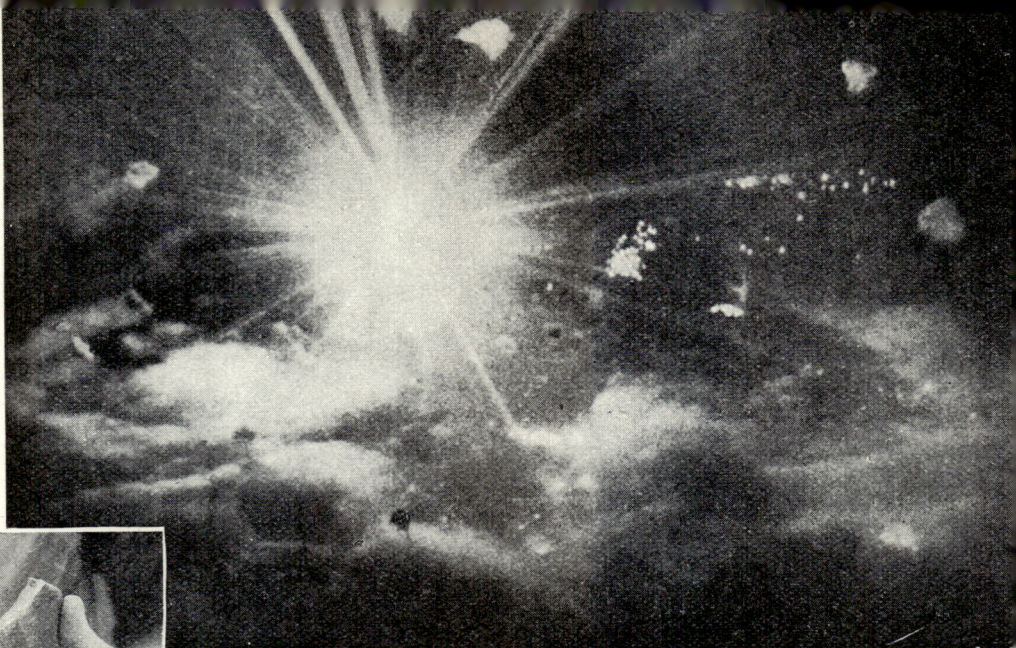

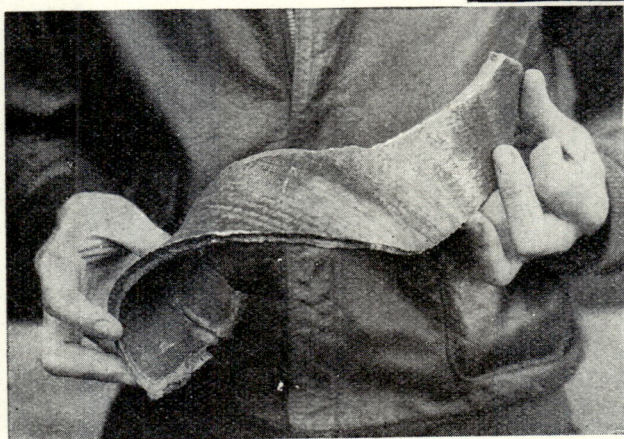

GERMANY'S A.A. DEFENCES

A flare shell (above) which, when it burst in the air, looked like an aircraft blowing up, was one device used by the German anti-aircraft defences in order to give raiders the impression that the flak was more effective than in fact it was. R.A.F. pilots called these flares 'scarecrows.' Left, a 10-lb. piece of metal found embedded in the wing of a Flying Fortress after a raid : it was part of a rocket shell fired by German twin-engined fighters.

Photos, British Official ; Associated Press

within the aircraft, called, in R.A.F. slang, the " gen-box." Working like a fluoroscope, this instrument projects the invisible rays upon a glass screen as visible rays which form a picture of the groundscape, and this enables the navigator or bomb-aimer to "see" through miles of darkness or cloud. Ships, industrial targets, and particular parts of cities can be identified and bombed even in bad visibility. American bombers, supplied with this British instrument (which Americans called the " magic eye "), were able to operate when they would otherwise have been grounded by weather. Hence came the term " bombing by instruments."

More powerful engines, with constant speed airscrews, using the new corundite sparking plug (with fused alumina instead of mica for its insulator and with a platinum wire point 1/300th of an inch thick) gave greater reliability and speed.

When the war began the 250-lb. and 500-lb. bombs were the most commonly used, and the one-ton bomb was almost the heaviest. The American heavy bombers were designed to drop the smaller sizes of bombs. The enemy dropped bombs weighing one ton and three-quarters on England during 1940–41. Before introducing precision bombing with large bombs, Bomber Command used the 2,000-lb. parachute blast bomb similar to the German " landmine." British four-engined bombers made possible the use of larger bombs and these were progressively developed. The 4,000-lb. bomb was first dropped on Naples on October 21, 1941. It was used from the United Kingdom first against the Matford Works at Poissy on April 2, 1942. It had to be flown there with the bomb doors open. That was soon remedied so that longer-range attacks could be made. The 8,000-lb. (" blockbuster ") bomb was first used against

Heavier Bombs Used

Flt.-Lt. WILLIAM REID (R.A.F.V.R.)

On November 3, 1943, Flt.-Lt. Reid's Lancaster was twice attacked, and he himself twice wounded, on its way to Dusseldorf. His navigator was killed, his wireless operator fatally wounded, and the machine severely damaged. But he kept on his course, delivered his bombs, and, semi-conscious, turned home. Awarded the V.C. for most conspicuous bravery.

Group-Capt. G. L. CHESHIRE (R.A.F.V.R.)

Holder of D.S.O. and double bar, and D.F.C., and awarded the V.C. in September 1944 for most conspicuous bravery in completing 100 missions, Cheshire led his squadron in many attacks on heavily defended areas, frequently releasing his bombs from below 2,000 ft. In an experimental attack on Munich in April 1944 he flew over the city for some time at 700 ft.

Pilot-Officer CYRIL BARTON (R.A.F.V.R.)

Posthumously awarded the V.C. for unsurpassed courage during a raid on Nuremberg on March 30, 1944. Inter-communication system and machine-guns were destroyed 70 miles before reaching the target and three of his crew baled out in error ; but he bombed the objective and brought his plane back to England without navigational aids —to die in crash-landing.

Photos, British Official ; Fox Photos ; L.N.A.

Karlsruhe on Sept. 2, 1942, and against Italy first on Nov. 28, 1942, at Turin. In 1944 the 12,000-lb. "factory-buster" blast bomb was first used against the Gnome-Le Rhône aero engine works at Limoges and next against the FW-190 aeroplane factory near Albert and the assembly plant and repair depot at Merlan-les-Mureaux, in the nights following February 8 and March 2 ; this huge bomb was used solely for precision bombing against such isolated targets until November 27, 1944, when it was employed in an area attack on industrial buildings in Munich. The 12,000-lb. ("earthquake") bomb was also developed (under Mr. B. M. Wallis, of Vickers-Armstrongs, the inventor of geodetic aircraft construction) as a streamlined armour-piercing bomb ; released from a height, this bomb fell faster than sound travels and could penetrate battleship armour, concrete submarine pens, flying bomb launching ramps and stores.

Daylight raids, such as that on the M.A.N. Diesel Works at Augsburg on April 17, 1942, when 7 out of 12 Lancasters were lost, were costly, so the technique of brilliant night illumination of targets was perfected, and towards the end of 1943 isolated factories were destroyed or damaged even more efficiently than by day, for the night bombers could fly lower with safety from flak, and could bomb accurately within an area less than 500 yards square.

Night Illumination of Targets

A special type of bomb was developed for the attack on May 17, 1943, upon the Moehne, Eder and Sorpe dams (see page 2660, and illus., p. 2659) ; it could be dropped from 100 feet (or less) so that its considerable forward impetus carried it onward to explode against the dam wall. The Sorpe dam resisted it, as it also resisted on October 15, 1944, the 12,000-lb. armour-piercing bomb. A new incendiary bomb throwing a 15-feet jet-flame came into use in 1944.

From the marshalling tactics adopted by Wing-Commander G. P. Gibson, V.C., during the attack against the dams in 1943 was evolved the Master Bomber form of attack. One very experienced pilot—the Master Bomber—controlled each such operation, flying low over the target to identify it, and to confirm that flare markers were dropped in the correct positions to ensure accurate bomb-aiming by the task force, before giving in radio

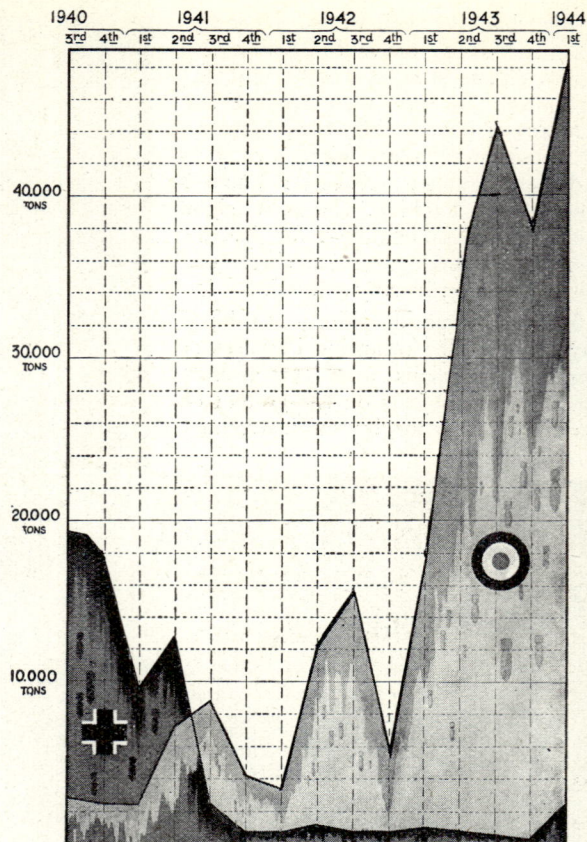

LUFTWAFFE AND R.A.F. BOMB TONNAGE
This graph illustrates more forcefully than words the decline in the tonnage of bombs dropped by the Luftwaffe (dark shading) and the rise quarter by quarter in that dropped by the R.A.F. on Germany alone (light shading). In the first quarter of 1943 the R.A.F. reached Germany's heaviest tonnage, and thereafter increased the weight of its attack.

TRAIL OF THE PATHFINDERS
The duty of pilots of the Pathfinder Force, commanded by D. C. T. Bennett, C.B.E., D.S.O. (right, below), promoted Air Vice-Marshal in December 1943, was to find the target and identify it with coloured flares. Here Bomber Command heavies are coming in over a marked target. Members of this force wore a special badge on the left breast-pocket flap (right).

code the order to bomb. The first fully planned Master Bomber attack was made in the moonlight night of August 17, 1943, against Peenemunde research station (see illus., p. 2658). This attack was led by Wing-Commander G. L. Cheshire (later awarded the V.C. : see p. 2963). It followed the discovery by photographic reconnaissance of peculiar-looking jet-propelled aircraft standing close to launching ramps whose appearance on the photographs confirmed intelligence reports and stories from Sweden of the flying bomb. This attack was followed by intensive photographic reconnaissances which located partly built launching sites in the Pas de Calais, against which Bomber Command, from November 1943 to June 1944, dropped more than 100,000 tons of bombs (including the 12,000-lb. A.P. type) in one of its greatest diversions from direct air blockade.

Bomber Command Operations Headquarters was built underground in the country, lit by fluorescent lighting, and air conditioned. Here the Commander-in-Chief held his staff conferences and

2964

R.A.F. PHOTOGRAPHIC RECONNAISSANCE

1. The Mark XI Vickers-Armstrong Supermarine Spitfire, an all-metal single seat, low wing monoplane used by both the R.A.F. and the U.S.A.A.F. for photographic reconnaissance duties. It had a Rolls-Royce Merlin engine of over 1,650 h.p., and was used to photograph the breached Moehne and Eder dams (see p. 2659), Berlin and other bomb damage, and to obtain information about ground dispositions previous to the Allied invasion of France.   2. Installing a camera in the fuselage of a Spitfire Mark XI.   3. A WAAF officer, watched by two Canadian pilots, examines photographs from a newly developed film. 4. A picture of Linosa Island, 27 miles N.E. of Lampedusa, built up from a number of reconnaissance photographs.   *Photos, British Official*

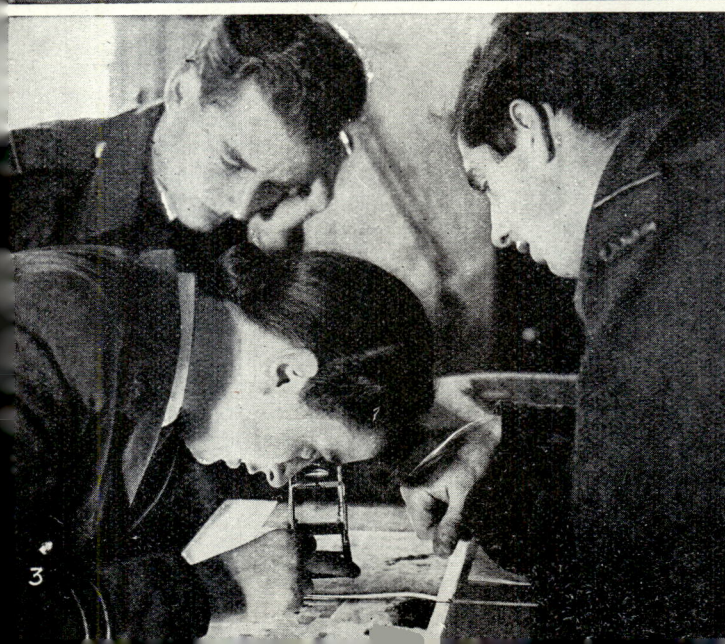

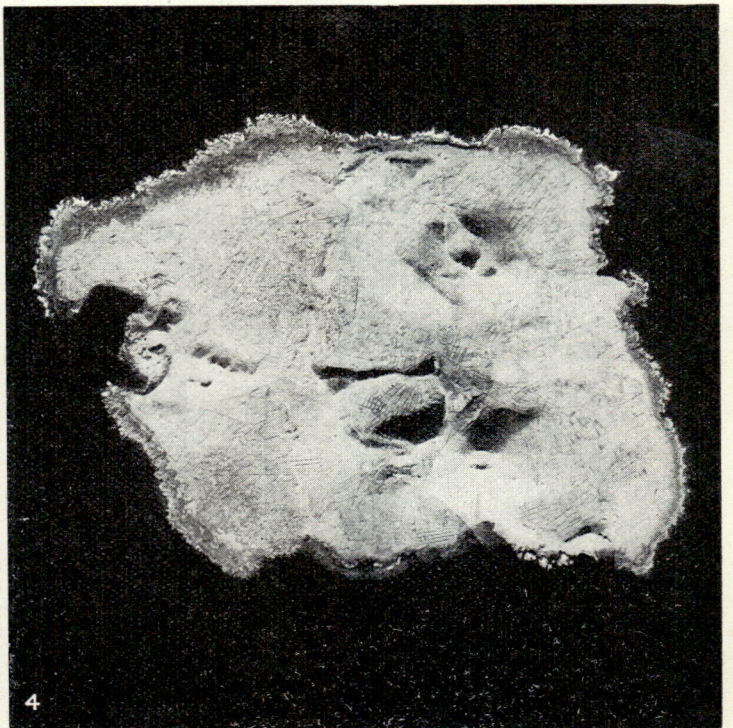

(see illus., p. 1926).

DEBUT OF THE R.A.F.'s 'FACTORY-BUSTER'

On the night of February 8, 1944, 12,000-lb. 'factory-buster' bombs were used for the first time in a raid by the R.A.F. on the Gnome-Le Rhône aero engine works at Limoges in France, built in 1939 as one of the four main repair depots of the French Air Force. These photographs, that on the left taken before the raid, that above after it, illustrate the effect of these bombs: twenty bays out of a total of 48 were totally destroyed, three others were severely damaged, and seventeen suffered roof displacement.

Photos, British Official

planned his assaults; from here his orders radiated to Group Commanders and thence to Stations and Squadrons (see illus., p. 1926). Broad direction of the campaign came from the Minister of Defence and the Chiefs of Staff Committee. The Ministry of Economic Warfare probed into German industrial economy to find where the enemy would suffer the greatest military difficulties from damage and loss through air attack. The targets were chosen by a Target Selection Committee, which indicated priority. From this target list the

Commander-in-Chief selected the best target or targets for his force for any given night, having regard to weather forecasts, time of year (long or short nights decided the question of range), the known or suspected disposition of enemy defences, and the state of the battle plan of large targets such as

the Ruhr, Hamburg or Berlin, Bomber Command's main industrial objectives.

The devastation caused in Coventry by the Luftwaffe was used as the unit of measurement of Bomber Command's attacks. Coventry was photographed from the air, and the photographs joined in a mosaic to form a map. The extent of **Coventry as Unit of Devastation** the damage was accurately assessed on the ground and transferred to a transparency page that overlaid the map, one colour showing total damage, another partial damage, and the unmarked portion no damage. Details of population, area and damage were stated in figures and percentages of built-up areas. All Germany's principal cities were similarly photographed, and the damage done to them was similarly assessed by Intelligence from examination of subsequent air photographs. The effect of attack against each built-up area could thus be seen visually in direct comparison with Coventry. This volume, bound in blue leather, was Air Chief Marshal Harris's blue book of the work of Bomber Command.

The enemy exerted himself to minimize the damage to his war potential by

LOADING A MOSQUITO WITH A 4,000-LB. BOMB

Until British factories began to produce Stirlings, Halifaxes, and Lancasters, 4,000 lbs. was the maximum load any bomber could carry. Here a Mosquito is being loaded with its single 4,000-lb. bomb. Pilots reported that the plane leapt into the air when its load was released 'like an express lift going up in a hurry.' Mosquitoes continued to be used on many missions long after heavier aircraft carrying bigger bombs were available for special targets. *Photo, Keystone*

MEXICAN PARADE IN SUPPORT OF THE ALLIES

In his address to Congress on September 2, 1943, President Camacho of Mexico stated that relations between Mexico and the United States had never been better, and this goodwill towards the nearest of the Allies was reflected in Mexico's feeling towards the rest of them. Here is part of a big parade organized in the little city of Cuernavaca to demonstrate its support of the war against the Axis. Though Mexico did not put any armed forces into the field, over 11,000 Mexicans enlisted in the U.S. forces, and her oil and other war materials were invaluable to the Allies.

BERLIN UNDER BOMBARDMENT

Berlin received one of its heaviest attacks of the war on April 29, 1944, when about 1,000 Fortresses and Liberators, escorted by about 1,000 fighters, dropped some 2,000 tons of bombs on the Reich capital at noon. Despite thick cloud, visual bombing was possible through gaps. Very strong opposition was met from some 200 enemy fighters as well as a violent rocket barrage over the city. The U.S.A.A.F. shot down 88 German machines (72 by bombers and 16 by fighters) for the loss of 63 bombers and 14 fighters. This photograph, taken during the raid, shows through cloud and cloud shadows Tempelhof Airport (near the top) ; just below and slightly to the right. smoke rising from direct hits on the big Tempelhof railway marshalling yards ; further below, direct hits on the Anhalter Station and the new Nazi Air Ministry.

Photo, U.S. Official

ONE LANCASTER —ONE BOMB

The introduction of precision bombing, and the construction of aircraft able to carry greater weights on long-range missions, made it possible for the R.A.F. to use heavier and heavier bombs. The first 4,000-pounder was dropped on Naples, October 21, 1941; the first 8,000-lb. 'blockbuster' on Karlsruhe railway centre, September 2, 1942; the first 12,000-lb. 'factory-buster' blast bomb on the Gnome—Le Rhône aero engine works at Limoges, February 8, 1944.

A further development was the 12,000-lb. streamlined, armour-piercing 'earthquake' bomb, here shown in position in the bomb-bay of a Lancaster, with armourers checking the installation before closing the bomb doors. It was used against concrete submarine pens, flying-bomb launching ramps, and similar well-protected objectives.

Speaking in the House of the sinking of the German battleship 'Tirpitz' on Nov. 12, 1944, Sir A. Sinclair, Secretary of State for Air, said, 'This brilliant feat of arms was accomplished by British crews, aiming with a British bombsight of extraordinary complexity, ingenuity and accuracy, a 12,000-lb. bomb of British design and manufacture from a British Lancaster — the only aircraft in the world which could carry that bomb.'

Photo, Sport & General

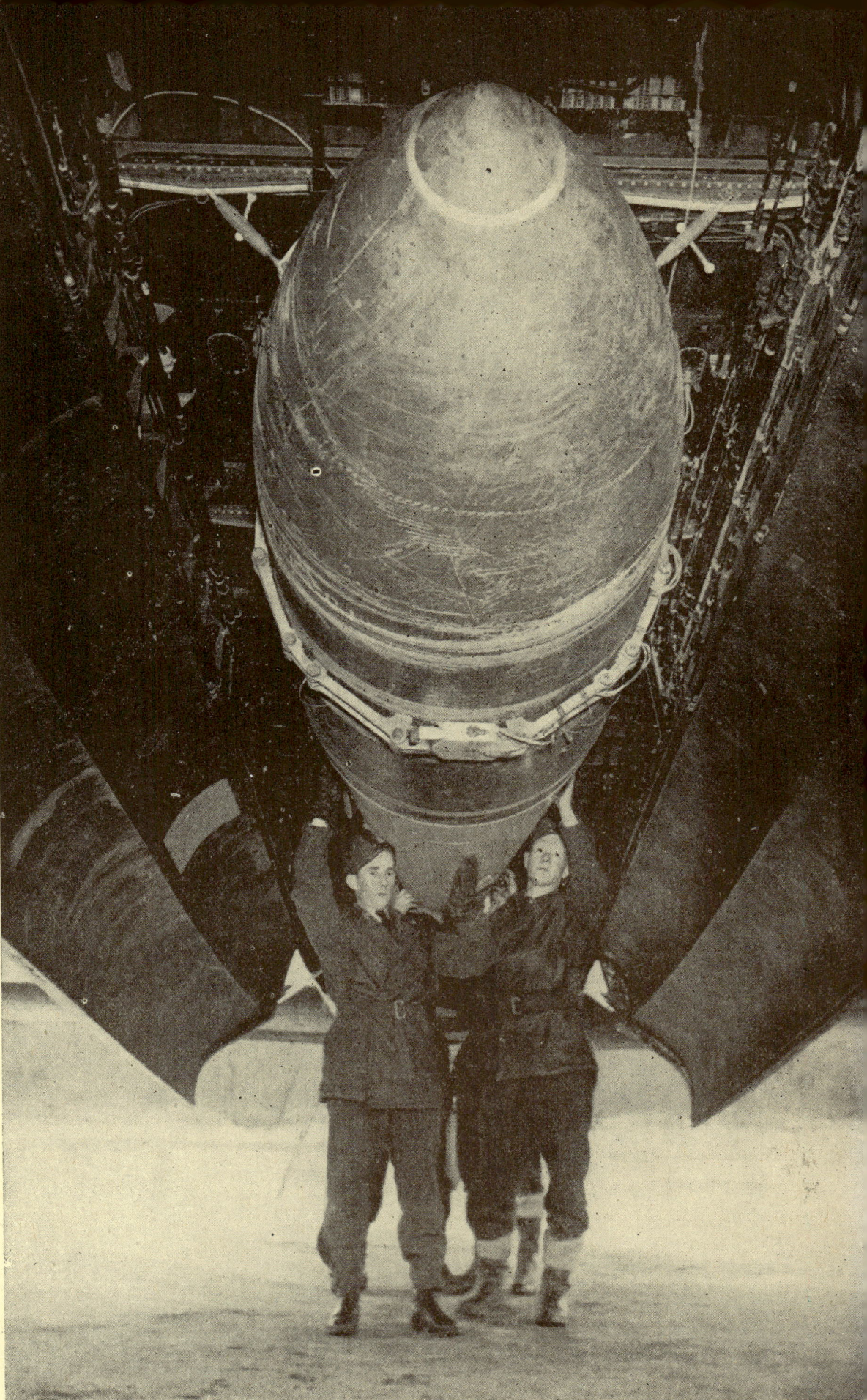

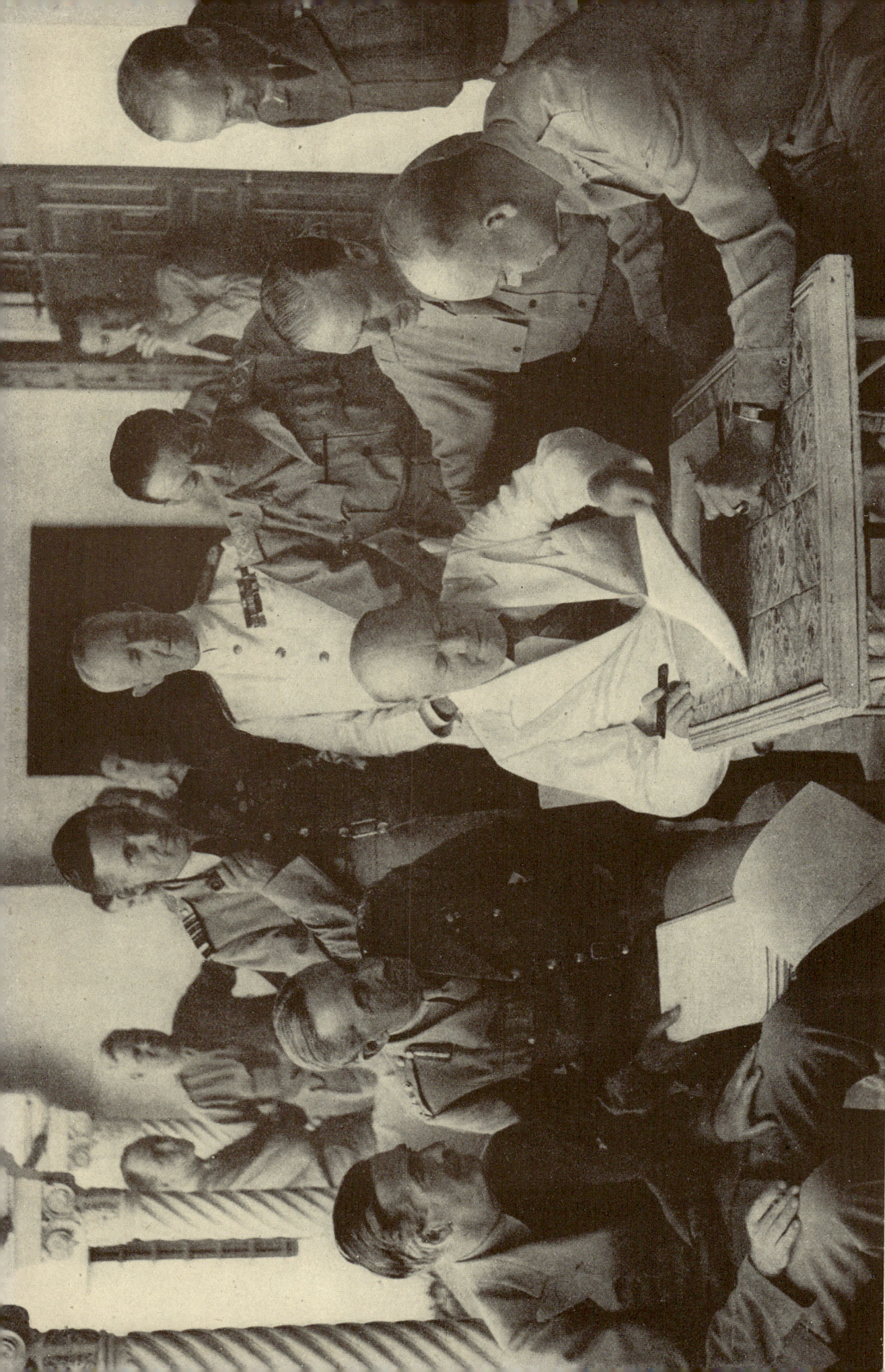

BRITISH PRIME MINISTER WITH ALLIED COMMANDERS IN NORTH AFRICA

Following his meeting with President Roosevelt in Washington from May 13-26, 1943, Mr. Churchill, accompanied by General George Catlett Marshall (Chief of Staff, U.S. Army), flew on May 27 to Gibraltar and on to Allied G.H.Q., North Africa. Mr. Anthony Eden, British Foreign Secretary, joined him at Algiers for conversations with the Allied military leaders. Here is the Prime Minister at Algiers in the centre of a group consisting of (left to right) Mr. Eden, Sir Alan Brooke (Chief of the Imperial General Staff), Air Chief Marshal Sir Arthur Tedder (Allied Air C.-in-C., Mediterranean), Admiral Sir Andrew Cunningham (Allied Naval C.-in-C., Mediterranean), General Sir Harold Alexander (Deputy Allied C.-in-C., North Africa), Gen. Marshall, Gen. Dwight D. Eisenhower (Allied C.-in-C., North Africa), and Gen. Sir Bernard Montgomery (C.-in-C., British 8th Army).

Photo, British Official

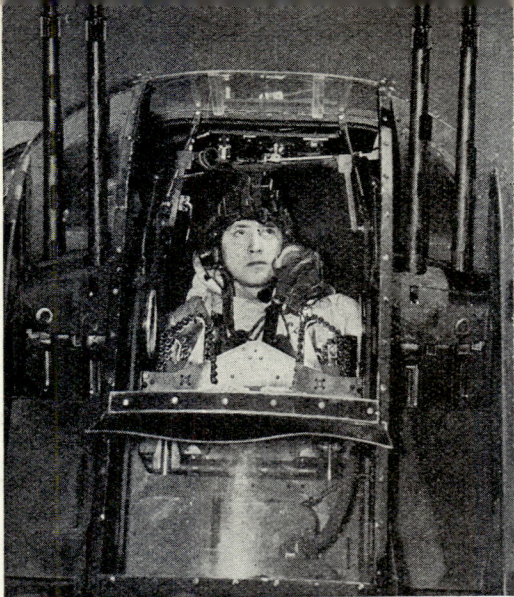

'TAIL-END CHARLIE' AND HIS GUNS

'Tail-end Charlie' was the R.A.F. nickname for the rear-gunner of a long-range bomber, who sometimes spent as much as ten hours alone in his turret. He could talk with the rest of the crew over the inter-communication telephone, and a door connected his turret with the fuselage or could be swung clear if he had to bale out. The rear guns were mounted to move vertically; the whole turret to move laterally. Here is a Lancaster rear-gunner ready for a flight (left); a Halifax's rear guns being tested during a night flight (right). *Photos, British Official; Topical*

rebuilding, removing, and dispersing industry, and by creating more underground factories. When photographic reconnaissance and intelligence reports indicated that a damaged area was again coming into use, the bombers returned to the attack and undid the work of reconstruction. The new industrial areas were sought and attacked.

The continuing assault forced the enemy to provide an increasing number of military and civil defence personnel, and it was estimated in 1943 that some

Enemy's Defence Personnel 3,000,000 were permanently employed in active air defence, civil defence, mine - sweeping, and essential repairs. As British bombing became more severe it was impossible for fire-fighters to work during the actual attack. The intensity of the bombing forced them underground, and when they emerged, the fires had taken firm hold. The columns of flame that swept upward sucked air to feed the conflagration. Hurricane winds up to 90 miles an hour swept through the debris-strewn streets, and it was impossible for men to hold firehoses in their hands. Often water supplies were smashed. In order to save parts of towns, defence workers were obliged to dynamite buildings to create urban fire-brakes across which the flames could not pass.

After the United States entered the war it was decided to send a bomber force to operate from the United Kingdom. Flying Fortress and Liberator bombers carried smaller bomb loads than the heavy aircraft of Bomber Command, but were more powerfully armed. They were designed and armed for day assaults. Their take off and landing speeds were faster than those of the British night bombers. To enable them to carry their biggest bomb loads it was necessary to site them as close as possible to their target areas and give them the best flying country for their difficult take off. Bomber Command vacated the excellent airfields in East Anglia and moved north into and around Yorkshire. But the American bombers did not accumulate as quickly as was expected, and for a period the value of the East Anglian airfields was lost. The heavy bombers of this U.S. Army 8th Air Force first attacked targets in enemy-occupied countries. Their initial German target was Wilhelmshaven naval base on January 27, 1943.

FLYING-BOMB EXPERIMENTS AT PEENEMUNDE

In the battle against the flying bomb, which came to its height in the summer of 1944, the Intelligence services, air reconnaissance squadrons, and photographic interpretation units played an important preliminary part. This photograph, released only in September 1944, was taken on November 8, 1943, and shows a flying-bomb ready on a launching ramp (indicated by arrow) at the experimental station of Peenemunde, bombed the previous August by the R.A.F. (See p. 2658.)

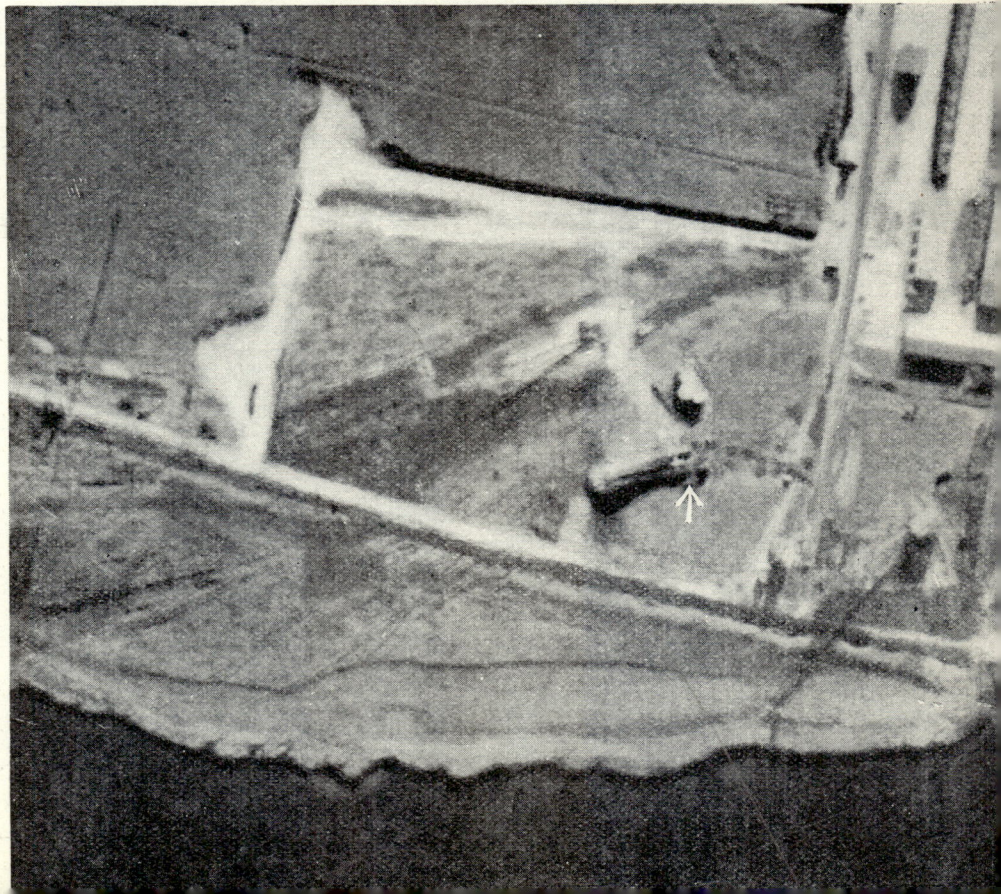

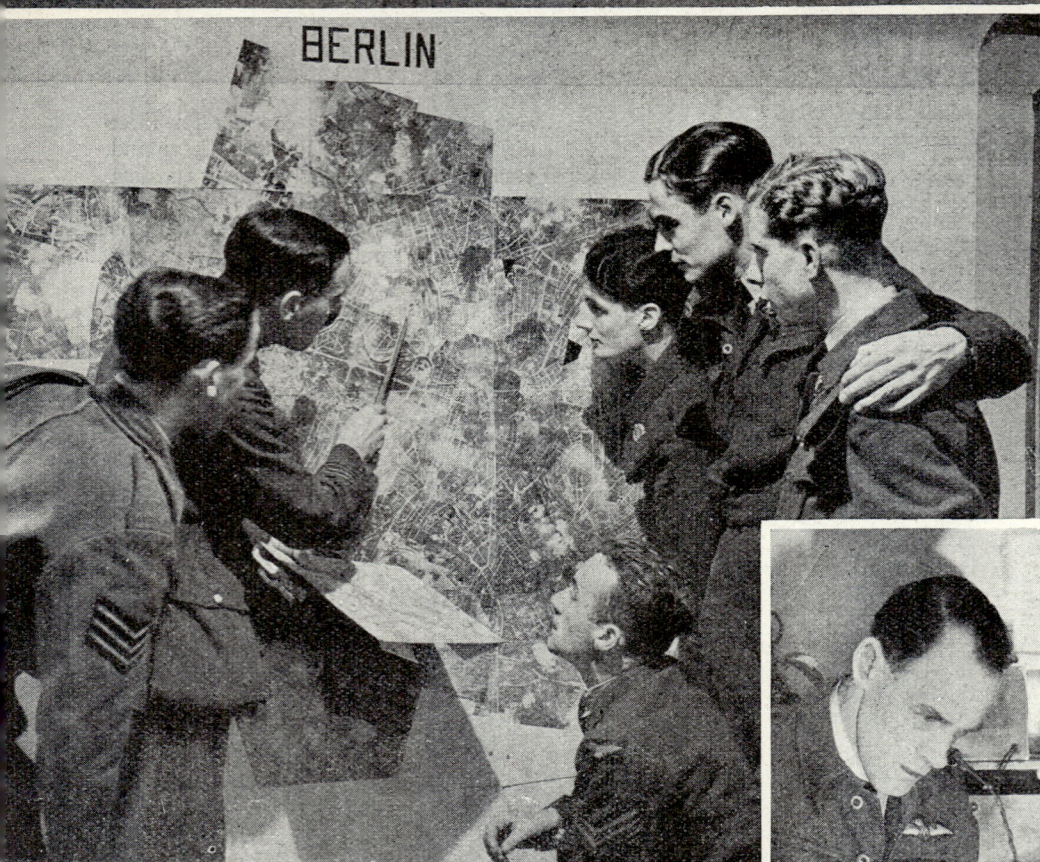

NIGHT TARGET: BERLIN

Between November 18, 1943 and February 15, 1944, the R.A.F. made fifteen heavy night raids on Berlin (see table in page 2974). 1. Lancasters taxi to the take-off point for a flight to Berlin. 2. An Intelligence Officer instructs pilots as to their primary target, using a large scale air map of the German capital. 3. W.A.A.F. telephone operator passes on directions to guide a returning bomber safely in to base. 4. Crew of a Stirling reports after completing a successful mission to Berlin.

Photos, British Official ; Associated Press ; Topical Press ; G.P.U.

DAYLIGHT RAIDS ON THE REICH CAPITAL

The effects of the heavy night raids made by the R.A.F. on Berlin during the winter of 1943–44 can be seen in the plan (right), where buildings destroyed have been blacked out. They include industrial, government and commercial buildings in the heart of the city. In March, 1944, the U.S. Air Forces took up the battle. Above, bombers of the U.S.A. 8th A.F. stream out on March 4, vapour trails behind them, to make their first daylight attack on Berlin by heavies. They had an escort of U.S.A. 9th A.F. and R.A.F. fighters.

Photos, British & U.S. Official

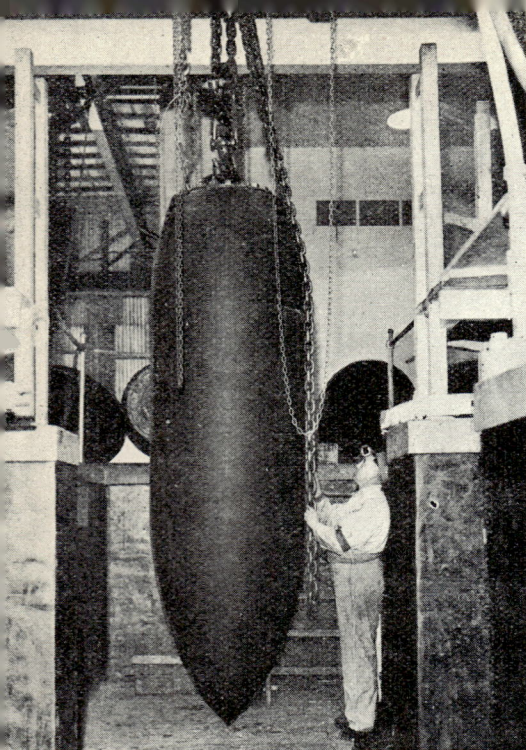

R.A.F.'s EARTHQUAKE BOMB

The second type of 12,000 lb. bomb used by the R.A.F. was a stream-lined, armour-piercing missile nicknamed the 'earthquake' bomb. Released from a height, it fell faster than sound travels, and could penetrate battleship armour and immense thicknesses of concrete. Above is a 12,000 lb. earthquake bomb being lifted into position for loading. Below, filling one of these missiles with explosive; and a finished 12,000-pounder ready to go into the bomb bay of a Lancaster.

HEAVY BOMBER ATTACKS IN BATTLE OF BERLIN FROM AUG. 1943 TO MAY 1944

Date	Target	Force	Bomb Tonnage	Planes Missing B	Planes Missing F	Planes Destroyed By B	Planes Destroyed By F	Day or Night Attack	Remarks
1943 Aug. 23	Berlin	RAF.BC.	1,700	58	—	—	—	N	Biggest attack on Berlin to date; lasted 50 mins.
Aug. 31	Berlin	do.	1,450	47	—	—	—	N	Heavy raid; lasted 45 mins.
Sep. 3	Berlin	do.	1,000	22	—	—	—	N	Attack lasted 20 mins. Lancaster force.
Nov. 18	Berlin and Ludwigshafen	do.	2,500 (on both targets)	32	—	—	—	N	Record force of nearly 1,000 bombers; the larger force went to Berlin and dropped 350 4,000-lb. bombs.
Nov. 22	Berlin	do.	2,300 plus	26	—	—	—	N	
Nov. 23	Berlin	do.	1,500 plus	20	—	—	—	N	
Nov. 26	Berlin and Stuttgart	do.	1,000 plus	32	—	—	—	N	All Lancaster force.
Dec. 2	Berlin	do.	1,500	41	—	—	—	N	
Dec. 16	Berlin	do.	1,500	30	—	—	—	N	
Dec. 23	Berlin	do.	1,000	17	—	—	—	N	
Dec. 29	Berlin	do.	2,000 plus	20	—	—	—	N	
1944 Jan. 1	Berlin and Hamburg	do.	1,000	27	—	—	—	N	
Jan. 2	Berlin	do.	1,000	27	—	—	—	N	Germans reported 730 bomber force.
Jan. 20	Berlin	do.	2,300 plus	35	—	—	—	N	Attack lasted 30 mins. Record load on Berlin.
Jan. 27	Berlin	do.	1,500 plus	34	—	—	—	N	Attack lasted 20 mins.
Jan. 28	Berlin	do.	1,503 plus	47	—	—	—	N	Record all Lancaster force.
Jan. 30	Berlin	do.	1,500 plus	33	—	—	—	N	
Feb. 15	Berlin, with diversionary attack on Frankfort-on-Oder	do.	2,500 plus	43	—	—	—	N	Record force of over 1,000 aircraft. Attack lasted 30 mins.
Mar. 4	Berlin	USA8AF bombers	67	14	23	6	9	D	First heavy bomber raid on Berlin by day. Escort of USA9AF and RAF fighters.
Mar. 6	Berlin	do.	1,650	68	11	93	83	D	Berlin's first severe day attack. Force of 1,500 bombers and fighters.
Mar. 8	Berlin	do.	1,073	38	15	42	83	D	750 bombers and 800 fighters.
Mar. 9	Berlin and Hanover	do.	775	7	1	—	—	D	Heavy clouds. No fighter opposition.
Mar. 22	Berlin	do.	1,430	13	9	—	1	D	Very strong force.
Mar. 24	Berlin, Kiel and other targets	RAF.BC.	2,500 plus	73	—	—	—	N	Over 1,000 aircraft in force.
April 29	Berlin	USA8AF	1,400	63	14	72	16	D	Large force with Allied escort.
May 7	Berlin, Muenster and Osnabrueck	do.	1,246	8	5	—	—	D	Strong force.
May 8	Berlin and Brunswick	do.	892	36	13	60	59	D	
May 19	Berlin and Brunswick	do.	914	26	19	53	72	D	Considerable strength attack.
May 24	Berlin	do.	1,081	32	13	48	29	D	Strong force.

NOTE : Attacks on targets within the urban area of Greater Berlin are given in the above table for heavy bombers only ; attacks by the R.A.F. Bomber Command Light Night Striking Force of Mosquitoes are not included. Attacks on targets definitely outside Greater Berlin, but within the Berlin district, such as the USA 8 AF attack on an aircraft factory at Rathenow, 35 miles from Berlin, on April 18, 1944 are excluded. The bomb tonnages given are approximate ; Air Ministry reports do not always state exactly what tonnage was dropped on the main target, and frequently there were diversionary targets and mine-laying operations ; casualties to aircraft also affect the actual tonnage dropped. But a total of 20,000 tons of bombs was certainly dropped on Berlin by R.A.F. Bomber Command between Nov. 18, 1943 and the end of January 1944.

With the capture of Foggia on September 27, 1943, a group of valuable airfields fell into Allied hands, and it became possible to base the U.S. Army 15th Air Force in Italy. This force struck into the south German, Austrian, Hungarian and Rumanian industrial areas. Industry around Vienna soon began to feel the power of these Fortress and Liberator bombers. Russia agreed to give U.S. bombers airfield facilities, and with bases in Britain, Italy, North Africa and Russia, U.S. bombers with fighter escort attacked distant targets on daylight shuttle raids.

During 1943 Bomber Command and the U.S. Army 8th Air Force dropped 157,000 and 55,000 tons respectively on enemy targets. That was Bomber Command's first year of real bombing,

and it dropped 136,000 tons on Germany alone. By the end of the year photographs showed that 27 per cent of Germany's built-up area was devastated.

Actual bombing proved that a far greater weight of bombs was required to cripple a nation's industry than had been thought before the war. (To that, in some measure, was due the escape of Britain in 1940–41.) The larger the target area, the more difficult it was to destroy. Barmen, a small town of about 50,000 inhabitants forming part of Wuppertal, was 98 per cent devastated by one 1,000-ton attack (night of May 29-30, 1943), but a city of 1,000,000 inhabitants could not be equally devastated by twenty such attacks: in later raids

Barmen 98 per cent Destroyed

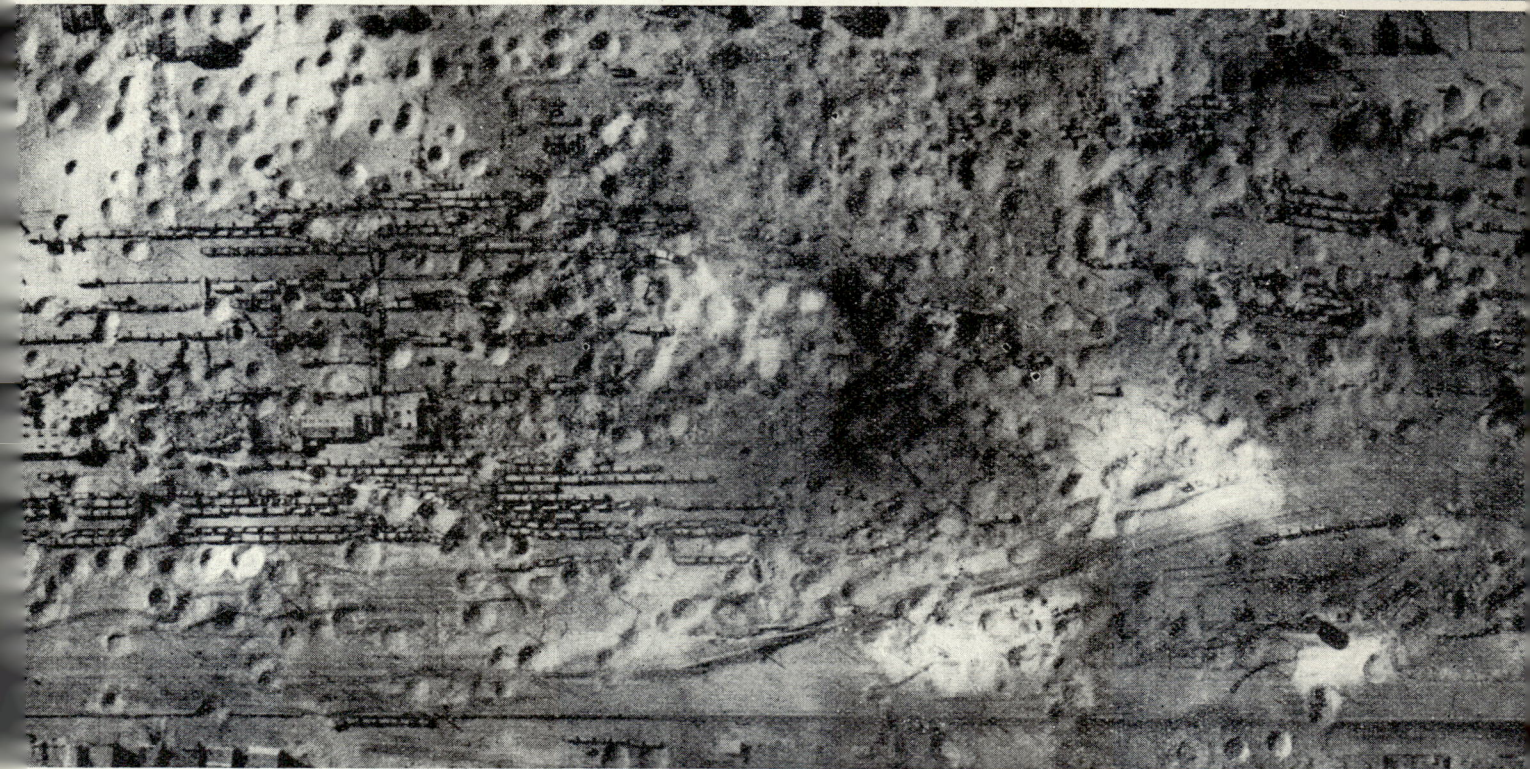

RAILWAY YARD BEFORE AND AFTER R.A.F. ATTACK

On the night of April 18-19, 1944, over 1,000 Bomber Command Halifaxes and Lancasters attacked railway targets in France, among them the yards of Juvisy-sur-Orge, near Paris. These two photographs are of Juvisy yards, the top taken before, the other on the afternoon after the R.A.F. attack. Workshops, repair depots, signalling apparatus, and other facilities have disappeared. Rolling stock and tracks have been thrown about like a child's toys. *Photos, British Official*

many bombs inevitably fall on partially devastated areas. So it became the practice in 1944 to send forces of precision bombers—either U.S. heavy day or British medium day-and-night bombers—to attack targets undamaged within devastated areas. The British bomber used was the Mosquito, which in 1943 carried one ton of bombs; its load was increased until, in 1944, it could fly one 4,000-lb. bomb as far as Berlin at over 30,000 feet, with its crew of two seated in a pressurized cabin; these aircraft formed the Light Night Striking Force of Bomber Command's Pathfinder Force, and up to late 1944 they contributed 2,200 tons to Berlin's bombing.

From July 24 to August 3, 1943, Hamburg received 11,000 tons and

suffered about 67 per cent damage. Eight of the new saturation raids were made against Berlin between March and November 1943, when the real battle of Berlin began. The assault on the German capital was interfered with by measures taken to hold up the use of the flying bomb, but Berlin received about 30,000 tons of bombs in nineteen attacks between November 18, 1943, and March 9, 1944; the last four of these attacks were made in daylight by the U.S.A. 8th A.F. Although badly damaged, Berlin was not knocked out.

Before the invasion of Normandy, Berlin received seventeen further attacks, in which between 10,000 and 15,000 tons of bombs were dropped; seven were major attacks, four by the 8th Air Force and three by Bomber Command; six British and four American smaller-scale attacks were made.

Berlin, a city of about 4,500,000 people, on present evidence, would take about 90,000 to 100,000 tons to encompass its destruction; this would mean 40,000 to 50,000 sorties with present aircraft, flying at least 60,000,000 miles

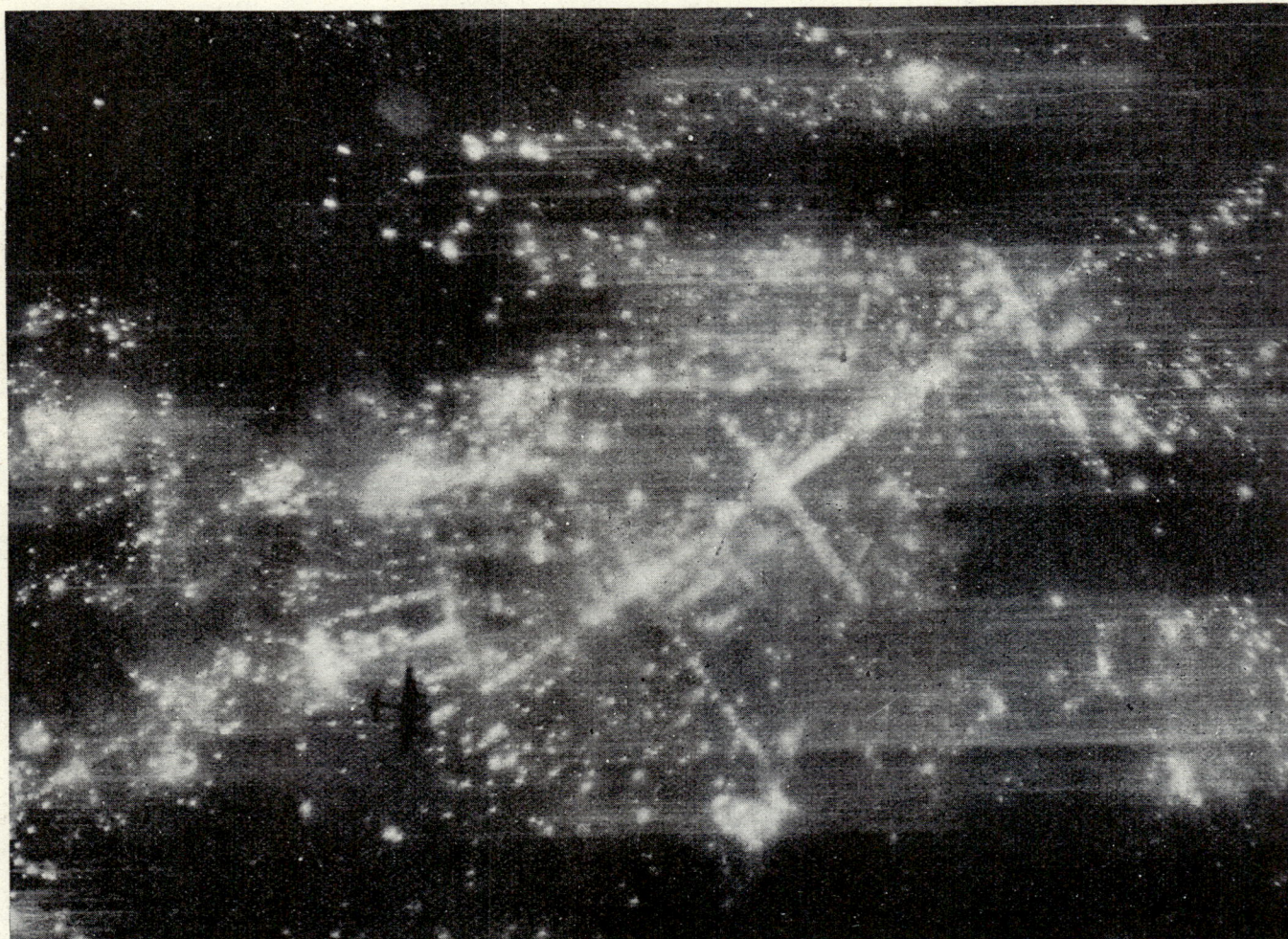

FIRES RAGED IN HANOVER

This photograph was taken during a heavy, concentrated fire attack on Hanover by a strong British bomber force on the night of October 8-9, 1943. Thousands of incendiaries were showered down. German A.R.P. organizations carried out extensive demolitions to prevent the fires from spreading. The ribbon of light across the picture is the blazing Sallestrasse. Bottom left is a Lancaster silhouetted against the glare of the fires.   *Photo, British Official*

and consuming about 15,000,000 gallons of petrol. No bomber forces have yet reached this scale of power. But it was not necessarily the policy of Allied bombing totally to destroy cities, except to support the armies in the field. The target was enemy industry, not the people's homes.

The important Focke-Wulf fighter assembly plant at Bremen was bombed by 107 Fortresses on April 17, 1943. **Focke-Wulf Plant Evacuated** Instead of rebuilding, the enemy evacuated plant and workers to Marienburg, a small Pomeranian-Polish frontier town. On October 9, 1943, American bombers damaged 70 per cent of Marienburg. The Germans began to rebuild the badly damaged plant. On April 9, 1944, American bombers destroyed nearly 70 per cent of the rebuilt factory. In attacks on those three days the 8th Air Force lost 76 bombers and eight escorting fighters, but 217 enemy

fighters were shot down in combat. The blow to the Luftwaffe in the air added to its industrial loss on the ground.

In Bomber Command's second experimental mass raid by 1,036 bombers in the night following June 1, 1942, the bombers did not locate the target, which was Krupp's Works, Essen, and unloaded all their bombs elsewhere. Bomber Command staff set out to remedy this failure. Attacks against Krupp's works by four-engined bombers in the nights following March 5 and 12 and April 3, 1943, damaged a quarter of the buildings. Attacks were made in the nights following April 30 and May 27, but it was not until July 25, 1943, that damage assessment reached 54 per cent. By December 1943 it was estimated that the works had suffered 40 per cent permanent reduction in output, plus six months' production loss from the remainder of the works. When repairs neared completion, Bomber

Command struck in the nights following March 26 and April 26, 1944, and photographic reconnaissance showed that only six of 200 large buildings in the works were then undamaged. Nothing better illustrates the rising power of British bombing—25 per cent effective against Germany's greatest industrial target in the spring of 1943 after failure in 1942, 54 per cent effective in the summer of 1943, and up to a possible 97 per cent in the spring of 1944.

From the opening attack on Essen on March 5, 1943, the assault on the widely scattered industrial area of the Ruhr continued for several months, and Bochum, Cologne, Dortmund, Duesseldorf, Muenchen-Gladbach, Muenchen-Rheydt and Wuppertal suffered great damage and curtailment of their heavy industries production.

The combination of developed technique and increased weight of attack was responsible for the results obtained. In 1942 it was possible to drop 1,400 tons of bombs only by making up a composite force; in 1943 Bomber Command alone could drop 2,300 tons in one attack; on April 10, 1944, a record load of 3,600 tons was dropped on rail targets in France and Belgium, and on April 20 a new record load of 4,500 tons was carried to rail centres in W. Europe. The time spent over the target was progressively reduced from 90 minutes to 30 minutes or less.

So with the U.S.A. 8th A.F.: its first attack, on August 17, 1942, against the railway marshalling yards at Rouen (see pages 2516-2518) was made with 12 Fortresses carrying 18 tons of bombs; on June 21, 1944, more than 1,000 Fortress and Liberator bombers dropped 1,300 tons of bombs on Berlin's railway system in a few minutes' attack.

For a long period Bomber Command's losses averaged about four-and-a-half per cent. American day bomber losses were also heavy. A **Enemy Fighter** direct assault upon **Production** enemy fighter assembly **Attacked** workshops was therefore undertaken by the American 8th and 15th Air Forces, mainly between July 1943 and March 1944. Tremendous air battles were fought over Germany and Austria with enemy fighters trying to keep the bombers from their targets. The fighter plants were still further dispersed. But

the bombers and their escort fighters won the decision and prevented the German plan to build defensive fighters from reaching its intended scale.

Then the two American air forces concentrated on the enemy oil industry. The 15th Air Force from Italy reduced the output of the Rumanian oilfields at Ploesti to less than one-quarter of its previous supply, and struck at the Austrian and Hungarian oilfields. The 8th Air Force and R.A.F. Bomber Command attacked central Europe's synthetic and natural oil supplies.

From the beginning of the air blockade, Bomber Command had struck at refineries, but at first (of necessity) on so small a scale as to be ineffective. Springtime in 1944 saw the position altered. By day the 8th Air Force hit the synthetic plants of Leuna, Magdeburg, and Politz, damaging the great sprawling works again and again. Bomber Command pathfinders located by night the Ruhr oil plants, lit them up with flares, marked them with target indicators, and the main forces bombed them. German oil output from all sources was once 15,000,000 tons a year. Allied air attacks greatly reduced that output.

If it be borne in mind that heavy

industries, oil, aircraft, submarine construction, tanks, guns, aluminium plants, instrument makers' factories, V-weapon producers, railway workshops, road lorries, half-track vehicles, clothing manufacturers, shipbuilding yards, engine manufacturers for road, rail, sea, and air transport, makers of ball bearings, sparking plugs, carburettors, magnetos, optical instruments and many other products had their output reduced and in some cases totally destroyed, while transport by railway, canal and road (by destruction of aqueducts and of bridges), river and sea (by laying of mines) was delayed and diverted, it will be understood how great was the contribution of strategic bombing to the blockade of German war industry; especially when the forces allocated thereto were comparatively small relative to the total air effort of the Allies on all fronts, certainly not much exceeding 15 per cent of Anglo-American air power, with almost no Russian air power at all. And by early 1945 about 1,000 enemy ships had been sunk by mines, over 60 per cent of which had been laid by aircraft mostly of Bomber Command, whose air-laid magnetic and acoustic mines had sunk more than 700 ships.

RUSSIAN BASES FOR AMERICAN BOMBERS

On June 2, 1944, it was announced that American bombers from Italy, after bombing a target in Rumania selected by the Russian High Command, had flown on and made a first landing at American air bases in Russia, whose preparation, decided on at Teheran (November 28-December 1, 1943), had been going on in secret since the previous February. Left, Lt.-Gen. Ira C. Eaker, Commanding Allied Air Forces in the Mediterranean from December, 1943, on a Russian aerodrome. Below, U.S. Flying Fortresses coming in to make their first landing in Russia.
Photos, Associated Press ; Pictorial Press

Chapter 297

LINES OF ALLIED STRATEGY IN 1943

Naval, military and air operations in which the United Nations were engaged in 1943 have already been described in detail area by area. Here Maj.-Gen. Sir Charles Gwynn examines the factors which determined Allied strategy as a whole, shows the links between the different campaigns, and explains their successful development in all fields as the year progressed

THE politico-strategic aim of the Allies was from the first not merely to halt the aggressor Powers but to bring about their complete defeat by offensive action. Yet at the time when offensive plans were conceived, the fortunes of the Allies were at their lowest ebb, and the primary necessity was to ensure the security of the bases from which offensives could be launched. The situation was complicated by the fact that the British Empire and the U.S.A. were engaged in war with Japan from which Russia stood aloof.

President Roosevelt and Mr. Churchill agreed that the defeat of Germany should take precedence over the defeat of Japan, but nevertheless the bases from which the offensive against Japan would be launched had to be defended and further Japanese aggression halted. Into this problem came also the support of China in her resistance to Japan, for apart from other considerations China might eventually provide the most important base from which a decisive offensive could be launched.

For the war against the Axis Powers and their satellites in Europe, there were three main potential offensive bases—Russia, the Middle East and Britain.

Of these Russia undoubtedly was of the most immediate importance, for only in Russia and by Russian armies could the bulk of Germany's army, on which her strength primarily depended, be fully engaged. Russia being geographically isolated, the difficulty of assisting her and of co-ordinating her operations with those of the other Allies was great; yet it was of supreme importance that not only should she be saved from the danger of defeat in detail, but that her offensive power should be developed.

From the Middle East base there was no possibility of opening a direct attack on Germany, but it provided a spring-

board for an attack on her Italian partner and for other operations in the Mediterranean theatre to which a certain number of German troops might be diverted increasingly according to the degree Italy weakened. The Middle East base also was essential for operations to restore the naval situation in the Mediterranean and to reopen this

TRAVELLER'S RETURN
Mr. Churchill's luggage being unloaded from the Liberator bomber 'Commando,' on his return to Britain after the Casablanca Conference, following which he had flown on to Egypt, Turkey, Cyprus and Tripoli. By the time he landed in Britain again he had covered 10,000 miles, nearly all in 'Commando,' in which he had been to Russia and the Middle East the previous August. The plane bears Russian and Turkish emblems. On March 28, 1945, Mr. Churchill announced that 'Commando' had been lost while flying to the U.S.A. *Photo, British Official*

all-important lateral line of sea communications.

Britain provided the main base of sea power for all western overseas operations and for the development of the air offensive against Germany. Furthermore, it was the assembly and training area for British and American forces and the sole springboard from which an amphibious attack might ultimately be launched on the western seaboard of Europe.

When, in June 1942, President Roosevelt and Mr. Churchill met at

Washington (*see illus.*, p. 2494), with Messrs. Soong and Litvinov representing China and Russia, the German summer offensive in Russia had started, and while the conference was in session news of Rommel's victories in Libya and of the fall of Tobruk arrived. Furthermore, although the threat of an invasion of Britain had passed, the U-boat menace was at its height which, if it did not threaten Britain with starvation, by its inroads on shipping immensely reduced the offensive potential of the U.S.A. and the Empire. Yet it must have been clear that successful defence necessitated counter-offensive action, apart from the problem of an ultimate offensive to complete the defeat of the enemy. Co-ordination of passive defence being obviously impracticable, each of the threatened countries, Russia, China and Britain, had in that respect to stand on its own feet. Mutual assistance therefore depended on the extent the counter-offensive potentialities of each could be increased by material aid, and by the extent counter-offensive action by each would cause the enemy to disperse or weaken his efforts.

Russia and Britain (especially in Egypt) stood in need of material aid which the U.S.A., not herself directly threatened and commanding immense industrial power, was in a position to supply; and its delivery was in the main dependent on Anglo-American sea power. China also was in desperate need of material, but the difficulty of supply was well-nigh insurmountable. Material aid provided by the U.S.A., and as far as practicable by Britain, was therefore a fundamental strategical factor in building both the immediate defensive and ultimate offensive Allied potential. This in its turn implied the closest co-operation between Britain and the U.S.A. in the anti-U-boat

ALLIED CHIEFS DEMAND UNCONDITIONAL SURRENDER

Mr. Churchill and Mr. Roosevelt at Casablanca in January 1943 where, with Marshal Stalin's concurrence, it was decided to demand unconditional surrender from the Axis. Seated also is Admiral Ernest J. King, C.-in-C., U.S. Navy. Standing, right to left, are Field-Marshal Sir John Dill, British Military Member, Joint Staff Mission to Washington ; Lord Louis Mountbatten, Chief of Combined Operations ; Lieut.-General Sir Hastings Ismay, Chief Staff Officer to the Minister of Defence (Mr. Churchill). *Photo, British Official*

war and in the development of shipping resources.

In other respects, assistance to Russia depended mainly on the extent to which the air offensive from Britain compelled a diversion of German air power and man power to anti-aircraft defence. There seemed little probability that Germany would divert any considerable elements of her army from Russia to subsidiary theatres ; and although she was compelled to retain a large force to protect her western seaboard, that did not materially reduce her offensive strength, for the troops so employed constituted a reserve that could be drawn on as required, being replaced by those that had become exhausted or depleted in the active theatres.

Nevertheless, at this first Washington Conference the project for the Anglo-American landings in French North-Africa in co-operation with a counter-**Washington Plans, June 1942** offensive from Egypt was approved. Its aims were (a) to expand the Middle East base and to drive all Italian and German troops out of Africa, (b) to restore the naval situation in the Mediterranean and (c) to open the way for the final defeat of Italy and for such other operations as might, for the benefit of Russia, create an ulcer Germany could not afford to neglect. Incidentally, it was hoped that the French troops in North Africa would be drawn into the Free French movement and lead to the foundation of a substantial French Army. It seems improbable that the project was designed to be

directly co-ordinated with Russian operations, but rather to increase the offensive potential of the Western Powers and to establish unity of action between them. On receipt of the bad news from Libya, President Roosevelt took immediate steps to accelerate the flow of material aid to the Middle East, not only to strengthen the immediate defensive position there, but with a view to the projected counter-offensive by the Eighth Army—an essential part of the North African plan.

The Washington Conference was followed by the visit of Mr. Churchill to Moscow in August. It can hardly be supposed that this meeting was designed to co-ordinate the more immediate Allied plans, but rather to ensure that ultimate aims coincided. By that date the German summer offensive had made alarming progress, and there seemed a serious danger that Russia might be deprived of her main sources of oil supply and thereby lose all ability to develop offensive power even if she were able to maintain a defensive struggle. Mr. Churchill has, however, stated that he found Marshal Stalin full of confidence, and there can be no doubt that the latter had already a major counter-offensive in view when winter provided favourable conditions and the great new armies under training were ready to come into action.

Since the projected counter-offensive in Egypt could not be launched till the late autumn when summer heat had passed and the necessary reinforcements of men and material **The Turning of the Tide** had arrived, it was clear that both in Russia and in the Middle East a defensive attitude would have to be maintained for some months, but that the counter-offensive in the two theatres would probably synchronize, although not on a deliberately co-ordinated plan. In the event, the Eighth Army's offensive, the landings in North Africa, and the Stalingrad offensive within a space of three weeks marked the turning of the tide. There was no seasonal suspension of operations during the winter of 1942–43, and the great campaigns of the latter year therefore really started in the autumn of 1942. Winter offensives in both theatres ran their course concurrently. The Russian offensive was brought to a pause partly by the reverse suffered in the failure of the attempt to isolate the German forces in the Donbas and partly by the spring thaw; while the surrender of Von Arnim's army completed the North African campaign.

In both campaigns disastrous defeats had been inflicted on the enemy ; in both cases the security of the bases had been ensured, and they had been greatly

NAVAL AND AIR CHIEFS AT CASABLANCA

Admiral E. J. King, C.-in-C. U.S. Navy, with Admiral of the Fleet Sir Dudley Pound, First Sea Lord and Chief of the Naval Staff, and (right) Lt.-General Henry H. Arnold, Commanding General of U.S. Army Air Forces, with Air Chief Marshal Sir Charles Portal, Chief of Air Staff of Great Britain, during the consultations on Allied strategy for the coming year held at Casablanca in January 1943.

extended and made suitable as springboards for further offensive operations. In particular, in Russia the great railway system running southwards from Moscow had been recaptured, providing much-needed lateral communications. The African campaign had secured naval and air bases required for amphibious operations against Italy, and had gone far to reopen the Mediterranean lateral route, although the Italian Fleet, and aircraft operating from Sicily and Sardinia, still rendered it precarious.

Furthermore, the disaster she had suffered in Russia made it difficult for Germany to fill the gap left by the annihilation of Von Arnim's army, while on the other hand the troops that Von Arnim took to Tunis might otherwise have been dispatched to Russia to mitigate the effects of winter disasters. These were not calculated results but, as often happens, well-designed operations even when independent produce as valuable results as fully co-ordinated plans could do.

The winter offensives having achieved their main object, plans for the summer campaign could be put in operation. At the Casablanca Conference in January between President Roosevelt and Mr. Churchill (see p. 2908), plans for the invasion of Sicily were made, although at that date the winter campaigns were still in progress, and their results could not yet be certainly foreseen, but they had made such a wonderful start that the strategy to be pursued could be laid down and mutual understanding ensured. In May the campaign in Tunisia ended, and when the President and Mr. Churchill met again at Washington in the same month, " we set before ourselves as our principal objective the knocking of Italy completely out of the war this year," explained Mr. Churchill later.

Casablanca, January 1943

THE AXIS BEGINS TO RETREAT

Compare this map showing the relative Axis and United Nations positions as a result of the battles of 1943 with the map of Russia in page 2355, which shows the farthest penetration eastward of the German armies, and that of Europe in page 2345. In the West, the Allies had driven the axis out of Africa, regained Corsica, and over-run Sicily, Sardinia, and southern Italy.

It may be noted that the Western Allies, having once cleared North Africa, could proceed with offensive operations unhampered by defensive considerations.

Allied Strategy for 1943

Russia, on the other hand, had still to consider the possibility of recovery and a renewal of the offensive by Germany. Moreover, it was evident that although the defeat of the German armies would be Russia's primary object there was little prospect of such defeat being immediately decisive in view of the vast spaces in which the enemy had room for evasive action, made all the easier by his possession of good railway communications. Recovery of her territory in German occupation was therefore a very important aim of Russian strategy, not only to strengthen her defensive and economic situation, but to deprive the enemy of room to manoeuvre. Yet the more territory that was recovered, the longer Russian communications would become. On all counts, therefore, Allied strategy for the remainder of 1943 aimed at closing the ring round Germany and wearing down her strength, rather than achieving immediate results which would force her to accept unconditional surrender.

The summer campaigns, which have already been described, may be summarized as follows :

The Russian campaign started with the great defensive battle in the Kursk salient, which must certainly be regarded as one of the decisive battles in history, for her defeat in it deprived Germany of all power of further aggression and opened the way for the Russian offensive (*see* Chapter 282). There is evidence that Marshal Stalin deliberately awaited the German attack, in order to launch his offensive when his opponent had exhausted his strength ; and he certainly took all precautions to meet the attack with a minimum expenditure of his own reserve power.

Thenceforward Russian strategy followed its own course, applying continuous pressure, recovering vast tracts of Russian territory, and by alternating

Germans in Russia Evade Final Defeat

blows inflicting heavy losses of men and material on the enemy. The German army was too huge a force to be defeated in one decisive battle, and the strategic aim was rather to split it up and defeat it in detail. That object was to a large extent attained, and it was only by long and skilfully executed retreats that the Germans evaded complete defeat. Apart from the immense improvement in her own position that

WELCOME TO TRIPOLI

On his homeward journey from the Middle East, Mr. Churchill landed at Castel Benito aerodrome, Tripolitania, on February 5, 1943. He was received by Generals Alexander and Montgomery, and drove through Tripoli, where he reviewed Imperial troops and addressed the Eighth Army. He is here shaking hands on his arrival with General Sir Bernard Montgomery. Below, Mr. Churchill, with General Montgomery, leaves the quarters in which he stayed at Tripoli. *Photos, British Official*

her offensive won and the proof it gave of her offensive power under both summer and winter conditions, Russia, by containing the mass of the German army, greatly facilitated the exploitation of the Allied victories in North Africa.

On their part the Allies, having secured the necessary base in North Africa, concentrated on the defeat of Italy, for which the capture of Sicily was a necessary preliminary step, since, as in all amphibious operations, air cover was an essential factor. The Sicilian landing was all the more notable as being the first large-scale opposed landing undertaken under modern armament conditions, and it provided much useful experience (*see* Chapter 283). Whether it would have been so completely successful had not the Russian campaign prevented the Germans from adequately filling the gap left by Von Arnim's army, may be doubted.

BRITISH COMMANDERS CONFER AT SEA

Following the Allied victory in Tunisia, Mr. Churchill went to Washington in May 1943. From May 13-26 he and President Roosevelt were planning how to knock Italy completely out of the war. Here Mr. Churchill is holding a preliminary conference on board the warship which took him to America with (left to right) Air Chief Marshal Sir Charles Portal, Admiral of the Fleet Sir Dudley Pound, General Sir Alan Brooke, and Field-Marshal Sir Archibald Wavell, C.-in-C., India.

The Allied advance in Sicily brought about Mussolini's downfall and gave proof of Italian willingness to surrender, but with the chaotic conditions prevailing Badoglio required some time to establish his position sufficiently to take the final step. He had to be assured of Allied support to meet German reaction (and that support was at first limited to the crossing of the Straits of Messina). Shortage of shipping, made all the more acute by losses suffered in North Africa and Sicily, rendered it impracticable immediately to stage a new amphibious operation on a scale large enough to strengthen Badoglio's hand.

Such reinforcements as the Germans sent to Italy were used to secure control over the north, and Kesselring was left to delay the Allied advance in the south with little Italian assistance. Badoglio's acceptance of Allied terms was announced on September 8 (see Hist. Doct. CCLXXII, p. 2866), and the Salerno landing came next day. By a narrow margin, Kesselring had insufficient force to deal with it. How nearly his counter-attacks came to success and how effectively his small army held up the Allies' advance towards Rome is told in Chapters 286 and 302. The Allies may have under-estimated the difficulties of the Italian terrain and expected

Disappointments in Italy

a more favourable climate, with the result the invasion of Italy was in some respects disappointing. It revealed, however, the inherent difficulty of amphibious operations which had been somewhat obscured by the comparatively easy success of the Sicilian landings, due largely to the feebleness of Italian resistance. It thus gave useful warning of the degree of preparation necessary before a landing in France could be attempted, and it went far to allay the uninstructed popular demand for an enterprise which, if prematurely launched, would certainly have resulted in disastrous failure.

Kesselring, without drawing much on German reserves, was able to check the Allied advance on Rome, and the most immediately serious results for the Germans of Badoglio's defection were that the airfields in southern Italy provided a base from which Austria and parts of Germany, previously inaccessible, could be bombed. The loss of Sardinia and Corsica also was a threat to southern France which made new demands for protective troops. Even more important, Italian troops in Greece and the Balkans had to be replaced by Germans—all the more so because the possession of a base in southern Italy opened up the possibility of an Allied landing on the east coast of the Adriatic; while the resistance movements in

those countries were stimulated by arms transported from Italian airfields. At the same time the Adriatic and the Gulf of Genoa no longer provided Kesselring with safe sea communications. The surrender of the Italian Fleet, —a potential danger although it had always been strangely ineffective—left the Allies undisputed masters of the Mediterranean, except in the Aegean, which was still commanded by Axis aircraft. On the whole, the Italian campaign, if at this stage disappointing in its tactical results, produced strategic effects of immense value to the Allied cause as a whole.

Concurrently with land operations east and south, the Allied air offensive based on Britain (see Chap. 296) was constantly growing in power, especially after the heavily armed American bombers made long-range day bombing practicable.

Allied Air Offensive Grows

Although there were no indications that bombing would by itself produce decisive results on German morale or on her war industries, it forced the Germans to assign increased parts of the Luftwaffe to defence and to divert an immense amount of manpower to repair work and anti-aircraft organization. The Luftwaffe weakened under the stress of dispersion and the inability to maintain production of aircraft and trained personnel on a scale to compensate for dispersion, while Allied air superiority steadily increased.

Yet it was perhaps in the war at sea that in 1943 the tide turned most

2982

decisively against Germany (*see* Chapter 284), and on sea power the contribution of the Western Allies to the common cause depended, in the west and in the Far East. Mr. Churchill had always given first priority to the anti-U-boat war, and in 1943 not only did new construction of shipping begin to overtake losses, but the linking of air and sea power both for protective and offensive action had begun to give results of far-reaching importance. The danger of raids by German surface warships still necessitated the retention of a high proportion of the Royal Navy's capital ships in Home waters, but this was compensated for by the growing power of the American Navy.

During 1942, and even in '43, Allied strategy in the Far East was designed to arrest Japanese aggression and to ensure the security of the bases and lines of communication essential to the ultimate development of a counter-offensive. The battles of the Coral Sea and Midway Island, the defeat of the Japanese landing at Milne Bay and the repulse of the attempt to capture Port Moresby were all essentially defensive victories (*see* Chapter 249). Even the landing on Guadalcanal (*see* Chapter 250), the advance across the Owen Stanley range, and the offensive in Arakan (*see* Chapter 270) had a definite defensive purpose. But during 1943, although Japan had not entirely abandoned further aggressive designs, and although operations in the Far East were limited by the priority given to the war with Germany, Allied strategy was offensive so far as resources permitted. This proved so successful that by the end of the year Japan in her distant outposts was on the defensive, and the Allies had extended the base for their ultimate offensive.

The dominating idea in Allied strategy in the Pacific theatre was to make a maximum use of air power to secure air superiority over a constantly extending area in which the Navy and convoys under its protection could operate in reasonable security from air attack, and into which the enemy's still superior Fleet would enter at its peril. In view of the limited number of aircraft carriers at the time available and the danger of exposing such vulnerable ships, this policy entailed the maximum use of shore-based aircraft and the necessity of securing successive bases from which they could operate. Consequently land and amphibious operations in the first instance were designed to secure advanced air bases, and each such operation had to be carried out within a range at which the co-operation of land-based fighter aircraft was possible.

Thus in New Guinea, although a continuous advance by land was, under immense difficulties, practicable, air support was essential, not only to cover lines of communication which perforce depended on sea transport, but to prevent the enemy reinforcing his detachments by sea (*see* Chapter 276). In the Solomon Islands, where each step involved a completely amphibious operation, the same limitations were

Difficulties of Pacific Campaign

FIRST MEETING OF THE 'BIG THREE'

Marshal Stalin, President Roosevelt and Mr. Churchill on the steps of the Soviet Embassy at Teheran, Persia, during the first joint meeting of the three leaders, November 28-December 1, 1943. They ' reached complete agreement as to the scope and timing of the operations which will be undertaken from the East, West and South.' Close behind them in this photograph stand (left to right) Field-Marshal Sir John Dill, Marshal Voroshilov, General Sir Alan Brooke and Admiral William D. Leahy, Chief of Staff to the President.   *Photo, British Official*

placed on the length of each step. (See Chapter 287.)

At one stage it seemed that this island-hopping procedure, however successful each hop might be, would be interminable. Nevertheless, by the end of the year advanced air bases had been secured which immensely increased the area in which an air umbrella could be provided, giving the Allied Navies greater liberty of action and denying the enemy power of maintaining communication with his advanced bases. These, under air attack, soon lost their offensive potentialities—Rabaul being a

Advanced Pacific Air Bases Secured

Britain, leaving many of the Solomons still in occupation by powerless Japanese forces. Thus by the close of the year Japan found the Allies steadily encroaching on her outer ring of bases, and she was unable to bring assistance to or maintain communication with them without risking a fleet action within range of Allied land-based aircraft. Rabaul she still held, but she found it impossible to use it as a naval base and was compelled instead to use Truk, 700 miles to the north in the Caroline Islands. She was also compelled for much the same reasons to abandon her foothold in the Aleutian Islands in the far north. Now clearly on

Mountbatten as its chief relieved the Commander-in-Chief in India of responsibility for operations against Japan and indicated the scale on which they would ultimately be carried out. Shortage of shipping and the prior claims of amphibious operations in the Mediterranean and those under preparation in Britain denied Lord Louis the resources required for amphibious operations on a large scale, and the barrier of roadless mountains made it difficult to reconquer Burma from India. Nevertheless, the organization was created and the seed sown for the development of an offensive policy. The air offensive against Japanese communications and establishments was steadily increased and air transport of war material to China was developed.

Furthermore, a scheme put forward by General Stilwell, General Chiang Kai-shek's American adviser, for opening a new road connecting the head of the Assam railway with the old Burma road at the Chinese frontier was approved. General Stilwell undertook to cover the road construction with his Chinese troops trained and equipped in India. To safeguard the Assam railway British and Indian troops were stationed on the frontier mainly in Manipur, and they also covered the improvement of roads leading across the mountains with a view to operations in north Burma. To divert Japanese forces from interference with General Stilwell's operations, the Arakan offensive was resumed, and General Wingate's Chindits, starting strategical use of guerilla warfare supplied by air transport, had much the same object. (See Chapter 270.)

LEASE-LEND AID FOR RUSSIA

The third agreement for the provision of armaments, food, and other supplies to Russia was signed in London on October 19, 1943, by (right to left) the Rt. Hon. Oliver Lyttelton (Great Britain), Mr. J. Winant, U.S. Ambassador (U.S.A.), M. Gusev, Soviet Ambassador (U.S.S.R.), and Mr. Vincent Massey, High Commissioner (Canada). Sir Alexander Cadogan, Permanent Under-Secretary of State for Foreign Affairs (Great Britain) and M. Borisenkev, Trade Delegate (U.S.S.R.) also signed the agreement.　　　　*Photo, P.N.A.*

notable case. Concurrently, the Allied naval strength, especially in aircraft carriers, grew steadily, and it became apparent that a more rapid procedure might be adopted. Instead of clearing Japanese occupied islands successively, it was realized that those detachments which could be neutralized and isolated by air and naval action might be bypassed, while other islands in the Japanese outer defences could be captured by amphibious operations under cover of carrier-borne and long-range shore-based aircraft.

By this method a footing was obtained in the Gilbert Islands and on New

the defensive, Japan had to meet General MacArthur's armies steadily progressing up the north coast of New Guinea, heading by that route towards the Philippines, while Admiral Nimitz by wider-flung amphibious operations was heading towards the various island groups that formed a protective ring to her Home waters.

The Allied offensive strategy taking shape at this stage was decided on in broad outline at the Quebec Conference held in August 1943, where the Japanese war was the main subject for discussion. The creation of the South-East Asia Command with Lord Louis

Thus in the Far East as in Europe the stage was set for the full development of the great offensive in 1944, the plans for which were settled at Teheran in December 1943 (see Hist. Doct. CCLXVI, p. 2636). These plans, of course, envisaged the continuance of the offensive during the winter both in Russia and Italy, but it was clearly not expected that the decisive stage of the war would be reached in Europe before the following summer, when the full power of the Western Allies could be thrown into the struggle. It may, however, be presumed that the outlook was so encouraging that it was agreed that the new strategic technique against Japan might be developed without detriment to the common cause.

Diary of the War
NOVEMBER and DECEMBER, 1943

November 1. Russians recaptured Perekop and Armiansk. R.A.F. damaged over 200 rivercraft along Irrawaddy (Burma). U.S. Marines landed on Bougainville; Japanese cruiser and 4 destroyers sunk in engagement off Empress Augusta Bay (Solomons).

November 2. Heavy attack by U.S.A. 15th A.F. on Wiener-Neustadt (Austria).

November 3. U.S.A. 8th A.F. made biggest raid of war to date on Wilhelmshaven; shattering night attack by Bomber Command on Duesseldorf. 5th Army captured Sessa Aurunca (Italy).

November 4. U.S. troops crossed Upper Volturno; 8th Army captured Isernia (Italy).

November 5. British troops crossed the Garigliano (Italy). U.S.A. 10th A.F. heavily bombed Akyab (Arakan).

November 6. Kiev, capital of Ukraine, carried by assault by Red Army.

November 6-7 (night). Japanese troops landed on Bougainville (Solomons).

November 7. 1st Ukrainian Army recaptured Fastov. 8th Army reached the Sangro river (Italy).

November 8. 1st Ukrainian Army recaptured over 60 localities including Makarov. Turin heavily bombed by day.

November 9. Red Army recaptured Borodianka and Leonovka. 8th Army captured Castiglione; Genoa and Villar Perosa heavily bombed (Italy). Agreement to establish UNRRA signed by 44 nations in Washington. General de Gaulle becomes sole president of French Committee of National Liberation.

November 10. 1st Ukrainian Army recaptured Ivankovo and Mirovka; Soviet marines landed in Crimea. Bomber Command night attack on Modane (France).

November 11. 1st Ukrainian Army recaptured over 100 places including Brusilov. Bomber Command made heavy night attack on Cannes (France). Successful attack by 200 Allied Liberators on Rabaul: Japanese cruiser and 2 destroyers sunk, cruiser and 11 destroyers probably sunk, 88 enemy planes destroyed for loss of 17 Allied planes.

November 12. Strong German parachute forces landed in Leros (Dodecanese). American troops withdrawn from Choiseul (Solomons).

November 16. Large formation of U.S. bombers attacked Knaben molybdenum mines and Ryukan power station (Norway). Anglo-Italian garrison on Leros surrendered. U.S. bombers attacked Hongkong and Swatow (China).

November 17. German counter-attack launched in Kiev bulge (U.S.S.R.). At night heavy concentrated attack by Bomber Command on Ludwigshafen (Germany).

November 18. Recapture of Rezhitza and Korosten by Red Army. Bomber Command made simultaneous major attacks on Berlin and Ludwigshafen (Germany). Yugoslav partisans announced capture of Jankovac.

November 19. Heavy night attack by Bomber Command on Leverkusen (Germany). British made first crossing of Sangro river (Italy).

November 21. Yugoslav partisans reported capture of Foca (Bosnia).

November 22. British and Canadian bombers dropped 2,300 tons of bombs on Berlin at night.

November 22-26. Cairo Conference (Roosevelt, Churchill, Chiang Kai-shek).

November 23. Second successive night attack in force by Bomber Command on Berlin (1,500 tons). U.S. troops captured Makin and Betio (Gilbert Islands).

November 24. 8th Army crossed Sangro for five miles inland from Adriatic (Italy). Heavy daylight attack by N.W.A.A.F. on Toulon (France).

November 25. Strong Bomber Command force made sharp concentrated night raid on Frankfort-on-Main. Changteh invested by Japanese (China). Four Japanese destroyers sunk, one damaged in Solomons engagement.

November 26. Russians reoccupied Gomel. 1,000 U.S. aircraft attacked Bremen; two major night attacks by Bomber Command on Berlin and Stuttgart. Australians captured Sattelberg (New Guinea).

November 27 and 28. Attacks by U.S.A. 10th A.F. on Rangoon (Burma).

November 28. 8th Army launched an offensive from Sangro bridge-head (Italy).

November 28-December 1. Teheran Conference (Stalin, Roosevelt, Churchill).

November 29. Violent German attacks with strong armoured forces in Kiev salient. Heavy daylight attack on Bremen by U.S. Fortresses. Australians captured Bonga and Gusika (New Guinea).

November 30. Russians evacuated Korosten. U.S. Fortresses bombed Solingen (Germany).

December 1. U.S. bombers again attacked Solingen. German "winter line" in Italy shattered. Yugoslav partisans announced capture of Bares.

December 2. Great force of Lancasters and Halifaxes dropped over 1,500 tons of bombs on Berlin. 5th Army, after heavier barrage than at Alamein, launched offensive in central Italy, and pushed forward two miles. Strong U.S. bomber formation attacked Marseilles (France).

December 3. Bomber Command in great strength made night attack on Leipzig. 8th Army captured Lanciano (Italy). Changteh fell to Japanese (China).

December 4. 8th Army captured San Vito and reached Moro river (Italy). U.S. task forces raid Marshalls and Nauru.

December 4-6. Roosevelt, Churchill and Inonu of Turkey met in Cairo.

December 5. First daylight raid on Calcutta: 500 civilian casualties.

December 6. Moro river crossed by 8th Army (Italy).

December 7. 5th Army captured peak of Monte Camino (Italy).

December 8. Australians captured Wareo (New Guinea). Nauru Island bombarded by U.S. task force.

December 9. 5th Army, after nine days' bitter fighting, in control of Monte Camino and Monte Maggiore (Italy). Chinese recaptured Changteh (China).

December 10. Red Army recaptured Znamenka.

December 11. Fierce tank battles in Kiev salient. Daylight attack on Emden by U.S.A. 8th A.F.

December 12. Arrival of Brazilian Military Mission in Algiers announced. Czech-Soviet alliance signed in Moscow.

December 13. All enemy attacks held in Kiev salient. 900 tons of bombs dropped on Kiel by U.S.A. 8th A.F.

December 14. Red Army recaptured Cherkassy after 5 days of bitter street fighting. Allied aircraft attacked aerodromes near Athens (Greece).

December 15. Strong U.S. bomber formations gave Innsbruck (Austria) its first raid; Bolzano also bombed. Evacuation of Allied troops and Greek civilians from Samos announced. Yugoslav partisans announced German occupation of Briboj and Rudo. Successful landings by U.S. 6th Army in New Britain. Australians captured Lakona (New Guinea). First trial of war criminals, Kharkov (U.S.S.R.).

December 16. Major night attack on Berlin by Bomber Command (1,500 tons).

December 18. General MacArthur announced Americans in control of Arawe Isthmus (New Britain).

December 19. U.S. Fortresses heavily raided Innsbruck (Austria); smaller force bombed Augsburg (Bavaria).

December 19-20 (night). Heavy attack on Bangkok by newly formed Eastern Air Command (Siam).

December 20. Over 500 U.S. Fortresses and Liberators made daylight attack on Bremen (1,200 tons); Bomber Command dropped 2,000 tons on Frankfort-on-Main, followed by Mosquito attack.

December 21. Yugoslav partisans captured Vojnie, near Zagreb. Recapture by Chinese of several towns in "Rice Bowl" area reported. 100 enemy planes, 16 destroyed, attacked Arawe (New Britain).

December 22. 5th Army captured Monte Cavallo (Italy).

December 23. French "rocket coast" bombed for fourth successive day by Allied bombers. R.A.F. night attack on Berlin: 1,000 tons of bombs dropped.

December 24. 1st Ukrainian Army went over to offensive in Kiev bulge; Gorodok recaptured by Red Army. Over 2,000 Allied aircraft attacked special military installations in Pas-de-Calais area: none lost. Commanders of European armies of liberation announced.

December 26. Battleship "Scharnhorst" sunk off Norway by Home Fleet.

December 27. Commanding ridge ("The Pimple") in Ramu Valley captured by Australians (New Guinea).

December 27 and 28. Three German destroyers and a German blockade-runner destroyed in the Bay of Biscay.

December 28. 1st Ukrainian Army recaptured Korostyshev and some 60 other localities. Canadians gained full possession of Ortona after 9 days of bitter fighting (Italy).

December 28 and 29. Cape Gloucester airfields stormed by U.S. Marines (New Britain).

December 29. 1st Ukrainian Army recaptured over 250 localities, including Korosten and Chernyakov. Bomber Command attacked Berlin (2,000 tons).

December 31. Zhitomir retaken by storm by Soviet troops.

Chapter 298

INDIA : ARSENAL OF ATTACK ON JAPAN

The year 1944 passed in India without any major event or catastrophe, except for the Japanese incursion into Assam (described in Chapter 299). In the political sphere, the release of Mr. Gandhi on health grounds was followed by further vain efforts among the Indian leaders to achieve unity among themselves. In the war sphere, Indians continued to serve with valour and distinction in all the services. In the industrial sphere, India's contribution grew in importance. For the history of India during 1943, see Chapter 267

THE year 1944 opened for India with the Japanese massing for an all-out attack on the north-eastern frontier. It ended with the steady advance of the United Nations forces—conspicuous among them the British Fourteenth Army (whose existence was revealed in an announcement from the S.E. Asia Command on January 11)—along the road to Mandalay. The enemy's onslaughts had been held and ultimately broken, two out of three Japanese divisions engaged on the Imphal-Kohima front alone being virtually wiped out. Behind the screen maintained by the gallantry of the British, Indian, Gurkha, African, American, and Chinese forces in the field, the Government and people of India under the leadership of the Viceroy, Field-Marshal Lord Wavell, continued to strengthen resources of the country as " bridgehead and arsenal " of the United Nations for waging war against Japan.

In this fifth year of war, the strain on India's economy and manpower brought to the fore problems which the Government tackled with an alert eye to the post-war future as well as to the immediate requirements of the war itself. Politically, there was much discussion ; but no solution of the stubborn problems of controversy was found.

In Bengal, a Province which, besides being the centre of vital industrial enterprises, shared with Assam the unenviable distinction of being closest to the war zone, Mr. R. G. Casey assumed office as Governor on January 22 (*see* p. 2803). He speedily made himself acquainted with conditions in the Province, examining particularly the effect of measures taken to cope with the distress caused by the famine of the previous year. Official reports at the end of January were encouraging : Bengal could expect a bumper rice crop. The Central Government had undertaken to supply Greater Calcutta's food-grain requirements on a rationed basis for thirteen months. The Government of Bengal had managed to set up a food-grain reserve of 100,000 tons. Under Mr. Casey's inspiring leadership, the Province during the year saw a progressive improvement in conditions ; but he was careful to insist that plans for procuring rice should be laid not for 1944 alone, but for several years ahead.

In April Mr. Casey warned those who maliciously advised cultivators not to sell to the Government. He urged the public to co-operate with the Government because the one way to defeat the Government's arrangements for averting famine would be denial of that co-operation. In July he was able to tell the instigators of hoarding that as the result of success in procuring rice, hoarders would hold on to stocks at the risk of incurring heavy losses.

The severity of Bengal's calamity, aggravated by human error, was symptomatic of a strain which was general in India though better borne elsewhere.

The new Viceroy had begun his term of office by laying stress on the need for close study of India's economic conditions, and the year opened with an historic event in the realm of science. On January 3 Professor A. V. Hill, Secretary **Royal Society Meets in Delhi** of the Royal Society, presided in New Delhi over the first meeting of that Society ever held outside Great Britain since its founding in 1662. This meeting preceded the opening by Lord Wavell of the annual Indian Science Congress at Delhi University. Professor Hill gave from the Prime Minister a message in which Mr. Churchill commended to the scientists of the world the task of directing knowledge to the purposes of peace and human good. To the notable list of Indian Fellows of the Society, Professor Hill then proceeded to admit the two latest elected to that honour : Sir Shanti Bhatnagar, chemist, who had invented an unbreakable container for air-dropped material which played an important part in the Chindit operations in Burma (*see* p. 2692) and was afterwards used in Allied operations everywhere, and Dr. Homi J. Bahba, physicist. Professor Hill's tour in India for the purpose of advising the Government on scientific and industrial

CHIANG KAI-SHEK IN INDIA

Following the Cairo Conference in November 1943, Generalissimo Chiang Kai-shek broke his return journey in India where he visited many of the centres in which Chinese soldiers were undergoing training by United States officers. Here the Chinese leader sits beside Admiral Lord Louis Mountbatten, Supreme Allied Commander, S.E. Asia, during a tour of inspection of a training centre in eastern India. Madame Chiang Kai-shek, who accompanied the Generalissimo to Cairo (see page 2638), sits beside the driver of the jeep. *Photo, Planet News*

GIFTS FOR THE VICEROY

On August 10, 1944 it was announced that Field-Marshal Lord Wavell, Viceroy of India, had recently toured the Manipur front, near the Assam-Burma border, and, accompanied by the Maharajah of Manipur, had visited Imphal, Kohima, and Bishenpur, and decorated men of the 14th Army. Lord Wavell also thanked the Naga hill men for their help against the Japanese, and is here seen accepting gifts from them at Kohima. *Photo, Indian Official*

3 G ³

THIS WAS NAGA VILLAGE, KOHIMA

Jail Hill, Hospital Hill, Garrison Hill, Naga Village, Treasury Ridge, Gun Spur, Aradura Spur . . . those were the names of places where the heroes of the defence of Kohima fought and fell. Here is Naga Village, after war had swept over it during the brief Japanese invasion of India in early 1944. Below, British and Gurkha troops moving up behind tanks during the pursuit of the Japanese which followed the clearing of the Kohima-Imphal road in June.

(Below) KOHIMA-IMPHAL ROAD WINDS ON TO TIDDIM

The road between Kohima and Imphal was cleared of the Japanese by June 22, 1944. The British continued operations during the monsoon season, pushing the enemy farther and farther back ; but it was not until the monsoon ended that on October 14 they were able to open a tank attack on Tiddim (Burma), captured on Oct. 19. This aerial photograph shows the road from Imphal to Tiddim winding through the hills. *Photos, British and Indian Official*.

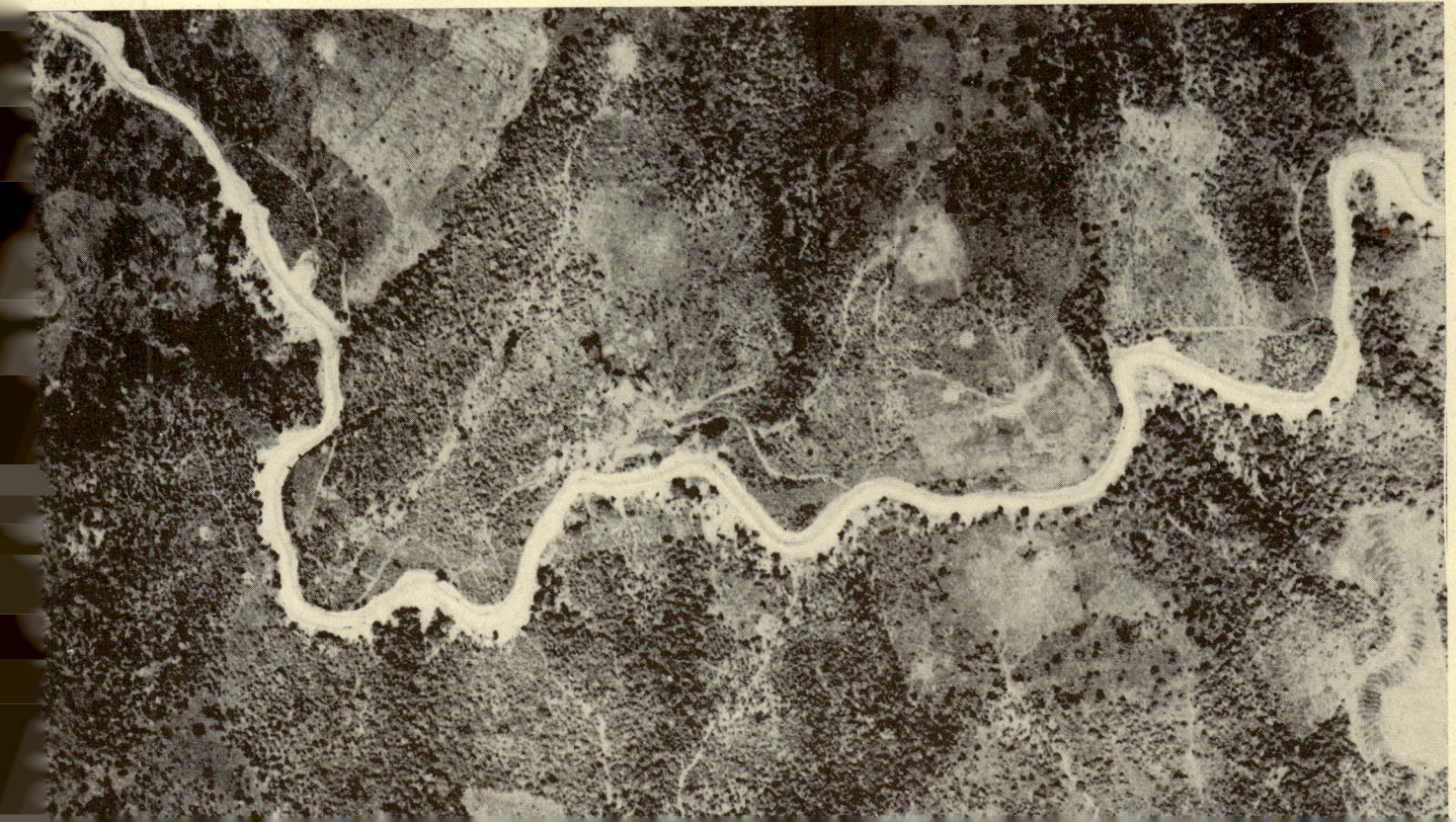

MYITKYINA AIRFIELD, BURMA, IN ALLIED HANDS AGAIN

After a twenty-day hard and daring march across mountainous jungle country that had been considered virtually impassable, three columns of American Rangers and Chinese troops under Brig.-Gen. Frank Merrill, launched a surprise attack which met only slight resistance and captured Myitkyina airfield (evacuated by the Allies two years previously) intact (May 17, 1944). The Japanese made a determined counter-attack a week later, but were beaten off. Here lies one of the Japanese attackers where he was shot down. In the background a C-47 transport plane takes off while another burns as the result of an attack five minutes before by four Zeros.

Photo, Associated Press

Sir ARDESHIR DALAL

Part author of the Bombay Plan, a scheme of development for Indian industry drawn up by Indian business men, a former Indian Civil Servant, and a member of the well-known firm of Tata, Sir Ardeshir was appointed by the Viceroy head of the new Department of Planning and Development whose creation was announced on June 1, 1944.

Sir S. S. BHATNAGAR

Sir Shanti Swarup Bhatnagar, O.B.E., D.Sc., Director of Scientific and Industrial Research, was at Delhi admitted a Fellow of the Royal Society in January 1944 during the first meeting of the Society ever held outside Britain since its foundation in 1662. Among his inventions was an unbreakable container for air-dropped material.

Photos, Indian Official

research produced from him some inspiring addresses both in India and, on his return, to the public of Great Britain.

Lord Wavell's first speech to the Central Legislature was made at the opening of the session on February 17. He reaffirmed in the most precise manner the Government's policy based on the Cripps proposals. The desire of the people of Great Britain and of the Government of the United Kingdom was to see India prosperous, united, completely self-governing, and a willing partner in the British Commonwealth. No fundamental constitutional change could be made until the war with Germany and Japan was ended, and when that happened full account would be taken of the interests of those who had loyally supported the war effort. Great Britain was bound in justice and honour to hand over India to an Indian rule which could maintain the peace and order and progress established by the British administration.

The Viceroy pointed out that the Cripps offer had not been made in panic, but in the hope that war so close to India might arouse a spirit of unity and co-operation overriding political differences in the hour of danger. It still stood after nearly two years as the solemn pledge of the Government that India should have full control of her own destiny. Referring to the detention of political leaders, the Viceroy pointed

Viceroy on Government Policy

out that any of them could secure release by the simple process of withdrawing from the " quit India " resolution of August 1942, and so co-operate in the tasks ahead. There was ample scope for political activity in attempting the task of " preliminary examination of the constitutional problems of India by an authoritative body of Indians." If such a body were to come into being the Government would give it every help.

In defining his own tasks, Lord Wavell put first, assistance to the South-East Asia Command in driving the enemy from the gates of India ; in stabilizing India as one of the principal bases for the war against Japan, the economic problems of India must be studied and solved.

The speech had little effect on the general attitude of the Congress Party and the Muslim League. It may be doubted whether the Viceroy expected anything else. His chief concern was

to make it clear that the Government's policy still stood, and that there were means of breaking down the impasse if Indian political leaders were disposed to co-operate in the war effort.

Meanwhile the Government proceeded to direct that effort and at the same time to plan India's post-war economy. India continued, therefore, on her paradoxical way. Her war effort, involving the raising of armies, expanding industrial manpower and technique, went ahead, and the unprecedented strain on her manpower and economy was courageously and effectively met by Government and people. Figures given to Parliament in London on January 16, 1945, showed that Indian casualties to November 30, 1944, totalled 152,597 (killed, 17,415 ; missing, 13,935 ; wounded, 35,224 ; prisoners, 76,023).

Indian Casualties

Yet the two chief political parties— at variance with one another—maintained aloofness from the war. The press reflected this Janus-like attitude : on political and constitutional issues, in the main it supported the recalcitrants ; with very few exceptions, it encouraged support of the United Nations wholeheartedly, albeit reserving to itself ample occasion for disparaging or refraining from acclaiming British achievements. This element of unreality in the Indian atmosphere was not new. It had developed with the technique of " non-co-operation." It had ample scope because, with the progressive transference of power from British to Indian hands in both political

TRAGEDY IN BOMBAY HARBOUR

On April 14, 1944, an accidental fire on board a ship carrying ammunition led to an explosion and more fires which put the whole port of Bombay out of use for several weeks, and the Victoria Dock itself for eight months. Some 750 persons were killed, 1,500 others injured. Here is the scene of desolation on the waterfront after the fires had been got under control by the local fire services, assisted by British, Indian, and American service personnel. *Photo, British Official*

INDIA ABROAD

Total Indian casualties to November 30, 1944, were 152,597, of whom 17,415 had been killed. Indian troops from British India and the native states had served in Abyssinia, North Africa, and Europe as well as in their own country and Burma. Right, a Gurkha wireless operator of the 8th Army on patrol near the river Senio in Italy ; below, a Sikh on guard in the mountains north-west of Arezzo, *Photos. British Official*

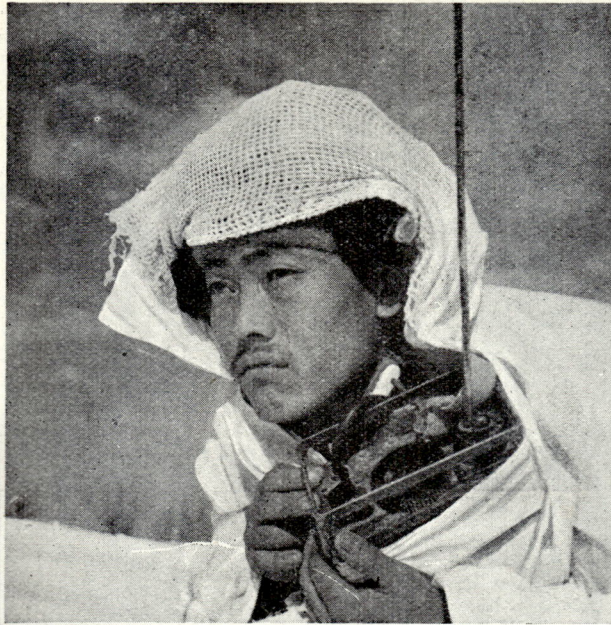

to a Committee of Indian economists and official representatives of the Central and Provincial Governments. The creation of a Department of Planning and Development was announced on June 1, an indication of the extent to which various branches of investigation had produced material for practical action. The publication early in the year of what came to be known as the Bombay Plan—a comprehensive if grandiose document drawn up by leading Indian industrialists—drew public attention in India and England to the lines on which Indian thought was running. By inviting one of the authors of the Bombay Plan—Sir Ardeshir Dalal—to be the first holder of the new portfolio the Viceroy took a decision which was widely commended.

Sir Ardeshir had graduated with high honours at Cambridge and then entered upon an interesting career in the I.C.S. After 22 years' official service he had joined the great firm of Tata, and in that employ he **Head of New Department of Planning** had become part author of the Bombay Plan. The Government's own reconstruction reports were on the point of completion and it was thought that in the person of Sir Ardeshir Dalal India would have an administrator who would be able to reconcile the imaginativeness of the Bombay Plan with the practical considerations the Government's own proposals would emphasize.

Ministry of Food in London paid a visit which resulted in a report being made to the Cabinet and also gave India useful guidance on her food problem.

Towards the end of the year a Technical Mission from the United Kingdom reported on the possibility of producing artificial fertilizers in India. It recommended the centralization of production in a single factory in the United Provinces, and the training of technical experts from India in establishments overseas. This report was duly referred

and administrative spheres, the Government's scrupulous observance of constitutional niceties deprived both Delhi and Whitehall of the function of correcting fallacies in argument.

Broadly speaking, Lord Wavell and his Government devoted themselves to the war effort and to the encouragement of the public mind in looking to the future. A number of technical experts from Great Britain and the United States of America were invited to advise on various matters in which the Government considered important advances could be made. On the food question, for example, Sir Henry French of the

DEFENDING INDIA AGAINST THE JAPANESE

The 14th Army which saved India from invasion by the Japanese and advanced deep into enemy-occupied Burma during 1944 was made up of divisions composed of both British and Indian troops. (The notable part played in the year's campaigns by the 5th, 7th, 17th and other Indian Divisions is described in Chapter 299.) Here a British officer is instructing a Sikh patrol operating in the mountains of the Assam-Burma borderlands. *Photo, Indian Official*

HEROES OF THE INDIAN ARMY WIN THE VICTORIA CROSS

Sepoy KEMAL RAM
(8th Punjab Regiment)

(Right) During a visit to the Allied armies in Italy, H.M. the King pinned the V.C. on the breast of Sepoy Kemal Ram who was awarded the decoration for silencing three machine-gun posts (two of them single-handed) near the river Gari in Italy on May 12, 1944.

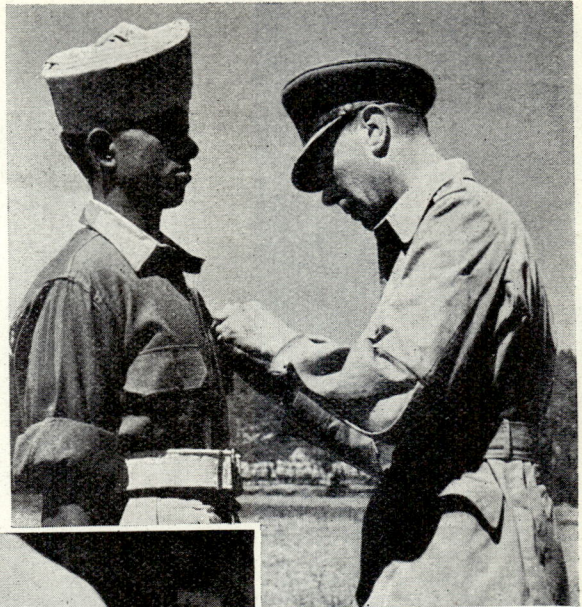

Rifleman GANJU LAMA
(7th Gurkha Rifles)

(Below) Rifleman Ganju Lama, though very seriously wounded, knocked out two enemy medium tanks unaided, and killed or wounded every member of their crews, during a counter-attack against Japanese who had broken into a British position near Ningthoukhong, Burma, in June 1944.

Naik YESHWANT GHADGE
(5th Mahratta L.I.)

Posthumously awarded the V.C. for gallantry in Italy on July 10, 1944. During an attack on a strongly defended position in the Gothic line, every member of his section, himself excepted, was killed or wounded. Unaided, he rushed the machine-gun post without hesitation, knocked out the gun and its firer with a hand grenade, shot one of the gun crew, and clubbed two others to death with the barrel of his tommy-gun.

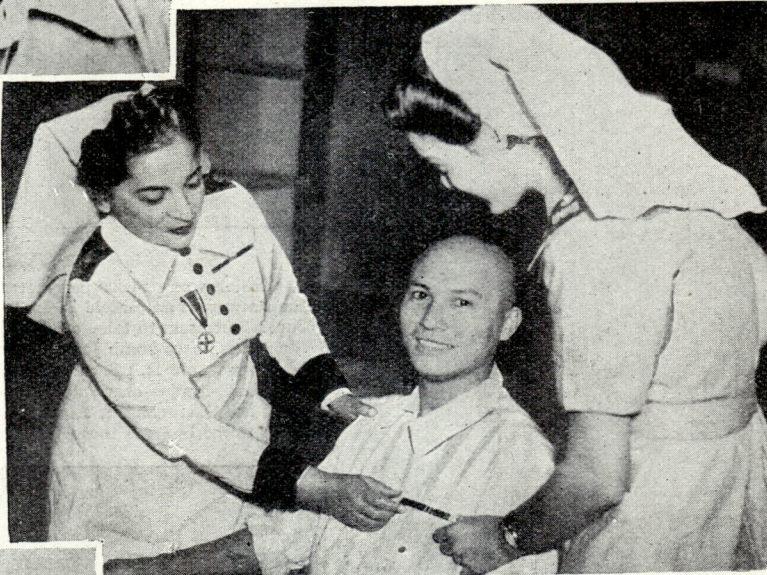

NETRABAHADUR THAPA
(Subadar, 5th Royal Gurkha Rifles)

Posthumously awarded the V.C. for his gallant defence of the exposed 'Mortar Bluff' piquet protecting the base at Bishenpur (Burma). With 41 men, he held on against some 200 Japanese through the night of June 25-26, 1944.

Naik NAND SINGH
(11th Sikh Regiment)

On the night of March 11-12, 1944, Naik Nand Singh, leading the platoon ordered to recapture at all costs a position covering the Maungdaw - Buthidaung road (Burma), by his determination, dash, and magnificent courage ensured the recovery of the position.

Naik AGANSING RAI
(5th Royal Gurkha Rifles)

'Mortar Bluff' piquet, lost after Subadar Netrabahadur Thapa was killed, was recaptured on June 26, 1944, together with 'Water' piquet close by, thanks to Naik Agansing Rai's magnificent display of initiative, outstanding bravery, and gallant leadership.

Rifleman TULBAHADUR PUN
(6th Gurkha Rifles)

On June 23, 1944, a battalion of the 6th Gurkha Rifles was ordered to attack the railway bridge at Mogaung (Burma). Every member of Rifleman Pun's platoon except himself was killed or wounded, but alone he charged and captured two machine-gun posts.

Sepoy BHANDARI RAM
(10th Baluch Regiment)

On November 22, 1944, though seriously wounded in face, chest, and leg, he continued to climb a precipitous slope under fire and destroyed single-handed a Japanese light machine-gun post which was holding up the advance of his platoon in East Mayu, Arakan.

Photos, British and Indian Official

ALLIED AIR POWER IN INDIA

1. Indian women carrying materials for the extension of the runway at an airfield in India to allow American B-29 Super-Fortresses to take off for China on the first stage of their mission to bomb Japan in June 1944. 2. Hydraulic lifter used at a R.A.F. airfield in India to load and unload. 3. Camel-drawn dray alongside an American transport plane near Karachi. 4. American P-47 Thunderbolt fighters being towed by jeeps through Karachi to a nearby air base.

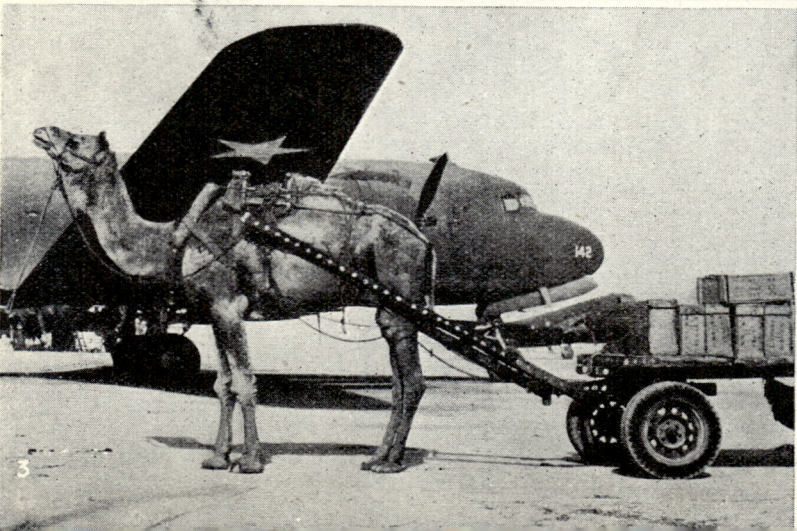

By the end of the year Sir Ardeshir announced the Government's intention to industrialize India at a rapid rate, " the profit motive being harnessed to the country's good." Industries like ordnance and munition factories would be owned by the Government; public utilities should be wholly or partially nationalized. The scope for private enterprise might be enlarged but generally greater Government control would be exercised over it in the future. A permanent Tariff Board would be set up to grant protection to Indian industries on a liberal basis. Manufacture of machinery would be undertaken. Steps would be taken to establish in the United Kingdom and the United States of America offices to facilitate negotiations between Indian industrialists and foreign manufacturers of machinery. Expansion of technical education in India would be supplemented by sending Indians to other countries for training.

The Government's proposals were based on an all-India plan for 15 years with a detailed phased plan for 5 years.

Development Proposals Development of electric power was an outstanding feature. The pace at which the growth of population had outstripped the increase in the productivity of the soil prompted attention to land development, crop improvement, and measures to combat the serious soil erosion which in some provinces, notably the Punjab, put a check on the efforts to match productivity of the land with the fertility of the people. In the special circumstances of the war the record of India was remarkable. The " Grow More Food Campaign " by the last month of the year had increased the total acreage under food from 195 million acres in 1939 to 206·3 million acres in 1944. These figures included an increase in the acreage under rice from 73·8 million acres to 80 million acres.

The general effect of the war on India's economy was not entirely ill. The rise in prices and wages, the demand for India's products and manufactures was reflected in the accumulation of sterling balances in London, thanks to the exceedingly favourable bargain made by the Government of India with the authorities at Whitehall. Moreover, the cultivator's prosperity enabled him to relieve himself of the burden of debt to a degree unknown before—some observers went so far as to say that the estimated indebtedness of the peasant to the moneylender of £800 million had been almost wiped out. Even if that statement was too optimistic, the spending power of cultivator and worker reached an uncommonly high level.

The shortage of consumer goods restricted the use of the money available, but outlets were found in increased railway travel and in Savings Certificates, despite the long-ingrained prejudices of the Indian people, which in time of trouble leads to the hoarding of money to a greater extent than in countries where banking facilities are better understood and appreciated.

Part of India's soil—the Andaman Islands—was still in enemy occupation. One of her provinces—Assam—experienced the travail of attack and invasion, but by the end of the year the Governor, Sir Andrew Clow, was able to congratulate the people not only on the defeat of the enemy but on the worthy part they themselves and particulaly their own Assam Rifles had played in the defence of their Province. On the north-west Frontier the wonted vigilant watch and ward continued, but the general story was one of quietness to which neighbourly relations with the Afghan Government made valuable contribution.

Hopes that political agreement could be established between the Congress Party and Muslim League rose in the summer when after his unconditional release from internment on health grounds on May 6 Mr. Gandhi offered to meet Mr. Jinnah. The two leaders started their talks in Bombay on September 9 but it was soon obvious that agreement would be difficult to achieve. Mr. Gandhi's explanation of the breakdown on September 27 was that the two men disagreed fundamentally in that Mr. Jinnah wanted to treat the 100 million Indian Muslims as a nation, and Mr. Gandhi wanted to insist on the unity of India. In short, Mr. Gandhi spoke of Muslim Indians, Mr. Jinnah of Indian Muslims. Mr. Jinnah's view was that Mr. Gandhi could speak only for himself. After this failure, Sir Tej Bahadur Sapru organized a non-party conference to examine and formulate a solution of the communal issue within a set period. The resultant conciliation committee could not secure the co-operation of Mr. Jinnah, but at the end of the year it was proceeding to explore the possibilities of a settlement. Realizing the opportunities offered by the policy of the Government, many Indian politicians even of the Congress Party and Muslim League would have liked to see an end of the differences which prevented approach to the task of constitution making. They described their state as one of " frustration." Meanwhile, Indian participants in the Governments, at the centre and in the Provinces, as well as Indians fighting in the field were creating for themselves reputations and experience likely to

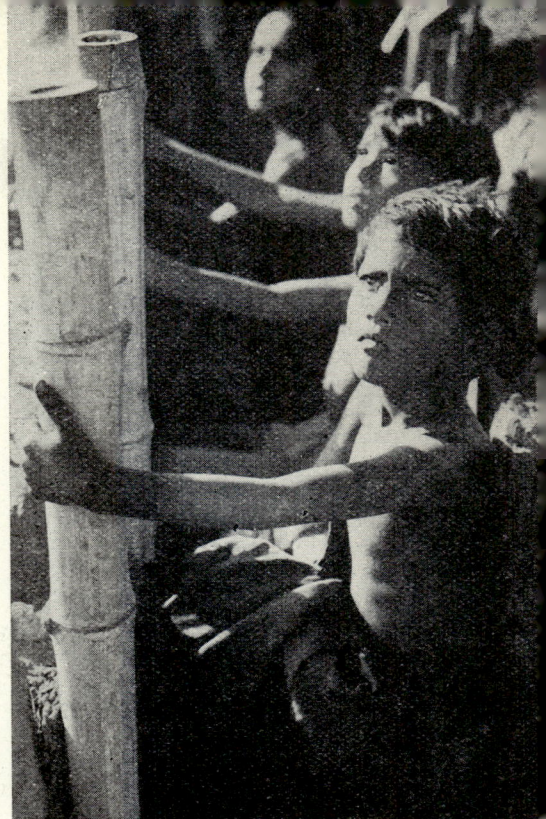

' ALERT ' IN INDIA

There is more interest than fear in the concentrated gaze of these Bengali children sheltering in a slit trench while Japanese Zeros pass overhead : in fact, they behaved much as did young Britain during the German ' blitz ' (see illus., p. 1201). Below, a member of the W.A.C. (I), serving with the R.A.F. in India, builds up a map of the Irrawaddy river from air reconnaissance photographs in order to assist Allied operations against the Japanese-held town of Myitkyina.
Photos, Indian Official

cause them to be looked to in preference to their "frustrated" elders.

The presence in India of more British troops than at any time in history created difficult issues. Normal facilities in housing and other ways had to be **Needs of** greatly supplemented, **British Troops** and questions of can-**in India** teen supply were raised. Statements made by visitors to India on their return to England tended to throw blame on the resident British—both official and non-official—but these statements underestimated the magnitude of the problem and overestimated the size of the British population, which in normal times is about 30,000 men, women, and children inclusive. Indeed, figures collected for the National Service Committee showed that of 12,000 non-official British men of military age, about 9,000 had been posted to the forces, thus leaving a very small number to bear the strain of expanded industrial development and other additional activities involved in the war. Moreover, of the British women it appeared that 2,000 had joined the Women's Auxiliary Service—the equivalent of the British ATS. Lord Munster, sent out by the Government to inquire into the whole subject, reported fully on the soldiers' requirements and brought the problem into its proper focus. He recommended continuous publicity at home by press and radio to make the troops feel that their achievements were not overlooked by their own

FAMINE VICTIMS

Famine in Bengal (see p. 2648) was abating as 1943 passed into 1944, but many of the victims were still in emergency hospitals established by the military. Here Maj.-Gen. D. Stuart, O.C. Military Forces, Famine Relief, Bengal, is talking to a child patient in the emergency hospital at Barisal.

countrymen. He advocated "background" instruction to troops on their way out to the East so that they would be able to take an informed interest in life out there. Standards of comfort at the reception camp in India, in the cleanliness of trains and in conditions of the transit camps should be raised. Additional leave camps, increased staff for the Soldiers and Sailors' Families Association and for philanthropic and voluntary bodies which looked after the welfare of troops, reorganization of the Canteen services, improvement in communications, more E.N.S.A. parties, many more doctors, trained nurses and V.A.D.s, more trained British cooks, more bands and musical instruments, more wireless receiving sets, more cinema projectors should be provided as soon as possible. The impression given by the report was that, although the authorities had not neglected the welfare of the troops, they had failed to appreciate the magnitude of the problem and had not taken a broad enough view of the measures required to overcome its admitted difficulties. Mr. Churchill's realization of the importance of the provision of adequate amenities for the troops was shown by his appointment of Lieutenant-General C. J. S. King as his personal representative in India to ensure that the Munster recommendations were speedily carried out.

The story of the year would not be complete without mention of the appalling tragedy which on April 14 overwhelmed Bombay Harbour. The accidental ignition of cotton in a lower hold of the s.s. "Fort Stikhine," a ship of 7,142 tons owned by the Ministry of War, whose cargo included ammunition, cotton, and lubricating oil (attributed to a careless smoker's dropped cigarette), caused widespread havoc in port and ashore. 231 Service personnel were killed or missing, and 476 injured; 510 civilians were killed or missing, and 1,000 injured, 500 of whom were detained in hospital. The damage done was estimated at about £24 million. For several weeks the Port of Bombay was unusable, and Victoria Dock itself, where the accident happened, was not restored to use till December 10. The fires raged for

REPRESENTING PREMIER
Lt.-Gen. C. J. S. King, sent to India by Mr. Churchill as his personal representative following Lord Munster's report on the needs of the British forces serving there. His mission was to see that Lord Munster's recommendations were put into effect.
Photos, Indian Official

days, and, in the words of an eye-witness, ships were tossed about like toys and litter from dock buildings was strewn along the entire water front. Human heroism and co-operation illumined the dark tragedy. One officer said, "You could see all—American Negro, British sailor, British Tommy, Indian troops and American sergeants—working together as one group of men without any kind of distinction . . . They were all perfectly co-operating . . . . It was magnificent. Nobody asked who was the senior. They went on with the job." The heroic work of the fire services, and British, American, and Indian troops prevented the fires from spreading westwards across Mahomed Ali Road (which would have involved the whole of Bombay) and to the nearby Alexander Dock, where lay three ships laden with ammunition and explosives. Several awards for gallantry were made by the Government to men who specially distinguished themselves. The commission set up to inquire into the fire found that there was no evidence of sabotage. Mistakes in handling an accidental outbreak led to the magnitude of the disaster.

Turning to overseas relationships, India continued to view with disapproval the policy of the Union of South Africa toward Indian resi-**India** dents in the Union. **and** Legislation introduced **South Africa** into the Natal Provincial Council restricting the rights of Indian residents in the occupation and acquisition of property was held to be contrary to the terms of the Pretoria Agreement reached on April 18 for the purpose of setting up conciliation machinery to deal with issues of land occupation and acquisition. The Government of India put into force the Reciprocity Act against nationals of the Union in India.

Another storm in the press was produced by publication of what was said to have been the opinion of Mr. William Phillips, personal representative of President Roosevelt, on the Indian Army. Mr. Phillips was alleged to have called Indian soldiers mercenaries. This alined British and Indian press on the same side with a rare solidarity.

2996

Chapter 299

FROM DEFENSIVE TO OFFENSIVE IN BURMA

1944 marked the turning point of the SEAC war against the Japanese. The early summer found Admiral Mountbatten's forces fighting against a dangerous Japanese attack, carried actually on to Indian soil. But by the end of the year they had marched to the gates of Mandalay. Out of the summer defensive battles grew the shape of great Allied offensives that continued, non-stop, into 1945. Chapter 270 describes operations in Burma during 1943

At the start of 1944 there were three isolated areas of fighting on the Burma front :—

1. In Arakan—the coastal strip on the Bay of Bengal ;

2. On the Chindwin River near Tiddim and north, up to Imphal ;

3. On the American General Stilwell's front in Northern Burma, where he was engaging the 18th Japanese Division in his attempt to reopen a land route to China.

In between these three battle areas—each at least 200 miles from the next—were almost impenetrable hills and jungle in which major military operations were impracticable. It was the existence of these three separate and scattered fronts that made the fighting in Burma seem, to those who tried to follow it at home, confused and unrelated, especially as each of the three areas successively became the scene of major operations, filling the communiqués with new unpronounceable names.

The beginning of the year found SEAC in a state of just having finished a major reshaping of its plans. As Supreme Commander, Admiral Lord Louis Mountbatten himself said later, " In view of my original association with combined operations a lot of people, myself included, jumped to the conclusion that large scale amphibious operations in South-East Asia would at

GENERAL GIFFARD AT IMPHAL
General Sir George J. Giffard, C.-in-C., 11th Army Group, S.-E. Asia, prepared the land operations in western Burma. He is seen here talking with men who fought on the Imphal front during a visit he paid to forward areas there.
Photos, British and Indian Official

once be the order of the day. It need now be no secret that all the landing ships and craft originally allotted to SEAC had to be withdrawn for more urgent operations in the West. The order to

us in Burma was to ' carry on with what we had left.' "

With the landing craft gone, SEAC had to make a new plan on a less ambitious scale, and Admiral Mountbatten decided to concentrate on driving the Japanese out of the north-east corner of Burma so as to help General Stilwell's forces to push their Ledo Road project on towards China.* This plan was based mainly on a large airborne " Chindit " expedition dropped behind the Japanese opposing Stilwell, and also on a general supporting engagement in the Arakan and Imphal sectors ; this engagement being designed to tie the Japanese down and prevent them from sending reinforcements to the north.

It so happened that the second half of the plan—the one for a general engagement—was made easy of achievement by the Japanese themselves, because they, too, had a battle scheme. This was nothing less than a wholesale advance into India, first through the coastal plains of Arakan, and then, later, through the Imphal plain to Kohima and so into the Brahmaputra Valley. This battle plan of theirs, though embarrassing at the time, was, in the long run, a good thing. The

---

* After the Japanese cut the Burma Road in April 1942, a road from Ledo in Assam to meet the Burma Road at Mongyu was planned. Built behind Stilwell's advancing troops, it came into use in January 1945.

GENERAL CHRISTISON
(15th Indian Corps)
Lieut.-Gen. A. F. Philip Christison, C.B., M.C., Commander of the 15th Indian Corps to which belonged the 5th and 7th Indian Divisions operating in Arakan in 1944, was appointed K.B.E. in September, 1944.

GENERAL BRIGGS
(5th Indian Division)
Maj.-Gen. H. R. Briggs, D.S.O. and bar, O.B.E., commanded the 5th Indian Division which fought in and held the Arakan coast strip during the Burma campaigns of 1944 (see map in page 2999).

GENERAL MESSERVY
(7th Indian Division)
Maj.-Gen. F. W. Messervy, Commander of the 7th Indian Division which held the ' box ' east of the Mayu range until relief reached them, although they were completely cut off from base except by air.

GENERAL LOMAX
(26th Indian Division)
Maj.-Gen. C. E. N. Lomax, C.B., D.S.O., M.C., commanded the 26th Indian Division (' Tiger Heads '), sent from Chittagong to the relief of Messervy's ' box ' near Sinzweya in the Kalapanzin valley.

GENERAL FESTING
(36th Division)
Maj.-Gen. F. W. Festing, D.S.O., commander of the 36th Division, which fought on the Arakan front and was then flown in to assist in the pursuit of the Japanese from Myitkyina to Mogaung (see map in p. 3003).

SUPPLIES DELIVERED 'DOWN THE CHIMNEY'

Maj.-Gen. Wingate's dictum, 'Have no lines of communication on the jungle floor; bring in the goods down the chimney' was successfully put into effect in support of the 7th Indian Division, isolated east of the Mayu hills in February 1944 and kept supplied by parachute until relief reached them. Here a plane is flying low over a dropping area. Left, men of the 7th Division retrieve air-dropped supplies. *Photos, British and Indian Official*

Japanese came to us instead of our going to them, a situation which probably resulted in fewer casualties for us, and more for the enemy, the rebound of whose defeat took us up to Mandalay.

Early in February the Japanese struck the first blow. It was in Arakan, where our troops were edging slowly south down the coastal plain, with the immediate object of capturing the transverse Maungdaw-Buthidaung road which runs from east to west—being carried through the district's backbone, the Mayu range, in a series of tunnels.

The Japanese High Command, seeing the danger of losing this vital cross-road, sent a force, by way of jungle tracks, in an outflanking movement which eventually brought them on to the important Ngakyedauk (Okeydoke) Pass, the only pass through the Mayu hills north of the Buthidaung-Maungdaw road. This pass carried our line of communication to the 7th Indian division operating to the east of the Mayu range, and was our "tender spot."

Once established on the pass, the Japanese plan, as was indicated in documents captured later, was to force the cut-off 7th Indian Division to withdraw through the pass (its only road back) and so be annihilated. They made a determined attempt to achieve this aim, an attempt which would undoubtedly have been even more dangerous had the Japanese been able to put in a stronger "infiltration force" behind our lines by way of the Kaladan Valley. This right hook, however, was blocked for them, by the presence in the Kaladan of the 81st West African Division. Nevertheless the Japanese forces which did get round and on to the pass were a severe threat to the 7th Indian Division, a threat intensified when the enemy managed to get a body of men on to the hills overlooking our main supply road to the whole front—the coast road from the north down towards Maungdaw.

There is no doubt that when they had reached this position the Japanese considered the battle of Arakan won. They had foreseen no other action on the part of the encircled 7th Indian Division but to retire and, in retiring, to be annihilated. **Japanese Claim Defeat of 7th Division** So sure of their victory were they that the Japanese claimed on Tokyo Radio that the last remnants of the 7th Division were fleeing in disorder towards Chittagong; that the Japanese were rapidly advancing into India, and would soon be in Delhi. But the 7th Indian Division did not retire. Under Major-General F. W. Messervy, it stayed where it was and went into an all round "hedgehog" defence.

At this stage our air power took a decisive hand and, throughout the rest of the battle, the Dakotas of Troop

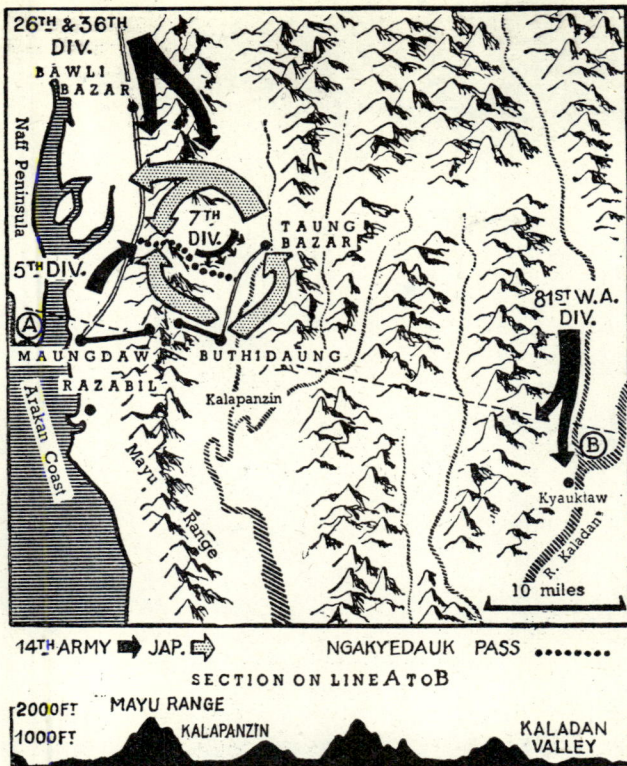

SOUTHERN BURMA FRONT

This diagrammatic map illustrates the situation of the 7th Indian Division, cut off in February 1944 in the valley east of the Mayu range by an encircling movement of Japanese troops which gave them temporary control of the Ngakyedauk Pass. More than half the Japanese forces employed in the operations were destroyed.
(Shaded arrows, Japanese ; black arrows, British.)

Carrier Command supplied all the needs of the Division by parachute drop. Such an emergency had been wisely foreseen by our planning staff and, at the start of the operation, ten days' rations for 40,000 men had already been packed by the 14th Army's " Q " Chief, Major-General A. Snelling. From the moment the 7th Division was cut off, the Dakota supply aircraft maintained an almost continuous shuttle service over the beleaguered troops. To protect the unarmed Dakotas, Spitfires of the 3rd Tactical Air Force flew an air umbrella which destroyed or badly damaged 65 Japanese fighters before the enemy was forced to withdraw his Air Force completely from the struggle, ten days after the Japanese had begun to develop their plan.

It was a great air victory, and at all material times afterwards we had complete air supremacy. The Dakotas, on

Allied Air Supremacy

which our troops were entirely dependent, operated unmolested— though within a quarter of an hour's flying distance of Jap fighter strips. In the whole operation, only one Dakota was lost—and she had delivered her load.

Arakan, indeed, carried forward logically, and demonstrated in battle, the soundness of the Wingate technique of land-air war. Casting about always to find a means to " overcome the advantage the Jap held in his jungle mobility," Wingate had said, " the vulnerable artery is the L of C winding through the jungle. Have no L of C on the jungle floor. Bring in the goods, like Father Christmas, down the chimney." The R.A.F. had never once failed during Wingate's first footslogging march into Burma in 1943 to deliver their loads " down the chimney." Upon this basis 14th Army was now building a completely new concept of jungle supply organization and Arakan was its first vindication.

Meanwhile, relief measures for the 7th Division were being taken by the 14th Army Commander, Lieut.-General William Slim, and the Commander of his 15th Corps, Lieut.-General A. F. P. Christison, to whose Corps both the 5th and 7th Indian Divisions then belonged. General Slim had previously held the 26th Indian Division (Major-General C. E. N. Lomax) at Chittagong to cover the road to India. This division was now ordered south, to smash its way through the ring of Japanese to relieve the beleaguered 7th.

Inside Messervy's " box," formidable hedgehog defences had been raised. Tanks and guns formed a protection, and later the " box " was ringed with barbed wire. Every man was told what the situation was and of the further steps being taken by the Corps Commander to meet it. From Supreme Commander Lord Louis Mountbatten came a heartening message telling them that he had directed powerful reinforcements towards them. Under the guns of the enemy on the surrounding hills, the men were conscious of the fact that a desperate battle called for every ounce of endurance that the British and Indian soldier could pull out. All day the sound of explosions reverberated round the hills as first one and then another ammunition or petrol dump blew up. Three times stocks of ammunition were reduced to a dangerously low level. Luckily, the Japanese did not realize this and the airmen quickly replaced each loss. But the enemy continued also to pour in on our men an unceasing torrent of mortar bombs, grenades, and shells of every calibre.

The casualty stations overflowed, while a depleted medical staff laboured to cope with the growing number of dysentery and malaria patients, as well as wounded. The devotion of the doctors and

Devoted Medical Staffs

their orderlies was truly moving. Some of them paid the final price of duty. It was impossible to hold every point in strength, and one night, in pitch darkness, the enemy overran the medical dressing station on the edge of the " box." The patients were bayoneted on their stretchers, and six doctors were shot dead.

MESSERVY'S 'BOX'

Map showing the position occupied by Major-General Messervy's 7th Indian Division in the Kalapanzin valley when they were cut off from contact with base by the rapid advance across the Mayu range of Japanese forces advancing from Buthidaung. Relief came from India, pushing the enemy back over the Ngakyedauk Pass and breaking his strength in the area.

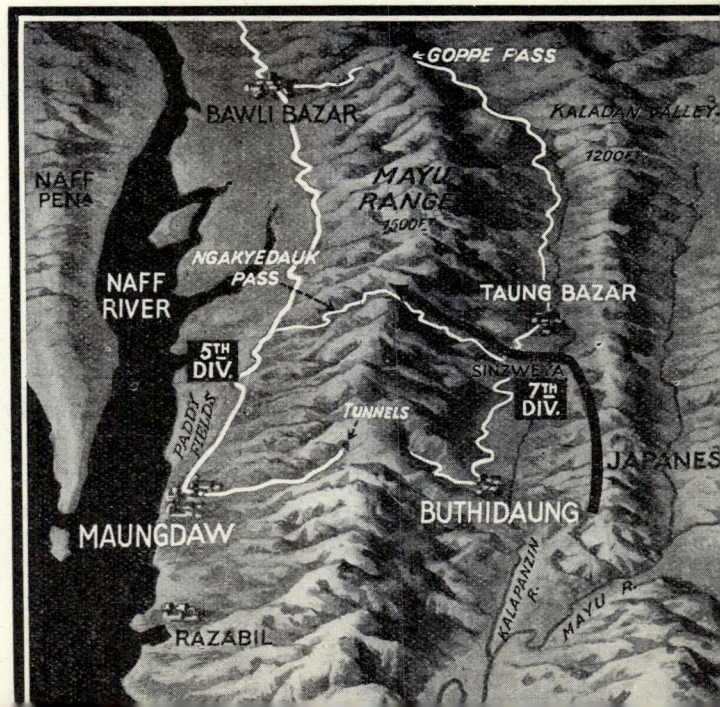

CLEARING THE ENEMY FROM ARAKAN

1. Men of the 14th Army clearing the ground of booby traps and burying enemy dead after they had driven the Japanese from Hill 1301 in the Mayu range. 2. Mule convoy, loaded with supplies for the 7th Indian Division climbs Ngakyedauk Pass. 3. One of the tanks which helped to drive the Japanese from the Ngakyedauk Pass and so open the way to the invested 7th Division in the Kalapanzin valley. 4. Damaged entrance to one of the tunnels which carry the Maungdaw-Buthidaung road through the Mayu hills, after its recapture by the British. *Photos, Indian Official*

While this grim fight was going on in the 7th Division "box," Lomax's "Tiger-heads" (26th Indian Division) were fighting their way to the rescue. This unit, including the Lincolns and the Wiltshires, broke resistance to the north of the "box," and drove the Japanese back over the "Okeydoke" Pass and into the Kalapanzin Valley. The British 36th Division (Major-Gen. F. W. Festing) was now also sent down to help, and the relieving force pushed the Japanese back against the 7th Division "box"— thus trapping the would-be trappers. The enemy—who had started out with only ten days' rations—were now exhausted, some of them having had no food for over a week. A great slaughter was then made of them. All told, 7,000 enemy dead were counted —and, by February 23, the Japanese "Chittagong" army was broken. Communication between the 5th and 7th Divisions across the Mayu range was restored, and one of the first men to cross the now cleared "Okeydoke" was Major-General H. R. Briggs, Commander of the 5th—coming to congratulate Major-General Messervy on the 7th's wonderful stand (*see* map p. 2999).

Thus ended No. 1 attempt to invade India. Said the Prime Minister in a special message to Mountbatten, "The enemy has been challenged and beaten in jungle warfare. His boastfulness has received a most salutary exposure."

The beaten enemy was not allowed respite in Arakan. He was pursued by Messervy and eventually the west to east road from Maungdaw to Buthidaung and its tunnels fell to us with the start of the monsoon in June. This enabled us to hold a fairly comfortable forward line during the rains which

'Tiger-heads' to the Rescue

make ground operations on this sector impossible, and our troops were well poised for a swoop south towards Akyab when the monsoon ended.

The Royal Air Force, operating from all-weather strips, made the monsoon uncomfortable for the Japanese, because, on every day on which flying was possible, they were out bombing and strafing the enemy's monsoon quarters.

The next centre of operations was 200 miles to the north-east, in the Chindwin-Imphal sector. Here, on March 17, 1944, the Japanese launched the second of their offensives against India.

The Japanese plan was audacious, far reaching, and simple. All told, a hundred thousand troops were to march to the assault, first to seize the British bastions at Imphal and Kohima and then to proceed another 30 miles northwards and put themselves astride the Bengal-Assam railway, the main supply road to General Stilwell. If all went well they would, by this time, have virtually done away with the 14th Army and left Stilwell out on a limb. India would then stretch before them, and their long-term plan was to move westwards to Calcutta—relying on "political unrest" in India to pave the way for their advance into Delhi.

Three Japanese divisions were committed immediately to this assault. They had with them an order of the day from General Mutaguchi which said : "This operation will engage the attention of the whole world and its success

GENERAL SCOONES
(4th Indian Corps)

GENERAL STOPFORD
(33rd Indian Corps)

Lieut.-Gen. Geoffrey A. Scoones, C.S.I., O.B.E., D.S.O., M.C., was caught in the Imphal Plain by the Japanese advance into Assam. The corps under Lieut.-Gen. Montague G. M. Stopford, C.B., D.S.O., M.C., was rushed across India to relieve Kohima. Both Commanders were made K.B.E. Sept., 1944.

may even lead to the conclusion of the war." One division—the elite 33rd—was already across the Chindwin not far from British outposts at Tiddim and Fort White, where the position had been static for some time. The British Division in this area was the 17th —the famous "Black Cats"—under Major-General David Cowan. They depended for their line of communication on the 164 miles of the Imphal-Tiddim road running due south from Imphal through almost impassable country. This road runs parallel to the Chindwin River, and a long line of communication parallel to a front has always, through military history, been the biggest of magnets for attacks.

The Japanese in their plan were attracted by this magnet. As their crack 33rd Division began to move up from the south to threaten Tiddim, other parties of troops crossed the Chindwin much farther north, and began to advance westwards to get across this road before the British 17th had had time to withdraw along it to the Imphal Plain. The 17th could have been left where it was and supplied by air on the Arakan basis, but this would have been a perpetual drain on Allied troop carrier aircraft resources, and Cowan was told to pull out his Division immediately, starting at night (March 13) to march northwards, having left Tiddim in flames. He took with him 4,000 mules and 2,000 vehicles and, in the darkness, covered 40 miles of the tricky mountain road before dawn. Behind his men pressed the enemy 33rd Division, and more Japanese troops while this was going on rushed across from the Chindwin to cut off Cowan's line of retreat, and the rest

Japanese Advance Westward

GENERAL GRACEY
(20th Indian Division)

GENERAL COWAN
(17th Indian Division)

GENERAL ROBERTS
(23rd Indian Division)

The 'Black Cats,' under Maj.-Gen. David T. Cowan, D.S.O., M.C., were manning the Tiddim outpost in Burma when the Japanese launched their Assam attack ; he made a masterly retreat on Imphal. Maj.-Gen. Douglas Gracey was guarding the Tamu-Palel road across the Kabaw valley ; he also succeeded in withdrawing to Imphal. Maj.-Gen. Ouvry L. Roberts, D.S.O., assisted the 17th in its hazardrous retreat. *Photos, British and Indian Official*

of its way back Cowan's Division had to fight—at the rear, the pursuing enemy 33rd, and at the head the road blocks designed to prevent it from reaching Imphal. Tokyo radio had already destroyed the 17th Division, and claimed that only the commander and 26 men had escaped to tell the tale.

Lieut.-General G. A. F. Scoones, commander of the 4th Indian Corps, sent the 23rd Indian Division (Major-General Ouvry L. Roberts) to assist the 17th's withdrawal, and, after much fighting, the 17th eventually reached the Imphal Plain, bringing all its mules and 90 per cent of its transport.

17th Division Reaches Imphal Plain

Meanwhile, other strong enemy forces were marching on Imphal from the south-east and from the east. They had crossed the Chindwin in two places—at Sittaung, 50 miles south-east of Imphal, and at Homalin, 50 miles due east of Imphal. The force which crossed at Sittaung was striking at the Imphal Plain by the shortest route—along a good road through our outpost at Tamu towards Palel and its airfield. Opposing it was Major-General Douglas Gracey's 20th Indian Division. Gracey's men, who had long been trained in jungle conditions, had orders to retreat slowly through the malaria bed known as Kabaw Valley. They fell back in a masterly and resolute manner, inflicting great losses on the enemy before they, too, safely reached the Imphal Plain in time to take up a position near Ukhrul. The Imphal Plain, a flat giant saucer 30 miles in diameter, now contained the main forces of the 4th Corps with two good airfields to supply it. The plain might be compared to an octopus, whose tentacles had been stretched out to the Japanese front on the Chindwin, along the roads to the south, south-east and north-east. When the Japanese attacked, the tentacles were slowly withdrawn, thus defeating phase one of the enemy plan. But at the end of March the Japanese had come up to the edges of the plain, now, in all senses, a fortress offering a solid wall of resistance.

To the north of Imphal ran a road, the Kohima Road, which wound 80 miles to Kohima, and then westward

for another 40 miles or so to the railway at Dimapur. A vital road this—the only connexion between 4th Corps and the railway running to the great base at Calcutta. Like the Tiddim road, this one ran parallel to the front, and the Japanese had not overlooked it. The Japanese 31st Division was given the job of penetrating through the Somra hills and debouching on to the Imphal-Kohima Road, thus cutting the last link between the 4th Corps in Imphal and the outside world. The Japanese were then to turn their attention on the garrison of Kohima itself, and, after taking the town, were to proceed north to cut the main railway.

The first part of this plan went to schedule. The Japanese surged over the Kohima ridge, cut the roads, and completely isolated Kohima itself, which stands 5,000 feet high in the hills and had no air strip. Kohima was then laid under a murderous barrage. The garrison was small—it mustered all told just over 3,000 men, including convalescent soldiers, civilians, and cooks. Against it was launched the full fury of the whole Japanese 31st Division.

For fourteen days and nights the defenders of Kohima held the bridgehead to India. The eyes of the world were upon them because the Japanese had already made their usual enormous radio claims, among which was the one true one that they stood at last upon Indian soil. In India itself, questions were naturally asked, and it was known that it very much depended upon the Kohima garrison whether the Japanese were to be kept out of the Brahmaputra Valley.

Defence of Kohima

Help was immediately sent to the invested town. From the far away Arakan battlefront, the 5th and 7th Indian Divisions were flown in, the 5th to Imphal and the 7th to Kohima. The British 2nd Division (The Crosskeys), which had been training in amphibious warfare, was rushed up at all speed from India. Some men of the Royal West Kents had forced their way into Kohima before the road was cut, and, knowing more help was on its way, they settled down to battle.

It is doubtful whether there is a more glorious stand in the annals of war than the defence of Kohima. The battle was murderous and the supply line was once again " in the air," and by parachute. While Lieut.-General M. G. M. Stopford's 33rd Corps was smashing down from Dimapur to Kohima, the men inside the town disputed every inch against overwhelming odds. They could not evacuate their wounded, and day and night they were under a drum fire of artillery. But the 33rd Corps, with the British 2nd Division, under Major-General J. M. L. Grover, as its spearhead, got through and, as they entered the ruined town, they saw parachutes festooned on every other tree, showing how well the air supply crews had done their job. Not a building was left undamaged and the dead lay unburied. In the ruins were grimy and bearded riflemen, so dazed after their ordeal as scarcely to realize that they were saved.

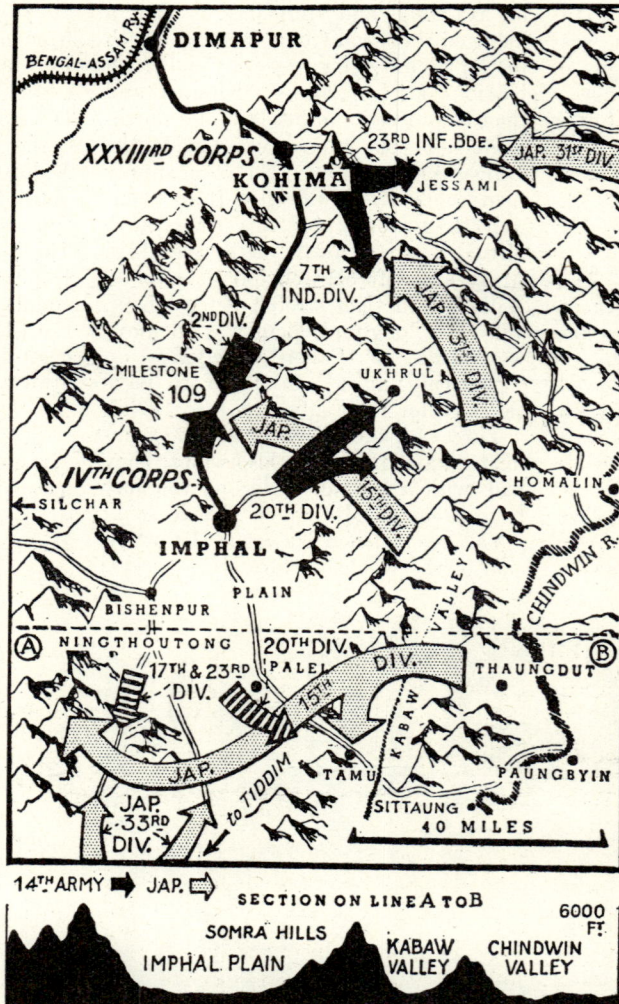

CENTRAL BURMA FRONT

The shaded arrows show the direction of the enemy's main thrusts in his attempt to invade India across the Assam border, the black arrows show the movements of British forces in the same area. The enemy opened the campaign in March 1944 and encroached on to Indian soil, but by August 25 the only live Japanese remaining in India were prisoners.

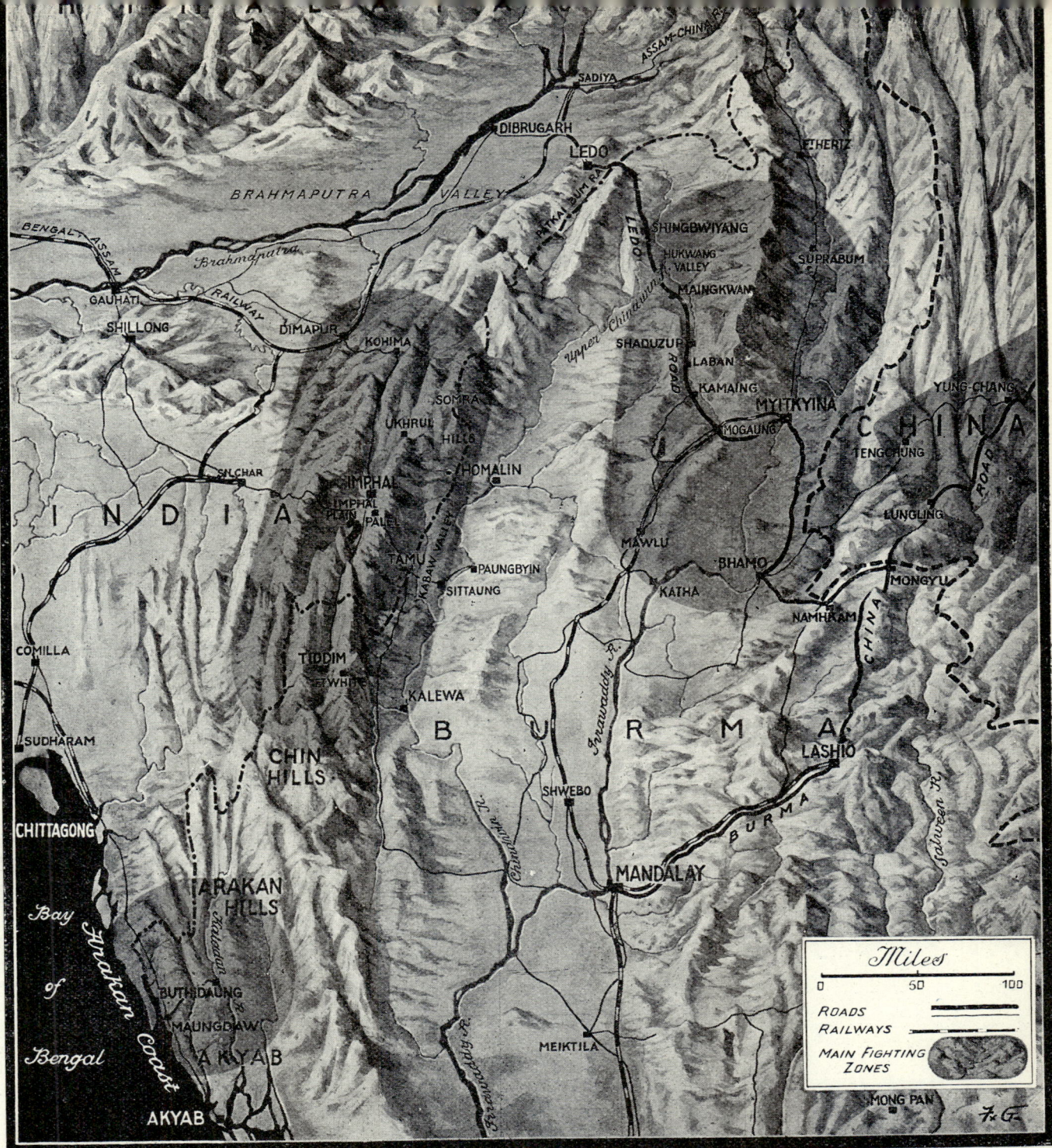

1944 BATTLE ZONES IN BURMA

This contour map gives an indication of the appearance from the air of the three widely separated fronts on which fighting was going on in Burma during 1944. Operations developed during February in the Arakan area, in March in the Kohima-Imphal zone bordering India, and were continuing throughout the year in the north-east, where General Stilwell's forces were fighting through the Hukwang valley clearing the way for the construction of the new Ledo road.

But the battle of Kohima was not over. The Japanese launched a last furious all-out effort to capture the town, because, without it, their battle plans were useless. They rained down shells and mortar bombs and, behind that shower of death, came the Japanese infantry. In one place, only the tennis court of the District Commissioner's bungalow separated the Japanese from the British lines. After many days of slaughter across this tennis court, the British managed to winch up a Lee tank over a gradient of 1 in 3 to fire over open sights into the enemy bunkers.

That tank did its job, but its burnt out shell remained in Kohima as a sign of the price of victory that its crew paid. This costly "stand-up" battle raged for days, and the names of the Royal Norfolks, The Queen's Royal Regiment and the Royal West Kents will always be associated with the name of Kohima. One platoon of the Royal West Kents was reduced to 4 men, all wounded—but the Japanese attack was held off and no enemy soldier ever set foot upon the Bengal-Assam Railway. Kohima was finally cleared of the enemy by May 14.

In Imphal, the main body of the 4th Corps was still completely besieged. It was, and to the end of the campaign remained, entirely dependent upon

RE-OPENING THE KOHIMA-IMPHAL ROAD

In March 1944 the Japanese got within striking distance of Imphal, and all but captured Kohima. But British counter-attacks from both places cleared the road between them by June 22. Operations to drive the enemy from his positions in the surrounding country continued during the monsoon. Here a British tank is crossing a river north of Imphal. Below, men of the West Yorks Regiment dismantle a Japanese road-block. *Photos, Indian Official*

supply by air, and Maj.-Gen. George E. Stratemeyer's Eastern Command here tackled successfully the biggest air supply problem that had so far been faced on any front. The Dakota Squadrons overcame the difficulties by sheer guts and perseverance. The Japanese on the hills surrounding Imphal saw the stream of troop carriers, day by day defeating their master plan by pouring in food, fuel, ammunition and men to the British Forces. On their return journeys the Dakotas bore out the wounded, and also 40,000 officers and men who were not, at that moment, needed on the garrison's ration strength.

By the end of May not one Japanese soldier was still above ground anywhere near the plain itself. The Third Tactical Air Force, with its dive-bombers, beat a ceaseless tattoo on all enemy positions, and the infantry completed what the bombs and the shells had started.

The crisis was over. The reinforced 4th Corps had been built up in the plains of Imphal for a break-out; and to the north, forces were getting ready at Kohima to smash their way south. Speed, however, **British Attack From Kohima** was needed. The full monsoon was "just around the corner," and the rains were already beginning to interfere with the Dakota flying. At all costs the road must be opened.

So, on June 2, the British attacked. The 2nd Division broke out southwards from Kohima in an impressive advance with armour and infantry advancing under the smoke and fire screen of guns, mortars, dive-bombers and fighters. The close air support was magnificent. Bomb-lines only thirty yards ahead of the British troops were allotted to the Vengeance dive-bombers and the attacks were duly made—with no mistakes. The 7th Indian Division and the 23rd Infantry Brigade (Brigadier L. E. C. Perowne) fanned out eastwards of Kohima to cut across the jungle tracks, which were the enemy Divisions' only lines of supply.

As the troops of 33rd Corps came down from the north, those of 4th Corps in Imphal struck northwards to meet them. In Mountbatten's war-room at Kandy the day-by-day progress of the two forces towards each other was read out, and was anxiously followed by the Supreme Commander and all his staff. By June 7, 70 miles separated the columns. On the 22nd the two forces met at milestone 109. The land route into Imphal was cleared for the waiting convoys of lorries, and the 31st and 15th Japanese Divisions had been pushed into the jungle, disorganized and beaten, to starve. (*See* map p. 3002.)

British and Indian patrols found gaunt, emaciated Japanese skeletons— hundreds at a time—dead of starvation. Around their necks were bags of rice which their dying stomachs could no longer digest. It was a grave Japanese disaster, involving something like 100,000 enemy casualties. The British had had casualties too, but they were nothing like those of the Japanese— in the whole year ending September, 1944, the British total of killed, wounded and missing was 27,000. The British also were able to evacuate their wounded and sick by air within a matter of hours. The Japanese had no such service, and their wounded and sick were cut off and left to die—even assisted to die by their comrades. The enemy High Command had gambled on capturing British foodstuffs and British stores at Imphal and Kohima. It had gambled with its eyes wide open, with no line of communication and no air support—and it had lost.

In India the news was flashed that the last Japanese had been driven from Indian soil. Military headquarters knew that the last possible offensive the enemy could launch towards the Brahmaputra Valley was broken. There would not, there could not be a comeback. Although the monsoon had now started, the stage was set for the offensive which was to take the British to Mandalay.

In the third battle area of Burma, Lieut.-General Stilwell was carrying on his Ledo Road offensive, assisted by a

Stilwell's Ledo Road Offensive

large airborne Chindit expedition under Major-General Orde Charles Wingate. The fighting here was proceeding at the same time as the Japanese Imphal offensive, and like the armies engaged in battle at the gateway to India, Wingate's expedition depended entirely upon air supply. No higher tribute can be paid to the R.A.F. and American Dakota squadrons than to say that both campaigns ended victoriously for the Allies.

In 1943 Wingate marched his Chindits into Burma—marched them over the Chindwin and the Irrawaddy, and then marched them back again (see p. 2692). For 1944 he had a far more audacious plan. This was to fly his main force into the heart of Burma and then to move freely along the enemy's lines of communication, establishing a series of strongholds—each stronghold having its own aerodrome. In this way a powerful force would be firmly established, with its own air support and with constant communications (also by air) with the 14th Army. That these islands of Allied-held territory were

AIR EVACUATION OF SICK AND WOUNDED

Transport planes brought in men and supplies to the Allied forces operating in north-east Burma and evacuated their sick and wounded. Here Chinese casualties from ' Merrill's Marauders ' are being loaded into a waiting plane, which will carry them back to base hospitals. Below, a patrol operating in north-east Burma : it consists of Allied-equipped and trained Chinese, and jungle-wise Kachins native to the area led by British and American officers.
Photos, Associated Press ; Keystone

to be 200 miles behind the Japanese lines did not worry Wingate. He foresaw that, with the supplies coming " down the chimney " and the wounded being constantly evacuated, he could maintain his force in action almost indefinitely, although in the middle of enemy-occupied Burma.

This audacious plan was devised at Quebec (August, 1943 : see page 2799) and had the immediate support of Mountbatten and the Americans. The Americans recruited a special air force for Wingate known as " The Air Commando " and this was placed under the command of Colonel Philip Coch-

rane, 33-year old U.S. fighter ace. The Air Commando consisted of a large number of gliders with their Dakota tows, which were to take in the initial shock troops, while the fighting side of the Commando was equipped with P.51 planes (Mustangs) fitted to carry bombs and rockets.

The combined *modus operandi* was laid down as follows :—

First, the Mustangs would co-operate with the 3rd T.A.F. in a large series of sweeps over all Japanese aerodromes in Burma. This was to destroy as many enemy aircraft as possible and so reduce chances of air interference to

N.E. BURMA COMMANDERS
Lieut.-Gen. Sun Li-Jen, Commander of the 1st Chinese Army, enjoys a joke with Brig.-Gen. Frank Merrill, Commander of 'Merrill's Marauders' who included hard-bitten U.S. troops from Guadalcanal. Between them is Colonel Edward McNally, American liaison officer with General Sun.
Photo, Keystone

the minimum. The plan was duly carried out with great success and, immediately before the Wingate "fly-in," Cochrane's P.51's discharged 1½ million pounds of explosives on enemy airfields and destroyed over 100 Japanese aircraft. (An incidental result of these successful sweeps was that the Japanese were robbed of the air cover they had been building up for their invasion of India, and so completely did the R.A.F., the Indian Air Force, and the U.S.A. 10th. A.F. dominate the skies over Arakan, Imphal, and Stilwell's front that Japanese aircraft scarcely appeared over any of the Burma battle zones in 1944. Many captured Japanese documents contained phrases such as, "Every day, all day, their aeroplanes are here—we do not have to ask if they are friendly or if they are enemy—we know : we know they are enemy because never, never do we see one of our own.")

Next came the fly-in. Two landing grounds, clearings in the jungle, had been earmarked by Wingate during his 1943 expedition—but they had not been closely reconnoitred or even fully photographed from the air for fear of arousing Japanese suspicions. Gliders were to take in British troops, whose job was to hold off any Japanese attack, and American aerodrome construction engineers to build landing strips for Dakotas. To emphasize the inter-Allied nature of "Operation Thursday," as it was called, the clearings were named "Broadway"

'Operation Thursday' Begins

and "Piccadilly"; a third strip was later called "Chowringhee" after the chief street of Calcutta.

On the evening of the fly-in there came a snag : last minute reconnaissance revealed that logs had been laid across the "Piccadilly" clearing. There was a hurried conference on the base aerodrome as to whether this meant that the Japanese had discovered the whole plan. It was an awful moment, for secrecy meant everything; but it was decided, and in the event rightly so, that the obstruction was a coincidence, and it was ruled that the operation should proceed. All the gliders, however, had to be routed to "Broadway."

On the night of Sunday, March 5, most of the high officers of South-East Asia Command were assembled on the Indian aerodrome to see the start of the Burma air invasion. Fighting troops and American engineers were loaded into the gliders along with the necessary equipment, which included a number of bulldozers. As the moon rose the first Dakota took off, towing its loaded glider behind it. The procession had started.

After a night flight of nearly 200 miles, the air armada arrived over "Broadway," and the gliders were cast off, one by one, to make their landings. Unluckily, the control glider had been forced down farther back, and, in the first uncontrolled landings, there was some confusion in which a number of the gliders were wrecked. There were casualties, and there were grim scenes as surgeons worked by the light of the moon, while search parties hunted in the jungle for men whose gliders had crashed beyond the perimeter of the clearing. But, of the 54 gliders which set out from India, 37 arrived at "Broadway," eight came down west of the Chindwin in friendly territory and another nine in the enemy zone—two within a hundred yards of Japanese H.Q. Our casualties were light, and most of the men forced down later regained our lines.

By the time the last glider was down, "Broadway" was ringed by a thin defensive circle of British troops. The next few hours would decide the fate of the Wingate expedition. But Wingate had chosen his area well. He had observed his own first precept, which was, "Strike where the enemy temporarily isn't." There were no Japanese forces, and no attack. Inside the defensive ring, the American construction engineers worked all through that night and the next day, uprooting trees and levelling the ground.

In twelve hours after the first glider had plunged down into darkness over this unprepared bit of jungle clearing,

"Broadway" air strip was completed. On the Monday evening—exactly 24 hours after the expedition started—the first Dakota, flown by the Commander of Troop Carrier Command, Brig.-General W. D. Old, landed at "Broadway." Two days later 3,000 men of Brigadier "Mad Mike" Calvert's Chindit brigade had safely disembarked.

Three nights after the fly-in there was a second landing nearby at the "Chowringhee" strip, and four columns of Brigadier W. D. A. Lentaigne's brigade were safely brought in. Thus, within a week of the start of "Operation Thursday," nearly a divisional strength of Chindits, comprising British, West African, Indian and Gurkha troops, had been landed without interference in the middle of Japanese-held Burma. They had been planted, to use Wingate's phrase, "in the very guts of the enemy."

More Landings in Japanese held Burma

It was his last as it was his finest exploit. Flying towards India after a tour of his forward positions, his plane was lost in a storm. A fire on a hill seen by an American pilot on the night of March 24 was the funeral pyre of Major-General Orde Charles Wingate. His battered topee—a topee as individual as its owner—was found thrown clear of the wreckage. With Wingate perished two British war correspondents—Stuart Emeny of the "News Chronicle" and Stanley Wills of the "Daily Herald." Wingate's command was taken over by

DEPUTY SUPREME COMMANDER
Lt.-Gen. Joseph W. Stilwell, Commander-in-Chief of U.S. Army Forces in India, Burma and China, and SEAC Deputy Supreme Commander, under Admiral Lord Louis Mountbatten, surveys Japanese positions in north-east Burma with Lieut.-Gen. Sun Li-Jen, commanding the 1st Chinese Army.
Photo, New York Times

LIEUT.-GENERAL WILLIAM J. SLIM

General Slim, appointed Commander of the British 14th Army in Burma in October 1943, had the task of withstanding determined Japanese attempts at the invasion of India which began in February 1944 in the Arakan district. The 14th Army broke the enemy's strength and drove what was left of his forces far back into Burma. General Slim was made K.C.B. in September 1944, and was invested with his new honour by the Viceroy of India, Lord Wavell, at a ceremony near Imphal in Assam on December 15, 1944.

Photo, Indian Official

ALLIED TROOPS CROSS THE MOGAUNG RIVER IN BURMA

The Chinese 22nd Division, fighting in north-east Burma, entered the Mogaung Valley (see map in page 3003) about March 22, 1944, capturing Shaduzup on March 24. Kamaing fell on June 16 after a seven-day siege. Mogaung itself was captured in a concentric attack by 'Chindits' from the east, Chinese from the south, and British and Gurkha troops from the north on June 25. Here, Chinese and American troops are crossing the Mogaung river by an improvised bridge made of empty petrol tins and planks lashed together. *Photo, Paul Popper*

RUNNING UP THE FLAG AT DOVER, SEPTEMBER 30, 1944

On September 30, 1944, scenes of great enthusiasm occurred in Dover, Folkestone, Deal and Ramsgate—the towns of "Hellfire Corner" which had been under shell-fire from German batteries in the Calais area since August 12, 1940—when the Mayor of Dover, Alderman J. R. Cairns, announced that all enemy long-range guns had been captured. Mr. Cairns, here hoisting Dover's flag on the town hall in celebration, sent messages to Mr. Mackenzie King (Canadian Premier), Field-Marshal Montgomery, and General Crerar (commanding the 1st Canadian Army) expressing the gratitude of the townsfolk to the Canadians who had ended their long ordeal.   *Photo, Planet News*

'SHIPS OF OVER SIXTY DIFFERENT TYPES TOOK PART IN THE OPERATION'

In describing on March 7, 1945 the fleet which carried the invasion armies to France in June 1944, Mr. A. V. Alexander, First Lord of the Admiralty, said, 'It included ships and craft for landing tanks and infantry, for giving close support fire, for landing guns and transport, for making smoke, and even floating kitchens and craft fitted with extended fire escape ladders to put men up cliffs. In all, 4,066 landing ships and craft of over 60 different types took part in the operation.' Many of these ships were specially designed and built, many were adapted merchant ships. This photograph, taken off one of the landing beaches some days after the initial landings, gives a visual idea of the mass and variety of shipping used in the invasion operations.

Photo, U.S. Official

Lentaigne (promoted Major-General), one of the column commanders of the 1943 Chindit march into Burma.

Such was the element of surprise of this Wingate plan that it was a week before the Japanese discovered what was going on. They launched an air attack against " Broadway," but it was too late. The strip was too well organized. R.A.F. Spitfires were already stationed on it for defence, and also it was ringed round with Bofors ack-ack guns. The raiders were beaten off.

Having concentrated, the Chindits then set forth to maraud the lines of communication of the Japanese 18th, the division opposing General Stilwell.

Lieut.-Gen. Joseph Stilwell, Mountbatten's American Deputy Supreme Commander, had been given S.E.A.C.'s No.

Restoring Land Link with China

1 task — that of restoring a land link with besieged China. " Vinegar Joe " Stilwell—" Uncle Joe " to his troops—had under him the 1st Chinese Army (Lieut.-Gen Sun Li-Jen), formed from the Chinese Divisions which had come out of Burma with Stilwell in the great retreat of 1942. These Chinese Divisions, refitted with British and American equipment, had been re-trained by the Americans, and had a number of American officers. Theirs was the role of capturing from the Japanese the ground over which the Ledo Road was to be built. Behind them were the American, British and Indian engineers who were to build the road as fast as the Chinese captured the land on which to build it. (See illus., p. 2704.)

The route which the road was following was from Ledo in Assam, at the railhead of the Bengal - Assam railway, over the 5,000-foot ranges of Patkai Bum, and then along the broad valley of the Upper Chindwin down the Hukwang and Mogaung Valleys in the direction of Mogaung, which it by-passed, turning eastward to Myitkyina and Bhamo, after which it would join the old Burma Road into China. All that existed for the first part of Stilwell's drive was a path for mules and a historic refugee trail but, beyond Shingbwiyang,

STILWELL'S MARCH AND CHINDIT LANDINGS

While the Japanese were attempting to invade India from western Burma in the early part of 1944, Stilwell from the north-east and the airborne Chindits from the centre were closing in on the Japanese in the Mogaung area. This map shows the moves made by the forces under Stilwell (black arrows) and by the Chindits (shaded arrows : the names of their landing strips are in italics).

there was a road of sorts leading through Shaduzup and Kamaing. The engineers were to make of this track and primitive road a 30-foot standard double track highway.

The method of the march was simple. First went the Chinese Divisions to drive the enemy before them. On either side in flanking movements sweeping deep into the hills moved Chinese patrols and Brig.-Gen. Frank Merrill's American

Marauders, which included veteran U.S. infantry assault troops from Guadalcanal. These forces, including a column of Gurkhas and Kachins, cut into the Japanese rear and created general confusion.

On the heels of the troops, and often alongside them, came Engineer Reconnaissance parties and with them the bull-dozers and the road-building gangs—gangs which had to be armed to fight off Japanese sneak raids. By the side of the road was also built the great oil pipe-line running all the way back to Calcutta, and designed, on completion, to allow tankers in Calcutta Harbour to pump petrol into the heart of China.

Opposing Stilwell in this diagonal drive across northeast Burma was the Japanese 18th Division, based on three key towns, Kamaing, Mogaung and Myitkyina. Its opposition was stiff.

When the Chindits launched their airborne invasion, Stilwell was at the entrance of the Mogaung Valley (March 19). The

Japanese Between Two Allied Forces

enemy 18th Division was drawn up in front of him—the Japanese depending for all their supplies and reinforcements on the railway which runs from Myitkyina down to Mandalay. It was on to this vital railway that the Chindits dropped. Overnight the whole strategic position in north-east Burma was changed. The Japanese, instead of fighting a fairly easy defensive fight with a good line of communication behind them, found themselves sandwiched between two Allied forces.

Brig. Calvert's Chindit Brigade got behind Mogaung, while another Chindit column, that of Brig. Bernard Fergusson (Black Watch), came in by foot over the Chindwin and marched right across the enemy's main line of communication. Fergusson and his column had made a magnificent march over 7,000-foot hills and through unmapped country. He came southwards from Ledo along Stilwell's right flank. His object was to attack the town of Indaw, one of the key places on the Japanese-held railway.

Mawlu. These Chindit strongholds—Aberdeen, White City, Blackpool and the rest—were constantly attacked by the Japanese, but the Chindits held on, stopping all enemy reinforcements and traffic by road block and ambush on the railway and on the roads. The effect of this "stopper" on the enemy lines of supply was soon felt by the Japanese 18th Division, and Stilwell pushed on through weaker opposition to invest Kamaing. But he still had to fight at Shaduzup and Laban, north of Kamaing, where his infantry cut up the Japanese garrisons.

He fought at Inkangtang, where he flung in heavy tanks, manned by Chinese crews, and overran well-entrenched enemy gun emplacements. Some of the Allied tanks got lost in the dense jungle and their crews

Air Aid for Lost Tank Crews

would probably have been forced to abandon them, but aircraft, carrying out photographic reconnaissance, took photographs of the surrounding country, which they dropped to the tank crews to show them the best way home to the main forces.

Two years to the day after he had been "run out of Burma" Uncle Joe came marching back.

Meanwhile the Chindits continued their large scale operations in the rear. Lentaigne, Fergusson, Calvert and Brodie led their columns up and down the Japanese lines of communication. To describe their exploits and fights would need a book—but always they were working to the master-plan: "help Stilwell and clear north-east Burma." To the men of the Leicester, Black Watch, Beds and Herts, Queen's, Yorks & Lancs, Essex Regt., Lancashire Fusiliers, South Staffs, King's Own, Cameronians, The King's and the Burma Rifles and their West African and Indian comrades, and the gunners and engineers who served with them, go undying glory. Praise, too, to the R.A.F. and U.S.A.A.F. men who flew them in, maintained them, and evacuated the sick and wounded. The work of the two Sunderland flying boats which shuttled back and forth to pick up 500 sick and wounded Chindits from Indawgyi lake in daylight.

WINGATE'S LAST OPERATION
Maj.-Gen. O. C. Wingate, organizer of the Chindits' airborne invasion of Burma in 1944, is here seen talking with Col. Philip J. Cochran, commander of the U.S. Air Commando which made the initial 'fly-in' on March 5. Right, plaque on the wooden cross erected in a forward area to the memory of Wingate and the men who were lost with him when their aircraft crashed on a Burmese hillside on March 24.
Photos, Planet News ; British Newsreels

One of Wingate's last messages before he was killed was to Bernard Fergusson; it described the march of his brigade as "Hannibal Eclipsed." It was Fergusson who set up the famous jungle stronghold of "Aberdeen," 35 miles west of Mawlu, on the main railway. Here a Chindit airstrip was built and Dakota contact with the outside world established.

Meanwhile Calvert's Brigade had set up another Chindit stronghold, the "White City" road block, also near

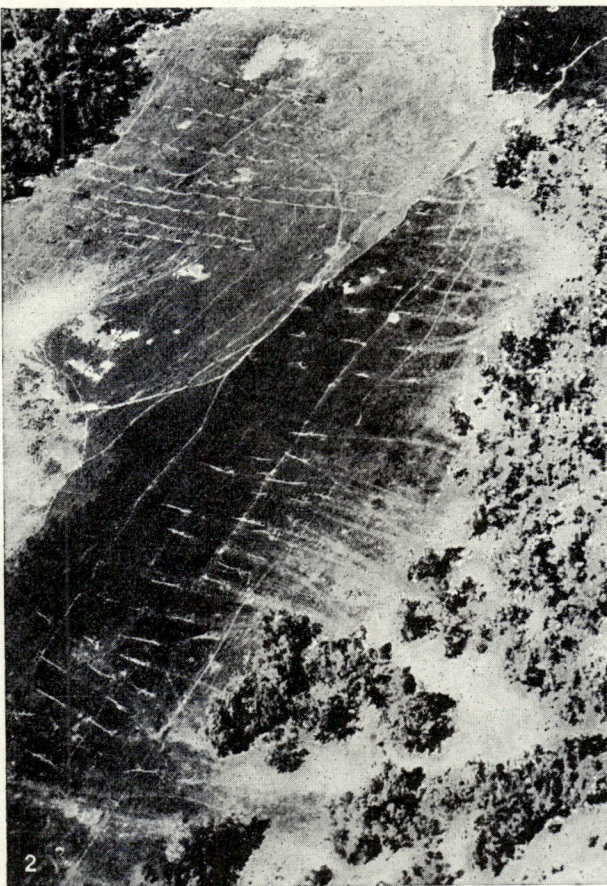

AIRBORNE LANDINGS IN BURMA

1. Sorting the ropes of gliders so that they can be hooked on to other gliders and to tow-planes preparatory to the 'fly-in' on March 5, 1944, of Col. Cochran's U.S. Air Commando, whose job it was to make an airstrip at 'Broadway' on which Dakota transport planes could land. 2. The clearing selected as 'Piccadilly' airstrip had had logs laid across it and could not be used (see p. 3006). 3. Men landed by glider (one that crashed lies behind them) wait for daylight to begin work on 'Broadway' airstrip. 4. Men of Cochran's Commando get to work preparing the airstrip, completed twelve hours after the first glider touched down. *Photos, U.S. Official; New York Times*

ALLIES RESUME OPERATIONS ON MYITKYINA AIRFIELD

Myitkyina airfied fell to a surprise attack by 'Merrill's Marauders' on May 17, 1944, after having been in Japanese hands for two years.   1. The airfield seen from the first glider-towing aircraft which touched down there after its recapture by the Allies.   2. Men and supplies for Stilwell's forces landed by gliders and transport planes at Myitkyina airfield.   3. Shelling the town of Myitkyina with a U.S. 75-mm. howitzer, brought in by air.   4. A crippled C47 transport plane is towed off the runway by midget bulldozers—specially constructed for airborne operations.

Photos, Paul Popper ; Associated Press

is typical of the dangers the airmen faced to keep faith with Wingate's men.

Farther north, relying on the 14th Army to keep the Kohima Japanese from his lines of communication, Stilwell

Stilwell's Chinese Troops Advance

was going all out and his Chinese troops were doing great things. One column, which had had less than ten weeks' training, killed 2,000 of the enemy in an advance of only 8 miles along the "road trace."

On May 17, as Stilwell's main forces closed in to take Kamaing, came the unexpected, electrifying news that another American-Chinese column had seized the Myitkyina airfield intact. On reaching the watershed of the Mogaung Valley, Stilwell had detached Merrill's Marauders and Chinese forces

Capt. J. N. RANDLE (Royal Norfolk Regt.)
Posthumously awarded the V.C. for gallantry at Kohima during the three days May 4-6, 1944. He was killed silencing a Japanese machine-gun unaided.

L/Cpl. J. P. HARMAN (Royal West Kents)
Posthumously awarded the V.C. for gallantry at Kohima on April 8, 1944. Single-handed he wiped out two machine-gun posts before he was killed.

Maj. F. G. BLAKER (Highland Light Infantry)
While attached to the 9th Gurkha Regt., he won the V.C. on July 9, 1944, when he led his company through jungle to seize a hill overlooking Taungni, Burma.

Maj. F. HOEY (Lincolnshire Regt.)
On Feb. 16, 1944, he led an attack in Ngakyedauk Pass. First to reach the objective, he killed all the defenders but was fatally wounded. Awarded the V.C.

Photos, Indian Official, News Chronicle, G.P.U.

Sgt. H. V. TURNER (West Yorks Regt.)
Posthumously awarded the V.C. for conspicuous gallantry at Ningthoukhong in Burma on June 7, 1944, when from a weakly held position he repelled Japanese attacks for two hours, going forward alone six times to hurl grenades at the enemy.

Capt. M. ALLMAND (6th Gurkha Rifles)
Won the V.C. and lost his life leading attacks on strong enemy positions at Pin Hmi road bridge and the railway bridge at Mogaung in June 1944. He was fatally wounded in a final charge, single-handed, on a Japanese machine-gun nest.

Lieut. A. G. HORWOOD (Queen's Royal Regt.)
While attached to the Northamptonshires, he ensured the success of operations at Kyauktaw (Arakan) by his cool, calculated actions on Jan. 18-20, 1944, and his magnificent bearing under fire. Mortally wounded, he was awarded the V.C. posthumously.

for an outflanking attack on Myitkyina, railhead of the Burma railway. They scaled the 7,000-foot Naun Hykit Pass, and by a forced march of twenty days, along secret paths, appeared suddenly on the Myitkyina airstrip. The Chinese actually seized the greater part of the town by surprise assault, but, in the confusion of the night, some units came under the fire of their own machine-gunners and a withdrawal was ordered. But they continued to dominate the railway station, and thus isolated Myitkyina from all communication with Mogaung, the next big station down the line. With Myitkyina airfield lost to the enemy, the pilots on the "hump" air line to China could breathe more freely: the chances of Japanese fighters jumping them were now slender.

At Mogaung itself, Calvert's Chindits launched a full scale attack from behind, and, in the town, effected a junction with the Chinese Division which had just

taken Kamaing. The Chindits had linked up with Stilwell—and all the Chindit brigades then passed to Stilwell's command.

The battle for Myitkyina was long drawn out, for, their escape barred by Lentaigne's forces, the Japanese fought for 78 days before Brig.-Gen. T. F. Wessel's American-Chinese forces occupied the town on August 4.

Stilwell and the Chindits had done a grand job and the Japanese were in retreat. The way was now open for the last lap of the drive to China. The

Chase to Mandalay Begins

British 36th Division (Maj.-Gen. F. W. Festing), flown in to Stilwell's Command, was the spearhead of the chase down the railway towards Mandalay—while the Chinese branched off to carry the road on to Bhamo and China. Already strong forces of their compatriots were advancing to meet them from the Salween river on the China side.

The British and American Governments' recognition of the great achievements of 1944 was shown by the knighthoods granted to Slim and his Corps Commanders—Scoones, Christison and Stopford—and by the full generalship given to Stilwell.

Maj.-Gen. LENTAIGNE   **Brigadier M. CALVERT**   **Brigadier B. FERGUSSON**
Brig. W. D. A. Lentaigne, D.S.O., column commander in the 1943 Chindit march, promoted Major-General, took over command of the Chindit forces after Wingate's death. Brig. 'Mad Mike' Calvert's Chindit brigade disembarked at 'Broadway' airstrip. Brig. Bernard Fergusson, D.S.O., led the Chindits who, supplied from the air, came in on foot across the Chindwin.

ALLIED INVASION OF FRANCE: HOME GUARD STAND DOWN

The Allied invasion of France took place at last on June 6, 1944.   A few hours after
it began—in very stormy and unseasonable weather—the Prime Minister informed
the House of Commons that the long-awaited operation had begun, and was going
better and with much smaller losses than had been expected.   So well did it go that
six months later it was possible for the Home Guard to be stood down : an occasion
made memorable by a broadcast from H.M. The King.

H.M. THE KING BROADCASTS TO THE NATION ON THE STAND-
DOWN OF THE HOME GUARD, DECEMBER 3, 1944.

OVER four years ago, in May 1940, our country was in
mortal danger.   The most powerful army the world
had ever seen had forced its way to within a few
miles of our coast.   From day to day we were threatened
with invasion.

In those days our Army had been gravely weakened.   A
call went out for men to enrol themselves in a new citizen
army, the Local Defence Volunteers, ready to use whatever
weapons could be found and to stand against the invader in
every village and every town.   Throughout Britain and
Northern Ireland the nation answered that summons, as
free men will always answer when freedom is in danger.
From fields and hills, from factories and mills, from shops
and offices, men of every age and every calling came forward
to train themselves for battle. . . .

In July 1940, the Local Defence Volunteers became the
Home Guard.   During those four years of continuing anxiety
that civilian army grew in strength ; under the competent
administration of the Territorial Army Associations, it soon
became a well-equipped and capable force, able to take over
many duties from regular soldiers preparing to go overseas.
I believe it is the voluntary spirit which has always made
the Home Guard so splendid and so powerful a comradeship
of arms.   The hope that this comradeship will long endure
was strong in me this afternoon while many thousands of
you marched past me in one of the most impressive and
memorable parades that I have ever seen.

For most of you—and, I must add, for your wives too—
your service in the Home Guard has not been easy.   I know
what it has meant, especially for older men.   Some of you
have stood for many hours on the gun sites, in desolate fields
or wind-swept beaches.   Many of you, after a long and hard
day's work, scarcely had time for food before you changed
into uniform for the evening parade.   Some of you had to
bicycle for long distances to the drill hall or the rifle range.

It was well known to the enemy that if he came to any
part of our land he would meet determined opposition, at
every point in his advance, from men who had good weapons
and, better still, knew how to use them.   In that way the
existence of the Home Guard helped much to ward off the
danger of invasion.   Then, too, our own plans for campaigns
in many parts of the world depended on our having a great
citizen force to help in the defence of the homeland.   As
anti-aircraft and coastal gunners, sentries at vulnerable
points, units for dealing with unexploded bombs, and in
many other ways, the Home Guard have played a full part
in the defence of their country. . . .

But you have gained something for yourselves.   You have
discovered in yourselves new capabilities.   You have found
how men from all kinds of homes and many different occupa-
tions can work together in a great cause, and how happy
they can be with each other.   That is a memory and a
knowledge which may help us all in the many peace-time
problems that we shall have to tackle before long.

I am very proud of what the Home Guard has done and I
give my heartfelt thanks to you all.   Officers, non-commis-
sioned officers, and men, you have served your country with
a steadfast devotion.   I know that your country will not
forget that service.

MR. CHURCHILL INFORMS THE HOUSE OF COMMONS ON JUNE
6, 1944, OF THE FALL OF ROME AND THE ALLIED INVASION
OF FRANCE.

THE House should, I think, take formal cognizance of the
liberation of Rome by the allied armies under the
command of General Alexander with General Clark, of the
United States Service, and General Oliver Leese in command
of the Fifth and Eighth Armies respectively.   This is a
memorable and glorious event which rewards the intense
fighting of the last five months in Italy. . . .

I have also to announce to the House that during the night
and the early hours of this morning the first of a series of
landings in force upon the European Continent has taken
place.   In this case the liberating assault fell upon the coast
of France.   An immense armada of upwards of 4,000 ships,
together with several thousand smaller craft, crossed the
Channel.   Massed airborne landings have been successfully
effected behind the enemy lines—and landings on the beaches
are proceeding at various points at the present time.   The
fire of the shore batteries has been largely quelled.   The
obstacles that were constructed in the sea have not proved
so difficult as was apprehended.

The Anglo-American allies are sustained by about 11,000
first-line aircraft, which can be drawn upon as may be
needed for the purposes of the battle. . . .   Reports are coming
in in rapid succession.   So far the commanders engaged report
that everything is proceeding according to plan.

And what a plan !   This vast operation is undoubtedly the
most complicated and difficult that has ever occurred.   It
involves tides, winds, waves, visibility both from the air and
the sea standpoint, and the combined employment of land,
air, and sea forces in the highest degree of intimacy and in
contact with conditions which could not and cannot be fully
foreseen.   There are already hopes that actual tactical
surprise has been attained, and we hope to furnish the enemy
with a succession of surprises during the course of the fighting.

The battle that has now begun will grow constantly in
scale and in intensity for many weeks to come, and I shall
not attempt to speculate upon its course.   This I may say,
however.   Complete unity prevails throughout the allied
armies.   There is a brotherhood in arms between us and our
friends of the United States.   There is complete confidence
in the supreme commander, General Eisenhower, and his
lieutenants, and also in the commander of the Expeditionary
Force, General Montgomery.   The ardour and spirit of the
troops, as I saw myself, embarking in these last few days
was splendid to witness.   Nothing that equipment, science,
and forethought could do has been neglected, and the whole
process of opening this great new front will be pursued with
the utmost resolution.

AT THE END OF THE SAME SITTING, MR. CHURCHILL MADE
THE FOLLOWING FURTHER STATEMENT :

I CAN state to the House that this operation is proceeding
in a thoroughly satisfactory manner.   Many dangers
and difficulties which at this time last night appeared extremely formidable are behind us.   The passage of the sea
has been made with far less loss than we apprehended.   The
resistance of the batteries has been greatly weakened by the
bombing of the Air Force, and the superior bombardment of
our ships quickly reduced their fire to dimensions which did
not affect the problem. . . .   The landings along the whole
front have been very effective, and troops have penetrated
in some cases several miles inland. . . . The landings of the
airborne troops . . . on a scale far larger than anything that
has been seen so far in the world . . . took place with extremely little loss and with great accuracy. . . . A very
great degree of risk had to be taken in respect of the weather.
But General Eisenhower's courage is equal to all the necessary
decisions that have to be taken in these extremely difficult
and uncontrollable matters.   The airborne troops are well
established and the landings and the follow-ups are all proceeding with much less loss—very much less—than we expected. . . . The enemy will now probably endeavour to
concentrate on this area, and in that event heavy fighting
will soon begin. . . . It is, therefore, a most serious time that
we enter upon.   Thank God, we enter upon it with our great
allies all in good heart and all in good friendship.

BRITISH SHIPBUILDING FACTS: EDUCATIONAL REFORM

Mr. Alexander's figures, comparing British ship production for the years 1939-1943
with that for 1914-1918, were the first clear indication of how tremendous had been
the effort to which Britain—and the civilized world—owed its survival.   The Education Act, passed after long and controversial debate in the House of Commons, implemented the intention of the country to equip its children with ability to appreciate,
use, and improve their national heritage

MR. A. V. ALEXANDER, FIRST LORD OF THE ADMIRALTY,
REVEALS THE FACTS OF BRITISH WARTIME SHIP CONSTRUC-
TION TO THE HOUSE OF COMMONS, NOVEMBER 1, 1944.

ALTHOUGH it would be wrong to assume that we are at
the end of real danger from attacks on our shipping,
especially by U-boats and mines, I think we have
now reached a stage of the war when the worst of our shipping
problems are over. . . .

But for the assistance, efficiency, and continuity of effort
in British shipyards, the country would not have survived
the most dangerous part of the war. . . . Some measure of
the immensity of the naval shipbuilding accomplished by the
United Kingdom in this war is shown by the following figures
of naval vessels completed between September, 1939 and
December, 1943 :

Major war vessels, including battleships, cruisers,
monitors, fleet escort carriers, destroyers, submarines,
frigates, sloops, corvettes, fleet minesweepers, fast cruising
minelayers, and depot ships of various kinds.

Numbers	634
Tonnage (S.D.)	1,183,501

Mosquito craft, including motor gunboats and torpedo
boats, various types of motor launches and motor minesweepers.

Numbers	1,260
Tonnage (S.D.)	120,358

Other naval vessels, including landing craft of all de-
scriptions, trawlers, and other miscellaneous craft.

Numbers	2,729
Tonnage (S.D.)	334,919

Side by side with this great programme of warship building,
the repair and maintenance of vessels already on active service has been carried on. Many classes of vessels have been
able to remain in harbour only for the very minimum period,
and wear and tear have increased accordingly. Damage
from action has been frequent, and there has been extraordinary damage from the worst Atlantic gales for years.
In addition we have had to force convoy after convoy through
the northern seas to Russia. . . .

Even at a very critical stage of the war the labour available in the contract shipyards was divided into 55 per cent
for naval construction and repairs, and the remainder for
mercantile needs. To achieve maximum importing capacity
the standard tramp of about 10,000 tons deadweight was
built, adapted later for special cargoes such as tanks, aircraft, and other bulky items. Again, some indications of
the magnitude of the effort put into merchant shipbuilding
in this war is given by the following figures showing the
number and tonnage of the ships constructed :

		No.	Thousand Gross Tons
1939, Sept.–Dec.		56	243
1940		182	810
1941		236	1,158
1942		259	1,302
1943		237	1,204

The tonnage of merchant vessels launched in the four
years 1915–18 was 3,770,170, whereas in the four years 1940–43
the tonnage was 4,415,668, and this in spite of the fact that
we have fewer yards and ships and less labour available than
in 1918, and in spite of the blackout and air-raid damage to
the yards and workers' homes. . . . We have been able
gradually to increase the proportion of faster ships in the
programme of merchant construction, and in particular to
undertake the programme of standardized cargo liners of
15 knots, furnished on " austerity " lines. . . .

We can contemplate the termination of the programme of
standardized types, and have already begun to turn to the
production of vessels more suited to the somewhat different
services likely to be required during the remaining stages
of the war. For example, we require smaller cargo vessels
capable of using Mediterranean and other smaller Continental
ports, and for the Far Eastern war we require faster ships
of the cargo liner type and specially designed coasters. . . .

THE EDUCATION ACT, 1944, WHICH CAME INTO FORCE ON
APRIL 1, 1945, ENACTED THE FOLLOWING AMONG ITS PRO-
VISIONS :

Ministry of Education. It shall be lawful for His Majesty
to appoint a Minister whose duty it shall be to promote the
education of the people of England and Wales. The department of which he is in charge shall be known as the Ministry
of Education.

Three Stages of Education. The statutory system of public
education shall be organized in three progressive stages to
be known as primary education, secondary education, and
further education.

Compulsory School Age. The expression " compulsory
school age " means any person between five years and fifteen
years. A person shall be deemed to be over compulsory
school age as soon as he has attained the age of fifteen years :
provided that, as soon as the Minister is satisfied that it has
become practicable, he shall lay before Parliament the draft
of an Order in Council substituting for references in this
section to the age of fifteen years, references to the age of
sixteen years.

Duty of Parents. It shall be the duty of the parent of
every child of compulsory school age to cause him to receive
efficient full-time education suitable to his age, ability, and
aptitude, either by regular attendance at school or otherwise.
Penalties enacted for failure to carry out this duty are : not
exceeding one pound for the first offence, five pounds for the
second, ten pounds or a month's imprisonment, or both, for
third and subsequent offences.

Religious Education. The school day in every county
school and in every voluntary school shall begin with collective worship on the part of all pupils in attendance at the
school. Religious instruction shall be given in every county
school and in every voluntary school. The collective worship
shall not be distinctive of any particular religious denomination, and the religious instruction shall be given in accordance
with an agreed syllabus, and shall not include any catechism
or formulary which is distinctive of any particular religious
denomination. If the parent of any pupil requests that he
be wholly or partly excused from attendance at religious
worship and instruction in the school, the pupil shall be
excused from such attendance accordingly.

County Colleges. Not later than three years after the
date of the commencement of the Act it shall be the duty
of every local education authority to establish and maintain
county colleges, that is to say centres approved by the Minister,
for providing for young persons such further education as
will enable them to develop their various aptitudes and
capacities and will prepare them for the responsibilities of
citizenship. It shall be the duty of the local education
authority to serve upon every young person residing in their
area who is not exempt from compulsory attendance for
further education a notice directing him to attend at a county
college for one whole day or two half-days in each forty-
four weeks in every year while he remains a young person.

School Meals. Regulations made by the Minister shall
impose upon local education authorities the duty of providing milk, meals and other refreshment for pupils at
schools and county colleges maintained by them.

Prohibition of Fees. No fees shall be charged in respect
of admission to any school maintained by a local education
authority or to any county college or in respect of education
provided in any such school or college.

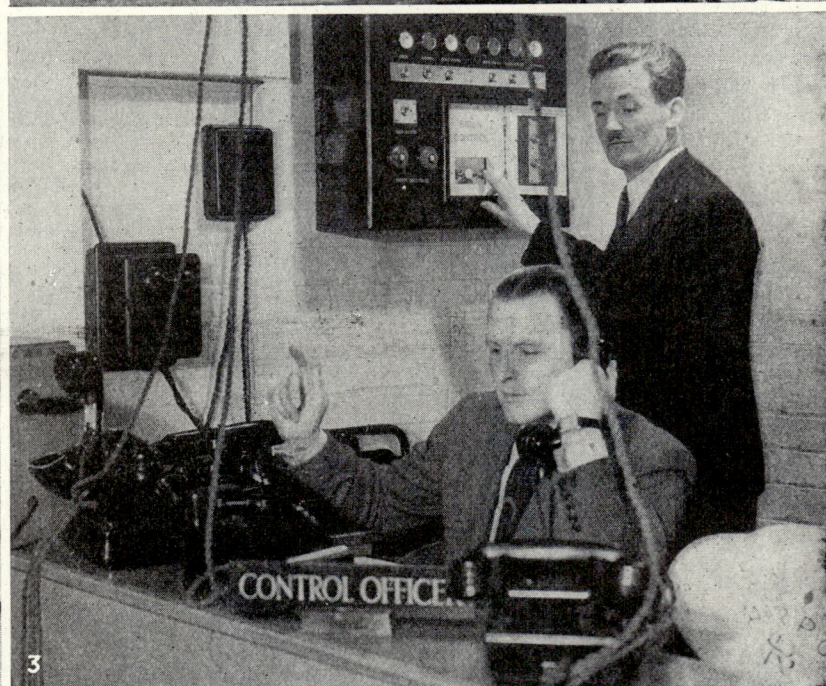

WORKERS AT WAR

1. Inspection of 'Barracuda' aircraft in course of construction. These torpedo-bombers, used with success by the Fleet Air Arm against enemy shipping in all zones, were designed and made by the Fairey Aviation Company. High-winged monoplanes (the wings could be folded) powered by a Rolls-Royce engine, they had a crew of three, carried bombs or mines, and could operate by day or night from carriers or land bases. 2. Dinner-time at the counter of a Ministry of Aircraft Production self-help canteen. 3. A.R.P. controller's desk in a factory : his assistant is about to press the button of the factory siren on receipt of a 'red' warning (meaning danger of air attack imminent). 4. Registering volunteer blood donors at a shoe factory. The blood so given saved thousands of lives of wounded.

3018

Chapter 300

INVASION YEAR IN GREAT BRITAIN

For the whole world, but perhaps particularly for everyone in Britain, 1944 was sharply divided by the invasion of Normandy on June 6. Though the majority of Britons realized that, as Mr. Herbert Morrison aptly remarked, "You cannot start a second front with a piece of chalk on a pavement," the year opened with a strong sense of waiting long-drawn-out. But the success of the landings in France produced the courage and hope necessary to withstand the enemy's attacks with new long-range weapons—and to continue post-war planning. Home affairs for 1943 were covered in Chapter 262

THE year 1944 opened for Britain with a sharp return of raiding from the air by the enemy. This was not unexpected, for in January it was announced that General Eisenhower had assumed command of the forces assembling for the invasion of Europe, and that Supreme Headquarters, Allied Expeditionary Force, was in London.

Beginning with a raid by some 90 planes (16 of which were destroyed) on the night of January 21–22, London experienced during the next ten weeks the heaviest air attacks it had undergone since the "blitz" of 1940–41. The enemy raiders were met with a barrage of an intensity never before put up—so violent that many people found it the most unnerving part of this series of attacks. The increased strength of the raids can be gathered from the casualties : December 1943, 10 killed, 41 injured ; January, 107 killed, 270 injured ; February, 961 killed, 1,712 injured—the highest figure since May 1941 ; March, 279 killed, 633 injured ; April, 146 killed, 226 injured. During the night of February 18–19, showers of incendiaries fell in the heart of London, some on the roof of Westminster Hall, many in Old Palace Yard. Incendiaries fell on Harrow School on February 22–23 : there were no casualties though some damage was done.

On the night of February 23–24, bombs fell close to the American headquarters in London : the London Library received a direct hit ;

St. James's Palace Blasted

Chatham House (the Royal Institute of International Affairs) and St. James's Theatre were damaged ; St. James's Palace and the Chapel Royal were severely blasted ; irreplaceable art treasures, including paintings by Rembrandt, Van Dyck, and Frans Hals, in the hands of King Street experts, were buried. Some half only of these valuables were recovered.

In the first three months of 1944, the Luftwaffe made some 20 attacks on Britain, using each time about 100 aircraft (on February 22, 175), and dropping a total of 2,400 tons of bombs (compared with 48,000 tons dropped by

Bomber Command on Germany). Some 150 enemy planes were shot down. German propaganda magnified the strength of each attack ten times, adding that Londoners were fleeing in panic from the city, and Civil Defence measures had failed completely.

Though the German picture was grossly distorted, this renewal of enemy bombing did lead to some heart-searching among civilians over the heavy Allied bombing of Germany—a feeling voiced in the House of Lords on February 9 by the Bishop of Chichester. While recognizing the legitimacy of concentrated attack on industrial and military objectives, he expressed concern as to whether the Government understood what "area bombing" was destroying. The Government spokesman, Viscount Cranborne, said firmly, " I can give the Bishop no hope that we shall abate our bombing policy. On the contrary, we shall continue it against proper and

suitable targets in increasing power and with more crushing effect until final victory is secure."

News taken as intimations that the invasion could not be far off included the announcement on March 20 that Frenchmen, Belgians, Netherlanders, Poles and Czechoslovaks had been receiving training in all phases of Civil Defence work ; and on April 7 that a special N.F.S. volunteer contingent would be available for fire-fighting overseas in support of the Army Fire Service. Tension grew when Mr. Cordell Hull, U.S. Secretary of State, informed the press on March 10 that Eire had rejected an American request for the removal of Axis consular and diplomatic representatives from Eire because their presence constituted a danger to the lives of American soldiers and to the success of Allied Military operations. Two days

Civil Defence Workers for Overseas

EMERGENCY LAUNDRY IN A BOMB-WRECKED STREET

The blast damage done by the flying-bomb attacks on London and South-East England that began on June 13 1944, caused a great deal of dust and dirt with which citizens in their wrecked houses found it impossible to deal. Much appreciated mobile laundries and baths, run by Women's Voluntary Services and other agencies, brought some cleanliness and comfort into the lives of these unfortunate people.   *Photo, Daily Mirror*

LONDON DAMAGE IN THE 'LITTLE BLITZ' OF 1944
Here is St. James's Palace with its windows blown out : this and much other damage was done in the area by bombs dropped during an enemy air raid on the night of February 23–24, 1944. Right, platforms six and seven at Paddington station after they had been hit by a bomb early on March 3, 1944.   *Photo, Associated Press*

departure from Great Britain of official carriers or diplomatic and consular representatives or any members of their official or domestic staff, excepting only the American and Soviet missions and those of the fighting Dominions.

But still the great moment delayed. On April 24, the Home Office announced that all travel from Britain, whether by sea or air, to any overseas destination would be suspended for military reasons from April 27 until further notice. But April dragged to its close, and May went slowly by. The Army Post Office issued a notice on May 19 that " during the

later, the British Home Office announced that, in view of Eire's rejection of the American request, which had the full support of the British Government, all travel, subject to certain restrictions, between Great Britain and the whole of Ireland must be suspended forthwith. Eire's appeals to the other Dominions for moral support against the United States met unqualified rebuffs. On April 5, the telephone service between Great Britain and all parts of Ireland was suspended, to prevent possible leakage of vital information ; the telegraph service was under strict censorship.

From April 1, a coastal belt about ten miles in depth extending from the Wash round the east and south coasts to

Closing of Coastal Areas

Land's End, and certain districts on the Firth of Forth, became " protected " areas, and all persons not resident on that date were prohibited from entering them ; a week later, the coast of South Wales and the Bristol Channel to Portishead, areas on the Clyde and the west and north coasts of Scotland were made " regulated " areas. In all these districts, all persons over 16 had to carry their identity cards and produce them to any constable or any members of the British or Allied forces ; the use of binoculars and telescopes was forbidden. Rumours there were of great concrete embankments, which disappeared overnight, on the north side of the Thames estuary, of strings of ammunition barges packed tightly end to end on the south side, of shipping so thick

in Weymouth Bay that no water was visible ; but on the whole both curiosity and informativeness were restrained with equal decency. (The preparations going forward in these areas are described in a later chapter.)

On April 7 Mr. Edward Stettinius, U.S. Under-Secretary of State, arrived in London and spent three weeks in Britain holding a series of informal discussions, covering all the fields in which Great Britain and the United States were collaborating, with Mr. Churchill, other members of the Cabinet, British officials, the Russian and French ambassadors to Britain, and the ministers of the various exiled Allied governments.

A thrill of expectancy swept through the country at the sudden announcement by the Foreign Office on April 17 that from midnight on April 17–18 and until further notice the Government would be unable to permit the transmission or receipt by diplomatic missions of any telegram not in plain language ; the dispatch or receipt of any diplomatic bag without censorship ; or the

coming months more men will be serving overseas than has been the case at any stage so far in this war," and urged correspondents to restrict their letters to one thin sheet in a thin envelope. An appeal for yachtsmen and men with motor-boat or steamboat experience to put their services at the disposal of the Royal Navy for short periods of duty was answered by 3,700 volunteers.

The days passed. The weather was abominable. Rain fell, storms raged. A feeling that there could be no invasion in 1944 began to set in, when on June 6 a communiqué issued by S.H.A.E.F. at 9.35 a.m. informed the world that an

Allied invasion of Northern France had begun. A few hours later Mr. Churchill said in the House of Commons, " I have to announce to the House that during the night and the early hours of this morning the first of a series of landings in force upon the European continent has taken place." (*See* Hist. Doct. CCLXXV, p. 3016.) The weather continued shockingly bad, and on that account the exhilaration produced by this long awaited news was tinged with much anxiety. However, on June 12 Mr. Churchill, accompanied by Field-Marshals Smuts and Sir Alan Brooke, visited the Normandy front; and on June 16 King George VI himself visited his troops in France. The Allies clearly were not going to be swept from the shores of Europe in the ignominious way prophesied by Hitler.

Diplomatic privileges were restored from midnight of June 19–20; protected areas on the Firth of Forth became regulated areas on July 29, other protected areas became regulated on August 25; orders still in force compelling immobilization of unattended motor vehicles and of

Diplomatic Privileges Restored

BACK TO 'CIVVY STREET'

Men released or transferred from the Services with at least six months' service received civilian clothes, available from October 16, 1944, besides such service apparel as they were allowed to retain. Here is a private of the Pioneer Corps with the clothes he has chosen. The suits were of normal design—the order imposing restrictions on the style of men's suits had been revoked on January 27, 1944.
Photo, Associated Press

vessels on inland waterways were rescinded on August 29; in September the ban on camping within ten miles of the British east and west coasts was revoked, except for some areas in Scotland.

The announcement on July 19 that " in view of the large reserves of air crews, Allied air supremacy on all fronts, and the present low casualty rate, the War Cabinet have decided to release large numbers of men designated for the R.A.F. air crews and a smaller but still large number of men of the R.A.F. Regiment for active service with the Army," and that substantial numbers of " hostilities only " naval ratings would be transferred for similar reasons to the land forces, caused a good deal of heartburning among men who had opted and been selected for the Air Force and the Navy; but a general sigh of relief went up from the nation, for it was a decisive indication that air and naval casualties in the initial landings and the build-up of the armies in France had been far lower than anticipated.

The successful invasion of Normandy had an immediate effect on the Home Guard which, through the anxious weeks preceding June 6, had been ready to oppose some last desperate throw by the enemy. (At that time the strength of the Home Guard was 1,727,000, of whom 142,246 were on A.A. duties, 7,000 with the coastal artillery, and 7,000 doing bomb disposal work; women members numbered 30,696.) But there was no descent either upon the coasts of Britain from the sea or in her hills and valleys from the air. Confident, apparently, in his " West Wall," the enemy waited.

All compulsory drill and training of the Home Guard were discontinued from September 11, and on November 1 it was stood down, remaining liable, however, to recall in case of emergency. On Sunday, December 3, the King, accompanied by the Queen and the Princesses, took the salute in Hyde Park at a great march past of 7,000 men

FRESH FRUIT—AT A PRICE

Owing to the scarcity of fresh fruit, street hawkers had no great difficulty in the summer of 1944 in selling pineapples at five guineas each, grapes at 16s. a pound, and peaches at 2s. each. These fruits, luxuries even in peace-time, were not controlled in price as were all foods which were necessities of life. *Photo, News Chronicle*

representing detachments, battalions, and batteries from all parts of Great Britain and Northern Ireland. On the same day stand-down parades were held throughout the country, and in the evening the King broadcast a message of thanks and appreciation. (*See* Hist. Doct. CCLXXIV, p. 3016.)

One week exactly after the invasion of Normandy, on the morning of June 13, the first flying bomb was spotted by the Royal Observer Corps near Dymchurch. Though the general public knew nothing of " Vergeltungswaffe Eins " (Reprisal-weapon One) except vague rumours of a " pilotless plane," the Government had known of the German experiments and their possible threat for nearly two years. The first public intimation in southern England that something queer was happening was an all-night alert with no barrage, no aeroplanes, and very few bomb explosions. For over three weeks, official reports stated merely that there had been enemy activity against " southern England." Londoners found themselves congratulated by correspondents outside the zone of attack on escaping this latest enemy frightfulness. But on July 6 the Prime Minister in a statement to the House made it clear that London was the principal recipient of these missiles.

Attacks by Reprisal-Weapon One

Evacuation from greater London was reopened on July 1, and during that month the eight deep shelters, ordered in 1941 at the height of the blitz and kept since in reserve, were opened.

London's Deep Shelters Opened

These shelters were more than 100 ft. underground; were bomb-proof, gas-proof, water-proof; could sleep each 8,500, and in emergency shelter 35,000: had restaurants, rest rooms, medical posts and sick bays; and were all air-conditioned. Shelterers crowded once more into the bunks in the tube stations, into the surface shelters in the streets. Anderson and Morrison shelters came into use again. London was a beleaguered city; but the picture painted by German propaganda of the whole of southern England as a scene of desolation and London abandoned by the Government was far from true. Life went on throughout the bombardment.

On August 2, Mr. Churchill again reviewed the position, mentioning the possibility that the enemy might also use long-range rockets, and strongly advising those who could stay or get away from London to do so. But his warning was overlooked, and evacuated people began to stream back to London when, on September 7, Mr. Duncan Sandys, chairman of the Flying-Bomb Counter-Measures Committee, began an official statement with the words: "Except possibly for a few last shots, the Battle of London is over. . . ."

Not a single London borough escaped flying-bomb damage. A later chapter is devoted to the development and effects of the flying bomb, and to the steps taken to combat it both before and after it began to be used. Here it will suffice to add that figures for London air raid damage issued in September after the worst of the flying-bomb attack had passed were: air raids, 1940-44: 84,000 houses destroyed, 142,000 still to be repaired, of which 42,000 were uninhabitable; flying-bomb attacks, 23,000 houses destroyed, 1,104,000 damaged (many slightly). Throughout Britain 202,000 houses had been destroyed or damaged beyond repair, 4,328,000 were damaged but repairable.

It was not till November 10 that the Prime Minister referred to actual attacks on Britain with long-range rockets—Vergeltungswaffe Zwei. The first of these had fallen in Chiswick on September 8, but absolute silence was preserved about them in the press. Even in enemy propaganda, they were mentioned only two days before the Premier referred to them, so uncertain had the Germans been about the range and effectiveness of their V2. Damage and casualties were caused, and south-eastern England was again the chief sufferer; but the practical effect on the course of the war of intermittent bombardment by this new terror weapon was nil.

OILFIELD IN ENGLAND

The existence of an oilfield in England was revealed on September 23, 1944—its situation at Eakring near Newark, Nottinghamshire, in December. Here is the head of one of the 238 wells in the field, which was about two miles by half a mile in extent. The oil-bearing stratum lay at 2,000-2,500 feet below ground. From the beginning of the war until its existence was divulged, it had produced about 78,000,000 gallons of oil. *Photo, L.N.A.*

Organized evacuation from greater London and southern England was suspended on September 7, except for expectant mothers, the infirm, blind persons and invalids. Day-time fireguard duties

War Time Regulations Relaxed

were discontinued, and night fireguard duties (except in London and south-east England) suspended from September 12. Blackout regulations were modified, beginning with the introduction of "half-lighting" of windows, except during alerts, on September 17. The Removal of Direction Signs Order, 1940 was revoked on October 9. From October 10, newspapers were allowed to publish details of the weather after two (instead of ten) days' delay, except in the case of snow or flood which was not to be mentioned for five days.

September 30 was a great day for south-east Kent. At 10 a.m. loud-speakers in the streets of Dover broadcast the message: "The Mayor has received official information that all the long-range guns on the other side of the Channel have been captured." The people of "Hellfire Corner"—Dover, Folkestone, Deal, Ramsgate—immediately assembled in the streets, dancing,

THIS WAS THE ONE DROP HAMMER . . .

Speaking on March 21, 1945, on the Distribution of Industry Bill, Mr. Oliver Lyttelton, Minister of Production, said, 'Would it surprise the House to know that at a certain time there was only one drop hammer which could forge the Spitfire crankshaft?' This was the hammer, at the Sheffield works of the English Steel Corporation. Two teams of eight men manned it. It was worked sixteen hours a day, and produced about ten crankshafts an hour. *Photo, News Chronicle*

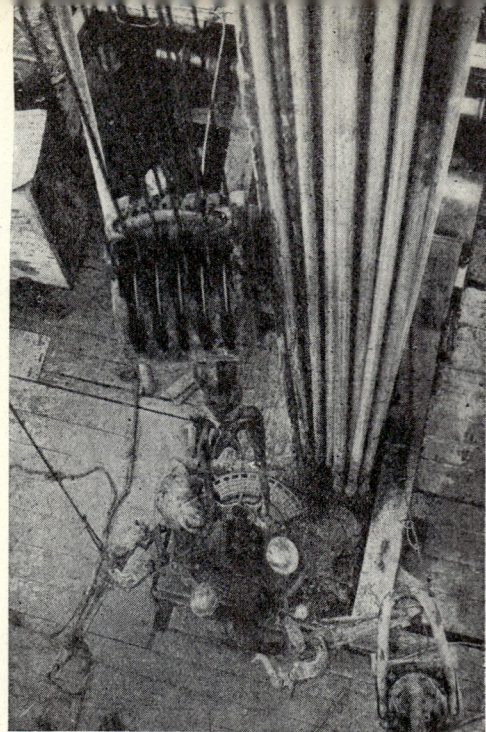

In the years when our Country was in mortal danger

THOMAS ATKINS

who served 4 July 1940 – 31 December 1944

gave generously of his time and powers to make himself ready for her defence by force of arms and with his life if need be.

George R.I.

THE HOME GUARD

MEN OF THE HOME GUARD ON ACTIVE SERVICE

In June 1944, 142,246 members of the Home Guard were on anti-aircraft duties, manning the rocket batteries. Development of rockets as a war weapon started in Britain in 1934; production on a large scale began in 1940. First used against low-flying aircraft, they were successfully employed from the spring of 1941 against high-flying night bombers. Left, certificate of service issued to every member of the Home Guard serving on November 1, 1944. Below, Home Guard units passing through Piccadilly Circus on their way to Hyde Park for the stand-down march past H.M. the King on December 3.

SEVEN SEA-FORTS THAT GUARDED THE THAMES

These sea-forts, built in the Thames estuary to keep the Port of London open, had as their primary task—carried out with complete success—the driving off of mine-laying aircraft. Standing on concrete piles 50 ft. above the water, they were 36 ft. square and 20 ft. deep, and were armed with 3.7-in. A.A. guns, Bofors guns, and lighter armaments. They were linked with the land by telephone and with each other by cat-walks. Four were manned by the Royal Navy; three by the Army. *Photo, Fox*

singing and cheering: they had been under bombardment since August 12, 1940, when the first German shell fell on Dover. Flags flew everywhere and special services were held in the churches. (*See illus. p. 3009.*)

The pushing back of the Germans made it possible during August and September to reduce the number of full-time members of both the N.F.S. and Civil Defence. (A call went out from S.H.A.E.F. later in the year for volunteers for a highly trained British Civil Defence Overseas Column.) Organized return of evacuated school children whose homes were in N. and W. England, the Midlands and Wales also began.

Four serious ammunition explosions occurred during the year. The first, at a northern railway station on February 4 during the loading of ammunition, resulted in ten deaths. On June 2 the leading truck of an ammunition train caught fire and blew up in a small Cambridgeshire town. Two were killed, twenty injured, the station was demolished, a wide area wrecked and damaged, 500 made homeless, and the 70-ton engine was lifted off the rails and reduced to a mass of wreckage. About the same time a fire started in an ammunition dump in East Anglia. Several major explosions took place, but the N.F.S extinguished the fire in eight hours and saved the bulk of the ammunition. The worst accident occurred on November 27 near Burton-on-Trent in part of a huge R.A.F. underground storage depot. Towns and villages over a wide area rocked; farms were wiped out—one was

Ammunition Explosions

engulfed in a crater 300 feet deep and 300 yards across; a cement works was demolished, hundreds of cattle killed, scores of houses stripped of their roofs, and several square miles of country devastated by subterranean explosions. The main part of the depot and the administrative buildings, however, were not seriously affected; the total loss of bombs was under 4,000 tons. The total death-roll was 70 (including six Italian co-operators); 13 were injured and detained in hospital.

The existence of an English oilfield was revealed in September—its situation near the village of Eakring, 7 miles from Newark, in December. Some thousand men were employed in the annual production of about 100,000 tons (26,000,000 gallons) of oil of excellent quality suitable for high grade lubricants. A pipe-line system a thousand miles long, constructed since 1941 at a cost of £7,000,000, had, by the end of 1944, carried 2,400,000,000 gallons of imported petrol from the ports to scores of secret underground storage tanks and then to the main centres of consumption, particularly airfields. Mr. Geoffrey Lloyd, chairman of the Oil Control Board, said in January 1945 that without this oil "grid" the "build-up of the Allied air offensive to anything like the desired scale would have been impracticable." During the invasion of the Continent, the pipe-lines carried petrol at the rate of 5 million gallons a day.

Not merely the Church of England, but the whole country and perhaps the whole world, suffered a blow in the death of Dr. William Temple, Archbishop of Canterbury, on October 25 at the early age of 63. This able, sincere, well-loved and energetic churchman had been appointed Primate of All England only on February 23, 1942, in the expectation that his wisdom would help more than the members of his own church during the peacemaking and after. His predecessor, Lord Lang, who had retired at 75 on account of advancing years, conducted the funeral ceremonies of his successor—an unprecedented event in church history.

"Statistics relating to the War Effort of the United Kingdom" (Cmd. 6564), a booklet published in November, contained many interesting figures, among them these: Between June 1939 and June 1944, the total number of men aged 14 to 64 and women aged 14 to 59 in the Services or in industrial employment in Great Britain rose from $18\frac{1}{2}$ to 22 millions. Of these, 10·3 millions were in the Services or whole-time Civil Defence or industries mainly concerned in the output of munitions. At the height of the enemy air attacks in 1941, the number of whole-time Civil Defence workers was 324,000, reduced to 225,000 by June 1944. The total male population between 14 and 64 was 16,010,000 in 1939; 15,910,000 in 1944. Of the total munitions supply made available to the British Commonwealth, the United Kingdom produced about 70 per cent, the Empire ten per cent, the United States 20 per cent (16 per cent lend-lease; four per cent cash purchase). By 1943, through increased home production, an adequate supply of food was being maintained while food imports were below pre-war level by 50 per cent. The total private income of persons and businesses rose from £4,560 million in 1938 to £8,075 million in 1943. Addition of pensions, unemployment relief, etc., and deduction of direct taxation and other

Statistics of the War Effort

compulsory payments brought these figures to £4,489 million and £6,798 million respectively. Personal expenditure on current goods and services increased from £4,138 million in 1938 to £5,049 million in 1943, the actual quantity of goods and services, however, being less than in 1938, and the increased expenditure being accounted for by higher indirect taxation. Annual savings increased from £351 million to £1,749 million.

The total cost of the war to Britain up to September 2 was £23,893,000,000, of which 44 per cent had been met by taxation. Daily expenditure from June to September was between £13,250,000 and £14,000,000.

Figures of lend-lease aid from Great Britain to the United States given by President Roosevelt to Congress were reprinted by H.M. Stationery Office on December 8. Up to December 1943, the Government of the British Commonwealth had expended 1,175,000,000 dollars (about £292,000,000) in reverse lend-lease. By June 30, 1944, the sum had risen to 3,348,000,000 dollars (about £830,000,000). It would have required a thousand ships to send across the Atlantic what the United States forces received from the United Kingdom. The percentage of total United States army requirements in the European theatre provided by the United

Lend-Lease from Britain to U.S.A.

PREFABRICATED HOMES FOR THE BOMBED-OUT

A great many houses were destroyed in Poplar, in the East End of London, during the heavy raids of 1940–41, and the borough suffered also from later raids and the flying-bombs. Poplar Council was among the first in London to put up temporary prefabricated bungalows to help rehouse its people. Here are two 'box bungalows' of wood and asbestos built in the Isle of Dogs. They had a living-room 19 ft. by 12 ft. with a built-in kitchen recess containing cooker, sink, and boiler, and two bedrooms each 11 ft. by 10 ft. *Photo, Daily Mirror*

Kingdom ranged as high as 63 per cent in the case of quartermasters' supplies, and 58 per cent for engineers' supplies. Great Britain built and equipped twenty hospital trains for the transport of American wounded in France. The "Queen Mary" and the "Queen Elizabeth" were given to carry American troops across the ocean. Sixteen million boxes of matches, 14,120,000 rounds of ammunitions, 11,000 telegraph poles, 37,250,000 cakes of soap, 7,800,000 lb. of salt and 20 per cent of the food for the United States forces in the United Kingdom were other specific items provided: in addition to which, as Sir Stafford Cripps, Minister of Aircraft Production, explained in a broadcast to the United States on March 11, whole areas in Britain were evacuated to make room for American troops, thousands of acres of agricultural land were cleared for American aerodromes, bases, training grounds, etc., and the fruits of British research in radar, aeroplane engines, and other scientific and technical fields were made available to the United States.

The Government's plan for releasing men from the armed forces after the conquest of Germany was set out in a white paper (Cmd. 6548) published in September. Men in Class A were to be released on grounds of age and length of service; in Class B, to be transferred to civilian reconstruction work on account of special qualifications. By reckoning two months' service as the equivalent of one year of age, the Government evolved a simple but ingenious method which would lead to the transfer to civil life of some men of all ages. But the paper made it clear that the number of men likely to be released depended entirely on requirements for the war against Japan and for the garrisoning of occupied countries. A little later the Government announced that women, married or

Plans for Release from the Forces

'BOOKSTALL' IN PARLIAMENT SQUARE

On October 24, 1944, Mr. A. P. Herbert, Independent Member for Oxford University, asked in the House, 'Is it now possible to remove the bookstall from Parliament Square without danger to the State?' Amid laughter, Sir James Grigg, Secretary of State for War, answered, 'Yes, Sir.' The 'bookstall,' seen here, was in fact a concrete blockhouse— one of a number put up in 1940 and camouflaged so cleverly that thousands of Londoners passed them daily oblivious of the deception. *Photo, Topical Press*

INVASION CONVOYS ROLL THROUGH LONDON

British, American, French and other Allied contingents rumbled across the country steadily in jeeps and lorries, on tanks and armoured cars, during the days which followed the first Allied landings in Normandy in June 1944. The people of England thus gained an idea of the masses of men and material that had been prepared for the great day. Here is a scene in a London suburb as Scottish troops pass through. *Photo, Planet News*

single, with household responsibilities, and those wishing to join their husbands on release from the forces; women over 60; and men over 65 were to be permitted if they wished to retire from industry immediately the European war ended, irrespective of the production on which they were engaged; and more consideration would be given to all other classes of industrial conscripts. Young men and women reaching the age of registration for employment would continue to register; but while young men would be liable to be called up for the forces, young women could volunteer for, but would not be directed into, the forces.

Possibly the most important piece of legislation of the year was the Education Act, which received the Royal Assent on August 3, to come into effect on April 1, 1945. (The principal provisions of this Act are given in Hist. Doct. CCLXXVII, p. 3017. Under this measure the public system of education was entirely reorganized, being divided into three stages, primary, secondary, and

further (part-time) education. School-leaving age was to be raised to 15. Religious instruction to an agreed syllabus and an act of worship were made part of the curriculum of every State school. Unfortunately, within a fortnight of the passing of this act, the Minister of Education (to give him his new title) issued an order retaining the school-leaving age at 14 at least until April 1, 1946, "owing to the impossibility in present circumstances of finding the additional teachers and providing the additional accommodation which would be required in order to raise the school-leaving age to 15 on April 1, 1945."

A white paper on "The Control of Land Use" (Cmd. 6537) published on June 23 stated that the Government accepted in principle the Uthwatt Committee's recommendations regarding the public acquisition of land in areas requiring redevelopment as a whole, but rejected the committee's detailed proposals for dealing with compensation and betterment owing to the undesira-

bility of providing substantially different treatment for owners of undeveloped land inside and outside town areas and of developed land, as recommended in the report; and the difficulties of giving effect to other of the recommendations. (*See* Hist. Doc. No. CCLVIII, p. 2371.) On the same day a Town and Country Planning Bill was introduced which, though severely criticized by Labour members as "one of a series of bad improvisations in planning," was passed into law. It empowered local planning authorities to acquire by a simpler and quicker procedure land needing to be redeveloped; land required to provide alternative accommodation for displaced persons or alternative open space; land for certain other planning purposes.

Town and Country Planning Act

An act to provide for Exchequer grants towards the extension of piped water supplies and sewerage in rural localities and to make it the duty of local authorities, "wherever practicable at a reasonable cost," to provide piped water supplies to every rural locality in its district in which there are houses or schools received the Royal Assent on July 27—one of several acts

LIEUT.-GENERAL SIR OLIVER W. H. LEESE, Bt., K.C.B., C.B.E., D.S.O.

On January 5, 1944, it was announced that General Leese, who commanded the 30th Corps of the 8th Army from El Alamein to Tunis (see pp. 2526, 2548) and in Sicily (see p. 2834), had been appointed to succeed General Montgomery as commander of the 8th Army in Italy (see Chapter 302). His transfer to the command of the 11th Army Group (including General Slim's 14th Army), in succession to General Sir George Giffard, and of the U.S. Forces in the India-Burma Theatre (A.L.F.S.E.A.—Allied Land Forces, S.-E. Asia) was announced in November 1944.

Photo, British Official : Crown Copyright

3 H 3

BUILDING SHIPS FOR THE BRITISH MERCHANT NAVY

The ocean-going merchant fleet, including tankers, under the British flag at the beginning of the war was $17\frac{1}{2}$ million gross tons of vessels of 1,600 gross tons and over—about the same as in 1914. At the end of 1943, despite production in British and Canadian yards, purchase, loan and capture of vessels, it was, through losses due to enemy action, only $15\frac{1}{2}$ million gross tons. Yet the total tonnage of merchant ships launched from British shipyards in 1940-43 was 4,415,668 (compared with 3,770,170 in 1915-18), and the work was carried out in spite of heavy naval demands, the blackout, and the large volume of repair work—at one period $2\frac{1}{2}$ million gross tons were on hand for repair. Further details are set out in Hist. Doc CCLXXVI, p. 3017. Here the hull of one of the standard tramps mentioned in this document is under construction on the stocks. Right, riveting deck plates after the launching of the hull. Top right, sixteen weeks after launching, tugs pull the ship into position for completion. *Direct colour photographs by Fox*

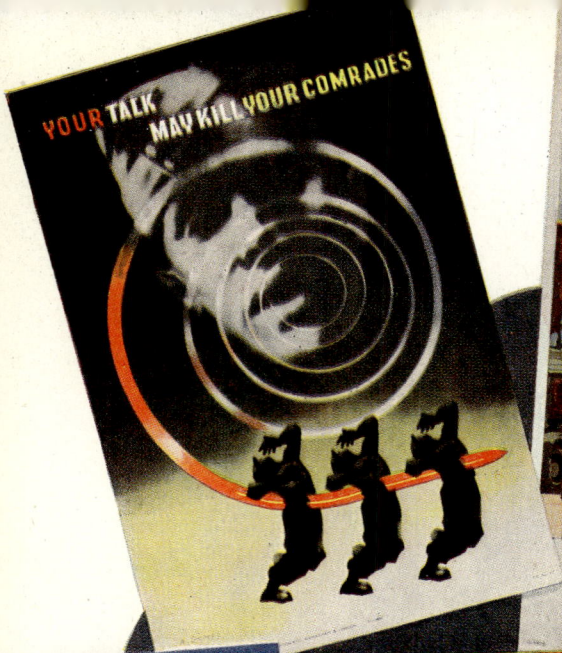

Feeding 45 Millions
UNLOADING

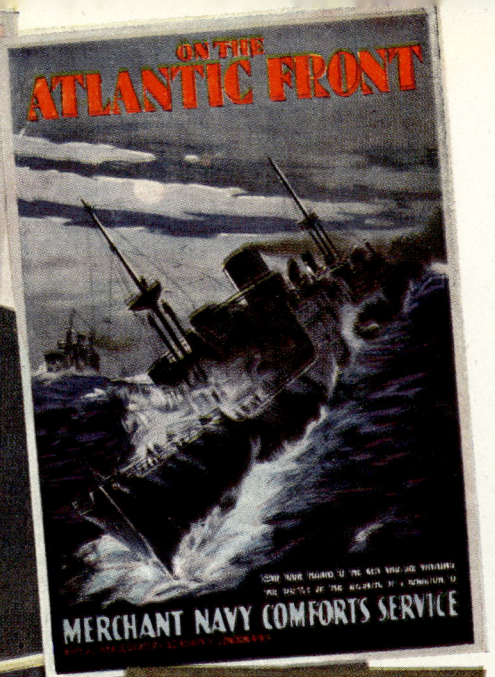

MERCHANT NAVY COMFORTS SERVICE

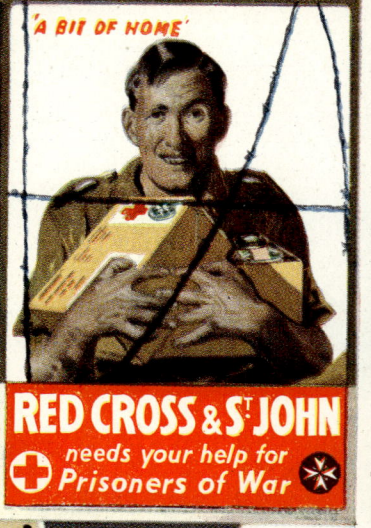

BACK THEM UP!

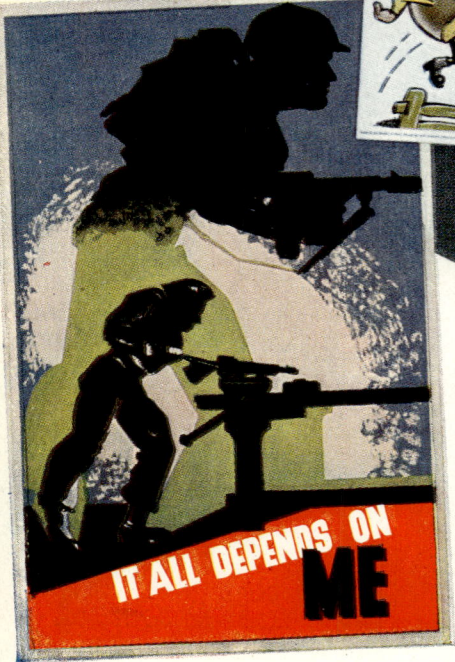

APPEALS TO BRITISH CITIZENS

Posters seen on the Home Front during 1943 and 1944 that reminded Britons of their wartime duties as citizens, both to themselves and to their fellows serving over and on the seas. Selections of posters in circulation in earlier phases of the war are reproduced in pages 538, 551, 828, 1489 and facing page 1735

signed by Princess Elizabeth during her first term as a Counsellor of State while the King was absent in Italy.

A scheme to provide without direct payment for everyone who desires it "the care of a family doctor, the skill of a consultant, laboratory services, treatment in hospital, the advice and treatment available in specialized clinics, dental and ophthalmic treatment, drugs and surgical appliances, midwifery, home nursing and all other services essential to health," was explained in a white paper published on February 17 (Cmd. 6502). Laymen received its provisions with interest and a good deal of approbation. Many younger members of the medical profession were favourable to it, but a number of the older practitioners greeted it with the same violent opposition as had been offered to the original health insurance scheme of 1911 by medical practitioners of that day.

Comprehensive social insurance schemes applying to the whole population and covering sickness and unemployment benefit, retirement pensions, death grants, and family and orphan allowances were set out in a white paper (Cmd. 6550) issued on September 26. Based largely on the report (*see* p. 2369), drawn up in 1942 by Sir William Beveridge (who was elected member of Parliament for Berwick-on-Tweed in a by-election held on October 17), the Government schemes envisaged slightly lower contributions from both workers and employers; proposed 5s. a week for each child after the first, plus allowances in kind—meals and milk at school (against Beveridge's 8s. a week); sickness and unemployment benefit at the same rate (40s. for married man, 24s. for single person), but for a limited period; full rate of retirement pension to be 35s. (instead of 40s.) for husband and wife, 20s. instead of 24s. for a single person, but to come into force immediately instead of after 20 years. Sir William Jowitt was named on October 9 as first Minister of the proposed Ministry of Social Insurance.

A further white paper (Cmd. 6551) covering industrial injuries departed entirely from previous practice, treating workmen's compensation not as a legal liability of the employer, but as a social service assimilated in many ways to the war pensions scheme. Benefit would be 35s. a week for 13 weeks, with 8s. 9d. for a wife and 5s. for the first child (other children would draw 5s. under the general scheme). Pension for 100 per cent disablement would be 40s. a week plus 10s. for a wife and 7s. 6d. for the

Social Security Plans

first child, these payments not to be subject to subsequent revision. Women were to receive the same basic rates as men. The cost of the scheme would be covered by contributions of 6d. a week for men, 4d. for women, half rates for children; the same from employers; plus an Exchequer contribution.

The need for a redistribution of seats was strongly felt by the House of Commons, and a conference appointed in February under the chairmanship of the Speaker resulted in the House of Commons (Redistribution of Seats) Act (Oct. 26), making temporary provision for a fuller representation of abnormally large constituencies, to be followed by a considered redistribution of seats based on a report by a boundary commission (appointed on November 8). As a temporary measure, Hendon (208,609 electors) and Romford (207,101) were given four members, Harrow three, and 17 other constituencies two, instead of in each case one member.

To prevent disfranchisement of civilians through change of residence owing to war circumstances, the Parliamentary Electors (Wartime Registration) Act of July 13 enacted that, pending the preparation of a new register under the Parliament (Meetings and Elections) Act of 1943, a citizen inscribed in the National Register as residing in a constituency on the qualifying date (later fixed as December 1, 1944) was to be included in the electoral register. All men and women in the Services were required to fill in declaration cards so that their names could be included in the new Service Register of Electors. Service voters on the register and in the United Kingdom during an election would be able to vote by post or in person. Registered Service voters abroad could appoint proxies at home to vote for them.

On the second reading on October 31 of the bill to prolong the life of Parliament, Mr. Churchill said, "In asking for a prolongation of the life of this Parliament for another year, I doubt very much whether the Parliament will last so long. We certainly cannot exclude the possibility that a desire to return to the party system will be strongly expressed" at the annual meetings of the various parties composing the Coalition—a prognostication which proved correct. "Let us assume that the German war ends in March, April or May . . . I have myself a clear view that it would be wrong to continue this Parliament beyond the period of the German war." The extension of a year was enacted: but all the parties began to get their house in order with a view to a contested election during 1945.

3027

EMERGENCY ENDED
The relaxing of fireguard duties and the passing of the blackout in September 1944 were followed by the dismantling of some of the emergency water tanks built to help fight enemy incendiary bombs.

EXIT BEACH DEFENCES
German prisoners of war clear barbed wire defences from a British beach. Following the revocation on October 9, 1944 of the Removal of Direction Signs Order, 1940, a name board is rehung at a G.W.R. station (below). *Photos, Associated Press; Topical*

THE MERCHANT NAVY CARRIES MEN AND SUPPLIES FOR OUR ARMIES IN FRANCE

Following the first landings in Normandy on June 6, 1944, supplies and personnel had to be moved across the Channel continuously—during the first three days alone, excluding assault forces, 38 convoys comprising 743 vessels made the journey. 1. Troop transports, and a tank landing craft await the order to disembark. 2. Discharging supplies from merchantmen on to the pierheads of a section of the prefabricated port at Arromanches. 3. Supply ship flung on to the beach by the 70 m.p.h. gale which swept the Channel on June 19. *Photos, British Official; Pictorial Press; Associated Press*

Chapter 301

THE MERCHANT NAVY'S PART IN INVASION

The invasion of Europe in June 1944 called for all the Allies possessed in military, naval, and air strength ; but it could never have been effected without the use of thousands of merchant vessels manned by tens of thousands of volunteer seamen. Their part in this momentous happening forms the main theme of this chapter, which includes also some account of the Merchant Navy's other 1944 activities. For the Merchant Navy's history in 1943, see Chap. 275

IN June 1940 Britain withdrew from the Continent of Europe the remnants of the army which had been sent across the Channel in 1939. Then began the great task of transforming Britain into the forward base from which the enemy astride Europe could be struck down. For four years, in a hundred thousand voyages, ships brought from four continents the materials of war and food for the sustenance of Britain's armed forces and people ; and all the time against constant menace on, over and under the sea, the building up of huge striking forces continued, and other maritime tasks were carried out concurrently in the Mediterranean and Arctic Seas and in the wide waters of the Far East.

Merchant ships made possible the assembly of the diverse and massive paraphernalia of invasion : and mer-

Merchant Navy's Triumph

chant ships carried it to the shores of Normandy on June 6, 1944. In a very special sense the invasion of Normandy was the Merchant Navy's triumph : it was the climax of four years' endeavour against an enemy as resourceful as he was cruel ; it was the fulfilment of the promise seamen made at Dunkirk, just four years before, that the Merchant Navy would return to Continental Europe. In May and June 1940 the Army was withdrawn by a strange collection of ships and craft of all sizes, from big cargo ships to little pleasure boats ; it was a glorious but hectic, haphazard affair. In June 1944 the Allied Armies were taken back by an even stranger armada, and the ordered precision was complete to the smallest detail.

The invasion of North Africa late in 1942 (*see* pages 2392 and 2539) was carried out with some 850 ships. For the invasion of France five thousand ships of all types were assembled : besides naval vessels, 4,066 ships and craft of over 60 different types— troop transports, big and little cargo vessels, cross-Channel ships, tankers large and small, hospital ships, and many types of specially built landing ships and landing craft. In the words of Mr. Leo T. Crowley, U.S. Foreign

Economic Administrator, " most of the ships and sailors were British."

Some one thousand of these vessels, totalling about 3,000,000 tons gross, were merchant ships, most of them specially adapted for their tasks, but all the same to be distinguished from men-of-war and from the assortment of invasion craft. More than two-thirds

MERCHANT NAVY POSTMAN
During the summer of 1944, hundreds of merchant vessels were plying between the ports of Britain and the beaches of Normandy. Every day mail for officers and men was delivered to ships in port by motor launch. The number of letters delivered at one port averaged 6,000 daily, and the postal launch's ' round ' took more than six hours. *Photo, British Newspaper Pool*

of that merchant tonnage employed in the initial phase was under British control. American merchant ships, mostly Liberty ships, numbered about 150.

Coastal ships of shallow draught had played a major rôle in the Dunkirk evacuation. In the triumphal return to France coastal ships were again in the forefront. In a list of just over 600 British ships (other than passenger liners, naval auxiliaries and smaller craft such as tugs) used during the first week of the invasion, no less than 400

were small coastwise vessels, coastal colliers, cross-Channel passenger ships and others of less than ocean-going size, the majority of them being humble cargo ships which normally plied between ports around the British Isles. Many were of less than 300 tons gross. Some were new, others over 40 years old —the " Edith," 230 tons, built in 1900, " Felspar," 800 tons (1908), " Rose," 260 tons (1901), " Kyle Bute," 800 tons (1900) and many more. They carried stores, ammunition, lorries and their drivers to the shores of France and the front line of battle. Fitted with strengthened masts and special derricks to unload their unfamiliar cargoes, often with 100 or more men on board vessels never designed to carry a passenger, many of the coasters beached themselves and waited for the next tide to float them off.

" In the past the ceaseless work of our coasters, year in, year out," declared the Minister of War Transport (Lord Leathers) later,

Service of the Coastal Ships

" has often been overshadowed by the more spectacular achievements of the deep-sea fleets, but without the hundreds of shallow-draught vessels . . . the landing of an Army with all its vehicles and equipment on the Normandy beaches would have been exceedingly difficult, if not impossible."

Some of the many types of special invasion craft—such as the 300 ft. L.S.T. (landing ship, tank), 160 ft. L.C.I. (landing craft, infantry) and others— made the journey to France under their own power, bearing tanks, vehicles and troops straight on to the beaches. The smaller assault vessels—L.C.A.s, L.C.M.s, L.C.P.s, among them—as well as such craft as the invaluable amphibian known as a " Duck " (D.U.K.W.), were brought across by merchant ships and lowered on to far from calm waters some distance off the beaches. The infantry assault ships began the invasion. They were quickly followed by the first groups of stores coasters, then by troopships, large cargo ships and more coastal vessels carrying vehicles ; and then more stores coasters—many of them flying French, Dutch, Belgian, Norwegian or Danish flags. To the music

BRITISH-BUILT SHIPS

A fast new cargo ship, built in a British yard, and specially designed to carry strategic cargoes—on this particular voyage, the deck cargo included small craft of different types. She was fitted with three 120-ton derricks. Left, stern view of an all-welded, prefabricated coastal tanker building in a British yard : she was specially planned to carry petrol, cased or in bulk. (See also colour photographs following p. 3026.)   *Photos, British Official*

of a shattering weight of Allied bombs, a sky-full of Allied aircraft, salvos of shells from battleships, cruisers and destroyers, and the answering fire from the enemy, 250,000 men were landed, together with their equipment, in the first 24 hours. After 36 hours, one observer said : " It seems as though we have been here for weeks. The entire place is alive with shipping. It reaches from the shore almost to the horizon."

Once the beach-head was secure, weather, always the chief risk, became the greatest obstacle to the success of the transport movement—on which the reinforcement and supply of the invading troops depended. No amount of valour and no amount of air support would have staved off a disastrous rout

if the flow of fresh troops and supplies had been stopped in the first few days. The weather proved a formidable enemy indeed : defying the season, it was rough from the first. For a fortnight a shuttle service back and forth across the Channel continued. Then there gathered a storm such as had not been seen in the Channel in June for 40 years. The gale lasted five days, with little respite. Unloading on the beaches ceased. The position was critical at that stage ; it would probably have been disastrous had the storm come sooner. It was retrieved by a superhuman effort when the wind and seas began to abate. By July 6, 1,000,000 men had been put ashore, together with more than 180,000 vehicles and 650,000 tons of stores. In the first 100 days, 2,200,000 men were landed with 4,000,000 tons of stores and 500,000 vehicles.

That achievement would have been impossible but for the most dramatic single feature of the whole Allied plan —the construction of two artificial harbours, one for the use of the British forces, the other for the Americans. It was known that the Germans would defend the " invasion ports " with all the strength they could muster, realizing that while the Allies might obtain a foothold along the coast they would probably be unable to sustain and enlarge it against a strong counter attack if they could unload supplies only on to beaches. With the aid of 60 blockships for part of the breakwaters, the British harbour—" compared to which Dover seems small " (as Mr. Churchill put it)—was constructed off the beaches

at Arromanches in less than a month. Within five days the blockships had been sunk in position and huge concrete caissons, floating breakwaters and piers were being towed, in 480-foot lengths, across the Channel where it approaches its widest—the Normandy beaches were 100 miles from the English ports. By June 18, the two harbours were half completed and coasters could be unloaded at any state of a 20-foot tide. The next day was the first day of the storm which brought havoc upon the port equipment making its slow passage from Britain. All the pier sections for the Americans' port were lost in mid-Channel, and the prefabricated port itself so severely damaged that it was never completed, but its loss was offset by the rapid fall of Cherbourg. At Arromanches, however, the great steel and concrete works stood fast—though not without damage —a trickle of supplies was kept up during the worst days of the storm, and by the middle of July the port was working to maximum capacity, ships of all sizes unloading on to huge pier-heads connected to the shore by four long steel roadways supported by steel and concrete floats. (The planning, designing and construction of the prefabricated ports is described in a later chapter.)

When the Merchant Navy carried to France the British Expeditionary Force of 1939, 174 ships were used, making about 400 voyages all told. Even that movement, begun within four days of the declaration of war, had to be carefully planned. But the voyages were from port to port, the ships could be loaded in normal fashion and dispatched to a rough time-table. The North African invasion called for a very different technique : opposition was expected, every group of ships had to be, to a large extent, a self-contained assault force, and every piece of equipment had to be available, not when it could be most conveniently unloaded, but when it was wanted by the force commander. Within a " master plan " for the operation as a whole, the working of each separate convoy could, however, be organized more or less as a self-contained problem of limited duration. Then in the invasion of Sicily—in which 2,700 ships and landing craft took part —and at Salerno in Italy more experience was gained of the " amphibious operations of peculiar complexity and hazard " which Mr. Churchill had foreshadowed. A new form of warfare was being perfected.

But the operations which began on June 6, 1944, were different, not merely because the scale of things was so much

Perfecting a New Form of Warfare

larger, nor because the enemy defences were more formidable and his opposition more determined, nor merely because the element of strategic surprise was missing (though of tactical surprises there were many). The combination of these things with the fact that, once begun, the movement had to be maintained continuously and at a high tempo made the Normandy invasion dwarf the previous ventures in complexity as well as magnitude.

Organization of the merchant ships was the responsibility of the Sea Transport Department of the Ministry of War Transport, working, of course, very closely with the Admiralty and other Service Departments and with the American authorities. The detailed work of planning began eighteen months in advance. Then came the fitting of ships of all sizes and types with special gear and equipment so as to avoid congestion in the repair yards, with its waste of ship-carrying-space. Special " register books " were compiled showing the particular information that would be needed about every vessel which might be called on to take part— speed, hold and hatch sizes, cargo-handling equipment, fuel consumption, stability and other details. Apart from landing craft, which were primarily

Eighteen Months' Planning

the Army's responsibility, other special vessels had to be designed and built, such as a special design of coastal tanker to carry petrol, cased or in bulk.

At a later stage the more intricate planning was begun. Every single ship was first " loaded on paper." Each vessel had its loading plan, on which each item of its cargo was marked so that, while no space would be wasted, yet every piece of equipment would be unloaded where and when it was wanted. Every single tin of petrol, every case of food or ammunition— not to mention tanks, guns and lorries —carried to the Normandy shores on the first outward voyages was assigned to a particular ship, and not only that, but to a particular " spot " in that ship. Since nearly every vessel carried a mixed cargo and since no two ships— not even sister ships—are exactly alike, the planners had an immense task. It was realized that planning in such detail as this, so different from the improvisation at Dunkirk, must be exact and complete.

The movements of the ships were worked out in advance in similar detail. Loading (which had to be spread over a considerable period), "standing by," taking up station, sailing, discharging, the return voyage . . . each phase was carried out by individual ships, and by ships forming a group,

REPAIR AND MAINTENANCE

Repair and maintenance of vessels constituted an immense labour in the shipbuilding yards. In five years, Merseyside alone repaired and refitted 600 naval ships and hundreds of merchantmen, the average time taken being three days per ship. Here workers are removing the damaged rudder of a 6,000-ton cargo ship.

according to a prearranged schedule. By means of special charts on which the different movements of the vessels could be seen in stages, it was possible to tell how the troops and supplies would arrive at each sector of the beaches, how the sailings would be staggered to provide for staggered discharging and how long each ship should

READY TO INVADE THE SOUTH COAST OF FRANCE

Over 800 ships of all types and of many nationalities took part in the invasion of the south of France on August 15, 1944. The jumping-off points were Sardinia, Corsica, Italy and North Africa. Landings were made over a considerable part of the coast between Nice and Marseilles. Here is a mass of varied shipping waiting in an Italian port for the signal to sail.

Photos, U.S. Official ; Central Press

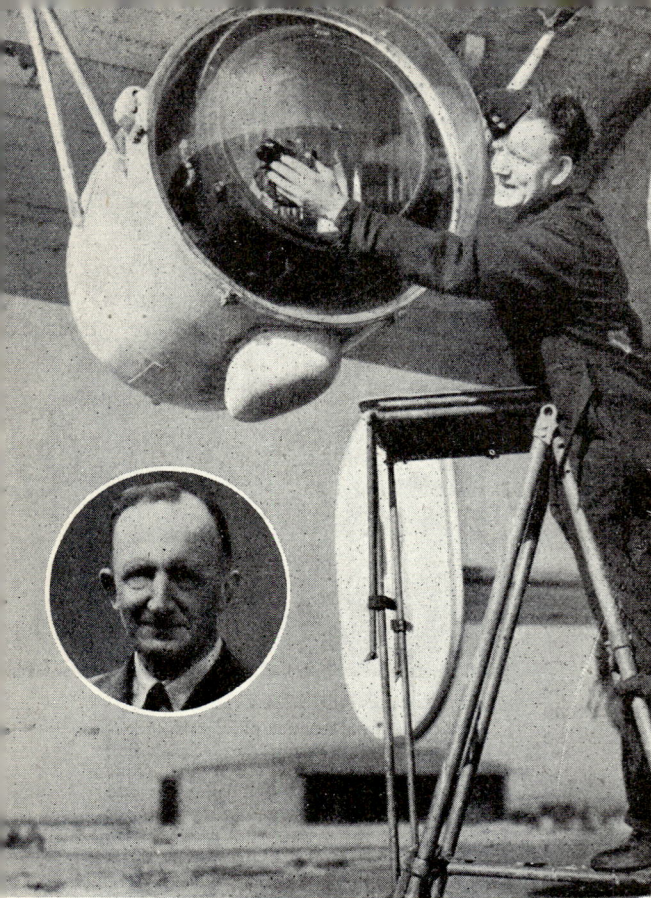

'LEIGH LIGHT' INVENTOR

The 'Leigh Light,' carried by Coastal Command aircraft, could throw on the water a beam many millions of candle-power in strength. It made possible night attack against submarines and was described as 'the keystone of success in the air offensive against U-boats in the Atlantic.' It was developed by Wing-Commander H. de V. Leigh, O.B.E., D.F.C., whose portrait appears inset.

Photos, British Official

take to cover each stage of the round voyage. Such was the sort of organization involved. Nothing, however, could be left to chance or mere theory. And so hundreds of exercises were carried out to show whether theoretical solutions evolved in conference would work in practice. "We grew so schedule-minded," one shipmaster has been quoted as saying, "that if we were five minutes out we thought the war was lost."

Considerable destruction of merchant

ships had to be allowed for: it was the most hazardous venture which had ever been undertaken. Yet it was possible to record in a special statement issued under the authority of Mr. Churchill and Mr. Roosevelt that, " despite attempts by a substantial force of U-boats to pass up-Channel from their bases in Norway and France," no merchant ship among the thousands moving across the Channel and coastwise during these vast man-oeuvres was sunk by U-boat —with one possible exception, and that loss may have been due to a mine. Indeed, during June 1944 the losses from U-boats reached " almost the lowest figures of the entire war."

But it was not only U-boats which had to be faced. There were the shore batteries, bombers, E-boats as well. And, perhaps as great a menace in the result, there was the weather, and its effect upon many of the small ships loaded for battle. In spite of the unmatched scale of the Normandy invasion, in spite of the unceasing traffic back and forth, in spite of the enemy's long and arduous preparations, the losses of merchant ships were less than in the landings in North Africa, in Sicily and at Salerno; in the first critical fortnight they amounted to less than one per cent of the total tonnage employed.

If the Merchant Navy formed the backbone of the invasion—it, after all, carried out the fundamental job—it is impressive that it was the one and only civilian group directly involved. Every Merchant Navy man, and there were some 50,000 of them taking part, was a volunteer. If the significance of that was generally missed—and certainly the seamen themselves gave no thought to that aspect—it was because of the tradition whose roots went even deeper than four years of war at sea. Eight months previously a special form of " articles " was drawn up for officers and seamen prepared to take part, so it was stated, in the invasion of Europe. Somewhat puzzled as to why such procedure should be necessary, no less than 90 per cent of the possible volunteers signed without more ado.

The " V-articles " were designed to avoid contract formalities which would otherwise have been necessary if, for instance, a seaman changed from one ship to another, and also to relieve masters of various accountancy problems in the midst of invasion. Their effect was to treat the seamen involved as a single combined force, instead of so many individual crews, and special " operational seamen's pools " were maintained at strategic ports so as to ensure that no ship of the shuttle service to France was held up by crew problems. Thanks to the success of the operations and to the strength and effectiveness of the covering air and naval forces, in the first month Merchant Navy casualties totalled less than a hundred; but a very different tale was to be anticipated when the seamen—many more than were needed—had volunteered for invasion eight months previously.

Two other sea landings in the war in Europe were accomplished in 1944. In January considerable forces were put ashore at Nettuno and Anzio in the rear

Merchant Navy Volunteers for Invasion

'ACE U-BOAT KILLER' BURIED AT SEA

Capt. F. J. Walker, C.B., D.S.O., R.N., commander of the Second Escort Group and among the most successful naval destroyers of enemy submarines, died of a heart attack in July 1944. Left, Mrs. Walker casts a wreath into the sea after the committal of her husband's body. Below, the crew of the sloop 'Wild Goose,' Second Escort Group, show her flag, designed by Able Seaman C. E. Woods, made by Yeoman W. L. J. Miller (third and fourth from the left).

BRITAIN'S LARGEST LINERS ON LEND-LEASE TO THE U.S.A.

President Roosevelt in his 17th Report to Congress on Lend-Lease Operations (reprinted in Britain on December 8, 1944) dealt with the aid received by the United States from the British Commonwealth. Among her services Britain placed at the disposal of America, for the transport of troops to the European theatre of war, her two largest and fastest liners, 'Queen Elizabeth' (above), completed in 1939, 85,000 gross tonnage, and 'Queen Mary' (below), completed in 1936, 81,235 gross tonnage. Between them they brought over more than 800,000 Americans. Troops are seen assembled on 'Queen Mary's' deck for boat drill. (See also illus. p. 2398.)   *Photos, British Official*

of the enemy lines south of Rome. Begun before dawn, the initial attack was a complete surprise to the enemy; though it was four months before the Anzio beach-head forces broke out to link up with the main Army, the landing itself was highly successful.

The Allies' sixth great assault by sea in the West was made on August 15 in the south of France, between Nice and Marseilles. With the **Landings in Southern France** help of large airborne forces, the landings were accomplished with greater ease and relatively smaller losses than any of the former amphibious operations. A 30-mile front was established within 12 hours and by the third day the beach-head embraced an area of about 500 square miles. The invasion fleet comprised about 800 ships—500 of them transports and landing craft.

Although there was a revival of activity in December, the U-boats throughout the year failed to stage an effective " come-back " from the crushing defeat which was the principal feature of the sea war in 1943 (*see* Chapter 275). The monthly statements from the Prime Minister and President Roosevelt became repetitive in their brief records of success in a battle which at one time had seriously threatened the very outcome of the war.

On every route the flow of supplies was maintained. In May it was revealed that during the previous six months ships of the United Nations had delivered nearly 1,250,000 tons of war equipment and material to Russia by the Arctic route, with a loss in ships of only two per cent. Losses of freight from enemy action and other causes were, in fact, less than 16 tons in every thousand delivered, while in the course of the voyages heavy damage had been inflicted on enemy forces.

It was not for want of trying that the Germans failed in their under-water attack upon the increasing tonnage of merchant ships plying across the Atlantic. The Allied escorting forces on the sea and above it were, indeed, able to keep up the offensive tactics which had been developed during the great convoy battles of the previous year. As one of the official statements put it, " several [U-boats] are now sent to the bottom for each merchant ship sunk, whereas formerly each U-boat accounted for a considerable number of merchant ships before being destroyed." This was due to the vigilance and the relentless attacks of the anti-U-boat forces, " including the scientists who support them in a brilliant manner."

The year opened with " a very satisfactory month," the merchant tonnage sunk being among the lowest of the war, while in February a larger number of U-boats was destroyed, and the losses from **U-Boats at Bay** U-boat action were the second lowest of the war. In one month it was revealed the losses of United Nations shipping were mainly incurred in far distant waters, where, presumably, escorts were generally weaker than in the Atlantic. The losses for May were " by far the lowest for any month of the war "—a fraction, indeed, of the losses inflicted on enemy shipping, petty in total compared with that of the Allies.

On August 9 it was announced that the number of German U-boats sunk during the war had by then exceeded 500—a figure which implied the loss to the enemy of about 20,000 skilled personnel. " It is therefore understandable," the statement added, " that the U-boats still operating are extremely cautious." At a time when it was vital to Germany to interfere with the steady stream of supplies to France, the efforts of her submarines were ineffective; seventeen were sunk in the Channel during June and July. The statement concluded:

TUG-BOATS ON WAR SERVICE
During the war, a new type of small, standard, 1,000 indicated h.p. tug (left) was designed which could be manufactured in sections and subsequently assembled at a shipyard, where the total time needed to make ready for launching was usually four-and-a-half days. A fleet of tug-boats was kept in readiness to salvage torpedoed vessels. Below, several of these rescue tugs refloat a cargo boat damaged by torpedo.
Photos, British Official ; Keystone

FIRST LIBERTY SHIP APPROACHES ANTWERP

The shores of the Scheldt river were freed of the enemy by November 8, 1944, but not until November 30 was it announced that Antwerp was open to Allied shipping and the first big Allied convoy had arrived in port. Over 90 minesweepers had been engaged for 24 days in clearing the approaches, 80 mines being swept on the first day alone. The opening of Antwerp, one of the finest ports in Europe, eased the problem of supply for Allied commanders, for it lies only 60 miles from the German frontier.   *Photo, British Official*

" The U-boat fleet is still of impressive size, nevertheless the U-boats remain the hunted rather than the hunters. They have been attacked from the Arctic to the Indian Ocean, aircraft playing a great part with the surface forces. This pressure will be maintained until all chances of revival of the U-boat campaign are killed, whatever may be the new devices and methods developed by the enemy.

" The Nazi claims of sinkings continue to be grossly exaggerated. For instance, their claim for June . . . was an exaggeration of a thousand per cent."

By August the enemy submarine bases in the Bay of Biscay had been neutralized (though the Germans were still in Lorient and St. Nazaire at the end of the year). The U-boat operations for that month were described as " sporadic and relatively ineffectual." " The losses by U-boats since the beginning of 1944, compared to former years, are almost negligible," Mr. Churchill stated in the House of Commons on August 2. The lull continued for three months, and the losses of Allied tonnage from U-boats in October touched the lowest point since the beginning of

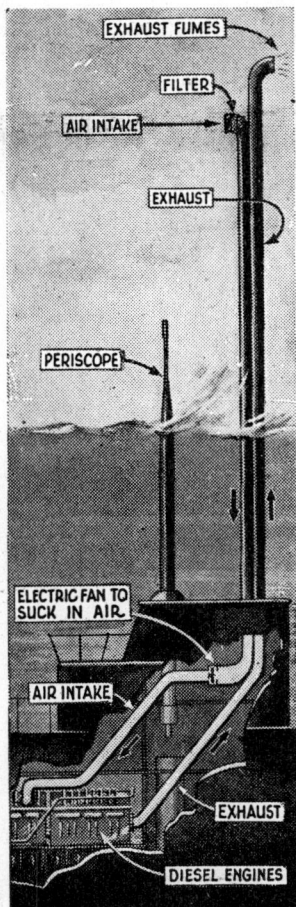

THE 'SNORT'
Diagram illustrating method of working of the Schnorkel Spirall device, nicknamed ' Snort,' the extendable air-shaft fitted to U-boats.

the war, an improvement on the outstanding record of May. While losses were again " very small " in November, the official report for that month contained a warning that improved types of U-boats might be thrown into the battle, and revealed that new devices had been introduced, including an extensible air intake and exhaust buoyed on the surface which enabled U-boats to remain submerged for long periods " and so penetrate into areas denied to them for the past three years." The new device, the Schnorkel Spirall, known as the " growler " gear and nicknamed " Snort," was also designed to offset the successes scored by Allied aircraft which attacked at night, with the help of flares and Leigh lights, while the submarines were charging their batteries (*see* also Chapter 304). The Germans claimed that it enabled submarines to stay under water for as long as a month.

The warnings of previous months were

followed by the statement that in December " German U-boat warfare flared into renewed activity." Allied merchant shipping suffered " increased losses," though German submarines continued to be sunk in widely separated parts of the Atlantic. Two enemy agents, Eric Gimpel, a German, and William Curtis Colepaugh, a U.S. national, landed by U-boat on the coast of Maine in November, were sentenced to be hanged as spies on February 14, 1945, by a military court in New York.

Many stories were told of individual battles in the war on the U-boats and of the successful protection of Atlantic convoys ; and accounts were issued of outstanding successes on the Arctic route. On May 19 the Admiralty announced that during an action fought inside the Arctic Circle over several days in conditions of intense cold and severe weather, two U-boats were sunk and others sunk or damaged ; the convoy, the largest sent to Russia to that date and carrying 250,000 tons of tanks, guns, ammunition, and aircraft, got through and returned home safely. In another Arctic Circle engagement which took place in April, three U-boats were sunk (one by the Second Escort Group commanded by Captain F. J. Walker, the Navy's " Ace U-boat killer " ; *see* pp. 2852 and 2854), others were damaged and six shadowing aircraft were destroyed ; the convoy suffered no loss or damage. November 4 brought the announcement that while

Convoys to Russia Get Through

attempting without success to interfere with a large and important Arctic convoy, three U-boats had been sunk and several others damaged.

Another outstanding exploit of the Second Escort Group was reported on March 19. In one offensive sweep in the North Atlantic the Group destroyed six German submarines during operations extending over 20 days, some by gunfire and others by depth charges. The last of the six had been attacked with depth charges by two of the sloops at intervals for more than five and a half hours when, shortly after H.M.S. "Starling" had fired her last "dustbin," it surfaced about a mile away. Within eight minutes the U-boat, abandoned by its crew, was sunk by "Starling's" gunfire. When the Escort Group reached port, to be given a naval welcome such as had not been known before, another of Walker's sloops, H.M.S. "Wild Goose," flew a flag commemorating seven U-boat "kills." Ships under Captain Walker's

More Success for the Second Escort Group

command had sunk no less than 20 U-boats, 15 by the famous Second Escort Group, when, on July 10, 1944, it was announced that this outstanding personality of the anti-U-boat campaign, four times awarded the D.S.O., had died in hospital from a heart attack. He was buried at sea. "Victory has been won and shall be won by such as he. May there never be wanting in this realm a succession of men of like spirit and discipline, imagination and valour, humble and unafraid. Not dust nor the light weight of a storm, but all the sea of the Western Approaches shall be his tomb," said Admiral Sir Max Horton, Commander-in-Chief, Western Approaches, from the pulpit of Liverpool Cathedral.

The Second Escort Group was faithful to its tradition. Two months later it was announced that four U-boats had been sunk during a recent patrol.

One of the strange incidents of the U-boat war was the stopping by a German submarine of the Portuguese liner " Serpa Pinto," carrying European refugees to Canada. The incident took place in mid-Atlantic on the night of May 26. The Germans threatened to torpedo the ship and 385 passengers and crew took to the boats. At dawn

the U-boat commander took on board the ship's master and told him a radio message had been sent to Berlin for instructions as to whether the ship should be sunk or not. Eventually orders were said to have come not to sink the vessel. The passengers were nine hours in the boats ; two of the crew and a 16 months old baby were drowned while transferring between the vessel and the lifeboats and two American citizens were taken prisoner by the submarine.

For sheer audacity it would be difficult to equal a story of blockade running by British ships—revealed in 1944—through the Skager Rak to Sweden.

Britain needed certain Swedish products in greater quantity than it was practicable to carry by air. And so the blockade runners were built. They had to be merchant vessels, so as not to compromise

British Blockade Runners

Swedish neutrality, and they were operated by Ellermans Wilson line, of Hull. Small, handy, and inconspicuous, though very fast, with a fair cargo capacity for their size, they were specially designed for the job, and they established a " shipping line " to Sweden, bordered by occupied countries,

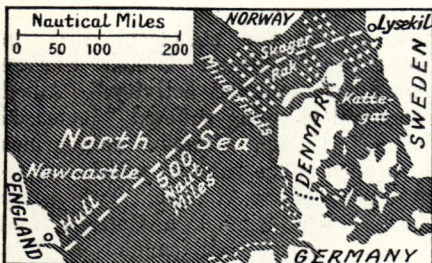

BRITISH SHIPS RUN THE GERMAN BLOCKADE

The map shows the run between Hull and Lysekil in Sweden, through the Skager Rak, of the ships of the blockade-running flotilla described in this page. Below, the Commodore of the flotilla on the bridge of ' Nonsuch ' with Captain D. Stokes, O.B.E., of Hull, on his right. To starboard is ' Hopewell,' named after a famous Hull whaler of other days. *Photo, Planet News*

SHIPS OF A CONVOY BOUND FOR RUSSIA

In a running action inside the Arctic Circle (see page 3035), British warships and naval aircraft sank two U-boats while defending a convoy carrying to Russia over 250,000 tons of war material. One U-boat was sunk by gunfire after being damaged by a Swordfish, the other by a Swordfish unaided. Both aircraft were part of a squadron operating from H.M.S. 'Chaser,' one of 38 escort-carriers transferred from the U.S. Navy to the Royal Navy. Here a Swordfish from 'Chaser' is circling ships of the convoy. *Photo, British Official*

washed by the waters of that "German lake," the Baltic, and barred from the outside world by Occupied Denmark.

The crews, about 20 in each ship, were specially selected and trained; their average age was about 25, and none of the masters was over 40. The

World's Most Adventurous Shipping Line service was started in the autumn of 1943 as soon as the nights were long enough for the purpose, and it was kept up throughout the winter. The Swedish end of the most adventurous shipping line ever established was at the little port of Lysekil, on the Kattegat. A warm welcome always awaited the officers and men (most of them from Hull) when they arrived in Sweden, on passages sometimes described as "uneventful." Britons and Swedes alike delighted at the irate impotence of the German Consul as he watched the loading and unloading of cargoes.

One only of the blockade runners was lost: the "Master Standfast" was captured by German warships (which were said to have invaded Swedish territorial waters) and her master (Captain C. R. W. Holdsworth) was killed. Like the audacious "Cossack" of "Altmark" fame, the names of all will take a worthy place in the records of Britain's maritime history—the "Gay Corsair" (Captain R. Tanton, O.B.E.); the "Gay Viking" (Captain H. Whitfield, O.B.E.); the "Hopewell" (Captain D. Stokes, O.B.E.); and the "Nonsuch" (Captain H. W. Jackson, O.B.E.).

Swedish-German trade by sea was reduced in stages during the year by various means until, towards the end of September, the stoppage was made virtually complete by the closing of Sweden's Baltic ports and territorial waters to foreign shipping.

Another "diplomatic move" in the sphere of shipping was taken about the same time when the United States authorities placed a ban upon the calling at Argentine ports of American ships northbound from South America.

Among the official announcements made during the year was the brief but grim revelation that an Allied ship carrying substantial numbers of American soldiers had been sunk by enemy action at night in European waters—when was not stated, for it was believed that the enemy did not know the fact of the sinking. About 1,000 men were reported missing; about the same number were rescued.

In spite of the reduced sinkings of United Nations shipping, in spite of the continuation of the American shipbuilding drive at a high level—16·3 million tons deadweight were built by U.S. Maritime Commission shipyards in 1944, compared with 19·2 million tons in 1943—yet by the end of the year there was no easing of the stringent tonnage position. By this time the merchant fleet controlled by the United Nations was probably not far short of the total tonnage owned in the world before the war—and it contained a much higher proportion of large cargo-carrying vessels. As Admiral Emory Land (U.S. War Shipping Administrator) put it, "the reduction in ship losses has given us no noticeable relief in shipping; rather it has made possible faster exploitation of military gains, which, in turn, has increased the need for ships."

Particularly was this so in the case of the war against Japan, with its extravagant demands on shipping due to the great distances involved. With every new landing in the Pacific—the Marshall **Shipping Demands of the Far East War** Islands, the Marianas, Palau Islands, and the Philippines were among the outstanding American sea-borne landing campaigns in 1944—not only had a great quantity of shipping to be assembled for the actual assaults, but the already long ocean supply lines were further stretched. And at the Quebec Conference in September (to and from which Mr. Churchill and his party travelled in the "Queen Mary") it was decided further to increase the tempo of the war in the Far East.

Chapter 302

THE ALLIES FORCE THE ROAD TO ROME

In a review of the Italian campaign, Field Marshal Sir Harold Alexander, C.-in-C. Allied Armies in Italy, said that when history came to be written it would be judged as one of the most brilliant and successful fought in the Second Great War. This chapter, by Squadron-Leader Derek Adkins, covering the Allied advance from Naples to Rome, shows that these words were no idle boast, for the country was of appalling difficulty, the defence skilled and stubborn. Earlier operations in Italy are described in Chapter 286

FOLLOWING the fall of Naples on October 1, 1943, the Allied 5th and 8th Armies were facing German forces on a front extending from Naples in the west, through Benevento and across the Apennines to San Severo and the mouth of the river Fortore in the east.

Allied progress was steady rather than spectacular. The limiting factor was not so much the scale of enemy opposition as the need for building up an adequate reserve. In the early stages of the campaign a high proportion of the forces put ashore was of necessity fighting troops, but the time had now come when it was essential to strike the right balance by bringing in administrative units and rearward services. The weather also was a handicap; it prevented all movement off the roads, which were extensively mined and cratered.

On the night of October 2–3, a Royal Marine Commando and specialist troops made a landing just south of Termoli near the mouth of the river Biferno on the Adriatic coast, and by nightfall of the 3rd Termoli was in British hands. A sharp counter-attack was beaten off and the Royal Marines then linked up with the British armoured brigade which had previously captured Foggia. Further strong detachments were landed on succeeding nights, and the enemy's immediate reaction by reinforcing this sector indicated how sensitive he was to any threat to this flank. Another German counter-attack on October 5, supported by a considerable weight of armour, gained a little ground over the Biferno river. The position was quickly restored, however, and the bridge-head consolidated and strengthened, while reinforcements continued to land at Termoli. Farther south, the Canadians were in contact with German patrols in the hills 30 miles west of Foggia.

By October 9, the 5th Army was firmly established along the line of the Volturno river, and small bridge-heads had been thrown across at several points. British infantry entered Capua on October 7 and consolidated their positions down to the sea. To the east the Americans fought their way steadily forward into the high ground north of Benevento, maintaining contact with the Canadians on their right. By this time, 2,000 tons of supplies were being discharged daily through the port of Naples.

During the night October 12–13, General Mark Clark launched a full-scale attack across the Volturno river, where the enemy occupied strong covering positions and appeared to have been reinforced. Resistance, as expected, was most determined. Nevertheless, on the 5th Army's right flank progress was good, and by dawn four American battalions were across the river just east of Capua. There was some bitter fighting, and several counter-attacks with armour. Farther east still, opposition was less severe, and the Americans forged quickly ahead. The attack in the British sector was in part forestalled by the Germans, and consequently was only a qualified success. A small bridge-head to the west of Capua was under continuous fire, but on October 15 a Guards Brigade succeeded in crossing the river by one of the American bridges to the east. Four miles down river from Capua another footing was gained at Grazzanise, and both these positions were subsequently consolidated and enlarged. On the coast the 46th Infantry Division landed (October 12–13), supported by two squadrons of Shermans (which had been ferried round by sea) and soon established a firm foothold with patrols up to the canal three miles to the north. A supporting bombardment by H.M. destroyers was also carried out. By October 16 the enemy had been forced back steadily from the river line, and all bridge-heads were being consolidated and improved.

Over on the 8th Army's front, the 78th Infantry Division crossed the Biferno river, and by October 16 patrols were working along the Adriatic coast ten miles north-west of Termoli. Farther inland, the Canadians continued to

Attack Across the Volturno

MONTGOMERY INSPECTS A ROYAL MARINE COMMANDO

Men of a Royal Marine Commando and special airborne troops carried out a successful landing behind the enemy lines at Termoli on the night of October 2-3, 1943. The German garrison was surprised and overcome, a number of prisoners were taken, including the commander of the German forces in the sector (captured in bed), and the town was occupied. Here General Montgomery is inspecting the Royal Marines who carried out the exploit. *Photo, British Official*

make good progress; they entered Campobasso on October 14, and the important junction of Vinchiaturo fell next day.

The enemy's gradual withdrawal brought him on to ground increasingly favourable for defence, and it became apparent that his next line of resistance would be formed by basing his right flank on the high ground east and south-east of Gaeta, while his left flank rested on the line of the river Trigno. There were also signs that the Germans had begun to flood the Pontine marshes.

By October 21, 8th Army patrols were already working their way along the Trigno, which they crossed about five miles from its mouth on the night of October 23–24 (anniversary of El Alamein). Farther south, the line ran through the mountains to a point ten miles south-west of Campobasso. The best going, however, was made by the Americans on the 5th Army's right flank, and between Pontelandolfo and Capua they pushed forward upwards of ten miles towards the Matese mountains. From Capua to the sea, in the British sector, progress was slower, although by October 23 a useful thrust was developing north-westwards astride the Capua–Cassino road. In the coastal belt the patrol line on October 22 ran parallel to the Volturno river at a distance of about five miles, but the need for strengthening the administrative side and the strain on the temporary bridging limited the development of any real threat to the enemy in this area. Bridging, in fact, became a major problem of the campaign, for the Germans had so far demolished some 600 bridges in Italy, including all those north of the Foggia–Salerno line.

In the face of steady and increasing pressure along the whole front, the enemy began to pull back his outposts on both coastal flanks. The 78th Division, supported by successful bombardment from H.M. destroyers "Queenborough" and "Raider," increased

Bridging Becomes a Major Problem

CROSSING THE RIVER VOLTURNO

During the night of October 12-13, 1943, in bright moonlight after heavy rains, British and American troops of the 5th Army launched an offensive across the Volturno river, preceded by a massed barrage. 1. Supplies arriving on the north bank of the river in the early morning light. 2. U.S. infantrymen haul their rubber assault boat over by means of a rope stretched from shore to shore. 3. American engineers watch British troops cross a pontoon bridge thrown across the river.
Photos, British Official; New York Times Photos.

their bridge-head over the Trigno and occupied Vasto on November 5, while Indian troops farther south pushed forward along the line of the river. In the mountainous central sector Isernia was occupied on November 4, and American and British forces on the 5th Army's front continued to advance slowly against considerable opposition. Petrella was taken on October 30, and by November 7 patrols were four miles forward of the line Mignano–Isernia, with U.S. Parachute Infantry troops in touch with the 8th Army in the latter town. On November 5 American troops, across ground of which " every foot was

EIGHTH ARMY FORCES THE SANGRO RIVER

This panorama of the Sangro river, from the snow-capped Gran Sasso Mountains on the left to its mouth on the right, gives an idea of the difficulties of the crossing, made by the 8th Army on November 24, 1943 during heavy rains. The river had risen five feet, and the surrounding land had become a quagmire. All the bridges were down (the remains of one of 19 spans can be seen), so that the passage had to be made on foot through water breast-high, or over improvised bridges.

studded with anti-personnel mines," captured Venafro by storm; while on the west coast patrols of the 7th Armoured Division reported that Mondragone was clear of the enemy by October 29. After reaching the line of the Garigliano, long-range patrols of the 46th Division found Minturno also clear of the enemy by November 5, but the village was reoccupied a fortnight later by the Germans, who launched numerous counter-attacks to avoid an enforced battle of movement along the approaches to Rome.

During the rest of the month the weather restricted operations along the whole front. Many of the rivers became flooded (the Trigno rose seven feet in three days), roads were impassable to wheeled traffic, and early falls of snow added to transport difficulties. In several cases Basuto Labour Companies

had to be called in to maintain supplies.

The enemy continued to dig in behind the Sangro river along the so-called "winter line," and considerably strengthened his defences north of the Garigliano. Demolitions were also reported at Pescara on the east coast and at Gaeta on the west. By November 9 patrols from the 78th Division were across the Sangro and in contact with the enemy north of the river on the 21st. By the end of the week a bridge-head six miles long and two miles wide had been firmly established. The construction by British and Indian sappers of three bridges across the Sangro in full flood was a feat of engi-

neering calling for considerable courage and technical skill. Higher up the river the 8th Indian Division consolidated their gains round Atessa, which they captured on November 13, and by the same date the Indians and Canadians had cleared the Vasto-Isernia road. In the central sector the 5th Division entered Alfedena on the 23rd.

On the 5th Army's front there was considerable fighting astride the Cassino road. Both Allied Corps were forced to give a little ground north of Venafro and south of Mignano on November 15, and the general line remained unchanged until the beginning of December. Towards the end of November the port of Bari was opened and began to receive a heavy quota of Allied shipping. (For its subsequent bombing by the Germans, see p. 2849.) During the night of Nov. 27–28 Gen. Montgomery

METHODICAL DESTRUCTION BY THE ENEMY

Bridges, railways, telegraph and telephone lines were systematically destroyed by the Germans as they retreated through Italy. Here (left) is the main railway line in the Teano valley after they had evacuated it, and (below) the specially constructed track-wrecker which achieved this demolition : weighing about 10 tons, it had a hook at the rear which ripped up the sleepers while it dropped 2 lb. charges of high explosive down the runways on either side on to the rails.

delivered what he described as a "colossal crack" from the Sangro bridge-head. The attack was preceded by a heavy artillery bombardment, and a break in the weather enabled the Tactical Air Force to give full support —83 light bomber and 319 fighter-bomber sorties being flown on November 29. The axis of the advance lay along the line Lanciano–Chieti, with the 78th Division to the right and the 8th Indian Division to the left. The New Zealand 2nd Division was held in reserve on the left flank. As expected, enemy resistance was bitter, and flame throwers and Mark IV tanks were used in street fighting, but by noon on the 30th Fossacesia and the whole ridge overlooking the valley of the Sangro were in Allied hands. "We have broken into and through the German winter line on the Adriatic axis," said General Montgomery. By December 3 the 78th

Division had reached S. Vito on the Adriatic coast after fierce fighting, while inland Lanciano had been captured.

The Americans, on the 5th Army front, moved forward to the assault on the afternoon of December 2 after a week's intensive patrol and artillery activity, culminating in a bombardment, heavier than that at El Alamein, by 650 Allied guns. The attack developed into a battle for the Mignano gap and continued unabated until the 18th when the key village of San Pietro, 8 miles S.E. of Cassino, was taken. French troops were brought in on the right flank of the American sector and made local advances through the hills to the north-west of Filignano. The enemy had been able to prepare formidable defences, and consequently progress was slow. The Germans fought desperately, realizing that with the village of San Pietro in Allied hands

they would be forced to fall back on a line covering Cassino, with their left flank resting in the mountains west of Alfedena and their right flank on the west bank of the Garigliano towards which British troops were advancing steadily.

Meanwhile, the 8th Army's penetration of his winter line caused the enemy some alarm, and he made efforts to bring up sufficient forces to stop any exploitation towards Pescara. The Canadians relieved the 78th Division and continued to advance to the river Moro. By December 6 they had several battalions across, and on the 11th were just south of Ortona. The New Zealanders, after entering Orsogna on the 3rd, were counter-attacked out of the town two days later. A series of attacks and counter-attacks followed in this area, the Germans making every effort to hold the high ground round Guardiagrele, the capture of which would have enabled the 8th Army to use it as a pivot for their subsequent advance

Enemy Attempts to Stop 8th Army

FIRST ALLIED CONVOY SAILS IN UNDER VESUVIUS

On October 8, 1943, a week after the Allied occupation of Naples, Col. Knox, U.S. Navy Secretary, said, 'Naples is an ungodly mess. The water-front is destroyed. Piers are blown up, 70 ships sunk in the harbour, the food supply exhausted, and the population without drinking water.' Allied bombing and German demolitions had made the harbour unusable ; but our engineers got to work on it, and in less than three weeks the first Allied convoy arrived in Naples.

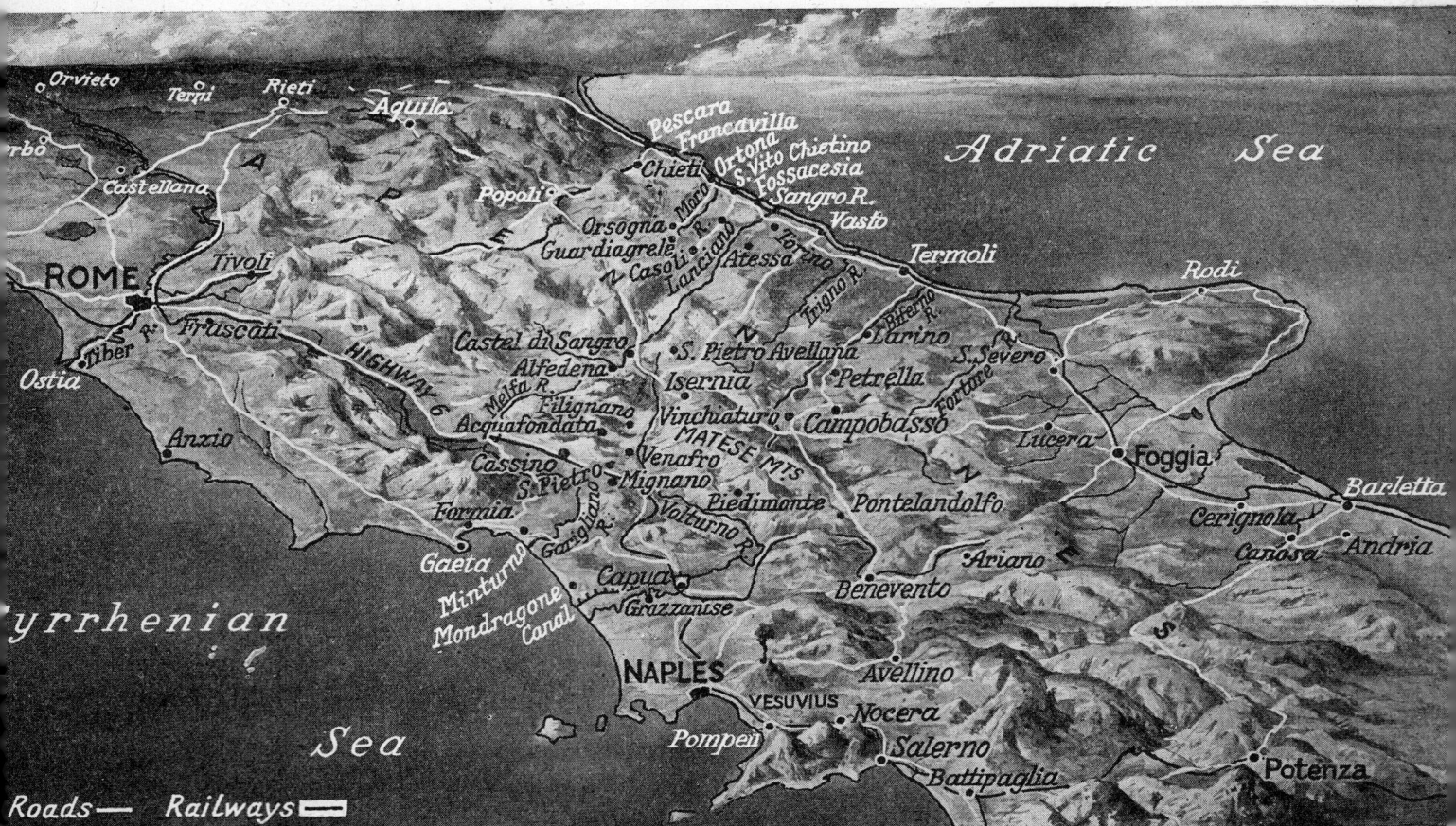

FROM NAPLES TO ROME

This relief map of the Italian peninsula between Naples and Rome shows the rugged nature of the country through which the 5th and 8th Armies fought their way against stubborn German resistance. No natural feature in Tunisia equalled the mountains of central Italy in difficulty—and the enemy here was better prepared. A detailed map of the Anzio area appears in p. 3048.

Specially drawn for the SECOND GREAT WAR *by Félix Gardon*

along the coast. The Imperial forces engaged in the struggle for the Ortona–Orsogna road inflicted considerable casualties on the enemy, and after December 15 there was a slight slackening in his defensive effort which enabled the Canadians and Indians to cut the lateral road in one place and the New Zealanders to cut it in another. There were, however, no conclusive results until the 28th when the Canadians threw the enemy out of Ortona after nine days of some of the fiercest fighting yet experienced in the campaign. German parachute troops, supported by tanks, fought desperately for every floor in every house in every street and no quarter was given by either side. German casualties were heavy—so were those of civilians in the town. Canadian losses also were considerable. Without pausing after their hard-won success, the leading Canadian brigade, pushed on up the Pescara road.

After San Pietro had been cleared of mines, the 5th Army resumed its advance, and on Christmas Day launched an assault into the mountains to the north-west. At the same time attacks

P.I.A.T. ANTI-TANK WEAPON

This Projector, Infantry, Anti-Tank, designed on unorthodox lines, weighed 33 lb., and fired a 2¾ lb. bomb which would penetrate four inches of armour plate. Fired from the shoulder, it was used in Italy with good results against tanks, pillboxes, and transport.

were renewed farther north against the enemy's mountain positions to the west of Filignano. There were indications that the enemy was making a cautious withdrawal from positions facing the right flank of the 5th Army, but the Germans stubbornly maintained the cohesion of their line along the whole western sector, and it became obvious that only heavy and unremitting Allied pressure would force them back on Cassino. On the night of December 30–31, a Commando raid was made two miles south-east of Minturno, supported by an attack by an infantry brigade across the river Garigliano. The action was successful, a bridge being destroyed and over thirty prisoners taken. The following night another attack was carried out several miles inland against one of the few remaining German positions east of the river.

January saw an intensification of the wintry weather with heavy snow in the central Apennines aggravating the supply problem to such an extent that the Royal Air Force was called upon to drop food to units temporarily isolated by snowdrifts. But in spite of conditions growing, if possible, worse, the Allied armies kept up the pressure. The Canadians continued their battle against undiminished opposition, while inland the Indians, who felt the cold

M.A.C. SHIP TAKES IN GRAIN AT A CANADIAN PORT

Originally to provide air-cover in the 500-mile gap in the Atlantic beyond the range of land-based aircraft until the
Allied acquisition of bases in the Azores (see p. 2656), a number of British merchant ships were fitted with flight decks
to carry defensive aircraft of the Fleet Air Arm. These Merchant Aircraft-Carriers (M.A.C. ships) were all grain-
carriers—the only type of merchant ship which can dispense with derricks, winches and other cargo appliances.
Their tiny flight decks—in one case, only 400 feet long—presented the pilots with many difficulties in taking off and
landing-on, but M.A.C. ships contributed to the reduction of ship losses from 1943 onwards.   *Photo, Keystone*

READY FOR THE ASSAULT ACROSS THE SANGRO RIVER

By November 20, 1943, the 8th Army had under its control twelve miles of the south bank of the Sangro River from its mouth on the Adriatic. Four days later, attacking in heavy rain, the British crossed the river and secured a bridgehead five miles long and one deep. General Montgomery described the crossing as 'a very tough business indeed': the troops, after living for a week in 'wet meadows that had become a bog,' had waded the swollen river breast-high despite a current running at 15 m.p.h. The sappers built and rebuilt bridges. Here Sherman tanks of 'B' Squadron are waiting to move to the assault. In the foreground is a stack of 4.5-in. shells.   *Photo, British Official*

SUPPLIES FOR THE ANZIO BEACH-HEAD FORCES

Porto d'Anzio, port of Nettuno, was captured on January 24, 1944, two days after the first Allied landings on the beaches of the area, and in spite of desultory bombing and constant shelling by the enemy, it was soon brought into service for landing supplies and embarking the wounded. Some thousands of tons of material were landed daily. Stores arrived in Liberty ships which anchored offshore, and unloaded their cargoes into Landing Craft Tanks, D.U.K.W.s, and Landing Ship Tanks. Here two L.S.T.s are unloading in the harbour. *Photo, British Official*

GERMAN PRISONERS COME IN FROM THE GUSTAV LINE

In spite of the almost suicidal tenacity with which the Germans defended the Gustav line in Italy against the Allied assault which began on May 11, 1944, a number of prisoners were taken—among them 1,500 of the 1st Parachutist Division by the British in and around Cassino, and 1,200 of the 71st Infantry Division (wiped out at Stalingrad and afterwards reconstituted) by the French in their advance to capture Ausonia. Here German prisoners under British guard are bringing in their own wounded to an Allied medical post.

Photo, British Official

severely, improved their positions two miles west of Ortona. In the Orsogna area New Zealand patrols maintained contact with the enemy on the outskirts of the town. The fighting everywhere showed that the Germans were making every effort to prevent a breakthrough and that until they were forced back on to a new main defence line they would fight delaying actions based on all intervening rivers.

On the 5th Army front the Germans reacted fiercely to the threat to their Cassino defences and launched bitter counter-attacks against any Allied gains. On the right flank heavy snow-falls limited activities to patrolling until January 12, when the French returned to the attack, occupying Acquafondata two days later. Meanwhile the Americans in the central sector, in conjunction with the British on their left, launched an attack on the night of January 4–5 on a front of some ten miles which resulted in the capture of Cervaro on the 12th, thus bringing their forward troops to within three miles of Cassino. Here they encountered a further obstacle in the river Rapido. The French then advanced a further two miles in the direction of Atina and reached a point

Converging on Cassino

FIFTH ARMY FIGHTS FOR SAN PIETRO
Key village to the Mignano gap, San Pietro fell to American assault troops of the 5th Army on December 18, 1943, after a bitter four-day battle. The little place, eight miles south-east of Cassino, had been turned by the Germans into a strongpoint, and was reduced to rubble by artillery fire and heavy bombing before the enemy was driven out of it. Here San Pietro is half-hidden by the smoke of fires started by bursting shells showered down on it by Allied guns. *Photo, Keystone*

four miles north-north-east of Cassino. The pressure was extended in the Garigliano area on the night of January 16–17 when British troops launched an attack across the river. Some troops were also landed from the sea north of the Garigliano's mouth. On the right they were held up, but in the coastal sector, on a front of ten miles inland from the sea, they had immediate success. Minturno was captured on the 20th and a general advance of three miles made, H.M.S. "Orion" and five destroyers giving supporting fire. On the 8th Army front an attack by the Canadians north-west of Ortona, also on the 17th, while gaining little ground, succeeded in distracting the enemy's attention from impending events to the south.

Heavy bombing put all fighter bases around Rome, except Guidonia, out of commission, and by disrupting communications prevented any large-scale movement of troops to the Anzio area, some thirty miles south of Rome.

Allied Landings at Anzio

There British and American formations landed successfully in the early morning of January 22 with gun support from H.M. and U.S. cruisers, gunboats and destroyers. For once the weather was favourable and the sea calm. The convoy was apparently unspotted, for the first landings at 2 a.m. completely surprised the enemy. What little air opposition there was, was encountered after the landings. The approach to the beaches presented a good deal of difficulty : it was through shallow water and over sandbars, and the landing forces had to use pontoons. Nevertheless, a beach-head some ten miles long and four miles deep was formed in

CANADIANS OF THE EIGHTH ARMY IN CAPTURED ORTONA
After nine days of some of the fiercest fighting of the war, Canadians gained full control of the ruined town of Ortona on December 28, 1943. German parachute troops serving as infantry resisted street by street with the greatest tenacity, and left the town thickly sprinkled with mines and booby-traps. Canadian and enemy casualties were heavy, and the civilians of the town suffered badly too. *Photo, British Official*

3$1^1$

ANZIO AND THE ROAD TO ROME

Allied landings in the Anzio-Nettuno area began at 2 a.m. on January 22, 1944. But though the Allied forces there soon advanced some miles inland, they were so vigorously opposed by the Germans that it was not until May 25 that they linked up with the 5th and 8th Armies advancing from the Cassino area. Shaded arc indicates the so-called Hitler defence zone.

Specially drawn for THE SECOND GREAT WAR *by Félix Gardon*

the Anzio-Nettuno area, and on the 25th an advance began, aimed to the north at Campoleone, astride the Rome–Naples railway, and to the north-east at Cisterna, some ten miles down the line. The general attack was launched on the 30th. Until the night of February 3–4 no major counter-attack was staged, but daily increasing resistance gave obvious indication of the enemy's intention to prevent, if possible, an Allied advance towards the Alban Hills, and to seal off the Allied forces in the Anzio-Nettuno beach-head or, preferably, drive them into the sea.

The enemy also made efforts to withstand any further penetration of the Gustav line (as the defences between the Garigliano and Cassino came to be known) on the main 5th Army front. The fighting developed into the bloodiest battles of loss and gain for both sides and continued unabated without conclusive results until May. During these months, owing chiefly to bad weather conditions, activity in the Adriatic sector of the 8th Army front was largely confined to patrolling and small-scale skirmishes, and something very near to a complete lull set in on both sides, so that the forward positions of the Allied line remained much what they had been at the end of January. Beyond the Gustav line it ran from Alfedena through Cassoli and Orsogna to Ortona.

Throughout February sustained enemy efforts to annihilate the forces in the Anzio beach-head met an equally sustained resistance. The Campoleone salient had to be abandoned, and this was followed by a slight withdrawal near Carroceto. For the most part the initiative remained with the Germans who, after a number of small-scale attacks, increased their air and artillery activity on February 16 as a prelude to a strong thrust from the direction of

Enemy Counter-Attacks at Anzio

LANDING AT ANZIO

Transport, guns, and men coming ashore from landing craft at Porto d'Anzio, the port of Nettuno, late in January, 1944. Left, a German shell bursts among a fleet of 'ducks' carrying troops and supplies to the beaches from transports offshore from Anzio. These amphibious wheeled trucks, officially D.U.K.W.s (from their factory serial letters), carried 20 men, or the equivalent in cargo. They swam to the beach, and then rolled up it. They were used at Reggio (see illus., p. 2869), Salerno, in the Normandy landings in June 1944, and in many operations in the Far East.

Photos, British Official ; Keystone

ALLIED BOMBARDMENT DESTROYS MONTE CASSINO MONASTERY AND ABBEY

The Allies reached the town of Cassino, vital point on the road to Rome, by February 2, 1944; but they failed to take it, for it was commanded by Monte Cassino on which stood the ancient monastery and abbey that was the cradle of the Benedictine Order, used by the Germans as an observation post and strongpoint, and destroyed by Allied bombing and shelling on February 15. Here the abbey is completely hidden by smoke from exploding bombs. Below, the remnants of the abbey after its capture by Polish troops on May 18. *Photos, British Official; Keystone*

DESOLATION FALLS ON THE CITY OF CASSINO

Fighting for the city of Cassino went on from February 2, 1944, when the Americans fought their way into its outskirts, until May 18, when it was captured in a final assault by British troops. A fortnight's savage street fighting in February left few buildings intact ; but some 1,400 tons of bombs were dropped on the city (less than one square mile in extent) on March 15 to destroy the walls that still concealed countless enemy guns. Above, 'Hangman's Hill' ; below , the ruined city under bombardment. (See also illus. in pp. 3064–65.) *Photos, Associated Press ; Planet.*

ALLIED WARNING TO ITALIANS

On February 13, 1944, American guns trained on the abbey of Monte Cassino fired 11,000 copies of this leaflet warning Italians to leave the precincts as the Allies were about to attack it. Two days later a rain of bombs and shells fell on the ancient buildings, founded by St. Benedict in 529, and reduced them to the mass of ruins shown in page 3049.
Photo, U.S. Official

Campoleone, co-ordinated with a move in the east of the beach-head, the whole attack being backed by a larger weight of artillery than the enemy had hitherto brought into play in either Africa or Italy. The net result, however, was a penetration of Allied positions to a depth of less than two miles astride the main Anzio–Rome road, the enemy losing many dead and nearly three thousand prisoners.

On the Gustav line, where the main 5th Army was operating still, American troops succeeded, by January 30, in moving twenty-three tanks across the Rapido, next day capturing the village of Cairo, some $2\frac{1}{2}$ miles north of Cassino. By February 2 they were in the northern outskirts of Cassino itself, where house-to-house fighting took place as Imperial troops advanced towards the monastery which the Germans were using as an observation post and strongpoint. (The monastery, cradle of the Benedictine Order, was founded by St. Benedict in 529, and became a national monument after the dissolution of the monasteries in Italy in 1866.) On the 13th, American guns trained on the abbey fired a " barrage " of 11,000 leaflets emphasizing the Allied desire to save the abbey, but warning those there (including Italians) that the time had come to attack it. Two days later the abbey was destroyed by bombing and shelling. But the position remained unchanged, with the Canadians holding about one-third of the town. On the night of March 14–15, the Canadians were secretly withdrawn and between 8.30 and noon on the 15th some 1,400 tons of bombs were dropped on the

Cassino Abbey Destroyed

town, followed by a murderous artillery barrage on the town and on the German pillboxes studding Monte Cassino and the ruins of the abbey above. Immediately this ceased, a formation under Lieut.-General Sir Bernard Freyberg, V.C., went in to the attack, and by dusk had taken two-thirds of the town. By next afternoon the castle on the heights overlooking the town from the west was in the hands of New Zealand infantrymen. An Indian formation, in pitch darkness and pouring rain, then began the assault on " Monastery Hill " (Monte Cassino itself), which lies somewhat less than a mile to the west of the town. After capturing their first objective, " Hangman's Hill," within a few hundred yards of the monastery, they became isolated from the town and eventually had to be withdrawn on the night of March 24–25.

The air bombardment on the first day of this offensive—the heaviest that had ever been made in the Mediterranean theatre—had somewhat of a boomerang effect, for it seriously impeded progress along the roads leading to the town and within Cassino itself. Although the river Rapido, which had become a torrent, was successfully bridged south of Cassino, it was only with great difficulty, owing to huge bomb craters, some filled with water, that three tanks managed to enter the southern outskirts of the town. Tanks entering from the north were stopped by mounds of rubble and debris.

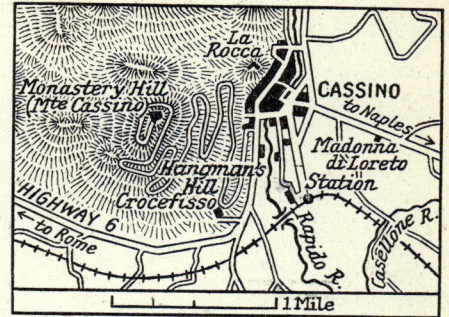

CASSINO AND ENVIRONS

This detail map shows how the city of Cassino, vital point on the road to Rome, and several miles of the road itself, were dominated by Monte Cassino, with the massive buildings of the Benedictine monastery and abbey crowning it, and by 'Hangman's Hill.'

The topographical difficulties of the battle were also considerable. " Monastery Hill," commanding as it did the entrance to the Liri valley (the only conceivable route to Rome), was the primary objective. But to outflank it from the north was nearly impossible, first, because it was bounded on that side by a ravine so deep that it proved impossible to cross it ; secondly, because if a wider northern flanking movement had been tried, it would have necessitated crossing Monte Cairo, a still more formidable peak, whose summit was covered in deep snow.

A further difficulty was that, to the south, where the natural obstacle was the river Rapido, any bridging expeditions immediately came under heavy

GERMAN STORES ROUND AN ALTAR

When the monastery of Monte Cassino was finally captured by the Poles on May 18, 1944, stores of food and ammunition were found round this altar among the ruins, which were littered with German dead and fragments of equipment. With the fall of Cassino and Monte Cassino monastery, the strong, heavily defended Gustav line ceased to exist, and the Germans were forced back on the so-called Adolf Hitler line. (See map in page 3048.)
Photo, British Official

3051

FOR EMERGENCY AIRFIELDS IN ITALY

To enable Allied planes to land, refuel, and rearm immediately behind the armies as they advanced, the Army Airfield Construction Groups worked steadily through North Africa and Italy. Here pressed steel plates, used for the surface of runways in Italy, are being unloaded at a site chosen for an emergency airfield. (Compare these plates, made necessary by Italian weather conditions, with the Somerfeld track used in dry North Africa and illustrated in page 2545.)
Photo, British Official

enfilade artillery fire from German gun positions sited at the foot of the mountains to the west. A direct assault on the monastery was therefore only possible to small parties of infantry who, operating over pathless and unfriendly slopes, were themselves dependent for maintenance on porters and mules, and supplies dropped from the air.

In the Anzio beach-head, after a lull, the enemy launched his third major attack on February 29, followed by other

Enemy's Third Major Attack at Anzio

smaller attacks. All were repulsed, with resultant heavy casualties to the Germans. The little port of Anzio, which had been under constant long-range shelling and desultory air bombardment, continued to discharge supplies at a satisfactory level varying between 2,000 and 5,000 tons daily—on March 10 the record total of 7,000 tons was reached. Further Allied reinforcements arrived, including fresh formations which took the place of some of those that had borne the brunt of the heavy fighting during the first few weeks. Activity in the field remained on a small scale until March 15 when elements of an American battalion took and held against fierce counter-attacks two strongpoints in the area immediately west of Case Carano, about five miles south-west of Cisterna. A few days later British troops carried out a successful raid three miles south-west of Carroceto station. The enemy reacted with harassing tactics and

probing attacks which continued intermittently throughout April and May without any definite success, although specific penetrations of Allied positions on occasion caused higher British casualties than German. During these weeks the enemy nevertheless remained principally on the defensive, which suited the plans of the Allies who were regrouping and preparing for a large-scale offensive against the Gustav Line. These preparations involved the transfer of the greater part of the 8th Army (under the command of Lieut.-Gen. Sir Oliver Leese, who succeeded Montgomery in January), with reinforcements, to the support of the 5th Army in the Gustav line sector, leaving 5th Corps to hold the Adriatic sector. Owing to complete Allied air superiority, the enemy remained unaware of these changes until the Allies were ready to attack on May 11.

Right up to that date, the position at Cassino remained substantially unchanged. Counter-attacks had been repulsed, and an exploration attempted of the warren of underground tunnels —some dating from the 16th century —which connected the Benedictine abbey with points in the surrounding country and served as shelters for the German defenders during air and artillery bombardments. The tunnels were however, found to be so blocked with debris that their exploration was abandoned. Patrolling, exchange of artillery and mortar fire, regrouping and reliefs had continued.

On May 11 at 11 p.m., the combined 5th and 8th Army attack opened on a thirty-mile front from above Cassino to the Tyrrhenian Sea. The disposition of Allied formation was as follows : Polish troops in the mountains north and north-west of Cassino ; British and Indian forces from Cassino to the Liri valley ; French in the mountains south of the Liri valley ; Americans in the coastal sector. By the evening of the 13th, the better part of two infantry divisions and a number of tanks were across the Rapido south of Cassino.

The French made particularly good progress : by the end of the same day they were within 2½ miles of San Ambrogio, having captured Monte Faito (2,550 ft.), an integral part of the Gustav line.

Second Allied Assault on Monte Cassino

The Americans secured Ventosa (12th) and Castelforte (13th) and began an attack north of Minturno. The French continued their spectacular advance, a dispatch of May 14 stating : " It is impossible to rate the French achievement too highly ; in three days they advanced seven miles, storming a series of mountains comparable in height and ruggedness to Scafell."

The bridge-head across the Rapido was steadily extended and built up with reserve formations, until on May 15 Indian troops were 400 yards short of Pignataro, which they captured next day, when, despite heavy opposition,

MEMORIAL AT ANZIO

This monument was erected by officers and men serving with the 2nd Battalion, The Sherwood Foresters, in memory of comrades who fell fighting in the Anzio beach-head between January 22 and June 3, 1944. The names of the places they helped to gain are recorded. *Photo, The Times*

GUSTAV LINE ATTACKED

At 11 p.m. on May 11, 1944, the 5th and 8th
Armies jointly attacked the Gustav line—
formidable by nature, and made more so by
German military engineering ingenuity. At
'zero hour' thousands of Allied guns delivered a 40-minute barrage much heavier
than that at El Alamein; then followed an
infantry attack, launched before moonrise
on a 30-mile front. 1. French troops, who
made a spectacular advance in the San
Ambrogio area, pass a disabled enemy tank
in a shattered village. 2. General Alexander,
C.-in-C. (right), and Lieut.-General Leese,
commanding the 8th Army, before the
assault. 3. British units wait by a railway,
destroyed by the Germans (see illus., p.
3040), for darkness to fall. 4. A 4·2-in.
mortar in action—one of a number which
took part in the night barrage—and its crew,
members of a Light A.A. Regiment, R.A.

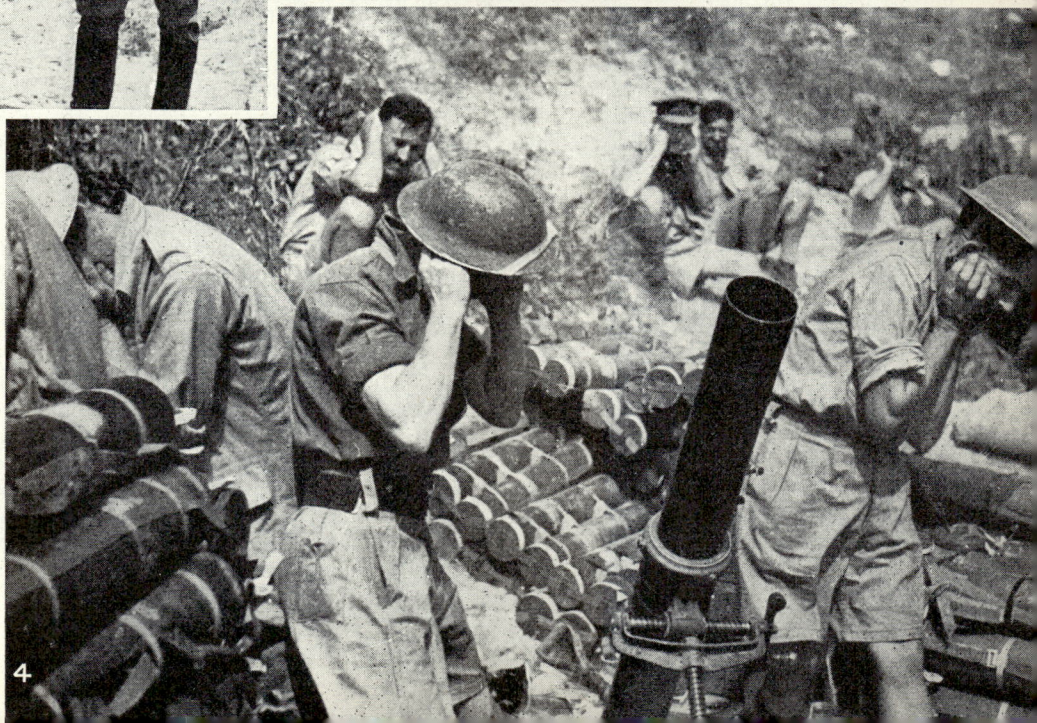

place of Juvenal and St. Thomas Aquinas) to British troops, and Piedimonte to the Poles; Indian troops took Roccasecca and Poles Monte Cairo—all on the 25th. Leading elements of a British armoured division were within ¾ mile of Arce by the 27th. The Canadians established a bridge-head over the Melfa on the 26th and took Ceprano two days later; while S. Giovanni and Pastena were in the hands of the French by the 26th. The Americans meanwhile had reached Priverno and Sezze. Prisoners since May 11 totalled 13,000.

The last week before the capture of Rome saw the penetration of the enemy's defences in the Alban Hills, the pivot on which the whole of his

ANZIO MEN MEET THE MAIN FIFTH ARMY AGAIN
Four months after the first landings at Anzio, the men who consolidated and held the beach-head broke through enemy resistance to link up with the main 5th Army advancing from the Gustav line. Here men of the two forces greet one another as they meet near Borga Grappa on May 25, 1945. Right, Lieut.-General Mark Clark, commanding the 5th Army, cheered by British and Americans on reaching the meeting place.   *Photos, British Official; British Newsreels*

the whole line of the Cassino–S. Giorgio road was crossed and fresh Dominion formations were brought in on the southern flank of the bridge-head.

On May 17 the two formations south of Cassino turned north-west towards Highway 6 and reduced the distance between themselves and Polish troops

End of the Gustav Line

who were then attacking in the hills to the north of the road, to about 2,000 yards. These Polish forces had been rebuffed in their first attempt to gain the heights to the north-west of Cassino, but they attacked again and by the 18th the 2nd Polish Corps, commanded by Lt.-Gen. Wladyslaw Anders (*see* page 2576), captured the long-coveted "Monastery Hill," while British forces entered the ruins of the town of Cassino itself. A special communiqué from General Alexander's H.Q. ended: "The Gustav line south of the Apennines has now ceased to exist." The Allied advance continued.

The impetus of the French attack to the south of the Liri disorganized the Germans, and they began to retreat. The French took full advantage of this and soon won control south of the river, capturing Esperia on the 17th. The Americans thrusting steadily westwards through difficult country and along the Appian Way, captured Itri and Fondi on the 20th. The same day they also cleared the Gaeta peninsula and captured the port of Gaeta.

Stiffening resistance against the Allied forces in contact with the Hitler line then decided General Alexander to launch concerted attacks from the main front and from the Anzio beach-head, the former to crack it open, the latter to cut the main lines of communication between Rome and the enemy facing the 8th Army in the Liri valley. The concerted offensive opened on the night of May 22–23, and by the 25th the Adolf Hitler line had been completely overrun, having been first broken by the Canadians who got armoured elements up to the east bank of the river Melfa, a tributary of the Liri. This gave them control of the Aquino–Pontecorvo road, and opened up country possible to tanks. To the left of the Canadians, the French also attacked; while the Americans on the coastal flank continued to thrust forward, reaching Terracina on the 24th. The following day an American engineer unit from the Anzio beach-head met a British reconnaissance patrol of the main 5th Army near Borga Grappa. American armoured elements in the beach-head also made substantial gains in the direction of Velletri, and Cisterna fell on the 25th. Cori was secured (26th) and Artena occupied without opposition by the 27th.

On the main front the follow-up went on apace. Pontecorvo fell to Canadian armoured cars, Aquino (birth-retreat hinged. The principal threat was initiated from the American sectors where, after encountering very stiff resistance south of Valmontone and Velletri, American forces during the night of May 31–June 1 broke through the German defences and gained access to the Hills. The advance developed rapidly. Both Velletri and Valmontone fell on 2nd, and at 9 a.m. on June 4 American reconnaissance units were in the city of Rome. The 8th Army also made steady progress, but their advance was hampered by demolitions and the naturally close country.

And so the first capital city held by the enemy fell to Allied forces 48 hours before the invasion of France. Neither Anzio nor Cassino was the 100 per cent success the Allied High Command had

Allies Enter Rome

hoped, but the beach-head had played a decisive part in the summer, and Cassino had been the key to the winter line. Both contributed to the Allies' main object, which was to destroy as many German divisions as possible and to register a first-class victory before the western front re-opened.

Chapter 303

TENSION IN THE MIDDLE EAST

*When, in 1944, the shadow of war receded from the Middle East, unrest grew.
As Mr. Kenneth Williams here shows, efforts towards Arab unity, popular
dissatisfaction due to inflation and other economic difficulties and, in Palestine,
the activities of a small number of Jewish terrorists which culminated in the
murder of Lord Moyne (British Minister Resident in the Middle East), were
among the causes. For the Middle East in 1943, see Chapter 266.*

THE year 1943 had ended for Egypt with a significant development. On Christmas Day the first Soviet Minister presented his credentials to King Farouk. In the Minister's staff was a Counsellor, a Russian Moslem, who was able to participate **EGYPT** in the spiritual life of Egypt in a way unknown to representatives of other European diplomatic missions.

Egyptians felt so far removed from the threat of war that there was considerable talk about revising the 1936 Anglo-Egyptian Treaty. The Premier, Nahas Pasha, himself an ardent Nationalist, could not ignore such speculation, but he publicly announced, on January 3, that the time was not ripe for modifying the treaty with Britain. Whether his words were as carefully listened to as they might have been is arguable; at any rate, there were currents beneath the seemingly smooth surface of things, and early in the year the University of Al Azhar had to be temporarily closed following political demonstrations by the easily effervescent students.

Three matters may be said to have dominated the Egyptian scene in 1944: the problem of Arab unity; change of government in Cairo; the difficulties of the local economic situation.

On February 9 it was announced that, after discussions with a representative of the King of the Yemen, Egypt and the Yemen wished for further collaboration and that they sought co-operation among all Arab countries. But two factors militated against Arab unity: the recurring problem of Palestine, and France's equivocal position in the Levant States. On both these heads, Egypt made her position clear: she protested several times to the U.S. Government against statements in a Senate committee in favour of creating a Jewish National State in Palestine, and, recognizing the independence of the two republics of the Levant, she opposed the imposition of treaties on them giving a predominant position to the French.

By the end of February, the Premier was telling the Egyptian Senate that

plans were going ahead for the discussion of Arab unity, and that a beginning would be made by inviting the independent Arab States—Iraq, Saudi Arabia, Syria, the Lebanon, and Transjordan—but that their Arab brothers in such lands as Morocco and Tunisia were not forgotten. On September 25, Nahas Pasha opened a preparatory Pan-Arab conference at Alexandria, at which Syria, the Lebanon, Iraq, and Transjordan as well as Egypt were represented. Saudi Arabia and the Yemen at first held back, Ibn Saud stating that no useful result could be secured unless Palestine were represented—a view supported by the Yemen. But on September 28 delegates arrived from these two states, demanding however that Palestine be represented. Musa el Alami, sent as

an observer by the Palestinian Arab parties, was invited to join the conference, which ended on October 7 with the signature by representatives of Egypt, Syria, the Lebanon, Transjordan, and Iraq of a protocol providing for the establishment of a League of Arab States. Saudi Arabia and the Yemen adhered to the protocol in January 1945. One of the articles stated that " the Conference holds that the engagements made by Britain, which comprise the cessation of Jewish immigration, the safeguarding of lands belonging to the Arabs, and the advance of Palestine towards independence, constitute rights acquired by the Arabs, and that their execution will be a step forward towards the desired goal. . . ." The Conference, while recognizing the horrors of persecution of the Jews in

LORD MOYNE ASSASSINATED

On November 5, 1944, Lord Moyne (left), British Minister of State in the Middle East, was shot at and killed in Cairo by two young Jewish terrorists from Palestine. His driver, Lance-Corporal A. H. Fuller, R.A.S.C., was also killed. The murderers were caught by an Egyptian constable, Mohamed Abdullah (right), and condemned to death on January 18, 1945. Above, part of the funeral procession of Lord Moyne and his driver.

Europe, felt that "nothing would be more arbitrary and unjust than to attempt to settle the question of the Jews in Europe by another injustice" to the Arabs of Palestine.

On October 8 King Farouk dismissed Nahas Pasha and his Government, and asked Ahmed Maher Pasha to form a Cabinet. Taking but a day to form his administration, the new Premier told the Press that his aim was to cleanse the country of the corruption and chaos of the "despotic rule just ended." Political personalities, such as Ali Maher Pasha and Makram Ebeid Pasha, who had been interned under the Wafdist regime, were set free; Makram Pasha, indeed, became Finance Minister in the new Cabinet. The Premier adopted a moderate tone in his statements on international affairs, and he relieved the fears of many foreign observers when he declared, on October 11, that he would assist the Allies to the utmost to gain victory, not only against Germany, but also against Japan. It was a notable and helpful pronouncement, for Egypt's interest in the Far Eastern war had not been marked, though Egypt and the Middle East were important, strategically, to the Allied campaign against Japan. Parliament was dissolved by royal decree on November 15, to reassemble, after the elections, on January 18, 1945.

New Egyptian Government

Two conferences of importance to the whole Middle East were held in Cairo under the auspices of the Middle East Supply Centre (set up in 1941 under the direction of the Ministry of War Transport to supervise civilian needs of territories, cut off from normal sources of supply, covering an area of 2,500,000 square miles and a population of 50 millions). The first, from February 7–10, which considered agricultural problems, was attended by over a hundred delegates. It discussed among other things soil erosion and land reclamation, and passed resolutions emphasizing the need for development of resources, full exchange of information, stimulation of production, irrigation and other post-war schemes.

The second, from April 24–29, concerned finance. War had brought prosperity to the Middle East in terms of cash, but there had been no corresponding increase in imports of goods, and Lord Moyne, British Minister Resident in the Middle East, opening the conference, said that price inflation was the immediate problem to be faced. As many of the statistics produced concerned military expenditure, the proceedings were held in secret.

Twenty-eight resolutions were passed, divided into three sections, dealing with taxation, loans and savings, price policy and price control. It was generally agreed that all Middle Eastern States should try to produce more, and

C.-IN-C. STARTS THE DRAW

On November 17, 1944, the Prime Minister announced in the House of Commons that a scheme had been worked out under which in every four weeks about 6,000 men with long overseas service would return home for four weeks' leave. Men were selected by ballot. Here General Sir Bernard Paget, C.-in-C. Middle East, is drawing the first name from the drum in the first ballot for leave from his command.

to create a better equilibrium of exchange among themselves.

But inflation had hit the region hard, and it was in the nature of things that the M.E.S.C., which came into existence partly to save shipping to the Middle East, partly to encourage local self-sufficiency, should, as a restrictive agent, receive some unpopularity. There was therefore considerable rejoicing when, on December 30, modifications in M.E.S.C. control of imports were announced, M.E.S.C. recommendations for import licences being no longer required for a large range of articles.

Full lighting was restored in Cairo and Upper Egypt on August 2, though "dim-out" was retained in the Suez Canal zone and along the coast.

At the beginning of 1944, Turkey was still disinclined to join the Allies, though she indicated her sympathy with them by such actions as the expulsion of the correspondent of the Domei agency on January 28, on the charge of having sent misleading information to Japan; and the indefinite suspension in February of the German "Turkische Post," for publishing anti-British material.

TURKEY

However, a British Military Mission, sent to implement for 1944 the supply

AUSTRALIAN CORN IN EGYPT

A ship loaded with bagged wheat from Adelaide, Australia, is here seen at the quayside in Port Tewfik, near Suez. Unloading went on at full pressure, 5,800 tons being discharged in 24 hours. Men of the British Army who kept cranes and other gear in good working order were responsible for this record feat. *Photos, British Official*

VON PAPEN LEAVES TURKEY
After Turkey stopped exporting chrome to Germany in April 1944, Von Papen, the German Ambassador, used threats to persuade her to change her decision. Instead, she broke off diplomatic and commercial relations. Here Von Papen smiles at well-wishers as he left Ankara for the last time.

arrangements made during Mr. Churchill's visit to Adana in January 1943 (see page 2639), left Ankara on February 8 after " inconclusive " talks lasting five weeks. As Mr. Churchill explained to the House of Commons on May 25, " The hopes we cherished of Turkey boldly entering the war in February or March, or at least according us the necessary bases for air action— these hopes faded. After giving £20,000,000's worth of British and American arms to Turkey in 1943 alone we have suspended the process and ceased to expect Turkey to range herself with the victorious united Powers, with whom, I think there is no doubt, her sympathies lie.

" The Turks, at the end of last year and the beginning of this year, magnified their danger. Their military men took **Churchill** the gloomiest view of **on Turkish** Russian prospects in **Hesitations** south Russia and the Crimea. They never dreamed that by the early summer the Red Army would be on the slopes of the Carpathians, drawn up along the Prut and Seret rivers, or that Odessa and Sevastopol would have been liberated. . . . Having over-rated their danger, our Turkish friends increased their demands for supplies to such a point that, having regard to the means of communication and transport alone,

the war would probably be over before these supplies could reach them. . . . It looks probable that . . . the great allies will be able to win the war in . . . south-east Europe without Turkey's being involved."

One particular source of Allied dissatisfaction was an increase of Turkey's supply of chrome to Germany, and a decrease of supply to Britain. Her annual production of chrome was some 100,000 tons. In 1943, the United Nations received 56,000 tons, Germany 47,000 tons. In the first two months of 1944, 14,800 tons went to Germany (against increased deliveries of arms), 1,870 tons to the United Nations. Allied protests led Turkey, on the personal initiative of President Inonu, to decide to suspend exports of chrome to Axis countries from April 21. As a result, the German Ambassador, Von Papen, was recalled to the Reich.

In May he returned to Ankara, protesting that by her action in regard to chrome, Turkey had violated the Clodius Agreement. Ankara's response was to have blackout tests throughout the country. In the same month, the Turkish authorities discovered a secret Pan-Turanian Society which had been working for the Nazis since 1940.

In June, it was learned that the British Government had protested strongly to Turkey against the transit from the Black Sea to the Aegean Sea of German vessels which stripped themselves of

naval equipment in order to pass through the Straits. The Turks convinced themselves of the correctness of the British allegations, and took the necessary action ; but the resignation of the Foreign Minister, M. Menemenjoglou (who, though certainly not pro-Nazi, was wedded to neutrality), was announced on the same day (June 15) that stricter supervision of shipping passing through the Dardanelles was announced.

Germany was perturbed, and at the end of July, the German Ambassador was warning the Turks that Britain intended to force them into the war. But on **Turkey** August 2 the Ankara **Breaks with** Government, in a de- **Germany** cision ratified unanimously by the Grand National Assembly, broke off diplomatic and commercial relations with Germany. Before the end of that month, the Turkish Government decided to end the mission of its Ambassador to Vichy. The Germans were in full retreat, and though some of them preferred internment in Turkey to return to Germany, the prestige of Von Papen (personally decorated by Hitler on his return to the Reich) had crumbled to nothing.

The Turks took these anti-German steps with little enthusiasm. Their chief fear still came from Russia, and the Soviets were outspoken in their view of the unimportance of Turkey's action in breaking with Germany. The

AMERICAN LEND-LEASE BOMBS FOR TURKEY
On May 25, 1944, Mr. Churchill revealed in the House of Commons that during 1943 £20,000,000 worth of British and American arms had been given to Turkey under the arrangement he made at Adana in January 1943. Here crates containing bombs shipped from the United States are being loaded by Turkish soldiers at Iskanderun (Alexandretta) into goods vans for transfer to storage dumps on Turkish aerodromes.
Photos, Keystone

Turks appeared to cling the more closely to their alliance with Britain as constituting their main hope of the future, though on November 1 the President spoke of relations with the Soviet as "very friendly." Yet the passivity that seemed to invest Turkey was stirred neither by the action of her Government nor by her fears. To the end of the year she pursued a leisurely course in ridding the land of German influence; it was not until December 11, for instance, that the Deutsche Bank and the Deutsche Orient Bank in Turkey were ordered to liquidate their business. Russian criticisms of what was considered in Moscow to be dilatory, indecisive action continued, and Turkey's sense of isolation remained.

An earthquake, which severely damaged a number of towns, occurred in Anatolia on February 1. About 7,000 houses were destroyed; 2,382 were killed; 1,490 injured.

During 1944 Iraq was mainly concerned with attainment of Arab unity. In the forefront of discussions, whether in Baghdad or in other **IRAQ** Arab capitals, was Nuri Pasha, the Prime Minister, who visited the heads of nearly all the Arab States. It was certainly largely owing to Iraq's efforts that the Pan-Arab Congress of September 25 met at Alexandria.

R.A.F. LAND TRANSPORT IN THE MIDDLE EAST

This omnibus, used by the R.A.F. for duty runs between Habbaniya, Iraq, and Damascus, Syria, had 12 gears, was of 90 h.p., weighed 30 tons, was 75 feet long and 11 feet high, and carried 40 passengers with their luggage. It was air-conditioned, had a kitchen, toilet accommodation, and iced water laid on. The car standing beside it (a Hillman Minx) gives a basis for computing its size. *Photo, British Official*

IRAQI PARACHUTISTS

During 1944 200 Iraqi tribesmen received training as parachute jumpers under British instructors, who taught them all phases of commando fighting from unarmed combat to the use of the most recent war weapons. But they continued to carry their traditional weapon, the kungar, a 15-inch long curved knife. Here are some of the recruits about to go on leave. *Photo, British Official*

On February 28, the Iraqi Government protested to the U.S. Government about statements made in a Senate committee on the creation of a Jewish State in Palestine, pointing out that the American desire that Palestine should become a Jewish State meant the hostility to the U.S.A. of every Arab in Asia and Africa, and was being used by Nazi propagandists to put Arab not only against Jew, but also against the whole democratic world. In April a number of men connected with Rashid Ali's revolt of 1941 (see page 1679) were brought back to Baghdad from Rhodesia. Kamil Shabid was condemned to death, others to terms of imprisonment. Nuri Pasha resigned the premiership in June, on account of ill-health; he was succeeded by Hamdi Pachachi. Diplomatic relations with Russia were established in September.

Under an agreement signed by representatives of the French Committee of National Liberation, Syria and the Lebanon, on December 22, 1943, most of **SYRIA AND** the powers previ- **THE LEBANON** ously exercised under mandate by France came on January 1, 1944, under the authority of the Syrian and Lebanese Governments. France retained authority over social insurance, educational and cultural services, and, for the duration of the war, over the special security troops—levies of native rank-and-file with French officers.

General Beynet, the new French Delegate-General, arrived in Beirut on March 9; the two States protested that he should be given a purely diplomatic designation, in view of their independence; but he retained the title. From the French point of **New French** view, the situation was **Delegate-** complicated by two **General** things: the League of Nations from which the French mandate in Syria and the Lebanon (like the British mandate in Palestine) derived, was no longer in effective being; and the French Committee of National Liberation (later in the year the provisional government of France) was holding in trust responsibilities as to which only a government based on a freely elected French assembly could, it felt, rightly make final decisions. In both Damascus and Beirut there were during the year minor clashes with the French.

Claiming the full prerogatives of sovereignty, Syria and the Lebanon announced in January that they were establishing legations in Algiers, Baghdad, Cairo, London, and Washington. They also took an active part in the moves towards establishing Arab unity; and they protested (February 29) against the attitude of American senators on the Zionist question. The Soviet Union formally recognized the Syrian Republic on June 28, and in September the United States recognized the inde-

LORD GORT TAKES OFFICE AS HIGH COMMISSIONER

Sir Harold MacMichael's term as High Commissioner of Palestine came to an end on September 3, 1944. He was succeeded by Field-Marshal Viscount Gort, V.C., as High Commissioner and C.-in-C., Palestine and Transjordan, who arrived by air at Lydda airport on October 31 and drove immediately to Jerusalem where he was sworn in. This photograph was taken in the ballroom of Government House, Jerusalem, during the swearing-in ceremonies. *Photo, British Official*

for certain crimes, including the carrying of arms or bombs. A curfew was imposed in Tel-Aviv, Jerusalem, and Haifa from March 26 to April 2, and 60 suspects were arrested in various towns (April 1–2). Rewards totalling £1,900 were offered for information leading to the recapture of six of the Stern Group who had escaped from detention in October 1943.

More policemen were killed on April 1. On May 10 a Jewish policeman was shot dead in Tel-Aviv, and on the 17th an attempt was made to wreck the broadcasting station at Ramallah. The Jewish community formally deplored the outrages; but a declaration issued by the Chief Rabbis in Palestine on May 22 demanding the establishment of a Jewish commonwealth in Palestine and the admittance of all Jews who wished to enter the country did not help the Government. **Jewish Attitude to Outrages**

In July, bombs exploded in the police headquarters and in the land registry in Jerusalem; and on August 8 the car of the High Commissioner was ambushed as Sir Harold MacMichael, who was wounded, was going to a farewell gathering—it having been announced in July that Lord Gort would succeed him as High Commissioner when his term of office ended on September 3.

pendence of the two countries by appointing Mr. George Wadsworth (till then Consul-General) Minister to Syria and the Lebanon.

In October, the French Council of Ministers, presided over by General de Gaulle, rejected the two States' request that France should relinquish control of the special security troops. Matters were not eased by General Beynet's statement to the Lebanese President in the same month—made, it transpired, on his own initiative and without instruction from Paris—that the resolution passed by the Pan-Arab Congress forbidding Arab States individually to enter into treaties which might be construed as inimical to Arab interests as a whole, made impossible the conclusion of a treaty with France, and that the French Provisional Government might therefore consider invalidated General Catroux's declaration of independence for Syria and the Lebanon. The state of tension had not relaxed, and there were no signs of improvement in the situation by the end of the year.

The history of Palestine in 1944 was marked by a series of terrorist outrages, culminating in the assassination of Lord Moyne, British Minister of State in the Middle East, in Cairo in November. Extremist Jews, impatient of the slow methods of the Jewish Agency for converting Palestine into a Jewish **PALESTINE**

State, staged incidents almost every month. The organizations involved were three: the Hagana, the Irgun Zvi Le'umi b'Eretz Israel (National Military Organization in the Land of Israel), and the "Stern Group." On February 3, plans were discovered for a bomb-plot in St. George's Cathedral in Jerusalem. On February 12, bombs exploded in the Immigration Offices in Jerusalem, Haifa, and Tel Aviv. Six days later in letters to the Hebrew Press Irgun Zvi Le'umi admitted responsibility for the crimes, saying "We have started the battle to open the gates of Palestine to persecuted European Jews." Before the end of February a British policeman was injured and police property damaged on Mount Carmel by bomb explosions; two policemen were shot and died at Haifa.

In face of activity so harmful to their cause, Zionists tried to close their ranks, and in March it was announced that, following a visit by three members of the Palestine Executive to Dr. Weizmann in London, Mr. Ben Gurion was willing to resume the chairmanship of the Jewish Agency Executive. The outrages went on. On March 23, C.I.D. headquarters at Haifa were wrecked by a heavy explosion. Three British constables were killed and three seriously injured. Part of the C.I.D. building at Jaffa was destroyed. On March 24, the Government reintroduced the death penalty (abolished in 1940)

APPEAL TO JEWISH WOMEN

'Women must be mobilized for military service' runs the text of this poster addressed to Jewish women in Palestine. The appeal met with a good response. The decision of the War Office to form a Jewish Brigade Group, to fight as a separate unit, was announced on September 20, 1944. *Photo, Keystone*

HELP FOR PERSIA'S DISTRIBUTIVE PROBLEMS

To ease the difficult problem of getting cereals from the producer to the consumer in Persia—a country more than six times the size of Great Britain, with few railways and little motor transport —Government collecting centres were set up, on the initiative of British and American advisers, to which farmers could bring and sell their produce. This was then stored until a convoy load had accumulated, when it was transported by British army lorries to more populated areas. Here is one such centre. *Photo, British Official*

But still the Jewish community failed to help actively in the arrest of the criminals. On August 21, a collective fine of £500 was imposed on a Jewish quarter of Jerusalem owing to its inhabitants' failure to help police investigation of the attempt on the High Commissioner's life. On September 27, four police stations at various places were attacked by night, police and civilian casualties resulting. Mr. T. J. Wilkin, assistant superintendent of police, was murdered in Jerusalem on September 29. Some 50 armed men raided the Department of Light Industries at Tel-Aviv (October 5–6) and stole textiles valued at £100,000.

So serious was the situation that the military were called in to co-operate with the civil authorities: this became **Terrorists Removed from Palestine** known when on October 10 a joint announcement was made by Mr. J. W. V. Shaw, Officer Administering the Government of Palestine, and General Sir Bernard Paget, C.-in-C., Middle East, deploring the effect of terrorist activities on the war effort, and calling on the Jewish community to assist the forces of law and order and not " allow the name of Yishuw to be prejudiced by acts which can bring only shame and dishonour on the

Jewish people as a whole." Nine days later the Government announced that 251 persons detained as terrorists had been removed from Palestine.

Field-Marshal Viscount Gort, V.C., arrived to take up his post as High Commissioner and C.-in-C. for Palestine on October 31. Lord Moyne was shot dead in Cairo by two Jewish terrorists, Eliahu Hakim (25) of Haifa and Ephraim Ben Zuri (20) of Tel-Aviv, on November 5. The murderers were arrested, tried before the Supreme Military Court in Cairo, and sentenced to death on January 18, 1945. This dastardly act appeared to shake the Jewish community from its passivity ; Dr. Weizmann went at once from London to Palestine, to exert his influence with his co-religionists there, for Lord Moyne's assassination was a serious setback to Zionist sympathies throughout the world. Mr. Churchill said in the House of Commons (November 17): " That is a shameful crime which has shocked the world and has affected none more strongly than those like myself who, in the past, have been consistent friends of the Jews. . . . If there is to be any hope of a peaceful and successful future for Zionism these wicked activities must cease, and those responsible for them must be destroyed, root and branch.

. . . Although the primary responsibility is that of the Government, full success depends on the wholehearted co-operation of the entire Jewish community."

The Jewish press strongly condemned the assassins of Lord Moyne. Arrests of terrorists by the Government continued. But the passing of a resolution on December 22 by the Jewish Elected Assembly in Palestine, appealing to the United Nations to agree to the opening of Palestine to Jewish immigration and the establishment of a Jewish State, did nothing to relieve the tension in the Holy Land.

The War Office announced on September 20 that the Government had decided to accede to the request of the Jewish Agency that a Jewish Brigade Group should be formed to take part in active operations. Brigadier E. S. Benjamin, already in the Middle East, was named a month later as commander.

On February 10 it was announced that the British and United States Legations in Teheran had been raised to Embassy status. Dr. Millspaugh, head of U.S. Mission of Financial Advisers **PERSIA** to the Persian Government (*see page 2645*), again, on June 27, threatened to resign the task of reorganizing the country's finances, following attacks in the press and other difficulties. Prices were indeed high, and all failings in administration were laid at the door of Teheran. Educated Persians seemed inclined to see little hope of improvement until foreign troops were removed from Persian soil, and the poorer classes began to sigh for the old days of Shah Riza Pahlavi—who died an exile in South Africa on July 26.

But criticism was not reserved exclusively for foreigners. There were many attacks on Sayyid Zia-ud-Din Tabatatai, the foreign-educated Persian of strong personality who, in the years following the First Great War, brought Riza Pahlavi into power, and returned to his country from Palestine in 1944. Some Persians would have liked to see him as Premier ; others, and particularly those in touch with Russian thought, considered him a menace.

On September 23 a Soviet mission, led by M. Kavtaradze, Soviet Vice-Commissar for Foreign Affairs, arrived in Teheran to discuss economic relations. M. Mohammed Said, who had replaced M. Soheily as Prime Minister in March, told the press on October 21 that the Soviet Government, the American Standard Oil Co., the Sinclair Oil Co., and the British Shell Co. had all been negotiating for oil concessions for months, but that Persia would grant no oil concessions during the war. This decision had the backing of the *Mejlis*. A press campaign, with which the extreme Left Wing party Tudeh was associated, began, and Moscow reported meetings in Teheran demanding the resignation of M. Said. M. Kavtaradze told the press in Teheran on October 29 that relations between Russia and Persia remained friendly, but that the "disloyal attitude taken by the Premier towards the Soviet Union precludes further co-operation." The following day M. Said broadcast a reply, asserting among other things that so long as foreign troops remained in Persia public opinion would consider any concession as given under duress, that the economic condition of the world was not clear, that the oil conference in Washington (July 25–August 8) had left the whole oil position in doubt, and that all reports from Persian representatives abroad urged that no concessions should be granted until after the war.

The British and American Governments took the view that the Persian Government was entirely within its rights in taking its decision.

In order to make clear that the stand adopted by the Teheran Government was not merely a personal one, M. Said resigned in November, to be succeeded

by M. Nurteza Qualikhan Bayatt, formerly Minister without Portfolio. M. Bayatt, backed by an almost unanimous *Mejlis*, was as firm in his refusal to grant concessions as his predecessor had been.

During the last few weeks of the year, accusation and counter-accusation continued. The Russians inspired fresh attacks on the Teheran administration, and Persian publicists replied with spirit. So affected were some Persians by what they called "synthetic demonstrations" in the north that they actually suggested moving the Government from Teheran, the capital, so that it would be less under the influence of foreign powers. M. Kavtaradze left Teheran on December 11, and on the 19th it was reported that M. Bayatt had proposed a compromise on the basis of the sale of oil to Russia without formal concessions.

All through the year, supplies of war material continued to go to Russia through Persia. "Paiforce" (Persia and Iraq Command), comprising the British 10th Army, a large Polish Army,

and the Iraqi Army, had been created in August 1942, to assure the defence of the Persian oilfields when the German threat to the Caucasus looked most serious (*see* map in p. 2355), and also to safeguard these essential deliveries. Lieut.-General Sir Arthur Smith succeeded Lieut.-General Pownall (*see* illus., p. 2642) as G.O.C.-in-C. of this command in February 1944. Paiforce included men of the Royal Engineers, R.A.S.C., Pioneer Corps with Indian battalions and locally enrolled labour, as well as famous infantry regiments. It was destined to see no fighting, but under conditions of extreme hardship it performed a most important role, improving port facilities, constructing roads, railways, and pipe-lines, and undertaking other duties of a like kind. On November 3, 1944, G.H.Q. Persia-Iraq Command was able to announce that stores sent to Russia through the Persian Gulf and Anglo-American supply lines for military and reconstruction purposes had reached a total of 4,000,000 tons.

SUPPLIES FOR RUSSIA CROSS PERSIA

On November 3, 1944, G.H.Q. Persia-Iraq Command announced that a total of 4,000,000 tons of military and reconstruction supplies had been sent to Russia through the Persian Gulf Anglo-American supply lines. Here a train is being assembled at the Persian Gulf port of Khorramshahr for transit to Russia. Below are the American-built docks at this port piled with merchandise unloaded from the string of Liberty ships alongside. *Photos, New York Times*

Diary of the War

JANUARY and FEBRUARY 1944

January 1, 1944. R.A.F. dropped over 1,000 tons on Berlin (night); repeated 2nd. Allied planes attacked Japanese warships at Kavieng (New Ireland).

January 2. 1st Ukrainian Army recaptured Radovel. General Eisenhower left the Mediterranean to take command of Supreme Headquarters, Allied Expeditionary Force (took up duties January 16). U.S. troops landed at Saidor (New Guinea). Enemy airfields in the Marshall Islands bombed; again 3rd.

January 3. Novograd-Volynsk recaptured by Russians. General Montgomery arrived in Britain to take command of the British Group of Armies in the Allied Expeditionary Force.

January 4. Belaya-Tserkov captured by 1st Ukrainian Army. Heavy daylight attacks by U.S. bombers on Kiel and Muenster. Over 1,250 Allied bombers attacked Pas-de-Calais (France).

January 4-5 (night). 5th Army launched attack (Italy).

January 5. Berdichev recaptured by Russians. 2nd Ukrainian Army launched offensive. R.A.F. dropped over 1,000 tons on Stettin (night). Lieut.-Gen. Leese appointed Commander, 8th Army.

January 6. Russians captured Rokitno (inside 1939 Polish frontier).

January 8. Kirovograd stormed by 2nd Ukrainian Army.

January 10. Two allied air attacks on Sofia (Bulgaria).

January 11. New Soviet offensive in Mozyr direction. Oschersleben, Halberstadt, and Brunswick (Germany) attacked by 1,200 U.S. aircraft. Maungdaw (Burma) recaptured by British.

January 12. Russians took Sarny. Cervaro captured by 5th Army (Italy).

January 14. Russians took Mozyr and Kalinkovichi. Bomber Command dropped 2,000 tons on Brunswick (night).

January 15. Soviet offensive opened on Leningrad front.

January 16. British attacked across Garigliano (Italy).

January 17. Strong Allied air attack on Rabaul (New Britain); 3 Japanese merchant ships sunk, 2 left sinking.

January 18. Italian railway yards attacked by Allied bombers. Secretary for War stated up to 15 German divisions engaged by Yugoslav Partisans.

January 19. Russians recaptured Krasnoye-Selo. Peterhof and Ropsha.

January 20. Russians recaptured Novgorod. R.A.F. dropped 2,300 tons on Berlin (night). British troops captured Minturno; heavy Allied bombing of airfields, railway yards (Italy). American bombers raided Paramushir (Japan).

January 21. Mga recaptured by Russians. Dawn-to-dusk Allied air offensive against Pas-de-Calais targets (France). First heavy Allied air attack on Magdeburg by Bomber Command (2,000 tons). Night attack on Britain by 90 German planes; 16 destroyed. General offensive launched on 5th Army front (Italy). Americans bombed Paramushir (Japan) and Meiktila (Burma).

January 22. Allied landing in Anzio-Nettuno area (Italy).

January 23. Nettuno captured; communications heavily bombed by Allied aircraft (Italy). 18 gun positions at Wewak (New Guinea), 17 at Rabaul (New Britain) silenced by Allied bombers.

January 24. Pushkin and Pavlovsk recaptured by Russians. Allies occupied Anzio; violent German counter-attacks against 5th Army main front (Italy).

January 26. Rabaul (New Britain) heavily bombed. Argentina broke off diplomatic relations with Axis.

January 27. Leningrad completely freed from enemy blockade. Major R.A.F. attack on Berlin (1,500 tons).

January 28. Lyuban recaptured by Russians. Major R.A.F. attack on Berlin.

January 29. Novo Sokolniki recaptured by Russians; new Russian attack launched in Ukraine. U.S. bombers attacked Frankfort-on-Main (1,800 tons.) Some 60 enemy machines dropped bombs in S.E. England, including London. Marshall Islands bombed and bombarded by U.S. carrier-borne force.

January 30. Heavy day raids on Brunswick and Hanover by U.S. bombers; major night attack on Berlin by Bomber Command.

January 31. First land fighting in Dutch New Guinea on Eilanden River. American landings in Marshall Islands.

February 1. Red Army captured Kingisepp. 5th Army broke through the Gustav Line (Italy). Americans captured Roi Island (Marshalls).

February 2. Americans fought their way into outskirts of Cassino (Italy).

February 3. Russians encircled 10 German divisions in Dnieper Bend; Red Army fighting inside Estonia. Over 1,100 American aircraft made daylight raid on Wilhelmshaven (Germany). Strong German counter-attack against Anzio beach-head (Italy). Determined Japanese attack in Arakan (Burma). Namur Island (Marshalls) captured by Americans. Two Allied air attacks on Wewak (New Guinea); 93 Japanese planes destroyed.

February 4. "Saturation" daylight attack on Frankfort-on-Main by U.S. bombers. Savage fighting in Cassino (Italy). U.S. Fortresses raided Toulon and the Anthéor Viaduct (France). About 70 enemy planes attacked S.E. England. Japanese occupied Taung Bazaar (Burma). China-based U.S. bombers attacked Bangkok (Siam). U.S. warships bombarded Paramushir (Japan).

February 5. Rovno and Lutsk recaptured by Red Army. Kwajalein (Marshalls) occupied by U.S. Forces. Japanese sealed Ngakyedauk Pass (Burma).

February 6. Apostolovo and Marganets recaptured by Red Army; Soviet bombers made night raid on Helsinki.

February 8. Red Army took Nikopol. Daylight attack by U.S. Fortresses on Frankfort-on-Main (Germany). R.A.F. dropped first 12,000-lb. bomb on Gnome-Rhône works at Limoges (France).

February 10. Strong U.S. Fortress formations bombed Brunswick by day. Night Allied air raid on Bangkok (Siam). South of Italy, Sicily and Sardinia restored to Italian Government.

February 11. Red Army recaptured Shepetovka. Heavy Allied air attack on Frankfort-on-Main. Taung Bazaar re-captured by British (Burma). Huon Peninsula (New Guinea) cleared of Japanese.

February 12. Red Army recaptured Luga. M. Paassikivi, former Finnish Premier, arrived in Stockholm; met Soviet ambassador there, 16th.

February 13. East bank of Lake Peipus cleared by Red Army. Some 60 enemy raiders attacked S.E. England.

February 14. Red Army recaptured Korsun. American and New Zealand forces landed on Green Islands (Solomons). Ponape (Carolines) bombed by Liberators.

February 15. R.A.F. dropped over 2,500 tons on Berlin (night). Monte Cassino bombed and shelled by Allies.

February 16. Helsinki (Finland) bombed by Soviet planes. Second major German attack against Anzio beach-head (Italy). 15 ships of Japanese convoy off Kavieng (New Ireland) sunk.

February 16 and 17. Powerful U.S. naval and air attacks against Truk (Carolines); 201 enemy planes destroyed, 19 ships sunk, 7 probably sunk.

February 18. Encircled German divisions in Dnieper Bend finally liquidated; Staraya Russa recaptured by Red Army. Sharpest German air raid on London since 1941. 5th Army launched major attack on Cassino (Italy). Allies bombed and bombarded Rabaul (New Britain) and Kavieng (New Ireland). Engebi (Marshalls) captured by U.S. Marines.

February 19. Nearly 1,000 Halifaxes attacked Leipzig (night).

February 20. Powerful American bomber attacks on Leipzig, Bernburg, Brunswick, Rostock, Gotha, Gutow and Oschersleben; 2,000 tons dropped by Bomber Command at night on Stuttgart. Sharp Luftwaffe attack on London.

February 21. Kholm recaptured by Russians. Brunswick, Hanover and other places heavily attacked by U.S. bombers. U.S. Government requests Eire to remove Axis representatives.

February 22. 3rd Ukrainian Army took Krivoi Rog by storm. U.S. bombers attacked Bernburg, Aschersleben, Halberstadt, and Regensburg (Germany). S.E. England attacked at night by 175 enemy planes. First Allied attack on Marianas.

February 23. Luftwaffe made sharp attack on London. Steyr (Austria) bombed by U.S. Liberators.

February 24. Russians took Dno and Rogachev. Gotha and Schweinfurt (Germany) and Steyr (Austria) attacked by U.S. bombers. Two night attacks on Schweinfurt by Bomber Command. Ngakyedauk Pass (Burma) freed of enemy. 100 tons dropped on Rabaul by Allies at night (New Britain).

February 25. Regensburg, Stuttgart, Augsburg, Fuerth, Zell-am-See attacked by U.S. bombers; 8-hour Allied day offensive against targets in N. France, Belgium and Holland. Severe double night air attack on Augsburg.

February 26. 600 Soviet bombers attacked Helsinki (Finland). Over 200 Allied planes (1 lost) bombed Rabaul.

February 29. Third major enemy offensive launched in Anzio beach-head. Americans landed on Los Negros (Admiralty Islands). Official statement on Finnish-Soviet relations issued in Moscow.

HOW ITALY'S THOUSANDS OF WRECKED BRIDGES WERE BY-PASSED

The Germans in their retreat through Italy blew up every bridge as they crossed it, thus adding greatly to the difficulties of the Allied advance through country that was by nature easily defensible. Here is a bridge near Campobasso (captured by the 8th Army on October 15, 1943) cut in two by the enemy. Generally, engineers had to repair the old bridge or construct a new one before the army could move on. Here, traffic was able to cross the valley by making the track to the left, rejoining the road on the other side of the bridge. *Photo, Canadian Official*

IN THE DESOLATE SHADOW OF HANGMAN'S HILL

For 5½ months, the 1st Parachutist Division held Cassino and Monte Cassino monastery, thus impeding the Allied advance towards Rome. In the final assault on May 18, 1944, the Polish 2nd Corps captured the monastery, while British infantry with New Zealand tanks secured the town. The 1st Parachutist Division lost half its strength. Here two of the 1,500 prisoners taken are being brought in through ruined Cassino. *Photo, British Official*

AMERICANS IN JEEPS REACH THE COLOSSEUM AT ROME

U.S. troops of the 5th Army broke through the Alban Hills and reached the outskirts of Rome by 7.30 a.m. on June 4, 1944. There was stiff fighting in the eastern and southern outskirts of the city, but by nightfall the German rearguard had been finally driven out. All Rome's famous cultural buildings and monuments were intact. The 5th Army received a tremendous welcome from the people. Here jeeps are driving past the Colosseum through a lane of cheerful onlookers.

Photo, British Official

Chapter 304

NAVAL EXPLOITS IN WESTERN WATERS

The largest naval operation in the west during 1944 was the Allied landing in Normandy, which is described in Chapter 311. Here is an account of the other naval activities of the year in the Atlantic and the Mediterranean, including the Navy's part in the landings at Anzio and in the South of France. Merchant shipping history for the same period will be found in Chapter 301. For naval operations in the west during 1943, see Chapter 284.

ALTHOUGH events proved the general feeling to be unduly optimistic, the war in the Western Hemisphere appeared at the beginning of 1944 to be starting its final phase, at sea as well as on land. Outside the Mediterranean, for the first few months, the traditional definition of naval life as being " long periods of boredom with short intervals of intense excitement " seemed justified in the public eye : an attitude immediately changed by the invasion of Normandy (described in Chapter 311). Inside the Mediterranean the inter-service co-operation was showing excellent results, although to the public these were slow in materializing.

Progress in the northward drive in Italy having met with unexpectedly strong opposition, the Army made a new landing near Net-

The Navy at Nettuno tuno, ahead of the fighting line, on January 22 (*see* page 3047) under strong and carefully organized cover by British and Canadian small craft and a powerful air "umbrella." The Nettuno beach was chosen for its convenience for landing, but the neighbouring small port of Anzio was a first objective and was soon captured. In spite of some delay on the beach, which spoiled the full element of surprise, the carefully worked out time-table was well kept and as far as the Navy was concerned the operation was a success in all its branches. The large convoy, awkward to handle as such landing convoys invariably were, was attacked by submarines and aircraft on passage, but the escort had no difficulty in dealing with them, although later in the fighting the enemy took toll of the ships supporting the Army by bombardment and sank the cruisers " Penelope " (H.M.S. " Pepperpot " of the Malta run —*see* page 2285) and " Spartan " (first mentioned on her loss) and the destroyers " Inglefield " (with 250,000 miles of war service to her credit) and " Janus " (which fought at Matapan).

A large force of German submarines which attempted to enter the Mediterranean in February was fought for eleven days and nights by H.M. destroyers and Coastal Command air-

craft in and around the Straits of Gibraltar. Three of them were sunk and several damaged ; later events confirmed the opinion that very few, if any, succeeded in getting through.

In the early months of the year the French naval forces were beginning to make their weight felt ; the ships had been refitted in British and American yards and their numbers increased by the transfer to the French flag of several small craft. The officers and men were as keen to have their revenge on Italy for the treachery of 1940 as they were to redress the wrongs inflicted by Germany. Retrained in new methods, and with discipline tightened, they did good service.

Though the enemy was still in force in the waters on either side of the northern half of Italy, the initiative had passed to the Allies. Enemy material, at any rate that seized from the Italian Navy, was decidedly inferior. Allied submarines, particularly the handier types of small tonnage, attacked every enemy target which presented itself

in any part of the Mediterranean with repeated success : the comparative insignificance of the individual vessels destroyed gave the public little idea of the ceaseless strain involved in these actions and their cumulative effect on enemy morale and material.

Slowly but surely the Allied line advanced up Italy, supported at every step on both coasts by the Navy's bombarding and inter-

Naval Support for Allied Armies

cepting forces, and the German bases far behind were under constant attack. The ports of Leghorn on the west and Ancona on the east were taken by Allied land forces in July after the Germans had done all the damage they could. Rear-Admiral T. H. Troubridge, R.N., commanded the naval section of the Combined Force which captured Elba in June in two days. On June 21, the 10,000-ton Italian cruiser " Bolzano," which fell into German hands after Italy's surrender, was sunk at Spezia by a " human torpedo " (*see* page 2847) manned by

BRITISH SUBMARINE FLOTILLA IN HARBOUR

Here is a British submarine flotilla alongside its parent ship, just visible on the left. Second from the right is H.M.S. 'Upright,' the submarine which during a year's tour of duty in the Mediterranean during the dark days of 1941-42, torpedoed and sank a floating dock—unique exploit for a submarine—and shot down an enemy aircraft.

Photo, British Official

Sub.-Lt. Malcolm Causer and Able Seaman Harry Smith, an exploit for which they were awarded the D.S.O. and C.G.M. respectively.

The famous 47,000-ton Italian liner "Rex," also in German hands, was set on fire by rocket planes and driven ashore sinking, subsequent attacks rendering her quite useless for further service. The old cruiser "Taranto," prepared to act as a blockship at Spezia, was sunk by air attack, and German communications between Italy and Yugoslavia, where the patriots had their hands very full, were reduced to a trickle by the combined operations of British destroyers, cruisers and light coastal forces with aircraft.

Enemy Communications attacked

At the end of October the Germans claimed that the hospital ships "Tuebin-

gen" and "Freiburg" had been sunk in the Adriatic. In the case of the "Tuebingen," on November 18 they made a new claim, giving a much later date. After investigation the British Government admitted that she had been sunk in error and made an apology, but pointed out that, in addition to the long list of enemy attacks on Allied hospital ships published earlier in the war, the "Amsterdam" had been deliberately sunk by a U-boat while returning from Normandy in August, although she was duly notified and fully marked.

In the eastern Mediterranean the Germans had considerable floating material, all originally Italian, but comparatively little opportunity of using it.

British submarines, assisted by those of various Allies, maintained a continuous pressure alone or in collaboration with aircraft, while the smaller vessels from destroyers downwards showed constant dash. The Allies were not yet ready to strike major blows; but in August, when Rumania and Bulgaria gave up the struggle, withdrawal by the Germans from the innumerable Greek islands in which they had established small garrisons became inevitable and was repeatedly harassed. Light cruisers and destroyers, using guns up to 4·7- and 6-inch, constantly bombarded islands with excellent effect, while light craft were always on the move. A hundred and fifty warships, mostly small, were employed — British, Canadian, South African, Greek, French and Polish. Enemy destroyers were helpless; their impressive "paper" qualities proved of little use when it came to hard active service, particularly in the winter months. They fought desperately but ineffectively and several were sunk.

In October, a rapid succession of landings on the islands and the Greek mainland, carried out with the assistance and under the cover of the Navy, in spite of great supply difficulties, proved most successful. Certain islands which had been heavily fortified were by-passed. The Navy bombarded the principal ones from time to time, saw that the blockade was maintained, and supplied Greek partisans with munitions. The unhappy lack of unity among the Greeks was immediately apparent, and parties ashore, including those covering the landing of famine relief supplies, sometimes found themselves attacked until parties of Royal Marines had to be landed, and on several occasions the ships had to support the army with their guns.

Once the Allies had landed in Northern France, the enemy must have expected a landing in Mediterranean France, though apparently he was confident that it would take place only after the Italian fighting line had been forced into north Italy. Even the "softening up" air operations against the naval base of Toulon, which afforded excellent cover for careful reconnaissance, he appears to have regarded only as a means of checking submarine attacks on supply lines. At the beginning of August, however, the concentration of tonnage could no longer be hidden and was reported by Berlin, which prophesied a new landing on the north-west Italian coast. Corsica,

Preparing to Land in South France

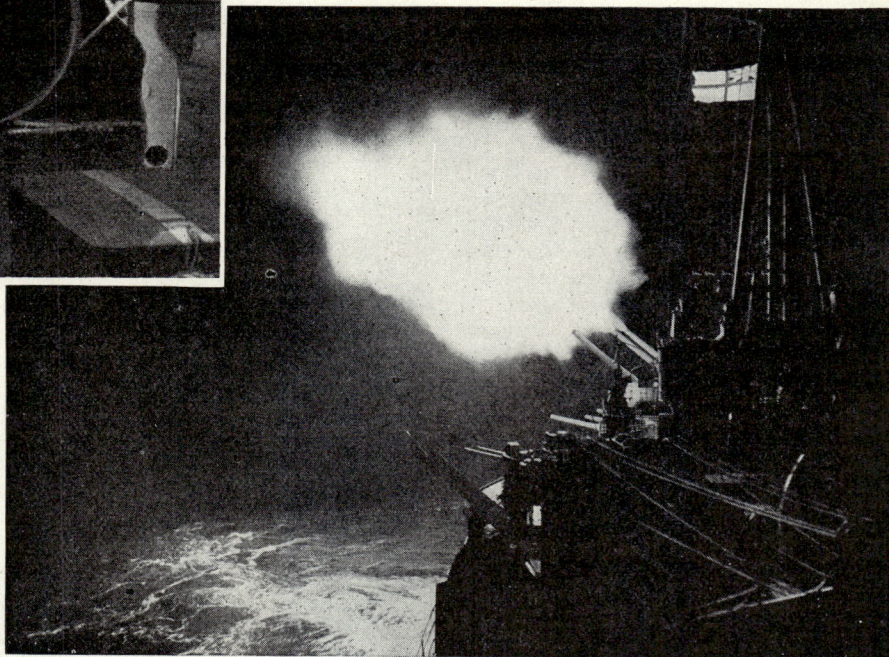

NAVAL SUPPORT AT ANZIO

The Royal Navy gave powerful support to the Allied armies as they fought their way up Italy. For instance, on January 28, 1944, the cruisers H.M.S. 'Mauritius' (seen here firing her 6-inch guns during a night engagement off Anzio) and 'Dido' and the new destroyer H.M.S. 'Kempenfelt' silenced German shore batteries, broke up enemy troop movements, and cut a supply train in two. Above, General Alexander (seated, left) and Admiral Troubridge at Anzio.

APPROACHING THE ISLAND OF ELBA

In the early hours of June 17, 1944, a detachment of the French army commanded by General de Lattre de Tassigny landed from an Allied invasion fleet (under Rear-Admiral T. H. Troubridge, R.N.) on the island of Elba, which lies between Corsica and Italy. By 10.30 a.m. on June 19, all organized resistance had ceased. Here are tank landing craft going inshore during the attack.

Photo, British Official

Sardinia, Italy and North Africa were the jumping-off points for the invasion fleet, which got under way on August 14. Eight German corvettes sailed right into it at sea and were promptly destroyed. Three hundred vessels of the Royal Navy, French, American, and other fleets covered the transports and landing craft numbering 500 ; 12,000 French sailors took part in the operations. On the 15th the landing was made with remarkably little loss.

Sub.-Lieut CAUSER   A.B. HARRY SMITH

On June 21, 1944, Sub.-Lieut. Malcolm Causer and Able Seaman Harry Smith entered the harbour of Spezia on a 'human torpedo' (see illus., p. 2847) and sank the 10,000 ton Italian cruiser 'Bolzano,' which had fallen into German hands after Italy's surrender. They were awarded the D.S.O. and C.G.M. respectively for this exploit.

Photos, Daily Mirror

Among the covering vessels were rocket craft—officially called Landing Craft Tank (Rocket). Information about

Landing Craft Tank (Rocket)

these vessels was not released till September, but it was then revealed that they had assisted at the landings in Sicily, at Reggio, Anzio and Nettuno, and in Normandy, as well as in the South of France. The raid on Dieppe in 1942 brought home forcibly the need, in tackling strongly defended beaches, for more fire support from the sea as infantry landed and crossed the beach than

could be given by existing weapons, and among the ideas put forward was the novel one of fitting a great number of rocket projectors in a Landing Craft Tank in such a way that they could be fired in tremendous salvos on to the beach, stunning the defenders just before the assault troops went in. The idea was not readily accepted. One L.C.T., however, was fitted with rocket projectors and was ready for trial in April 1943. The trial was an anxious one, but the rockets went off, the craft did not sink, and the only casualty was an officer closely concerned in the invention whose hair, eyebrows and moustache were singed off by the flash of the rockets.

The fire from a rocket craft was roughly equivalent to the fire of thirty regiments of artillery or thirty cruisers each mounted with twelve 6-inch guns when related to the time over which the bombardment took place. When the salvo was fired there was a vivid flash and the rockets rushed through the air, to detonate a few seconds later on the beach with an appalling crash. All opposition from one battery of 80 millimetre cannon concealed in a Sicilian wood ceased after one attack by rocket craft. When a rocket craft went into action, the ship's company, with the exception of the commanding officer who controlled the firing mechanism from a protected position on the bridge, went below decks. As the salvos were fired there was a deafening roar, and a blinding flash enveloped the steel deck. The decks would have become red-hot from the backfire except for the automatic water spray. After a succession of salvos the water sprayed reached boiling point. During the tests all those taking part wore asbestos suits. The practice shoot preceding the Sicilian invasion

took place off a little island in the Mediterranean.

Six craft were adapted and took part in the landing in Sicily, where it was reported that the impact so shocked some of the Italian garrisons that they surrendered without resistance. Many more were ordered for the invasion of Normandy, designed to carry an even greater number of rockets, all of which could be fired in a period of some thirty seconds at a considerable range.

Stiff resistance was encountered at Toulon but combined attacks, with particular attention to the bombing of the scuttled French battleship "Strasbourg" (which was used as a fort for her 13-inch guns) forced the last of the German garrison to

French Fleet Re-enters Toulon

surrender on August 28. On September 15 the French battle fleet, accompanied by the British cruiser "Sirius" (see illus. p. 2947), flying the flag of Admiral Sir John Cunningham, Allied C.-in-C. Naval Forces, Mediterranean, and the American cruiser "Philadelphia," flying the flag of Admiral Davidson, re-entered the port. Its harbours could not yet be used efficiently for supplies on account of the damage done by Allied bombing from sea and air, and by the retreating Germans ; but they were steadily improved, although the enemy control of northern Italy remained a constant threat to the supply services. The enemy used both full-sized and one-man submarines against them, but their success was not great and their casualties were heavy.

The German occupation of Norway remained a serious threat. Not only was Germany securing invaluable supplies, although she lost increasing quantities as the year progressed, but the U-boat bases on the Norwegian coast were a continuing menace to Atlantic shipping and to the convoy route to north Russia. The battleship "Tirpitz" was the backbone of that menace, and although most of the actual attacks were carried out by German submarines and aircraft, her existence demanded that Britain should keep big ships in home waters, when they might have been more advantageously employed elsewhere. Repeated attempts were made to destroy, or at least to cripple her (*see* pp. 2850 and 2853), but her usual moorings close under the cliffs in Alten Fjord made

her a particularly difficult target. On April 3, 42 Barracuda torpedo-bombers of the Fleet Air Arm dropped 40 tons of H.E. on her, scoring at least 24 hits. When the attack ended "Tirpitz" was adrift, shrouded in smoke, and burning fiercely amidships. Naval aircraft carried out several low-level attacks on "Tirpitz" and other naval units on August 22, 23, 24 and 29. Thereafter, the R.A.F. took over the attack, and their exploits, ultimately successful in sinking her, are described in Chapter 315. Her end, the last real capital ship which Germany possessed, greatly simplified the problems of the Admiralty.

Although "Tirpitz" had been the main object of attack in Norwegian waters, the German supply route was still of great importance and was made more and more dangerous. Submarines, destroyers, light coastal forces and what the Americans would call task forces—escort carriers covered by surface ships of various kinds—caused heavy losses to the enemy. The task forces from the Home Fleet proved particularly successful as they combined attacks on shore installations with those on shipping and convoying craft. The stream of munitions still went to Russia by the northern route (*see*

'TIRPITZ' HIT BY BARRACUDAS OF THE FLEET AIR ARM

Two forces of Barracuda torpedo-bombers, supported by Corsair, Hellcat, Seafire and Wildcat fighters, dropped 40 tons of high explosive on the German battleship 'Tirpitz' on April 3, 1944, as she lay in the shelter of Alten Fjord, Norway. The attack appeared to take 'Tirpitz' by surprise, and no air opposition was met. Violent explosions and flames as high as the ship's mainmast were observed on board. Here clouds of smoke and flame rise from the damaged battleship. Left, a loaded Barracuda in flight. Below, a Wildcat takes off from H.M.S. 'Ravager.' *Photos, British Official ; Chas. E. Brown ; Planet News*

ROCKET SHIP IN ACTION

Early experimental raids on enemy occupied coasts made it clear that some new kind of fire support from the sea was needed to cover infantry landings. The Landing Craft Tank (Rocket) was the result. It was fitted with a great number of rocket projectors which could be fired on to the beach in tremendous salvos, stunning the defenders just before assault troops went in. They were first used at the landings in Sicily. *Photo, Planet News*

Chapter 301), the escort being varied according to the changing conditions, but generally consisting of cruisers, destroyers, escort craft and mine-sweepers and an increasing number of escort carriers. Towards the end of the year, the flag officers in command took to using the carriers as their flagships, an innovation generally regarded as eminently successful. When Finland surrendered and the Russians worked round into northern Norway, while Sweden's attitude towards the Axis stiffened, the enemy's sea communications became more and more important, and Allied attacks were intensified.

As the Red Armies advanced, Russian naval bases on the Baltic and the Black Seas were re-captured in steady succession, enabling Russian submarines, and in the Baltic Russian surface vessels, to join the British Fleet in the destruction of German transports and supply ships. In December the R.A.F. bombed Gdynia, which had become the principal German naval base since the heavy bombing of Wilhelmshaven and Kiel, and, owing to the position in the Baltic, and the loss of bases in France, the bulk of the German Navy was transferred to Denmark and southern Norway.

Russian Naval Bases Recaptured

Anti-submarine measures attained a very gratifying measure of success, which tended to grow steadily until almost the end of the year. Submarine attacks in the Atlantic still depended on "wolf-pack" methods, but with greatly reduced results: many months showed more submarines than merchantmen destroyed. This was contrived only by unremitting care and watchfulness. Convoying and air patrol continued without diminution, although the organization of larger convoys economized in escort vessels, and British and American yards were able to change over from building patrol craft to producing other vessels in more urgent demand, especially landing craft of all types. The good results obtained were

'ISLAND FORTS' PROTECT EAST COAST SHIPPING

The waters off England's east coast are always busy with small shipping, to protect which from enemy air attack a number of 'island forts' were put up. They consisted of two concrete towers, 50 feet high from the base, connected by a steel superstructure on which A.A. guns were mounted. Commissioned as H.M. ships, they were manned by Royal Marines under R.N.V.R. officers with naval ratings for technical duties. (See also illustration in page 3024.)

ALLIED WARSHIPS OFF THE NORMANDY BEACHES

H.M. ships and ships of the United States and other Allied Navies not only escorted the vessels carrying men and materials to the Normandy beaches from June 6, 1944, onwards, but also assisted the forces after they had got ashore by long-range shelling. 1. The Allied Naval C.-in-C., Admiral Sir Bertram Ramsay, watches the sailing of the great invasion fleet from the bridge of a torpedo boat. 2. The cruiser H.M.S. 'Glasgow' during the three-hour bombardment of Cherbourg by an Anglo-American naval force on June 25; behind her lies the U.S. cruiser 'Quincy.' 3. The battleship H.M.S. 'Rodney' shelling enemy positions in the neighbourhood of Caen. 4. Fresh canisters of cordite and other ammunition being transferred to H.M.S. 'Glasgow' on her return to a British port after her action off the French coast.

Photos, British Official; British Newspaper Pool

REFUELLING A BATTLESHIP AT SEA

The changeover from coal to oil as fuel in the Royal Navy made it possible, by the maintenance of a fleet of tankers each carrying 12,000 tons of crude oil, for H.M. ships to refuel at need at sea instead of having to come in to harbour. Here H.M.S. 'Warspite' refuels at sea from a tanker which has come out to her in answer to her call for oil. *Photo, British Official*

due to more adequate material, more thorough training and experience, perfect co-operation between ships and aircraft, and world-wide organization.

The increased use of escort carriers (the use of Merchant Aircraft Carriers, shown in page 3043, declined in 1944) combined with the preoccupation of the Luftwaffe elsewhere to diminish air attacks on merchantmen. But though air attack in the Atlantic became rare, it was delivered, when it happened, with great determination. Attacks were most common on the north-bound convoy route between Gibraltar and the United Kingdom.

Air attack helped by the Leigh Light (*see* page 3032) accounted for many U-boats caught charging their batteries on the surface. In the autumn the German Admiralty announced a new appliance which would permit U-boats to defy air attack by charging their batteries submerged, and which came to be called the "growler" gear, a collapsible air intake buoyed on the surface (*see* page 3035).

Success Against U-Boats

But while this gear saved submarines from being surface targets for aircraft, the noise of even the improved Diesel engines recharging the batteries was much louder than the purr of the electric motor propelling the ship submerged, so that the Asdic became much more effective and attack by depth charges was facilitated. The noise also gave warning from a long distance of submarines manœuvring into position to attack convoys and permitted avoiding action to be taken. Another serious factor for the U-boat crews was the terrible strain of long

periods submerged, living on "tinned air."

The relaxation of the submarine blockade for a large part of the year had been of the greatest value to the Allies in building up supplies, both munitions and those required by Britain while tonnage was withdrawn for the invasion of northern France. This had been in active preparation since 1942 and demanded the most perfect co-operation between the three Services. The immensity of the preparations kept the Admiralty employed for a very long time. They involved not only co-operation with the heads of the other fighting forces but also with the Ministry of War Transport and the ship-owners. Vessels of all types had to be employed, a very large number manned by crews whose gallantry and

dash were much greater than their sea experience. Endless rehearsals were necessary to ensure the perfect timing and station-keeping which was essential and which had to be the responsibility of the young officers themselves—for direct control by seniors was impossible —and the Communications Branch.

The lessons of previous landings, particularly those which had involved delays and casualties, had to be carefully adapted to the different conditions of northern France and an immense amount of floating material had to be fitted for its new purpose (*see* Chapter 301). And with all the careful preparations beforehand, allowance had to be made for conditions causing delay as, indeed, they did for twenty-four hours.

Before the Invasion of Normandy

Naval ships of all kinds were employed. First 309 British, 16 Canadian and 22 American minesweepers cleared the approach channels for the trans-

THIRTEEN BRITISH WARSHIPS FOR THE RUSSIAN NAVY

After the surrender of Italy, the Soviet Government asked for Italian ships. In view of the unsuitability of these for use in northern waters, early in 1944 Britain transferred to Russia 20,000 tons of merchant shipping, the battleship 'Royal Sovereign' (here being handed over to her Russian crew), eight ex-American destroyers (and a non-operative destroyer of the same class for spare parts), and four modern submarines. The United States supplied the same amount of merchant shipping and the cruiser 'Milwaukee.' *Photo, British Official*

ALLIED FLEETS ASSIST SOUTH OF FRANCE LANDINGS

British, United States and French warships supported the Allied landings in the south of France, which began on August 15, 1944. Here the U.S. battleship 'Nevada' is bombarding enemy shore positions. Above, the escort carriers H.M.S. 'Pursuer' (foreground), H.M.S. 'Attacker' and H.M.S. 'Khedive' (three of the 38 escort carriers transferred from the U.S. to the Royal Navy in 1942) and other ships of the Royal Navy off the south coast of France. *Photos, British Official*

ports and naval ships. On the lessons learned in Allied attack on fortified islands in the Pacific, the heaviest metal, as well as the lighter quick-firing guns, was used for bombarding prepared positions. Among the ships engaged were H.M. battleships "Warspite," "Ramillies," "Nelson" and "Rodney," mounting 15- and 16-inch guns, the U.S. battleships "Nevada," "Texas" and "Arkansas," and the 15-inch British monitors "Erebus," "Roberts" and "Abercrombie." Six-inch and 8-inch gun cruisers of the British, U.S., Polish and French Navies took their full part, together with destroyers and small naval craft of every kind. During the first three weeks over 50 British warships—fleet and "Hunt" class destroyers, frigates, corvettes, trawlers and light coastal craft—combined into an inshore force under Capt. M. L. Power on the destroyer "Kempenfelt," fought off attempts by the enemy to break into the landing areas.

Considering the nature of the operations, and the inevitably long fore-knowledge by the enemy that they

were impending, the losses on and after the landings on June 6 were light. The Royal Navy lost the destroyers "Boadicea" (Lt.-Com. F. W. Hawkins) and "Swift" (Lt.-Com. J. R. Gower), the frigates "Mourne" (Lt.-Com. R. S. Holland), "Blackwood" (Lt.-Com. L. T. Sly) and "Lawford" (Lt.-Com. M. C. Morris), the trawler "Lord Austin" (Lt. E. S. T. Robinson) and the auxiliary "Minster" (Act. Lt.-Cdr. W. Jackson). Norway lost the destroyer "Svenner." United States losses were the destroyers "Corry," "Meredith" and "Glennon," the naval transport "Susan B. Anthony," the minesweeper "Tide," the frigate "Rich" and the fleet tug "Partridge." In addition were the ships used as blockships: these included the old British battleship "Centurion," which had long been used as a target, the French "Courbet," which dated from 1911, and the Polish (ex-H.M.) cruiser "Dragon," which had been severely damaged. (*See* Chapter 307.)

The striking success of the actual invasion did not see the end of the Navy's activities on the north-west

coast of Europe. Not only was it necessary to keep a careful guard against attack from both the occupied French coast and the North, but also to prevent senior German officers slipping back to safety.

The Germans still had a number of destroyers south of the invasion area and these were always liable to cause trouble. On August 6 H.M. cruiser "Bellona" (Capt. C. F. W. Norris) with the destroyers H.M.S. "Ashanti," H.M.S. "Tartar," H.M.C.S. "Haida" and H.M.C.S. "Iroquois" encountered two enemy convoys off St. Nazaire. The first consisted of seven ships and every one was sunk after the British had secured the inshore position, H.M. ships suffering a few casualties. The second fled back to port. In two brisk night actions on August 23, off the French coast between Brest and Lorient, the cruiser H.M.S. "Mauritius" and the destroyers H.M.S. "Una" and H.M.C.S. "Iroquois" sank eight enemy vessels, suffering no damage or casualties, though under fire from enemy shore batteries. Many other exciting actions occurred and some losses were sustained. The advances along the French, Belgian and Dutch coasts were largely the business of the Army, but the Navy gave full co-operation, both with ships and with land forces and Commandos of the Royal Marines; and all the time the material available in European waters was being steadily reduced by the withdrawal of ships of nearly every type to be prepared for service in the Far East.

Actions off the West of France

Chapter 305

RUSSIANS RECONQUER THE UKRAINE

There was no pause between the autumn campaign of 1943 in Russia, described in Chapter 291, and the subsequent winter campaign—the second opening on December 14 with an attack in the direction of Nevel, the same day on which the first ended with the capture of Cherkassy. Major-General Sir Charles Gwynn here deals with operations in the Ukraine, leaving the contemporary Crimea and Leningrad campaigns for consideration in Chapter 310

THE situation on the Russian front by the latter half of December 1943 is shown in the map in page 3076. The winter campaign may be said to have opened in the north centre of the long front when, on December 14, Bagramyan's 1st Baltic Army took the offensive in the Nevel sector along the main Leningrad-Vitebsk railway south-west of Veliki Luki. The immediate object of this offensive was to isolate Vitebsk from the north. But presumably it had, by striking at a sensitive point on the German front, the further purpose of containing German reserves and preventing their transference to the fronts of the main offensive. Bagramyan had a rapid success, capturing Gorodok on the 24th, after ten days of fierce fighting, and thus outflanking Vitebsk. The German defences were, however, exceptionally strong on this front, and although heavy pressure was maintained no deep penetrations were effected.

On December 24 the main offensive, which aimed at the destruction of the German armies in the western Ukraine **Vatutin Returns to the Attack** and the liberation of that great territory, really started. On that date Vatutin, having worn down Von Manstein's Army and shattered his Panzer Divisions, turned suddenly from the defensive to the attack. It was an amazing feat of generalship, recalling the course of the great Kursk salient battle of the summer and postulating a wonderfully courageous and skilful husbanding of reserves under critical conditions even at the expense of giving ground.

Vatutin had great and rapid success: in six days' fighting ground had been gained to a depth of 30 to 60 miles on a 180-mile front, and Von Manstein's badly mauled force was in full retreat. Korosten had been recovered (December 29), and Zhitomir was taken on the 31st. Berdichev, a key railway junction south of Zhitomir, was outflanked by the capture of Kazatin farther to the south-east. It was evident that Vatutin's main thrust was directed towards Vinnitsa on the upper Bug which covered approaches to the Odessa-Lwow railway in the neighbourhood of Zhemerinka.

This railway was the main line of communication for all the German forces in the Ukraine, and clearly Von Manstein would fight desperately to protect it.

On January 5 he lost Berdichev, (*see* illus., p. 2925), but succeeded in rallying in the Vinnitsa area, where he was protected against outflanking movements by the Bug and could also bring up reserves quickly by railway from both west and east. He was therefore able to initiate about January 12 a series of counter-

GENERAL IVAN BAGRAMYAN

On December 19, 1943, the Soviet High Command announced that troops of the 1st Baltic Army under General Bagramyan had launched an offensive five days earlier in the area south of Nevel (which had been captured on October 7), and, after fierce fighting, had broken through a strongly fortified defence line on a 50-mile front to a depth of 19 miles, liberating over five hundred localities.

Photo, Pictorial Press

attacks which for a long period checked any further Russian advance in the direction of Zhemerinka. But although Vatutin was compelled by the strength of Von Manstein's counter-attacks to stand on the defensive in this region, he had already struck in other directions. From the Korosten area he had advanced south-westwards, capturing on January 3 Novograd-Volyusk on the Korosten-Tarnopol railway; and he

had pushed south from Fastov to capture on January 4 Belaya-Tserkov, a strongly held town which had been the base for Von Manstein's first counter-attack after his loss of Kiev.

Vatutin was at the time criticized for dispersing his effort in three directions instead of concentrating for his main blow; but he probably counted on Von Manstein's **Russians Meet Stubborn Resistance** drawing reserves to the Vinnitsa front, leaving his northern sector lightly held. It must be remembered, too, that Vatutin was entirely dependent on road transport. That may have imposed limitations on the size of the force that could be used in any one direction, especially as roads that would stand up to heavy traffic in the prevailing mild weather were few, and they all radiated from Kiev. In any case, Vatutin's plans worked out well. His right made rapid progress and by the middle of January was close to the important railway centre of Shepetovka; while on his extreme right Sarny, on the Kiev-Brest-Litovsk railway which skirts the southern side of the Pripet marshes, was captured (January 12). This was an important success, for it cut the Rovno-Vilna railway which had given the Germans valuable lateral communications across the Pripet.

The drive from his left front which captured Belaya-Tserkov may have had the defensive purpose of making the base of the Kiev salient more secure against counter-attacks, but it probably from the first also envisaged co-operation with Koniev's army, which had taken the offensive westwards from the base of the Kremenchug bridge-head and on January 8 had captured the important town of Kirovograd. Both these drives continued to make steady progress against stubborn resistance—on the Belaya-Tserkov front, in particular, strong counter-attacks were defeated in the neighbourhood of Uman; but nothing spectacular was achieved until the first week in February.

Meantime, north of the Pripet marshes on January 11, Rokossovsky had resumed his offensive west of the upper Dnieper, and in a few days had captured Mozyr and Kalinkovichi, where the

Gomel-Brest-Litovsk railway crosses the Mozyr-Vitebsk line; thus greatly improving his lateral communication with Vatutin's Army across the Pripet marshes.

Farther north, on the Veliki Luki front, the important strong point and railway junction of Novo Sokolniki on the Vitebsk-Leningrad line was captured by Popov (January 29). Much more important, on January 18 a major break-through on the Leningrad front was announced. (For the great northern offensive of which this was the start, *see* Chapter 310.)

Novo Sokolniki Captured

Little was heard of the southern front during the last half of January. Although some progress was reported towards Rovno, beyond Belaya-Tserkov, and on Koniev's Kirovograd front, it seemed that German counter-attacks at Vinnitsa and Uman had largely succeeded in stabilizing the front, and that the Leningrad offensive had become the main Russian effort.

But on February 3 came the sensational news that Vatutin and Koniev, resuming their offensive from the Belaya-Tserkov and Kirovograd fronts respectively, had by amazingly swift and deep thrusts joined hands in the Zvenigorodka - Shpola area, thereby completely encircling ten German divisions (some 100,000–120,000 men) which had been clinging to the Dnieper about Kanyev up-stream of Cherkassy. It had for some time been evident that this force was in a pronounced salient and it was difficult to see its purpose. Possibly it retained its position in hopes that it might ultimately form the right wing of a counter-offensive towards Kiev, and meanwhile it apparently relied on the strongly fortified town of Smyela and the marshy nature of the country surrounding it to provide security against Koniev's attacks. Now, however, not only was the force encircled, but Koniev by brilliant outflanking

MUD ON THE DNIEPER FRONT

The unusually mild weather made movement in Russia peculiarly difficult during the winter of 1943-44. The battles along the Dnieper, for instance, were fought in country devoid of roads and deep in mud. Here a mud-spattered German soldier is attempting to free a vehicle from the clinging clay. *Photo, New York Times*

tactics, through marshes the Germans had deemed impassable, had captured Smyela. An attempt to retreat rapidly by breaking through the encircling ring was the only course open to the Germans. But, hampered by masses of transport, and subject to attack from the air and by guerillas, the retreat was brought to a standstill in the area round Korsun, with the Russians closing in on all sides. The position was desperate, but Von Manstein attempted to save it by rushing up reserves to attack the ring from outside, thus forcing the Russians to face in two directions.

Fiercely as Von Manstein attacked, his efforts were unavailing; and the Korsun divisions, running short of material despite attempts to supply them by air, became less and less capable of co-ordinated action. By degrees they were split up into small groups, although not till February 18 were they finally annihilated with the loss of 55,000 killed, 18,200 prisoners and all their material. This was a crushing defeat for Von Manstein; moreover, the Russians had shown, especially in the original encircling thrusts, astonishing mobility in spite of mud and rain. The Germans, on the other hand, were ill-equipped for

Korsun Pocket Annihilated

RECONQUEST OF THE UKRAINE

The area in darkest shading on this map had been reconquered by the Russians by the middle of December 1943. The great Ukraine offensive which began at that time carried them by the middle of April 1944 across the area in lightest shading into the foothills of the Carpathians.

Specially drawn for THE SECOND GREAT WAR *by Félix Gardon*

LIQUIDATION OF THE 'KORSUN POCKET'

On February 3, 1944, Vatutin and Koniev encircled ten German divisions in the Kanyev-Korsun area. Von Manstein attacked from the west in an attempt to relieve his surrounded men, but in vain, and by February 18 the 'pocket' was annihilated. 1. Marshal Rotmistrov, commanding powerful Russian armoured units, watches a battle between Soviet tanks and German troops. 2. A Junkers-52 drops supplies to the encircled Germans. 3. Abandoned enemy transport in the Korsun pocket. 4. Some of the 18,200 prisoners taken.

Photos, Pictorial Press ; Planet News

SOVIET ARMOUR IN ACTION IN THE UKRAINE

Tank forces of the 1st Ukrainian Army, striking from the Sarny and Novograd-Volynsk areas, tore deep gaps in the enemy defences at Lutsk, which they took by storm, and Rovno, which they captured in an outflanking movement—both victories achieved on February 5, 1944. Here a tank of the 1st Ukrainian Army is seen firing during a night attack. Other tanks can just be distinguished in the background.

Photo, Pictorial Press

such conditions; in particular their Tiger tanks were frequently bogged; at best they lacked manoeuvrability and were no match for the Russian armour, which was lighter and better designed and had broader tracks and greater clearance. Throughout the winter fighting the disparity was always evident.

While the Korsun struggle was still in progress, the Germans were suffering other serious reverses. On February 5 the recapture of Lutsk and of Rovno, capital of Polyesye, and for long centre of German administration of "occupied Eastern territories," was announced, proving that Vatutin's right wing had penetrated some 50 miles farther than had been suspected. Apparently in this marshy area the Germans had concentrated their defence on roads, believing that attacks would be confined to them; but by making use of their cavalry, as Rokossovsky had also done in his Mozyr offensive, the Russians were able to outflank the enemy's centres of resistance, compelling their evacuation. Rearguards left to cover withdrawals suffered heavily and much material was lost. Russian gains in this direction were all the more important as they indicated the possibility of a wide outflanking to the west of Von Manstein's position at Vinnitsa. Vatutin's divergent offensives had by this time justified themselves.

Vatutin's Tactics Justified

The Germans suffered an equally serious defeat on the front of Malinovsky's 3rd Ukrainian Army. An Order of the Day on February 6 announced that Malinovsky, who had apparently taken over from Koniev the Nikopol-Krivoi Rog front, had captured Apostolovo and was in the outskirts of Nikopol. Hitler issued an order that Nikopol must be held at all costs. But on February 8 another Order of the Day announced that Tolbukhin's 4th Ukrainian Army had wiped out the bridge-head on the east bank of the Dnieper at Nikopol, driving the garrison into the river and with great loss, and, in co-operation with Malinovsky, had captured Nikopol itself; in all destroying some 7 divisions. Tolbukhin's reappearance in the Soviet Orders of the Day was interesting, as it showed that his army had been left to guard the line of the lower Dnieper and to maintain watch over the Crimea. The capture of Nikopol and its manganese ore was a heavy blow to German war industries, but the enemy made great efforts to retain his hold on Krivoi Rog and its valuable iron mines.

As a proof that Vatutin's front at this time was not altogether static and that danger was threatening Von Manstein's communications west of Vinnitsa, the important strongpoint and railway centre of Shepetovka, which the Germans had been using as a supply base, was captured on February 11 by troops under Chernyakhovsky, evidently one of Vatutin's principal subordinates.

The annihilation of the Korsun pocket on February 18 closed a disastrous fortnight for the Germans, and in subsequent days they were given no respite. On the 22nd Malinovsky took Krivoi Rog by storm; and on the 24th an Order of the Day announced that Rokossovsky had struck again and captured Rogachev, one of the principal German strongpoints on the upper Dnieper. This latter was a remarkable feat, for the town was protected on the east by the Dnieper and on the west by its tributary the Prut, on neither of which was the ice strong enough to carry artillery. But the attack had been organized in complete secrecy and the Germans, confident in the strength of their position, were taken by surprise.

Germans Surprised at Rogachev

March brought still greater disasters to the enemy on these widely separated sections of their front. On March 5 an Order of the Day announced that Marshal Zhukov had taken over command of the 1st Ukrainian front in relief of Vatutin, who was ill, and had broken through on a front of 110 miles to a depth 15–30 miles, routing four tank and eight infantry divisions despite continued unfavourable weather. The general direction of the attack was from Shepetovka towards Tarnopol, and it had reached and cut the main Tarnopol-Odessa line, thus interrupting the main communications with Poland of all enemy troops in the Ukraine, and in particular those of Von Manstein's strong force in the Vinnitsa-Proskurov area.

While this was happening Malinovsky had been pressing south from Krivoi Rog, clearing the west bank of the lower Dnieper, and with the obvious intention of reaching the lower Bug and the great port of Nikolaiev at its mouth. An Order of the Day of the 9th announced that a fresh wave of his offensive had broken through the German front and had crossed the Inguletz, a tributary which joins the Dnieper close up-stream of Kherson and had been strongly fortified by the Germans as a second position west of the Dnieper. Three German tank and six infantry divisions were heavily defeated in these operations, and the offensive continued.

Then on March 10 an Order of the Day announced that Koniev's 2nd Ukrainian Army had captured Uman and Kristinovka. (This **German Troops' First Panic Flight** indicated that Koniev had extended his front to take over what had been Vatutin's left wing.) In some ways this was the greatest disaster of all, because for the first time German troops really cracked and fled in panic. Moreover, the Uman region had been strongly held, for the force which had failed to rescue the Korsun pocket had fallen back to it to re-organize. When Koniev's attack developed, it was covered by a tremendous weight of artillery which threw the Germans into some disorder, although they recovered sufficiently to counter-attack. But the Russian infantry and

armour were not to be stopped and, penetrating deeply, reached an area where German tank reserves were assembled ready to seal off any break-through. Here once again weather exerted great influence. The spring thaw, which had thoroughly set in early in March, had reduced the ground to a bog, and the German tank crews, finding their machines virtually immobilized, were seized with panic and deserted them. Soon the whole front under attack broke down in rout, abandoning a great mass of intact equipment.

From now on it was evident that the Germans on the whole front from Vinnitsa to the mouth of the Dnieper were bound to retreat, if not to the Dniester at least to the Bug, and the offensive of the 2nd and 3rd Ukrainian Armies took on more and more the character of pursuit. On the 1st Ukrainian front Zhukov met stiffer resistance, for the Germans fought hard to retain Tarnopol and the Vinnitsa-Proskurov sector which, strongly held and fortified, protected the lines of the upper Bug and upper Dniester, together with the railway system connecting Poland with eastern Rumania —still a valuable link with the armies in the south though not comparable with that which had been provided by the main Odessa-Tarnopol line.

Malinovsky's main axis of pursuit was at first southwards towards Kherson and Nikolaiev, turning defence lines facing eastward and catching the Germans in flank as they endeavoured to retreat to **Banks of the Dnieper Cleared** the Bug. By March 13 he had cleared the whole of the west bank of the Dnieper, capturing Berislavl and Kherson, and on his right he had crossed the Ingul, a tributary of the Bug, and was pressing on to the lower reaches of the latter river. In these operations he had broken up the 6th German Army formed to replace the 6th Army lost at Stalingrad. Parts of it were surrounded and annihilated, and by the middle of the month higher control was lost, the troops being ordered to make the best of their way westwards. But south of the railways running west from Kirovograd the Germans made a stand on the lower Bug, and it was not till the end of the month that Malinovsky forced a crossing and was able to capture Nikolaiev (March 28) after a bitter fight.

Meanwhile Koniev continued his pursuit after his Uman victory. Thrusting west and south-west with the evident intention of outflanking the whole German group opposing Malinovsky in the Dnieper bend and cutting them off from Von Manstein's northern group,

RUSSIAN LONG-RANGE GUNS IN THE PRIPET MARSH AREA

Polyesye, the district lying in the triangle between Brest-Litovsk, Mogilev and Kiev, and consisting of forest, marsh, lake and meadow, presented many difficulties to the contending German and Russian forces, especially during the mild winter of 1943-44. Here a heavy long-range gun mounted on a caterpillar chassis is being hauled across snow-covered Polyesye by a tracked lorry.

Photo, Pictorial Press

ON THE RUMANIAN FRONTIER

Marshal Koniev's 2nd Ukrainian Army reached the River Prut, state frontier of the U.S.S.R., on March 26, 1944, on a 55-mile front. On April 2 the Red Army crossed the river. 1. Russian troops being ferried across the Prut: Soviet tanks, guns, and infantry poured into Rumania by barge, float and raft. 2. Soviet soldiers on Rumanian soil chat with local fishermen. 3. Red Army guards at a temporary bridge across the Seret—one of a number built by Soviet sappers—near Botosani, captured on April 8.

Photos, Pictorial Press

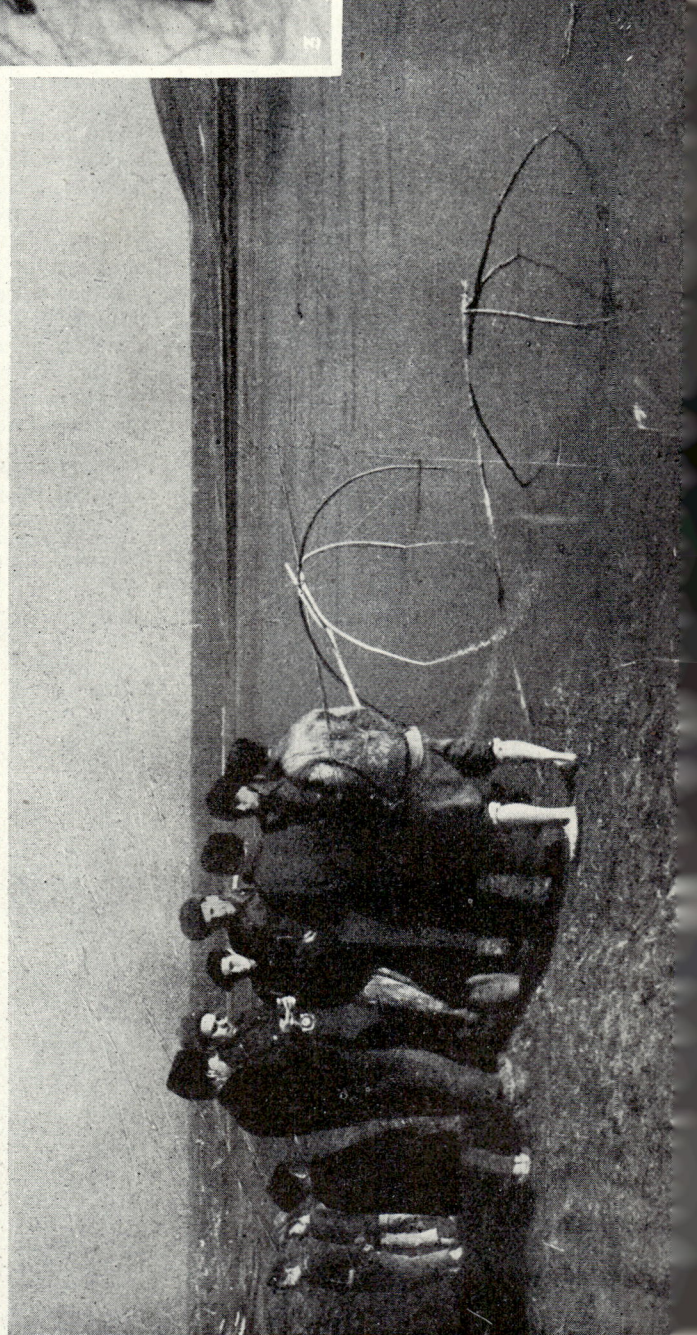

he crossed the middle Bug on a 60-mile front. Pressing on, by March 16 he had cut the main Odessa-Lwow railway to capture Vapnyarka, while on his left he was swinging south towards the railway running west from Kirovograd. By the 20th his right had captured Mogilev-Podolski on the Dniester, which was crossed on a 50-mile front; and two days later his left had taken Pervomaisk, which had formed the northern anchorage of the German's rallying line on the lower Bug. His centre reached the Prut on a wide front from Jassy northwards by the end of the month, by which time his left, pressing southwards, had crossed all railways leading to Jassy from the east.

With this great threat rapidly developing, the Germans facing Malinovsky on the lower Bug and those that had escaped from Nikolaiev were bound to **The Red Army Recaptures Odessa** retreat as fast as they could towards Odessa and the lower Dniester, abandoning among other places the fortress of Ochakov which commands the entrance to the Dnieper-Bug estuary, thus enabling the Russians to use the great port of Nikolaiev.

For a few days it seemed as if the Germans would make a determined attempt to hold Odessa and to establish a front covering the Jassy-Odessa railway, which crosses the Dniester at Tiraspol; for Malinovsky near the coast, and Koniev between Jassy and Tiraspol, were meeting stiffening resistance. By a brilliant outflanking move, however, Malinovsky cut the railway at Razjelnaya on April 5. With their front thus broken, the Germans east of the Dniester fell back on the Odessa defences, but Malinovsky gave them no time to recover and the great city, which in Russian hands in 1941 had stood a long siege, was now evacuated under conditions which indicated great demoralization. Some of the Germans escaped by sea, leaving their Rumanian allies and others for whom shipping was not available to get away if they could across the broad Dniester estuary, over which there was only a train ferry. The recapture of Odessa (April 10) was a glorious climax to the campaign on this section of the front, more especially since it had been brought about by the cumulative destruction of very strong German forces, and it yielded great booty. But the spring was now well advanced and, in addition to mud, melting snow in the Carpathians was bringing the Dniester, Prut and Seret down in flood.

Moreover, Von Kleist, who had been given command of the southern group when it had been cut off from Von Manstein's northern force, had been reinforced chiefly by Rumanian troops. It was consequently impossible for the Russians to exploit their success much further.

To complete the picture of the situation on the southern section of the front before it was finally stabilized in the spring, a very brief account will suffice. Malinovsky **Russians Thrust to the Carpathians** carried his advance up to the line of the Dniester and captured Tiraspol (April 12), but though he established small bridge-heads across the river, he was unable, in face of violent counter-attacks by Von Kleist, and while the flood was at its height, to extend them sufficiently for the deployment of large forces. Koniev's southern drive, although he crossed the Prut and Seret, closely threatening Jassy and cutting the railway that runs north on the west bank of the latter river, was also brought to a standstill. Von Kleist organized a strong defensive front stretching from the Carpathian foothills in the Seret valley, through Jassy and Kishinev to Benderi on the Dniester opposite Tiraspol. He had, however, been entirely cut off from Von Manstein's armies in the north and all his communications ran through Rumania. Heavy fighting on this front continued spasmodically till well on into the summer, arising from Russian attempts to extend their bridge-heads across the Dniester and to make progress in the Carpathian foothills. Jassy and

RUSSIAN FLAG FLIES IN ODESSA AGAIN

Odessa, evacuated by the Red Army on October 17, 1941, was recaptured by the 3rd Ukrainian Army under General Malinovsky on April 10, 1944. The victory was saluted by 24 salvos from 324 of Moscow's guns, and by a special salute of 12 salvos from 120 guns of the Black Sea Fleet. Here the Soviet flag is being hung from the balcony of the Lunacharsky Theatre. Above, citizens help in dismantling a defence post erected by the Germans. *Photos, Pictorial Press*

Kishinev were also under pressure, but Von Kleist maintained a very active defence and frequently counter-attacked strongly. His right flank was well protected by the Dniester in flood and his left by the Carpathians, where swollen mountain torrents limited the scale of operations.

We may now turn again to Zhukov's operations against Von Manstein. Zhukov's object in his offensive from the Shepetovka region, striking west and south towards the upper reaches of the Bug and Dniester and threatening the communications westwards of Von Manstein's armies on the Vinnitsa-Proskurov front, was clearly to destroy

on the Bug. Both armies advanced and cut the Odessa railway, Koniev near Vapnyarka (March 16) and Zhukov at Zhemerinka (March 18). Two days later Vinnitsa fell to Zhukov, who continued to compress Manstein's Vinnitsa-Proskurov group (completely separated by Koniev's advance from Von Kleist's armies) into a salient increasingly contracting and in danger north of the upper Dniester. By March 25 he had captured Proskurov and had reached the Dniester in the west, while his left in contact with Koniev's right was clearing the north bank of the river in the direction of Kamenets Podolski, captured on the 26th. Some of the Germans

and from the Stanislavov region. For a time the enemy forces in what became known as the Skala Kettle seemed likely to share the same fate as those at Korsun ; but eventually a considerable part did escape and, although some 26,000 men had been killed in the Kettle, only some 7,000 prisoners were taken in the final round-up, completed about April 15, on which date the capture of Tarnopol was announced.

This marked nearly the end of Zhukov's offensive, for not only were further operations hampered by mud and swollen rivers, but it was evident that Von Manstein had received considerable reinforcements. From his bases at Lwow and Stanislavov he was delivering powerful counter-attacks which brought the Russians to a standstill on the front running from Brody (on the Rovno-Lwow railway), west of Tarnopol, east of Stanislavov, and thence into the northern approaches to the Carpathian passes. On this front, especially in the Stanislavov area, heavy fighting continued during the spring, chiefly brought about by Von Manstein's counter-attacks, but not much ground changed hands.

The winter offensive in the Ukraine had achieved wonderful results, particularly as the exceptionally mild winter had been very unfavourable to the Russians, and the Germans had always the advantage of an intact railway system in their rear. The great river lines of the Dnieper, Bug, Dniester, Prut and Seret had been crossed despite elaborate fortifications prepared by the Todt organization. Immensely valuable territory had been recovered and disastrous losses of men and material had been inflicted on the enemy, whose forces had finally been split into two widely separated groups on the defensive. Both groups had, however, escaped the complete destruction which had at one time threatened them, and in that respect complete success had eluded the Red Army, despite its immense exertions of summer, autumn, winter and well on into the spring.

Results of Ukraine Offensive

GERMAN AIR AMBULANCE ON THE RUSSIAN FRONT
Fieschler ' Stork ' aircraft, which could land in a very small space, were used by the Germans on the Russian front to pick up their wounded and transport them to ambulance posts in the rear. (Compare with British evacuation of wounded by air from Burma, see page 3005.) Here the stretcher on which lies a wounded man is being lifted from a ' Stork ' at the reception point.
Photo, Sport and General

those armies or to drive them back into the Carpathians. Tarnopol and Proskurov on the Lwow-Odessa railway were the first great strongpoints to be encountered in the line of his advance, while farther south Stanislavov and Cernauti stood on important railway communications with Hungary and Rumania. Although Zhukov's main break-through was in the west, he maintained heavy pressure south of Berdichev and towards Vinnitsa. By March 12 there was street fighting in Tarnopol and the Russians were closing in on Proskurov, though the Germans fought back hard.

By that time, too, Koniev's victory at Uman and advance across the Bug enabled his right to co-operate with Zhukov's left at Vinnitsa, threatening the flank of the Germans opposing him

no doubt made their escape southwards into the Carpathians, but a large group was surrounded north of the Dniester. The situation was extremely confused, for the Germans appear to have been split up into groups far behind the Russian thrust southwards towards the Carpathians, which by the end of the month had captured Kolomyja (29th) and Cernauti (30th) on the upper Prut, cutting the main railway from Rumania into Poland. By April 8 advanced troops had penetrated the passes up to the frontier of the former Czechoslovak province of Ruthenia.

The surrounded Germans in the rear were, however, fighting desperately, attempting to cut their way out westwards, and in this they were assisted by violent rescue attempts made by Von Manstein south-west of Tarnopol

The great part played by Marshal Vatutin, whose untimely death (April 14) was announced just as the campaign was drawing to a close, is generally recognized. Perhaps the most brilliant of a number of brilliant commanders, he had a boldness in conception and a resolution in action that were inspiring ; and his great ability was never more conspicuous than when he was compelled to stand temporarily on the defensive while preparing for a riposte against an exhausted opponent.